Riding with the Revolution

Historical Materialism Book Series

The Historical Materialism Book Series is a major publishing initiative of the radical left. The capitalist crisis of the twenty-first century has been met by a resurgence of interest in critical Marxist theory. At the same time, the publishing institutions committed to Marxism have contracted markedly since the high point of the 1970s. The Historical Materialism Book Series is dedicated to addressing this situation by making available important works of Marxist theory. The aim of the series is to publish important theoretical contributions as the basis for vigorous intellectual debate and exchange on the left.

The peer-reviewed series publishes original monographs, translated texts, and reprints of classics across the bounds of academic disciplinary agendas and across the divisions of the left. The series is particularly concerned to encourage the internationalization of Marxist debate and aims to translate significant studies from beyond the English-speaking world.

For a full list of titles in the Historical Materialism Book Series available in paperback from Haymarket Books, visit: www.haymarketbooks.org/ series_collections/1-historical-materialism.

Riding with the Revolution

The American Left in the Mexican Revolution, 1900–1925

Dan La Botz

Haymarket Books
Chicago, IL

First published in 2024 by Brill Academic Publishers, The Netherlands
© 2024 Koninklijke Brill NV, Leiden, The Netherlands

Published in paperback in 2025 by
Haymarket Books
P.O. Box 180165
Chicago, IL 60618
773-583-7884
www.haymarketbooks.org

ISBN: 979-8-88890-536-4

Distributed to the trade in the US through Consortium Book Sales and
Distribution (www.cbsd.com) and internationally through Ingram
Publisher Services International (www.ingramcontent.com).

This book was published with the generous support of Lannan
Foundation, Wallace Action Fund, and the Marguerite Casey Foundation.

Special discounts are available for bulk purchases by organizations and
institutions. Please call 773-583-7884 or email info@haymarketbooks.org
for more information.

Cover art and design by David Mabb. Cover art is a development of
*Painting 41, Rhythm 69 (William Morris Block Printed Pattern Book, with
Hans Richter Storyboard, developed from Richter's Rhythmus 25 and Kazimir
Malevich's film script Artistic and Scientific Film—Painting and Architectural
Concerns—Approaching the New Plastic Architectural System)*. Paint and
wallpaper on canvas (2007).

Printed in the United States.

Library of Congress Cataloging-in-Publication data is available.

Contents

Preface

I initially began to study the groups and movements discussed in this book because of a certain personal, autobiographical interest in the subject. Like many of the people discussed here, I was an anti-war activist, though 50 years after they were. I grew up on the US-Mexico border, became a Spanish speaker, and like the subjects of my book I worked with Mexican socialist and labour organisations in international solidarity. Like them, I edited or wrote for several socialist and labour newspapers. Finally, like them, I hoped that working-class internationalism might overcome capitalism and war. My projects, like theirs, failed to achieve that hoped-for revolutionary transformation. No doubt my own experiences stimulated my interest in the US left and its relationship with the Mexican Revolution.

When I began to write this book some 25 years ago, my thought was that it would be simply a book about international labour solidarity, in particular the role of American leftists in the Mexican Revolution. I was intrigued to find that a group of American war resisters, beginning in 1917, should have gone to Mexico and ended up with some other foreigners and a handful of Mexicans organising the Industrial Workers of the World and founding the Mexican Communist Party. I found it both a fascinating example of transnational and international solidarity and labour organising, as well as a romantic story of idealism and adventure. The book today is, I believe, still all of that.

The more I worked with this material, however – letters in archives, newspapers of all sorts, memoirs, institutional documents, police reports, and of course the developing secondary literature – the clearer it became that it was also a record of experiments in the social laboratory of the era of industrial capitalism in North America in the early twentieth century. And in particular it was a study of the theory and practice of internationalism by American labour and left organisations. We have in the quarter century from about 1900 to 1925 in Mexico an opportunity to examine several labour and leftist strategies at work as groups from the United States, each using its own political theories and methods, analysed, planned, and then acted to carry out their strategic goals.

We see in this history how American Protestant social gospel missionaries, the Socialist Party of America – with its reformist majority and its revolutionary left wing – the revolutionary syndicalists of the Industrial Workers of the World, and the Farmer Labor Party members, as well as the revolutionary socialists of the early Communist Party each attempted to intervene in the Mexican Revolution and with what results. While originally focused on the US war resisters in Mexico between 1917 and 1921, I have also included the organisers that the Communist International sent just a few years later. We must follow all of their activities too in order to understand the trajectory of the American left in Mexico in those years. The one missing modern left political tendency, Stalinism, or to be more exact, bureaucratic collectivism, did not play a role in Latin America until the 1930s, which falls outside the purview of this book.

I should say a word too about my other activities involving Mexico. While in Mexico doing my research, Robin Alexander, International Affairs Director of the United Electrical Workers Union (UE), asked me to produce a newsletter for the Frente Auténtico de Trabjao (FAT) of Mexico and the UE of the United States, so I became the editor and principal writer of *Mexican Labor News and Analysis*. During that period, I also occasionally accompanied UE delegations as an authority on Mexican labour history, as a journalist, or sometimes also as an interpreter. So, for 20 years, like the subjects of my dissertation, I too was an American leftist and labour activist engaged in international work, in solidarity with the working people of Mexico.

I have continued to write about contemporary Mexican economy, labour, and politics, with some articles appearing in publications such as the Solidarity website, *Dollars & Sense*, *Against the Current*, *New Politics*, *Labor Notes*, *Jacobin*, *Viento Sur*, and others. There is no doubt that my own experiences in Mexico collaborating at times with the FAT, with the Partido Revolucionario de los Trabjadores (PRT), or with the Zapatista Army of National Liberation (EZLN) allowed me to better understand the experiences and the thinking of the men and women who are the subjects of this book. Today, as a member of the socialist group Solidarity and of the Democratic Socialists of America (DSA), I continue to be involved in international work, still involved with my comrades in striving to establish international alliances that can advance the working class and the struggle for socialism.

Acknowledgements

Much of the material for this book began as my doctoral dissertation, ' "Slackers": American War Resisters and Communists in Mexico, 1917–1927', written for the History Department of the University of Cincinnati and completed in 1998 with the support of Fulbright and Taft Fellowships. Professor Ann Twinam, then one of my advisors at the University of Cincinnati and now at the University of Texas at Austin, worked to help me earn the Fulbright.

I conducted the research for the dissertation while I was associated with the Centro de Investigación y Estudios Superiores en Antropología Social (CIESAS) and was assigned to work with Daniela Spenser, an authority on the history of the Communist International in Mexico and on the relations between the governments of the United States, Mexico, and the Soviet Union. Daniela and I shared documents with each other: I shared documents from US archives and she shared documents from Russian archives. We became both colleagues and friends. I owe a great debt to professors Twinam and Spenser who were both enormously helpful.

Benedikt Behrens, a historian of the University of Hamburg kindly shared with me documents from the private archive of Francisco Olivares. My thanks also to the late Ben Watanabe, a leader of the General Workers' Union of Tokyo, Japan, for his help with Katayama's Japanese autobiography. Two Latin Americanists, the late James D. Cockcroft, a historian, and sociologist Samuel Farber, read and commented on parts of the manuscript. Over the years, I also learned from his book as well as conversations and correspondence with Professor Barry Carr of La Trobe University.

While involved in my research in Mexico and for years afterwards, I also worked closely with Robin Alexander, the International Affairs Director then for the United Electrical Workers Union (UE), for 20 years – 1994–2014 – on the monthly newsletter, *Mexican Labor News and Analysis*. I have no doubt that my immersion in Mexican political and labour affairs for twenty years helped enrich my understanding of those who decades earlier had been engaged in Mexico in promoting international labour solidarity.

For 25 years after finishing the dissertation, I continued to research and write on the American left's involvement in the Mexican Revolution. The journal *Against the Current* published some of my articles on this topic. My thanks to the librarians and archivists of more than a dozen institutions in Mexico and the United States who helped me find the documents I sought.

I also wish to express my gratitude to Sebastian Budgen and Danny Hayward from Historical Materialism for their support and to the anonymous reader they assigned to read my manuscript who made several useful suggestions for editing my draft.

Finally, thanks to my wife Sherry Baron, herself a model of dedication to workers and their health and safety on the job and in their communities, as well as a paragon of patience and a great companion who has supported me many times over the last 25 years and encouraged me to finish this book. Thanks for everything, Sher.

Abbreviations

AFL	American Federation of Labor
Casa	House of the World Worker – Casa del Obrero Mundial
CGT	General Confederation of Workers – Confederación General de Trabajadores
CLP	Communist Labor Party
COM	House of the World Worker – Casa del Obrero Mundial
CPA	Communist Party of America
CPPA	Conference for Progressive Political Action
CPUSA	Communist Party of the United States of America
CROM	Regional Confederation of Mexican Workers – Confederación Regional de Obreros Mexicanos
CTRM	Confederaton of Workers of the Mexican Region – Confederación de Trabajadores de la Región Mexicana
FLP	Farmer Labor Party
FSODF	Federation of Union of Workers of the Federal District
FSORM	Federation of Unions of Workers of the Mexican Republic – Federación de Sindicatos Obreros de la República Mexicana
IAM	International Association of Machinists (US)
ISR	International Socialist Review
IWW	Industrial Workers of the World, Wobblies
KRESINTERN	Communist Peasant International
LCAEV	League of Agrarian Communities of the State of Veracruz – La Liga de Comunidades Agrarias del Estado de Veracruz
SPA	Socialist Party of America
Wobblies	Members of the Industrial Workers of the World

Pseudonyms

Because several of the individuals who feature in this book use a variety of pseudonyms, it will be helpful to list them.

Pseudonym followed by real name.

Alfred Albrecht	Bertram Wolfe
Arthur Albright	Bertram Wolfe
Mike Gold	Irwin Granich
Manuel Gómez	Charles Francis Phillips
Carl Johnson	Karl Jansen
Martin Paley	Herman Levine
M. Paley	Herman Levine
Mischa Poltiolevsky	Herman Levine
Jesús Ramirez	Charles Francis Phillips
Charles E. Scott	Karl Jansen
Frank N. Seaman	Charles Francis Phillips
Charles Shipman	Charles Francis Phillips
Edgar Woog	Alfred Stirner

The American Left and the Mexican Revolution – A Testing of Political Theories and Strategies

In this book, I follow the lives of a number of individuals associated with a variety of organisations – Protestant Churches of the social gospel, the American Federation of Labor, the Socialist Party, anarchist groups and the Communist Party – all of them in the broadest sense on the left of the political spectrum in the United States. Most would have described themselves as internationalists, though their concepts of internationalism varied greatly. Many of the individuals are quite famous figures in American history: Samuel Gompers and Eugene Debs, for example; then there are other well-known personalities in the history of American Socialism and Communism, such as John Reed, Louis Fraina (Lewis Corey), and Bertram Wolfe. Linked to the Americans in Mexico, we also find several international figures: Manabendra Nath Roy, Alexander Borodin, and Sen Katayama. In the period between 1900 and 1925, most of these organisations and individuals became allied with one faction or another of the revolutionary forces in Mexico and some – though not all – eventually became admirers of the new Mexican revolutionary government that emerged in 1920. So, this is a collective biography of the small groups of people who in these years worked individually or together in Mexico to turn the revolution in the direction they desired. It is also a history of these individuals and groups who tested the theories and the strategies of their organisations in the great laboratory of the Mexican Revolution providing us with a remarkable record of experiments in internationalism, some of the reformist variety and others of the revolutionary sort.

Why focus on the Americans when there were others from Latin America, Europe, and Asia who were also involved in the Mexican Revolution in those years in one way or another? (The first draft of this book had chapters dealing with many South Americans who were touched by, linked intellectually to, or somehow associated with the Mexican Revolution: José Ingenieros, Manuel Ugarte, Victor Raúl Haya de la Torre, José Carlos Mariateguí, and Julio Antonio Mella.) While it is true that other foreigners also either participated or took a great interest in the Mexican Revolution, the relationship between the Americans and Mexicans was most important for several reasons. First, because the two countries are contiguous, travel by railroad or steamship was easy after 1900, and Americans tended to go to Mexico first for work in the mines and oil fields and later to evade the draft and the war. At the same time Mexicans went to the United States to work in the fields or the mines or were forced into exile to escape the revolution or political enemies. The migrations in both directions continued throughout this period of the first quarter of the twentieth century and the economic, political, social, and cultural influences were significant. Even when other foreigners were present in Mexico, they often worked closely with the numerically dominant Americans, even though it is true that groups such as the Spaniards were large and influential, as were some of the Latin American groups.

I have divided the organisations of the Americans in Mexico into two groups operating in two different time periods and with fundamentally different methods. Part I deals with the first period, beginning around 1900 when, with the completion of the US and Mexican railroad systems and their connection at Laredo and later other points, Mexico became more fully a part of the US-dominated North American political economy, with industry encouraging and facilitating the movement of Americans and Mexicans to each other's countries, as the enormous US and other foreign investment transformed the Mexican economy while also deepening the social pressures within Mexico that would lead to the Mexican Revolution in 1910.[1]

The dramatic growth of industrial capitalism in the first two decades of the twentieth century had a tremendous impact on the society and politics of both countries. The end of the Civil War in the United States led to the victory of industrial capitalism and finance and the creation of what was virtually a new Constitution and a new state. In America, following the era of Robber Barons and political bossism, Progressives – upper- and middle-class reformers generally sharing the racial prejudices of American culture – were transforming the country from top to bottom, bringing greater government regulation, establishing more state intervention, and developing social programmes to lift up the masses of immigrants from Eastern and Southern Europe as well as Black people migrating from the South into northern cities. At about the same time in Mexico, Porfirio Díaz and his circle, *los científicos*, also established a stronger state that unified the country's provinces, attracted foreign investment from Europe and America, and began the modernisation of the country.

The expansion of American capitalism, linked to Europe, Latin America, and Asia, created a path of industry and commerce on which the world's expanding working class travelled, challenging capital as it went. With the opening of the

---

1 Hart 1989, p. 6.

twentieth century, new struggles for democracy and socialism swept Europe, as well as the Americas and Asia. Strikes spread across Europe and Russia, as they also broke out throughout the United States, while the dictatorship of Porfirio Díaz faced the first tremors of the coming revolution as anarchists led rebellions, workers participated massively in strikes in metal mining and in textiles, as liberal reformers began to agitate for political democracy.

Most of the first group of Americans to take an active political interest in Mexico became involved between 1900 and 1921 and were based in the US and usually directed their activity toward the US. While they mostly attempted to influence American public opinion, once the revolution broke out and then developed, they also attempted to influence the course of the revolution itself. The first group that I examine were the American Protestant missionaries influenced by the Social Gospel such as George B. Winson, Mary McOuat Wallace, and Samuel Guy Inman; they had been in Mexico but most left at the outbreak of the revolution in 1910, fleeing the violence. I then turn to the Socialist Party figures involved with Mexico – John Kenneth Turner, John Reed, and Eugene Debs. The Socialists first offered their support to the anarchists of the Mexican Liberal Party and later to the liberal Francisco Madero. I look too at the role of Samuel Gompers of the AFL and what we might call American labour imperialism. I also briefly discuss the Progressive journalist Lincoln Steffens before taking up the anarchists: Emma Goldman, William C. Owen, Voltairine de Cleyre. All of these people, who are discussed in Part I, investigated, wrote about, and interpreted events in Mexico, primarily with an eye to influencing American public opinion as well as pressuring the US government in an attempt to change its policies. While Turner and Reed actually went to Mexico to investigate conditions and report on them, they did not stay long, returning to write and publish their books. Turner and the Los Angeles chapter of the Socialist Party did support and aid Ricardo Flores Magón and the Mexican Liberal Party. Still, these Americans mostly operating in the US did not become directly involved in organising in Mexico.

Second, we have the groups of Americans who went to Mexico and worked in Mexico with Mexican leftists, workers, and social movements between 1921 and 1925. They are taken up in Part II. By 1917 things had changed dramatically. In Mexico, Venustiano Carranza's Constitutionalists were winning out over the Conventionists of Pancho Villa and Emiliano Zapata. The Russian February Revolution of 1917 overthrew the Tsar and made it possible for President Woodrow Wilson to lead the United States into the World War in April of 1917 on the side of the Triple Entente Alliance of Britain, France, and Russia. But then in Russia in October 1917 the Bolsheviks seized power and thrust it into the hands of the *soviets* or workers' councils and refused to continue the war.

It was in that context of the United States at war and revolutions roiling Russia and Mexico, that the first group of American socialist war resisters, known as 'slackers', crossed the border into Mexico, living there between April 1917 and the expulsion of most of them in 1921, among them Roberto Haberman, Linn A.E. Gale, Charles Francis Phillips, Eleanor Parker, Irwin Granich, Hendrik Glintenkamp, Herman Levine, and Evelyn Trent. Phillips became involved with the Indian nationalist M.N. Roy and the Russian Mikhail Borodin in the organisation of the Mexican Communist Party. Just as the first group of Americans were expelled, another group made up of Communists from the US arrived in Mexico, staying from 1921 until the departure of the last of them in 1927. In this group were the Italian American Louis Fraina (Lewis Corey), the Japanese Sen Katayama, and again Charles Francis Phillips. A little later came American Bertram Wolfe.

These two groups of Americans, unlike the earlier pre-1917 group, not only took up residence in Mexico but also worked there with other foreigners and with Mexican leftists, workers, and peasants to organise with peasant leagues, labour unions, feminist groups, and the Mexican Communist Party. Also, in this period we find John 'José' W. Kelley of the International Association of Machinists and the Farmer Labor Party active in Mexico, collaborating with the Mexican government and the unions that it supported.

While there was a good deal of overlap in the politics and activities of all of those who took an interest in Mexico, still their actual strategies and practices were distinctly different. Through the biographies of those involved, we look here at each political tendency's ideology, its concept of social and political action, its view of the role of the working class, its relationship to the capitalist class and other classes, its conception of how social change would take place, and we examine the ultimate goal to which each group aspired. We see here the strengths and weaknesses of these various leftist approaches and we have therefore an opportunity to draw lessons from them, with the caveat that times and circumstances change and the application of the lessons to another period brings its own specific challenges.

Each of the tendencies we examine here had its own ideology, its own organisational approach, its own strategy and often its own tactical repertoire applied during Mexico's revolutionary period. Let me sketch out first the main developments of the revolution and then briefly describe the different organisations and their approaches before plunging into the story in all of its complexity and detail.

1   The Mexican Revolution: A Brief Account

The Mexican Revolution is often dated from 1910 to 1920, the date when major violence had ended and a new government came to power, but it is also sometimes dated from 1910 to 1940, the latter being the year when the original goals of the revolution may be said to have been fulfilled, even if not to everyone's satisfaction. The principal goals were land reform, labour rights, and lay public education, all of which were incorporated in the Constitution of 1917, though not achieved until the 1930s. The Revolution and the following civil war were fought out to determine just how far the revolution would go in transforming the old order, at the centre of which were the questions of property and labour. The Mexican Revolution overthrew an economic order based on mining and haciendas and the government that represented those who owned them; it replaced that order and its government with a new state, one that, while authoritarian and capitalist, responded to a greater degree to the subaltern groups of the society.

Here is how it happened. Porfirio Díaz, the dictator of Mexico came to power in 1876. He and his inner circle of wealthy landowners and businessmen ruled the country in their own interest, taking land from the mestizo and indigenous peasantry to expand their haciendas. Most of the country's peasants were reduced to landless day labourers earning miserable wages. Díaz encouraged American, British, and French financiers and industrialists to invest in Mexico, and they did, modernising the mines, building railroads, and developing the petroleum industry. To maintain his power, Díaz used the national army, *los federales*, and his militia, *los rurales*, to suppress rebellions of indigenous people such as the Yaquis as well as putting down peasant uprisings and worker strikes. Díaz modernised Mexico at the cost of the nation's working people, exacerbating the already great economic inequalities. The result was that by the beginning of the twentieth century, Mexico had become a powder keg and all that was needed was a match to set it off.

In 1906, Ricardo Flores Magón and his anarchist Mexican Liberal Party, followers of the ideas of Mikhail Bakunin, carried out insurrections in an attempt to detonate a revolution. While the insurrections failed disastrously, they were accompanied by mass strikes at the Cananea copper mine and in the Río Blanco textile mills that threatened the ruling elite. The rebellion of 1906 was suppressed, but its reverberations continued to be felt for years. Just as the Russian Revolution of 1905 was the 'dress rehearsal' of the revolution of 1917, so too the 1906 insurrections and strikes proved to be a preparatory exercise for the Revolution of 1910.

The wealthy landlord and industrialist Francisco Madero initiated the Revolution of 1910 when he decided to challenge Díaz in the election scheduled for that year. Díaz imprisoned Madero, but the challenger escaped and called for a revolutionary uprising on 10 November 1910. Though Madero's campaign began with a call for political reform, it became a peasant revolution whose principal demand was agrarian reform, that is, the distribution of land to the peasants and indigenous people from whom it had been taken. Initially and rapidly successful in 1911, Madero's liberal revolution was overthrown within the year and Madero himself murdered by the counter-revolutionary Victoriano Huerta. But several regional revolutionary leaders – Venustiano Carranza, Pablo González, Francisco 'Pancho' Villa and Emiliano Zapata – rebelled against the new dictator and overthrew him in July 1914.

The revolution had been victorious twice, but now the revolutionary forces themselves divided into the wealthy state-builders, the Constitutionalists, led by Carranza and Álvaro Obregón, who were opposed by the plebian Conventionists led by Villa and Zapata. The Constitutionalists emerged victorious, Zapata was assassinated, and Villa retired to his ranch in Chihuahua, but then Carranza and Obregón fell out in what one might see as a struggle between the bourgeois and Jacobin wings of the revolution. After a brief contest, Obregón, the Jacobin, took charge while Carranza was assassinated. The victors of this last stage of the civil war, Obregón, Plutarco Elías Calles, and Adolfo de la Huerta – known as the Sonoran dynasty – began the construction of the new state. Obregón became president in 1920, but de la Huerta led a rebellion against the other two triumvirs. He failed and was crushed. Calles succeeded Obregón as president in 1924, and when the latter decided to run for president for a second time, he was assassinated in 1928. Calles would continue to be the power behind the throne until 1934, after the period under consideration here ends. He was succeeded by Lázaro Cárdenas, opening a new period that completed the nationalist revolution.

All of the Americans and other foreigners who attempted to intervene in and influence the Mexican Revolution in this period found themselves confronting a rising Mexican nationalist sentiment and a new nationalist state that was a political chameleon often taking on the colour of its surroundings. The new revolutionary government sometimes appeared to be extremely conservative and at other times reformist, Socialist, syndicalist, or even Communist. And many people were fooled, at least for a while. As one historian wrote of the new government, 'The conservative elements came to believe that there would be a return to the old time, and the radicals showed up at the national palace to run up the red and black flag'.[2] The revolution was in reality Bona-

---

2   Puente 1994, p. 75.

partist in character – that is a *caudillo*, a military man on a horse – Carranza and then Obregón – rising above the country's contending social classes.[3] No class proved strong enough to take power for itself – and the new government was particularly inclined to mimetic adaptations as it sought to keep each of the rival classes – peasants, workers, petite bourgeoisie and haute bourgeoisie – in a state of subordination.

At the same time, like some invasive species the new state thrust its roots down into the cities, towns and villages, into the factories, the *ranchos*, and the indigenous *ejidos*, and out of the soil of the popular classes came the new regime's caciques, spreading across the country like desert flowers after a rain. Or, to change metaphors, a pyramid of generals – often describing themselves as socialists and managing local political bosses – stood atop a vast base of impoverished peasants and workers whose constant agitation threatened at any moment to bring the whole structure down; and so, if one wished to change the new state, it became necessary to organise amongst those at the base of the pyramid. It was into this unstable situation that American and other foreign political and labour organisations attempted to insert themselves in order to influence the future direction of Mexico, of the Americas, and of the world.

2   The American Left Turns to Mexico, 1900–17

Before the Mexican Revolution broke out in 1910, Protestant missionaries from the United States had begun to take an interest in and express concern about the conditions of Mexican working people, and the ministers and lay workers would later support the liberal wing of the revolution led by Francisco Madero and then would back Carranza. American labour and left organisations such as the American Federation of Labor (AFL) and the Socialist Party of America (SPA) initially supported the Mexican Liberal Party (PLM) led by Ricardo Flores Magón. Socialist Party members in Los Angeles played a key role in building US opposition to the Mexican dictator Porfirio Díaz. The AFL and SPA backed the PLM because of the party's name, its initial reformist programme, and its early publications that suggested it was primarily a labour-left opponent of the dictator Díaz. As the PLM's anarchist politics became clearer and when a genuine liberal capitalist leadership appeared in the form of Francisco Madero, the US left, with the exception of the anarchists and the Industrial Workers of the World (IWW), virtually abandoned Flores Magón and the PLM and turned to

---

3   Aguilar Mora, 1982, *passim*.

Madero. After 1911 and certainly by 1914, the politics of both the US and the Mexican organisations and their projects had developed and become more distinct. The left, which had initially been united in its support for the revolution, divided into its constituent parts: Progressive and Socialist reformers, revolutionary syndicalists, and anarchists, and the Communists and the Farmer Labor Party. Each of these groups had a distinct vision, strategy, and practice of intervention in Mexico, each competing for the fulfilment of its policy. Let me summarise their various views.

The American Federation of Labor led by Samuel Gompers had, by the time of the Mexican Revolution, a 20-year history that made clear its acceptance of the capitalist system and its partnership with capital. Moreover, Gompers had thrown the AFL's political support to the Democratic Party and strongly backed Woodrow Wilson's vision and strategy in world affairs. Just as the United States government and its dollar diplomacy provided sword and shield for US investments, so Gompers and the AFL attempted to extend US-style, class-collaborationist labour unionism throughout Latin America. Gompers had already extended the US labour organisation to Canada and had carried his model to Puerto Rico. With the outbreak of the Mexican Revolution, he would work with the post-revolutionary Mexican government to extend his sort of unionism to Mexico as well, while also cooperating with the Mexican government and its loyal unions in the fight against anarchist, syndicalist, and later Communist labour organisations. In 1918, Gompers and Puerto Rican and Mexican allies created the Pan-American Federation of Labor with the goal of extending American business unionism to the entire hemisphere, from the Hudson Bay to Tierra del Fuego.

The Socialist Party of America, whose most prominent figure during the era of the Mexican Revolution was Eugene V. Debs, held the view that socialism was possible in the United States and could be achieved through a combination of political and economic action, that is, through elections and union organisation. These were the politics of the Second International and of its leading organisation, the German Social Democratic Party led by Karl Kautsky. At the same time, Debs and other SPA leaders believed, in accordance with social-democratic doctrine, that socialism was impossible in Mexico, which had not yet achieved a capitalist level of development. The task, therefore, was to support a political force that would bring capitalism and bourgeois democracy to Mexico, and that force was at first mistakenly identified as Ricardo Flores Magón and the Mexican Liberal Party, but then the SPA turned to suppot Francisco I. Madero's Democratic Party and later Venustiano Carranza's Constitutionalists.

The SPA's left wing, as exemplified by John Reed, identified with Mexican workers' and peasants' struggles from below and at first found their champion in Francisco 'Pancho' Villa, the brilliant military leader of the revolutionary armies of northern Mexico. Villa's army of miners, railroad workers, small ranchers, day labourers, and the drifters of the northern plains seemed to represent the Mexican incarnation of Marx's proletariat with little to lose but their chains. Reed and the SPA left wing, just emerging at that time, without a clear analysis, programme, or strategy, found its own yearning for a radical movement in Villa, just as those same radicals had found their American champions in the strikes of the Industrial Workers of the World. They ignored Villa's initial alliance with the capitalist state-builders like Madero and Carranza, his friendly relations with US mining companies, and his flirtation with the Wilson administration. They admired Villa romantically as the heroic leader of the mounted proletariat, sweeping across northern Mexico, a worker's movement, inchoate but class-conscious at its base. Reed went off to ride with them, to write about them, and to champion them.

The US anarchist movement, whose central figure was Emma Goldman, first supported the anarchist Mexican Liberal Party led by Ricardo Flores Magón and then the peasant movement in Morelos and the South of Mexico led by Emiliano Zapata. Goldman and friends had opened the anarchist offices in St. Louis, Missouri to Ricardo Flores Magón and other PLM leaders when they fled into exile. Somewhat later, other anarchists such as Voltairine de Cleyre and William C. Owen recognised the anti-working class and anti-peasant politics of Madero and Carranza and saw problems with Villa, while Zapata and his movement seemed to them to exemplify the revolutionary people organising autonomous producers' communities, the seeds of a future libertarian communist society. The anarchist analysis of Mexican society and politics, and especially of Carranza, proved to be far more insightful than that of the Socialists, though the anarchists completely misunderstood Zapata and the Morelos movement, projecting onto the traditionalist peasants and their conservative, Catholic agrarian community the anarchists' own libertarian communist ideology. In any case, the anarchists by and large proved to be unable to establish a strong connection to the Mexican movement, their intervention was limited largely to good will, small financial contributions, and a small-scale, armed anarchist foray.

The Industrial Workers of the World (IWW), a revolutionary syndicalist organisation that used on-the-job action and strikes to build industrial unions, was committed to organising both men and women workers of all nationalities and races, no matter what their work, with the ultimate goal of using the general strike to overthrow capitalism and usher in a socialist society. The IWW, whose members were known as Wobblies, organised immigrant factory workers and the armies of labourers, who mined metal, cut timber, harvested crops, and travelled North America on the vast railroad networks of Canada, the United States and Mexico. The iww reached Mexico even before the revolution and became strong in the period between 1914 and 1925. The American progressive journalist Lincoln Steffens wrote in December 1915, 'The iwws are getting control of labour here. That will be a big factor in the future of Mexico'.[4] While that was an exaggeration, wartime persecution in the US pushed more Wobblies, war resisters, draft dodgers, and leftists over the border by 1917. iww members, both Mexicans and Americans, then became the leadership of various groups of workers in Mexico with its strongest presence in the *Faja de Oro*, the oil-rich region on the Gulf Coast, the centre of which was the city of Tampico.

The iww's concentration on industrial workers to the exclusion of all else (in a society where 80 percent of the population lived by agriculture) and its opposition to political action in a nation in the midst of a political revolution meant that it had little ability to compete in the society at large with the dominant Mexican revolutionary nationalist parties or with the more wide-ranging anarchist organisations who also organised peasants, or later with the Communists with whom it competed for the industrial workers' loyalty. The iww could lead massive strikes in Tampico and organised in some mines in northern Mexico, but it was otherwise largely disconnected from Mexico's revolutionary upheaval.

3   The American Left, the Russian Revolution, and Mexico

The slaughter of World War I created around the world at first a movement of resistance and then a new revolutionary left.[5] Following the Russian October Revolution of 1917, the eyes of workers and leftists around the world turned toward the east.[6] The Bolshevik Party, later called the Communist Party, which had led the October Revolution, and the *soviets* or workers' councils which had formed the foundation of worker and peasant power, became mythic ideals – mythic because virtually no one had any idea what either 'Bolshevik' or *'soviet'* actually meant.[7] By 1919, however, the newly formed Communist International had sent Mikhail Borodin to Latin America and he made contact with US

---

4   Steffens 1938, vol. 1, p. 364.
5   Prezioso 2017, *passim*.
6   Ferro 1967, *passim*.
7   Serge 1984, p. 104.

and foreign activists in Mexico, sowing the first seeds of Communism in Latin America. The Communist International sent other organisers in the early 1920s and the small Mexican Communists Party soon established relations with leaders and activists among workers and peasants, but government repression, the rise of Mexican nationalism, and the weakness of the international meant that this revolutionary socialist tendency proved capable of establishing only a small, struggling Communist Party.

In the early 1920s, the Farmer Labor Party and the International Association of Machinists, which formed an important part of it, also made an intervention in Mexico. Some FLP activists saw the Mexican revolutionary government of Álvaro Obregón and Plutarco Elías Calles as a farmer-labour government in power. The identification with the new Mexican state led them to support the government and its efforts to subordinate the Mexican unions to the new revolutionary leadership. The FLP activists worked on both sides of the border, with the workers in Mexico to strengthen their unions and with unions in the United States to demand recognition and preferential treatment for the Mexican government. While the effort was brief, lasting only a couple of years, it demonstrated the Farmer Labor Party's tendency to look toward government to solve the problems of working people – even when that government tended toward populist authoritarianism and worked to suppress the left unions and worker movements. While the IAM organiser John 'José' Kelley was a dynamo of energy, still his small project does not compare in importance to the work of the early Communists. Yet the Communists would find much of their work largely swept away by the Mexican Revolution's nationalism.

By 1927, Russia had suffered a counter-revolution that rapidly overturned the institutions of workers' power, a process completed by 1937. Stalin became the dictator of Soviet Russia and the actual leader of the Communist International. Communist Party politics around the world became subordinated to the Stalinist ruling class's domestic and foreign policy. We do not deal here with the Stalinist Communist period, but the PCM's political vicissitudes, its constant twists and turns – from Third Period sectarianism and ultra-leftism, to the Popular Front alliance with bourgeois politicians, to the alliance with Hitler, to the return to the Popular Front once more – tended to make party building difficult.[8] In the late 1930s, the Communists' Popular Front policy led to their dual subordination, first, to Stalin and the Soviet Union, and second, to a lesser extent, to the Mexican government of Lázaro Cárdenas, though that did not protect the Communists from repression through the Cold War period of the

8   La Botz, 2018, *passim*.

1940s and 1950s. In the 1960s the Mexican Communists revived, turned toward Eurocommunism, that is, toward social democracy, and then in the 1980s its members euthanised the party and entered the reformist Party of the Democratic Revolution.

One might perhaps like to think that the US left's labour solidarity always tended to further the cause of workers' power and of the struggle for international socialism, that is, one might like to look at the labour left rather ecumenically and argue that everyone did their little bit to advance the cause. In fact, the various left organisations, divided on questions of strategy and end goals, could not collaborate and several of the US left's interventions in Mexico led to serious failures while others contributed to disasters, as you will read in the following pages in some detail. Ricardo Flores Magón's politically ill-conceived invasion of Baja California from the United States with the support of US-based IWWs, other leftists, and soldiers of fortune would prove a fiasco that destroyed his reputation and ruined the PLM organisation. Eugene Debs's and the Socialist Party's support for Madero and later for Carranza put them on the side of the new capitalist government in Mexico, even as that state fought and destroyed the plebian forces of Villa and Zapata and the leftist labour unions. American anarchists supported their co-thinkers in Mexico but found that Mexican anarchists had succumbed to rising Mexican nationalism. And while the IWW led massive strikes on the Gulf Coast for a few years, the unions loyal to the new Mexican government ultimately won the battle for control of the working class in that period. The Farmer Labor Party, like the Socialists, put itself on the side of the Bonapartist regime in Mexico, an authoritarian capitalist state, even as that government worked to crush the anarchist and Communist left. Finally, the Communists of the early 1920s, though they represented a genuinely revolutionary socialist impulse, proved to be too small to have much of an impact and, despite their generally correct analysis of the developments, ultimately proved incapable of fully understanding and politically navigating the nationalist revolution that was underway all around it. Their support of the Obregón government during the de la Huerta rebellion failed to save the party and fundamentally compromised its principles. The American left had not always advanced the causes of democracy and socialism, but in any case, the weight of any or even all of the foreign leftist forces in Mexico, from the AFL to the Communists, was simply insignificant compared to the power of the enormous social and political Revolution that had thrust up the generals who now became presidents – sometimes calling themselves socialists – as they created a new capitalist state in Mexico.

Politics is always about vision and strategy. The key point for socialists is always the political independence of working-class movements from the capitalist class, and by the 1930s also from the bureaucratic Communist class. The failure to establish that principal of political independence either in the United States or in Mexico would inevitably lead to failure and sometimes to catastrophic failure for some groups. But politics is also about organisation and power, and small organisations, if they cannot grow quickly enough, become irrelevant to the tidal movements of history. The Socialist Party's left wing and the Communists came closest to the ideal of working-class political independence and to international labour solidarity, but the former remained undeveloped and trapped in the reformist Socialist Party, while the latter was in the 1920s simply too small and still too immature to have a significant impact. By the time the period we discuss here had ended, the Mexican Revolution had produced a new nationalist government with which the left could not compete, while the Russian Revolution had created a new ruling class that used the Communist International to serve itself and the Soviet Union's national goals.

PART 1

The American Left Supports the Mexican Revolution

∴

American Protestantism, Progressivism, and the Mexican Revolution

Protestant Christianity and the American Progressive movement are two of the most important and often neglected influences of the left on the Mexican Revolution. Starting in the 1870s, missionaries carried Protestantism to Mexico while US government officials, diplomats, and businessmen in Mexico provided the first contacts with American Progressivism. Mexican exiles in the United States were also exposed to Protestant and Progressive America during the period from 1900 to 1920, and they absorbed the socio-political views and concepts that would later influence Mexico's revolutionary movement, its labour unions, and its leftists. We examine in this chapter how these two movements understood and attempted to influence Mexican society and US policy toward Mexico.

America was fundamentally a Protestant country, and even Catholics and Jews often found themselves protestanised, that is, acculturated and assimilated and finally transformed into modern individualists competing in the capitalist struggle and consuming in the capitalist market – even if they subsequently went on to become socialist collectivists. Protestantism in America played a large part in the development of secularism and in the creation of a democratic society, as well as in the development of the notion of individual rights, and a particular conception of humanism based on individual opportunity and self-fulfilment. Protestantism, particularly that strain of Protestantism that believed in human perfectibility,[1] drove American reform movements – abolition of slavery, women's rights, prison and insane asylum reform, abstention from the consumption of alcohol, workers' rights, urban reform, and socialism – also contributed to the rise of Progressivism.

Progressivism in the United States was an upper- and middle-class reform movement concerned with financial and corporate power and its abuse, with political bossism and its corruption, and with the state of the working class and particularly immigrants. These American bourgeois and petit-bourgeois reformers sought to use the capitalist state to solve their own economic problems of profitability, to break the populist power of party bosses (usually Demo-

---

1 Passmore 2000, Chapters 6 and 7.

crats but sometimes Republicans or Socialists), and to bring discipline to the working classes, in particular through Americanisation programmes aimed at the assimilation of Eastern and Southern European immigrants and blacks. Progressives advocated state intervention in and regulation of the capitalist economy, while at the centre of American Progressivism was the notion that capital and labour had to be partners in reforming the political and economic system.[2]

Protestantism and Progressivism dominated late nineteenth- and early twentieth-century American life and they formed the social, cultural, and intellectual context for the rise of the progressive, labour, and socialist left in the United States during the period under consideration here, from 1900 to 1925. Those two ideologies carried by missionaries and by businesspeople would also, though to a lesser degree, influence Mexican culture and Mexican leftists. The impact of both Protestantism and Progressivism was broad and yet quite significant, and at the same time it was in the end contradictory, since a reformed American government would still come into conflict with a reformed Mexican government led by nationalists who wanted to assert their country's sovereignty.[3]

One could argue that American imperialism carried Protestantism to Mexico, since, as John Mason Hart has noted, when American corporations invested in Mexico after 1870, so too did the American Protestant missionaries.[4] Yet at the same time, it was the Mexican anti-Catholic Liberal Party,[5] which believed in religious toleration as part of the process of establishing a democratic society, that encouraged the American missionaries. And leaders like liberal Mexican President Sebastián Lerdo de Tejada (in office 1872–76) welcomed and supported the Protestant missionaries in their efforts. When he became president in 1876, Porfirio Díaz continued the policy, even after he made peace and formed an alliance with the Catholic Church. The Liberals, who were admirers of nations like Great Britain and the United States, hoped that the Protestants' presence in Mexico 'would help to create a new national consciousness'.[6] And so it did, though it was not necessarily the consciousness that the Liberals initially hoped for.

---

2   On American Progressivism see: Hofstadter 1955; Croly 1909; Weinstein 1968; Kolko 1963; Sklar 1988; Williams 1966.

3   Ridge 2012, *passim*.

4   Hart 2002, p. 43.

5   This Mexican Liberal Party of the 1850s to 1870s should not be confused with another party of the same name led by Ricardo Flores Magón in the early twentieth century.

6   González Navarro 1994, vol. 2, p. 24.

Beginning in the 1870s, hundreds of American missionaries from the major Protestant denominations, from the various Bible societies, and from several sects as well went to Mexico – generally to the northern states – buying land, building churches, organising Sunday schools as well as primary and high schools, establishing presses and periodicals, and publishing millions of pieces of literature.[7] By 1913 one could find in Mexico Episcopalian, Presbyterians, Methodists, Baptists, Disciples of Christ, Friends (Quakers), and Adventists proselytising and leading congregations in prayer.[8] The missionaries' influence extended throughout the North of Mexico, from the US-Mexico border south to Zacatecas and between the Pacific Ocean and the Gulf of Mexico, that is, throughout the entire northern region known to geographers as Arid Mexico, though America Protestants could also be found proselytising in Veracruz and Mexico City. Many of the early Protestant churches and schools were built near the northern railroad lines and amidst the mining communities and ranches. By the time of the Mexican Revolution of 1910 there were still just 700 Protestant congregations and only 75,000 Protestants in Mexico[9] while the country had 15 million inhabitants most of whom were nominally Roman Catholic, though there were also many who practised indigenous religions. Nevertheless, while the numbers were small, the influence of the Protestants was very significant.

Who joined the Protestant churches in Mexico? The missionaries tended to have most success among 'certain social layers in transition: mine workers, textile industry workers, the hired hands of the agricultural sector, casual labourers, and some small rural landowners'.[10] The Protestant churches made little or no headway with the indigenous villages or peons on the haciendas, nor with the bourgeoisie or the oligarchs, but rather they were most successful with those 'who had precarious economic situations because of their link to capitalism and the nascent class of wage-earners'.[11] Some of the Protestant converts, coming as they did from the working class, participated in or even became leaders of the workers' mutual societies and labour unions.[12] The Prot-

---

7   Baldwin 1990, p. 24, Table 1; Winton 1913, pp. 182–3.

8   Baldwin 1990, p. 35, Table 2. In addition to the Protestants, members of the Church of Jesus Christ of Latter Day Saints, went to Mexico as colonisers, buying land and establishing Mormon communities. Ludlow 1992. The Mormons, however, did not carry the same social values as the Protestants.

9   Baldwin 1990, pp. 58 and 87.

10   Bastian 1993, p. 15.

11   Ibid.

12   Bastian 1993, pp. 63–73.

estant missionaries' activities often anticipated and later paralleled those of the various labour and left organisations that followed.

The first Protestant missionaries who went to Mexico in the 1870s and 1880s tended to be quite conservative. They had no criticisms of the dictatorship of Porfirio Díaz, the president whose government tolerated and even encouraged them. Indeed, they expressed their approval of Díaz who kept order and put down the occasional rebellion. One is struck in reading the letters of the earliest missionaries by their apparent lack of interest in Mexico's situation; they express no concern about the lack of political democracy or the atrocious social conditions. Their letters deal almost solely with buying land, building churches, and proselytising. If they mention conversations with people in Mexico, they are always with other Americans or wealthy Mexicans. Yet even in those early years the missionaries introduced into Mexico elements that had not existed in Mexico before and that had an impact, such as the women's missionary organisations, schools that taught the poor how to read and write, and later hospitals that treated patients even from the lower classes.[13]

After 1900, however, American Protestantism in the United State became profoundly social, political, and reformist. Some of the Protestant churches of the United States in the late nineteenth and early twentieth century had in response to the savage capitalism of the Gilded Age broken with the laissez-faire economic model and criticised the American plutocracy. They developed a new theology with economic and political implications called the Social Gospel.[14] The great railroad strike of 1877 and other industrial conflicts, the growth of the cities and of the sweatshops, and the widening gulf between rich and poor led Protestant pastors and theologians to argue that the church had to play a role not only in saving souls but also in solving these problems. While the pastors preached the new morality, the institutional church had to provide social services for the poor.[15] Pastors, lay leaders, and entire congregations took up 'the social question', that is, the issue of the inequality of wealth and poverty and the state of the working class and the poor in America. Washington Gladden, a Congregationalist pastor and one of the early advocates of the Social Gospel, wrote in 1908, for example:

> The redemption of the social order is, then, the problem now before us. Can it be accomplished? President [Theodore] Roosevelt thinks that it

---

13   Ada M.C. Drees 1913, *passim.*
14   Hopkins 1940, *passim.*
15   Degler 1940, pp. 338–51.

can, and those who stand with him and support him assume that the existing competitive régime can be moralised and made to represent the interests of equity and fair dealing. If this can be done, nothing more is needed. If it cannot be done, the existing régime must make way for something better. The conviction that it can be done is finding expression just now in the vigorous efforts that are being made to amend and strengthen the laws which restrain plunderers and oppressors, so that opportunities may be equalised and the paths to success be kept open for men of all ranks and capacities. This is simple justice, and for this the church of God must stand with all the might of her influence.[16]

This Christian minister's statement – that 'If it cannot be done, the existing régime must make way for something better' – represented a new development in American Protestantism. Gladden then expatiated on the role that the Christian church – that is the Protestant church – has to play in establishing racial equality, in bringing about economic justice, in ending political corruption, and in inaugurating an era of world peace. Such notions of social reform, once transported by the missionaries to Mexico, found a ready audience among many during the era of the Porfirian dictatorship.

Walter Rauschenbusch, the Baptist pastor and theologian, wrote one of the classic theological texts of the Social Gospel, *The Social Principles of Jesus* published in 1917. More radical than Gladden, Rauschenbusch went further; he argued that it might be necessary to overturn the political and economic elite. In one passage he wrote:

Every demand of God for righteousness in the history of Israel had been resisted by those in power. What title, then, did they have to the rights they claimed? Unless they fulfilled the function of true leaders, why should they not be put out of power and brought to justice?[17]

Rauschenbusch could certainly be interpreted here as calling for the overthrow of the existing economic and political leadership of the country who had enriched themselves at the expense of the people. And indeed, he was. While this was not actually a call for class struggle and revolution, it was a powerful demand for profound reform. The Protestant Social Gospel of the early twentieth century called upon Christians to stand up against oppression

---

16   Gladden 1908, see Chapter VII.
17   Rauschenbusch 1917, p. 102.

and exploitation, to stand with working people and the poor, and to take up what Rauschenbusch called a 'revolutionary mission to society'.[18] So, in the early years of the twentieth century, Christian ministers in Mexico carried with them this new theology, which dominated the principal Protestant denominations of the era.

While Gladden and Rauschenbusch and the Christian socialists were not translated into Spanish at the time, no doubt many of the Protestant ministers who went to Mexico had studied Gladden and Rauschenbusch and other such Social Gospel theologians in the seminary. With these ideas so important in the Protestant churches in the United States in the period from 1900 to the 1920s, the Social Gospel principles were also carried to Mexico. This new Protestantism tended to become a civic religion that carried with it something that resembled a social and political programme which included public education, improvement in the lives of workers, respect for individual rights and human rights, the notion of the equality of women, and, of course, temperance, along with the famous Protestant work ethic, and also an end to corruption in politics, but above all it expressed a concern for the well-being of society as a whole, and especially the downtrodden and the poor.[19] There had also developed in the United States out of this Social Gospel a Christian socialist movement.[20] Christian socialists supported the unions, their strikes and boycott, called for social reforms and even socialism, and some Christian socialist ministers and lay people joined the Socialist Party.

Missionaries, consciously or unconsciously, actively or passively, brought the Social Gospel to Mexico.[21] Historian John Mason Hart notes in *Revolutionary Mexico: The Coming and Process of the Mexican Revolution* that, 'In the late 1890s deepening workers' unrest led to increasingly frequent strikes, sometimes linked to radical Protestantism. The violence at Cananea and Río Blanco began with Protestant anti-Catholicism, secular humanism, and PLM [Mexican Liberal Party] anarchism in the same meeting halls.'[22]

While there is no doubt that some of the missionaries shared the view of US political leaders and American corporate executives that the United States, racially superior, politically more progressive, and technologically more advanced, should guide Mexican development,[23] at the same time the mis-

---

18   Rauschenbusch 1917, p. 185.
19   Bastian 1993, pp. 303–15.
20   Weinstein, 1967, pp. 19–23.
21   Bastian 1993, p. 158.
22   Hart 1987, p. 357.
23   González 2004, pp. 94–6.

sionaries' Protestant theology also carried other ideals and values that would influence Mexico's emerging nationalist ideology. We see the impact of this new theology on the missionaries who had worked in Mexico and the education being given by the churches and Bible societies to those planning to work in Mexico. We have, for example, George B. Winton's *Mexico To-Day: Social, Political, and Religious Conditions* which was published in 1913, a few years into the Mexican Revolution, as part of the Forward Mission Study Courses of the Missionary Education Movement, a book intended to be used in the education of missionaries. Winton makes it clear in the preface to the book that he places himself on the side of the Mexican Revolution (at the time he was writing the book, that is the Madero revolution):

> The Mexican people are engaged in a struggle for freedom. Political independence has been achieved; liberal freedom of conscience is at last realised; a liberal constitution guarantees human rights. But the burden of popular ignorance and of industrial helplessness has not yet been lifted. That load must be taken off. It has grown insufferable. The paroxysms that are now shaking the country to its centre are but blind struggles after this liberty.[24]

Winton, exaggerating the actual success that had been achieved, sees the Mexican Revolution as part of a global movement for democracy, writing, 'The day of government by the people, the plain people, the common people is dawning in all the world'.[25] He calls on Americans to help Mexico:

> Mexico needs help, especially the help of her nearest neighbours to the north. To know her condition, to sympathise, to lend a hand in the work of education and in the spread of the true religion, is far better than to criticise and to threaten her with armed intervention.[26]

Winton went on to provide a comprehensive critical analysis of Mexico. While he condemned the Aztecs, the Spanish, and the French for their violent conquests, Winton justified the American depredations – the incorporation of Texas into the United States and the US-Mexico War – and even found some merit in Porfirio Díaz's long, dictatorial reign, but he is also a sharp critic of

---

24   Winton 1913, p. ix.
25   Winton 1913, p. 26.
26   Winton 1913, pp. ix–x.

Mexico's political, economic, and social conditions at the time that he was writing. While finding virtue in some Spanish landlords who could sometimes be kind, he goes on to criticise the system of debt peonage:

> On the great plantations conditions prevailed almost identical with those in the south of our own country during slavery days. The peons of a hacienda were enslaved in a somewhat worse way than if they had been bought as chattels. Chattel slaves are always well cared for because they are actual property. Peonage was a kind of industrial slavery in which it was the man's labour that was pawned and not his person. Hence the master, unless he was a man of heart, felt no responsibility for the well-being, physical or moral, of the hand on his place. This manner of life went on let it not be forgotten, for three hundred years. No wonder that it scored furrows in the social fabric of Mexico so deep that a hundred years of freedom and of industrial improvement have not wiped them all out.[27]

To grasp this issue was, of course, to grasp the central question of the Mexican Revolution and to place oneself on the side of the revolutionaries against the *ancien régime*.

Winton also took up the question of the despoliation of the Indians' communal land.

> In recent years lumber and mining syndicates, many of them involving foreign capital, have fought, and by various means have obtained, possession of much land which had been community holdings of Indian villages ... In many places the poor Indians have been cheated and exploited. This form of abuse greatly discredited the later years of the Díaz administration.[28]

Landlords, both the historic caste of *criollos*, people of Spanish descent, and foreign corporations, had been responsible for grabbing up the land of mestizo and indigenous peasants. One should remember that Winton is writing to a public made up of American and Canadian missionaries, many from the American Midwest, not long after the populist movement of farmers had challenged bankers, railroads, and grain elevator operators. Many of his American readers could well understand and sympathise with the farmers' grievances that he described.

---

27   Winton 1913, pp. 28–9.
28   Winton 1913, pp. 67–8.

Winton also provides long descriptions of the deplorable conditions of Mexican women of the working classes. Women were considered and treated as 'inferiors', they spent their lives as 'domestic drudges', which kept them ignorant. Women of the poorer classes were 'slaves to the most cumbersome form of housework', particularly the grinding of corn for tortillas.[29] Many of his readers, of course, would be women planning to do missionary work in Latin America and anxious to organise women's groups in the Protestant churches; and certainly, they must have been moved to sympathy by his depictions.

Of course, as a Protestant, Winton also provides a devastating description of the Mexican Catholic Church: preoccupied with wealth and politics, corrupt and immoral, idolatrous and ultimately not really Christian, as well as holding the Catholic Church largely responsible for keeping the country in ignorance and poverty.[30] With these descriptions of land, labour, and the Catholic Church, Winton provides his Protestant missionary readership with an understandable reason and a justification for the Mexican Revolution. His arguments suggest that the American and Canadian people should support the Mexican people as they struggle for a more just society.

Winton saw what had happened in Mexico as what historians would later call 'a revolution of rising expectations'.

> The very improvement in the economic conditions of the labouring classes made the people restless. For centuries they had expected nothing and had been resigned in a dull way to their hard lot. Now at last better things began to seem possible. Wages had risen .... They began to question and to investigate. It seemed to them especially inexplicable that a few men should have a great deal more land than they need or could improve, while others by the score were at hand, wanting land, ready to till it, but unable to get hold of it. Equally puzzling was the difference when they began to note between the proportionate burden of taxation borne by the rich and the poor. The poor man was taxed heavily, while the rich man lightly.[31]

Winton also presented to his readers the intellectual, social, and political excitement of the revolution, the publication of newspapers with various political perspectives, the discussions in their pages, as well as the development of a variety of organisations. He describes in particular the workers' experience:

29   Winton 1913, pp. 133–9.
30   Winton 1913, pp. 81–111.
31   Winton 1913, pp. 58–9.

Modern factories of many kinds have been established in different sections of the country and the working people are going through various stages of adjustment to their new conditions, including the organization of labour unions, of mutual benefit societies, and like agencies. This effort at coöperation and organization has been a most wholesome influence.[32]

As a result, workers had won higher wages, better living conditions, and 'time and spirit' for social activities.

Winton gives the flavour, the exhilaration of the workers' experience, and the personal as well as the social value of such worker self-organisation:

The various social organizations – labor unions, mutual insurance societies, debating clubs, masonic and other lodges – have had stormy careers. Not seldom they have completely wrecked on the rock of disagreements among their members. But the discipline of trying to adjust themselves to the demands of such social experiments, the effort at self-command and at mutual surrender for a common cause, has been of incalculable value to the people. It has helped to teach them that if a man is to be a sovereign citizen, he must begin my mastery of himself ... It has set the common good in its true light as more important than the welfare or gratification of any individual – as essential even to the welfare of each as well as all.[33]

The political and intellectual transformation then taking place in Mexico could be partly attributed to the Protestant church with its schools and its women's organisations, and it also rebounded to those same churches. As Winton writes,

The recent political disturbances have been distinctively popular movements – excepting, of course, the coup of Díaz and Huerta against Madero. They have profoundly stirred popular thought. They put a premium on reading and intelligence. One result is that mission schools are crowded as never before.[34]

Winton encouraged missionaries to seize the moment:

---

32   Winton 1913, pp. 156–7.
33   Winton 1913, pp. 157–8.
34   Winton 1913, p. 168.

> The long submerged and disregarded common people of Mexico are com-
> ing to a consciousness of themselves. They are longing for light and help.
> Never before was the way so wide open for the Christian teacher.[35]

Winton opposed military intervention in Mexico – 'That would be terrible, disastrous' – and called instead upon the Protestant churches to send 'to our needy
neighbour teachers, evangelists, friends'.[36]

Other missionaries developed similar analyses. A few years later, in November of 1916, Mary McOuat Wallace, who had been a missionary in Mexico, wrote
an article titled 'Misunderstood Mexico' for the *Bulletin* of the Presbyterian
Church's Board of Missions. Wallace went further than Winton in her support
for the Mexican Revolution. Her analysis of the Mexican situation was more
critical of US imperialism, sympathised with revolutionary general Francisco
'Pancho' Villa, and praised Gen. Venustiano Carranza, then claiming the title of
President of Mexico.

Wallace's critique of both European and US imperialism was succinct and
incisive:

> Anyone who understands the land and the people at all must confess that
> Mexico has been crushed, oppressed and miserably treated since the days
> of Cortez. Spain, France and the United States of America have each given
> her a whack in his own brutal way and for his own ungodly gains. Soldiers
> of fortune of many nations have gone to Mexico to exploit her for their
> own selfish ends, taking all they could get, and giving, or leaving, little in
> return. They have not even left an impress of good manners or good mor-
> als or pleasant memories.

> Not long ago, Mexico was nearly as large as the United States. Little by
> little (the Mexicans say *poco a poco*) slices have been carved off. Califor-
> nia and Texas, Colorado and Utah, Nevada and Oklahoma, New Mexico
> and Arizona and once upon a time, quite a chunk of Wyoming and Kan-
> sas belonged to Mexico.[37]

No wonder, wrote Wallace, that Mexicans were suspicious when General Pershing and his troops crossed the Mexican border supposedly to find and capture
Pancho Villa.

---

35   Winton 1913, p. 170.
36   Winton 1913, p. 172.
37   Wallace 1916, p. 1.

She argued paternalistically and sententiously for assistance to Mexico, writing:

> Do we remember that we are in the best sense Mexico's keeper? Do we feel that it is a waste of time to help our nearest neighbours? Is our faith in Mexico and her oppressed masses so strong that it is contagious, or is it weak and ineffective? Do we believe that all men, even Mexican peons, were created free and equal? Or do we in unholy self-conceit think our own dear baby worth six of Mexico's less favored little ones but still precious in His sight?[38]

Wallace warned that if American Protestants did not help Mexico, then the violence of Mexico might spill across the Rio Grande River into the United States.

In her pamphlet, the missionary praised the role that Protestants were playing in the revolutionary government in Mexico:

> Gen. Carranza is bitterly opposed to the Roman Catholic Church which has held sway in his country for three centuries. We do not approve of bitterness in anything, least of all in religion, but it is *his* country, *his* church, *his* people, all of which he understands and knows through and through, far better than we can ever hope to know them. Whatever mistakes Carranza is making, he shows most excellent judgment in his choice of men for prominent political positions. A number of these men are Protestants, not in name only, but are leading earnest, active, Christian lives. True democracy and Protestant Christianity go hand in hand. Carranza is working for a democracy and Mexico is bound to have Protestant Christianity when she becomes a true democracy.[39]

Wallace then went on to write that Carranza's Secretary of Education was a Protestant and to mention several other Protestants in leadership positions in the state governments, most of them heads of education departments or superintendents of schools. She concluded that discussion writing, 'There are scores of Protestants who are serving their country in various capacities, and General Carranza certainly knows a good man when he sees him, be he Catholic or Protestant. It seems as if President Carranza must come out right when he has so many good men back of him'.[40]

---

38 Wallace 1916, p. 2.
39 Wallace 1916, p. 3.
40 Wallace 1916, p. 4.

By 1919, at least some in the American Protestant establishment had not only become supporters of the Mexican Revolution sympathetic to Carranza's Constitutionalists, but virtual publicists for Carranza, most important among them, Samuel Guy Inman. Inman, who would become famous as a defender of Mexico's liberal revolution, had been born and raised on a farm in Trinity, Texas and when a young man went off to study at Texas Christian University. In 1902 he took a position as a social worker with the Disciples of Christ Church in New York City, spending three years working in the tenements of lower Manhattan while also earning a BA at Columbia University.

The Disciples of Christ then sent him as a missionary to work in Monterrey, Mexico, then known as the Chicago of Mexico because of its heavy industry. Later he moved to Piedras Negras, Coahuila, on the border just across from Eagle Pass, Texas; there he established the People's Institute.[41] An article in the *Bulletin* of the Pan-American Union described it: 'The People's Institute is unique among Mexican institutions. It combines the work of the social settlement, the public library, the Charities Organization Society, the Society for the Prevention of Cruelty to Animals, and all the other benevolent, educational, and reform organisations of the ordinary American city'.[42] At Inman's institute Protestantism and Progressivism came together to promote a radical transformation of Mexico. Piedras Negras was also the headquarters of General and President Venustiano Carranza, the leader of the Constitutionalist forces during the last years of the Mexican Revolution, providing Inman opportunities to meet and talk with the revolutionary chief.[43]

In 1915, Inman accepted the position of chief executive of the Committee for Cooperation in Latin America, an organisation representing thirty American and Canadian Protestant church agencies. While conducting many tours of Latin American to meet with both Protestant missionaries and Latin American government officials, he also authored several books and became an acknowledged expert on Mexico as well as a popular writer and lecturer on US-Mexican relations. He undertook to defend the liberal wing of the Mexican Revolution led by Francisco Madero and then by Carranza, arguing for what today would be called a policy of engagement rather than military intervention. At US Senate hearings in 1919 organised by Senator Albert Bacon Fall who worked closely with Edward L. Doheny and other American oilmen of the Association of Producers of Oil in Mexico, Fall fought to defend US oil and mining interests, fre-

41   Woods 1964.
42   Inman 1919, p. 221.
43   Inman 1919, *passim*.

quently calling for US military intervention in Mexico. The main issue was that Carranza's government had adopted a new Constitution in 1917, Article 27 of which upheld Mexico's right to the country's subsoil, that is, its mineral rights. The hearing pitted Fall against Inman.[44] Inman appeared as the Progressive David standing up to Fall, the imperialist Goliath threatening the Mexican people.

As one historian writes, 'He [Inman] barely escaped a citation of contempt from the subcommittee, was almost accused of treason, was denounced as a propagandist for Carranza, criticised for being unfaithful in his duties to his Protestant church employers, and unfairly appraised by Fall as being ignorant of Mexican affairs'. Inman came out of the encounter scarred and bruised, but undaunted, and within a few months after the hearings he was to be morally vindicated by the discovery of illegal collusion between Fall and Doheny in American oil fields, the scandal known as Teapot Dome.[45]

Inman published his book *Intervention in Mexico* in 1919, but Doheny bought up virtually all copies, thus removing the book from circulation. Like Winton and Wallace before him, Inman criticised Mexico *ancien régime* based on the exploitation of landlords and the church, but also the avaricious foreign investors, writing:

> ... the Mexicans are an exploited people. The land baron and the priest have continued their unholy alliance from the days of the Conquistadores till the present, playing alternately the one into the hands of the other, to keep the people in ignorance, superstition, and debt, so that the exploitation by both *padre* and *amo* [priest and master], would be sure and easy. Foreign capitalists, with their immense concession have usually been willing to join in the system of exploitation.[46]

Inman argued that instead of decrying the chaos and violence in Mexico, 'It would seem, rather, that we ought to rejoice that the people have finally found the strength to protest against their wrong'.[47]

In *Intervention in Mexico* Inman argued that a genuine revolution had been carried out that had achieved free elections, the liberation of the peons, improved conditions for skilled workers, brought some reform to the Catholic

44   Woods 1964.
45   Woods 1964.
46   Inman 1919, pp. 44–5.
47   Inman 1919, p. 45.

Church, and established a more representative government. He contended that the people and the government of the United States should recognise that, 'There has recently been a real social revolution in Mexico, and there can be no turning back'. He asserted that, 'The time for armed intervention has passed, if it has ever been'. So, argued Inman, 'our Government should back up the Carranza Government in a strong, consistent, continuous way, aiding it in securing necessary funds for rehabilitation, for larger educational development, for the pursuit of bandits, and for strengthening the general program which the Carranza government has outlined for the great problem of reconstruction'.[48]

Inman believed that intervention would be both wrong and pointless because, 'This is a question not of stopping a fight, but of solving a problem. It is not a revolution to be crushed, but an evolution to be guided'. He believed that the natural guide for the Mexican Revolution's new government was the United States government of Woodrow Wilson.[49] Inman, like his Protestant missionary predecessors in Mexico, believed that guidance should be given primarily through education, including vocational education. He pointed for example at Henry Ford who was preparing to open auto and tractor plants in Mexico and had already begun training Mexicans in Detroit. In fact, Buick opened a factory in Mexico in 1921 and Ford followed in 1925. American Protestantism and capitalism, thought Inman, would lift up Mexico and its people.

During the period between 1915 and 1919, the American Protestant churches had generally come to support for the Constitutionalists rather than the plebeian Conventionists Emiliano Zapata and Francisco 'Pancho' Villa. The Protestants had come to the same position as that of the AFL and the Socialist Party. The Progressive movement, from its corporate and political elements to its labour and left groups came to the common view that Carranza and the Constitutionalists with their desire for a reformed political system and a more progressive capitalism represented the best chance for both Mexico and the United States.

Inman had wanted the United States to back Carranza, but by 1920 it was already too late for that, as he had been assassinated and Álvaro Obregón had become president. With that the most violent phase of the Mexican Revolution came to an end and so too did the prominent political role of American missionaries in Mexico. Yet one could say that many of the goals of the progressive Protestant missionaries had been fulfilled: The Díaz dictatorship had been overthrown by the liberal Madero-Carranza revolution. Under Obregón

---

48   Inman 1919, pp. 60–1.
49   Inman 1919, pp. 204–10.

Mexico and the United States reached a modus vivendi, even if the United States had not achieved the tutelary partnership that the Protestants had hoped for.

While it may be true that American imperialism brought Protestantism to Mexico, it is also true that Protestantism in Mexico contributed to the development of a progressive ideology that was often both radical and democratic. Or put another way, American imperialism, at least in Mexico at that time, whether intentionally or not, also tended to promote both corporate capitalism and social reform. The Protestant missionaries of the late nineteenth century brought to Mexico a set of values that laid the basis for what we might call *a pre-revolutionary cultural and intellectual transformation*, that is the development of a set of ideas, beliefs, and sentiments that contributed to the construction of what became the Mexican nationalist revolutionary ideology. Those values included the idea of representative government, of the regulatory state, of equality before the law, of the equality of women, of the importance of education, of the rights of unions and workers, and of the importance of abstaining from the consumption of alcohol. The Protestant church was for many men and women in northern Mexico often the first step to the left, the first move for them personally toward becoming revolutionary leaders. Many who first took up the Bible later took up the gun.

When the revolution broke out then, first in the Magonista insurrections of 1906 and then more seriously in the mass uprising of the Maderista revolution in 1910, it is not surprising that the Protestant churches in Mexico by and large rallied to the revolution. And many individual Mexican Protestants entered the ranks of the revolutionary organisations. The inner circle of the Mexican Liberal Party (PLM), led by Ricardo Flores Magón, was anarchist and atheist, but a good number of its sympathisers had been Protestants, while Francisco I. Madero's liberal programme attracted many more Protestants.[50] Carranza too attracted Protestants to his banner. There was no such thing in southern Mexico, where Emiliano Zapata's Revolutionary Army of the South was made up of famously pious Catholic soldier-peasants who wore cards bearing images of the Virgin of Guadalupe on their *sombreros*. But after all the factional battles were over and the dead buried, it was the Sonoran dynasty of the North, where Protestantism had been a crucial influence, that ultimately won the Mexican Revolution and took power.

---

50   Bastian 1993, pp. 234–5.

1   America's Model of Modernisation

During and after the US Civil War (1861–65), in which the industrial capitalist North defeated the slave plantation economy of the South, American capitalism underwent a tremendous expansion: a national railroad network was constructed, industrial centres in the Great Lakes region expanded enormously, immigrants from Europe populated the expanding cities of the East Coast and the Midwest, and the great 'Robber Barons' of industry and banking created a new aristocracy that could afford to buy the Congress and put in place presidents and cabinet secretaries who represented their interests. The Pennsylvania Railroad developed the bureaucratic structure that became the organisational model for hundreds of other corporations, while Frederick W. Taylor introduced 'scientific management' of the workforce with the goal of greater efficiency and productivity, and, naturally, greater profits.[51] 'The incorporation of America', as one author called it, led to the rise of a new middle class of corporate executives, managers, and technicians, while at the same time transforming and subordinating the old middle class of lawyers, professors and religious ministers. The rise of the corporation affected every aspect of American society and culture.[52]

One result of all of this was the rise of Progressivism, a flexible ideology held by upper- and middle-class reformers who hoped to regulate capitalism and reform politics so as to dampen the excesses threatening to divide and disrupt the society and to jeopardize profit-making, above all the conflicts between labour and capital. While it was the Robber Barons who first drove the economic invasion of Mexico, by the turn of the century the corporate managers in Mexico had been touched by the Progressive ideals of efficiency and uplift. The scientific managers would provide the efficiency with their machines and the uplift, that is, the education and training of the working class, made up of the immigrants in America and the peons in Mexico. Some thought they could not only make themselves rich by investing in Mexico, but also modernise Mexico, improve its people, and make their lives better.

During this period before the Revolution, Mexicans' attitudes toward the United States were ambivalent: wary but also welcoming. Since Mexico's defeat in the US-Mexican War of 1846–48 and the loss of half of the nation's territory to the United States, Mexicans were well aware of the power of the United States and the danger of US expansionism. Mexican intellectuals, entrepreneurs, and

---

51   Haber 1964, *passim.*
52   Trachtenberg 1962, *passim.*

political leaders saw two alternatives: either to establish a secure, dependent relationship or carry out an economic development that would make their country more powerful and better able to defend itself.[53] Under Porfirio Díaz, the country would do both, because renegotiating Mexico's dependency and carrying out industrialisation, it turned out, were part of the same process. Díaz attempted to prevent further depredations by the United States by also inviting British and French capitalists to invest in Mexico, hoping that way to play off one imperial power against the other. The United States, however, was the closest, was growing rapidly and overtaking Great Britain as the greatest productive power on the planet, and it soon established vast economic interests in the country to the south.

By the 1890s, American companies had invested hundreds of millions of dollars in Mexico in a variety of industries: mining, railroads, oil, agriculture, and lumber.[54] Tens of thousands of Americans, the best estimate is 40,000, most of them engaged in business there as investors, managers, or skilled workers moved to and lived in Mexico City or Guadalajara, though others lived on ranches or in the company towns of the mining or oil industry.[55] Often American investors had Mexican partners, they certainly had Mexican lawyers, and they sometimes had to work with and pay off Mexican politicians, so a good number of upper-class Mexicans benefitted directly from American investment. US corporations also hired thousands of Mexican workers who benefitted in terms of jobs and better wages than in other sectors, even if many also came to feel mistreated and exploited. Some Mexicans of all social classes came to admire American industry and its technology. Much of Mexico's elite came to believe that the country was being uplifted and modernised by America's economic involvement.

While American capitalists invested in industry in Mexico: developing mines, building railroads, and drilling oil wells, their greatest economic influence, however, may have been in agriculture. American farmers in the arid Southwest had developed agricultural techniques that in the late nineteenth century had an important impact on Mexico. Mexican landowners in Sonora, just across the border from Arizona, imported and appropriated modern agricultural methods that had first been developed in the United States and then by American companies in northern Mexico. These included the digging of canals for large-scale irrigation, the development of improved seeds, the establish-

---

53   Córdova 1975, p. 31.
54   Hart 2002, *passim*.
55   González 2004, p. 43.

ment of experimental agricultural stations, and increased farm mechanisation. Álvaro Obregón, future revolutionary general and then president of Mexico from 1920–24, was a garbanzo (chick pea) farmer in Sonora who applied these methods in his fields.[56] The Sonorans who ultimately emerged in the 1920s as the leading group of the Mexican Revolution saw their goal in large part as modernising Mexico along the lines that they had known in their home state and had first seen across the border in California and Arizona.

Mexicans also went to the United States during the first two decades of the twentieth century, mostly as refugees from the revolution and civil wars seeking shelter and then work. Eventually one million Mexicans emigrated to the United States in that period, among them a good number of revolutionary exiles. Many crossed over into Texas or California, like Ricardo and Enrique Magón who set up their headquarters in St. Louis, Missouri, and later in Los Angeles, California, others travelled on revolutionary economic and diplomatic missions to New York City or Washington, D.C.[57] José Vasconcelos, wrote in his memoir *Ulises Criollo* that in the United States, 'Even though we were "greasers", we enjoyed greater human rights than in the country of Santa Anna'.[58] The United States – even while seen as imperialist – was for many Mexican Revolutionaries a model of democracy and freedom. Vasconcelos remembered crossing the border as a young revolutionary intellectual: 'We really entered, in those times, through the open door, the land of the free, the prototype of our dreams as democrats'.[59] Of course the United States ceased to be a sanctuary for the revolutionary followers of Ricardo Flores Magón when US President William Howard Taft and Mexican President Porfirio Díaz decided to join together to suppress the anarchist revolutionaries, imprisoning them on one side of the border or the other. Many others, however, found the United States hospitable.

While it is true that some Mexicans opposed the American bankers, industrialists, and skilled workers who invested in or worked in Mexico, seeing them as invaders who were taking over the nation's economy, many others admired or at least envied the Americans for their business acumen, their wealth and success, and for their methods and culture. As Alan Knight has written, 'The whole notion of a Mexican backlash against foreign penetration (whether on the part of exploited workers or a frustrated national bourgeoisie) is greatly exaggerated

---

56   Aguilar Camín 1995, pp. 132–6.
57   Pani 1936, pp. 268–98.
58   Vasconcelos 1993, vol. 1, p. 335.
59   Ibid. The Spanish reads: 'entrabamos de verdad, en aquellos tiempos y por puerta franca, *the land of the free*, prototipo de nuestros sueños de demócratas'.

and errs in regarding Mexican and foreign interests as locked into a zero-sum game'. Many Mexicans, especially those in the North, like the Madero family, 'sought to emulate American enterprise, not to liquidate it'.[60]

Mexico's revolutionary leaders also often appreciated the Americans. Francisco 'Pancho' Villa, for example, liked and got along well with the American mining companies and their American employees in Mexico.[61] While during the revolution and civil wars Mexicans murdered many Spanish and Chinese businessmen and foremen, they seldom killed Americans, perhaps because they feared the United States, but more likely because they did not see the Americans as their oppressors in the same way as they did the Spanish, or as unfair competitors as they did the Chinese. The Americans, however much Mexicans resented their economic domination and their racism, also represented models of industry and economic prosperity, potential economic allies, and a possible future for their country.

One can readily see why such ideas would be of particular interest and utility to the revolutionary builders of a new state. As Knight writes, in the Mexico of the dictator Porfirio Díaz, France too provided a model for Mexicans, but 'the closer, almost overwhelming example of the United States was more potent still'. He goes on:

> A somewhat fearful admiration of American economic might was common among educated Mexican, both Porfiristas and their opponents. In particular (I would argue) [Mexican] northerners, who were most directly familiar with the American model, sought to emulate it south of the border. Though this might involve a degree of nationalist resistance to American economic penetration, it involved yet more collaboration and the attempted inculcation of American values – hard work, thrift, hygiene, entrepreneurialism, initiative. Sometimes this emulation even implied the classic liaison between Protestantism and the progressive, capitalist ethos.[62]

Some Mexican workers were in the pre-revolutionary period anti-imperialist, but others often valued the American investment that had provided them with employment at wages much higher than they could make either in the rural countryside or in other industrial jobs. With the coming of the Mexican Revolu-

60   Knight 1986, vol. 1, p. 69.
61   Katz 1998, p. 71.
62   Knight 1986, vol. 1, p. 69.

tion in 1910, the outbreak of war in Europe in 1914, then the US entry into the war in 1917, relations between the Americans and the Mexicans became much more complicated. American politicians, financiers, and industrialists feared that Mexico would become an ally of Germany, especially after the Zimmerman telegram, the secret communiqué from the German to the Mexican government proposing that in exchange for a military alliance Mexico could reclaim its enormous lost territories in America. Then after the Bolshevik or Soviet Russian Revolution of 1917, American conservatives in government and business feared that Mexico might follow Russia in its expropriating and collectivising socialist experiment. This fear was strengthened when Mexico adopted its Constitution of 1917 with Article 27 that declared that Mexico owned the country's subsoil, thus threatening the oil and mining interests. All of this led to tremendous tensions between the two countries, yet the United States still remained a model for the new Mexican state-builders such as Carranza and Obregón.

2 American Labour Unionism

The American union movement arrived in Mexico in the early twentieth century and had an impact on workers similar to that of Progressivism's influence on government and business. Mexican workers adopted the organisational models, union strategies, and political theories that American leftists and labour unionists had imported into Mexico. The American brought to Mexico experiences from the Populist farmers' movement of the nineteenth century to the labour movement of the early twentieth century. Their reformist and revolutionary ideas became the subject of discussion not only in the ephemeral newspapers of the labour movement and the left, and not only among revolutionary nationalist and anarchists, Socialists and later Communists, but also among Mexican intellectuals such as anthropologist Manuel Gamio[63] and philosopher José Vasconcelos, as well as revolutionary generals such as Salvador Alvarado.

Vasconcelos, the philosopher who had joined the radical Convention of Zapata and Villa and later worked in the Obregón government even went so far as to suggest that American radicals had largely created the ideology of the new Mexican revolutionary government. There is a remarkable passage in Vasconcelos's *Ulises Criollo* about the influence of the American left and labour movement in Mexico that is worth quoting at length:

---

63 Gamio 1922, cited in Gamio 1975, pp. 40–6.

... even though we didn't realise it, the revolutionary ideology that per-
meated the country was a reflection of the union movement of America.
The agitators crossed the border coming down to provoke uprisings like
that at Cananea, repressed in turn by US soldiers, with the consent of
the Porfirian government. The doctrines that failed in the nation to the
north for lack of a propitious environment had a material repercussion in
oppressed and desperate Mexico. What we couldn't express ourselves in
a rally or in the newspaper took refuge in a conspiracy. The great majority of the secondary leaders of the rebellion since 1910 until today [1936]
have been men of rudimentary culture who have ingested the ideology
of the Industrial Workers of the World, first, and of the American Federation of Labor afterwards, when Calles promoted yellow [reformist] unionism, a simulated revolutionary labour unionism. American magazines
of progressive thought, daily newspapers full of information circulated in
Mexico and disseminated the stories of [Mexican] government abuses,
about which one couldn't talk in our own territory. While from the United
States, the refugees of previous rebellions, headed up by the Flores Magón
[brothers] and supported by Yankee workers' organizations, maintained
a violent campaign against the despotism of Díaz.[64]

Vasconcelos is one of the few Mexican intellectuals who credit the role of
Americans in contributing to the ideology of the Mexican Revolution and there
is much truth in his view. Surprisingly the major intellectual historians of the
Revolution, those concerned with the development of Mexico's revolutionary
and post-revolutionary thought generally omit entirely the influence of American Protestantism, Progressivism, and labour unionism.[65] We do not spend
more time on this issue here, since this large and complicated topic forms the
subject matter of the rest of this book.

3   American Progressivism in the Creation of the New State

The American Progressives' influence on Mexico is perhaps clearest after 1917,
as the violent period of the revolution began to come to a close and the

---

64   Vasconcelos 1993, vol. 1, p. 323.
65   Surprisingly, Arnaldo Córdova does not mention the impact of Protestantism in his magis-
      terial *La ideología de la Revolución Mexicana: La formación del Nuevo regimen* (1973); nor
      does Jesús Silva Herzog in *Trayectoría de la Revolución Mexicana y otros ensayos* (1994
      [1963]); nor Abelardo Villegas in *El pensamiento mexicano en el siglo XX* (1993).

new Sonoran dynasty commenced constructing a new state. When Salvador Alvarado, one of the Sonorans,[66] wrote his book *La Reconstrucción de México* (The Reconstruction of Mexico), a three-volume, 1,000-page plan for the future of his country, he drew heavily on American progressive thought. His book frequently looked to Americans such as Henry George, Booker T. Washington, and Woodrow Wilson for guidance. Alvarado called for a 'single tax on land' as described in the work of Henry George and Nicholas N. Young.[67] He called for 'state socialism' rather than revolutionary socialism, following the recommendations of the moderate American Socialists W.E. Walling and H.W. Laidler and he gave the example of the Non-Partisan League of North Dakota.[68]

To deal with the issue of Mexico's indigenous people, Alvarado looked to a variety of American influences. First, he mentions the teachers of Alaska who cared for and taught, who 'adopted and adapted' the indigenous people there.[69] Second, he took up the example of Booker T. Washington, the founder of the Tuskegee Institute, who educated American Negroes of both sexes.[70] And then he turned to Woodrow Wilson, the conservative critic of Reconstruction in America, who in his book *The History of the American People*, warned of the dangers of northern whites manipulating the Negroes, seeing it as a warning to Mexicans regarding the possible manipulation of their indigenous people.[71]

To deal with education problems, Alvarado recommended the George Peabody Teachers College of Nashville, Tennessee and the US government's vocational education programs; while to handle municipal issues, Alvarado suggested that Mexico look to the Galveston Plan for commission government. While all of this, of course, was developed more than a decade after the Revolution's first shots in 1906, and though not all of the Mexican revolutionaries shared Alvarado's enthusiasm for the Americans' example, still his writings demonstrate that American Protestantism, Populism, and Progressivism had long had an influence on Mexican Revolutionaries, finding their fullest expression as the violent period of the revolution was winding down and ideas for the construction of a new state were needed.

The Mexican Revolution, a profoundly nationalist process and development, took place in a continuous interaction with American businesspeople, with the US government and US military, with American Protestants and Progressives,

---

66   Born in Sinaloa but raised in Sonora.
67   Alvarado 1985, vol. 1, p. 113, pp. 181–8, pp. 194–7, pp. 206–7.
68   Alvarado 1985, vol. 1, pp. 162–3.
69   Alvarado 1985, vol. 2, pp. 46–7.
70   Alvarado 1985, vol. 2, p. 50.
71   Alvarado 1985, vol. 2, pp. 54–5.

as well as with the left and the labour movement. The Protestant-Progressive *Weltanschauung*, that is, a modernist and developmentalist worldview, had a tremendous impact on Mexico. In the early stage of the revolution, it provided a political programme for the reform of the society, while after the revolution it provided a theory of the state as social arbitrator and regulator. In both stages, the idea of class collaboration was central, and the notion of the importance of the working class in establishing a social pact was also recognised. Without the Americans' Protestant and Progressive example, it is hard to imagine the modernising bourgeoisie of people like the Maderos and even harder to conceive of the Sonoran dynasty that took power in 1920. The Protestant missionaries and the Progressive businesspeople and professionals did not ride with the revolution, but they inspired some of reformist and revolutionary riders of the time. We return now to the beginnings of the Mexican Revolution between 1900 and 1906 and to the first interaction between Mexican revolutionaries and the American left.

The Mexican Anarchists of the PLM and the American Left

The revolutionary movement in Mexico may be said to have begun with the furious reaction of a group of young Liberals to the pronouncements of Mexican Bishop Montes de Oca y Obregón, who, speaking in Paris in 1900, announced that, with the blessing of President Porfirio Díaz, the Catholic Church of Mexico was flourishing as never before. Moreover, said the prelate, the Reform Laws of the 1850s, which had led to the seizure of church property a half century before, were now just former fires reduced to ashes. The Bishop exaggerated, but his praise of Díaz enraged many of the young Liberals in Mexico's mostly upper- and middle-class intellectual milieu because it seemed to prove once and for all that Liberalism's historic values could not and would not be defended by Díaz.

The Church, symbol and, to a great extent, substance of the old order, whose wealth had been broken by Benito Juárez's Liberal Revolution in the 1850s, had made its peace with President Porfirio Díaz and gradually seen much of its authority restored. Though it had lost much of its land and wealth, Roman Catholicism had recouped its position as one of the most powerful institutions of Mexican society. The Catholic Church retained its grip on education; in the Liberals' view, promoting superstition, not science. The Liberals' dream of a government representing the educated classes and of a laissez-faire capitalist society based on competition had never really come to be; autocracy, crony capitalism, and monopoly flourished. The Liberals' Constitution of 1857, which had established a federal republic was being trampled underfoot and the Catholic Church's influence restored. The Liberal attempt to create a Republic and a free-market economy had led instead to Díaz's virtual monarchy, resting on an oligarchy, that in turn was based upon the domination of local political bosses over the country's small businessmen, workers, and peasants.

Mexico had become a dictatorship under the former liberal general, Porfirio Díaz who had held power since 1871, that is, for almost thirty years. Díaz and his inner circle of wealthy landowners, industrialists and politicians known as the Liberal Union or more commonly as *los científicos*, had gathered economic and political power into their own hands, dispossessing the Indians and peasants, exploiting the workers, while at the same time excluding many other large and small businessmen and virtually the entire middle class from power at all levels. Díaz and his clique had also encouraged investment by foreign capitalists from the United States, Great Britain, and France, who now dominated the railroads and mining. Díaz had turned the Congress into a rubber stamp, the state governors into his lieutenants, and his local political bosses dominated the cities and towns. His army, *los Federales*, and his rural police, *los Rurales*, had succeeded not only in suppressing rebellion but also in stifling criticism by shutting down the opposition press. While there was a growing but quiet opposition among a sector of the modernising bourgeoisie, especially in the North, the miserable and largely landless peasants who made up 85 percent of the population had no voice, and the new industrial working class making up another eight to 15 percent of the population had yet to succeed in organising itself. Finally, Díaz had made peace with the Church, which once again used the temple and the classroom to control the minds of the Mexican people. The Bishop was not only right that the Church had regained some of its power, said the young Liberals, but more important the Constitution of 1857 was dead, and Mexico's people had been politically disenfranchised and largely economically dispossessed.[1]

There had been many local rebellions against Díaz over the years, by Indian and peasant communities or sometimes by townsfolk, but in reaction to the Bishop's Paris speech, now for the first time in a generation there arose among a group of men (they were nearly all men at first) in an attempt to revive the historic Liberal positions and to organise a popular national movement for reform. Like all the other movements of the late nineteenth and early twentieth century, this new movement would invoke the Liberal Party tradition of Benito Juárez who had fought the Conservatives in the great Reform of the 1850s and then led the resistance to the French Intervention in the 1860s. While classical liberalism meant republican government and laissez-faire capitalism, opposition groups sometimes used the term to defend everything from democracy and civil rights to peasant communal land holdings and labour unions. The new Mexican radical movements of the opening of the twentieth century would all use the rhetoric of liberalism, even as they fought for other ideals.

1   The PLM and *Regeneración*: Resistance to the Dictator

Whether in direct response to the Bishop's speech, or coincidentally simultaneous with it, Camilo Arriaga, a wealthy mining engineer and former Congressman, published the manifesto 'Invitation to the Liberal Party' on 30 August. He

---

1   Knight 1986, Vol. I, pp. 15–36; Cockcroft 1983, pp. 85–114; Hart 2002, pp. 71–268; Guerra 1992, Vol. II, pp. 9–25.

invited liberals to join in creating a political party to defend and promote their ideals. Arriaga himself set an example by founding the 'Ponciano Arriaga' Liberal Club named after his grandfather a leading liberal of the Juárez era. At the same time, the brothers Ricardo and Jesús Flores Magón of San Antonio Eloxochitlán, Teotitlán del Camino, Oaxaca began on 7 August to publish in Mexico City a new newspaper named *Regeneración* (Regeneration). The paper's purpose, said the authors, was to denounce miscarriages of justice in the courts, and it soon became an advocate of the new Liberal Party founded by Arriaga. By October, the Flores Magón brothers' paper was condemning 'obstacles to the enjoyment of democratic rights', and by November the paper was arguing that the 'people are sovereign and authority is its servant. It is the people who have the right to claim submission and obedience of its servant'. On the last day of the year, *Regeneración* added to its masthead the slogan: 'an independent newspaper of combat'.[2]

When the Liberal Party's founding convention took place in San Luis Potosí, on 5 February 1901, Ricardo Flores Magón attended as the delegate of the Mexico City Liberal Students Committee, which he had organised and also as the publisher of *Regeneración*.[3] The Convention delegates, mostly professionals, teachers, and students, came from cities and towns that were historic bastions of liberalism, some from older Liberal Clubs or Masonic lodges.[4] Several women, 'pioneering feminists' attended the convention as well.[5] The young radicals, however, turned the Liberal movement in a new direction. Ricardo Flores Magón took an active role in the convention and was immediately recognised as one of the new movement's leaders. Later that month his paper published the Liberal Party platform that had been adopted by the convention, a document remarkable for its thoroughly moderate and reformist positions. The PLM called for respect for the laws, a liberal and civic education, honesty among public officials, and the end to the practice of putting individual personalities above the Constitution and Reform Laws. There appeared to be nothing radical about the movement's pronouncements.

While the platform was mild, the group's attitude was radical. 'What was notable, nevertheless, in those days', writes historian Arnaldo Córdova, 'was the

---

2 Córdova 1975, p. 91; Parés 1990, pp. 17–19.
3 The Liberal Convention took place on 5 February 1901 in San Luis Potosí, founding the new Liberal Party. The Mexican Liberal Party was not founded until 28 September 1905 in St. Louis, Missouri. In reality, one evolved into the other and they are fundamentally the same organisation, so from the Convention of 1901, I have simply called this organisation the PLM.
4 Guerra 1992, Vol. 2, pp. 19–21.
5 Akers Chacón, 2018, pp. 125–7.

posture of frank and open opposition to the dictatorship'.[6] One of the Liberal convention's resolutions, for example, called upon its affiliated clubs to initiate a vigorous press and campaign against the arbitrary despotism. In March 1901, *Regeneración* published the manifesto of the 'Ponciano Arriaga' Liberal Club, stating that, 'Faith in justice, respect for the rights of others, and the worship of democracy will make us strong, heroic, independent and worthy, and we will show how to fetter obscurantism, to chain up the ambitious and traitorous clergy, and to remove forever from the government of the Republic unworthy functionaries, servile adulators, and insufferable despots'.[7] The new Liberal Party appeared not as a traditional party primarily interested only in electoral politics, but rather as an organising centre of a movement of resistance against the government.

The Liberal Convention put great emphasis on the party's organisation, establishing a 'central leadership' (*centro director*), which at sometime in the indefinite future be elected, but would, for the time being, be the 'Ponciano Arriaga' Liberal Club. The resolutions would the 'force of law' (*fuerza de ley*), as would other decisions deriving from them. As historian François-Xavier Guerra writes, 'In spite of all of the provisions for internal democracy that were adopted in other resolutions, the reality of the predominance of the central leadership continued to be total ...'.[8] In fact, there would never be any elections for the central leadership of either the Liberals or the future Mexican Liberal Party.

The Díaz government's spies took note of the new organisation and the government responded at once. In May of 1901, Mexican Liberal Party leaders Ricardo and Jesús Flores Magón and Antonio Sota y Gama were arrested on a variety of minor charges and jailed by the Díaz government, no doubt with the hope of discouraging the little band of radicals. Despite the repression, in November of 1901 Camilo Arriaga and José María Facha wrote and mailed to the other liberal clubs a list of issues to be taken up by the Second Congress to be held in San Luis Potosí in February of 1905 (though that convention was never held). They mentioned several of the party's fundamental concerns: fulfilling the Reform laws, ensuring freedom of the press, guaranteeing the right to vote, and getting rid of the political bosses in towns and cities.

The important new element, however, was point 5: 'Practical and legal measures to favor and improve the condition of the workers on the rural plantations and to resolve the problems of land and agriculture'. The Mexican Liberal Party (PLM), in this mailing to its members, had suddenly recognised and seized

---

6   Córdova 1975, p. 93.
7   Ibid.
8   Guerra 1992, Vol. 2, p. 20.

upon the issues which would agitate Mexico for the next forty years: oppressed workers, landless peasants, and the need for agrarian reform. Until that time, few in Mexico had understood and articulated the importance of the land question. From that moment forward, no one in Mexico could afford to neglect the question of agrarian reform and nothing would be settled until the country's peasants once again had their land.[9]

The Second Congress for which that circular was written never took place because Arriaga and other members of the 'Ponciano Arriaga' Club of the PLM were arrested and jailed in January 1902. Ricardo Flores Magón, who had by then been released from jail, began to publish another newspaper *El Hijo del Ahuizote*, and also turned it into a vehicle for attacking the Díaz regime. Other PLM leaders published half a dozen similar papers in various cities in northern Mexico. For a year the PLM leaders, always in and out of jail, continued to propagandise against the government and to organise their party and the opposition movement. Then, on 16 April 1903, Díaz's police moved in and closed the PLM newspapers, arrested several of the PLM leaders, and incarcerated the lot of them in the Belén Prison. Among those arrested were Ricardo and Enrique Flores Magón, Alfonso Cravioto, Santiago R. De la Vega, Santiago De la Hoz, Rosalío Bustamante, and Macías Valadés.

2   Belén Prison: A Turning Point

The Belén imprisonment was a turning point for the young men who formed the Mexican Liberal Party. It was in Belén that the principal leaders – while also communicating clandestinely with other Liberals being held in other prisons – reached a number of key decisions about both the politics and the organisation of the PLM. First, the leaders agreed that they were revolutionary anarchists in the tradition of the Russian Mikhail Bakunin but concurred that they should keep their anarchism a secret behind a liberal façade. Second, the group agreed that in an effort to maintain the support of the genuine liberals, they would put forward, at least at first, a non-threatening labour and agrarian programme;

---

9   Córdova 1975, pp. 113–22, pp. 125–35. Early Mexican anarchist writers had developed a critique of Mexican landownership and the state of the peasantry, most notably José María González. See Hart 1984, pp. 81–98. His writings, however, were not widely distributed or well known. Wistano Luis Orozco in his *Legislación y jurisprudencia sobre terrenos baldíos* (1895) had taken up the question in depth. And Andrés Molina Enríquez would not publish his important book *Los grandes problemas nacionales* (*The Great National Problems*) until 1909 (Córdova 1973, pp. 113–22 and pp. 125–35).

only gradually would they make explicit their programme of 'libertarian Socialism', that is, anarchism. Third, they decided that upon their release from prison they would go to the United States and establish there a *Junta de Organización*, an organising centre and leadership in exile. There they would resume publication of *Regeneración* as the PLM's official voice and they would write and publish a revolutionary programme that spoke to the needs of peasants and workers. Finally, they would organise trusted members into revolutionary cells capable of carrying out an armed insurrection. And, they stipulated, if the first uprising should fail, they would continue to attempt other such uprisings in order to spread the movement.[10]

The PLM leaders, who until the Belén imprisonment of 1903 had led a peaceful, movement of resistance committed to bringing about political reform largely through education and the press, had suddenly adopted a plan to become a revolutionary organisation aiming to overthrow the government through armed force. Many had been anarchists, followers of Mikhail Bakunin, but now they collectively and officially – though secretly – adopted this political identity. That they did so is not surprising in the context of Latin American history. Anarchism became the dominant left ideology throughout Latin America in the late nineteenth and early twentieth century. Bakunin's revolutionary anarchism, blocked in the more industrial Northern and Western regions of Europe – Germany, France, Belgium and Holland – by the dominance of Marxist socialism, found fertile ground in the less industrialised regions of southern Europe, in Greece, Italy, and Spain. Principally through migration, but also through the activities of anarchist seamen who distributed the movement's literature, anarchism spread from Spain to Cuba, Mexico, Argentina and Uruguay, and Brazil, as well as other countries in Latin America. In Mexico it was Ricardo Flores Magón who in Belén prison fought for and won the PLM leadership to agree to a programme of 'libertarian Socialism without any phase of State Socialism'. That is, to a programme of anarchism.

Flores Magón was hardly the first socialist or anarchist in Mexico. European anarchist ideas had reached Mexico in the late 1860s following the end of the Reform movement and the War against the French Intervention led by President Benito Juárez. The Greek immigrant Plotino C. Rhodakanaty was among the first to bring the new European revolutionary ideas to Mexico, though imported European newspapers and books more commonly spread the anarchist and socialist message.[11] For Mexicans, Spanish anarchism was linguistically

---

10   Cockcroft 1968, pp. 114–15.
11   Lida 2001, pp. 103–49.

and culturally the most accessible version of European revolutionary theories. Some upper-class Mexicans who could read and write French had access to the French socialist literature, though at the time there were virtually no good translations of Marx's writing anywhere in either Spanish or French. Still Marx's ideas about capitalism and socialism were conveyed through popular pamphlets and journalism. Groups of Mexican anarchists and socialists published newspapers and brochures and got them into the hands of the few literate workers and rural leaders. Already by the end of the 1860s to the 1880s some workers' mutual associations and unions and peasant leagues espousing socialism or anarchism existed, and one led an uprising in the Chalco region and in the Sierra Gorda of San Luis Potosí under the banner of anarchism or libertarian socialism.[12]

The PLM leaders had similarly been influenced by European anarchism and socialism at the end of the nineteenth century. Historian James Cockcroft describes the radical education of several of the future PLM leaders in his classic *Intellectual Precursors of the Mexican Revolution, 1900–1913*. Camilo Arriaga, who might be called the PLM founder, played a central role in diffusing anarchist ideas among many of those who would come to be the leaders and cadres of the PLM. Arriaga came from a wealthy northern mining family with a long history in Liberal politics, who were supporters of Porfirio Díaz. While studying at the Escuela Nacional Preparatoria in Mexico City in the mid-1870s, Arriaga began to read Proudhon, Marx, Engels, Bakunin and other European socialists and anarchists. Later he went to France where he acquired a large library of anarchist and socialist books and pamphlets.

After returning from France, Arriaga earned his degree in engineering in the mid-1880s and went to work in his family's mines while also serving as a representative first in the state and then in the national Congress. Towards the end of the century, he became increasingly critical of the Díaz regime and part of what was seen as the liberal opposition to the dictator. From Mexico City, Arriaga returned to San Luis Potosí where his home, with its library of left literature, became the centre of a group of young radicals that included Antonio Soto y Gama, Benjamín Millán, Humberto Macias Valadés, and Rosalío Bustamante. Together these young idealists read and commented on the classics of European socialism. It was with that group that Arriaga founded the 'Ponciano Arriaga' Liberal Club, one of the strongest PLM centres.[13] Though Arriaga would later become a supporter of Francisco Madero, and a Liberal

---

12   García Cantú 1969, pp. 33–78.
13   Cockcroft 1968, pp. 64–70.

in the more traditional sense of the word, he played a key role in creating the milieu that fostered the new Mexican anarchism.

3   The Founders of the PLM and Their Views

While it was in Belén Prison that the PLM leaders affirmed their anarchist philosophy and vowed to form a revolutionary organisation, they had all had earlier exposure to anarchist ideas. Ricardo, Jesús, and Enrique Flores Magón were sons of a comfortably well-off family from Oaxaca of distinguished liberal credentials. Their father had fought against the US invasion of Mexico in 1847, in the war of Reform with Benito Juáurez against the conservatives, and against the French Intervention with General Porfirio Díaz in the battle of Puebla on 2 April 1867 where Maximilian and the French suffered their final defeat. The family was proud of its patriotic and liberal heritage. Like Arriaga, Ricardo went off to Mexico City to study at the Escuela Nacional Preparatoria and then to the Escuela Nacional de Jurisprudencia, the law school. While there, he became involved in the student protests of 1892 against the third term election of Porfirio Díaz in 1892 and was arrested and jailed for his activities. Three years later, Ricardo gave up his career in law and went off to join the painter Joaquín Claussel who was publishing *El Demócrata*. Leaving that paper, between 1897 and 1900 Ricardo worked in the family's import-export business before going off to Mexico City again in 1900 with his brother Jesús to found their own publication, *Regeneración*. Sometime during those years as a student and young adult, Ricardo had begun to read the writing of European anarchists such as the Russian Peter Kropotkin, the French Jean Grave, and the Italian Enrico Malatesta. By the opening of the twentieth century, though still describing himself in public as a Liberal, Ricardo Flores Magón had become a convinced anarchist.[14]

Other leaders of the PLM, many of whom were from well-off or middle-class families and had professional educations, experienced similar intellectual trajectories. Soto y Gama, for example, was the son of a provincial lawyer and his wife, a modest middle-class family of 14 children. The father was a loyal Liberal and in his living room hung a large photo of Sebastián Lerdo de Tejada, the author of the laws that had taken from the Catholic Church its vast landholdings. As a young man Soto y Gama read Kropotkin, Jacques Élisée Reclus, Bakunin, Charles Malato, Pierre-Joseph Proudhon, and Karl Marx. The Span-

---

14   Cockcroft 1968, pp. 84–7.

ish anarchist publishing house Maucci had set up a press in Mexico and made copies of books by those authors available at just 25 centavos each. According to historian Cockcroft, Soto y Gama viewed the First Liberal Convention of the Liberal Clubs 'as an excellent façade behind which he and other young radical could develop their Anarchist and Socialist ideas'. With some exaggeration Soto y Gama claimed, 'All of us were Anarchists through and through'.[15]

Juan Sarabia, another early PLM leader, who came from a poorer family, also became familiar with radical literature by 1900. Son of a poor musician who was the leader of a military band in San Luis Potosí, the young Sarabia attended the Instituto Científico y Literario del Estado, but rebelled against its 'exaggerated scholasticism'. His father sent him to work in a cobbler's shop for while and then took him to Mexico City where the boy studied printing in a night school. After his father's sudden death in 1895, though only 14 years old, he supported his mother and sister by working in a local library, but finding the pay too low, went off to work in the El Cabezón mine in Guanajuato. Later his mother found him work in the San Luis Potosí-Zacatecas telegraph office, but he was laid off because he was still underage. Having to earn a living for his family, he went off to work at the Fundición de Morales, a foundry a couple of miles outside of San Luis Potosí. After recovering from an attack of pneumonia and a case of small-pox, he next found work in the tax department. While working, Sarabia read the works of Jules Verne, Victor Hugo, Leo Tolstoy, Émile Zola, Maxim Gorky, and Kropotkin. He also wrote poetry and published some of his poems in a local newspaper. With financial assistance from Arriaga, he quit his government job and became the publisher of El Demócrata. While not a convinced anarchist like the others, Sarabia was familiar with anarchist writings.[16]

As a whole, the Mexican Liberal Party leadership was made up of young intellectuals and activist men whose families generally came out of the Liberal tradition; several of whom had adopted anarchism as their personal philo-sophy. Through their participation in the Mexican Liberal Party, they worked to establish the organisation that they believed would lead a revolution to cre-ate a libertarian socialist or anarchist society. Some of the leaders, however, held other views. Lázaro Gutiérrez de Lara, Antonio I. Villarreal, and Manuel Sarabia considered themselves to be socialists in the European Marxist tradi-tion, while Juan Sarabia might best be characterised simply as a democratic reformer. While several of the leaders of the PLM were anarchists or socialists, the majority of the members of the PLM were not necessarily of the same mind.

---

15   Cockcroft 1968, pp. 71–7.
16   Cockcroft 1968, pp. 77–82.

Some were liberals, some socialists, and probably most were simply men and women, activists who wanted a more democratic Mexico.[17]

4   The Influence of Mikhail Bakunin

While they had been exposed to various political philosophies of the left, it was in Belén Prison that the PLM founders became anarchists. Inspiring the group was the political philosophy and organisational model of Bakunin, the Russian anarchist. Born in 1814, the son of a Russian nobleman and Czarist ambassador, Bakunin developed his anarchist philosophy in the midst of his participation in the European Revolution of 1848 and through his interpretation of the experience of the Paris Commune of 1871. Unlike Marx's conception of socialism, which was based on the idea of working-class power and the need for a workers' political party struggling to expand democracy in order to take state power, Bakunin's anarchism privileged no particular social class and had no interest in creating a political party or a revolutionary government. He advocated instead the creation of a small, elite, secret organisation of revolutionaries capable of leading a broader revolutionary movement of various social classes.[18]

During the period of the 1840s Bakunin typically saw nationalist and peasant movements as the vehicle of revolutionary change. He rejected the idea of seizing state power or creating a new state and called instead for the destruction of the state and its replacement by a cooperative society. Bakunin believed that a revolution would be led by a secret organisation that would direct a mass movement. The notion of an open debate about ideals, principles, and strategies by a democratic mass movement was alien to him. He argued instead that an anarchist elite working covertly would ignite the movement through the 'propaganda of the deed' and then steer it through its clandestine organisation. Bakunin wrote in his 'Letter to a Frenchman' in 1870,

> We have for better or worse built a small party: small, in the number of men who joined it with full knowledge of what we stand for; immense, if we take into account those who instinctively relate to us, if we take into account the popular masses, whose needs and aspirations we reflect more

---

17   Hart 1988, p. 119. He asserts that this is clearly the case because when Francisco Madero initiated the Mexican Revolution in November 1910, the majority of PLM members deserted and joined the organisation of Madero.

18   Draper 1990, pp. 130–75.

truly than does any other group. All of us must now embark on stormy revolutionary seas, and from this very moment we must spread our principles, not with words *but with deeds, for this is the most popular, the most potent, and the most irresistible form of propaganda.* Let us say less about principles, whenever circumstances and revolutionary policy demand it – i.e., during our momentary weakness in relation to the enemy – but let us at all times and under all circumstances be adamantly consistent in our action. For in this lies the salvation of the revolution.[19]

Anarchists believed that their deeds – assassinations of political leaders, armed assaults on centres of power, uprisings large or small – would convince the masses to follow 'instinctively'.

At the centre, guiding these actions and then the movements that followed would be a secret society of revolutionary leaders. Secrecy, centralisation of power, and leadership from the top-down formed the core of Bakunin's politics. As Bakunin wrote about his planned revolution in Bohemia in his famous 'Confession' of 1851:

> All clubs, newspapers, and all manifestations of an anarchy of mere talk were to be abolished, all submitted to one dictatorial power; the young people and all able-bodied men divided into categories according to their character, ability, and inclination were to be sent throughout the country to provide a provisional revolutionary and military organization. The secret society directing the revolution was to consist of three groups, independent of and unknown to each other: one for the townspeople, another for the youth, and a third for the peasants.

Each of these societies was to adapt its action to the social character of the locality to which it was assigned. Each was to be organised on strict hierarchical lines, and under absolute discipline. These three societies were to be directed by a secret central committee composed of three or, at the most, five persons. In case the revolution was successful, the secret societies were not to be liquidated; on the contrary, they were to be strengthened and expanded, to take their place in the ranks of the revolutionary hierarchy.[20]

After their imprisonment in Belén in 1903, the Magonistas adopted this political philosophy and strategy. The revolution would have no specific class char-

---

19   Bakunin 1971, pp. 195–6.
20   Bakunin 1971, pp. 69–70.

acter but simply aimed to organise the people, and it would be led by a secret group of revolutionaries, the leaders of the PLM.

5   The Revolutionary PLM

The PLM leadership arrived in the US border town of Laredo, Texas in January 1904, becoming out of necessity a bi-national or transnational revolutionary movement operating in two countries. There they established their *Junta* or leadership committee made up of Ricardo Flores Magón (president), Juan Sarabia (vice-president), Antonio I. Villarreal, Enrique Flores Magón, Librado Rivera, Manuel Sarabia, and Rosalío Bustamante. While women had been early participants, they played no role in the party's top leadership.[21] The party's principal public activity remained publishing propaganda. With the financial assistance of Arriaga, the PLM was able by 5 November 1904 to begin again to publish *Regeneración*, now in its fourth year of irregular publication. By September 1905 the paper was publishing 20,000 copies and would later publish as many as 30,000.

The PLM, which had never considered itself a political party in the ordinary electoral sense, but rather a movement of resistance, now transformed itself into a revolutionary organisation. Affiliated organisations were asked to meet regularly, to maintain the utmost secrecy, and to communicate regularly with the *Junta*, providing reports of local activity in their areas. The leaders began to establish membership lists meant to be kept secret from the authorities. The local groups were instructed to acquire arms and create armed units prepared for insurrection.[22] Now located in Texas, the PLM began organising Mexicans and Mexican-Americans in the cities and mining towns throughout the Southwest of the United States as well as in Mexico. As a matter of necessity, the PLM had become a bi-national revolutionary movement with a network that stretched along the porous border from Texas and Arizona through Sonora, Durango, Chihuahua, Nuevo León, and San Luis Potosí down to Veracruz and Mexico City.

Laredo's convenient location on the border unfortunately also made it vulnerable to Díaz's agents. After an attack on the life of Ricardo Flores Magón by a man armed with a knife, together with an attempt by Pinkerton private

---

21   Akers Chacón 2018, p. 127, claims that, 'By 1911 a corps of female leaders took up leadership positions within the organisation ...' with many female speakers and writers, but there were no women in the top leadership deciding the group's strategy.

22   Torres Parés 1989, pp. 27–9.

detectives to arrest his brother Enrique, the PLM leadership decided that they should move farther from the border. Fearing that they would surely be killed or kidnapped by Díaz's agents in the border town of Laredo, in February 1905 the PLM *Junta* moved its headquarters to St. Louis, Missouri in the very centre of the United States. There Ricardo Flores Magón and other PLM leaders came into contact with the American anarchist Emma Goldman and the Spanish anarchist Florencio Bazora.[23]

Sharing a common anarchist philosophy and politics, Goldman and the Mexican revolutionaries established warm relations that would lay the foundation for organisational solidarity between the anarchist revolutionary movements in both countries. The international politics and practices of the Mexican Liberal Party first began then not out of theory but out of the necessity of fleeing Mexico to avoid being arrested or possibly murdered by the Díaz government's police agents and developed out of their contacts with the American anarchists. Based on this experience, the Mexican anarchist movement would gradually construct an entire internationalist politics and strategy.

6   The Encounter with the Working Class

While in Texas and Missouri, the PLM leadership had its first real encounter with the Mexican working class. Though Mexico was not a modern industrial nation, between Díaz's rise to power and the outbreak of the Revolution in 1910, it had become a thoroughly capitalist nation with important industrial enclaves. Hacienda owners, now often producing products such as sugar and henequen for both a national and international market, had succeeded for the most part in destroying the traditional Indian and mestizo communities, taking their land, and reducing former peasants to day labourers. Many mines had been modernised and employed thousands of workers. Several large textile mills had been constructed, tended by other thousands of laborers. At the same time, the country had built a national network of railroads that had in turn given a fillip to mining and industry, leading to the growth of an industrial working class. The 1910 census revealed that Mexico had a population of 15 million and that most were in the labouring classes. Some 96.6 percent of rural households held no land; 80 percent of the population, labourers and their

----

23   Some historians have suggested that Goldman and Bazora converted Magón and other
      PLM leaders to anarchism, but as Cockcroft, Torres Parés and others have shown, the PLM
      leaders were already familiar with anarchist writings and had become anarchists years
      before arriving in St. Louis.

families, worked for some 20,000 landlords, entirely dependent upon agricultural wages. Estimates of the size of the Mexican industrial working class range
between 8 and 15 percent of the population; historians using the census of 1910
and other materials have counted 107,000 mine workers and 624,000 manufacturing workers.[24]

Mexican Working Class – 1910

Extractive Industries (mining)	100,000
Manufacturing	613,000
Gas, electricity, and combustible production	10,000
Railroads	18,000
Total industrial workers	741,000

*Source – Mexican Census of 1910

Another historian breaks it down this way: 195,000 workers and 500,000 artisans.[25]

During this same period in the United States, after the end of the Civil War
(1861–65), money from San Francisco and New York had poured into the Southwest and particularly into railroads and mining.[26] California, Nevada, Arizona,
Colorado, and Utah became the centre of hard rock metal mining in the United
States, and companies such as Guggenheim (later American Smelting and
Refining Company – ASARCO), Anaconda, and Phelps-Dodge that owned and
operated the mines and smelters also had similar operations in the northern
states of Sonora, Durango and Chihuahua in Mexico. In the United States, the
American mining and smelting companies and the railroads that served them
employed tens of thousands of workers, many of them Mexicans, both US
citizens of Mexican descent and newer Mexican immigrants, while they also
employed thousands of Mexicans and hundreds of Americans in their Mexican
operations.

The PLM leaders did not so much turn to the working class as stumble
upon it.[27] For the PLM, now headquartered in the United States and with

---

24   Cockcroft 1983, pp. 86–96.
25   Meyer 1973, p. 16.
26   Brechin 1999, pp. 13–70.
27   Akers Chacón 2018, pp. 131–47, calls this a 'turn to the working class'.

most of its members working either in Northern Mexico or in the United States, the Mexican industrial workers appeared as their natural milieu and consequently became the principal objects of their propaganda and organisation, even though for such anarchists the working class held no special place in their theory. Unlike Central Mexico, where the peasantry was far and away the largest social class, in Northern Mexico the class structure was different. Northern Mexico's population was made up of some peasants, modern farmers, and many ranchers large and small, as well as industrial workers employed on the railroads, in the mines, and in foundries and factories. During the period from 1884 to 1894, the number of active American mines in Mexico increased from 40 to 13,696.[28] Mexico's most important metallurgical plants, located in Nuevo León, Sonora, Durango, San Luis Potosí, Aguascalientes, Chihuahua and Monterrey, were modern mills and factories comparable with any in the world. They employed 15,000 industrial workers.

Mexican workers in both Northern Mexico and the United States had succeeded in establishing unions, though their existence was often tenuous as government and management in both countries did everything in their power to destroy them. In Northern Mexico, workers had despite government repression established unions such as the Great League of Railroad Workers with 10,000 members and the Iron and Foundry Workers of Chihuahua with hundreds of members. The largest and most important branch of industry, mining, however, had not yet been organised. In the United States, Mexican workers were sometimes members of the AFL, the Railway Brotherhoods, the Western Federation of Miners, or the Industrial Workers of the World (IWW). Many Mexicans also participated in the Socialist Party in the Southwest of the United States.[29] Mexican workers took an active role in the US and in Mexico in union organisation campaigns and in the strikes, which especially in mining often became bloody battles. PLM members in the United States often worked in the mines and joined the IWW or the Western Federation of Miners.[30]

The PLM strategy for organising workers then did not flow from their anarchist theory but was rather the result of its experience among the workers. Baca Calderón, one of the leaders of a Liberal club in Cananea, an American-owned company town in northern Mexico that was the home of the great copper mine of the same name, wrote to Villarreal in April of 1906,

28   Hart 2002, p. 152.
29   Gómez-Quiñones 1994, pp. 66–70.
30   Guerra YEAR?, vol. 2, pp. 12–21; Taylor 1993, pp. 159 and 167.

... all of the miners here are aware in the most practical way that the dictatorship is their worst enemy and at all times they feel a just desire to overthrow it. With regard to this, an idea has occurred to me: to found a miners union, without an oppositional character or any declared politics, at least for now. Afterwards, we will invite all of the miners of the Republic to found their own unions so that together we can create the Miners League of the United States of Mexico. All of these unions would have the obligation to collect funds to support the class as the leadership indicates when the situation requires it. These unions, in the end, will opt to join the Liberal Party in mass and with resolve.[31]

Calderón's letter to Villarreal lays out an idea that became a strategic concept of the PLM by 1906, not only at Cananea, but in other industrial centres as well. PLM cadres began to help organise unions and where possible worked not only to recruit their leaders but also to affiliate the unions themselves to the PLM. In several industrial towns, especially in the state of Chihuahua, the PLM succeeded in bringing together workers in PLM clubs that functioned like union organising committees or in other cases brought workers directly into actual unions.[32] The PLM's labour strategy then had two elements. First, the PLM attempted to recruit workers to join the PLM, and, if they seemed trustworthy, to its secret armed revolutionary organisations. Second, the PLM members supported workers in their attempts to organise unions, with the idea of getting the unions as a whole to support the PLM. There is, however, no suggestion that the PLM will be a workers' organisation or that workers will have a decision-making role.

In Cananea, Calderón, Ibarra and Diéguez brought workers into their liberal club, the Unión Liberal Humanidad (the Humanity Liberal Union), with the goal both of recruiting them to the PLM and organising a union as part of a national Miners League that they envisioned. The club succeeded in recruiting about 25 members. At the time Cananea, a joint venture of the Anaconda Copper Company and industrialist William C. Green's Cananea Consolidated Copper Company, employed 7,500 workers. Managers, supervisors, and technicians were often Americans, but 5,360 of the workers were Mexicans. When in June the company raised the possibility of bringing in subcontractors to do much of the work and laying off some of the current workforce, the miners began to protest, confronting the American bosses. In the resulting melee two

---

31   Hart 1988, p. 123.
32   Hart 1988, pp. 47–53.

American supervisors and three Mexicans were killed. After two or three days of strike and rioting, the workers movement was broken when Díaz sent in 2,000 soldiers seconded by five Arizona rangers who crossed the border leading a group of American vigilantes. In the end somewhere between 30 and 100 Mexican miners were killed in the suppression of the strike.[33]

While the strike had taken them by surprise, the PLM members rallied to it and two of PLM's local leaders, Calderón and Diéguez, who had been working for some time to organise a miners' union throughout the region, were asked to take leadership of the strike. The PLM leaders, however, hesitated to do so because, as they saw it, their objective was a revolution to overthrow Díaz, not merely the organisation of a union or a strike. And they hesitated to take responsibility for a movement that had already led to riots, deaths, and property damage.[34] Whether they wanted to take responsibility for it or not, the Díaz government and the company blamed them. The company suggested that they should be executed, but the Díaz government sentenced them to fifteen years in the San Juan de Ulúa prison, a virtual death sentence.

The PLM was also active in the Puebla-Orizaba industrial zone that overlapped the states of Puebla and Veracruz, the site of Mexico's great textile industry that in 1910 employed 32,000 workers. The workers conditions were difficult. For example, The French owned Industrial Company of Orizaba, established in 1895, employed some 6,000 workers who worked 13 hours a day for low pay given in scrip usable only at the expensive company store. PLM cadres, José Neira, Manuel Ávila, and Juan Olivares began to organise in the Puebla-Orizaba industrial region around 1905, working first among the legal mutual societies of Río Blanco, Nogales and Santa Rosa in the state of Veracruz. Neira was particularly fortunate to find that in Río Blanco a Protestant minister named José Rumbia was already criticising both 'the Catholic Church and the bourgeoisie'. After his sermons, Rumbia allowed Neira to speak to the workers about politics. In Rio Blanco, Neira succeeded in recruiting 27 workers as the local organising committee of the Great Circle of Free Workers (GCOL). The GCOL based itself on the PLM programme and workers who joined understood that they were affiliated with the broader movement. The three PLM cadres succeeded in organising 80 GCOL local union groups in textile plants in Veracruz, Puebla, Oaxaca, Tlaxcala, the State of Mexico, Querétaro, Hidalgo and the Federal District (Mexico City). The GCOL grew strong enough that during November it carried on negotiations with the Centro Industrial Mexicano, the textile employers association.

---

33   Hart 1988, pp. 123–4.
34   Torres Parés 1989, pp. 45–6.

When employers announced a wage cut on 4 December 1906, nearly 7,000 workers in 34 plants in Puebla and Tlaxcala went out on strike. The employers responded with a lockout at 93 factories throwing tens of thousands of workers out on the street. Díaz came to the employers' aid, immediately issuing a proclamation prohibiting strikes. Attempting to starve the workers into submission, the bosses also closed the company stores. The strikers turned to President Díaz for mediation and he issued a decision that most workers found acceptable.

In Orizaba, however, 2,000 workers at the Río Blanco plant, a minority of the total workforce, rejected the president's decision and refused to return to work. Moreover, they called for an end to the Díaz dictatorship. When the employer closed the company store, a woman named Margarita Martínez led an assault on the store in an attempt to get food for the workers, but company men and police beat back the attack, injuring many workers. Workers then burned the store and marched to Nogales and Santa Rosa where they sacked local businesses and burned pawnshops. On their way back to Río Bravo a Mexican Army battalion intercepted the strikers. The officers ordered their men to fire into crowds of men, women and children, killing scores. In the aftermath, more than 200 workers were arrested and imprisoned. Nevertheless, fighting between strikers and soldiers went on through the night. On 8 January, with the town occupied by 800 *federales*, 150 police, and 60 *rurales*, and with hundreds of workers jailed, the government and the company succeeded in restoring order. Two hundred workers had been killed, and 400 jailed. Twenty-five soldiers were also killed and more than 30 wounded. Some 1,500 workers in Orizaba were fired. The movement was defeated but, remarkably, not crushed; there would be repeated strikes in those textile mills over the next three years.[35]

The PLM had not organised and led the Cananea and Río Blanco strikes, but its members had participated in them and attempted to use them insofar as possible to build the revolutionary movement. The PLM's participation suggests that while the party had developed a strategic orientation to the working class, we might say that it did not have a working-class programme or practice. The PLM leaders and activists do not seem to have understood the distinctive nature of unions as institutions or of their economic, social, and political dimensions. While some PLM members were union activists and leaders, the leaders do not seem to have thought about using strikes and other forms of pressure to create stable union organisations, to negotiate contracts with improvements in wages and benefits, or to make other social gains of democratic reforms which would

---

35   Torres Parés 1989, pp. 53–4; Hart 1988, pp. 126–32.

benefit the working class and society as a whole. Nor is that strange. The PLM leaders tended to operate within a very short timeframe; they clearly expected to incite a revolution within months or certainly within a few years, not in decades. As anarchists, they believed that inspired by the propaganda of heroic deeds, the people would rise in revolt and rapidly adopt an anarchist worldview and set to work creating an anarchist society. Rather than seeing unions as central to the building of a revolutionary working-class movement, they saw them as adjuncts to the clandestine organisation of an armed insurrection. One can only wonder what might have been accomplished if the PLM had developed its alliance with the WFM and the IWW and Mexican miners' organisations and built a miners' movement with the economic power to disrupt the economies of both Mexico and the United States.

7   The 1906 Insurrection

The great strikes of 1906 and 1907, even if not organised by the party, coincided with and formed part of the Mexican Liberal Party's planned insurrection of 1906. The Díaz government, informed by his spies that something big was afoot for the fall of 1906, worked to interrupt the revolutionaries' schemes. The dictator repeatedly had PLM members arrested and closed their printing presses when they were operating in Mexico and when the group fled to the United States in 1905, he continued to pursue them. On 12 October, shortly after the group established itself in St. Louis, agents of the Pinkerton Detective Agency, operating without warrants and without having been deputised, entered the office of *Regeneración*. They confiscated the printing press and other equipment, took the organisation's files, and arrested Juan Sarabia and Ricardo and Eduardo Flores Magón on charges of libel and defamation. The charges were made by Esperón y de la Flor, a Oaxaca political boss who had apparently been sent to St. Louis by Díaz himself. The three key PLM leaders were held in jail pending the payment of a $10,000 bond.

The 1905 arrests represented another turning point in the PLM's politics and strategy. The effort to raise the $10,000 bond and free the men from jail became the basis for a joint campaign by Mexican and US left organisations. In Mexico, of course, the PLM's supporters did the work of publicising the matter and raising money, while in the United States it was socialist, anarchist, and labour organisations which came to the prisoners' aid. By December the US and Mexican groups had raised the bond and the three men were freed. The solidarity that arose between the Mexican and US organisations while working on the campaign would later lead the PLM leadership to develop an internationalist labour strategy which looked to foreign workers' organisations to play an important supporting role in the coming Mexican Revolution. At the moment, however, the PLM leaders' first concern was the insurrection. Fearing further harassment, such as the revocation of their bond, on the eve of the insurrection Ricardo Flores Magón and Juan Sarabia fled to Canada, first to Toronto in March and then on to Quebec in May. Antonio I. Villarreal and Manuel Sarabia were left in charge of *Regeneración* and of writing the Programme for the uprising and organisational preparations went forward.[36]

For the purposes of the insurrection, the PLM organised Mexico into five zones. Each zone was under the command of a trusted PLM cadre called a *delegado* (a delegate), and under the delegate was the guerrilla leader. The guerrilla unit members knew only their leaders and sub-leaders who were democratically elected by them. The five delegates were not to communicate with each other until the insurrection, which was to be initiated at the command of the *delegado general*, the military commander, responsible to the *Junta*. At the time the PLM had 44 guerrilla units, some as large as 200 or 300 men, but most around 50, which had to one degree or another armed themselves.[37] Altogether the PLM had perhaps 2,500 fighters dispersed across a vast area that included several states and many locales.

8   The Liberal Party Programme of 1906

In preparation for the insurrection to take place on the first of July, 1906, the PLM published the Programme of the Liberal Party in a press run of 25,000 copies.[38] The PLM programme combined elements of Mexico's traditional liberalism with a complete plan for urban and rural labour reforms. First, the programme called for a return to a genuine Republic by limiting the president and governors to one four-year term and establishing freedom of the press. Municipal political bosses were to be removed and the municipal government strengthened. Taxes on luxuries should be increased and those on necessities reduced. Obligatory military service was to be ended and in its place a volunteer national guard established. Military trials were not to be permitted in times of peace. The PLM also demanded improvements in education with an expansion of primary schools, increases in teachers' salaries and education obligatory up

---

36   Cockcroft 1968, pp. 124–9.
37   Torres Parés 1980, pp. 54–7; Hart 1988, pp. 121–32.
38   'Programa del Partido Liberal' in Zertuche Muñoz YEAR?, pp. 81–95.

to age 14. Churches were to pay taxes like any other business, the property they owned under the names of their agents was to be nationalised in accordance with the Reform laws, and church schools were to be closed.

What was novel about the programme were the proposals for dealing with the questions of labour and the land, proposals that constituted a comprehensive platform of labour rights and protections. The labour programme called for the establishment of the eight-hour day with a basic minimum wage of a peso a day, but varying from region to region so as to provide workers with a living wage. Piece rate wages were to be brought into line with the daily minimum wage. Domestic work and homework, that is, industrial work done in the home, was to be regulated by the government. Sunday was to be made an obligatory day of rest. Child labour under the age of 14 was to be prohibited. Employers were to maintain mines, factories, workshops and other workplaces in conditions that protected the safety and health of workers. Rural workers were to be given sanitary housing conditions. And all workers should receive compensation for workplace accidents. All existing day-labour debts to employers were to be annulled and measures adopted to protect sharecroppers. Renters were to be compensated for any improvements made on the landlord's property. Workers should not be paid in scrip, deductions could not be made from workers' wages, and the company store was to be abolished. Mexican employers should be allowed to hire only a minority of foreign workers and foreign and Mexican workers should receive the same pay for the same work. Surprisingly for a group that espoused an anarchist and internationalist philosophy and program, it also called for the prohibition of Chinese immigration, a common demand of both Mexican and American unions at the time.[39]

The land programme introduced the principle of usufruct: the land for those who work it. Landowners were to be required to make all of their land productive. Land left idle was to be taken over by the state and distributed in this way: First to Mexicans living and working abroad who wished to return were to be repatriated at government expense and given land to cultivate. Second, anyone

---

39   Chinese immigrants in northern Mexico had established businesses that competed with Mexicans leading to demands to end Chinese immigration. Pancho Villa, leader of the revolutionary movement in the North of Mexico, also hated the Chinese and permitted his troops to kill them. Katz 1998, p. 630. The PLM editors of *Regeneración* wrote about the Cananea mining town that 'the people have to put up with the insolence of the three thousand Yankees who live in Cananea and with the disgusting filth of the two thousand Chinese there, part of whom have monopolised the grocery business, while the others give themselves to their parasitic and ignoble lives'. Lomnitz 2014, p. 133.

who asked for land should be given it based simply on the understanding that they would work the land themselves and not sell it. A maximum acreage to be owned by anyone person was to be established. To make all of this possible the government would establish an agrarian bank that would make loans to be paid back in instalments over time. The programme also had other advanced ideas such as calling for the protection of the indigenous people, ending all differences between legitimate and illegitimate children so that they should enjoy the same rights, and transforming prisons into penal colonies based on the principle of rehabilitation. The PLM also called for establishing closer ties with the other nations of Latin America.

The PLM programme ended by asserting that when the party had 'triumphed' it would ensure that the wealth of corrupt officials would be taken from them and distributed especially to the Yaqui and Maya indigenous groups and to other groups and individuals who had been dispossessed of their land. Second, the first national congress meeting after the triumph would annul all of Díaz's changes in the Constitution of 1857 and other laws detrimental to Mexican society. Finally, the PLM announced that it would inform other governments around the world that Mexico would not be responsible for any debts or other obligations incurred by the Díaz government.

As historian François-Xavier Guerra observes, the Programme of 1906 also suggests that it will be the Mexican Liberal Party leader of the 'liberal people' who will represent the people's will. Guerra emphasises this point not because of the PLM's importance, but because on the 'eve of the Revolution', the PLM leadership makes this 'transfer of the will of the people to the minorities [i.e. the PLM leadership], a transfer that has been the essence of liberal politics in the nineteenth century and will continue to be in the revolutionary governments'.[40]

The PLM programme of 1906 represented an important development of the organisation's politics, moving from broad generalities about democracy and equality to speaking directly and specifically to the issues facing various social groups. While it was clearly intended to speak to Mexicans of all classes who wanted greater democracy and civil rights, the PLM programme of 1906 was addressed in particular to the country's labouring classes, its industrial workers, rural day labourers, and peasants. While the PLM leadership was anarchist, they published what was in fact a liberal manifesto to appeal to all social groups from the bourgeoisie and the petty bourgeoisie to workers and peasants. They had adopted and published what Adolfo Gilly has characterised as 'a radical

---

40   Guerra 1992, vol. II, p. 54.

nationalist and democratic program'.[41] It was a programme that in many ways anticipated and would inspire the future political developments and programs of the Mexican Revolution that was to come in the period from 1910 to 1940.

In addition to the Platform, in September 1906 the PLM also issued a Proclamation to the Nation, sent from headquarters in the United States to the *delegados*, the local guerrilla leaders, in which for the first time the party declared itself to be in open rebellion against the government of Porfirio Díaz. The document explained that under Díaz things were getting worse every day, that attempts at peaceful change had failed, and that, as so often happens in history, the dictator had forced the people to rebel. They PLM promised that its members would not lay down their arms until the revolution had triumphed. The PLM's military units were told that, once the revolution began, they should set to work without waiting for further instructions, implementing the programme as they moved throughout the country, closing company stores and instituting the eight-hour day and peso-a-day wage.[42] With that programme in hand, the insurrection was launched in October 1906.

Everywhere it was attempted – in Douglas, Arizona; Ciudad Jiménez, Coahuila; Acayucán, Veracruz; Ciudad Juárez, Chihuahua; and in other cities, towns and villages – the insurrection was 'an unmitigated disaster'.[43] The principal reason for the failure was police infiltration and mail surveillance. The federal, state, and local authorities knew virtually everything about the PLM leaders' plans. The authorities either arrested the leading local revolutionaries in anticipation of the insurrection, or, waiting for the day of the insurrection, had enough police and soldiers to quickly crush the *insurrectos*. The biggest fiasco took place in the key border cities of Ciudad Juarez, Chihuahua and its sister city El Paso, Texas. Control of the major border crossing was of strategic importance since it would have allowed the PLM to bring in more fighters, guns, and supplies from the United States. But, as Chihuahua Governor Enrique C. Creel explained in a letter to Díaz, he had succeeded in luring the revolutionaries into a trap by having troops stationed there suggest to the rebels that they would join the rebellion. Falling into that trap on 19 October were Juan Sarabia, the PLM's vice-president, and two other PLM cadres, César Canales and J. de la Torre. At the same time in El Paso private detectives captured PLM leaders Antonio I. Villarreal and Lauro Aguirre as well as the journalist J. Cano. The capture of the PLM leaders weakened the organisation severely and confounded the insur-

---

41   Gilly 1971, p. 51.
42   Hart 1988, p. 56.
43   Lomnitz 2014, p. 194.

rection. The PLM organisation was shattered everywhere and the PLM press was shutdown. Ricardo Flores Magón managed to escape to Sacramento, California.[44] As François-Xavier Guerra, writes, 'the insurrection was a failure that showed the limits of the conspiratorial strategy'.[45]

9   Economic Crisis, Another Insurrection, and Anarchism

Yet, remarkably, the PLM leadership did not view the insurrection as a failure, did not abandon their strategy, and would launch another uprising of exactly the same sort on a large scale in 1908. The PLM leaders saw the insurrection as a kind of propaganda of the deed on a large scale. Their idea was that their armed insurrection would set off a broader rebellion leading to a full-scale revolution. We might compare the anarchist view to the Marxist concept of insurrection. For Marxists, the insurrection is the culmination of a long historical period of organising involving the creation of a revolutionary organisation, the establishment of labour unions and labour political parties, the rise of workers' councils either in neighbourhoods or workplaces, the development of massive national confrontations with state power, and finally a revolutionary military organisation capable of overthrowing the state and bringing the working class to power. Such was the experience, for example, of the Bolsheviks in Russia.[46] But whereas for the Marxists the insurrection is the final stage, for the anarchists it is the first stage.

Certainly, their different theories of insurrection have to do with their respective conceptions of the relationship between what Marxists call the objective and subjective conditions. Marxists believe that economic and political situations change and develop and that at certain moments – generally as a result of economic crisis, political crisis, or war – a revolution is put on the agenda of history as a possibility. For Marxists, the balance of forces in society and particularly the state of organisation of the working class and its evolving consciousness of its situation are central. Anarchists on the other hand generally hold that in a world of permanent exploitation and oppression, revolution is always on the agenda and that achieving it is principally a matter of changing the consciousness of the people through propaganda and example. For the Marxist, the objective and subjective exist in a reciprocal relationship, influen-

44   Hart 1988, p. 57.
45   Guerra 1992, vol. 2, pp. 59 and 61.
46   The classic account of the Marxist theory of insurrection is to be found in Trotsky 1957, esp. Chapter 6.

cing each other. For the anarchist, the subjective is really the only significant factor. Anarchism is voluntarism – the will is all. Given their anarchist outlook, the PLM leaders believed that they had only to continue publishing *Regeneración*, building their organisation, arming their members and launching new insurrections. The PLM continued with this strategy until Francisco Madero launched the Mexican Revolution in November of 1910.

The failure of the1906 insurrection led to a split in the group between Ricardo Flores Magón and some of the other long-time members such as Camilo Arriaga and Juana B. Gutiérrez, and of several others from the old Club Ponciano Arriaga. The fight was bitter. Ricardo condemned his opponents in violent language, suggesting that Arriaga was nothing but a 'lazy aristocrat' and that Juana Gutiérrez was a 'lesbian – a degenerate'.[47] Ricardo called upon his supporters to come together around 'key points, most particularly around the need for immediate revolution'.[48]

The split with Arriaga and the others led Ricardo to conclude that the most important thing was the preservation of the revolutionary leadership, of the *Junta*. As Lomnitz writes, 'Ricardo's experience under pressure, then, was that without the junta, the movement dissolved into factionalism and disorganisation and could even drift into unsavory reformist alliances. Therefore, the junta had to be preserved'.[49] The *Junta* and its newspaper *Regeneración*. One cannot help but be struck by similarities to Vladimir Lenin's conception of the revolutionary party, but there is a difference. For Lenin, at least in theory, the party acted as the leadership of the working class to which it was responsible. The Leninist party's discipline was centralist, but in theory also democratic: democratic centralism. There were in the case of the PLM no such niceties. Ricardo led the *Junta* and the *Junta* led the revolution.

Another implication of Ricardo's conclusion was that the preservation of the *Junta* was all important, and therefore the leadership should not risk a return to Mexico.[50] Again, one thinks of Lenin and other Bolshevik leaders who facing arrest and perhaps death in Russia operated from Switzerland, other European countries, or even as far away as New York. But the Russian socialists also knew that when the revolution broke out, they had to return to Russia to lead it. Ricardo Flores Magón would never be able to decide that it was safe enough to return, and that would be a tragic weakness.

---

47   Lomnitz 2014, pp. 202–3.
48   Lomnitz, 2014, p. 201.
49   Lomnitz 2014, p. 207.
50   Lomnitz 2014, p. 207.

10   The Economic Crisis of 1907

The PLM's repeated attempted insurrections took place in the midst of a worsening general situation in Mexico as a result of the world economic crisis of 1907. The Mexican economic crisis that had actually begun in 1906 and lasted until 1908 had led to plant closings, layoffs, wage cuts, and general social misery in much of Mexico. So, from 1906 through 1910 there were, independent of PLM organising, waves of strikes in the mines and textile plants as well as an important railroad strike. The economic situation only exacerbated the dissatisfaction with the regime. While the PLM's insurrections might not succeed in detonating the revolution, they continued to demonstrate the great discontent that existed in the country and the growing willingness of the Mexican people to stand up against the government and even to take up arms in a struggle to overthrow it.

As conditions worsened after the 1907 economic crisis, Ricardo and the other PLM leaders came to believe that Mexico was ripe for revolution. As Lomnitz writes, 'Behind the junta's understanding of the causes of its failure there was a vision: Mexicans all over the country were thought to be fed up with the dictatorship and ready to rebel'.[51] The Mexican revolutionaries in the United States rejected the idea of waiting for the 1910 elections, a political process in which they had no hope. They began to organise for an insurrection in 1908, creating political clubs and resistance groups in Los Angeles and all of Southern California,[52] and throughout the American Southwest and the north of Mexico and even some deeper in Mexico.[53] These groups would take their cues from the *Junta* as the date approached.

After arriving in Los Angeles in 1907, the PLM's message had gradually become more explicitly anarchist. Ricardo Flores Magón had initially believed that he and his colleagues should portray themselves as liberals, keeping their anarchist principles a secret. In a fascinating undated private letter probably written in the summer of 1908 and sent to two of his closest collaborators, his brother Enrique and co-thinker Praxedis Guerrero, Ricardo explained why he had not earlier raised an anarchist program:

> If from the beginning we had called ourselves anarchists, nobody, except for a few, would have listened to us. Without calling ourselves anarch-

---

51   Lomnitz 2014, pp. 232–3.
52   Akers Chacón, 2018, pp. 181–205.
53   Lomnitz 2014, p. 249.

ists we have gone along sparking in many people's brains ideas of hatred against the possessing class and against the governmental caste. No liberal party in the world has the anti-capitalist tendencies of that which is about to revolutionise Mexico, and that has been achieved without saying that we are anarchists, and we should not have achieved it, even if we had not called ourselves anarchists, as we are, but had called ourselves simply socialists. It is all, then a question of tactics.[54]

Ricardo suggested that while claiming to be liberals, the PLM would promote anarchist measures:

We must give the land to the people in the course of the revolution ... We must also give the people possession of the factories, the mines, etc. In order that the whole country doesn't come down on top of us, we must continue the same tactic that we have attempted with some success: we must continue calling ourselves liberals in the course of the revolution, but in reality, we will go on propagandising anarchy and carrying out anarchist acts. We will go on expropriating the bourgeoisie and returning [the wealth] to the people.[55]

Ricardo called for the workers to take over both the fields and the factories, to work them collectively, and – come the revolution – to continue producing for the revolutionary movement and the new social order. The revolution would destroy the value of the existing currency, but peasants and workers would keep records of production and exchange goods among themselves without the use of money.

During this period, Ricardo Flores Magón and the PLM, who had always been sympathetic to Mexico's indigenous people, began to conceive of the indigenous as providing an example for their anarchist revolution. As Justin Akers Chacón writes, 'By 1908, they came to understand the indigenous campesinos and rural workers as "primitive Communists" who had occupied the front lines in the struggle against Díaz through ongoing resistance to the atomisation of their ancestral lands. They, in effect were the most intransigent opponents of capitalist expansion and natural allies within the revolutionary camp'.[56]

---

54   . Flores Magón 1989, pp. 380–1.
55   . Flores Magón 1989, p. 381.
56   Akers Chacón 2018, p. 144.

As the date for the insurrection of 1908 approached, the party's anarchist positions began to emerge ever more clearly. The PLM newspapers, the new *Revolución* beginning in 1907 and again after 1910 *Regeneración*, began publishing articles by Ricardo Flores Magón opposing an electoral or parliamentary strategy and advocating armed revolution, a war of the poor against the rich in which the people would seize the land and establish a cooperative society. Incendiary articles called for using bullets, not ballots. Alongside his own articles Ricardo Flores Magón ran excerpts from the books of the Russian anarchist Peter Kropotkin. There was no longer any doubt where the PLM stood. PLM newspapers, such as *Reforma* and *Libertad y Justicia* in Austin, Texas, called on workers and peasants to 'destroy the factory, block up the mine, devastate the farm, and resist the attack of the Cossacks with rifle bullets'. The PLM had now become an openly anti-capitalist party, an anarchist party aiming at a libertarian communist revolution.[57] Just before its 1908 revolt, the PLM board's anarchist majority voted to remove the socialists Villarreal and Manuel Sarabia from the board; though no longer a leader of the group, Juan Sarabia continued to be a trusted figure.

11　　　Persecution and International Solidarity

In response to the 1906 insurrection and the 1906 and 1907 strikes the Díaz government had determined that it had to eliminate the Mexican Liberal Party leadership once and for all. Since 1905 Díaz had set the Mexican state's embassy and consulates working with the Furlong Detective Agency that had conducted surveillance of the PLM's leaders and their activities. The US and Mexican governments cooperated to seize the mail between PLM leaders and their followers in both countries. In pursuing the PLM leaders over the rest of the decade, the Mexican government often had the assistance of the US Departments of State, War, Treasury, Commerce, Labour, Justice and Immigration. There existed as well a tacit understanding between Díaz and US Presidents Theodore Roosevelt and William Howard Taft that the PLM was an enemy of the governments of both nations and detrimental to their business interests. The top leaders of both Mexico and the United States cooperated to ensure that the Mexican anarchists were put out of commission.[58]

In 1907 Díaz's organisation acted, repeating more or less the scenario that had taken place in St. Louis. Directed by Enrique Creel, the former governor of

---

57　　Cockcroft 1968, pp. 162–3.
58　　Cockroft 1968, p. 128; Lomnitz 2014, p. 225.

Chihuahua who had been appointed the Mexican Ambassador to the United States, sent Furlong Agency detectives and local police officers, operating without a warrant, to the PLM headquarters in Los Angeles and arrested Ricardo Flores Magón, Librado Rivera, and Antonio I. Villarreal. The three revolutionaries fought off the detectives and police officers but were beaten into submission. While no charges were brought against them at the time, the PLM leaders' case was eventually combined with the unrelated case of two other PLM members, Tomás D. Espinosa and Ildefonso R. Martínez, who had been charged in Douglas, Arizona in December of 1906 with violating the neutrality law. All five men were charged with a conspiracy to launch a military expedition against Mexico from the then Territory of Arizona.[59] Ricardo Flores Magón and the others would remain in jail until 1910.

The American left and labour movements immediately moved to support the jailed Mexican revolutionaries as they had done before. In May of 1908 the Socialist Party of America's national convention voted a resolution in support of Ricardo Flores Magón and the other PLM members. The SPA's most influential newspaper, *The Appeal to Reason*, devoted virtually the entire 13 March 1909 issue to the PLM prisoners with a lead story by Ricardo Magón himself that had been smuggled out of his jail cell. The Los Angeles Socialist Party branch rallied immediately to the PLM cause with writer John Kenneth Turner playing a leading role. The wealthy socialist Elizabeth Darling Trowbridge provided financial support for the defence and socialist lawyers Job Harriman and A.R. Holston came forward to serve as the Mexican revolutionaries' defence attorneys.[60]

The Los Angeles Labour Council also came out in support of the Mexican revolutionaries in March, comparing Díaz's use of the American courts to arrest Flores Magón with George III's attempts to arrest George Washington. The Western Federation of Miners (WFM) voted to provide financial assistance, while the United Mine Workers (UMW) and the AFL also voted resolutions of support. Veteran organiser 'Mother' Mary Jones convinced the UMW to put up $1,000 and other miners' organisations to give another $3,000. When Samuel Gompers and the AFL Executive Council met with President Theodore Roosevelt, they gave him a letter dealing with the PLM prisoners' unjust arrest. In Chicago, the Political Refugee Defence League published the AFL's letter and began to circulate a petition demanding the release of Magón and the others. The League established a Mexican Political Refugee Committee with labour organiser John Murray as Chair and social worker and urban reformer

---

59   MacLachlan 1991, p. 22.
60   MacLachlan 1991, pp. 22–5.

Jane Addams as Treasurer. Thus, Flores Magón and the other political prisoners became a *cause celebre* not only of the American labour movement, but found their plight taken up by mainstream American progressives such as the influential Addams.[61]

The American labour organisations also used their political pull to get the matter taken up by the US Congress. Murray contacted William B. Wilson, a Democratic Party Congressman from Pennsylvania who was a former UMW official. Wilson, who chaired the House Rules Committee, was persuaded to hold Congressional hearings on the Mexican political prisoners in 1910. The solidarity on all sides – from the socialists, the unions, and the progressives – was remarkable.

To encourage such solidarity from American workers, the PLM leaders wrote and published in February 1908 in Emma Goldman's *Mother Earth* their 'Manifesto to the American People'. While avoiding criticism of the Roosevelt administration, the PLM leaders expressed their disappointment at being treated so shabbily in what they had thought was the 'free fatherland of George Washington'. They wondered if they might not be in Czarist Russia or 'the darkest heart of equatorial Africa' (then ruled by the empires of France and the King of Belgium and the scene of brutal exploitation, repression, and genocidal mass murder). The Manifesto expressed the PLM leaders' supposed disillusionment that corrupt officials could undermine the US Constitution.

In the Manifesto Ricardo Flores Magón and his comrades told the story of their persecution by Mexican and American authorities and explained why they had come 'to the decision to end by a revolution a state and condition of things that is offensive to civilisation and the most rudimentary humanitarian principles'. They then explained their programme of 1906 in broad outline, but changed the emphasis, suggesting that only the working class could actually carry out such a democratic and social programme. And, they suggested, such a struggle for democracy and social justice would become international.

> We think that political liberty is a beautiful lie so long as it has not for its basis economic liberty, and toward the conquest of that liberty our steps are directed. We are of the opinion that the social problem looming up on the horizon of humanity as a formidable great unknown, must be solved by the workingmen themselves, and it is for this reason and purpose that with all our forces, and with all our love we demand that the proletariat of Mexico organise and by so doing enable itself to take part in the tre-

---

61   Ibid.

mendous struggle that alone will liberate the proletariat of the world, the struggle which some day – may be in the near future – will place the goods of this earth within reach and power of all human beings.

Proclaiming 'we are revolutionists', the anarchists called upon the workers of the United States and the world's other nations to come to their assistance:

> Workers of the world! Our cause is your cause. The cause of the prolet-ariat knows no frontiers. The interests of the working people are the same in all lands under all climates, and all latitudes of our globe. Help us! ... Remember that only by unity of action and solidarity of effort the workers will emancipate themselves.[62]

The Manifesto, written and published simultaneously with the outpouring of solidarity from American labour and left organisations, represented the devel-opment of an internationalist labour outlook and strategy which the PLM had not expressed before, at least not at any length. For the first time, the PLM spoke in the terms of the socialist and anarchist movements about a worldwide work-ers' movement for the liberation of all humanity.

Solidarity among Mexican and US workers was not a new development. Dur-ing the end of the nineteenth century and the beginning of the twentieth, the Mexican border was porous, border controls were few, and both US and Mex-ican workers, especially in mining and on the railroads might work on either side of the border. The Knights of Labor, the American Federation of Labor, and the Industrial Workers of the World had all organised workers on both sides of the border at one time or another. US and Mexican workers had joined together in the US to strike and to organise unions. All of that had gone on for more than a generation.[63]

What was new about the PLM position was to link such bi-national labour solidarity to the idea of the Mexican revolution. And, equally novel and import-ant, the Mexican revolution was linked to the worldwide struggle against cap-ital. While the Socialist International and the Socialist Party of America called for an international socialist revolution, that idea, with the exception of a few tenuous contacts between the American and Mexican Socialist parties had never before been linked in practice to solidarity with Mexican workers. The PLM was now raising the idea of international proletarian revolution on the

---

62   Flores Magón 1908, pp. 546–54.
63   Gómez Quiñones 1994, pp. 63–177.

basis of an actual on-going revolutionary movement – if not yet a revolution – in Mexico. Yet, in fact, the manifesto did not express Ricardo Flores Magón's or the PLM leaderhip's genuine views.

12   The PLM's Conception of International Solidarity

In his private correspondence with PLM leaders, Ricardo Flores Magón explained his actual anarchist view of international labour solidarity. First, he called for the stimulation of anarchist immigration and of travel abroad by Mexican revolutionaries to win support for the coming Mexican Revolution.

> There will be new problems, but I don't think they will be hard to solve, with the workers themselves interested in the issues. In addition, many Spanish and Italian anarchists will come to see what's going on, and they will help a great deal. It seems to me that it would be good if one of us were to travel around during the revolution in order to inspire those comrades and urge them to give us a hand, inviting them to come to agitate the masses and to lead them in everything that may be necessary. I think that many would come and we could even defray the costs of their trip and they would spill out over the entire country a whole swarm of comrades.[64]

International labour solidarity is conceived of as an anarchist project, to be led and organised by anarchist militants from the Latin countries. At the same time, he feared – once the revolution was successful – becoming involved in regular international diplomatic relations and advocated instead a kind of international labour diplomacy. As he wrote to his comrades:

> We must not send representatives to foreign governments, because then we would enter into a sea of compromises that would deprive the revolution of its special character. We should cultivate international relations, not with the governments but rather with the workers' organisations of the world whether they be simply labour unionists, socialists or anarchists.[65]

---

64   Flores Magón 1989, p. 383.
65   Flores Magón 1989, p. 381.

By 1908, Flores Magón had come to see the prospects of the coming Mexican revolution in terms of its relationship to the anarchist movements of Spain and Italy, and to the anarchists, labour unions, and socialist organisations of other countries. Yet the Magonistas, though they received significant support from US labour and left organisations, did not place great hopes in the American workers. Ricardo wrote to his brother Enrique,

> Americans are incapable of feeling either enthusiasm or indignation. This is really a nation of pigs. Look at the socialists, how they cracked in such a cowardly way in their campaign for freedom of speech. Look at the brilliant American Federation of Labor, which with its million and a half members can't stop the judges when they declare injunctions against the unions or when they send organisers to places where there is no organised labour movement [sic]. These attacks on socialists and unions are tremendous, but they don't move the people. Those without work are chopped up and dispersed as in Russia; Roosevelt asks Congress to empower the administrator of the mails to exercise censorship over the newspapers: the nation is being militarised by giant steps but in spite of everything the Anglo-Saxon pachyderm doesn't become excited, doesn't become indignant, doesn't vibrate. If their domestic troubles don't agitate the Americans, can we expect them to care about ours?[66]

Then too, there was the Americans' racism. Ricardo wrote regarding the lack of adequate support from the Chicago labour movement,

> The group in Chicago doesn't defend us, it exists only to defend the Russians. And we are poor Mexicans. We are revolutionaries and our ideals are advanced; but we are Mexicans. This is our fault. Our skin isn't white and not everyone is capable of comprehending that also beneath our skin there are nerves, a heart, and a brain.[67]

Clearly the Magonistas had little hope that the American working class, which they perceived as conservative, timid, and racist, would offer much support to the anarchist revolution that they were working to foster in Mexico. Yet the American working class was by far the largest working class in North America, far larger than the Canadian and Mexican working classes, so if they, the Amer-

---

66   Flores Magón 1989, pp. 372–9.
67   Flores Magón 1989, pp. 412–14.

ican workers, were excluded because of their political weaknesses, then we are really talking about a minority of the continental working class taking charge. And, of course, the PLM never gave up its opposition to Chinese immigrants; there was no place for solidarity with them. All of this has to make one wonder just how sincere the Magonistas were in their call for an international working-class movement.

13   The Madero Revolution of 1910

In November 1910 an unlikely rival revolutionary leader suddenly wreaked havoc with Flores Magón's plans for revolution in Mexico. Francisco I. Madero, a candidate for president who had been imprisoned by Díaz, called for a revolutionary insurrection to take place on 10 November 1910. His call for revolution would reach a scale much larger than anything that the Magonistas had known and would split the PLM organisation down the middle.

Madero, a wealthy landowner and industrialist from northern Mexico, educated in Mexico, France, and the United States, came from one of the country's dozen wealthiest families, 'the cream of the enterprising, northern Mexican landed elite'.[68] He had been an early supporter of the Ricardo Flores Magón, *Regeneración*, and the Liberal Party. Camilo Arriaga, a friend of Madero's, had even succeeded in getting him to contribute $2,000 toward the publication of *Regeneración*. Madero wrote to Magón in early 1905 that he believed that *Regeneración* would help in the 'regeneration of the Fatherland by arousing Mexicans in noble indignation against their tyrants'. He went so far as to say that he found 'all of your ideas congenial'. Madero and Ricardo Flores Magón even collaborated in the draft of a manifesto urging Coahuila voters to exercise their rights in the gubernatorial campaign of 1905. Madero and Arriaga, however, both balked at the idea of armed revolution toward which the PLM was gravitating.

Madero represented a part of the capitalist class that had another political project for Mexico, one far different from that of Ricardo Flores Magón's. Madero was a member and a representative figure of a section of the Mexican bourgeoisie who felt that Porfirio Díaz's inner circle of *los científicos* and foreign industrialists had excluded them from their fair share of both power and of profits. These capitalists, bankers, industrialists and commercial farmers and ranchers, many located mostly in northern Mexico represented a modernising

---

68   Knight 1986, vol. 1, p. 55. Knight emphasises the northern financiers.

bourgeoisie that wanted to break the power of Díaz in order to expand their own influence and control over the Mexican economy and society.[69] This modernising bourgeoisie of the North found a broad supportive social base in Mexico's 'rising middle class' both urban and rural.[70] Though it is true that this was a heterogeneous movement with a largely middle-class base and eventually a following among workers and peasants, it was the modernising bourgeoisie of the North that led it. While Madero had initially felt that he shared with the PLM the common goal of reforming the Díaz regime, overtime it became clear to him that he and Magón were not only on diverging paths but also represented alternative and antagonistic visions of the sort of society that should be created once the dictator was overthrown.

Madero had become involved in politics following the violent repression of political dissidents in 1903 by Bernardo Reyes, the governor of Nuevo León. In response, Madero founded the Benito Juárez Liberal Club, ran for local office and lost, but then began to put his money into the organisation of other liberal clubs and the establishment of opposition newspapers such as *El Demócrata*. Madero and his friends in the Benito Juárez Liberal Club became involved in the Coahuila gubernatorial elections of 1905 but were again defeated. It was at this time that he also contributed financially to *Regeneración*. Then, Porfirio Díaz, in an interview with American journalist James Creelman published in *Pearson's Magazine* in February 1908, suggested that Mexico was ready for democracy, that the 1910 elections would be free and fair, and he implied that he was ready to step down.

Believing that the time to act had come, Madero decided to put forth his own vision of a post-Díaz Mexico in a book that would launch his own bid for the presidency. Madero's book, *Political Succession and Effective Suffrage*, published in 1910, argued that militarism had been the bane of Mexico's history. Madero argued that military leaders had repeatedly throughout the country's history established dictatorial power, Díaz being the most recent. Militarism had distorted Mexico's history; the country, he argued, must return to a civilian and democratic government. The book called for the organisation of a party standing for democracy with the slogan 'Effective Suffrage and No Reelection'.[71] The phenomenal success of his book launched Madero's national

69   Cockcroft 1983, pp. 96–7.
70   Knight 1986, vol. 1, p. 63. Knight discusses particularly the 'rising middle class' but acknowledges the very wealthy landlords, industrialists, and many corporate directors and managers who formed the leaders and cadres of the movement.
71   Francisco Madero, *La sucesión presidencial*, at: http://www.memoriapoliticademexico.org/Textos/6Revolucion/1910LSP.pdf

political campaign for the presidency as the head of the very democratic movement that he had called for.

At the same time that he was writing his book, Madero was organising his campaign. In January of 1909 he founded the Anti-Reelectionist or Democratic Party and by May he had established the Anti-reelectionist headquarters in Mexico City. In June he hired the brilliant young philosopher José Vasconcelos to edit the party's paper *El Anti-Reeleccionista*. Madero began to campaign for the presidency, travelling throughout the country and speaking to crowds of thousands. He was not the only candidate. There was also Díaz who, after all, had decided to run again. The other major opposition candidate Bernardo Reyes, was also running as the genuine Liberal, initially with a stronger organisation, though within a year Madero had caught up with and surpassed him.

While the core of the Madero movement was a section of the *haute bourgeoisie*, its strongest social base was among the eight percent of Mexicans who could be called middle class, mostly a classical petty bourgeoisie made up of small businessmen, merchants, and professionals but also including some corporate employees, directors and managers. By and large, Madero's followers approved of Díaz's economic programme, but objected to the dictatorship. As Alan Knight writes, 'Maderismo was ... the expression of a rising middle class, comfortably well off, and demanding its place in the political sun'. Yet the labouring classes also supported Madero in large numbers. Workers – miners, railroad workers, textile workers, printers and electricians – backed Madero, and the support of artisans may have been even greater.[72]

Madero courted the working class, speaking in the mill towns of Puebla, Veracruz, and the Federal District. His supporter, José Vasconcelos, the famous writer, recorded that, rather than attempt to win over the middle-class political activists, 'On the contrary, we began to organise mass meetings in the populous poor neighbourhoods, especially with the working class, and our success surprised us and began to alarm the government'.[73] Madero's modest but progressive labour programme called for pensions, accident compensation, and free association, that is, for the right to organise unions. This was enough to attract workers' support. Historians agree that most workers were far more likely to be supporters of the Liberal Madero than of the more radical Mexican Liberal Party.[74] Workers supporting Madero developed their own 'popular lib-

---

72   Knight 1986, vol. 1, pp. 55–71. Quotation on p. 63.
73   Vasconcelos 1993, p. 312.
74   Lear 2001, p. 129.

eralism' that 'equated the struggle against tyranny in the political sphere with that in the workplace', though they seldom raised specific demands.[75]

Díaz at first harassed Madero, threatening his financial and business interests, but by June, with Madero drawing large crowds, the dictator had decided that more serious measures were needed. Madero was arrested on charges of insulting the president and fomenting rebellion. The authorities also rounded up and jailed somewhere between 5,000 and 60,000 other members of the Anti-reelectionist movement and closed down the Anti-reelectionist press. Díaz naturally went on to win the primary elections. Having been defeated in the election, Madero was released from prison on bail and confined to the city of San Luis Potosí, but in October 1910 he escaped from his guards, took the train to the border, and walked across the international bridge into Laredo. Once opposed to violent revolution as unnecessary and unpatriotic, he now set about to organise one.[76] At once he set up his political headquarters in San Antonio, Texas, began purchasing guns in the United States, and published his revolutionary manifesto, the Plan of San Luis Potosí.[77] Madero's Plan, declared the recent national elections to be null and void, refused to recognise the results and called for the revolutionary overthrow of Díaz and the establishment of democracy in Mexico. While primarily a document demanding political democracy, it also called for the 'restitution to its former owners of land that had been taken from them in an arbitrary fashion'.[78] The phrase was powerful enough to begin to set in motion a peasant revolution that would eventually turn the country upside down. The proclamation called on the Mexican people to rise in revolution on 10 November 1910 at 6:00 p.m.[79]

While a few groups did rise up, some even a couple of days before the appointed hour, the organisational infrastructure for the rebellion had not yet been created and the revolution was postponed as fighting units were organised, arms collected, and plans laid. Finally, on 11 February 1911, Madero himself left the United States and entered Mexico at the head of 130 fighters, attacking Casas Grandes, Chihuahua. He personally led the first major action of the revolution that would bring him to power in less than six months. While the early battles were all defeats, the Federal Army commanders failed to follow up on their successes and the Maderistas learned from their mistakes. Madero behaved courageously enhancing his public image and inspiring his troops.

---

75   Lear 2001, p. 130.
76   Cockcroft 1968, p. 159 and p. 175.
77   González Ramírez 1954, pp. 37–8.
78   Ibid.
79   Knight 1986, vol. 1, pp. 71–7 and pp. 183–8.

14   Madero's Revolution Absorbs the PLM

Five days before Madero's revolution was scheduled to begin on 10 November 1910 as he had announced in the Plan de San Luis Potosí, the PLM issued a new manifesto urging its members to join in any pro-Madero uprisings, but to fight independently for the 'economic revolution'. PLM members were warned that Madero's was a 'conservative party' and that they should not make 'common cause' with his 'personalist' movement. Members were assured that the PLM had not signed and never would sign any agreement with the Madero Anti-Reelectionist movement. A new set of 'General Instructions' intended to guide members actions in the course of the 1910 insurrection reminded them that they might join with Madero's force in combat, but not in any political alliance.[80] While sharing a common enemy in the Díaz government, the PLM made it clear that they did not view Madero as an ally but rather as an enemy, a class enemy.

To explain his differences with the Madero revolution, Ricardo Flores Magón published the 'Manifesto to the Workers of the World', the first major revision of the PLM platform since the Program of 1906. The Manifesto began by explaining in broad terms the goals of the PLM:

> The Mexican Liberal Party is taking part in the current insurrection with the deliberate and firm goal of expropriating the land and the means of production in order to hand them over to the people, that is, to each and every one of the inhabitants of Mexico, regardless of their sex. We consider this step essential in order to open the way for the real emancipation of the Mexican people.[81]

Then he attempted to put the Mexican Revolution in an international context.

> This great struggle of the two social classes in Mexico is the first act of the great universal tragedy that very soon will have as its theater the surface of the entire plant, and whose final act will be the triumph of the generous formula Liberty, Equality, Fraternity which the bourgeois political revolutions have not been able to realise in fact, because they have not dared to shatter the back bone of tyranny: capitalism and authoritarianism.

---

80   Cockcroft 1968, p. 176.
81   Zertuche Muñoz 1995, p. 112.

Comrades of the entire world: the solution to the social problem is in the hands of the disinherited of the whole earth, and it requires the practice of only one great virtue: solidarity.[82]

Ricardo also called for a 'world protest against the intervention of [foreign] powers in Mexican affairs ...'.[83]

The PLM, with its underground organisation – scores of local groups throughout the country, veteran fighters, and caches of arms – contributed to some of the important struggles of the 1910 insurrection between November 1910 and February 1911. Then between February and June it was simply swept up in the rising tide of Madero's much broader and larger revolutionary movement with its myriad fighting groups and armies first of hundreds and then of thousands.[84] The PLM had twice attempted in 1906 and 1908 to detonate the revolution, and now the revolution had finally arrived, but with the PLM headquartered in the United States, with little money, and too few leaders and cadres, the PLM leadership found it difficult to have much impact on the course of the unfolding events, though they did have a strong organisation in Chihuahua where the first major actions took place. Ricardo's belief that the *Junta* must be protected and so could not return to Mexico, made it extremely difficult for him and his comrades to provide their personal leadership at the crucial moment.

15   The PLM as Revolutionary Vanguard

Throughout these years the PLM Junta, the small revolutionary leadership committee, had continued to lead the organisation. It was in this respect an anarchist organisation in the Bakuninist tradition, attempting through the propaganda of the deed to inspire a mass movement. The Junta, a self-appointed leadership body from the beginning, expelled those with whom it did not agree and coopted onto the body new members, as it needed them. The PLM then was

---

82   Zertuche Muñoz 1995, p. 113.
83   Ibid.
84   There is a difference of opinion on the importance of the PLM between James Cockcroft who argues that they contributed important groups of fighters and helped win significant initial victories (Cockcroft 1968, pp. 177–83) and Knight who argues that their role was minor or even negligible (Knight 1986, vol. 1, pp. 229–30). For Knight, the proof of the pudding is in the eating. He writes: 'After all, it was the 1910 Maderista revolt which turned into a revolution, not the PLM insurrections of 1906 or 1908' (Knight 1986, p. 130).

not in any sense a democratic organisation; there were no regular party conventions, no votes on the officers, no referenda on issues. One might argue that the unrelenting repression of the Díaz dictatorship made such democratic procedures impossible. Perhaps. But PLM's leadership and many of its followers lived and worked in the United States, many others might have easily crossed the border into the United States, as there were few border controls in that era, and held a convention there. Surely it would have faced difficulties from both the American authorities and the private detective agencies. But the revolutionary syndicalist IWW, the Socialist Party, and some American anarchist groups held political meetings in the United States, and so too might have the PLM. For the PLM to have done so would probably have involved the creation of a legal organisation and another parallel illegal organisation, an organisational strategy successfully employed by socialist parties in other countries. The point is that some sort of more democratic structure and procedures were possible. The truth of the matter, however, is that Ricardo Flores Magón had no interest in creating a democratic organisation, believing that he and his Bakuninist co-thinkers must lead the movement.

Even the *Junta* and the PLM's inner circle could not tolerate differences. Ricardo Flores Magón, the preeminent leader of the PLM, would organise and carry out over the years a series of expulsions of those individuals or groups that he believed had deviated from the anarchist revolutionary path, while others who developed independent views found that they had to leave to create new organisations or to join other parties. Some of these divisions were certainly politically justifiable, such as the split with the socialist in the PLM who had very quickly come to support Madero.[85] Ricardo's brother Jesús Flores Magón, Marueal Sarabia, and Lázaro Gutiérrez de Lara, leaders of the socialist faction, wanted to join the Madero movement and to participate in the democratic political opening that followed Madero's victory. In a personal meeting, Ricardo refused their proposal to join them in Madero's movement.[86] He was a revolutionary and he rejected participation in a bourgeois party, which Madero's organisation certainly was. Later several former Magonistas would become part of Madero's new capitalist state, including Enrique Flores Magón who became Secretary of the Interior, that is head of the state's repressive forces. It was from that office that Jesús Magón began to publish a new version of *Regeneración*, claiming the mantel of the PLM for Madero and relentlessly attacking the anarchist PLM in Los Angeles.[87]

---

85   Lomnitz 2014, pp. 275–99.
86   Lomnitz 2014, pp. 292–3.
87   Lomnitz 2014, pp. 302–3.

While the split with the socialist was justifiable politically, other splits and expulsions, such as that of fellow anarchist Juan Mancaleano who had come from the House of the World Worker (Casa) in Mexico City to Los Angeles and became involved with *Regeneración*, had no ideological foundation but resulted simply from the lack of an ability to incorporate others into the PLM project.[88] In any case, without any democratic structures or processes, and without any representation in the organisation of minority views, every difference of opinion was likely to lead to an expulsion or a split.

These political and organisational issues were exacerbated by Ricardo Flores Magón's character and personality. During his years in the United States, very difficult times of persecution, poverty, and danger, where he personally experienced the racism of American society, he became ever more irascible, doctrinaire, intolerant, an authoritarian.[89] He called his political opponents in the radical movement pimps, pederasts, lesbians, perverts, and degenerates. At other times he glorified violence and revenge.[90] He would go on to order the assassination of former colleagues who had become Socialists. As Claudio Lomnitz writes, 'The strategy of dealing so viciously with internal fractures and dissent was undoubtedly connected to the urge to place a strategic goal – armed revolution – above any other personal or ethical considerations. Following the failed revolution of 1906, this would become a recurrent practice in the Liberal [PLM] ranks'.[91]

While calling for an uprising in Mexico from Los Angeles, Ricardo Flores Magón himself declined to cross the border to lead the revolution, leading to accusations of cowardice from both his enemies and some PLM members.[92] He was compared to Madero, who after all had not launched his revolution from the United States but had returned to Mexico to issue the call and himself and then led his forces into battle. All of those were mistakes, but without a doubt his worst error in judgement was authorising a joint PLM-IWW invasion of Baja California.

88   Lomnitz 2014, pp. 436–41.
89   Lomnitz 2014, pp. 200–7.
90   Lomnitz 2014, pp. 203, 255, 259, 306, 376, 381, 393, and 396.
91   Lomnitz 2014, p. 204.
92   Lomnitz 2014, pp. 257–60.

16   The PLM Attack on Baja California

With Madero's democratic revolution threatening to eclipse the PLM's anarchist movement, the Magonistas decided to launch a dramatic offensive: an invasion of Baja California from their base in the United States. The Magonistas had
been hampered by the fact that their leadership remained in Los Angeles while
the revolution was developing in Mexico; it was absolutely essential that they
establish a headquarters on Mexican territory if they were to play a role in the
developing revolutionary movement. At that time, northern Baja California to
which there were no highways, was virtually unreachable by land from Central Mexico, was very sparsely populated with only 50,000 inhabitants in the
whole peninsula, and had only a small number of government troops defending it. It was quite vulnerable to attack. Many of the Magonistas' Mexican and
Mexican-American members were located along both sides of the border and
the PLM had an ally in the revolutionary syndicalist Industrial Workers of the
World (IWW) that had members in California and Arizona. So, it was decided
by the PLM *Junta* to violate US law and launch an invasion of Baja California
from the United States.

The PLM *Junta* sent a few men to reconnoiter the Baja California border
in December 1910. Then on 29 January 1911 two PLM members – José María
Leyva and Simón Berthold Chacón, both Mexican citizens – led a force of sixty
men from Caléxico, California (in the United States) to nearby Mexicali, Baja
California (in Mexico). The town was small. Both leaders were committed and
experienced PLM cadres. Leyva, who had been born in El Fuerte, Sinaloa, had
been involved in the Cananea strike of 1906 and in 1908 had participated in
an attack on Las Vacas, Coahuila. In Los Angeles he had joined the Hodcarri-
ers Union, working in construction. Berthold, born in Nacozari, Sonora, son of
a German father and a Mexican mother, was a well-known Socialist activist in
Los Angeles. The PLM quickly took Mexicali. From there the PLM troops moved
on to Tijuana, population 150, and to Tecate and Ensenada, which together with
other villages in the region had a total population of 1,500.[93]

The PLM found little support among the residents of Baja California for its
radical revolution, but there was enthusiasm for their revolution on the American side of the border among Socialists and anarchists. The American writer,
Jack London, then a Socialist, issued a personal manifesto that was distributed
at a meeting in the Labor Temple of Los Angeles organised by the IWW in support of the Mexican Revolution. London wrote:

---

93   Taylor 1993, vol. 1, pp. 199–200.

We socialists, anarchists, chicken thieves, outlaws and undesirable citizens of the United States are with you heart and soul in your efforts to
overthrow slavery and autocracy in Mexico ... All the names you are being
called, we have been called. And when graft and greed get up and begin to
call names, honest men, brave men, patriotic men and martyrs can expect
nothing less than to be called chicken thieves and outlaws ... I subscribe
myself as a chicken thief and a revolutionary.[94]

Emma Goldman, the famous American anarchist, visited Los Angeles and San
Diego during the months of the PLM invasion giving speeches in support of the
rebels. And Joe Hill, the American Wobbly, visited the PLM held territory in Baja
California in late April where he witnessed conflict in May between PLM troops
and Mexican *federales*.[95] For America's far left, the PLM-IWW alliance and invasion of Baja California was the cause of the hour, an expression of international
working-class solidarity, and the chance for a libertarian revolution in Mexico.

The PLM's Mexican forces numbering perhaps a hundred were initially sup-
plemented by about an equal number of IWW members many of whom came
from Holtville, a town in the Imperial Valley 125 miles east of San Diego. Soon,
however, they were joined by 'various soldiers of fortune, deserters from the US
Army and Marines, vagabonds, unemployed miners, vaqueros, bandits, etc.'.[96]
At its peak, the PLM army in Baja may have numbered 500, but it was hardly a
unified force. Over the next several months there would be constant tensions
between the Mexican and foreign fighters, between the PLM and IWW idealists on the one hand and the soldiers of fortune and political opportunists on
the other. The PLM had difficult in maintaining control militarily and politically over its forces in Baja California, some of whom occasionally carried out
unauthorised attacks on Mexican towns.

The PLM-IWW invaders seemed to lose sight of the mission, which was to
establish a foothold in Mexico in order to launch a broader libertarian revolution, and some now wanted to create a utopian community. After the capture
of the tiny town of Tijuana in May, one of the American commanders began to
establish cardrooms for poker and faro to attract tourists and provide income
and jobs. The IWW members dreamed of establishing in Tijuana a commune
that might provide a model of a communist workers society. At other times
though, the invasion force became dominated by the foreigners who elected

94   Labor 2013, pp. 317–18.
95   Adler 2012, pp. 170–7.
96   Taylor 1993, p. 201.

one or another soldier of fortune as their leader, some of whom entered into arrangements with American businessmen and politicians who had an interest either in investing in Baja California or in seizing it for the United States. Neither the Wild West utopia nor the businessmen's petty imperialism was advancing the PLM's libertarian revolution.

Madero, meanwhile, infuriated by *Regeneración*'s attacks on him, had decided that he would never be able to work with the anarchist wing of the PLM and that he could not tolerate the existence of their toehold in Mexico. It was impossible, however, to send his revolutionary army against the PLM's soldiers who had also risen in the rebellion against Porfirio Díaz. So, Madero negotiated with the US government to send by rail from El Paso, Texas to Caléxico, California some1,500 veterans of Díaz's federal army, officers and soldiers who had gone over to the Madero revolution commanded by General Manuel Gordillo Escudero. They would now be used to suppress the anarchist invasion. At the same time, Madero sent several former Magonistas, members of the socialist wing of the PLM who had joined his revolution – Jesús Flores Magón (brother of the rebels Enrique and Ricardo), Juan Sarabia, José María Leyva and Jesús Gonzéz Monroy – to try to negotiate peace with the PLM. The peace negotiations failed and Ricardo Flores Magón issued an order that his former friends and comrades Juan Sarabia and Lázaro Gutiérrez be assassinated, though his organisation could not carry out the threat.[97] General Gordillo's federal troops moved in, taking Caléxico without a shot being fired and then proceeded to Tijuana, where his forces numbering 600 men aided by 150 mostly Mexican volunteers from San Diego won the battle against a much smaller PLM force. The American Wobblies and other volunteers who had joined the PLM crossed the border and straggled back into the United States where they were arrested by the US military, while the rank-and-file Mexican radicals disappeared into the countryside.

Madero sent a 'peace delegation' made up of Jesús Flores Magón, José María Leyva, Juan Sarabia, and Jesús Gonzales Monroy, which met with the PLM Junta in Los Angeles on 14 June 1911. Madero's ambassadors supposedly offered Ricardo Flores Magón the vice-presidency under Madero if he would give up his independent revolutionary organisation, which he refused.[98] One has to think that it was unlikely that Madero would have fulfilled his promise to give the vice-presidency to Ricardo Flores Magón and impossible to imagine the anarchist ever occupying such a position.

97   Lomnitz 2014, p. 381.
98   Akers Chacón 2018, p. 269.

The PLM invasion of Baja California proved to be both a military failure and a far worse political fiasco. Ricardo Flores Magón and his *Junta* failed to exert military or political control over the forces they had dispatched to Baja California. They could not control the leadership and could not keep the forces on mission, which was to establish a PLM base there. Ricardo Flores Magón himself had declined to go to Mexico and to lead the revolutionary movement of which he was the head. Not only did some think him a coward, but his absence also contributed to the defeat of the mission by failing to provide personal leadership. The fact that the majority of PLM-IWW troops were in fact American radicals or foreign soldiers of fortune, and the involvement of some of the soldiers of fortune with American businessmen and politicians, discredited the PLM in the eyes of many Mexicans. Though Flores Magón surely never had any intention to separate Baja California from Mexico or to annex it to the United States, the damage to the group's reputation had been done; they were now seen by many as filibusters, that is, as adventurers in league with American imperialism.[99] Ricardo Flores Magón's invasion of Baja California also drove deeper the wedge between the anarchist and the socialist wings of the PLM, exacerbating the differences between the two. And, finally, it brought down on the group the most severe government repression that it had suffered.[100]

17   A New Wave of Repression

As Madero's forces were driving the PLM out of Baja California, US government officials arrested Ricardo and Enrique Flores Magón, Librado Rivera and other PLM leaders and activists on charges of violating the neutrality laws. Ricardo Flores Magón and the others were released on bail. The grand jury handed down on 8 July 1911 indictments against the PLM leaders on several counts of conspiracy to 'hire and retain persons in the United States to enter service of foreign people as soldiers'.[101] The PLM's socialist attorney Job Harriman managed to delay the trial for a year. On this occasion, there was far less solidarity than in the past. The American Federation of Labor, the Socialist Party of America, and the Progressives had deserted Ricardo Flores Magón and the PLM and had become supporters of Madero's liberal revolution. Only Emma Goldman and the anarchists and the Industrial Workers of the World stood by the Mexican revolutionaries.

99   Taylor 1993, pp. 222–7; Lomnitz 2014, pp. 319–29.
100   Akers Chacón 2018, pp. 245–69. He offers a more sympathetic account of the events.
101   MacLachlan 1991, p. 41.

The PLM leaders' trial took place in July 1912 in a hostile political atmosphere shortly after the confessed bombing of the Los Angeles Times Building in 1911 by ironworkers John and James McNamara who had been sentenced to fifteen years in prison. The *Los Angeles Times* had worked to convince the public that unions, anarchists, socialists and bombers were the same and represented a common threat to the established order and public safety. The trial of the Magonistas itself was quite unfair. During the trial the government brought to the stand dubious witnesses who fabricated evidence about the PLM members' activities, while the government would not pay to transport PLM witnesses to the trial. Outside the courtroom, allegations were made that industrialist John D. Spreckles had paid for the Mexicans' defence, a charge (the veracity of which is unclear) that was obviously intended to discredit the PLM in the eyes of its own supporters. The jury found all five men guilty of conspiracy, four on three counts and one on two counts, and the judge sentenced them to one year and eleven months in the federal penitentiary at McNeil Island, Washington.[102] The arrest, trial, conviction and imprisonment of Ricardo Flores Magón, the PLM's leading figure, and two of his most important lieutenants, removed them from the scene at a crucial moment. Their sentences shortened by four months for good behaviour, they were not released until 19 January 1914, by which time the situation in Mexico had changed dramatically.

18   The Split in the PLM: Anarchists vs. Socialists

The Madero revolution's success directly challenged the PLM's leadership and had quickly led to a split in the PLM that reached from top to bottom. The PLM's attacks on Madero, the proclamation of its anarchist program, and the invasion of Baja California had only exacerbated the divisions between the two groups. Precipitating the split was the case of Prisciliano G. Silva, a PLM military leader who had come to the aid of Madero's troops in Chihuahua but refused to recognise Madero as his leader. Madero had Silva arrested and disarmed, the beginning of the Madero policy of disarming or otherwise neutralising PLM troops.[103] Ricardo Flores Magón responded with the article 'Francisco I. Madero Is a Traitor to the Cause of Freedom' published in the 25 February 1911 issue of *Regeneración*. Magón wrote, 'Mexicans: your "Provisional President", as he fancies himself, has begun to deliver blows against freedom. What will

102   MacLachlan 1991, pp. 44–7.
103   Cockcroft 1968, p. 182.

happen when the "Provisional" becomes actual?'[104] The bitter conflict between Ricardo Flores Magón and Madero led to a split in the PLM.

The PLM, while dominated by the Bakunin anarchists like Ricardo and Enrique Flores Magón, had always had some members who considered themselves to be socialists rather than anarchists. Now, with the Madero rebellion gathering momentum, the socialist wing led by Lázaro Gutiérrez de Lara and Antonio I. Villarreal split off and went off to join the Madero forces. Gutiérrez de Lara and other socialist in the Mexican Liberal Party (PLM) had a substantially different intellectual formation than the anarchists, having been educated in the European socialist tradition. Socialism as an organised political tendency had first arrived in Mexico in 1888 with the German immigrant Pablo Zierold who worked in the Levien company workshop producing musical instruments. Zierold, who after coming to Mexico had remained in contact with August Bebel, Karl Liebknecht, and Rosa Luxemburg, both translated socialist articles and wrote pamphlets about socialism. He was a founder in August 1911 in Mexico of the Socialist Workers Party (PSO), later simply called the Socialist Party (PS). The party took its organisational and political ideas from the Spanish socialist movement where Marxist rhetoric provided a cover for reformist politics.

During the Madero regime, the small PS met in a private house or in the tailor shop of one of its members. Among those who attended the meetings were Aquiles Serdán, Serapio Rendón and Lázaro Gutiérrez de Lara.[105] Mexican socialists were educated in the approach of German, Spanish, and other European socialist parties with their evolutionary rhetoric, their emphasis on organising unions and a socialist party that could win elections, a process which they believed would make possible a gradual, peaceful conquest of power.[106] Nevertheless, given Mexican conditions, most importantly the dictatorship that made virtually impossible the building of unions or of reformist working-class political parties, the Socialists had joined the PLM and participated in its insurrections. Reformist socialism had mounted up, picked up its guns, and become part of a revolutionary movement, but its goal was the creation of a modern capitalist and democratic society in which a socialist labour movement could eventually grow.

The PLM socialists had accepted Ricardo Flores Magón's leadership for a decade, but when Madero's democratic movement appeared and found a national

---

104   Cockcroft 1968, p. 183.
105   García Cantú 1969, p. 130.
106   Schorske 1972, *passim*. See also: Kautsky 1971 and Kautsky 1909.

response, the socialists of the PLM moved on and joined the larger and more politically moderate movement. Their relationship with the Socialist Party of America may have facilitated that movement, though it is not clear how much the American Socialists influenced the Mexicans at that moment. Gutiérrez de Lara and others who left the PLM to join Madero did not simply become Maderistas, however; they remained socialists, even though they were now critical supporters of Madero's democratic revolution.

After the Madero forces' military victory in the spring of 1911 and his subsequent election to the presidency in November, the Mexican socialists – Juan Sarabia, Antonio I. Villarreal, Gutiérrez de Lara, and Soto y Gama – focused on organising in the Mexican working class, which sometimes put them at odds with the Madero government. The four organised a large demonstration on 3 September 1911 to protest a government crackdown on the transport workers. They also participated in a demonstration on 15 January 1912 organised by Ezequiel Chávez (also called Pérez) to support Madero, but Gutiérrez de Lara spoke out on the need for socialism. He also organised a labour group in Zacatecas and another in Nuevo León explicitly linked to the Socialist Party.[107]

While founded in the image of European social democracy, under the impact of the Mexican situation and Mexican and American left and labour organisations, the PS evolved and turned in a different direction. After an intense debate on the issue in the pages of the party's paper *El Socialista*, the organisation voted to reject parliamentary politics in favour of economic action, that is, the organisation of unions and strikes. The example of the IWW active in the mining regions of northern Mexico and of the Spanish anarchists in Mexico City may have helped to turn the PS away from electoral politics and toward revolutionary syndicalism. The anarchists of Europe, however, also influenced the party. While in Europe in 1910 to escape the repression in Mexico and the United States, Manuel Sarabia made contact with Jean Grave the French anarchist and publisher of *Les Temps Nouveaux*, for which Sarabia wrote some articles on the Mexican Revolution. He also renewed contacts with the Spanish-speaking left in New York, publishing verse and articles in *Cultura Proletaria*.[108]

The Socialist Party of Mexico, with its base among the former PLM members and its many contacts in the labour movement – among miners, textile workers, and various other groups in Mexico City – became a significant current in the *Casa del Obrero Mundial* (COM or Casa – House of the World Worker), the principal labour organisation established in the wake of the revolution. Between its

107   Torres Parés 1989, pp. 136–7.
108   Torres Parés 1989, p. 137.

founding in 1912 and its demise in 1918, the Casa was the principal labour organisation in Mexico with chapters in Mexico City and several industrial cities and towns. Socialists such as Soto y Gama, Santiago R. de la Vega, Rafael Quintero, and a comrade Pioquinto contributed to the Casa newspaper *El Sindicalista*. Santibañez who had become editor of the PS newspaper *El Socialista* wrote at the time:

> Given the state of revolution in which the country finds itself, we will not deal with political issues ... We will defend the working class and we will contribute to its intellectual and economic betterment, understanding that a people that doesn't advance disappears.[109]

The Mexican socialists appear by 1912 to have become revolutionary syndicalists, breaking with Madero and turning their backs on political parties while organising radical unions in a way that paralleled developments in other parts of the world, particularly in France and in the United States.

The Socialists' attitude toward the Madero government, at least in retrospect, can be seen clearly in *The Mexican People: Their Struggle for Freedom* written by Gutiérrez de Lara with the assistance of American socialist fellow traveller, journalist, and screenplay writer Edgcumb Pinchon and published shortly after the overthrow of the Madero government and assassination of Madero himself in 1913. The authors devote most of the book's 360 pages to presenting the Mexican Revolution as the culmination of a 400-year long struggle for freedom and social justice, relegating the Díaz regime and the revolution to the last 60 pages of the book. Gutiérrez de Lara and Pinchon credit the Mexican Liberal Party with representing the most important expression of that historic process in the first years of the twentieth century. They praise the PLM, recount the importance of the Cananea strike, describe the repression it faced, and recall the solidarity it received from the Socialist Party and the American unions, though they do not mention its anarchist politics.[110]

Gutiérrez de Lara had left the PLM to support Madero, yet his discussion and analysis of the Madero government is scathing and even contemptuous. The Mexican socialist now argued that once in power Madero was fundamentally no different than Díaz, using his office to enrich himself and his family through his connections to foreign corporations such as Standard Oil, one of the largest corporations in the United States.

---

109   Torres Parés 1989, p. 140.
110   Gutiérrez de Lara 1914, pp. 341–4.

The new administration in short, represented neither the principles of the Revolution, nor even the theoretical reformism of Madero. It represented simply the private interests of the Madero clan. It is not a matter of surprise, therefore, that throughout this régime not a single measure was instituted tending toward the amelioration of the vast evils endured by the people since the Díaz *cuartelazo* [barracks rebellion] of 1876.[111]

The authors go on to discuss Madero's failure to carry out either agrarian reform or to bring free elections and democracy.[112] Madero as president, they write, was an utter failure:

Exponent of the Revolution by the will of the masses he found himself in fact merely the *deus ex machina* of the Scientificos [*sic*]. And he had neither the knowledge, will, nor understanding to extricate himself from his false position. Such was the man who had ridden to power on the crest of the Revolution. A constitutional President under false pretenses, his whole subsequent career was a denial of the popular cause.[113]

The Mexican People was also tainted by antisemitism, arguing that Madero was a Jew, since some of his ancestors were Portuguese Jews, though the family had long been Catholic.[114] There are also gratuitous references to 'Jewish bankers'.[115] Then too, there is anti-Asian racism. They argue that Madero had behaved disgracefully by attempting to form an alliance with Japan, thus invoking the contemporary fear of the 'Yellow Peril', without actually using the words.[116]

Yet, they write, Madero's regime served a useful purpose by exposing what his personalistic and self-aggrandising politics actually mean. Now, they believe, the Mexican people understand better and demand both land and their rights.

In this clarified attitude of the Mexican people lies the great hope of the present Revolution. No man henceforth can ride on their backs to power. They will go forward unwaveringly, irresistibly, until they have established

---

111   Gutiérrez de Lara 1914, p. 348.
112   Gutiérrez de Lara 1914, pp. 348–9.
113   Gutiérrez de Lara 1914, p. 347.
114   Gutiérrez de Lara 1914, p. 344.
115   Gutiérrez de Lara 1914, pp. 224 and 244.
116   Gutiérrez de Lara 1914, pp. 353–7.

the new social order. They have learned democracy's great lesson, *that the individual cannot assume the functions of the collectivity*.[117]

Thanks to this policy of the Maderos, the policy of Díaz before them, the Mexican people are engaged to-day in a clear-cut, uncompromising *Revolution*, and are not as they might have been, the partially contented victims of a capitalist *reform*.[118]

The Mexican people, they argued, will now demand a real revolution, one that will end forever the rule of dictators and establish a democratic society. Their vision deserve quotation at length:

Ultimately must come a new Restoration – a new birth of Mexican democracy – but in happier conditions than in the restoration of Juárez .... If the workers of the world are true to their trust, the heroic struggle for democracy maintained by the Mexican people for the past one hundred years will end, and that shortly, in superb accomplishment.[119]

Gutiérrez de Lara and the other socialists, as their history and these excerpts so well show, joined Madero's democratic movement, but as genuine social democrats, they never simply became supporters of Madero. While initially backing him, once he was in power and repressed the labour movement, they organised demonstrations against the government. They published newspapers that criticised his policies and proposed pro-union and socialist alternatives. When Madero had been overthrown, they published a scathing critique of his administration and its policies. What is surprising about this socialist critique of the Madero regime is that while raising the ideas of an international proletariat and a struggle between the proletariat and capital, the authors never argue for and hardly mention the word 'socialism'.[120] There is only one use of the word socialism in a chapter dealing with the political struggles of the 1820s and 1830s. One suspects that they omit the word because they are writing for an American audience.

Ricardo Flores Magón and the other anarchist leaders of the PLM, released in early January, had become disconnected from the actual developments taking place in Mexico. The PLM socialists had joined Madero. Their old friends

---

117   Gutiérrez de Lara 1914, p. 349.
118   Gutiérrez de Lara 1914, p. 340.
119   Gutiérrez de Lara 1914, p. 358.
120   Gutiérrez de Lara 1914, p. 90.

in the Socialist Party of America, such as Turner, had first supported Madero and then after Victoriano Huerta's usurpation of the presidential throne and assassination of Madero, they had become supporters of Venustian Carranza. The PLM leaders lived in poverty and continued to work for their anarchist revolution. When they had reestablished themselves in Los Angeles, they returned to the publication of their version of *Regeneración*, though they no longer had a clear political strategy for the PLM as their calls for insurrection had once provided. Unable to organise and lead a revolutionary force, they were reduced to commenting on developments and the actions of others.

As was to be expected, they opposed World War I as a capitalist war and argued that workers had no country to fight for. Together with the war they opposed militarism and conscription and called for resistance in various forms. As the Wilson administration brought the United States into the war in 1917, and even before, all of these positions would become the basis for new legal charges against the PLM anarchists, leading to further arrests, trials, and imprisonment. Meanwhile, whenever they could get the money together, they published *Regeneración*, filling its pages with anarchist manifestos.

The anarchists responded to a series of violent events from Texas to Russia. In 1915, Ricardo Flores Magón, writing in *Regeneración* defended the Plan de San Diego uprising in Texas where a group of rebels had called for the separation of Texas from the United States. Texas had been part of Mexico until 1836, but after becoming independent until 1845 and then incorporated into the United States, white people of American origin had dominated Texas politically and economically, and white racism toward the various peoples of colour in the state was notorious. The Texas Plan de San Diego rebels, fed up with all that, had, in fact, been inspired by the Magonistas who had corresponded with various groups bearing some variant of the name 'Tierra y Libertad' in that state. Basilio Ramos led an armed band north from Matamoros into Texas in January of 1915 where *juntas* had already been organised in some areas. He and his allies formed the Liberating Army for Races and Peoples and issued the Plan de San Diego calling for freedom for blacks that lived under Jim Crow and for a distribution of land, mentioning in particular the America Indian people. Soon small groups of armed men were moving through the Texas countryside carrying out raids, burning bridges, destroying railroad facilities, and putting fear into the hearts of white Texans. The Plan de San Diego, coinciding with the Mexican Revolution and clearly inspired by its more radical elements, with is call for an alliance of Mexicans, blacks, and Indians, was clearly a white man's nightmare.[121]

121   Johnson 2003, pp. 60–70; Justin Akers Chacón 2018, pp. 216–24.

The press naturally vilified the rebels while the white landowners mobilised, and the Democratic Party's political machine took responsibility for organising the repression, through the Law and Order League, vigilante groups, and the Texas Rangers. Some vigilantes shot Mexicans on sight; some white Texans burned alive the rebels that they caught. In the end the authorities and the vigilantes killed altogether between 300 and 5,000 Mexicans and others. Thousands of others fled the area, some to Mexico.[122] Ricardo Flores Magón was either unaware of the degree to which his politics had inspired the uprising or he wished to avoid having to take responsibility for it. Based on newspaper reports, he attributed a fight over a woman in a bar between a Mexican man and an American for having detonated the uprising, though he understood that Mexicans had long-held legitimate grievances. Still, he described it as a spontaneous uprising, rather than the organised rebellion, which in fact it was. In his article of 2 October 1915, he defended the rebels, who, he said, were not bandits, but rather 'a natural movement of men who, on seeing their existence threatened, defended themselves as they could'. Rather than killing 'revolutionaries of Texas', he argued that the Texas Rangers and the vigilantes should be shot.[123]

When Ricardo Flores Magón and the other anarchists emerged from prison, the Mexican Revolution had become a civil war between the Conventionist of Pancho Villa and Emiliano Zapata, on the one hand, and the Constitutionalists of Venustiano Carranza on the other. The anarchist wing of the PLM had opposed Madero and they loathed Carranza who they characterised as a capitalist exploiter and oppressor, a strikebreaker (for his smashing of the Mexico City general strike of 1916) and an enemy of the people.[124] Ricardo Flores Magón and his comrades now embraced Zapata and his Liberating Army of the South, defending him from the calumnies of Carranza and publishing the Zapatistas' 'Manifesto to the Mexican People', ending with its call, 'Land for all, ripping it from the grip of those who today possess it'.[125]

Finally, Ricardo Flores Magón welcomed the Russian Revolution of October 1917 as the opening of the world revolution and praised Vladimir Lenin as 'the most brilliant revolutionary leader of the time' and the Bolsheviks as 'the real internationalists'.[126] Though soon Ricardo, like other anarchists – once

122   Heber Johnson 2003, pp. 108–22.
123   Flores Magón 1991, pp. 357–8.
124   Flores Magón 1991, pp. 355–96.
125   Flores Magón 1991, pp. 394–404.
126   Flores Magón 1991, p. 435.

he became clear that Lenin was a Marxist – opposed the Bolshevik's 'tyranny', while defending Russia against foreign invasion.[127]

The Magonista leaders were once again arrested on 16 February 1916, on charges of violation of the Espionage Act. The case went on for a year and a half, but on 4 February 1918, the US Circuit Court of Appeals found Ricardo and Enrique Flores Magón guilty. Ricardo faced additional charges for a manifesto in the final issues of *Regeneración* that called for workers to strike against the war. 'The worker goes on strike with no regard for patriotic interests – he is conscious that the fatherland is not his property, but rather the property of the rich'. In the end Enrique was sentenced to three years, Librado Rivera to 15 years, and Ricardo to 21 years.[128]

Ricardo Flores Magón spent his last days in Leavenworth prison, suffering from diabetes and other illnesses. He attempted to make peace with his brother and fellow prisoner Enrique who had become a supporter of Madero. Ricardo died of a heart attack on 21 November 1922 at the age of 48. The anarchist movement, for which he had worked all of his life, was in decline, repressed by governments around the world, superseded by reformist parties and unions, and on the far left eclipsed by the rise of Communism in Russia.

James D. Cockcroft has argued that the Mexican Liberal Party constituted a 'vanguard political-military organization'.[129] The question here is: What is one's notion of the vanguard organisation? A vanguard organisation is not simply a self-declared leadership of the working class, but rather a group that is firmly and deeply rooted in the working class. If it is to be a democratic socialist vanguard, then it must also be democratically controlled by its working-class membership. Ricardo Flores Magón believed his group could lead the people in insurrections that would overthrow Díaz and establish libertarian communism in Mexico. A centrally controlled Bakuninist organisation dominated by one man, its relationship with the Mexican working class had developed almost accidentally and remained limited and shallow, while the struggle for workers' power was not one of its central goals. The PLM represented the most intransigent group against Díaz in the early years of the revolution, but it was never a vanguard of the working class.[130]

---

127   Lomnitz 2014, p. 483.
128   Lomnitz 2014, pp. 444–5.
129   Cockcroft 1983, p. 113.
130   While I argue that Ricardo Flores Magón was an authoritarian and that the PLM was neither a revolutionary vanguard nor an internationalist organisation, given its leaders' anti-Chinese and antisemitic view, two recent histories (Lytle Hernández and Heatherton) offer a more sympathetic view. See my review of their books: "Book Review Essay:

19   Mexican and Russian Anarchists Compared

We might pause for a moment to compare the experience of the Mexican and Russian anarchists who were active during the same period. The experience of the Mexican anarchists in the Mexican Revolution in the period from 1905 to 1917 paralleled that of the Russian anarchists during the Russian Revolution from 1917 to 1924. In both countries, anarchism had an important presence early on, but the anarchists failed to create movements with the organisational strength that would have allowed them to persist and to have a long-term impact on revolutionary developments. Nor did they have the ability to withstand state repression in either country. Both the Mexican and Russian anarchist movements had been crushed by the ruling parties by the mid-1920s.

Russia might almost be called the home of anarchism, were it not for the role of its French founder Pierre-Joseph Proudhon. The two leading figures of modern anarchism, Mikhail Bakunin and Peter Kropotkin, had been born in Czarist Russia and anarchist groups inspired by them were active throughout the empire in the late nineteenth century. The Marxists of the Russian Social Democratic Labour Party (RSDLP) with its Menshevik and Bolshevik factions proved to be more effective organisers than the anarchists. The RSDLP dominated the left and established a real base of support in the urban working class. The anarchists, who were few and fractured into competing sects, did have a following, but they failed to build a mass movement of workers or peasants before the outbreak of the revolution. By the time the Russian Revolution occurred in October 1917, the Bolshevik faction of the Social Democrats completely dominated the left and much of the labour movement while the anarchists' presence was negligible.[131]

In both countries with the outbreak of revolution, other, better organised and more powerful political parties took centre stage, pushing the anarchists into the wings. The anarchists in both countries were opponents not only of the old regime, but also of the new one. In Mexico, the launching of the Madero Revolution in November 1910 eclipsed the Magonistas, while in Russia the outbreak of the February and then the October revolutions of 1917 found the anarchists marginalised by Socialists and the Social Revolutionary peasant party. Though the Magonistas fought alongside the Maderistas against the dictatorship of Porfirio Díaz, Ricardo Flores Magón, as we have seen, cri-

ticised the bourgeois character of Madero's revolution and would not support it. Similarly in Russia most anarchists would have nothing to do with the
Bolshevik-led socialist revolution, arguing that it was creating an oppressive
socialist state and within a couple of years declaring that it was a state capitalist regime.

After the Bolsheviks took power, some anarchists joined them, though most
remained independent, and some moved into violent opposition to the new
Soviet state. The Bolsheviks, changing their name to Communists, described
Soviet Russia as a workers' state, but the anarchists argued that it was a new
dictatorship and organised to overthrow it. Without the political or labour
organisations to challenge the Communists, the anarchists turned to terrorism,
attempting to assassinate Communist leaders. The Communists, who headed
the new Soviet government, created a political police force known by its Russian initials as the Cheka, which arrested, imprisoned and killed, among others,
hundreds of the government's anarchist opponents.[132]

No longer able to survive in the cities, many of the Russian anarchists fled
to Ukraine to join the anarchist Black Army of Nestor Makhno. Makhno was a
brilliant military commander, comparable in that regard to Mexico's Pancho
Villa. Makhno's army fought the White Armies to defend a regional experiment in anarchism. While maintaining his political and military independence,
Makhno did join with the Bolshevik's Red Army to make common cause against
the counter-revolutionary White Armies of generals Wrangel and Denikin, but
he refused to recognise the authority of the Soviet Republic or to subordinate
his forces to the Red Army. He would not put his army under the Bolshevik
Leon Trotsky's command. Once the White Armies had been defeated, Trotsky,
founder and leader of the Soviet Red Army, crushed Makhno's forces in November 1920.[133] With Makhno's defeat anarchism in Russia ceased to be a force or
even much of a presence except in the country's prisons.

Between 1918 and the mid-1920s the anarchists became a rivulet in the great
stream of one and a half million Russians flowing out of the country across the
Western borders of the Soviet Russia or through the Crimea to Constantinople.
Many went first to Germany and then on to France, while some reached the
United States or Latin America. Russian anarchism lived on in Berlin, Paris,
New York, Buenos Aires, and Rio de Janeiro, though it virtually disappeared in
its homeland.[134] With the Stalinist counter-revolution between 1927 and 1937,

---

132   Serge 1984, *passim*.
133   Arshinov 1974, *passim*.
134   Hassell 1991, *passim*.

virtually all left activists, both revolutionary socialists and the few remaining anarchists, in the Soviet Union would either die in prison or be murdered by the state.[135]

20   Conclusion

The various developments of the early 1910s in Mexico, the eruption of the Madero revolution, the split between socialists and anarchists in the PLM, and the rise of Zapata in the South and Villa in the North, seriously complicated the question of American solidarity with the Mexican revolution. Throughout the period from 1905 to 1910, American leftists, the AFL, the United Mine Workers, the Western Federation of Miners, and the IWW, as well as some American progressives, at first supported the Mexican Liberal Party as it struggled to survive the attacks of both the Mexican and the US government. To support the PLM was at first to support the only organisation in the field fighting the dictatorship, and moreover to back a group that had developed a programme for labour rights and standards. With the coming of the Madero revolution in 1910 and its success by mid-1911, American leftists, labour unions and progressives faced new questions. How would the unions and the left interpret the issue of solidarity with Mexico's workers and peasants? Would they now continue to support the Mexican Liberal Party? Or would they support the new Madero government? Or would they support Zapata? And what about Villa? What form would solidarity take in the new period?

Ricardo Flores Magón, the Mexican Liberal Party, and their anarchist politics dominated the first stage of the Mexican pre-revolutionary period from 1900 to 1910 and it was with the Magonistas that American labour unionists, socialists, and anarchists identified in those years. The broad American support for the PLM was based in large part on its moderate programme of 1906, a document that talked only about social reforms and not about social revolution. When Francisco I. Madero's democratic revolution began in November 1910, the broad American labour left and the Progressives did not initially see any difference between Madero's Anti-Reelectionist Party and the PLM. But when in 1911 Flores Magón issued his 'Manifesto to the Workers of the World', together with attacks on Madero and his movement, the differences became absolutely clear. The AFL, the Socialist Party, and the Progressives moved to support Madero, while only the American anarchists and the IWW continued to support the Magonistas.

---

135 Shteppa 1962, *passim.*

The collusion between the Mexican and US governments in repeatedly arresting and jailing the Flores Magón brothers and other PLM leaders made it difficult for the anarchist revolutionaries to maintain their own organisation and to establish and maintain solidarity with those in the American left. Their imprisonment removed the PLM's top leaders from the political scene between 1907 and 1910 and again between 1912 and 1914, crucial years in which the Mexican revolutionary movement grew and its political currents defined themselves. Imprisoned in the United States, the Magonistas failed to establish their own revolutionary headquarters in Mexico, while after he went into exile in 1904, Ricardo Flores Magón never again set foot in the land of his birth. To these issues must be added the misconceived and poorly managed invasion of Baja California, which most clearly demonstrated the weaknesses of both the PLM and of its American allies. In Mexico, the invasion discredited them in the eyes of many of their countrymen and in the United States it provided a pretext for indicting, trying, and imprisoning them.

Throughout these years American labour unionists in the AFL and the IWW, as well as the Socialist Party, supported the Mexican Revolution against Porfirio Díaz. American leftists of all stripes believed that by doing so they were supporting a fight for democracy and for socialism. American workers and leftists spoke out, distributed leaflets, published pamphlets and books, held meetings, engaged in demonstrations of support, and in some cases actually joined the revolutionary movements, scores of Americans fighting with both the Magonistas and the Maderistas. One could hardly doubt the internationalism of those who risked their lives to cross the border and to ride and fight with those they considered to be their brothers and sisters on the other side of the border. Once the Mexican revolutionaries divided, however, into those who believed that an anarchist or libertarian communism was possible at once and those socialists who thought a capitalist democracy would have to precede a socialist society, the movement was seriously weakened. When, however, the Mexican Socialists, former PLM members, experienced Madero in power, they began to evolve into revolutionary syndicalists. The splits in the Mexican revolutionary movement led also to changes in its relationship to the American left. We look now in greater detail at how the American left understood the Mexican Revolution in the chapters that follow.

Eugene Debs, the Socialist Party, and the Mexican Revolution

The Socialist Party of America, the most important leftist organisation in the United States at the time of the Mexican Revolution, played a significant role in organising support for the Mexican Revolution. Over a period of 20 years, Socialist Party leaders such as Eugene V. Debs, Victor Berger, John Kenneth Turner, and John Reed all played significant parts in the debates over the revolution and over the question of which organisation or leader to support. As on so many questions, the Socialist Party – known for being a big tent – found it impossible to arrive at a consensus, though its more moderate leaders and views prevailed.

Eugene Victor Debs was America's most impressive Socialist figure: founder of the American Railway Union and of the Industrial Workers of the World; founder of the Socialist Party and its repeated candidate for president; he was jailed for his role in the Pullman strike in 1894 and for his opposition to World War I in 1918, and while he never became a Communist, he strongly defended the Russian Soviet Revolution. If any man or woman seemed to stand for socialism in the United States, surely it was Debs.

Yet in his unofficial but all-important role as spokesman of the Socialist Party on the Mexican Revolution, Debs played a conservative role which would have long-term consequences both for the Mexican revolutionary movement and for the American working-class organisations. In 1911 Debs chose to reject the anarchist insurgents in Mexico and support instead the bourgeois liberal revolution of Francisco I. Madero. Debs rejected the anarchist call for the peasants to seize the land and the workers to seize the factories, arguing that such demands were premature. Debs's decision paralleled a similar one by Samuel Gompers that helped to isolate the Mexican Liberal Party anarchists, and led the Socialists to establish ties with the new Mexican capitalist state. Debs's decision would have long-lasting implications for US-Mexican labour solidarity. One could argue that they represent the first manifestation of what would be the unfortunate tendency of American labour leftists to be drawn into relations with the state in Mexico and with state-supported unions, a policy that continued until the end of the twentieth century.

What was it, one wonders, that made it so difficult for Debs and his Socialist Party comrades to understand the revolution in Mexico? For surely Debs had

gotten it wrong: without the peasant movement to seize the land and the workers' demands for power in the factories, the Mexican revolution would never
have accomplished the reforms that were instituted by the new capitalist government. Only the revolutionary movement made reform possible in Mexico,
and Debs did not see that. And Debs was the very best expression of his party,
but unfortunately his party lacked an international perspective in North America, and it was that which prevented it and him from understanding Mexico.

1   An Inconsistent Record

At the end of the first decade of the twentieth century, the Socialist Party had
become a small but very real power in American politics. Scores of Socialist
newspapers in a variety of languages appealing to immigrant voters had helped
to elect the Socialist Party mayors who headed up city government in dozens of
cities. The Socialist Party in 1912 had 100,000 members and its presidential candidate Eugene V. Debs won nearly a million votes in the national election. The
Socialist Party's positions on the Mexican Revolution of 1910 and on the US military interventions in Mexico in 1914 and 1917 mattered and had an important
impact on American society.

The American Socialist Party, almost since its founding in 1900, had discussed and debated foreign policy issues, above all militarism and imperialism.
The American Socialist response to those issues and the party's record of support for workers in other countries, however, had not always been consistent in
the period preceding the Mexican Revolution. During the Spanish-American
War of 1898, nearly all American Socialists supported the Cuban and Filipino
people's right to self-determination and generally opposed the war and the
acquisition of Cuba, Puerto Rico, and the Philippines. The American left rejected the idea that the search for resources and markets abroad justified the
taking of a colonial empire. American Socialists argued that the root cause of
the war was capitalism and the workers' lack of class consciousness.

American Socialists, however, were much less clear about the issue of US
intervention in the Caribbean between 1900 and 1911. American socialists, like
their European comrades, tended to believe in necessary and inevitable stages
of economic development from savagery and barbarism through slavery and
feudalism to capitalism and then socialism. Consequently, while they opposed
imperialism, they believed that capitalism would have a progressive impact
on what they saw as the backward countries and peoples of the Caribbean,
laying the foundations for labour unionism and socialism. 'While socialists bit-
terly attacked US intervention and investment in this region, their belief that

national development would follow the European and North American pattern allowed them to endorse the "progressive" aspects of American imperialism'.[1] In general, throughout the period the Socialist Party of America through its magazines and newspapers had little to say about US imperialism in the Caribbean, putting its emphasis on domestic issues. The ambiguities of the Socialist Party's positions on the role of the United States in the Caribbean would also be expressed in its positions on Mexico.

2   A Socialist Comrade in Mexico

The Socialist Party of America (SPA) began to take an interest in Mexico about the same time that it made contact with the Mexican Liberal Party. In 1905 a member of the SPA moved to Mexico, perhaps to work there, and wrote a couple of articles for the *International Socialist Review* (*ISR*), the first articles on Mexico since the journal's founding in 1900. The correspondent, apparently a rank-and-file member of the party, remained anonymous, no doubt to protect himself and the unions and the political organisation with which he had come in contact and about which he wrote.

'The government continues to dole out the national resources of the country to foreign money-bags while Mexican workers grovel in filth, disease and ignorance, for lack of access to these same resources', wrote the nameless correspondent. 'One thing is hopeful and that is, that however ignorant the working classes are they do not harbor any illusions concerning the identity of their interest with those of their employers'. He continued. 'On this point at least the most ignorant peon seems to be rather in advance of the average American trades unionist'.

The *ISR*'s correspondent described the low wages and miserable conditions of workers such as servant girls, tailors, shoemakers, and seamstresses, and mentioned the problem of working-class alcoholism. But he also noted the beginnings of labour organisation. 'In the city of Mexico, the workers are beginning to organise mutual aid societies which in some ways resemble our trades unions', he reported. 'In Guadalajara an attempt was made to organise the workers ... but was dispersed by the police'.

The anonymous author informed the *ISR*'s readers that, 'The Republican form of government [in Mexico] is a farce'. 'Capacious prisons of solid stone await to receive anyone who dares to speak or write a word of opposition to

---

1   Christopulos 1980, p. 67.

the governing power', he wrote. 'If socialists wish to reach these people it must be done through secret organisations and underground publications'. Finally, he suggested that:

> The industrial development of the United States and Mexico is so closely allied that the socialist movements of the two countries must necessarily have much in common. If there are any socialists in Mexico we should get into communication and see what can be done toward organization.[2]

Presuming that some American or European socialists must be living in Mexico, he asked them to contact the *ISR*.

The same correspondent contributed a second article nine months later in which he noted that, 'A small paper began to be published, *"El Obrero Socialista"*, [The Socialist Worker] under the direction of Señor Román Morales assisted by a small but resolute group of comrades. Later they organised "[La] Liga Socialista de Guadalajara" which holds regular weekly meetings'. The author's tone and description of events makes it clear that he was in touch with and probably working with this small socialist group.

The *ISR*'s anonymous correspondent described a special meeting held by La Liga Socialista to commemorate 'Red Sunday' in Russia, the day on which the Czar's troops had in 1905 fired on Father Gapon and the workers. 'On the walls were shields bearing the names and nationality of some of the world's most prominent socialists and friends of labour: among them I recall "Father" Gapon, Maxim Gorki, Karl Marx, Wilhelm Liebknecht, Enrico Ferri, Frederick Engels, Jean Jaurès, Emile Vandervelde, Tom Mann, Pablo Iglesias, Ella Wheeler Wilcox, and "Mother" Jones'. This was, wrote the *ISR*'s correspondent, 'the first public socialist meeting ever held in this Republic'. The police did not interfere. The author of the article concluded, 'The Mexican proletariat is beginning to realise the sublime idea of international working-class solidarity'.[3] The SPA's contact through its correspondent with this small group of socialists was apparently ephemeral, for there is no further mention of it after 1906.

While this initial coverage of the Mexican situation represented a good beginning, to the best of my knowledge the national SPA, a party with tens of thousands of members, created no budget for Mexican work, assigned no staff member to be responsible for contacts with Mexico, and sent no organiser to Mexico to establish a formal relationship with whatever socialist or other left-

---

2 'Conditions in Mexico' 1905, pp. 675–7.
3 'Mexico' 1906, p. 498.

ist group existed. Socialist contacts with Mexican radicals therefore developed rather haphazardly.

3   The Socialists and the Mexican Liberal Party

The Socialist Party in Southern California became involved early in international solidarity with the Mexican Liberal Party (PLM) which had established its headquarters in Los Angeles. When the Mexican revolutionary leaders Ricardo Flores Magón, Librado Rivera, Antonio I. Villarreal, and Manuel Sarabia were arrested in Los Angeles in 1907, and later charged with violating US neutrality laws – the government alleged they had planned an invasion of Mexico from St. Louis – the Socialist Party in Los Angeles immediately began a campaign for their release.

Socialists in Los Angeles, among them Job Harriman, John Murray, John Kenneth Turner, his wife Ethel Duffy Turner, and Elizabeth Darling Trowbridge organised the Mexican Revolutionists Defence League, and each of them made a valuable contribution to the defence of the Mexican revolutionaries.[4] Labour lawyer Job Harriman, vice-presidential running-mate of Eugene V. Debs in the presidential election campaign of 1900 and Socialist candidate for mayor of Los Angeles in 1911, represented Mexican Liberal Party leaders in court. The Socialist Party of Los Angeles took the issue to the Socialist Party national convention of May 1908 which passed a resolution in support of the jailed Mexican Revolutionaries. The issue was also brought before the International Socialist Bureau in Europe. Socialist activists in Los Angeles took the matter before the Los Angeles Labor Council and won support there for the PLM leaders on the grounds that they had been fighting for the working class.

John Murray was the son of a well-to-do family from New York who had become a socialist and union activist and who had earlier organised the Political Refugee Defence League of Chicago to defend Russian political refugees. When he learned of the plight of the PLM leaders, he expanded the group's work to include the Mexican exiles in Los Angeles. In 1908 he moved to Los Angeles, joined the Socialist group there, and became involved in the local Defence League. On 8 May 1908, the Socialists and their Defence League sent Murray to Mexico, ostensibly to investigate the PLM's accusations about the Mexican dictatorship, but probably also to carry messages for the PLM leaders in prison to their followers in Mexico.

---

4 'John Kenneth Turner' 1994, vol. 8, s.v.

John Kenneth and Ethel Duffy Turner were both Socialist Party activists and radical journalists who turned their skills to writing newspaper articles for the labour and socialist press about the Mexican prisoners. Elizabeth Darling Trowbridge was a Boston heiress who had joined the Socialist Party and used her fortune to support humanitarian causes. As a member of the Defence League, she paid for the Murrays' and later for Turner's trip to Mexico. Trowbridge fell in love with PLM leader Manuel Sarabia and married him in 1909, after which they published radical newspapers along the border.

After Murray returned from Mexico with tales of the terrible conditions there, Turner decided that he too would make an investigative trip. Turner had been born in Portland, Oregon on 5 April 1879, the descendent of pioneers, his Methodist minister grandfather having led a wagon train from Kentucky to Oregon in 1849. His father was a printer for the Portland *Oregonian*, and John Kenneth had followed his father into the news business. The young Turner became a Socialist when he was sixteen, and a year later established his own muckraking newspaper, *Stockton Saturday Night*. After working for a while as a schoolteacher, in 1904 Turner entered the University of California at Berkeley where he met Ethel E. Duffy and they married just a year later. Leaving San Francisco after the great earthquake of 1906, they travelled first to Portland and then to Los Angeles. Turner got a job at the Los Angeles *Express* newspaper, and the young couple both joined the Socialist Party. Through the Socialist Party, Turner met Job Harriman and became interested in Ricardo Flores Magón and the PLM.

Turner, who did not then speak Spanish well, arranged to travel with Lázaro Gutiérrez de Lara, one of the Mexican Liberal Party's principal leaders. Gutiérrez de Lara had been born into a wealthy and politically connected Mexico City family, had become an attorney, worked for the Mexican Secretary of Foreign Relations, and then became a judge. While living in Mexico City he met Ricardo Flores Magón and became a member of the Mexican Liberal Party. During the PLM's attempted insurrection of 1906, he was arrested in Sonora for speaking in support of the strikers at the Cananea copper mine. Eventually freed through the efforts of his family, Gutiérrez de Lara fled to Los Angeles to join the PLM *Junta* and became the editor of the group's newspaper *Revolución*.

In making the trip to Mexico, Turner posed as a wealthy American businessman who intended to invest in tobacco and henequen plantations in Mexico. Gutiérrez de Lara, acted as Turner's friend, financial advisor, and interpreter. Elizabeth Trowbridge put up the money for the trip and the two men left for Mexico in August 1908. Turner and Gutiérrez de Lara eventually travelled not only to Mexico City and Mérida but were also put up as guests on several haciendas. The two had opportunities to talk with the hacienda owners, managers, foremen, and workers. The *hacendados* explained to Turner how the systems of debt peonage and contract labour functioned, and Turner saw the working and living conditions of the labourers with his own eyes. Returning to the United States in January of 1909, Turner began to write a series of articles for *American Magazine* (formerly *Leslie's*) with a circulation of approximately 300,000. The first of the series, 'Slaves of Yucatan', appeared in the October 1909 issue, followed by two other instalments in November and December. But in January *American Magazine* dropped the series without explanation, and Turner then turned over the rest of the instalments to the Socialist Party's *Appeal to Reason*, which had an even larger circulation, 750,000, but had less influence beyond the left. Other chapters were published in the *International Socialist Review* and *Pacific Monthly*.

Turner's articles in *American Magazine* 'created a sensation in Mexico, the United States, and England', the series was favourably reviewed in the press, and Turner became something of a celebrity.[5] Now famous, Turner testified before a joint committee of the House of Representatives in Washington in June 1910 on the persecution of Mexican political refugees in the United States. While Turner's articles were appearing, the Mexican Revolution broke out in November 1910. But Turner was unable to find a trade publisher for the book version of the articles and turned to the Socialist publishing house Charles H. Kerr and Company of Chicago, which brought out the book in January of 1911. *Barbarous Mexico* became the principal source of information on Mexico for labour activists, leftists, and many liberals interested in the Mexican Revolution.

John Murray writing for *The Call* of New York and John Kenneth Turner for *The Appeal to Reason* also produced dozens of articles which would inform and educate the Socialist Party and its periphery. In March of 1909 the *International Socialist Review* published the first of several articles by John Murray on the conditions in Mexico. Like Turner, Murray emphasised the existence of slavery or quasi-slavery based on debt peonage in Mexico. In the first article in the series, Murray wrote that in Mexico he met secretly with a Mexican revolutionary who told him, 'We still have slaves in Mexico. Over half the population, eight million souls, sweat under this system of peonage'.[6] In other articles in the series Murray also described the repression under the Díaz regime with articles on the prison system and political prisoners.[7]

Turner's 'The American Partners of Díaz' published by the *ISR* in December 1910 was a powerful summary of his forthcoming book *Barbarous Mexico*.

---

5   Turner 1984, p. xvi.
6   Murray, March 1909, pp. 641–59.
7   Murray, April 1909, pp. 737–52; Murray, May 1909, pp. 863–5.

The article began, 'The United States is a partner in the slavery of Mexico'. The American people were not Díaz's partners, said Turner, but the US government and US corporations such as the Morgan-Guggenheim copper merger, the Standard Oil Company, the American Sugar Trust, the Continental Rubber Company, Well-Fargo Express Company, E.N. Brown of the National Railways of Mexico, Harriman and the Southern Pacific Railroad were Díaz's partners in slavery. Turner expressed his support for Mexican revolutionaries and opposed the role of the US government in stationing troops on the Mexican border to protect American interests in Mexico.[8]

Turner's *Barbarous Mexico* played an enormously important role in laying the foundations for international labour solidarity with Mexico. The genius of Turner was in the way he placed the struggle against the Díaz dictatorship in Mexico in the tradition of American abolitionism, a tradition which only 45 years after the Civil War still resonated in many sectors of American society. Turner condemned the Mexican government and US corporations for their role in supporting debt peonage slavery. His articles and book, read by hundreds of thousands, turned many Americans against the Díaz regime and won supporters for the revolutionary cause.

But in making this appeal to the American people on the issue of slavery, Turner recognised that he would have a problem because of the American people's racist attitudes regarding the Indians. Many Americans tended to look upon the Indians found in the United States as racially and culturally inferior savages, incapable of building genuine civilisations or of becoming part of one. The Indians, many Americans believed, were incapable of working as the Anglo-Saxon people did. Turner himself may have even shared this prejudice, but in any case, he knew that he could not defend Mexican Indians to the American people with their racial attitudes.

So, in dealing with the two principal enslaved Indian groups, Turner's first job is to argue that they are hardly really Indians at all. Turner writes:

> The Mayas are Indians – and yet they are not Indians. They are not like the Indians of the United States, and they are called Indians only because their homes were in the western hemisphere when the Europeans came. The Mayas had a civilization of their own when the Europeans 'discovered' them, and it was a civilization admittedly as high as that of the most advanced Aztecs or the Incas of Peru.[9]

---

8   Turner, December 1910, pp. 321–8.
9   Turner 1984, p. 8.

Turner wants his readers to see the Mayas physically as also quite different than the American notion of an Indian. 'The Mayas are a peculiar people' writes Turner. 'They look like no other people on the face of the earth'. But he then goes on to describe them in terms which might have reminded his readers of youths and maidens on a Greek vase or in a British neo-classical painting.

> They are not large in stature, but their features are remarkably finely chiseled and their bodies give a strong impression of elegance and grace. Their skins are olive, their foreheads high, their faces slightly aquiline. The women of all classes in Mérida wear long, flowing white gowns unbound at the waist and embroidered about the hem and perhaps also about the bust in some bright colour – green, blue or purple.[10]

Turner presents us with an idealised and classicised vision of the Maya before taking us to meet them as slaves working in the fields and living in squalid quarters.

Similarly, when he describes the Yaqui Indians of Sonora in Northern Mexico, Turner is at pains to distance the Yaqui from Indians in the United States (though some of them lived in US territory). The Yaquis are called Indians, but like the Mayas of Yucatan, they are Indians, and they are not Indians.

> In the United States we would not call them Indians, for they are workers. As far back as their history can be traced, they have never been savages. They have been an agricultural people. They tilled the soil, discovered and developed mines, constructed systems of irrigation, built adobe towns, maintained public schools, had an organised government and their own mint.[11]

Turner's description makes the Yaqui town – excepting its adobe houses – sound like some New England village. Turner also gives a physical description of the Yaqui which makes them little short of gods:

> The Yaqui certainly has an admirable physical development. During my journeys in Mexico, I learned to pick him out at a glance, by his broad shoulders, his deep chest, his sinewy legs, his rugged face. The typical Yaqui is almost a giant, the race a race of athletes.[12]

---

10   Turner 1984, p. 9.
11   Turner 1984, p. 28.
12   Turner 1984, p. 29.

Tall, lean and lanky – and colourless – the Yaqui was almost a Yankee. Turner, perhaps because he shared their prejudices, accommodated to the anti-Indian prejudices of his readers, turning the Maya and the Yaqui Indians into virtual Europeans.

Having sanitised and ennobled the Mexican Indians, Turner could then launch his attack on the practice of enslaving them. In Mexico chattel slavery was illegal, and Mexican plantation owners did not call their system slavery. But Turner made a convincing argument that it was indeed chattel slavery nonetheless. He began with the henequen haciendas of the Yucatan. 'The masters of Yucatan do not call their system slavery;' wrote Turner, 'they call it enforced service for debt. But the fact that it is not service for debt is proven by the habit of transferring the slaves from one master to another, not on any basis of debt, but on the basis of the market price of a man'.[13] Yucatan hacienda owners explained to him that they did not even keep accurate records of the debt. Rather the Yucatan plantation owners bought and sold their slaves for about 400 pesos apiece.

Similarly on the tobacco plantations in the Valle Nacional of Oaxaca, Turner found slavery called by another name. 'Just as in Yucatan, the slavery of Valle Nacional is merely peonage, or labour for debt, carried to the extreme, although outwardly it takes a slightly different form – that of contract labour', wrote Turner.

Once he had made the case that the system was indeed slavery, whatever it was called, Turner then turned to all the traditional arguments against slavery which had been made by the American abolitionist movement in the period leading to the civil war. Turner made an indictment that must have reminded his readers of the indictments made in the nineteenth century against the slavery that Americans had once known from Virginia to Texas:

> The slaves of the Yucatan get no money. They are half starved. They are worked almost to death. They are beaten. A large percentage of them are locked up every night in a house resembling a jail. If they are sick, they must still work, and if they are so sick that it is impossible for them to work, they are seldom permitted the services of a physician. The women are compelled to marry, compelled to marry men of their plantation only, and sometimes are compelled to marry certain men not of their choice. There are no schools for the children. Indeed, the entire lives of these people are ordered at the whim of a master, and if the master wishes to

---

13   Turner 1984, p. 9.

kill them, he may do so with impunity. I heard numerous stories of slaves being beaten to death, but I never heard of an instance in which the murderer was punished or even arrested.[14]

Turner said the 'slaveholders club' had 250 members, dominated by the '50 henequen kings'. These slave owners, some of whom owned plantations of tens or even hundreds of thousands of acres (thousands of square miles) owned 8,000 Yaqui Indians from Sonora, between 100,000 and 125,000 native Mayas, and about 3,000 Chinese or Koreans. Interestingly, though he writes with compassion about the Yaqui and Maya slaves, Turner never gives a sympathetic description of one of the Chinese or Korean slaves.

Not only did Turner not portray the Chinese slaves sympathetically, he actually used them in his narrative as boogiemen. The Yaqui Indians were being deported from Sonora and sold into slavery in the Yucatan, and Turner described the break-up of families, the separation of husbands and wives, parents and children. 'Conjugal fidelity', wrote Turner, 'was the cardinal virtue of the Yaqui home', and in Catholic Mexico divorce and remarriage were illegal, yet, Turner explains, the planters forced Indians to remarry against their will with Chinese men. While it was certainly horrible that the women were forced into marriage against their wills, Turner plays on the racial aspect:

> The Yaqui woman feels as keenly the brutal snatching away of her babe as would the cultivated American woman. The heart-strings of the Yaqui wife are no more proof against a violent and unwished-for separation from her husband than would be the heart-strings of the refined mistress of a beautiful American home .... To a Yaqui woman a native of Asia is no less repugnant than he is to an American woman, yet one of the first barbarities the henequen planter imposes upon the Yaqui slave woman, freshly robbed of the lawful husband of her bosom, is to compel her to marry a Chinaman and live with him![15]

Turner's racial prejudice and sexual stereotypes merge here to appeal to the lowest sentiments of his readers, many of whom presumably shared his biases.

Turner's racist attitudes toward the Chinese come as no great surprise, for such views were common among labour unionists and Socialists especially in California and shared by some of his friends in the Mexican Liberal

---

14   Turner 1984, p. 15.
15   Turner 1984, pp. 49–51.

Party.[16] Racism towards African Americans was even more common in the Socialist Party. The Socialist Party had at times in newspapers like the *Appeal to Reason* called for socialism and segregation, two separate but equal socialist societies: one white and one black.

Turner accommodated to his readers' racist attitudes toward American Indians, portrayed the Chinese peons in Mexico in racist terms, and depicted women too often as helpless victims, often victims of sexual advances or assaults portrayed in lurid terms. At the same time, Turner succeeded in his indictment of the Díaz regime for permitting and condoning slavery. Thus, in those terms, Turner's *Barbarous Mexico* armed a generation of anarchists, socialists and labour unionists with arguments against Mexico's *ancien régime* and in support of the revolutionary movement.

4   The Socialist Congressman against War with Mexico

The Socialist Party not only propagandised against US intervention in its magazines, it also took the fight to the US Congress. In 1910 simultaneously with the outbreak of the Mexican Revolution, Victor Berger, the leader of the Socialist Party in Milwaukee, Wisconsin had been elected to Congress. On 5 April 1911 freshman Congressman Berger introduced in the House of Representatives a 'Joint Resolution Relative to the Mexican Situation' opposing US military intervention. This Socialist resolution, unique in American history and of enormous importance in terms of international labour solidarity, merits citation in full:

> Whereas the despotism and brutality of the Mexican governing class has goaded the poor and oppressed of that country into a revolution in which they are struggling for liberty and the establishment of a political republic not only in name but in fact; and
>
> Whereas a state of civil war has for some time prevailed in Mexico – a war between a rich and powerful oligarchy and a liberty loving, oppressed, and despoiled people – and although there has been no attempt to invade the United States or even threaten it, the United States Army, by an Executive order, is now mobilised on the Mexican border threatening an invasion of Mexico; and

---

16   The Mexican Liberal Party, for example, opposed Chinese immigration to Mexico, just as the AFL did to the United States. See: Zertuche Muñoz 1994, p. 85.

Whereas this threat of invasion is used by the ruling class of that country to fortify its position in power against the progressive party and to jeopardise the national existence of Mexico: Therefore, be it

Resolved by the Senate and House of Representatives of the United States of America in Congress assembled, That the Senate and house of Representatives of the United States of America in Congress assembled unhesitatingly affirm the American doctrine of self-government and the principle that no people are bound to or ought to submit to another government's opinion or understanding of their interests, and furthermore declare that the United States Army should be withdrawn from the frontier and the Navy from the coast of Mexico, and that the intention and policy of the United State should be to remain neutral in the pending conflict, and not to invade, take possession of, or annex the country of Mexico.

Sec. 2. That the President immediately submit to Congress all documents and reports upon which the Executive order for mobilization was based, if not inconsistent with the public interest.[17]

Even though the sole Socialist Congressman's Resolution must have been primarily propagandistic, it nonetheless represents a high point in international labour solidarity. The Socialist Party went on record as opposing the US policy of military intimidation and attempted to mobilise the legislature against the executive in order to stop that policy. Berger also presented a petition of some 90,000 signatures opposing the US military mobilisation, while the Socialist Party discouraged military enlistment. Taken altogether, this was a model anti-imperialist campaign – though Berger would later reverse his position.

5   Why Support Mexican Workers?

Why should Americans support Mexican workers and peasants? Probably at the urging of the Los Angeles Socialists, Eugene V. Debs corresponded with Ricardo Flores Magón and lobbied Senator Robert M. La Follette on behalf of the imprisoned PLM leaders.[18] Debs in the letter to Senator La Follette wrote:

There are fourteen million peon slaves in Mexico, and there is a billion of American capital invested in that country. The average wage is 37 1/2 cents

---

17   '62 Congress', 1911.
18   Debs 1990, vol. 1, p. 299.

a day in Mexican money. The railroads, mines, smelters, cotton industries, etc. are mainly owned by American capitalists. They are having their
industries developed and operated on the basis of peon labour. That is
one of the reasons why there are over two millions of idle workingmen in
the United States, and why millions of others are getting such miserable
wages.[19]

Debs suggests that La Follette should take an interest in this cause not only for
humanitarian reasons, but also because Mexican workers' low wages attracted American industry to Mexico, causing unemployment in the United States.
Debs' argument would be adopted by the US labour movement and be repeated
throughout the twentieth century.

The *Appeal to Reason*, the Socialist Party newspaper in the Midwest with
a circulation between 500,000 and 750,000, argued similarly that American
workers should support the Mexican revolution so that cheap Mexican labour
would not be an alternative to American labour. The *Appeal* asked its readers
in 1909, even before the revolution had begun,

> Will we help our Mexican comrades rise or will we allow them to go down
> and pull us down to their level? ... There is no question of altruism or
> benevolence involved. We are not asking help for the Mexican refugees
> out of charity, but from an enlightened sense of self-interest.[20]

In another article the *Appeal* made the same point even more forcefully:

> The fourteen million half-naked, degenerate wretches employed at two-
> bits a day are employed in competition with American workers and this
> accounts in large part for the stagnation of industry and the great army of
> unemployed in the United States.[21]

Ricardo Flores Magón and the Mexican anarchists made virtually the same
argument for US workers' support for the Mexican revolution:

> If the Economic Revolution is crushed, the American workingmen will
> suffer the consequences, for an immigration of Mexican workingmen

---

19   Ibid.
20   Christopulos 1980, p. 81, citing *Appeal to Reason*, 20 February 1909.
21   Christopulos 1980, p. 90, citing *Appeal to Reason*, 27 March 1909.

still greater than the one that has been taking place during the last ten or fifteen years, will take place, and the salaries in this country will be lower still. But that is not all; the crushed Revolution means a victorious Capitalism. The wealth of the magnates of American industry will flow into Mexico, ... a field for all the adventurers and all the exploiters; the manufacturers of the United States would be transplanted to Mexico, that would become an ideal land for business because of the cheapness of salaries, and the American working men will find their factories and firms in this country closed down because it will be more profitable to their bosses to open their business where they will pay twenty-five to fifty cents a day for the same kind of work for which they would have to pay two or three dollars a day in this country [i.e., the United States].[22]

Both the Socialist Party of America and the Mexican Liberal Party attempted to appeal to the American workers fear of unemployment and low wages by arguing that the Mexican Revolution would raise the wages of Mexican workers and therefore end their economic competition with Americans. Not all appeals, of course, were to economic self-interest; the Socialist also appealed to ideals such as the 'brotherhood of man' and the ideal of international labour solidarity.

6   The Socialist Dilemma: Magón or Madero?

After the outbreak of the Mexican Revolution, in January of 1911, Turner published in *ISR* 'The Revolution in Mexico' in which he defended the revolution and opposed US intervention. 'Why is there a revolution in Mexico?' Turner asked. He answered that it was because the Mexicans 'have manhood in their blood, because they are unwilling to be slaves, because they are ruled by a despot and they want democracy, because there is no way to progress under a despotism except through revolution'. Turner wrote that he believed that US troops would probably be sent to Mexico, 'ostensibly to protect American lives and property, actually to hold Díaz, the Mexican partner of Wall Street, chief slave-driver of "Barbarous Mexico" on his throne'. Turner concluded, 'If, under such circumstances the American people are quiescent, I shall be ashamed that I am an American'.

---

22   Flores Magón et al. 1915, pp. 85–8.

But perhaps the most interesting thing about Turner's article was that it began to signal a change in the attitude of American Socialist toward the Mexican revolutionaries. Turner wrote:

> If Madero wins, his party will undoubtedly free the slaves, ameliorate the conditions of the peons, pass a few labour laws, and establish free speech, free press and actual elections. As these things would constitute a tremendous step forward, I, personally, wish the revolution every success, whether in the end it is dominated by the Liberal party [i.e., the Magonistas], or, as now, by the Anti-Reelectionists [i.e., the Maderistas].[23]

While indicating that he might prefer the Magonistas who would 'go further' in making fundamental economic changes, Turner made it clear that he could live with Madero. Turner's position indicated the beginning of a change in the line of the Socialist Party from its alliance with the PLM to support for Madero. But the position was still not clearly defined.

Yet, only a few months later in May 1911, the ISR published the demands of the Mexican Liberal Party: 'As a means of obtaining economic liberty, the Liberal Party proposes to rise up in arms against the political and capitalistic tyranny which is oppressing and degrading the Mexican people: to wrest from the power of the capitalists the land which has been appropriated by them, in order to deliver it, regardless of sex, to millions of human beings who compose the Mexican nation'. This manifesto, with its emphasis on the seizure and redistribution of land ran counter to Madero's emphasis on political democracy. Where did the Socialists stand? With Magón or Madero, with the anarcho-communists or the bourgeois liberals?

The answer to the question came from the most prominent and important leader of the Socialist Party, Eugene V. Debs.[24] Debs in an article titled 'The Crisis in Mexico' firmly rejected the position of the Magonistas and the Mexican Liberal Party. First, Debs called upon the Mexican Liberal Party to explicitly proclaim the anarchist programme which they had by then adopted but still attempted at times to hide from the public. Debs argued that anarchism rather than furthering the revolution, 'would put off the revolutionary end they have in view'. Debs rejected the idea that the Mexican people should seize the land, mills, factories, mines, railroads and other machinery of production. Debs

---

23   Turner 1911, p. 421.
24   The two principal biographers of Debs hardly discuss his role in US-Mexican relations. See: Salvatore 1982 and Ginger 1970. The best discussion can be found in: Christopulos 1980.

asked 'what would the masses in their present ignorant and unorganised state do with them after having obtained them? It would simply add calamity to their calamities, granting that this impossible feat were capable of achievement'.[25]

Second, Debs argued that the Mexican Liberal Party underestimated the power of the capitalist class worldwide and overestimated the possible benefits of international solidarity. Debs reminded the PLM that 'the rich control all the armies and navies of the world'. In the event of an anarchist revolution in Mexico, the revolutionaries would face not only the Mexican capitalist class, but also the United States and its military. Debs put little hope in international labour solidarity to save another Mexican Revolution.

> Let not the Mexican revolutionists depend too much on the 'International Committee of the Mexican Liberal party Junta' which they propose organising 'in all the principal cities of the United States and Europe'. That some effective co-operation may thus be secured is entirely probable, but our Mexican comrades who saw their own leaders thrown into American prisons with scarcely a protest except among the Socialists are apt to be disappointed if they rely to any great extent upon the enslaved working classes of other countries whose energies are all absorbed in their own struggle for existence.[26]

International solidarity while important in principle, could offer little at this stage of development of the radical forces.

Debs argued that rather than calling upon the workers to take over the land and the factories, 'The right course for the Mexican revolutionists to pursue in this crisis, in my opinion, is to lay the foundation for economic and political organization of the dispossessed and enslaved masses, throughout the Republic'. Without explicitly stating his support for Madero, Debs wrote:

> The overthrow of Díaz will mean at least, I take it, the right to organise the working class and this is the work that should be taken in hand with all the energy that can be brought to bear upon it.
>
> Here is virgin soil for industrial unionism and all the workers should be organised as speedily as possible within one great industrial organization and at the same time united politically within the Socialist party.[27]

---

25   Debs, July 1911, p. 23.
26   Ibid.
27   Ibid.

Debs suggested, without yet explicitly saying so, that Madero's victory meant the creation of a bourgeois democracy which would make possible the organisation of workers in unions and a Socialist party, and that – not anarchist revolution – was the task of the day.

In part, Debs condemned the PLM because of its rejection of the politics of the Socialist Party of America and the Socialist International and its ties to other anarchist organisations. As he wrote, 'they align themselves with the anarchists and virtually repudiate and renounce the international Socialist movement. If this is their attitude I must confess I do not understand it; if it is their attitude, their dream of establishing anarchist-communism in Mexico at this stage of its industrial and social development will be rudely dispelled before many days'.[28] Debs concluded his article calling upon the PLM to 'align themselves with the international working class movement, accept its principles, adopt its program, and then proceed with all their energy to educate and organise, economically and politically, the masses of Mexican peons and wage slaves' and thus 'blaze the way direct to emancipation'.[29]

Debs's article represented a turning point in the relations between the Socialist Party and the Mexican Liberal Party. Debs for the first time labelled the PLM as an anarchist group and explicitly rejected their anarchist program. Based on what has been called 'the evolutionary theory' of the Socialist Party, Debs foresaw that Mexico would have to pass through a stage of capitalism and bourgeois democracy before socialism became possible.[30] Clearly, Debs thought it preposterous that Mexican workers at that stage of their nation's economic and political development, and the workers' own level of consciousness, could successfully seize the means of production. Finally, Debs saw the enormous power of the capitalists worldwide and put little faith in international solidarity. Debs's article also implicitly endorsed the Madero revolution, the only other force in the field in Mexico. Madero's democratic revolution represented the appropriate stage for Mexican development.

An editorial in the same issue the *ISR* endorsed Debs's view and went somewhat further. The editorial argued that if the anarchists continued to call for a social revolution 'they will also give the ruling classes just the excuse they want to set up a military despotism as relentless as that of Díaz and ten times as strong. Have patience, comrades!' Consequently, American Socialists should eschew support for the Mexican anarchists, for it would only bring on repression.

---

28   Ibid.
29   Debs, July 1911, p. 24.
30   Pittenger 1993, *passim*.

The editorialist argued that under Madero's democratic revolution capitalists and socialists had a division of labour in Mexico:

> The capitalists have their necessary work to do in developing the natural resources of Mexico and organising its industry along modern lines. We have our work to do meanwhile in developing a revolutionary proletariat out of the children of the peons.[31]

After the appearance of Debs's article and the *ISR* editorial, the Socialists generally ceased to support the Mexican Liberal Party. Debs's break with Magón and the PLM came at the same time as that of the American Federation of Labor's (which we discuss in another chapter). Both the SPA and the AFL broke with the Magonistas because the anarchists opposed Madero's government. Thus, the PLM lost the support simultaneously of both the AFL and the SPA.

Debs, drawing conclusions very similar to those of Gompers, played a central role in the course of future US and Mexican socialist and union contacts. Debs's break with the anarchists was a particularly unfortunate decision for the Magonistas who were now largely isolated, and in terms of US-Mexican working-class internationalism, it ended more than a decade long alliance with the PLM. After Debs broke with the Mexican anarchists, the US Socialist and labour movement found that they had thereafter to work through the state-supported union movements, such as the House of the World Worker (COM) and later the Regional Confederation of Mexican Workers (CROM). The Socialists had turned their backs on Mexico's revolutionaries and embraced its reformists.

The positions taken both by Gompers and the AFL and by Debs and the Socialists also helped to deepen and solidify the divisions within the Mexican Liberal Party between its anarchist and socialist wings. The Mexican Liberal Party's anarchist leaders, Ricardo Flores Magón, his brother Enrique, and Librado Rivera broke with the PLN socialists, led by Juan Sarabia, Antonia I. Villareal, and Lázaro Gutiérrez de Lara. The PLM socialists moved to become supporters of the liberal Madero. Thus, Debs's decision also helped indirectly to cohere a social democratic tendency in Mexico.

But the Socialist Party was no monolith and the *ISR* continued to publish articles from opposing points of view. William C. Owen, the English anarchist and editor of the English language section of the PLM's newspaper *Regeneración*, wrote an article for the party's *International Socialist Review* in May 1912, in which he argued that 'the economic problem remains unsolved and it is evid-

---

31   'Editorial', July 1911, p. 47.

ent that Madero has neither the wish nor the capacity to solve it'. Owen argued that the Mexican peasants knew better than Madero. 'The peasant's answer is burn the public records, seize the lands and fight'. The peasant, wrote Owen, 'has magnificent traditions which embody the great principles of mutual aid and labour solidarity, and these have become instinctive with him owing to his communal past'.[32]

At the same time, the *ISR* published articles by conservative Socialists who saw no possibility of stopping US intervention, and in fact looked forward to the progressive work that would be done by American capitalists once they took power in Mexico. Herbert Sturges wrote an article in which he foresaw that American capitalists would force the US government to intervene in Mexico and eventually absorb the entire country. 'Socialist protest may serve to mitigate the horrors of war, and to induce less severity against the conquered prisoners', wrote Sturges. 'But no amount of working-class protest can prevent the intervention itself'. Sturges argued that 'Mexico undoubtedly needs industrial development, and the only ones who seem able and ready to manage this successfully, taking into consideration the whole world situation, are the capitalists of the United States'. Socialists might regret that neither the workers in the US nor those in Mexico were prepared to take on the tasks of economic development. 'But the fact is that we are not sufficiently organised to do this, and must leave it to the capitalists'.[33] Sturges's article not only defended capitalists in general, but justified the role of US capitalists in Mexico, thus apologising for US imperialism.

While the Socialist Party as a whole remained a consistent opponent of US intervention in Mexico, its views on the best future for Mexico were, at best, quite contradictory. The publication of articles by Turner, Debs, Owen and Sturges showed what could be called either the diversity of views or perhaps better the political confusion within the Socialist Party.

7   American Socialists Make Contact with Their Mexican Comrades

In March of 1912, the Socialist Party of Mexico sent its first delegate to the Socialist Party of America convention held in Indianapolis. That delegate came from the newly organised Socialist Party of Mexico led by Paul Zierold. Zierold was a German-born worker who had immigrated to Mexico where he became a

---

32   Owen, May 1912, p. 742.
33   Sturges 1912, pp. 332–5.

piano tuner. Zierold lived in Toluca where he established relations with the glass bottle workers union of the Toluca brewery. During his long career as a socialist activist, Zierold corresponded with August Bebel, Wilhelm Liebknecht and Rosa Luxemburg. Supposedly, a son of August Bebel, the leader of the German Social Democratic Party, worked in the Toluca brewery as did some other Germans. Zierold, working with the brewers and other workers and intellectuals, eventually brought together 11 men, two others with German names, and organised the Partido Socialista Obrero (Socialist Workers Party – PSO) based on the statutes of the Spanish Socialist Party on 20 August 1911. The party, said Zierold, could fit in a coach.

A year later the PSO began the publication of a newspaper, *El Socialista* (The Socialist), which carried in its banner Marx's famous phrase, 'The emancipation of the workers must be the task of the workers themselves'. Juan Sarabia, a former leader of the Mexican Liberal Party, became the editor of the newspaper. Another important PLM leader, Lázaro Gutiérrez de Lara, also attended the PSO meetings. In addition to the newspaper, the PSO also published several pamphlets, most of them introductions to socialism.[34]

Paul Zierold wrote in 1913 to the *International Socialist Review* to explain that, 'As soon as Díaz and his administration fell, a few Socialists united to organise the first Socialist Party of Mexico'. Zierold described the awakening of the Mexican workers, their organisation of unions and strikes. 'Each day brings new converts to the doctrine of Socialism', he wrote. 'At present there are published six Socialist periodicals in various parts of the republic. Without doubt before long a Socialist Party of great importance will be established in Mexico'. Zierold informed the *ISR*'s readers that 'the Socialists of Mexico sincerely desire a connecting link and an extension of co-operation to their Socialist brethren in the United States'.

But no more is heard of the Socialist Party of Mexico in the pages of the *ISR*, and presumably because of the revolution and civil wars in Mexico, it proved impossible to maintain contact. One of the founding members of the PSO, however, was Adolfo Santibañez who would still be active in 1917 when the American war resisters and draft dodgers known as 'the slackers', a number of whom were socialists, began to arrive in Mexico. In 1919 Santibañez and the American slacker socialists would be involved in the re-organisation of the Socialist Party of Mexico and the founding of the Mexican Communist Party.

---

34   García Cantú 1969, pp. 146–9.

8   The Socialist Party Reaction to the US Invasion of Mexico

The Socialist Party vigorously opposed and vehemently condemned Woodrow
Wilson's invasion of Veracruz in April 1914. Mary E. Marcy, in an article titled
'Whose War Is This?' published in June of 1915, immediately after the invasion,
argued that neither the Mexicans nor the Americans had anything to gain from
a US war on Mexico. In the tradition of international socialism, she argued that,
'If we are working men or working women, we HAVE NO COUNTRY .... The work-
ing men and women of ALL countries are OUR countrymen'. Moreover, wrote
Marcy, 'American working men have no quarrel with Mexican working men.
Their interests are our interests'. Marcy argued that,

> The CLASS WAR – the war of the propertyless and exploited working class
> against those who live off their labour – this is the ONLY WAR worthwhile.
> This is the ONLY war that can benefit OUR CLASS because it will give every
> working man and woman the right to work and to have the FULL VALUE
> OF HIS PRODUCT!
>   The only war in which we should engage is the working-class war,
> which will abolish Poverty from the face of the earth![35]

Marcy's article was accompanied by an article by Manuel Sarabia in which,
after giving a long historical background of the revolution, Sarabia argued that,
'The Mexicans must be left alone to work out their own salvation'.[36]
     In addition to those two articles, there was a letter from 'I.D.', a 'US Mar-
ine', written to his sister, presumably a member of the Socialist Party who had
passed it on to the *ISR*. He wrote to tell his sister that he was still alive and
in good health, but commented on the number of Marines killed by friendly
fire, that is, accidentally killed by their own comrades. The Marine described
how the invaders had killed 300 Mexicans and how one naval bombardment
had hit a school and killed 100 children. 'Everywhere you look you would see a
dead Spick, and the street all over blood', wrote the Marine. 'Sad sight to look
upon'.[37] The *ISR*, like many other Socialist newspapers, took a firm stand against
the war.

---

35   Marcy, March 1914, pp. 729–31.
36   Sarabia, June 1914, p. 735.
37   I.D., June 1914, p. 731.

9   Which Faction to Support?

The Socialist Party became increasingly unsure of its position on the factions in Mexico, especially after the Victoriano Huerta's coup overthrew and assassinated Madero, followed by the outbreak of civil war in Mexico in 1915 between the Conventionists of Villa and Zapata and the Constitutionalists of Carranza. David Bruce expressed the Socialists confusion in his article 'Bleeding Mexico' in April of 1916. 'Madero's rising', wrote Bruce, 'was in no sense a rising of the people'. Madero was assassinated, and then, said Bruce, 'Came other leaders – Huerta, Gutierrez, Carranza, Villa, Zapata. None of these are leaders of the people'. Bruce argued that 'a people must free itself'.[38] Thus Bruce fell into complete idealism, for the freeing of the people in the abstract could never be done by any real people in the concrete. Bruce expressed the Socialist Party's utter confusion in the face of Mexican factionalism.

Socialists could be found who favoured almost any of the leading figures. American Socialists frequently judged Mexican revolutionaries in terms of their support for organised labour. Some Socialists, for example, supported Francisco 'Pancho' Villa because they believed that he was sympathetic to the union movement. *The Appeal to Reason*, the socialist newspaper with the largest circulation, printed in bold face on its front page a letter from Pancho Villa to US President Woodrow Wilson in which the Mexican revolutionary demanded the release of Mother Jones from a Colorado jail, before Villa would discuss releasing the imprisoned Mexican landowner, Luis Terrazas. Villa wrote to Wilson that he would consider freeing Terrazas if Wilson would

> show the same regard for humanity toward one of your own citizens, a woman past eighty years, who is being illegally deprived of her liberty, by Gen. Chase, commander-in-chief of the Colorado division of the Rockefeller forces. I refer to Mother Jones .... I may take the liberty to remind you that about two years ago Mother Jones made an organising trip for the Western Federation of Miners through Mexico, under the full protection of President Madero ... Will you do as much for Mother Jones?[39]

In fact, though many of Villa's troops were miners or railroad workers, Villa had little relations to unions as such, and had not worked out a labour programme. But such gestures as Villa's letter to Wilson won support from Socialists and labour unionists.

---

38   Bruce, April 1916, p. 584.
39   Villa, 21 March 1914, p. 1.

John Kenneth Turner, passed through a brief period of support for Zapata. He explained in a 1914 editorial for a Marxist magazine that he was for Zapata because the land question was the overriding issue:

> I am for Zapata. Not for Zapata personally – I am for no man personally – but for the things and the people that Zapata stands for.
>   Zapata stands for the abolition of farm slavery through the parcelling out of the lands to the Mexican people.
>   ....
>   Zapata is but one of thousands upon thousands. These people do not care particularly what individual sits in the castle of Chapultepec [then the presidential residence and office]. They know that nothing can help them until they have the lands.[40]

But Turner soon gave up on Zapata and went over to Carranza.

Turner endorsed Carranza because of the Constitutionalists alliance with the House of the World Worker. As Turner wrote,

> The organised wage-workers are for Carranza to a man. Carranza has assisted the workers to organise and has helped them win their strike. One year ago, May 1, Carranza presided over an International Labour Day celebration of working men in the Mexican capital; he is probably the first head of any government ever to have done so radical a thing.[41]

Turner was not Debs, and his position did not represent the position of the Socialist Party. But, in fact, by 1916 many Socialist leaders and AFL leaders looked toward Carranza as the best hope of the Mexican Revolution. The *ISR* reflected this slide toward Carranza by running articles in late 1916 and early 1917 by Carranza's publicist Modesto C. Rolland.[42]

By 1916, not only was the Socialist Party bewildered about who it supported in Mexico, but it had also grown confused about its opposition to military intervention. Turner condemned Wilson in no uncertain terms. 'WILSON IS THE COMMANDER-IN-CHIEF OF THE ARMY AND NAVY OF THE UNITED STATES AND THE ARMY IS MASSACRING MEXICANS ON MEXICAN SOIL, he wrote'.[43] But, the *International Socialist Review*'s editors praised the Democratic Party

---

40   Turner, June 1914, p. 325.
41   Turner, May 1916, p. 655.
42   Rolland, September 1916, pp. 149–52; Rolland, July 1917, pp. 48–50.
43   Turner, May 1916, p. 655.

president for keeping the peace. The *ISR* editorialist saw the punitive expedition as the alternative to war. 'To howl suspicions of militarism against a president who had kept the working class of America out of war during a hair-trigger period is a species of treachery to the working class that does no good', wrote the *ISR* editorialist.[44] Though Wilson had ordered an invasion of Mexico by General 'Black Jack' Pershing and an army of 10,000 men, the *ISR* praised Wilson as a peacemaker, a strange position for a Socialist Party ostensibly opposed in principle to imperialism and war.

Victor Berger, the leader of the Milwaukee Socialists, went even further, endorsing Wilson's military invasion explicitly through his newspaper *The Milwaukee Leader*, the first time since 1898 that virtually any socialist publication had endorsed US military action against a foreign power. The *Leader*'s editorial read:

> The invasion of the United States by Mexican bandits ... left no alternative to the government at Washington excepting to use military force ... to pursue the murderers ....
>
> President Wilson ... could not have avoided a punitive expedition.[45]

The position of Berger and the *ISR* editorialist supporting Wilson's invasion of Mexico was *not* the official position of the Socialist Party. The Socialist National Executive Committee charged Wilson with capitulating to capitalist interests and condemned the invasion. 'Workers, you have the power to prevent all wars', read the NEC statement. 'You have no enemy but the same enemy which the Mexican Workers seek to overthrow. Use your power to prevent not only war with Mexico, but to prevent that preparation for war which leads to war'.[46] Nevertheless, it was clear from the Milwaukee Socialists position that the previous unanimity of the Socialist Party on opposition to war with Mexico had broken down.

10   Conclusion

The Socialist Party of America, generally speaking, supported the Mexican Revolution and opposed US military intervention. The Socialists, like the American Federation of Labor, early on established a comradely relationship with

---

44   'Doings', August 1916, p. 271.
45   Cited in Christopulos 1980, pp. 246–7.
46   Christopulos 1980, p. 248.

the Mexican Liberal Party (PLM) and engaged in an active legal, financial and propagandistic defence of the Mexican Revolutionaries. However, after Francisco I. Madero's anti-reelectionist movement succeeded in driving the dictator Porfirio Díaz from Mexico, the Socialists broke with the Mexican Liberal Party on the grounds that its anarchist politics could not succeed in liberating and would actually frustrate the aspirations of Mexican working people.

Eugene V. Debs, the most prominent figure and the most important leader of the Socialist Party, took the leading role in condemning and breaking with the PLM because of what he saw as its premature demands for abolishing capitalism and establishing a socialist society. Debs's and the Socialist Party's views were informed by the party's theory of the necessary stages of economic development as well as by their analysis of the actual events taking place in Mexico. The Socialist Party leadership believed that Mexico would have to pass through a stage of capitalist development before a socialist revolution came on the agenda. Debs tacitly endorsed Madero's government as the best hope for union and socialist organisation in Mexico. Debs and the Socialist Party took the position that the revolution was over and that Mexican radicals should now settle down to the long and patient task of education and organisation. Coming at the same time as the AFL's break with the PLM, Debs's statement left the PLM with no allies but those in the Industrial Workers of the World and the anarchist movement of Emma Goldman.

Debs's position of a tacit endorsement of the Madero regime was fundamentally flawed, for Madero's government either could not or would not resolve the central question of the peasants' demand for the land, the key issue of the revolution. Only continued armed and revolutionary struggle was likely to push the landlords and a new revolutionary government to distribute the land. Moreover, by breaking with the Magonistas, Debs left the Socialist Party of America without an interlocutor in Mexico, except for the new bourgeois government and its state-sponsored labour federations (COM and CROM). At the same time, Debs and the AFL by deserting Magón and the PLM exposed them to repression by the US government, though Debs did later soften his position somewhat and call upon Socialists to defend the civil rights of the Magonistas, even if differing with their economic and political programme.

Perhaps most important, the position taken by Debs and the SPA, which paralleled that taken by Samuel Gompers and the AFL, meant that from that point forward, most approaches by US labour organisations to the Mexican labour movement would be through the Mexican state. After Debs broke with the Magonistas, US unions and Socialists tended to approach Mexican workers through the Mexican President. President Madero arranged for Mother Jones to tour on behalf of the Western Federation of Miners. President Carranza supported John Murray and the American Federation of Labor in their meetings with the House of the World Worker. Later Presidents Obregón and Calles would invite Gompers to Mexico City and oversee the AFL's relations to the Regional Confederation of Mexican Workers. While it surely may not have been his intention, Debs's break with the PLM led the US Socialist and labour union movement to work through the Mexican state. The Industrial Workers of the World, however, would continue to try to relate to Mexico's independent left-wing unions, which were not controlled by the government.

The SPA, after the overthrow of Madero in 1913, became ever more confused about developments in Mexico, in part because it had no Mexican socialist or labour organisation with which to communicate. Without connections to some real organisation or movement in Mexico, the Socialists, both nationally and on the local level, veered wildly between Pancho Villa and Zapata one day and Carranza the next. Socialists had no clear idea about what they wanted to see happen in Mexico, though they tended to endorse bourgeois democracy over more radical developments (as in the case of Debs endorsement of Madero over Magón, and Turner's settling for Carranza over Zapata).

The Socialist Party of America did make contact with the small Socialist Party of Mexico led by Paul Zierold and Adolfo Santibañez, but despite the expression of the best intentions on both sides, the American Socialists never committed any personnel or resources to establishing genuine international ties to that organisation. Without guidance from the leadership of the SPA, Socialists who went to Mexico between 1910 and 1917 made their own decisions and formed their own ties to a variety of organisations and individuals (John Murray to the House of the World Worker, Roberto Haberman to Felipe Carrillo Puerto and the Socialist Party of the Southeast). At the same time because their party had no clear direction, the Socialists tended to become agents of the American Federation of Labor, as happened with both Murray and Haberman.

Gompers, unlike the Socialists, knew exactly what he wanted in Mexico: a stable capitalist democracy and a labour organisation modelled on – and if possible controlled by – the AFL, and he recruited Socialists like Murray and Haberman to work for him to construct such an alternative. Similarly, Emma Goldman, William C. Owens, Voltairine de Cleyre and the anarchists knew what they wanted: peasant seizure of the land, worker seizure of the factories, and the organisation of anarcho-communism. Gompers found his ally in Mexico in the government and the government-supported Regional Confederation of Mexican Workers (CROM) led by Luis N. Morones. Goldman and the anarchists found their allies in Ricardo Flores Magón and Emiliano Zapata. Only the Socialist Party had neither a programme nor a party to work with in Mexico.

Perhaps the most disturbing and depressing feature of the vicissitudes of the Socialist Party's positions on Mexico was the gradual development within the Socialist Party of America of a conservative group which was no longer staunchly anti-interventionist. Victor Berger and the *Milwaukee Leader*'s support for Wilson's invasion of Mexico represented the first step toward support for US imperialism in Mexico and Latin America. By 1916 the Socialist Party had also broken from an earlier position of criticism of the Border Patrol and US Army mobilisations and had endorsed specious national calls for self-defence on the US-Mexican border.[47] The change in Socialist policy on Mexico anticipated the movement of some Socialist Party intellectuals into the Woodrow Wilson war camp in 1917. Within the apparent pacifism, anti-militarism and anti-imperialism of the Socialist Party there already existed at the time of the Mexican Revolution, a group evolving toward support for the US government's and the US corporations' imperial interests.

The Socialist Party, the largest and most important group on the American left from 1900 to 1920, proved incapable of building any enduring international labour solidarity during the period of the Mexican Revolution and the First World War. The anarchists on the other hand developed a clear political analysis of the situation though they proved incapable of building a significant movement of solidarity with their comrades in Mexico. It is to them that we now turn.

---

47   Christopulos 1980, p. 315.

American Anarchists and the Mexican Revolution

Emma Goldman, the most famous figure in American anarchism, first made contact with Ricardo and Enrique Flores Magón and other leaders of the Mexican Liberal Party (PLM) in 1905 when they were in exile in Saint Louis, Missouri, a year before they launched their first uprising. Goldman had long talks with the Magonistas and though she is often credited with playing an important role in converting them to anarchism, in fact they were already convinced Bakuninist anarchists. Rather than her converting the Magonistas, it was they who converted her into supporters of their revolutionary movement in Mexico. Their political alliance and personal friendships would endure until the death of Ricardo in 1918, and in the mid-1920s Enrique and Goldman were still corresponding.

Five years after Goldman's meeting with the Magonistas, the Mexican Revolution broke out, an enormous decades-long peasant and worker rebellion inspiring two generations of American radicals and labour activists who saw in it the struggle of the underdogs for social and economic justice. As Goldman wrote in her autobiography, *Living My Life*:

> The revolution in Mexico was the expression of a people awakened to the great economic and political wrongs in their lands. The struggle inspired large numbers of militant workers in America, among them many anarchists and i.w.w.s [members of the Industrial Workers of the World], to help their Mexican brothers across the border. Thoughtful persons on the Coast, intellectuals as well as proletarians, were imbued with the spirit behind the revolution.[1]

By then Goldman and other anarchists had already been involved for years in solidarity with the Mexican revolutionists. For ten years, from 1907 until the suppression of *Mother Earth* by the US government in 1917, Emma Goldman and her collaborators wrote scores of articles dealing with Mexico, the government of dictator Porfirio Díaz, and with the revolution. Two of *Mother Earth*'s contributors, William C. Owen and Voltairine de Cleyre, went on to develop an anarchist analysis of the revolution that went to the very heart of the mat-

---

1 Goldman 1970, p. 479.

ter. As anarchists, they rejected bourgeois political leaders such as Francisco Madero and Venustiano Carranza and threw their support to Emiliano Zapata and the peasants and Indians of Morelos and other areas of Mexico. Their view would inform American anarchist thinking about Mexico for a decade or more.

The American anarchists saw the Mexican Revolution as the greatest revolutionary event since the Paris Commune of 1871, at least until the outbreak of the Russian Revolution in 1917. They argued that the Indian peasants with their communal traditions had raised the struggle for human liberation to a new level through their direct action in taking and redistributing the land. But in addition to offering such a political analysis, the anarchists of Goldman's *Mother Earth* also promoted international labour solidarity among US and Mexican workers, supported the Mexican Liberal Party, opposed the US government's attempt to jail PLM leaders, and organised a movement against US military intervention in Mexico.

For the American anarchists the Mexican Revolution represented the cutting edge of a worldwide anarchist revolution, and they took up the Mexican cause with enormous enthusiasm. Emma Goldman herself carried out a speaking tour on behalf of the Magonistas in Southern California in May of 1912. Other anarchists spoke and wrote on the Mexican Revolution in English, Spanish, Italian and Czech. The American anarchists took the matter of Mexico to the Canadian and British unions. Several attempted to put themselves at the service of the Mexican Revolution in one fashion or another. The British-born anarchist William C. Owen went to work with Ricardo Flores Magón on his newspaper *Regeneración* in Los Angeles. Influenced by anarchist publications and ideas, radicals like labour organiser Charles Cline set off across Texas to join the revolutionary movement in Northern Mexico. Some anarchists participated in the invasion of Baja California by forces of the Mexican Liberal Party and the Industrial Workers of the World. Other American anarchists joined Zapata's forces, such as George Duval who spent two years with the Zapatistas in Morelos.[2]

Goldman's magazine *Mother Earth* provides a record of the development of the anarchists' thinking about and activities in support of the Mexican Revolution. The anarchists' interest and involvement in the revolution began as a campaign of international solidarity with the Mexican Liberal Party. While *Mother Earth* carried two short pieces on Mexico in 1907, the first major article on Mexico appeared in February of 1908, the PLM's 'Manifesto to the American People'.

---

2 Duval, June 1915, pp. 142–3.

The Manifesto, several printed pages long and written from the Los Angeles County Jail in 1907 by Ricardo Flores Magón and his co-thinkers, was an appeal to the American people for support by the Mexican revolutionaries.

> Workers of the world! Our cause is your cause. The cause of the proletariat knows no frontiers. The interests of the working people are the same in all lands under all climates, and all latitudes of our globe. Help us! ... Remember that only by unity of action and solidarity of effort the workers will emancipate themselves.[3]

By the very act of printing the PLM Manifesto, to say nothing of their other activities, the anarchists put themselves in danger of the same sort of repression.

Shortly before the outbreak of the Mexican Revolution, the British anarchist William C. Owen wrote one of the first articles in *Mother Earth* in defence of the Mexican political exiles, who were constantly being arrested or jailed in the United States or extradited to Mexico where they would be jailed or killed. In what was the first or certainly one of the first anarchist articles on the Mexican Revolution, Owen wrote that US immigration laws and the extradition treaty with Mexico were 'a net placed in the hands of Díaz for the capture of his political enemies, and it is high time that these conditions, which represent an arbitrary use of authority as evil as anything found in Russia, should be taken up and investigated without fear or favor'.[4] He concluded, 'There should be a general call to stop, and *muy pronto*, the Russianising of this country'.[5] (Written before the Russian Revolution of 1917, the reference here, of course, is to Tsarist Russia.)

Owen's was among the first of dozens of such articles in *Mother Earth* and other anarchist publications.[6] From these first articles by Ricardo Flores Magón and William C. Owen grew an increasing collaboration and sympathy between the Mexican Liberal Party and the American anarchists.

---

3 Flores Magón et al., February 1908, p. 553.
4 Owen, February 1910, p. 394.
5 Owen, February 1910, p. 396.
6 Similar articles appeared in such anarchist publications as Alexander Berkman's *Blast!* and *The Agitator*. For example, the letters from Emma Goldman and Ricardo Flores Magón to *The Agitator*, 13 March 1911. All these papers can be found in the Emma Goldman Archives, Berkeley, California.

1   William C. Owen

Once the revolution broke out, the anarchists rushed to its defence, but more important perhaps, they also developed an analysis of the nature of the Mexican revolution and its goals which armed their American anarchist followers. While Emma Goldman herself and many other anarchists participated in this process of analysing the Mexican Revolution in the pages of *Mother Earth*, it was British anarchist Owen and the American anarchist Voltairine de Cleyre who primarily developed that analysis during 1911 and 1912.[7] At a time when the revolution was either derided as another Latin American coup d'état by some or hailed as a movement for political democracy by others, their emphasis on the social and economic character of the revolution represented a revelation. In a series of brilliant articles, the two anarchists grasped the fundamental character of the Mexican Revolution as a peasant upheaval directed toward the communal ownership of land.

William C. Owen was born on 16 February 1854 in Dinapore, India, the son of a wealthy British family but orphaned at birth. Raised in England, he studied law, and in 1882 migrated to the United States, living in New York and California and working as a journalist and teacher. He joined the socialists of the International Workingmen's Association, read *The Commonweal*, the newspaper of the Socialist League and corresponded with William Morris, the socialist artist and writer who was active in that organisation. Together with the Italian Francesco Saverio Merlino, Owen first discovered the Socialist League of the United States, but then came upon the writings of Peter Kropotkin and soon became his translator, beginning Owen's turn toward anarchism. After a visit with Kropotkin in England in 1892, he returned to the United States to become a journalist for the League for Prison Reform in 1893 and wrote among other things a pamphlet titled 'Crime and Criminals'. He began to work with the anarchist newspapers *Free Society* and *Mother Earth*, the newspaper of Emma Goldman, the leading American anarchist.

Owen developed his own particular anarchist philosophy. He considered himself to be an individualist as opposed to a collective anarchist, meaning that he was opposed to any form of social organisation whatsoever that might stifle the free activity of the individual. He strongly not only rejected Marxist socialism with its idea that a society could be both collectivised and democratic but also opposed the centralism of the syndicalists of the IWW. Unlike some anarchists, Owen did not accept Marx's analysis of capitalism but was

---

7   Avrich 1978, pp. 225–31.

more influenced by Henry George and his theory of 'land monopoly'. For Owen, the monopoly of land laid the basis for capitalism and for other economic and political monopolies. Through the abolition of the landlord class's land monopoly, Owen believed, society could achieve 'equality of opportunity', which was for Owen the goal. Unlike George, Owen did not see any role for the state in bringing about a fairer distribution of wealth. Owen also rejected Marx's idea of class struggle as standing at the centre of society, arguing that social problems were the problems of the whole society. He did not privilege the working class or unions, but rather encouraged anarchists and other revolutionaries to use education combined with action to move society to reorganise itself. He argued for direct action by the people against the powers that oppressed them.[8]

After reading the socialist John Kenneth Turner's book *Barbarous Mexico*, Owen began to take an interest in Mexico and particularly in the Mexican Liberal Party led by Ricardo Flores Magón. He developed his views on the Mexican Revolution and its significance in Goldman's *Mother Earth* and later in his own newspaper *Land and Liberty*.[9] Becoming directly involved in work with the Mexican revolutionaries from 1910 to 1912, Owen worked on the staff of *Regeneración*, the Spanish language newspaper of the Mexican Liberal Party edited by Ricardo Flores Magón, for which Own edited the English page.[10]

In *Barbarous Mexico* Turner had revealed the scandalous fact that chattel slavery existed in Mexico at the opening of the twentieth century. Taking that as his starting point, Owen began to make his analysis in his article 'Viva Mexico' in April 1911, arguing that the Mexican Revolution 'proposes to abolish chattel and wage slavery'. By combining the struggle against chattel slavery with the struggle against the system of capitalism and wage labour which socialists and anarchists called 'wage slavery', Owen shifted the argument to the left. The Mexican Revolution, if it really was a struggle against wage slavery, had the possibility of becoming a socialist or anarchist revolution.

Owen was surely influenced by the Russian anarchist Peter Kropotkin and his anarchist study of the French Revolution, a history 'from below' which emphasised the self-activity of the sans-culottes and the peasants. Kropotkin argued that even that most famous 'bourgeois revolution' had, under the pressure of the lower classes, tended toward anarchism and communism. Kropotkin had written of the year 1791 and 1792 that 'the revolutionary education of the

---

8   Owen discusses these issues in various articles in issue 16 of *Land and Liberty* published
     in 1914 and 1915.
9   Avrich 1995, p. 486, note 90.
10   Gómez-Quiñones 1977, p. 58.

people was being accomplished by the Revolution itself, and that the masses were by degrees emboldened to demand measures imbued with a communist spirit, which to some extend would have contributed to efface the economic inequalities'.[11]

Owen went on to challenge those who would characterise the Mexican Revolution as simply another Latin American *coup d'état*, arguing that in fact, 'an entire nation is in revolt'. The revolt was not a localised affair, but was rather 'nation-wide', and Mexico was a big nation. One test of a real revolution, argued Owen, was that it appeared not simply in the big cities but throughout the countryside. The French Revolution of 1789 or the Russian Revolution of 1905 had involved 'spontaneous outbreaks at a thousand and one scattered country points. Tested thus the Mexican movement bears all the marks of a genuine revolution'. Owen's Mexican Revolution was no *coup d'état* and no merely political revolution either; it was a nation-wide upheaval, a people in revolt, a social revolution to abolish slavery and wage slavery. Owen concluded his article by returning to the slavery issue and elevating it to the status of a global issue: 'The question is not Mexican but international; slavery and freedom are again at death grips'.[12]

Owen returned to the Mexican Revolution again in June of 1911 in another article, this time titled 'Mexico's Hour of Need'. By this time the profound differences between Francisco I. Madero, the wealthy liberal who had called for the national insurrection on 20 November 1910, and the anarchists of the Mexican Liberal Party led by the Flores Magón brothers had become apparent, and Owen addressed those political differences. While Owens stood on the side the Flores Magón and the PLM, his emphasis was on the role of Mexico's peasants themselves.

Owen argued in this article that the primary factor in the revolution was the peasants' opposition to the landlord. Wherever the Revolution goes, said Owen, the peasants burn the records, just as they did in the French Revolution. 'Not a Mexican peon but knows that the land monopolist is his enemy, who strikes him through the [government] official and the machinery of law', wrote Owen. The Mexican peon, then, was a natural anarchist, a natural opponent of government records and government officials.[13]

Just as Kropotkin had shown in the case of the French Revolution that the driving force was the 'direct action of the serfs', Owen argues that the peasants

11   Kropotkin 1909, vol. 1, p. 241.
12   Owen, April 1911, pp. 42–6.
13   Owen, June 1911, p. 106.

were the agents of the Mexican Revolution. As he writes 'the Mexican Revolution is spontaneous; proceeding from the bosom of the people; engendered by their economic needs and social aspirations; absolutely apart from the political ambitions of Madero and other representatives of privilege'.[14]

The real revolution, Owen claimed, had little or nothing to do with politics. 'In the almost invariable burning of the records; in the not infrequent execution of public officials; in the leaderless uprisings of plantation serfs and the constant multiplication of guerrilla bands, is to be read the true story of the Mexican Revolution'.[15] Owen stressed the Mexican Revolution's agrarian, peasant character, a rebellion of a simple people. 'For the hundredth time I emphasise my conviction that the simpler nations – living close to nature and not having lost their grip of elemental facts – invariably start these revolutions and fight them to the bitter end'.[16]

This interpretation of the Mexican Revolution marked a profound difference between anarchists and socialists. An anarchist like Owen believed that the simple peasants living close to nature represented the most revolutionary social class, while socialists believed the industrial working class had to play the leading role in a social revolution. While the anarchists stressed the importance of the social revolution, the socialists emphasised the importance of the struggle for state power, the political revolution. These differences in interpretation of the revolution would lead also to strategic and tactical differences between anarchists and socialists, and eventually to a complete split between them over the question of Mexico.

As an anarchist, Owen believed in the spontaneous uprising of the masses and rejected the idea of a leading role for a political party, even that of his allies in the Mexican Liberal Party. 'The Mexican Liberal Party has not made this revolution; could not have made it. That, however, it has interpreted the revolution correctly I have no doubt. That it will fight to the last ditch to prevent the people from being cheated of their victory I know'.[17]

Owen suggested that the role of an anarchist organisation was to interpret events, provide guidance, and offer solidarity. But the anarchists could not direct a movement that represented what was an elemental, natural force. Owen's articles provided anarchists with an interpretation of the Mexican Revolution far different from that of the Socialists and progressives with whom they some-

---

14   Ibid.
15   Ibid.
16   Ibid.
17   Owen, June 1911, p. 107.

times worked in coalitions to stop the US government's repression of the PLM and to oppose US military intervention.

2   Voltairine de Cleyre

Voltairine de Cleyre deepened the anarchist interpretation of the Mexican Revolution. She was already one of the best-known American anarchist writers and lecturers in the opening decade of the twentieth century. Born in the town of Leslie in rural Michigan on 17 November 1866 to Hector and Harriet de Claire, her father, a socialist and freethinker, named her after his idol Voltaire. The family was quite poor and her father worked as an itinerant tailor, wandering throughout Michigan to find work. Voltairine attended a convent school where she received a very good education and developed a lifelong hatred of the Catholic Church.

Freethinkers, that is, those atheists and agnostics who rejected religion, actually represented a small social movement in the late nineteenth and early twentieth century both in Europe and America. After she left the convent school at age 17, de Cleyre moved to Grand Rapids and became a writer for 'free thought', that is, for rationalist, agnostic and atheist, newspapers and magazines – *The Progressive Age*, *The Freethinkers' Magazine*, *the Truth Seeker*, *Free Thought* – and then a speaker on the movement's lecture circuit first in Michigan and then in Ohio and Pennsylvania. As her biographer Paul Avrich explains, she was an especially effective speaker because like the runaway slaves on the abolitionist lecture circuit a generation before, she could speak from personal experiences. She had spent four years in a convent and escaped to tell the truth about how young lives were 'murdered by the church'.[18]

Expanding her speaking tours, she travelled as far west as Kansas and as far East as Philadelphia and Boston, and in the course of her lectures came in contact with the socialists and anarchists who were often active in free thought organisations. While participating in a Memorial Meeting for Tom Paine in Linesville, Pennsylvania in December 1887, she heard Clarence Darrow deliver a lecture on socialism. She decided that she was a socialist, and her talks on individual conscience and religious liberty began to be tinged with socialism. Soon, however, she was converted to anarchism. Conversations with Russian Jewish anarchists played an important part in her conversion, though perhaps more important was the 11 November 1887 execution of the men convicted of the

---

18   Avrich 1978, pp. 40–1.

bombing at Chicago's Haymarket: Albert Parsons, August Spies, George Engel and Adolf Fischer.

On 4 May 1886, Chicago police had fired into a picket line at a strike at the McCormick Reaper Works, leading to the calling of a protest meeting at Haymarket Square. As the meeting was breaking up, police showed up and demanded that the meeting stop and the crowd disperse. At that moment, someone threw a bomb, killing a police officer and wounding some 70 others, six of whom later died. The police then opened fire on the workers, killing four and wounding many others. The authorities indicted eight men and brought them to trial, charged with the bombing. Six of them had not been present; evidence indicated that two others clearly had nothing to do with the bombing. No evidence was produced to connect any of the men with the bombing and no bomb thrower was ever identified. The combination of a biased judge, a packed jury, perjured testimony, and the public hysteria resulted in a guilty verdict for all eight. Appeals and petitions for clemency failed. Three of the eight were given long prison terms and five were sentenced to death. One of them, Lingg, committed suicide. The other four, Parsons, Spies, Engel and Fisher, were hanged on 11 November.

The Haymarket events had a profound impact on the American labour movement, putting an end to the period of strikes and rapid union organisation by the Knights of Labor that had opened in the mid-1870s. The defeat of the Knights of Labor was a defeat for its idealism and its inclusive organising approach; out of the wreckage of the radical labour movement arose the more moderate and narrow alliance of craft unions, the American Federation of Labor led by Samuel Gompers. At the same time, the Haymarket hardened the small anarchist movement, making the anarchists even more intransigent in their opposition to the state.

The Haymarket executions deeply moved de Cleyre, as they did other idealists of her generation, making her a convinced anarchist and leading her to participate nearly every year in the memorial services for the Haymarket martyrs.[19] The following year, in 1899, de Cleyre moved to Philadelphia which would be her home until 1910. There, living in poverty, she gave piano lessons and taught English to hundreds of Russian Jewish immigrants, many of them cigar makers and garment workers. A native speaker of English and of French perfected in the convent school, she now also developed 'a respectable command of both written and spoken Yiddish'.[20] Under the tutelage of her older friend Dyer

---

19   Avrich 1978, pp. 44–9.
20   Avrich 1978, p. 78.

D. Lum, a long-time union activist and anarchist, she developed her anarchist views, rejecting individualist and collectivist (or communist) anarchism in
favour of mutualism and voluntary cooperation.[21] De Cleyre had a child, Harry,
by her lover James B. Elliott, but she was economically, physically, and emotion-
ally unprepared to take on the responsibility of motherhood and gave him to
Elliott's family.[22] In 1894 de Cleyre had an opportunity to travel to England and
Scotland, meeting with anarchists there, including Jean Grave, one of the leading French anarchists. Returning to the United States she translated his book
Moribund Society and Anarchy.[23]

During the years 1890 to 1910 de Cleyre became recognised for her essays
and lectures as one of the outstanding figures of American anarchism, if not
as famous as Emma Goldman, the movement's outstanding leader in those
years, she was equally admired. While originally an anarchist pacifist, state
violence against the poor, the Spanish-American War, and the growth of militarism and imperialism changed her mind. By the time that the Mexican
Revolution broke out in 1910, she had become an advocate of revolution. As
Emma Goldman wrote, 'Voltairine began her public career as a pacifist, and for
many years she sternly set her face against revolutionary methods. But greater
familiarity with European developments, the Russian Revolution of 1905, the
rapid growth of capitalism in her own country, with its resultant violence and
injustice, and particularly the Mexican Revolution, subsequently changed her
attitude'.[24]

3   De Cleyre's Mexican Revolution

In the summer of 1911, Voltairine de Cleyre's first article on the Mexican Revolution, 'The Mexican Revolt', appeared in *Mother Earth*. De Cleyre followed closely the views laid out earlier by Owen but added other dimensions to them as
well. Like Owen, she rejected the idea that this was a merely political revolution
and emphasised its social character. Her article opens with the words: 'At last
we see a genuine awakening of a people, not to political demands alone, but
to economic ones – fundamentally economic ones'.[25] For anarchists like Owen
and de Cleyre, the real test of a revolution was its economic character. Polit-

---

21   Avrich 1978, pp. 51–9.
22   Avrich 1978, pp. 71–3.
23   Avrich 1978, pp. 117 and 122.
24   Goldman 1970, pp. 504–5.
25   de Cleyre, August 1911, p. 167.

ics was superficial; economics profound. Like Owen, she praised the Mexicans who 'hew down the landmarks, burn the records of the title-deeds'.[26] She wrote, 'they have driven off the paper-title men, and are working the ground on hundreds of ranches'.[27] But to this de Cleyre added a new element, the notion that the Mexican Revolution and the principle of the direct expropriation of the land represented a new and higher stage of revolutionary action. She wrote, 'the Slaves of Our Times, in a nation-wide revolt, have smitten the Beast of Property in Land. And once a great human demand is so made, it is never let go again. Future revolts will go on from there; they will never fall behind it'.[28]

The Mexican Revolution with its demand for the land would be the benchmark by which future revolutions were measured, she was sure. In December of 1911, de Cleyre published in *Mother Earth* the first of three instalments of an article titled 'The Mexican Revolution', based on a lecture she had delivered in Chicago two months before. This article represented the most ambitious anarchist analysis of the Mexican Revolution so far, and the most insightful. First de Cleyre began by putting the Mexican Revolution in the context of international events: 'The Mexican revolution is one of the prominent manifestations of [a] world-wide economic revolt .... It holds as important a place in the present disruption and reconstruction of economic institutions as the great revolution of France held in the eighteenth century movement'.[29] By placing the Mexican Revolution at the centre of a worldwide revolutionary movement, de Cleyre had elevated its significance and changed the perspective from which one analysed it. By comparing it to the French Revolution's role in world history, she had given it a world historical significance. Mexico thus became the concern of everyone, and certainly of all revolutionaries.

As Owen had done, and as she had done in her earlier essays, she argued that land was the central issue. But now she made a stronger claim: because land was the central and indeed the only issue, either that problem would be solved, or the revolution would be smashed. The revolution 'will end', she wrote, 'only when that bitterness is assuaged by very great alteration in the land-holding system, or until the people have been absolutely crushed into subjection by a strong military power, whether that power be a native or a foreign one'.[30] She predicted that 'the Mexican revolution will go on to the solution of Mexico's

---

26   Ibid.
27   de Cleyre, August 1911, p. 168.
28   Ibid.
29   de Cleyre, December 1911, pp. 302–3.
30   de Cleyre, December 1911, p. 303.

land question with a rapidity and directness of purpose not witnessed in any previous upheaval'.[31]

De Cleyre now added another element previously unmentioned by anarchist writers, the particular character of the Mexican rural people. The Mexican peasants were: 'primitively agricultural for an immemorial period, communistic in many of their social customs, and like all Indians invincible haters of authority'.[32] The Indians had traditionally been a 'communistic' people. 'The habits of mutual aid which always arise among sparsely settled communities are instinctive with them', wrote de Cleyre.[33] This was clearly a partial misunderstanding; for the communal traditions of Mexico's Indians were as strong or probably stronger not where population was scarce, but where the population was most dense, that is, in Central and Southern Mexico. Nevertheless, indigenous communal traditions were an important factor. The Indians, moreover, wrote de Cleyre, had '[n]o legal machinery ... no tax gatherer, no justice, no jailer'.[34] In addition, the 'mestiza [sic] or mixed breed population, have followed the communistic instincts and customs of their Indian forebear[er]s; while from the Latin side of their make-up, they have certain tendencies which work well together with their Indian hatred of authority'.[35]

Mexican President Porfirio Díaz, through his economic development programmes granting concessions to foreign capitalists and corporations, had devastated traditional Indian and mestizo life. 'The government took no note of the ancient tribal rights or customs, and those who received the concessions proceeded to enforce their property rights'.[36] Díaz passed laws that took away vacant lands, that is what were formerly common lands, from those who could not produce a land title. The Madero family and the Terrazas family and others had seized thousands of square miles of territory. Here, suggested de Cleyre, was the cause of the revolution. Land, the theft of the Indians' communistically held land, was the source of the revolution, and until that problem was resolved, the revolution would not end.

---

31   Ibid.
32   de Cleyre, December 1911, p. 304.
33   de Cleyre, December 1911, p. 305.
34   Ibid.
35   de Cleyre, December 1911, p. 307.
36   de Cleyre, December 1911, p. 306.

4   De Cleyre's Zapata

De Cleyre identified Emiliano Zapata as the leader of the forces who were carrying out the expropriation of the landlords' estates. 'Zapata has divided up the great estates of Morelos from end to end, telling the peasants to take possession', she wrote. 'They have done so. They are in possession and have already harvested their crops'.[37] This was the thing, as de Cleyre saw it. In a particularly perceptive passage, she writes:

> [Not] all of this fighting [is] revolutionary; not by any means. Some is reactionary, some probably the satisfaction of personal grudge, much no doubt the expression of general turbulency of a very unconscious nature. But granting all that may be thrown in the balance, the main thing, the mighty thing, the regenerative revolution is the REAPPROPRIATION OF THE LAND BY THE PEASANTS. Thousands upon thousands of them are doing it.
>
> Ignorant peasants; peasants who know nothing about the jargon of land reformers or of Socialists.
>
> Yes: that's just the glory of it! Just the fact that it *is* done by ignorant people; that is people ignorant of book theories; but *not* ignorant, not so ignorant by half, of life on the land, as some of the theory-spinners of the city.[38]

A real revolution, de Cleyre seems to be saying, follows a logic of its own. Whether this is a logic determined by the underlying economic system, in this case, the system of landed property, or the logic of a fundamentally communistic human nature is not clear from this passage.

In the final section of her essay, de Cleyre anticipated the critics of communal land ownership who would argue that such a system would fail to bring about economic development. De Cleyre asserted that Díaz had brought about the development of the corporations at the expense of the people. De Cleyre defended the Indian and mestizo appropriation of the soil arguing that 'however primitive their agricultural methods may be, one thing is sure: that they are more economical than any system which heaps up fortunes by des-

---

37   de Cleyre, December 1911, p. 338.
38   de Cleyre, December 1911, pp. 340–1.

troying men'.[39] Moreover, argued de Cleyre, the Indians had different values than the Anglo-Saxons. 'An Indian has a different idea of what he is alive for than an Anglo-Saxon has', wrote de Cleyre. 'And so have the Latin peoples'.[40] The Anglo-Saxon wants to 'be busy', to create what is useful and profitable, while the Indian and Latin peoples want 'to live', by enjoying a sensuous existence, creating beautiful things as part of nature. These are cultural ideals that caused conflict in a capitalist world, but which de Cleyre believed would be valued under anarchism.

The political revolution and the election victory of Madero could never bring stability to Mexico, argued de Cleyre, at least as long as they failed to resolve the land question. Given that the land question continued to be the central issue, she believed only three outcomes were possible: a military dictatorship, a US intervention, or a successful peasant revolution. Whatever the outcome, said de Cleyre, she honoured the Mexican peasant revolutionaries and their struggle for the land.

A few months later, de Cleyre returned to these themes once again in an article on the Paris Commune of 1871 titled 'The Commune is Risen' published in *Mother Earth* in March of 1912. After surveying the world's revolutionary movements in Western Europe, Russia, China, and elsewhere she concluded giving the place of honour to the Mexican Revolution. She wrote, 'under the Mexican sun, we know men are revolting for *something*; for the great, common, fundamental economic right, before which all others fade – the *right of man to the earth*'.[41] She ended her last article on Mexico before her premature death with the words, 'the Great Ghost has risen, crying across the world, *Vive la Commune!*'[42] The Paris Commune lived on in the Mexican Revolution, in the forces of Zapata and the peasants of Morelos.[43] Voltairine de Cleyre died in Chicago of meningitis on 20 June 1912.

---

39   de Cleyre, December 1911, p. 376.
40   Ibid.
41   de Cleyre, March 1912, p. 4.
42   de Cleyre, March 1912, p. 15.
43   *Mother Earth* published one other major piece of analysis of the Mexican Revolution, M. Baginski's 'The Significance of the Mexican Revolution' (Baginski, December 1913), written during the Huerta dictatorship, which was understandably much more pessimistic but added nothing new to the Owen-Voltairine analysis.

5   Anarchists versus Socialists

The anarchists' social revolutionary interpretation of the Mexican Revolution helped to sustain the anarchists' campaigns for solidarity with the Mexican peasants and workers in New York, Chicago, Los Angeles and other cities. But at the same time, this radical analysis led inevitably to conflicts with the American Federation of Labor and the Socialist Party, which had thrown in their lot first with Madero and then later with Carranza.

After 1911, when the Socialist Party opted for Madero, the anarchists became implacable critics. The Socialist Party's position derived logically from the evolutionary, gradualist politics of both the Socialist Party of the United States and the Second or Socialist International.[44] The Socialists' position was that the overthrow of Porfirio Díaz had ended a period of political dictatorship and economic feudalism and had thus opened the way for an era of bourgeois democracy and capitalist economic expansion in which industry and the working class would grow, while the people would enjoy democracy and labour unions and socialists would be able to organise. For this reason, Socialists supported the Madero government, or later the Carranza government, on the grounds that they opened a period of economic expansion, political liberty, and labour union rights. Socialism, in this view, was obviously not on the agenda in backward Mexico, and much less possible was some sort of libertarian communism.

The anarchists characterised the Socialist Party's position on the Mexican Revolution as 'so cowardly, contemptible and disgusting as to deserve the severest chastisement by the entire international revolutionary proletariat.'[45] This harsh condemnation came in part from differences between the Socialist Party and the anarchists over the invasion of the cities of Mexicali and Tijuana in Baja California by the joint forces of the Mexican Liberal Party and the Industrial Workers of the World. *Mother Earth* quoted the views of Socialist Party Congressman Victor Berger (speaking through his secretary W.G. Ghent):

> The 'insurrectos' [who had taken Baja California] are not Socialists, but are, in the main opposed to Socialism. Their movement is not predominantly a Mexican movement. It is a movement originating in the United States and its promoters and followers are a mixture of men of every creed except Socialism. Some of them are merely vague utopians. Some

---

44   Pittenger 1993, *passim.*
45   'Observations', July 1911, p. 131.

of them are so-called 'direct actionists'. Others are avowedly Anarchists. Still others are revolutionists by temperament and would as readily revolt against a Socialist administration as against a capitalist administration. The Socialist Party can afford to have no connection with this movement.[46]

The anarchists, of course, held exactly the opposite view. 'But for the i.w.w. boys and the Anarchists who joined the Mexican revolution from its very inception, the revolutionary traditions of the international proletariat would have been shamefully destroyed', they wrote.[47] The anarchists argued that the Socialists had cut themselves off from and turned against 'the most significant social events since the Paris Commune'.[48] Even worse, in the view of the anarchists, the Socialist Party had thus adopted a counter-revolutionary position. 'They are working with Madero, with Wall Street, and Washington against the Mexican revolution – for political considerations. But they will only gain the contempt and condemnation of the revolutionary element everywhere'.[49]

The anarchists attacked the Socialist newspaper *The Appeal to Reason* for 'an infamous article beginning: "the Mexican Revolution is at an end"'. And they attacked Eugene V. Debs, the Socialist Party's presidential candidate and most popular socialist leader, for calling for the Mexican Revolution to be brought to an end to prevent more bloodshed.[50] The anarchists were appalled to find that 'Madero, the henchman of the Mexican Revolution, enjoys the co-operation of the party of Eugene Debs'.[51] Owen, after analysing the Socialists reformist campaign in Los Angeles and commenting on their tepid attitude toward the Mexican Revolution, declared, 'the Socialist party is not a friend, but an enemy'.[52] Thus, by the end of 1911, anarchists and Socialists had broken completely and definitively over the issue of the nature of the Mexican Revolution.

---

46   'Observations', July 1911, pp. 131–2.
47   'Observations', July 1911, p. 133.
48   Ibid.
49   Ibid.
50   'Observations', August 1911, p. 162.
51   'Observations', July 1911, p. 133.
52   Owen, September 1911, p. 202.

6   Against US Military Intervention

Nevertheless, when in April 1914 the United States bombarded the city of Veracruz on the Mexican Gulf coast and then landed troops there, both rank-and-file Socialists and anarchists worked to oppose US military intervention in Mexico, even if they often did so separately. The anarchists laid out their anti-interventionist arguments in two articles published in *Mother Earth* in May of 1914, just after the US invasion and occupation of the port of Veracruz, Mexico. The anarchists feared, the occupation of Veracruz might be the opening of a general war with Mexico, so their arguments were not simply against the invasion, which they of course opposed, but against a full-scale war.

First, the anarchists saw the US attack on Mexico as a struggle between two state powers, and therefore an issue in which working people could have no interest. 'The American military invasion of Mexico is the act of a big ruffian bullying a smaller one', declared *Mother Earth* in an unsigned article, possibly written by editor Emma Goldman.[53] US and Mexican workers had no quarrel with each other, in fact, the anarchists argued, workers should be allies across the border:

> The working class of this country especially have not the slightest reason for war with the Mexican people. Their cause is a common one, both suffering from oppression and exploitation of a rapacious predatory class, whose official governmental representatives for the time being are Wilson and Huerta. The Wilson-Huerta war is a quarrel between two thieves. Let them fight it out themselves. American workingmen should refuse to slaughter or be slaughtered to protect the profits of American capitalists pressed from the blood of the Mexican peons.[54]

The article continued to argue that war should be turned into a rebellion against the military authorities: 'But if they should be forced to bear arms against the Mexican workers, they would do well to emulate the example of the Italian anti-militarist Augusto Masetti. When drafted for the war against Tripoli and ordered to kill his proletarian brothers, Masetti turned his gun against his Colonel and shot him in full view of his regiment'.[55] Rather than fighting peasants and workers in Mexico, argued *Mother Earth*, American workers should join the fight against the bosses in their own country. 'It is not in Mexico but

---

53   'Observations', May 1914, p. 67.
54   Ibid.
55   'Observations', May 1914, pp. 67–8.

in Colorado that the real American war is being waged. It is there that American workers have a most vital interest. It is the war of labour against capital, against the very interests are inciting the American people to slaughter in Mexico'.[56] The paper's editorialist called for a 'General Strike' against US military intervention in Mexico.

In the same issue, Leonard D. Abbott's article 'Let Us Make War Against War!' also argued that, 'We have no real quarrel with Mexico', and supported William 'Big Bill' Haywood's statement that a general strike would be labour's most effective protest against a capitalist war. But Abbott added another argument, urging his readers to refuse to serve in the military, 'a working man or a liberal does not need to wait for a general strike to make effective his protest against war. His duty is quite clear. As yet, fortunately, we are not plagued in this country by the systems of conscription and of enforced military service that have been established in many European countries .... All we need to do is to refuse to join the army'.[57]

To Wilson's invasion of Mexico, the anarchists opposed a programme of conscientious objection to military service, mutiny in the military, and the general strike. Perhaps partly because of the protests organised by anarchists, Socialists, labour unionists, and liberals and pacifists, there was no general US invasion of Mexico during the course of the Mexican Revolution. Certainly, there was a widespread movement against US intervention in which the anarchists played a small part. Little wonder, given their fierce anti-militarism and anti-imperialism, that after the United States entered World War I, the US governments suppressed *Mother Earth* in August 1917 and in 1919 deported Emma Goldman, Alexander Berkman, and other anarchists.

7   International Labour Solidarity

The American anarchists organised an international campaign for the defence of Mexican revolutionaries, for the victory of the Mexican revolution, and against US military intervention in Mexico. Their efforts involved anarchist, Socialist and labour organisations in several countries, among them Cuba, Canada, and England, as well as Mexico and the United States. With shoestring operations, the anarchists organised meetings, published pamphlets, and carried out protest demonstrations.

---

56   'Observations', May 1914, p. 68.
57   Abbott, May 1914, p. 82.

Cuba and Mexico have had a long and close association based on history, trade and culture, and so it is not surprising that one of the first international connections was between Cuba and Mexico. In 1908, *Mother Earth* carried an appeal by Cuban anarchists in opposition to the government of Porfirio Díaz. 'We, the proletarians of Cuba, feel it our duty to acquaint the world with the crimes committed against liberty and humanity by Porfirio Díaz', read the Cuban appeal. 'We call upon all workingmen to voice their solidarity with the oppressed of Mexico, and to take steps to end the brutal reaction in that unfortunate country'.[58]

The anarchists in New York created the Mexican Revolution Conference in the spring of 1911 and organised a demonstration in support of the revolution at Cooper Union on June 26 of that year.[59] In Chicago, the anarchists created the Mexican Liberal Defence League. In April of 1912, Voltairine de Cleyre wrote a report for *Mother Earth* on the activities of the League. As treasurer, de Cleyre reported that she had collected a total of $247.96 from various cities, which was sent on to the *Junta* of the Mexican Liberal Party in Los Angeles. While the sums of money were small, the anarchists were very active. Most of their activities were educational. De Cleyre reported that the Chicago anarchists had distributed 4,000 copies of a leaflet titled 'The Mexican Revolt', among Chicago labour unions. The anarchists also sold 200 copies of Owen's pamphlet on the Mexican Revolution. De Cleyre or other anarchists spoke at the Scandinavian Liberty League, at IWW Local 85, and at the Open Forum.[60]

In a cosmopolitan and polyglot city like Chicago, educational work had to be carried on in many languages. Ludovico Caminita, a visiting Italian anarchist, spoke on the Mexican Revolution to Italian speaking audiences. Through his speeches, the Chicago anarchists also met some Spanish anarchists with whom they began to work.[61] Voltairine also helped her friend Josef Kučera produce a pamphlet on the Mexican Revolution in Czech, *Revoluce v Mexiku*, as well as writing articles herself for the Chicago Czech anarchist newspaper *Volné listy*.[62]

The Chicago group's work also had an international dimension. De Cleyre's comrade Honoré Jaxon, a Canadian, visited England and distributed a statement on the Mexican Revolution to the Standing Orders Committee of the British Trade Unions. He also arranged interviews in the Manchester *Labour Leader* and other British newspapers. Jaxon returned from England to Canada where

---

58   Cuban anarchists, 1908, 'Mexico', *Mother Earth*, p. 172.
59   'Observations', June 1911, p. 99.
60   de Cleyre, April 1912, pp. 60–2.
61   Ibid.
62   Kučera 1911, cited in Avrich 1978, p. 230, fn. 36.

he lectured on the 'struggle of the Mexican proletariat' before the Trades and Labour Councils of Montreal, Quebec, and Toronto. In addition, he arranged interviews on the Mexican Revolution with newspapers of those three cities, as well as with journalists in Winnipeg.[63]

8   William C. Owen and *Land and Liberty*

William C. Owen had joined the staff of Ricardo Flores Magón's newspaper *Regeneración* in 1910, working for the paper until 1912. In 1914 he moved from Los Angeles to Northern California where he and his comrade W.D. Guernsey created the Bakunin Institute in the East Bay community of Hayward to promote their anarchist views. There, beginning in the spring of 1914, working in a 'remote country house', Own edited, wrote and published his tabloid newspaper *Land and Liberty*. While particularly concerned about the Mexican Revolution and aiming to promote solidarity with Mexico's working people, it also carried articles dealing with other national and international issues, as well as with arguments about the superiority of anarchism to capitalism, socialism, and syndicalism. Owen was particularly concerned about the question of US intervention in Mexico, condemning newspaper magnate William Randolph Hearst and *Los Angeles Times* editor Harrison Gray Otis, for promoting war with Mexico, and excoriating President Woodrow Wilson for invading Mexico.[64] Owen still saw Mexico as standing at the centre of the worldwide struggle for social justice. Jo (Charles Joseph Antoine) Labadie, a leftist labour activist in Hudson, Michigan wrote to *Land and Liberty*, 'Mexico is now the point of the wedge that divides the landlord from his power over the people and is the point of a world-wide push'.[65]

As opponents of intervention and activists in solidarity with Mexico's working people, Owens and his readers were interested in who supported American intervention and why. In early 1914, Owens published a letter from Lucy E. Parsons, the anarchist labour activist and widow of Haymarket martyr Albert Parsons, in which she argued that not only capitalists but also the corporate middle class supported Mexican intervention. Parsons wrote, 'You will find, for example, thousands of Standard Oil employees more anxious than Rockefeller himself for intervention in Mexico, because all their business future is bound up with the continuance of a system that enables them to exploit the Mexican peon as that company is now preparing to exploit the chinese [*sic*] coolie. Their tastes and social standing are those of the financial magnates'.[66]

Another group interested in American intervention were US property owners and corporate employees actually involved in work in Mexico. A 'San Diego correspondent' wrote to the paper about the American refugees from Mexico who had shown up there, presumably American corporate employees or property owners who had fled the revolutionary violence in general and the attacks on Americans in particular. 'The truth about the majority of these refugees is that they are as cold-blooded a lot of sharks as ever existed. They went to Mexico to pile up fortunes from the sweat and blood of the peons, and if the Mexicans had killed them, they would merely have got their just dues'.[67]

What about the American working class? Where did it stand? In another letter to the editor, a reader called George W. Stamm wrote, 'Everywhere the American worker is largely indifferent to the struggle in Mexico'. Stamm argued that American workers mistakenly thought that the great fortunes of the growing capitalist class were made only off his or her labour. 'He thinks these fortunes are made from his own underpaid work, whereas the greater part of them is coming, more and more, from foreign countries, from the cheap labour of the natives of the still underdeveloped nations, applied to their practically virgin resources'. Stamm argued that the Panama Canal had opened up the virtually untouched resources of Mexico and the Pacific Coast. 'That is the game the American worker is up against, and it is time for him to begin to understand it'.[68]

If they did understand the Mexican Revolution and wanted to support the Mexican people, what were Americans to do? Owen reported to his readers that in early 1914 he had received several letters from readers who wanted 'to go to Mexico and fight for Land and Liberty'. In answer to their questions for information and guidance, Owen wrote, 'Our advice has always been that the Mexicans be left to fight their own battles; that we who wish the Government of the United States to refrain from interfering keep our own hands off'. The Mexicans, he wrote, have proved themselves to be 'excellent fighters, and foreigners who go into their country, ignorant of its customs and language, are sure to be looked upon with suspicion and to be more of a nuisance than they are worth'. Rather than going to Mexico to fight, Owen proposed that Americans could show solidarity by explaining to Americans what was going on in Mexico.

---

66   Parsons, April 1914, p. 3.
67   Owen, May 1914, p. 2.
68   Stamm, April 1914, p. 3.

'The propaganda of explanation is still in its first infancy', he wrote. 'Nineteen-twentieths of our people are still unaware that the Mexican peon is fighting the battle they themselves will have to fight, for life must win security'.[69]

On 15 July 1914, the usurper General Victoriano Huerta, defeated by the revolutionary armies of Obregón, Carranza, Villa, Zapata and others, gave up and fled the capital. Owen wrote in a brief note in *Land and Liberty*, 'Huerta has gone and we now come to another phase of the Mexican problem – Carranza & Co., as agents for the benevolent dictator (in the interest of the North American plutocracy) Woodrow Wilson. It is now that the hornet's nest will begin to hum'. Owen correctly understood that Carranza was no friend of Mexico's working people, but he failed to understand that Carranza was a dedicated nationalist who would fight to defend the country's sovereignty and to renegotiate better terms in exchange for its subordination to the United States.[70]

9 The World War

The outbreak of the World War in early August of 1914 forced Owen, as it forced everyone else in politics, to reorient himself and to rethink his positions. Owen's *Land and Liberty*, originally conceived of primarily as promoting solidarity with the underdogs of the Mexican Revolution, was transformed within a few months to a magazine dedicated principally to discussions of the world war. At first, in the September 1914 issue of *Land and Liberty*, Owen accepted the war as an inevitable result of Europe's 'class, racial and religious hatreds', economic pressures, and of the drive of nations for more territory. He placed responsibility for the war on Germany, which because of its location at the centre of Europe in the midst of hostile empires had become militaristic.

'Circumstances made Germany and armed camp, and living in the camp, the nation grew military in all its thoughts'. Given the rise of German militarism, he argued that all nations were being drawn into the war by fear. 'This war has its roots in FEAR – each nation is afraid, and justly, of the other; the individuals of each nation, thanks to the ruthless commercial war which ravages us all the time, are afraid of one another'. In this situation, he spoke out for the rights of oppressed nations – Mexico, India, Ireland, Belgium, and Serbia – to defend themselves against invaders. Finally, he saw the World War as an opportunity for revolutionaries. 'This war ... should be but the prelude to an infinitely

---

69   Owen, September 1914, p. 11.
70   Owen, August 1914a, p. 4.

more gigantic struggle and should usher us immediately into the true revolutionary era'. Rejecting pacifism, he wrote, 'This is not time to lisp of peace and mediation. It is the time to set the teeth and spread the nostrils wide in our determination to win a life worth living'.[71]

In his October issue Owen continued to emphasise the responsibility of Germany for the war and excoriated the German Socialists for their support of their government. He reported sympathetically the position of the Anarchist Group of San Francisco, 'The Anarchists believe it imperative that the world should understand that this is a government-made war; that it is the natural consequence of building up huge governmental machines which hold the fate of nations in the hollows of their hands and, by creating and defending vast industrial and political monopolies, rules'. Owen also cited the anarchists' new pamphlet, *The Social Revolution* which declared that, 'Democratic America and England are not one whit better than is autocratic Russia. Republican France shows us precisely the same picture as does Imperial Germany'.[72] Owen himself lashed out at Woodrow Wilson for his invasion of Veracruz, Mexico on behalf of 'unscrupulous monopolists', warning: 'He has ordered out and will order out the federal troops whenever the privileges of our plutocracy are seriously threatened. Should we finally decide to invade Mexico he will enforce the Dick conscription law'.[73]

10   Owen Comes Out for England and the Allies

Owen's initial position resembled that of revolutionary socialists and anarchists in various countries of the world, but by November 1914, he had abandoned the revolutionary internationalist position, announcing his support for England and its allies France and Russia against Germany. In doing so, Owen acknowledged that he was following the lead of the Russian anarchist Peter Kropotkin who in a letter published in the anarchist magazine *Freedom* in the fall of 1914, argued that the idea of a general strike against war was an illusion that had hypnotised the anarchists. Since no general strike was going to take place anarchists and working people generally should participate in the military to defeat German militarism. 'I consider that the duty of everyone who cherishes the ideals of human progress, and especially those that were inscribed by the European proletarians on the banner of the International Workingmen's

---

71   Owen, September 1914, pp. 1–2.
72   Owen, October 1914a, pp. 6–7.
73   Owen, October 1914b, pp. 1–2.

Association is to do everything in one's power, according to one's capacities, to crush down the invasion of the Germans into Western Europe', wrote Kropotkin.[74] Alexander Berkman writing for *Mother Earth* replied, 'We unconditionally condemn *all* capitalist wars ...'. Later in February of 1916, Kropotkin helped to initiate and garner anarchist support for the *Manifesto of the Sixteen*, warning of the dangers of German victory and expressing their support for the Allies in the First World War.[75] Kropotkin and a few other leading anarchists, historically opponents of political parties and governments, of militarism and warfare, now gave up those principles.

Agreeing with Kropotkin's position, Owen now argued that the war was not the result of capitalism, but rather the result of militarism as embodied in the German state. Capitalists he stated have no desire for war, since war interferes with commerce, but militarist states want war to expand their territory. Working from his theory of land monopolies as the basis of all social ills, he argues that the land monopolist is an invader and taker of the land of others. German militarism and war, he suggested, represented the land monopolist writ large. Owen explained, 'I do not believe that Belgium invited invasion. I do not believe that either the French or the British wanted war. I do not believe that Germany was defending herself against Russia ...'. Owen made his position quite clear: 'In my judgment, and I have examined the evidence with greatest care – this war is an invasion, plotted for years and put most deliberately into effect by the Kaiser and his military clique'.

The German invasion of other nations had caused the war and, argued Owen, working people had a right and duty to resist. Owen explicitly broke with the socialist and anarchist tradition of internationalism, writing, 'Great as are the worker's wrongs, it is not true that, as a class, he has neither home nor country. It is not true that he has nothing to lose but his chains. It is not true that it makes no difference to him whether he lies under Prussian military rule, as an inhabitant of an annexed and conquered country, or as a citizen of a land that has known how to defend itself'. Owen asks how San Francisco's workers would respond if invaded by Japan? 'Would the workers shrug their shoulders indifferently, saying it was no concern of theirs? Of course, they would not. Of course, they would fly to arms, and he who tempted to convince them that their action was foolish would find it going hard with him'. Owen now used the example of Mexico and its right to self-defence against the United States to argue for

---

74   Kropotkin, November 1914, pp. 273–80 and Woodcock 1962, p. 217.
75   Kropotkin played a key role in influencing other anarchists, such as the Frenchman Jean
      Grave to support the war. See: Patsouras 1978, pp. 87–8.

the right of the Allies to resist and to crush Germany.[76] Emma Goldman in the December 1914 issue of *Mother Earth* attacked Owen for his pro-English and pro-war position, criticisms which Owens brushed off without responding to her arguments.[77]

Within a few months of the outbreak of the war, Owen had completely revised his position; rejecting Marxist and anarchist theories of capitalism and imperialism, he developed his own understanding of the war. He denied that capitalism and the corporations were behind the war as Marxists and many anarchists believed, arguing instead that capitalist actually opposed the war because it interrupted and interfered with business. This was not a commercial war, he argued, but a state war. States made war when they became dominated by a philosophy and practice of militarism, as embodied in Germany.

By February 1915, Owen had gone farther and was not only supporting the allies but also actually singing the praises of England, arguing that England was not an imperial power. Owen wrote, 'England has been no saint, but neither is she today the military criminal her foes are painting her. Free trade converted her nearly a century ago into a trading power and to free trade she owes her richest colonies and that supremacy at sea which she enjoys. Her rule over those colonies is largely nominal, and the proof is given by the alacrity with which they rush habitually from all four quarters of the globe'. Not only is England not an imperial power, but she is not a militaristic nation, says Owen. 'Great Britain stands along among the European powers in her refusal to adopt conscription and she fights today only because her back has been thrust ... against the wall. She would bring about universal disarmament tomorrow if she had the power and lead the world in that evolution from militarism to industrialism which has to come'.[78] (In March of 1916, little more than a year later, Great Britain introduced military conscription.)

Owen in reviewing J.A. Crumb's book *Germany and England* argued that England was a force for democracy and peace, even in her colonies. 'England has the most extensive empire on record; an empire which, in Canada, Australia, Africa and even in India itself, she has been endeavouring to democratise. For her, therefore, the leisurely securities of peace are the one necessity, and inevitably she leans toward the compromises of parliamentarianism, toward arbitration, peace conferences, Pacifisim, disarmament proposals, religious toleration, etc., etc.'. Germany on the other hand was all militarism, war, and invasion.

76   Owen, November 1914, pp. 1–4.
77   Owen, January 1915, pp. 1–3.
78   Owen, February 1915, pp. 3–4.

Surprisingly, while supporting Mexico's right to independence from interference from the United States, Owen had never been a supporter of Ireland's
independence from England. *Land and Liberty* had from early on run articles
supporting the Ulster Protestants who stood opposed to Irish independence.
Owen wrote in the August 1914 issue published before the outbreak of the
war that 'Ulster is voicing the world-wide dissatisfaction with what is called
Democracy, the cornerstone of which is majority absolutism'.[79] Now, with the
outbreak of the war, and concerned about the possibility of Ireland taking
advantage of England's war with Germany to fight for its independence, he ran
an article by P.J. Healy of San Francisco arguing that Ireland would be foolish
to try to separate from England. Healy wrote, 'The war is a most excellent lesson to those Irishmen who think they could maintain and absolutely separate,
independent, and sovereign government in Ireland. Let them look at the mon-
strous and barbarous outrage that has overwhelmed Belgium, a country fully as
able to maintain its independence as Ireland would be if she were left to look
out for herself'. Healy went on to argue that in any case attempts to separate
Ireland from England would be futile. 'Ireland is the keystone in the arch of the
British Empire, and the British people will never consent to its removal. So, the
Irish may just as well admit the stern fact that Ireland is indissolubly connected
with England and that, so long as men to turn plowshares into machine guns,
there will be a justification for the connection'.[80]

Owen's opposition to Germany and support for Great Britain in the war led
him to become an adversary of unions and strikes too. Opposition to unions
flowed from Owen's belief that Great Britain and her allies must be bigger
and stronger economically than Germany to win the war, while unions' strikes
interfered with the war effort. Owen wrote, 'As all the world has heard, Great
Britain labours under one enormous disadvantage in this war, being severely
handicapped by the rebelliousness of labour. In the Clyde and Tyne districts,
that small section of workers on which the country must depend for repairs
for its fleet is taking advantage of the public necessity and playing exclusively
for its own hand'. He quoted the British Director of Transport who accused the
Clyde shipyard workers of being able to make enough in three days to keep
them drunk for the rest of the week. He criticised the workers for being 'selfish'
and 'unintelligent' and added that by striking they were hurting trade unionism
by alienating it from the nation.[81] So the anarchist defender of Zapata became
a patriotic advocate of the victory of the British Empire.

---

79   Owen, August 1914b, pp. 3–4.
80   Owen, July 1915a, pp. 11–15.
81   Owen, July 1915b, p. 6.

11   Pancho Villa: A Modern Robin Hood

Interestingly, while Owen had repudiated the anarchist position on the World War, he remained an opponent of US imperialism in Mexico. In 1916 Francisco 'Pancho' Villa carried out a raid on Columbus, New Mexico in retaliation for the US government having assisted his enemy Venustiano Carranza. Villa's attack on US soil was followed almost immediately by President Woodrow Wilson sending General 'Black Jack' Pershing to Mexico with a 'punitive expedition'. Consequently, there was a great deal of controversy surrounding Pancho Villa who was usually dismissed in the American press, even by some of the left press as an ignorant, violent bandit.[82] While Owen's political views on the international situation had moved in a more conservative direction, he remained steadfast in his opposition to United States intervention in Mexico. In a contribution to this controversy, Owen wrote an article titled 'A Modern Robin Hood' for the *New Review*, the theoretical journal of the left wing of the Socialist Party of America. Owen opposed US intervention, arguing that 'our government's sole and sovereign aim was the protection of the enormous properties Americans had acquired in Mexico'.[83] Owen added that if Americans really wanted to understand what would come from US intervention in Mexico, they should study that 'chapter of United States history which deals with the extermination of the North American Indian'. Wrote Owen, 'It is against his blood brother beyond the Rio Grande that we are now advancing; against fully ten millions of his brothers. What is really on the *tapis* [on the carpet, that is, on the floor for debate] is the greatest Indian war on record'.[84]

Opposition to US intervention was widespread among the anarchists and most Socialists, as well as among many labour unionists and liberals. While the anti-war position was common on the left, what was original in Owen's argument was the claim that war on Mexico was another American war against the Indians. Whether or not mestizo Mexico could be equated with indigenous peoples, there was a poignancy to the argument that the continental conquest was continuing, now moving south. And another thing that made Owen's contribution particularly important was his defence of Pancho Villa, the man who had just invaded the United States. This is somewhat surprising, given that Ricardo Flores Magón and the Mexican Liberal Party had never forgiven Villa for having at first supported Madero and helped him to disarm PLM fighting

---

82   Steffens, for example, called Villa a 'bandit' and supported Carranza. Steffens, May 1916, pp. 533–47.

83   Owen, June 1916, p. 177.

84   Ibid.

units in Mexico. Owen, however, now came to Villa's defence, writing, 'Villa is, and has been for many years, a bandit. Mexico is full of bandits, as are the United States, England, Germany, and all civilised countries. But Villa has been a bandit of the mediaeval, Robin Hood type; a proletarian bandit, who made it his specialty to levy on the rich and divvy with the poor. Robin Hoods have always been popular with the masses, but modern civilisation has shoved them to one side and given us in their stead the subtler gentry who rob under cover of the law'.[85]

Owen admitted that Villa was violent, a 'free-handed spender' who had no doubt engaged in 'many grotesque extravagances'. He also conceded that he might have gotten 'a bad attack of swollen head', after being courted by entrepreneurs, financiers and the US government who were looking for an alternative to Carranza. 'But', wrote Owen, 'these are only passing follies, and the permanent character is the thing we must get at it we are to form a just estimate of Villa'. Owen continued: 'That character I am convinced – and I have talked with men who know him well – is basically proletarian, and nothing else; i.w.w., if you like to look at it that way; in closely-sympathetic touch with men in the rough, with the primarily virile instincts, with all that smug respectability abhors, with the very things to which such a government as that of the United States is constitutionally opposed'.[86] Owen contrasted Villa's and Zapata's radical nationalism to the views of Madero. 'Madero sincerely admired us [the United States] and our institutions, and events proved that he had no hold on the masses. Villa and Zapata instinctively hate us, and I, for my part, believe that their hold on the masses is proportionately great by reason of this very fact'.[87] On this question, Owen was clearly wrong. Villa had begun his revolutionary activity as a great admirer of American corporations, American bosses and workers, and even the US government. Only after the US dropped support for him had Villa changed his mind.[88] At the same time, Owen is no doubt correct that there was a strong sentiment opposed to US imperialism among the Mexican people.

Owen not only opposed US intervention, but he supported Mexican efforts to expel the US Army. The Mexicans 'have a most decided objection to our absorption of their country, and to our imposing on them a civilization by no means to their taste', wrote Owen. 'Curiously enough I sympathise with them in this'. Owen expressed little hope that the people of the United States would stop

85   Ibid.
86   Owen, June 1916, p. 178.
87   Owen, June 1916, p. 177.
88   Katz 1998, pp. 541 and 552.

the US intervention, that, he said would take a revolutionary movement in the United States. The Mexicans, he hoped, would 'show themselves the stronger and kick us out'.[89]

Owen continued to publish articles supporting the Mexican revolution's radical wing and condemning Woodrow Wilson and the United States government for their intervention in Mexico. At the same time, he had also developed a set of positions on the World War, on England and its empire – support for England and the Allies – that stood in stark contrast to his positions on Mexico. Moreover, it must have been clear to him that Wilson would eventually lead the United States into the war as an ally of England against Germany, an upshot that would bring his contradictory positions into high relief. Fearing deportation for his work on behalf of the Magonistas' Mexican Liberal Party and perhaps recognising the emerging contradictions in his position on Mexico and the World War, Owen fled to England where he wrote for the anarchist newspaper *Freedom*, supported England and the allies in the war, and after the revolution fiercely attacked Vladimir Lenin and the Bolshevik leadership of the Russian Revolution of October 1917.

Owen's support for the Allies in the World War was not characteristic of the anarchist movement, and his idiosyncratic positions seemed to have no impact on anarchist solidarity with the Mexican Revolution. Anarchists in the United States were still involved in solidarity with the Mexican revolutionaries in 1916. The anarchists helped create the Workers' International Defence League, with branches in Los Angeles, San Francisco, Chicago and New York. While it took up many other causes as well, this organisation focused much of its attention on the Mexican Liberal Party and the defence of the Flores Magón brothers and their comrades. The anarchists worked in a united front, as reported by Edgcumb Pinchon, general secretary of the Los Angeles branch: 'There is a permanent organisation 'in the service of all who require defence and aid in the struggle for economic justice'. It is identified with no faction. On its Executive Committee are men and women of Organised labour, Socialists and Single Taxers, Industrial Workers of the World and Anarchists – and rebels without a label. And these are of many nationalities – American, British, German, French, Italian, Russian, Jewish, and Mexican'.[90] Such organisation in solidarity with the Mexican Revolution continued until the suppression of the anarchist movement in June of 1917 by the government of President Woodrow Wilson.

---

89   Owen, June 1916, p. 178.
90   'The Arrest', April 1916, p. 492.

12   The Rangel-Cline Case

While most anarchists limited their support for the Mexican Revolution to keeping informed about developments, defending the Mexican people's right to determine their own fate, and perhaps throwing a quarter in the hat for the Mexican solidarity campaign, some went further. During this period, the American anarchists devoted nearly four years to the defence of a group of fourteen Mexican and US anarchists who were arrested in Texas, several of whom were held on charges of murder. Known as the Rangel-Cline case, the matter involved several members of the Mexican Liberal Party (PLM) and the American labour organiser Charles Cline.

Cline had had a remarkable career as a labour activist. He was a member of the Hotel and Restaurant Employees Union, Local 7 of Pueblo, Colorado and of the International Slate and Tile Workers Unions, as well as several other unions in St. Louis, New York City and Boston. In addition, he was also a member of the National Industrial Union of the Industrial Workers of the World. During his career, he had participated in the Hotel and Restaurant Employees strikes of 1903 and 1904, the Southern Pacific Machine Shop strike of 1911, and the Louisiana Lumber strike of 1912. 'By reason of his capacity as a speaker and organiser', wrote Goldman's *Mother Earth*, 'he is regarded as a very dangerous character by the lumber barons of Louisiana and Texas'.[91] Then in 1913, Cline had aligned himself with the Mexican Liberal Party and was on his way with 13 of its members to join the revolution when he was arrested.

Mother Earth gave this version of the story. On 11 September 1913, 13 Mexican men, Mexican Liberal Party members and Charles Cline, a member of the Industrial Workers of the World, left Carrizo Springs, Texas heading toward Mexico intending to cross the border 'peacefully' and join the Mexican Revolution. Between 1910 and 1916 hundreds of Americans had crossed the border to join the revolutionary forces of Madero and Villa, the Magonistas, or later of Venustiano Carranza and the Constitutionalists. Some were anarchists or socialists, some soldiers of fortune, and others dilettante adventurers. The US and Texas governments sometimes took the attitude that as long as such groups were not organised and did not constitute an armed invasion, that they were legal. At other times the US government viewed such activities as a violation of the US neutrality laws, which forbid the organisation of an invasion force on American soil, in which case the government had the violators arrested.

---

91   'The Rangel', June 1914, p. 112.

Unknown to the Rangel-Cline group, as the rode toward the border, they were being followed by four Texas sheriffs.

The party camped for the night at Capanes Wind Mill in Dimmit County, not far from Carrizo Springs. In the morning of 12 September, as they were breaking camp, Silvestre Lomas, one of the Mexicans who had been active in the labour movement in both Mexico and the United States, was shot through the back of the head and died. The anarchist group, responding to the attack, discovered several deputy sheriffs and took two of them prisoner as two others fled. The PLM men later said that they intended to release the two hostages when they reached the Mexican border.

The two prisoners, Dimmit County Sheriff Eugene Buck and Deputy Sheriff Candelario Ortiz were put in the charge of PLM member José Guerra. As they rode along, Sheriff Ortiz allegedly went for Guerra's gun, and in response Guerra shot and killed Ortiz, supposedly in self-defence. The PLM party then continued on its way until confronted by a group of sheriffs who demanded the release of Sheriff Buck. After some negotiation, Sheriff Jesse J. Campbell signed an agreement granting the PLM men permission to continue on to Mexico without further problems from the police in exchange for handing over Sheriff Buck. The PLM group turned over Buck and continued on toward Mexico.

The night of 12 September, the group camped in a ravine, still on the Texas side of the river. Campbell and the other officers, meanwhile, had returned to Carrizo Springs, raised a posse, and then later that same night followed the PLM group to the ravine where they opened fire upon the sleeping revolutionaries. The sheriffs succeeded in overpowering the PLM men, wounding Juan Rincón, Leonardo L. Vázquez, and José Abraham Cisneros. Rincón died of his wounds. Guerra was either killed or escaped but was never heard from again.

The prosecution accused Jesús M. Rangel and Charles Cline of being the leaders of the group, but also indicted twelve others for murder and other crimes. All fourteen men were tried, found guilty, and sentenced to prison for terms varying from six years to 25 years, to life. In prison, two of the revolutionaries were murdered. Lucio R. Ortiz was murdered in Penal Camp No. 1 at Parry Landing, Texas in 1915, and Eugenio Alzaldo was murdered at Penal Camp No. 3, also at Perry Landing, Texas in August of 1916. One of the PLM men, J.A. Serrato, succeeded in breaking out of the penitentiary, crossed the border into Mexico, and joined the revolution.[92]

---

92 'Appeal', December 1913, pp. 304–7; 'Observations', February 1914, pp. 55–6; 'Tyranny', February 1914, pp. 377–9; 'The Rangel', June 1914, pp. 111–15; 'The Rangel', August 1914, pp. 201–2; 'Mexican', October 1916, pp. 304–6.

The anarchists conducted a four-year campaign for the release of these men who embodied their notion of international labour solidarity. 'These cases offer the first opportunity that the American labour movement has had to give a practical demonstration to the Mexican worker that the American worker is not indifferent to his Mexican brother', declared *Mother Earth* in an unsigned article. 'We now have the opportunity of showing in a definite form that we really believe that "An injury to one is an injury to all".'[93]

While defending Rangel, Cline and the others, *Mother Earth* hoped to turn the defence campaign into a movement which would help to organise Mexican and Mexican American workers in the Southwest of the United States. The anarchists' argument merits citation at length:

> We have said that the American Federation of Labor, the Western Federation of Miners, the United Mine Workers and the Industrial Workers of the World have practically failed in the organization of these men. Right now, the strength of the Building Trades organization on the west coast is seriously endangered because of the influx of the Mexican workers who can do the unskilled work of the concrete worker, etc. Unless these men are organised and brought in, and made part and parcel of the American labour movement, the strength of those organizations which have been developed as a result of years of struggle is in danger. The same can be said of the railroad service, the mining industry and manifold other lines. These cases [the Rangel-Cline cases] open the door for an immense propaganda among the workers, who, if they remain apart from you are a menace, but who, if you can incorporate them into your bodies, can give you an enormous strength.[94]

The anarchist argument as given here is that the defence of the Mexican Revolution and of its most radical wing constitutes a bridge to Mexican immigrant workers in the United States who will join and work with an organisation that has proven that it stands on the side of Mexico's working people.

Mother Earth carried at least half-a dozen articles on the Rangel-Cline case during the years from 1913 to 1916, while anarchists formed Rangel-Cline defence committees, raised money, wrote leaflets and pamphlets, and spoke at public meetings. The anarchists' work on the Rangel-Cline case inevitably involved not only the defence of the 14 victims, but also two other causes:

---

93   'The Rangel', June 1914, p. 114.
94   'The Rangel', June 1914, p. 115.

the organisation of the unskilled worker and support for the peasant revolution in Mexico. Defence of Rangel and Cline was inseparable from the defence
of the oppressed and exploited Mexican workers on both sides of the border; the cause was one. Whether in those years the anarchists' defence of the
Rangel-Cline cases had any impact on labour organising is impossible to know;
there were just too many things going on at the time to make an assessment.
The idealistic approach to the Mexican worker may have been the right one,
though throughout those years Mexican workers were turning from anarchism and seeking solutions through political reform, as we demonstrate in subsequent chapters. All of those involved in the incidents of 1913 were eventually
pardoned by Texas's first woman governor, Democrat Miriam A. Ferguson in
1926.

13   Conclusion

For over a decade, from 1905 to 1917, Emma Goldman, William C. Owen, Voltair-
ine de Cleyre and other American anarchists supported the Mexican Liberal
Party and the Mexican Revolution and Emiliano Zapata and his Liberating
Army of the South. American anarchists engaged in all sorts of educational
work, protest movements, defence campaigns and fundraising efforts for the
Mexican revolutionary movement. A few anarchists even crossed the bor-
der and joined the revolution. Owen, living at the PLM's headquarters in Los
Angeles, editing *Regeneración*'s English language page, and writing for *Mother
Earth*, provided for two years a crucial organisational link between the two
groups.

   Owen and de Cleyre provided the anarchists with an analysis of the Mexican Revolution that was both congruent with the anarchist worldview and
fit the facts on the ground in Mexico. While progressives, Socialists and the
AFL saw the Mexican Revolution as primarily a political revolution, a revolution for democracy, the anarchists better understood its economic and social
goals. Though there was on the part of Owen and de Cleyre a romanticising of
the revolution and particularly of the Indian peasants, still they had grasped
the fundamental character of the revolution – a peasant revolution to reclaim
the land – in a way that virtually no other political groups of that time had.
Certainly, contemporary historians have tended to agree with Owen and de
Cleyre that the Mexican Revolution was fundamentally a nation-wide peasant
upheaval, which could not end until the land question was resolved. This view
was systematically argued by Frank Tannenbaum, an erstwhile member of the
Industrial Workers of the World (IWW), who spent time in Mexico in the 1920s,

in his classic *Peace by Revolution: Mexico After 1910*, and taken up again more recently by British historian Alan Knight in *The Mexican Revolution*.[95] This is certainly the dominant position among Latin Americanists today.

Another aspect of the anarchist interpretation, that is, that the Mexican Revolution represented part of a worldwide revolutionary process, has been defended by John Mason Hart in his book *Revolutionary Mexico: The Coming and Process of the Mexican Revolution*.[96] The anarchists' emphasis on the importance of indigenous communalism as a kind of proto-socialism has also been emphasised by Adolfo Gilly in his books *The Mexican Revolution* (*La revolución interrumpida*) and especially in *El cardenismo, una utopía mexicana* (Cardenism, a Mexican Utopia).[97] Owen's support of Pancho Villa, a modern Robin Hood, anticipates the work of Eric Hobsbawm on *Primitive Rebels*.[98] Moreover, their emphasis on the role of the peasants (which they learned from Kropotkin's history of the French Revolution) anticipated by 50 years the 'bottom-up social history' of the 1960s inspired by E.P. Thompson in England and by Jesse Lemisch in the United States. Finally, the correctness of the anarchists' analysis is confirmed by the Mexican Revolution's resolution when in the 1930s President Lázaro Cárdenas distributed millions of acres of land to the Mexican peasants, finally bringing the revolution to an end.

The anarchists, of course, were not primarily intellectual interpreters of events; they were revolutionaries. They were attempting to understand the Mexican Revolution and to draw out its lessons both to make possible the building of solidarity among American leftists and unions and to spread what they saw as the emerging anarchist ideal in the Zapatista commune to inspire American workers and other workers around the world. The American anarchists saw Zapata as a leader of a movement to be emulated. Later some historians, such as James D. Cockcroft, would argue that the Zapatistas, like the PLM before them, represented a 'vanguard political and military organization' of the working classes.[99] Yet in reality, while they were uncompromising in their fight for their land, the Zapatistas offered no vision, programme, or strategy that could lead and inspire the Mexican working class and the labouring people more generally.[100] And despite their efforts, the American anarchists of the 1910s had little influence on either the American labour movement or on US politics and foreign policy.

---

95   Tannenbaum 1966; Knight 1986.
96   Hart 1989.
97   Gilly 1971; Gilly 1994.
98   Hobsbawm 2010.
99   Cockcroft 1983, p. 113.
100   Gilly 1971, pp. 115–70.

The American anarchist movement was too small, too fragmented, and its influence too dilute. While the anarchists often worked with the IWW, they did not share that organisation's dominant view that a strongly centralised organisation was necessary to defeat the powerful corporations and the government, and consequently they had little influence in the unions.[101] They had even less impact on the AFL, with its business union politics and its pragmatic fight to monopolise jobs and control wages. And of course, they became harsh critics and opponents of the Socialist Party of America, the most important left organisation of the era. In terms of politics and public opinion, the anarchists had been under attack since the 1880s, seen as foreign, anti-American, and violent advocates of nihilism. They became virtual pariahs with the anarchist Leon Czolgosz's assassination of President William McKinley at the Pan-American Exhibition in 1901. Woodrow Wilson and Attorney General A. Mitchel Palmer renewed the attack on the anarchist during and after World War I. Small and weak, the anarchists' clear analysis of the Mexican Revolution was never matched by an equal capacity for action.

---

101   Brissenden 1919, pp. 295–304. The IWW had been centralist for some time, but the centralists won a decisive victory at a convention in 1913.

CHAPTER 5

Riding with Pancho Villa: The Radical Socialism of John Reed

John Reed, as we would say today, embedded himself in the army of Francisco 'Pancho' Villa, one of the few American Socialists who actually rode with the revolution. His articles on Mexico and his book *Insurgent Mexico* brought to his readers both a picture of ordinary Mexican people in revolution and a depiction of Pancho Villa, one of the revolution's most important leaders. Reed interpreted the revolution to American farmers and workers in terms based on their own experience so that they could identify with the working people of Mexico. While his book *Insurgent Mexico* was a wonderful piece of journalism, it did not ultimately play a decisive role in the debates; still its sympathetic and humanistic portrayal of the revolution at the grassroots warrants a fresh reading and analysis.

After the overthrow of Francisco I.Madero in February 1913, the Socialist Party found itself facing again the question of what leader and what party it supported in Mexico, especially in the first several months before Venustiano Carranza, the so-called 'First Chief' of the Revolution, had been able to establish his reputation as the successor to Madero and the leader of the various forces in the field under Generals Álvaro Obregón, Francisco 'Pancho' Villa, and many others. Mexico at that moment was politically something of a mystery. What was the Revolution now in this new stage? Who was doing the fighting? Why had they risen up? And what were the goals of the Revolution? Those were the questions facing the Socialist Party's members when in late 1913 the socialist and reporter John Reed, then only 26 years old, went off to cover the Mexican Revolution as a writer for *Metropolitan* magazine and as a correspondent for the *New York World*. Reed's articles and book would help to shape not only Socialists' and unionists' views, but also those of the broader American public.

Already having been involved in the most radical wing of the Socialist and labour movements in the United States, Reed's sympathies were with the revolution before he left and, once he arrived in Mexico, he virtually joined the insurgent army. During 1913 and 1914, Reed rode, ate, slept, caroused, and did everything (as far as we know) but shoot with the Mexican revolutionaries led by General Francisco 'Pancho' Villa as they fought against President Victoriano Huerta, the usurper who had overthrown and murdered Francisco I. Madero.

In his short time riding with them, Reed came to love the Mexican revolutionaries of the North and above all the ordinary working people, both the *pacíficos*, that is, the civilian non-combatants, and those who made up the troops.

Reed's articles later edited and published as the book *Insurgent Mexico* attempted to show what the revolution was all about and to explain what it meant in such a way as to overcome the racial prejudices and other biases of his American readers. If John Kenneth Turner's *Barbarous Mexico* had revealed to Americans the truth about exploitation and political oppression in Mexico, it was Reed's *Insurgent Mexico* that showed American readers for the first time in depth the ordinary Mexican man or woman who, driven by those horrendous conditions, had risen up in revolution, a revolution that Reed argued was entirely justified and whose ideals were noble. Reed explained, or, more correctly he allowed the men and women of *la tropa*, poor and ignorant as they might be, to explain the high ideals of the more democratic and egalitarian society in which they believed, even if – as they and he could see – it would be extremely difficult to achieve.

1   The Education of a Radical

John Reed was born on 22 October 1887, the son of a wealthy family of Portland, Oregon, his grandparents and parents having made their money in commerce. After a sickly and protected childhood in Portland, his parents sent him off to the 'distinctly upper class' *Morristown School* of New Jersey where one teacher found that he brought 'a newer point of view and a marked eagerness in all he did', while another described him as 'turned too much toward mischief and disorder'.[1] At the private high school Reed began to become a writer, producing short stories and poems for the *Morristonian* and then founding the comic school newspaper *The Rooster*. He also managed the school's football and baseball teams and won a letter on the track team. During a visit home, he found that his father, a progressive and a Jury Commissioner of the Federal District Courts, had become involved in the investigation of corruption and fraud in Portland that involved businessmen, politicians, and government officials. His father's work on the investigations provided young Jack Reed with his first exposure to contemporary American politics and left him highly critical of the country's democracy. His father's example of investigating to find out the

---

1   Rosenstone 1975, p. 26.

truth – even though there had been rumours and threats – provided young Jack with a demonstration of personal courage in the pursuit of political principle.[2]

In the fall of 1906, Reed entered Harvard, which president Charles W. Eliot had transformed from a small provincial college of 1,000 to a major American university with a student body of 4,000, a school of international renown. Its faculty included such luminaries as philosophers William James and Josiah Royce, and it had country's broadest selection of electives. Socially, Harvard was a labyrinth of clubs with implicit and recondite rules that governed the social life of the campus. A brash freshman with no respect for what was 'cricket', Reed failed to make an impression in the social clubs, became bored with his classes, though he easily passed them, and turned to writing, first for the Harvard *Lampoon* and then for the *Harvard Monthly* and the *Harvard Advocate*. By 1908 the various winds of change in America – populism, progressivism, and socialism – had begun to have an impact on the Harvard student body. Small groups of students began to meet to read Anatole France and Karl Marx.[3] Students began to criticise the college's lack of relevance, and writing in the *Advocate*, one student called upon teachers to 'become constructive and radical, [to] set our faces to the new dawn and [to] make us look at the light of unrisen suns'.[4]

As the new political climate spread on campus, Reed threw himself into a number of the new clubs: the Cosmopolitan Club that fostered relations between American-born and foreign students, the Dramatic Club that promoted the writing of original plays, and the Socialist Club founded in 1908 by nine undergraduates. Soon the Socialist Club had attracted thirty members and sometimes brought together another 50, though its influence was even broader. During Reed's last two years at college, says his biographer Robert A. Rosenstone, 'the Socialist Club was a potent force'. Reed and its other members wrote for the campus newspapers and revived moribund clubs as well as creating new ones such as the Harvard Men's League for Women's Suffrage and the Anarchist Club. The Harvard members wrote a platform for the Cambridge Socialist Party and proposed legislation that was presented to the Massachusetts Assembly. The future journalist and influential opinion-maker Walter Lippmann, a member of the club, criticised the Department of Economics for presenting Marxism only as a dead theory and not as 'a living thing in our midst'. Other young socialists accused the university of 'not paying employees living wages' while students also successfully petitioned the faculty for a class on socialism.[5]

----

2   Rosenstone 1975, pp. 3–35.
3   Rosenstone 1975, pp. 36–43.
4   Rosenstone 1975, p. 43.
5   Rosenstone 1975, pp. 43–5.

After graduating from college, Reed spent several months in England, France, and Spain, especially delighting in life on the Left Bank in Paris. When he returned to the United States in 1911, he settled down in Manhattan, finding a job at *The American Magazine* through the help of his family friend and his mentor the famous muckraker Lincoln Steffens. Reed was soon trying to make it as a freelance writer. Initially frustrated by rejection of his creative and critical articles by the mainstream magazines, Reed had a breakthrough when his pieces began to be accepted by mainstream magazines such as *The Saturday Evening Post*, *Colliers*, and *The Century*.

Within a year he had gravitated to Greenwich Village where the first American Bohemian scene had begun to emerge among young people critical of Puritanism, capitalism, and consumerism and in search of a life of beauty and freedom. When he came across *The Masses*, the avant-garde and left-wing magazine founded in 1911 by Piet Vlag and involving a group of radical Socialist and anarchist writers and talented graphic artists, Reed recognised at once that he had found his aesthetic and political home. Max Eastman, the socialist and feminist, who had become editor-in-chief, immediately recognised Reed's talent, and the young journalist was soon not only writing for the magazine, but in 1913 also became a member of the editorial board. Thus, Reed found himself at the centre of the most advanced artistic, intellectual, and political currents of American society in the remarkably creative decade of the 1910s.[6]

What were the politics of the Greenwich Village bohemians of *The Masses* amongst whom Reed found himself? Max Eastman had taken over editorship of *The Masses* in 1913 with the goal of turning it from the politics of reform to those of revolution. Eastman came from a literary family of reformers. He and sister Crystal Eastman were feminists, a view that also prevailed in the magazine. The magazine advocated birth control, the use of contraceptives, and free love. Eastman insisted that the prose and the art in *The Masses* have a realistic style combined with a cosmopolitan outlook and a whimsical attitude. As he wrote:

> I did not harp incessantly on propaganda. I tried to have plenty of things in every number which had nothing to do with socialism, and some of whose values were wholly comprised in themselves – some items, if you will, of art for art's sake.
>
> Aside from enhancing life, that seems to me the wisest way to conduct propaganda. The cherished idea is there, and it is there in clear and hon-

---

6   Rosenstone 1975, pp. 76–116.

est form. But it is not so drummed upon that only those already interested will listen. Loyalty to principle takes the place of zealotry, and enlightenment that of indoctrination.[7]

Eastman believed in the Marxist idea that the working class would make the revolution, and so *The Masses* was not simply pro-labour but a supporter of the Industrial Workers of the World (IWW), the revolutionary syndicalist union. Eastman wrote in one of his memoirs:

> ... the militant leaders of the working class without a single exception took the magazine into their hearts. Bill Haywood, Carlo Tresca, and Elizabeth Gurley Flynn, leading a strike in Paterson, New Jersey; Ettor Giovannitti in jail in Lawrence, Massachusetts; Schmidt and Kaplan in jail in California; Mother Jones and John Lawson battling the mine owners in West Virginia; Frank Tannenbaum marshaling the unemployed; William Z. Foster, starting a little syndicalist movement in Chicago; every agitator who really intended to overthrow capitalism and inaugurate a working-class millennium in the United States felt that he had a body of friends and colleagues in the writers and artists of *The Masses*. Our magazine provided for the first time in America, a meeting ground for revolutionary labour and the radical intelligentsia. It acquired, in spite of its gay laughter, the character of a crusade.[8]

American radical Joseph Freeman, a reader and fan of *The Masses* at that time wrote,

> *The Masses* ... seemed to reconcile our warring selves. Palgrave was Beauty; Marx was Justice; the *Masses* was both. It not only discussed politics and economics from a revolutionary viewpoint, but published drawings and poems which themselves combined Beauty and Justice. They attacked capitalism, they called for freedom. The magazine did not separate the struggle of the working class, we thought, from the yearning for Beauty.[9]

This was the place Reed came from, the place where working class struggle joined the fight for Justice and Beauty.

---

7   Eastman 1948, pp. 414–15.
8   Eastman 1948, p. 409.
9   Freeman 1936, p. 63.

The Masses opposed World War I when it broke out in August of 1914 and opposed the US entry into the war in April of 1917. For opposing military conscription, the US government shut down *The Masses* in 1917, and its staff – including John Reed – was put on trial in 1918 for violation of the Espionage Act, though none was convicted. This was the magazine that supported John Reed in what he called a participatory journalism that led him to go to Mexico to ride with Pancho Villa and find out what the revolution was all about.

But before he went to Mexico, Reed had significant contact with and involvement in the far left. Reed, living in the village and working for *The Masses*, had met William D. 'Big Bill' Haywood, the one-eyed, burly, battered, and intransigent leader of the Industrial Workers of the World, at a gathering in an apartment in the Village. Haywood spent hours describing and explaining the strike for the eight-hour day by 25,000 silk workers in nearby Paterson, New Jersey, a strike that had been virtually blacked out in the mainstream press. The Paterson police were attempting to beat the strikers into submission, while city officials filed charges of sedition against those who criticised the local government. Haywood believed that the strikers needed to get their story before the world if they were to win, and so Reed decided he would go to Paterson to publicise the strike.

No sooner had he arrived in Paterson than Reed was arrested for refusing to get off the street and jailed with the IWW leader and Italian newspaper editor Carlo Tresca, Haywood, and other Wobbly organisers. Reed's arrest brought publicity to the strike immediately and his articles such as 'War in Paterson' explained the strike to his readers in the Village and beyond. 'There's a war in Paterson', he wrote. 'But it's a curious kind of war. All the violence is the work of one side – the Mill Owners'.[10] Not content to merely write about the conflict, Reed soon became one of the principal organisers of 'The Paterson Pageant', a benefit for the strikers staged in Madison Garden. For Reed, partisan journalism and activism in the cause of the working class were one, and they had now become his vocation.[11]

During the organisation of the Pageant, Reed fell in love with Mabel Dodge, a wealthy, sophisticated woman eight years older than he, whose salon was the gathering place for everyone who was anyone in the Village. After a trip to France and Italy together, the returned home to Manhattan, but – poorly

---

10   Reed 1987, pp. 117–32.
11   Rosenstone 1975, pp. 117–32.

matched temperamentally – their relationship fell apart and Reed fled to Boston.[12] Anxious to both get away from New York and Dodge and to throw himself into a new project, in the fall of 1913 Reed accepted an assignment from *Metropolitan* magazine to cover the Mexican Revolution. The articles that he wrote for *Metropolitan* and other magazines and newspapers, later reworked into his book *Insurgent Mexico*, were what might be called impressionistic journalism, for he aimed to catch the essence of the experiences he was describing, not to document them. To do so he was often willing to combine people or events or even to create fictional characters and actions in order to capture the feel of the moment., Building on the style of Jack London and anticipating such great writers as Ernest Hemingway and John Steinbeck, *Insurgent Mexico* is a minor masterpiece of American literature.

2   *Insurgent Mexico*

Insurgent Mexico is the story of Reed's travels with the revolutionary armies of northern Mexico in late 1913 as they battle Huerta's *Federales* and Orozco's *Colorados*, who were even more hated because they were former revolutionaries, traitors who had gone over to Huerta. Reed rode with the armies across the vast landscape of the north of Mexico, plains, deserts, and mountains, from hacienda to hacienda, some of them more than a million acres in size, and always with the wealthy hacendado's *casa grande*, often a virtual fortress, at the centre. Reed rode with the revolutionaries into battle, joined them in their *fiestas* with the *pacíficos*, the civilian non-combatants, and slept beside the soldiers at night in rooms filled with the odour of sweat, *aguardiente*, and tobacco.

In the course of his extraordinary travelogue, Reed described the military train, the cavalry, the camp followers, and the lives of the ordinary people of the region, and as he wrote he painted miniature portraits of individual leaders and rank-and-file fighters. The revolution's violence was everywhere, death and destruction, dynamite, machine guns, and massacres, the slaughter of prisoners, the widows and orphans. He painted a vast canvas, a Bosch-like landscape with swirling scenes, dramatic contrasts, and tableaus of tragedy and comedy as well as many wonderful little cameos. The young master writer's word-paintings told his readers what the revolution was and why it was right that there should be a revolution, and he suggested that they should sympathise

---

12   Rosenstone 1975, pp. 133–48.

with the country's underdogs as they attempted to carry the revolution through to a just end. And Reed even suggested what that end might look like.

Like John Kenneth Turner and the socialists who had supported Ricardo Flores Magón and the anarchists of the Mexican Liberal Party (PLM) almost 15 years earlier, Reed, also a socialist, risked his life to tell the story of Pancho Villa and the revolution in northern Mexico. Reed went to Mexico as a reporter to cover the revolution, but soon found himself riding with the revolution and becoming a part of it. Towards the beginning of the book Captain Fernando touches him on the arm and asks, 'Will you sleep with the *compañeros*?' Reed does not reply but walks with Fernando to the stone storehouse where the men are singing or sleeping.

> They didn't distinguish me at first, but soon one of the card-players said: 'Here comes Meester!' At that the others roused, and woke the rest. 'That's right – it's good to sleep with the *hombres* – take this place, *amigo* – here's my saddle – here there is no crookedness – here a man goes straight ...'.

> 'May you pass a happy night, *compañero*', they said. 'Till morning, then'.

So, Reed became an '*amigo*', a '*compañero*', and one of the '*hombres*' himself. He put down his blanket and lay down on the floor 'very happily'. 'I slept better than I had before in Mexico', he wrote.[13] Now not simply a reporter but part of the revolution, Reed was content. He wrote a little further on that, though Americans insisted that Mexicans were 'fundamentally dishonest', he found them to be trustworthy. Though he was surrounded by the poor and had valuable belongings and money, no one ever stole from him, and, moreover, they gave him tobacco, which was scarce. Not only did Reed sleep among the soldiers, but he also accompanied them to the *fiestas* where they make 'the meester' drink and dance with them.

Reed was riding with the revolution, but would he also fight alongside the men? At one point a man named Julian Reyes challenges him:

> 'Are you going to fight with us?'
> 'No', I said. 'I am a correspondent. I am forbidden to fight'.
> 'It is a lie', he cried. 'You don't fight because you are afraid to fight. In the face of God, our Cause is Just'.
> 'Yes, I know that. But my orders are not to fight'.

---

13   Reed 1969, pp. 42–3.

'What do I care for orders?' he shrieked. 'We want no correspondents.
   We want no words printed in a book. We want rifles and killing, and if
   we die, we shall be caught up among the saints! Coward! Huertista!'
'That's enough!' cried someone, and I looked up to see Longinos
   Güereca standing over me. 'Julian Reyes, you know nothing. This *compañero* comes thousands of miles by the sea and by the land to tell
   his countrymen the truth of the fight for Liberty. He goes into battle
   without arms, he's braver than you are, because you have a rifle. Get
   out now, and don't bother him anymore'.[14]

Reed through Longinos thus explains to the reader how he saw his role, not
as a fighter, but as one making what was perhaps an equally important contribution to the revolution, telling the truth about it to the American public and
the world. After all, the American public opinion could affect US government
policy, and that could in the end decide the fate of the revolution. For Reed,
that truth is not a political or sociological analysis or a tract, but a journalistic,
sometime semi-fictional, but nevertheless accurate and faithful portrayal of the
people of Mexico in the midst of revolution. It is the picture of poverty with
dignity and resistance with courage that he puts forward as evidence of the
legitimacy of the upheaval.

   Not surprisingly, not all of the soldiers trusted Reed. At one point a man
named Salazar touches him on the arm and says:

> *Oiga, señor!* I have found out who you are. You are an agent of American
> business men who have vast interests in Mexico. I know *all* about Amer-
> ican business. You are an agent of the trusts. You come down her to spy
> upon the movement of our troops, and then you will secretly send them
> word. Is it not true?

An argument breaks out among the soldiers, but that then leads to another dispute about the men's loyalty to different leaders. Reed has used the description
of the man who challenged him to tell his readers about American imperialism, without ever using that word, while at the same time showing us that he
has no simple-minded ideas about the unanimity of opinion among the revolutionaries. Quite the contrary, throughout the book Reed described the various
rival leaders and their bands, as well as the larger and more important political divisions between Villa and the First Chief of the revolution, Venustiano

---

14   Reed 1969, pp. 51–2.

Carranza. Unlike some later American writers who would describe the Soviet Union, China, or Cuba in glowing and uncritical terms, Reed never simplified the revolution and its leaders, but always presented the revolution with all of its contradictions and limitations and the leaders with all of their faults.

Riding and living with the revolutionaries and travelling through the North of Mexico, Reed became completely identified with the country and its struggle. At one point, riding at sunset through the desert, Reed exclaims, 'It was a land to love – this Mexico – a land to fight for'.[15] He goes on:

> The ballad-singers suddenly began the interminable song of 'The Bull Fight', in which the Federal chiefs are the bulls and the Maderista generals the *torreros*; and as I looked at the gay, lovable, humble *hombres* who had given so much of their lives and of their comfort to the brave fight, I couldn't help but think of the little speech Villa made to the foreigners who left Chihuahua in the first refugee trains:
>
> 'This is the latest news for you to take to your people. There shall be no more palaces in Mexico. The *tortillas* of the poor are better than the bread of the rich. Come! ...'[16]

At another point, later in the story, Reed describes himself lying in the field with a group of 'ragged soldiers, living close together', singing ballads. He wrote, 'I felt my whole feeling going out to these gentle, simple people, so lovable they were ...'.[17] Reed, it is clear, has fallen in love with Mexico, with *los hombres*, with the revolution. Much of *Insurgent Mexico* is spent describing these ordinary people that Reed found so compelling.

The most frequently repeated image of *Insurgent Mexico* is that of groups of women, wearing black, walking to and from the well for water. This recurring Biblical image of the women at the well, one well known to American Protestants raised on scripture, makes the Mexican desert another Holy Land and humanises, dignifies, and universalises the Mexican people. The women water carriers are only one example of Reed's many sensitive depictions of women who he shows not only fetching the water, but also grinding the corn, preparing the meals, nursing the infants and tending to the children, as well as sometimes being abused by men or at other time fighting beside them – and even in one instance leading the male revolutionaries. Early on in the story Reed wrote, for example:

---

15   Reed 1969, p. 57.
16   Ibid, author's ellipses.
17   Reed 1969, p. 233, author's ellipses.

Three young girls crossed the square in single file, balancing *ollas* of water on their heads, shouting to each other in the raucous voices of Mexican women. At one house a woman crouched, nursing her baby; next door another kneeled to the interminable labour of grinding corn-meal in a stone trough. The menfolk squatted before little corn-husk fires, bundled in their faded serapes, smoking their *hojas* as they watched the women work.[18]

In another passage, when he goes to a dance, he described the women: 'The girls were dumpy and dull, Indian-faced and awkward, bowed at the shoulder from much grinding of corn and washing of clothes'.[19] His harshly critical judgement of their appearance is mitigated by his tender sympathy for their lives and bodies worn by hard work. But not all women are drudges. He described also 'a sullen, Indian-faced woman, riding side-saddle, who wore two cartridge-belts. She rode with the *hombres* – slept with them in the *cuartels*'.[20] Women, it often seems, are working longer and harder than the men, though he also depicted the men sometimes ploughing or roping cattle.

Life is hard and the revolution is harder, but the humble people it seems are nearly always kind and generous. At every door, though the people have only tortillas, beans, and coffee, and not enough for themselves and their families, one is welcomed and invited in to eat. Why this picture of ordinary life and labour? Because for Reed, this is what the revolution is about: the Mexican common people and their desire for a life of economic security, peace, and dignity.

The central theme of Reed's book is the meaning of the revolution. Throughout the book Reed pauses to ask one or another fighter the reason for the revolution, its importance, and its goals. They answer are given in words that have the ring of American radicalism and populism, answers that Reed has chosen carefully to both reflect the Mexican revolutionaries and to speak to his American readers. When Reed was writing, more than half of all Americans were still farmers, and early on in his book he chooses a farmer to speak to the question of the meaning of the evolution in a passage that deserves to be quoted in full:

... I shall not soon forget the hunger-pinched body and bare feet of an old man with the face of a saint, who said slowly: 'The Revolution is good. When it is done, we shall starve never, never, never, if God is served. But

18   Reed 1969, p. 16.
19   Reed 1969, p. 49.
20   Reed 1969, p. 45.

it is long, and we have no food to eat, or clothes to wear. For the master has gone away from the hacienda, and we have no tools or animals to do our work with, and the soldiers take all of our corn and drive away the cattle ...'

'Why don't the *pacíficos* fight?'

He shrugged his shoulders. 'Now they do not need us. They have no rifles for us, or horses. They are winning. And who shall feed them if we do not plant the corn? No, señor. But if the Revolution loses, then there will be no more *pacíficos*. Then we will rise, with our knives and our horsewhips .... The Revolution will not lose ...'.[21]

The revolution, as Reed has his respondent explain, springs from the suffering and the needs of the ordinary people, mostly farmers, who to the last man and woman will be willing to rise up when and if necessary. The goal of the revolution here is simple: enough to eat. In another passage several pages later, we have another more radical vision of the meaning of the revolution.

Captain Fernando leaned over and patted my arm. 'Now you are with the men (*los hombres*). When we win the Revolution, it will be a government by the men, – not by the rich. We are riding over the lands of the men. They used to belong to the rich, but now they belong to me and to the *compañeros*'.
'And you will be the army?' I asked.
'When the Revolution is won', was the astonishing reply, 'there will be no more army. The men are sick of armies. It is by armies that Don Porfirio robbed us'.[22]

When Reed asks him, 'But if the United States should invade Mexico?', Fernando replies:

... you have more money and more soldiers. But the men would protect us. We need no army. The men would be fighting for their houses and their women.[23]

---

21   Reed 1969, p. ??, author's ellipses.
22   Reed 1969, p. 36.
23   Ibid.

Reed has allowed Captain Fernando to present what is a very radical idea – the confiscation and redistribution of land from the rich to the poor – as simply a matter of fact, a fact of the revolution, and one that, having learned how the rich have treated the poor, the reader is likely to sympathise with. The road of revolution Reed suggests lies through the expropriation and redistribution of land to poor farmers. But, not only that: the government shall be one of ordinary working people and there will be no more state with its bodies of armed men.

The meaning of the revolution also appears in social legislation that actually distributes the land. Reed quotes a proclamation by the Governor of Sonora in which the meaning of the Revolution becomes more specific and institutionalised in an agrarian reform law that begins:

> Considering that the principal cause of discontent among the people in our State, which forced them to spring to arms in the year 1910, was the absolute lack of individual property; and that the rural classes have no means of subsistence in the present, nor any hope for the future, except to serve as peons on the haciendas of the great land owners, who have monopolised the soil of the state ....

And the proclamation ends:

> Therefore, the Government of the State of Durango declares it a public necessity that the inhabitants of the towns and villages be the owners of the agricultural lands .... [Author's ellipses.]

A man named Martínez then comments: 'That is the Mexican Revolution'. And Reed himself comments,

> 'It's just what Villa's doing in Chihuahua', I said. 'It's great. All you fellows can have a farm now'.[24]

So, Reed explains the Mexican Revolution to Americans as the great Jeffersonian ideal of the yeoman farmer, free and independent or as the Populists' vision of a country where farmers will be secure.

But the revolution is also about individual freedom. Reed asks someone else, Isidro Amayo about the meaning of the revolution:

---

24   Reed 1969, p. 77.

'We are fighting', said Isidro Amayo, 'for Libertad'.
'What do you mean by Libertad?'
'Libertad is when I can *do what I want!*'
'But suppose it hurts somebody else?'
He shot back at me Benito Juárez's great sentence:
'Peace is respect for the rights of others'.[25]

Reed goes on to comment that Amayo's definition, so often seen as 'an instance of Mexican irresponsibility', is superior to the American definition where Liberty is 'the right to do what the courts want'.[26] So the revolution was not only about the collective expropriation and redistribution of the land, but also about personal freedom.

On another occasion, Reed offers his own observation about the Mexican Revolution:

There wasn't one of these men who had any religion at all, although once they had all been strict Catholics. But three years of war have taught the Mexican people many things. There will never be another Porfirio Díaz; there will never be another Orozco Revolution; and the Catholic Church in Mexico will never again be the voice of God.[27]

The Revolution, continuing the Reform of the 1850s, was also about breaking the power of the Church and its hold on the property as well as the minds and souls of the people.

3   Reed's Pancho Villa

At the opening of the twentieth century, American Socialists and anarchists had at first supported Ricardo Flores Magón and the PLM, then later the Socialists had backed Francisco I. Madero, though many radicals became supporters of Emiliano Zapata and the Liberating Army of the South. But Reed backs Villa as the man who is both brilliantly leading the revolutionary struggles in the North but also, he argues, building a new government and putting in place revolutionary policies. While we know today that Villa was a different figure

---

25   Reed 1969, p. 40.
26   Ibid.
27   Reed 1969, p. 66.

than the legendary hero that Reed describes,[28] what is important for us is how Reed understood and portrayed Villa to the American public and particularly to the American left.

Reed recounted the legend of Villa, who had killed an official who raped his sister and became an outlaw after he stole cattle form a rich *hacendado*. For Reed, as for so many others who met and described him, Villa was a force of nature.

> Villa was the son of ignorant peons. He had never been to school. He hadn't the slightest conception of the complexity of civilization, and when he finally came back to it, a mature man of extraordinary native shrewdness, he encountered the twentieth century with the naïve simplicity of a savage.[29]

True, wrote Reed, Villa rustled cattle, looted haciendas, and robbed from the mines, but

> In time of famine he fed whole districts, and took care of entire villages evicted by the soldiers under Porfirio Díaz's outrageous land law. Everywhere he was known as The Friend of the Poor. He was the Mexican Robin Hood.[30]

Reed described Villa's loyalty to Madero, even after Madero imprisoned Villa in a penitentiary in Mexico City. Villa, who, 'For a long time … had passionately wanted an education', learned to read and write and in nine months could read the newspapers and write 'a very fair hand'.[31] Freed from prison, Villa went to live in El Paso, Texas, until Huerta usurped power, and then he returned, 'to conquer Mexico with four companions, three lead horses, two pounds of sugar and coffee, and a pound of salt'. And 'within one month he had raised an army of 3,000 men' and soon thereafter had defeated the *Federales* and conquered the vast state of Chihuahua.

Reed devoted the chapter 'A Peon in Politics' to describing Villa's political practice. He wrote, 'Villa proclaimed himself military governor of the State of

---

28   Two contemporary biographies by Friedrich Katz and Paco Ignacio Taibo II suggest that Villa was less a Robin Hood as a young man and more a politician as a mature man than Reed realised. Katz 1998 and Taibo II 2006.

29   Reed 1969, p. 117.

30   Reed 1969, p. 118.

31   Reed 1969, p. 120.

Chihuahua, and began the extraordinary experiment – extraordinary because he knew nothing about it – of creating a government for 300,000 people out of his head'. His policies represented the practical solutions to immediate problems in a manner that tended to ignore institutions, tradition and past practices. When his advisors suggested that Chihuahua should issue bonds to finance the Revolution, according to Reed Villa replied, 'Why, if all they need is money, let's print some'. So, money was printed and used to pay the army and, to prevent inflation, prices were fixed. He also demanded that all Mexicans exchange their silver and old bills for the new money, and, writes Reed, they did.[32]

'Villa's great passion was schools', Reed wrote. 'He believed that land for the people and schools would settle every question of civilization'. In Chihuahua City, with a population of 40,000, Villa at one time or another established over 50 schools. The principle was important, though Reed had nothing to say about the buildings, who taught in the schools, or what the students learned – or how long these institutions lasted in a revolution that would go on for another six years.[33]

Reed sympathetically described Villa's expulsion of the Spaniards from Mexico, against the advice of the American consul who suggested that Washington would not approve.

> 'Señor Consul', answered Villa, 'we Mexicans have had three hundred years of the Spaniards. They have not changed in character since the *Conquistadores*. They disrupted the Indian empire and enslaved the people. We did not ask them to mingle their blood with ours. Twice we drove them out of Mexico and allowed them to return with the same rights as Mexicans, and they used these rights to steal away our land, to make people slaves, and to take up arms against the cause of liberty. They supported Porfirio Díaz. They were perniciously active in politics. It was the Spaniards who framed the plot that put Huerta in the palace. When Madero was murdered the Spaniards in every State in the Republic held banquets of rejoicing. They thrust on us the greatest superstition the world has ever known – the Catholic Church. They ought to be killed for that alone. I consider we are being very generous with them'.[34]

---

32   Reed 1969, p. 122.
33   Reed 1969, p. 127.
34   Reed 1969, pp. 128–9.

Reed also showed Villa taking military command of the economy. 'No sooner had he taken over the government of Chihuahua', wrote Reed, 'than he put his army to work running the electric light plant, the street railways, the telephone, the water works and the Terrazzas (*sic*) flour mill. He delegated soldiers to administer the great haciendas which he had confiscated'.

Villa, Reed wrote, expropriated and nationalised the land of the great landlords. 'The rich Mexicans who had oppressed the people and opposed the Revolution, he expelled promptly from the State and confiscated their vast holdings. By a simple stroke of the pen the 17,000,000 acres and innumerable business enterprises of the Terrazzas (*sic*) family became property of the Constitutional government, as well as the great lands of the Creel family and the magnificent palaces which were their town houses'.[35] Then Villa, 'being a peon, and feeling with them' issued a proclamation, 'giving sixty-two and one-half acres out of the confiscated lands to every male citizen of the State, and declaring these lands inalienable for any cause for a period of ten years'.[36] (The idea of women's economic and political rights would only be taken up a few years later.)

Villa projects a future Mexico without armies and warfare, for 'Armies are the greatest support of tyranny. There can be no dictator without an army'. Villa tells Reed.

> We will put the army to work. In all parts of the Republic, we will establish military colonies composed of the veterans of the Revolution. The State will give them grants of agricultural lands and establish big industrial enterprises to give them work.

The soldiers, says Villa will work three days a week, and for three days they will teach the citizens how to fight so that they can defend the country.[37]

Reed ended the little chapter titled 'The Dream of Pancho Villa' with Villa's own vision of a happy future for his men and himself.

> My ambition is to live my life in one of those military colonies among my *compañeros* whom I love, who have suffered so long and so deeply with me. I think I would like the government to establish a leather factory there where we could make good saddles and bridles, because I know how to do

---

35   Reed 1969, p. 129.
36   Reed 1969, p. 139.
37   Reed 1969, p. 145.

that; and the rest of the time I would like to work on my little farm, rais-ing cattle, and corn. It would be fine, I think, to help make Mexico a happy place.

Reed presented his readers with a Villa who acts as the embodiment of the general will of the people. 'That was always Villa's power – he could explain things to the great mass of ordinary people in a way that they immediately understood'.[38] Villa has no theory, no ideology, he is certainly not a socialist, yet when he acts to solve the problems facing the people, he expropriates, nationalises, and distributes land with no concern for the previous govern-ment and its laws, no respect for capitalism and its markets or private property. Though Reed never says so, he depicted a revolutionary dedicated to agrarian reform who was a socialist in practice, one might say an unconscious social-ist.

Friedrich Katz in his definitive biography *The Life and Times of Pancho Villa*[39] argues that Villa had, as Reed suggested, created some sort of socialism in Chi-huahua, an authoritarian socialism. Katz writes that in Villa's Chihuahua there was no banditry and no disorder, in general no looting, robbery or murder. While 'Villista society was not democratic' and there 'were no elections', still Villa's army was a collection of bands rooted in local communities, and, as Katz writes, 'They were largely dependent on popular support'. Katz concludes from his study that, 'there were strong elements of socialism in its social democratic sense in Villista Chihuahua – that is of state ownership and state influence on the economy, as well as a commitment to the welfare state'. He quotes Duval West, Woodrow Wilson's special envoy to Mexico as writing in 1915, that Villa's ideology was 'that the property of the rich ought to be administered by the gov-ernment for the benefit of the masses, and even if not clearly articulated, the socialist ideal appeared to dominate the movement'.[40] So Reed had with his impressionistic journalism gotten it right.

While Reed was a great admirer of Villa as general and as governor, Reed clearly had great misgivings about Venustiano Carranza, the 'First Chief' of the Constitutionalist forces whom he had met, interviewed, and described as 'an aristocrat, descended from the dominant Spanish race; a great land-owner, as his family had always been great land-owners; and one of those Mexican nobles who, like a few French nobles such as Lafayette in the French Revolution, threw

---

38   Reed 1969, p. 229.
39   Katz 1998.
40   Katz 1998, pp. 429–30.

themselves heart and soul into the struggle for liberty'. Reed goes on, 'he armed the peons who worked upon his great estates, and led them into war like any feudal overlord ...' He portrayed Carranza as militarily cautious, protecting his troops, biding his time, and failing to say anything about the all-important land question. Reed saw Carranza, correctly, as a man who was a fervent national-ist, but had little interest in his country's lower classes.[41] An assessment with which most modern historians would agree.

After his reporting and writing on the Mexican Revolution, Reed went to Europe, interviewed Karl Liebknecht and travelled through Central Europe. Disappointed in the collapse of the Socialist or Second International, Reed endorsed Woodrow Wilson for president believing that he would carry out his promise to keep the country out of war. When Wilson failed to do so, at a meet-ing of the People's Council, Reed said, 'This is not my war, and I will not support it. This is not my war, and I will have nothing to do with it'.[42] In August of 1917, Reed went with his lover Louise Bryant to Russia, and the two journalists were witnesses to the Russian Revolutions of October 1917. Reed actually went to work for the Soviet government's Commissariat of Foreign Affairs, through which work he met both Vladimir Lenin and Leon Trotsky, the two principal revolutionary leaders. Based on his experience and observations, Reed wrote *10 Days That Shook the World*, published in 1919, which became a classic account of the revolution widely read by the American left.

Returning to the United States, Reed faced indictment in *The Masses* case but was bailed out and then two trials of that case ended in hung juries. Speaking out against war, in favour of the Russian Revolution, and against intervention in Russia, he was indicted anew for inciting to riot, but was acquitted. Working with the left wing of the Socialist Party he became the editor of its publication *The New York Communist*. At the Socialist Party's national convention in August of 1919, the left wing, including Reed was expelled. The left wing then split between to hostile factions, the Communist Party of America and the Com-munist Labour Party with which Reed was affiliated. Using a false passport, he went to Soviet Russia in the winter of 1919–20, spent some time observing conditions and talking with people like anarchist Emma Goodman and Com-munist Angelica Balabanoff, and then attempted to return to the United States. Arrested in Finland, he was tortured, became sick, and eventually returned to Soviet Russia which allowed him to participate as an American delegate to the Second Congress of the Communist International. After that Congress, he

---

41   Reed 1969, pp. 263–78.
42   Homberger 1986, p. 122.

travelled to Baku for the Congress of the Toilers of the East where, having contracted Typhus, he died surrounded by American friends Louise Bryant, war resister Charles Francis Phillips, and Louis Fraina, leader of the rival American Communist faction.

CHAPTER 6

Lincoln Steffens: An American Progressive in Mexico

Lincoln Steffens was in the 1910s a leading literary light of American Progressivism best known for his muckraking journalism published in popular magazines such as *McClure's* and *Everybody's* and above all for his book *Shame of the Cities*, an exposé of bossism, machine politics, and corruption in the United States published in 1904. The book created a sensation and made him one of the foremost progressive writers of the era. Sentimental, sententious, and didactic, Steffens at that time blamed corruption on no particular class but rather concluded that, 'The misgovernment of the American people is the misgovernment by the American people'.[1] Steffens message was that Americans could create a society where all – millionaires and paupers, the powerful and the powerless – could together create a better society for all. Later he would change his mind and become more critical, but that was the theme of his early work.

His book *The Upbuilders*, for example, showed how men as different as W.S. U'Ren, a blacksmith from Colorado and Rudolph Spreckles, the president of the First National Bank of San Francisco could both bring reform to their respective cities.[2] Steffens' principal idea at the time was the notion that class collaboration between capitalist and working people fighting together against corruption could bring about progressive social change for all, change that would benefit most the underdogs of society. But only a few years later Steffens had begun to change his views, blaming America's problems on the privileged, the banks, and the corporations.

Steffens was born in Los Angeles, California to the son of a wealthy banker and businessman,[3] who consequently had a privileged upbringing as a child. As a young man he attended the University of California at Berkeley where he earned his bachelor's degree in history and then went off to study at the universities of Heidelberg, Munich, and Leipzig as well as at the Sorbonne. He arrived at the conclusion that 'there was no scientific basis for ethics'. As one historian wrote, 'he adopted an experimental approach to life. He would gather

---

1   Steffens 1957, p. 2.
2   Steffens 1909, *passim*.
3   'Joseph Steffens' 1912, p. 1.

facts, verify them, form a theory; then usually, discard it, starting the process all over again'.[4] One could say that Steffens was an American pragmatist who sought solutions to problems rather than being guided by a political ideology. He became a reporter on Wall Street finance and business and then took up the study of corruption in American cities.

Back on the Wall Street beat for a second time, by 1906 Steffens revised his thinking, concluding that big business was really the problem with American political life. The banks, insurance companies, and railroads dominated the country and corrupted its political life.

> In short, what I got out of my second period in Wall Street was this per-
> ception that everything I looked into in organised society was really a
> dictatorship, in this sense, that it was an organization of the privileged for
> the control of privileges, of the sources of privilege, and of the thoughts
> and acts of the unprivileged; and that neither the privileged nor the
> unprivileged, neither the bosses nor the bossed, understood this or meant
> it.[5]

Steffens came to the conclusion that, 'The cure for the evils of political demo-
cracy is economic democracy'.[6] What exactly that meant he did not know, but he began to search for the answer.

At the same time, though he excoriated the privileged, Steffens also became enormously popular, including among those with privilege. 'In the years preceding World War I, Steffens achieved a unique reputation. He was widely read and discussed. Everybody knew and liked him – politicians, journalists, radic-
als, poets, underworld characters; Theodore Roosevelt and President Woodrow Wilson lent their ears to him'.[7] His entrée among the elite gave him access to information and opinions and also gave him the aura of one of the political cognoscenti, a man in the know.

Steffens took his popularity and opposition to privilege with him to Mexico in December 1914 where he was at once a retrospective critic of the dictatorship of Porfirio Díaz and soon a supporter of Venustiano Carranza's revolution. At the same time, the Mexican Revolution into which he went as a journalist had an important impact on Steffens who became increasingly radical.

---

4 von Mohrenschildt 1945, p. 32.
5 Steffens 1958, vol. 2, p. 591.
6 von Mohrenschildt 1945, p. 33.
7 Ibid.

Steffens, who spoke very little Spanish and who upon arrival knew next to nothing about Mexican history and culture, came briefly through his writing for popular magazines to play the role of an important interpreter of Mexico to the American people. Even before he went to Mexico, he was an opponent of US armed intervention in the southern neighbour and virtually as soon as he arrived in the country, he became a supporter of the revolution. After just one day in Veracruz, he wrote to his sister Laura:

> It's 'the' revolution; not only the Mexican revolution; it's not only the Mexican revolution, but the very same they had in France and long for in England and Germany and Russia. Americans are disgusted at the inconvenience to them, the injury to their business, and they go wild in descriptions of the base character of the Mexicans. But I find that the Mexicans want important things; things which we all ought to want: economic, not alone political independence and liberty.[8]

His support for the Mexican Revolution and his opposition to a US military intervention placed him on this issue among the broad left together with the Socialist Party, the American Federation of Labor, and the Industrial Workers of the World.

Steffens the journalist now became Steffens the lobbyist. Hoping to influence President Wilson and persuade him to support Carranza, in August of 1915 Steffens wrote to Wilson's close friend and advisor Colonel Edward M. House regarding the decrees that the Carranza government was issuing:

> These decrees are not political – they are economic. In large measure they are permissive. They tell the Mexican people what they may do with the resources of Mexico, and they go into effect only as the people act upon them. Thus, while they are autocratic in form and emanate from an oligarchy, they are really laying the foundation of an economic democracy: something the world has never seen before. In other words, the revolution is coming rapidly to an end, with Carranza and the Carranzistas [sic.] on top.[9]

Steffens went on, 'I cannot understand why our Administration does not recognise the Carranza government'.[10]

---

8   Steffens 1938, vol. 1, p. 351.
9   Steffens 1938, vol. 1, p. 357.
10   Steffens 1938, vol. 1, p. 358.

While Steffens had correctly grasped that Carranza was going to bring the revolution to an end and that he would come out on top – though it would take four more years – the journalist failed to understand that Carranza was not creating an economic democracy but rather laying the basis for a strong oligarchic state and a more modern capitalism. And remarkably Steffens apparently did not understand that House, Wilson and especially the American Congress were at odds with Carranza precisely because he threatened to take Mexico's resources – agricultural land, mines, and oil fields – away from American investors. Wilson's ostensible reason for not recognising the Carranza government was that it had not held democratic elections, so Steffens, writing in September 1915, tried to persuade House that while 'Carranza does not want to set up right away a complete, representative government', he would 'proceed gradually, holding little local elections first, say, in the towns; then in the counties, and then perhaps in states, and last of all, a national election for a congress and a president'.[11] In reality, Carranza had little if any interest in democracy, less than his predecessor Francisco Madero, and principally wanted to establish his faction's control of the army and the government.

In his magazine articles, books, and later in his famous autobiography, 'Steffens presented himself as a charming American naïf who in this world of municipal corruption and capitalist greed had somehow come out wise'.[12] In his private letters to his sisters Laura and Lou and to other relatives and friends, he was more explicit about his opposition to American capitalism and his anti-imperialism. On Christmas Day 1915, Steffens wrote to his sister and brother-in-law, Lou and Allen Suggett, summing up the revolution 'in a word':

> The second-class leaders of it are confiscating and taking to themselves the lands and concessions and privileges which corrupted the old gang, so they'll soon feel the effect upon themselves of owning a lot of 'good things'. Meanwhile, the revolution is running over the foreign ad Mexican capitalists, like a steam-roller. I know this, because they tell me so themselves. They think I'm sorry, but really, it's a joy to hear them holler. So, the thing is getting on. And don't misunderstand me, there still is hope that some good, fundamental reforms will result.[13]

11   Steffens 1938, vol. 1, p. 359.
12   Kazin 1974, p. 3.
13   Steffens 1938, vol. 1, p. 366.

While First Chief Venustiano Carranza was initially chilly toward the American journalist, Steffens gradually won the revolutionary's confidence. Steffens spent a good deal of time between 1914 and 1916 in Mexico, much of it either at the headquarters of Carranza or travelling in Carranza's private railroad car as the Mexican revolutionary leader toured the country.[14] Just as John Reed had ridden with Pancho Villa, so Steffens rode with Carranza, but he rode in style in the Pullman cars. Steffens took meals with Carranza, his generals, and government officials; at whistle-stops he listened to Carranza's usually short, dull speeches, and observed the crowds of humble people who brought Carranza both small gifts like chickens together with their requests for assistance for their communities or themselves. During his travels, Steffens picked up gossip and observed corrupt practices among Carranza's coterie of top generals and foremost political leaders. Naturally, Steffens also spoke with American diplomats and businesspeople that he met along the way, most of them hostile to Carranza's government.

In 1916, Steffens was back in Mexico. For Carranza it was a crucial year, the year that the tide turned and his forces seemed likely to soon bring the revolution to an end and establish a single central government. At the same time, it was also a year of mounting tensions with the United States as Pancho Villa's raid on Columbus, New Mexico led President Wilson to dispatch Brigadier General John J. Pershing's punitive expedition into Mexico, the second American military intervention in Mexico since the revolution began. The American oilmen and the Catholic Church continually demanded that the United States take strong action, and for many of them that meant a large-scale invasion and occupation of Mexico. Steffens wrote in defence of the revolution and against any American war to crush it. Unlike his young protégé John Reed, Steffens did not have much of an eye for ordinary individuals; he wrote about representative figures such as the 'American concessionaire' or the 'peasant woman', or he wrote about important figures, such as Carranza. Unlike Reed's wonderful word portrait paintings, Steffens engaged in argument, arguments in favour of national sovereignty, revolutionary change, and peace.

In a long article in *Everybody's Magazine* published in May of 1916, Steffens described the Mexican situation, how after the US occupation of Veracruz, all Americans knew 'the hate, the watchful, waiting hate of the Mexican for the American'. He wanted Americans to know that an invasion of Mexico and an attempt to conquer Mexico would not be easy. He quoted a young Mexican officer who told him:

---

14   Steffens, May 1916.

> Hate you? The Mexican hate for you Gringos would put joy into the supreme passion of rape, fire into the flames of arson, virtue into robbery, and a crown of glory on death and defeat at war with you.[15]

Steffens, who sympathised with Mexico and the Mexicans, wanted to make their passion understandable to the Americans who read him and did so by providing some historical context.

> The enmity in Mexico against the 'Colossus of the North', as they call the United States, is all sorts of hate held by all sorts of people there. It is reasonable and unreasonable; it is thought and felt; it is open-eyed and it is blind; it is suspicion and experience. It is racial, religious, economic, and it is historical. We did take away from Mexico Texas, New Mexico, California, the whole of our great Southwest; and their school histories tell their story of it; and their story is one of good American excuses to cover a bad slaveholder's conspiracy with traitorous Spanish and Mexican aristocrats.[16]

Steffens also wanted them to understand that Mexicans believed that all the United States and its people had been and remained enemies of Mexico.

> [Americans] belonged to, thrived with, and liked the old Díaz regime, and are openly or secretly against the Mexican revolutionary movement. They think that the American ambassador, Henry Lane Wilson, as in the plot to overthrow and kill Madero, was the prophet of their revolt. They know that leading Americans, with other foreigners, were with and for Huerta, the military autocrat, and failing him, are asking now for Villa, or any other 'strong man', like Díaz, like a czar, like an American boss, any tyrant that will put down the Mexican people, make them go back to work for their American and other masters. They may need, but they don't want, the American boss system in politics and the rising American industrial organization which turns out a few rich and many poor. That's what they are fighting against. The have other ideals, and, better or worse, they prefer theirs. We, sure of the superior excellence of ours, we continue to thrust ours upon them, our ideals, our ideas, our virtues, and also (as they see) our vices, and our methods, and our corruption; and all for their good. This is the height of our offending: our philanthropy.

---

15   Steffens, May 1916.
16   Steffens, May 1916.

Steffens was writing this just as Villa attacked Columbus, New Mexico, raising the possibility of another American invasion, and perhaps an actual full-blown war. He feared it would be a holocaust and he appealed to his American readers' humanity. His anti-war tirade was direct, powerful, and frightening. He warned of genocide:

> A war with Mexico is very likely to be a war of extermination. The people, the common people, all go to war there, the women and children along with the men. The women and children forage and do the camp work, but when their men drop, the women frequently pick up the rifles and continue the fire. So, the Mexican people will be at our battles with them. We can get at them. And we'll defeat them. Every intelligent Mexican I ever spoke with about it, admitted that in the end we would be victorious.

> But also, they say, and the Americans who know this people say, that before the end we shall have to slaughter the Mexican race as we did the Indians. If that is so, I say that our victory would be a disgrace to us and a disaster to the world, and that the man and the interests, American, Spanish, Mexican, British, German, and Roman [Catholic], that are risking such a monumental crime they cannot have thought out what they are praying and plotting and lying and paying out good money for.[17]

Steffens condemned the Americans and other foreigners who wanted war with Mexico in order to protect their business interests and also denounced Mexicans like Villa who were willing to risk or provoke a war. As he wrote, 'It's treason we're talking about: international treason; treason to Mexico in Mexico and treason to the United States in the United States'.[18]

While riding in his berth in Carranza's train, Steffens came to believe that he had come to know and understand the Mexican leader and his staff. 'Señor Carranza and his inner circle of advisers are as sincere, as honest, as determined, and as perplexed a group of radical reformers as I ever saw (or heard or read about) in power'. Steffens believed that Carranza was honest, as was testified to by an American businessman who told Steffens that he and others had tried to bribe Carranza and failed. Among the First Chief's subordinates there was graft, but Steffens was prepared to forgive it.

---

17   Steffens, May 1916, p. 533.
18   Steffens, May 1916, p. 533.

There is dishonesty in the Carranza party; lot of it. The stealing and graft-
ing is most confusing. But it is petty, and my experience in American
cities suggests that it is inevitable. When you break down as this Mexican
earthquake has done, the big orderly system of regular 'honest' graft, the
anarchy of petty graft takes its place. The universal desire for easy money
is freed, and all sorts and conditions of men go to stealing directly, rawly
cash. It's a stage of democracy apparently. Our cities are just coming out
of it; Mexico is just having now her Tweed days.[19]

Steffens declared that, 'Carranza was not a dictator and I think he doesn't want
to be'. On the contrary the journalist thought, 'The First Chief is building his
power slowly but steadily, but he is trying to build it democratically'.[20] At the
same time the Steffens observed, 'They are giving all, all of their power to Carranza and he is going around collecting it'. He wrote, quite contradictorily, 'He is
the head now of an oligarchy; his power is military ... Military power brooks no
free speech, no difference, and under the martial law of revolutionary Mexico
public opinion seems unanimous'. Steffens warns, 'This is impossible. It can't
last'.[21]

While expressing both his admiration and his reservations and concerns,
Steffens argued that the Carranza revolution represented a revolution of world
significance. He stated that, 'Carranza and his inner circle of advisers are planning ways and means of putting a stop or a check to the big grafts: the great
mining and oil concessions, and the enormous land grafts'. Steffens went on,

> The Carranzistas have a theory. They think their theory is the theory of the
> Mexican Revolution. Their theory is that the problem of civilised society
> is not poverty, but riches; that the solution of it is not to cure or nurse the
> poor, but to prevent the accumulations of enormous individual wealth;
> and so, their policy is to find out and close up the hole through which most
> or some of the products of labour lead through the workers, intellectual
> and physical, into the possession of philanthropists. Thus, it is economic,
> not political democracy and equality they are working for. In a word, they
> are trying to change the rules of the game, their game, our game, the game
> as it is played all over the world.[22]

19   Steffens, May 1916, p. 535.
20   Steffens, May 1916, p. 536.
21   Steffens, May 1916, p. 537.
22   Steffens, May 1916, p. 539.

Steffens made the remarkable claim that in Mexico, an alternative to the world economic model was being developed. And he liked it.

During his Mexican sojourn, Steffens, mistook the First Chief's radical rhetoric as he travelled the country to solidify his base, for a genuine radical social program. The American journalist became convinced that Carranza represented the best future for Mexico. Yet at the same time, Steffens remained a supporter of Woodrow Wilson, believing that the American president was fundamentally on the side of peace in Mexico. After the US invasion of Veracruz and just before the invasion of Chihuahua, Steffens wrote of Wilson, 'He has shown by his whole Mexican policy that he has understood what they were struggling for down there and he has trusted us, the people, to understand why he has stood against intervention and its consequences'.[23] Trusting in both Carranza and Wilson, Steffens saw his role as bringing them together.

As tensions rose after the US landing and occupation of Veracruz, Steffens tried urgently to contact Wilson through his advisor Colonel House and through Congressional Democrats. Steffens warned House that, 'The [Catholic] Church and other privileged interests here and abroad and in Mexico are desperately bent upon robbing Carranza and the revolution of their victory'.[24] Steffens even attempted to have himself appointed as Wilson's emissary to Carranza, but neither Wilson nor Secretary of State Robert Lansing would receive him at that time.

Riding on Carranza's train, Steffens became persuaded that he was having a profound influence on the Mexican revolutionaries. Steffens bragged to family and friends, 'I'm putting ideas into the heads of the Mexican leaders and they like them, and me. In fact, I'm pretty well in on the inside of the Mexican Revolution ...'.[25] Steffens' delusions and self-aggrandisement knew no bounds. He suggested at the time that he had had an important influence on the writing of Article 27 of the Constitution of 1917, which declared the nation to be the owner of the nation's subsoil. In his *Autobiography* published in 1931 he went further, making a preposterous claim: 'The American State Department, and some diplomats and secret service men, and a lot of American business men in Mexico have held it against me that I was the author of the famous Article 27 which has given them so much trouble'.[26] The article in fact had its roots in Spanish law, in earlier Mexican constitutions, in Andrés Molina Enríquez's

---

23   Ibid.
24   Stein 1975, p. 200.
25   Stein 1975, p. 201.
26   Steffens 1958, p. 726.

seminal book of 1909 *The Great National Problems* and in Luis Cabrera's important 1912 essay 'The Reconstitution of the Ejidos' and Zapata's Plan de Ayala.[27]
The whole thrust of the enormous revolution had been about deciding that
issue, which had been at the centre of years of both political debates and violent confrontations. Yet Steffens, ignorant of all of that and with his enormous
ego and incredible vanity, apparently actually believed that his whisperings in
the ears of Carranza had led to Mexico's most significant social reform.

Pancho Villa's raid on Columbus, New Mexico on 9 March 1916 followed by
General Pershing's 'Punitive Expedition' into Mexico less than a week later, led
a number of US political leaders to call for an all-out war with Mexico. And as
time went on, the threat of war did not diminish. In an attempt to avert a conflict with Mexico, Steffens, collaborating with Charles A. Douglas, Carranza's
American attorney in Washington, made repeated attempts to reach President
Wilson. Steffens believed that he had better information about Mexico than
that being presented to Wilson by the State Department or even by Wilson's
man in Mexico, former Minnesota governor John Lind. After repeated failures
to get a meeting with Wilson, In June Steffens finally succeeded and was invited
to talk with the president in his library in the White House. As Steffens later
wrote in his autobiography:

> I told him that members of his cabinet had said that war with Mexico was
> inevitable because he, the president was convinced that Carranza wanted
> and was forcing it. This was misinformation. Carranza did not want war
> but was convinced that he, Wilson, did.

Asked by Wilson if he believed in Carranza, Steffens answered that he believed
in him, 'As an honest man and a liberal. Not as a revolutionist'. According
to Steffens, Wilson told him, 'You have given me information, very valuable
information, information which prevents a war .... Yes, there will be no war
with Mexico'. But as historian Harry H. Stein writes, 'The danger of war had
actually subsided after the Mexican released the captured American soldiers
on June 28'. Steffens, however, was convinced that it was his efforts that had
prevented the outbreak of all-out war.[28]

Convinced that under the pressure of the oilmen and the Catholic Church a
US-Mexico war might still break out, Steffens carried out an exhausting cross-
country American tour between October and December 1916, speaking to stu-

---

27   Molina Enríquez 1991 and Cabrera 1994.
28   Stein 1975, p. 198.

dents, chambers of commerce, Rotary Clubs, and political organisations. He told his listeners that the cause of Mexico's 'ignorant peons is the cause of humanity'.[29] Steffens' two years of writing and speaking about Mexico made a significant contribution to the defence of Mexico, but he had also contributed to strengthening the more conservative wing of the revolution represented by Carranza. Steffens looked to strong leaders to resolve a nation's problems, and Carranza fit the bill. And so did Wilson.

Steffens' continued confidence in Woodrow Wilson, after the invasions of Veracruz and Chihuahua, was remarkable. In February 1918, he wrote to Charles A. Douglas regarding Wilson's 'recent peace message to Congress', which he believed carried 'an obvious meaning for Mexico and all the other Latin American Countries':

> He is declaring for the right of all nations, large and small, to work out for themselves, each in own destiny its own way and in its own good time. This means not only Belgium and Finland, Russia and France, India and China; it must mean Mexico, too. And it does. It means Mexico and Cuba, Puerto Rico and the Philippines. It means all of the Americas. And I believe President Wilson intends it so.
>
> I wish President Carranza could believe this.
>
> Mr. Wilson is making war on Imperialism. Not only German Imperialism. He is turned the war against German Imperialism into a war against all Imperialism: German, British, Russian, French, Italian *and* American. And I assert that this is not only implied in his messages; it is in his mind.[30]

Surely when Douglas passed on Steffens' letters or their contents to Carranza, the Mexican President, who was a fervent and stalwart nationalist, he must have been astounded. How, after two invasions of his country, constant political pressure and threats of war, could one believe that Wilson was an anti-imperialist and friend of Mexico? An objective observer would have seen that Wilson was destroying European imperialism and colonialism, but in order to make the United States dominant in the world economy. As Wilson himself said to a convention of salesmen in Detroit in July 1916, 'Lift your eyes to the horizons of the business and with the inspiration of the thought that you are Americ-

---

29   Ibid.
30   Steffens 1938, vol. 2, pp. 1304–5.

ans and are meant to carry liberty and justice and the principle of humanity wherever you go, go out and sell goods that will make the world more comfortable and more happy, and convert them to the principles of America'.[31] As Perry Anderson wrote, 'Wilson gave voice to every chord of presumption in the imperial repertoire: at messianic pitch. Religion, capitalism, democracy, peace and the might of the United States were one'.[32] Steffens failed to grasp that Wilson was positioning the United States to become the great world imperial power, and that is precisely what, at that time, made him a progressive and not a socialist. Yet another revolution would change his mind again and like John Reed he would end up finding his Mecca in Moscow.

Leaving Mexico behind, Steffens suddenly turned his attention from Mexico to Russia. When the Russian Revolution broke out in February 1917, Steffens travelled there to see for himself and to report. His visit to Russia resembled his earlier travels to Mexico.

> Of all the Americans who went to report revolutionary Russia, Steffens was undoubtedly the least qualified observer. His ignorance of the Russian language, history, political leaders, was abysmal .... Nor did Steffens in subsequent years every try to fill these lacunae, not even when he became America's foremost propagandist for the Bolshevik cause.[33]

Still, Steffens proved to be a keen observer of the process who predicted the fall of Prince Georgy Lvov and then Alexander Kerensky as well as the rise of Vladimir Lenin and the Bolsheviks. In and out of Russia several times between 1917 and 1923, Steffens became a fervent defender of the Russian Revolution, 'America's foremost propagandist of the Bolshevik cause'.[34] It was he who made the famous quip in the studio of artist Jo Davidson: 'I have seen the future, and it works'.[35]

Steffens summed up his views on Soviet Russia in his *Autobiography*, it was a view that apologised for and justified an authoritarian socialism from above:

> Soviet Russia was a revolutionary government with an evolutionary plan. Their plan was, not by direct action to resist such evils as poverty and riches, graft, privilege, tyranny, and war, but to seek out and remove the

---

31   Wilson 1981, cited in Anderson 2013, pp. 9–10.
32   Anderson 2013, p. 9.
33   von Mohrenschildt 1945, p. 35.
34   Ibid.
35   von Mohrenschild 1945, p. 37.

causes of them. They were not practicing what we and they preached. They were not trying to establish political democracy, legal liberty, and negotiated peace – not now. They were at present only laying a basis for these good things. They had set up a dictatorship, supported by a small, trained minority, to make and maintain for a few generations a scientific rearrangement of economic forces which would result in economic democracy first and political democracy last.[36]

This argument, that the Soviet Union's ultimate goal justified its temporary authoritarianism, dominated the international left from the 1930s until the collapse of the Soviet Union in 1991. Steffens had helped to create this mistaken and misleading interpretation of events.

Just as he had during the Mexican Revolution, Steffens wrote extensively on Russia and toured the United States and Europe speaking before all sorts of groups about the Revolution and its significance. Unfortunately, as von Mohrenschildt wrote, 'Psychologically, the major effect of his Russian experience was to blunt Steffens' critical faculties'. Until the end of his life, Steffens 'accepted the leaders' interpretation and never doubted it after'. He had an enormous impact, especially through his *Autobiography*, which has been called 'the key book of the depression'.[37] Just as he had been a supporter of Lenin's Russia he was, until his death in August of 1936, also a supporter of Stalin's repressive regime. 'Soviet Russia became for Steffens a new religion, admitting no doubts, no criticism'. In that way he contributed to the American liberals' acceptance and even admiration of the dictator Stalin and his totalitarian regime during the Great Depression decade.

---

36   Steffens 1958, vol. 2, pp. 795–6.
37   von Mohrenschildt 1945, p. 39.

CHAPTER 7

American Labour Imperialism: Samuel Gompers and the American Federation of Labor

Samuel Gompers founded the American Federation of Labor in 1886, bringing together craft unions and establishing a model of worker organisation that has come to be called 'business unionism', that is, the idea that unions should work to improve workers' live by establishing an alliance with the corporations and the capitalist class. He fought to defend business unionism against the Socialist Party and the revolutionary syndicalists of the Industrial Workers of the World (IWW) and later against the Communists. At the same time, he worked with the National Civic Federation to create a partnership with the corporations and banks. While initially averse to politics, Gompers' AFL formed an alliance with the Democratic Party in 1906 and, when Woodrow Wilson was elected president in 1913, gradually brought the AFL unions into line with his administration's foreign policy. In the 1910s and early 1920s, Gompers worked, under the shield of the US government, to extend the business union model to the entire North American economy – to Canada, Puerto Rico, and Mexico – and eventually to all of the Americas. He would have liked, no doubt, for the AFL to become the model of labour unionism around the world.[1]

The AFL was the most important labour organisation in the United States, so the US left's relationship to the Mexican Revolution can only be fully understood in light of the evolving position of Gompers and the AFL on the question of imperialism, beginning with the Spanish-American War of 1898. In the early years of the twentieth century, Gompers came to a position regarding the role of the United States in world affairs that coincided virtually completely with that put forward by President Woodrow Wilson. Both came to oppose imperialism and colonialism of the British, French, or Spanish sort based on the acquisition of foreign territory, but to favour the US economic expansion with the goal of the domination first of Latin America and eventually of the world. Mexico could be considered the first test of Wilson's and Gompers' broader policy vision as well as their first common project.

Within that broader context, it is important to understand the role played by Gompers and the AFL both in first supporting the Mexican Liberal Party

---

1 Buhle 1999, pp. 17–90.

(PLM) of Ricardo Flores Magón and later in backing Francisco I. Madero's revolution and the new Mexican state beginning in 1911. The AFL would eventually become a strong supporter of Mexico's revolutionary governments and of its state-controlled unions. In fact, the AFL would strongly support Mexico's dominant labour federation, the Regional Confederation of Mexican Workers (CROM) and draw it into an AFL-dominated transnational labour organisation in the Americas, the Pan-American Federation of Labor (PAFL). Gompers and his Mexico team – John Murray, Santiago Iglesias, and James Lord – worked to turn Mexican unions away from anarchism and later Communism and in the direction of business unionism. And then they worked to extend these policies to all of Latin America. Gompers' collaboration with the Wilson government on the question of Mexico during the Mexican Revolution and World War I, together with the AFL's involvement in Mexico could be called *labour imperialism*, an ideology and political practice based on the attempt to impose AFL hegemony and the business union model on Latin American unions that would have a long-lasting effect on the AFL and later the AFL-CIO and their relationship to the US State Department, the Mexican state, and Mexican unions.

1   The American Federation of Labor

The American Federation of Labor was the product of a working-class defeat that led to a turn to the right. The Knights of Labor, the insurgent, democratic, and inclusive labour movement that arose after the Civil War, carried out campaigns for unionisation, led great strikes, and fought for the eight-hour day, but had then been defeated after the Haymarket affair of May 1886. Daniel De Leon's Marxist union federation, the Socialist Trade & Labor Alliance (ST&LA), became marginalised (the latter in part through its own sectarianism) by the end of the nineteenth century. The employers, the courts, and the police destroyed radical labour unionism in the United States, leading Samuel Gompers and a group of union officials to seek another, more moderate path, one grounded on the acceptance of capitalism, a neutral attitude toward parties and government, and a strategy focused on the organisation of skilled workers rather than the unionisation of all workers.

Gompers, a cigar roller, and his colleagues who were also skilled workers, aimed to create a labour monopoly that could control jobs and wages for those skilled workers like themselves that the employers would find it difficult to replace. As for the rest of the working class, that is, most of the working class, well, there was not much that could be done for it in their view. Gompers saw the AFL as a partner with the American capitalist class, as particular unions were with partners with certain companies in their industries, a view that came to be called 'business unionism'. The health of the American corporation then would be reflected in the health of the American labour movement, and vice versa. Leftist critics referred to Gompers and his associates as the 'Labour lieutenants of capital'[2] or as 'junior partners' in capitalism, but Gompers and the AFL leadership preferred being junior partners to what they saw as the alternative, that is, following the Knights of Labor into noble martyrdom and certain extinction.

Though he had once been trained in Marxism, Gompers had rejected a socialist view of unions engaged in a class struggle for socialism for what came to be called 'pure and simple' trade unionism that only sought to improve the AFL members' wages and working conditions within the American capitalist system. Under his leadership, the AFL did not seek to alter fundamentally either the economic or the political system. As he said, the AFL's demand was simply, 'More'. Though it was not simply more money, but a whole programme of reform, which he summed up in his most famous remarks:

> We want more school houses and less jails; more books and less arsenals; more learning and less vice; more constant work and less crime; more leisure and less greed; more justice and less revenge; in fact, more of the opportunities to cultivate our better natures, to make manhood more noble, womanhood more beautiful and childhood more happy and bright. These in brief are the primary demands made by the Trade Unions in the name of labour. These are the demands made by labour upon modern society and in their consideration is involved the fate of civilization.[3]

Labour wanted more, indeed a lot more, and not simply in the workplace, but it did not demand a different economic or political system.

The AFL during the late nineteenth and early twentieth centuries thus became a federation of a trade or craft unions, representing mostly skilled, white, male workers, though it did also include some industrial unions such as the miners and needle trades unions. With few exceptions, such as among the miners, black workers were generally excluded from the unions but where some had become union members they were kept in segregated locals. The AFL was particularly strong in the building trades and in transportation where its affiliates included carpenters, electricians, and teamsters. (The sixteen Rail-

---

2   Daniel De Leon probably coined the term. De Leon 1900.
3   Samuel Gompers, 'Address', 28 August 1893.

road Brotherhoods, while not all part of the AFL, were organised on the same principle of craft unionism.) Originally committed to the idea that labour had no political party of its own and no permanent favourites among the bosses' parties, Gompers pledged that the unions would 'reward our friends and punish our enemies'. By and large, this meant support for the Democratic Party, especially of city officials who promised that they would not break strikes; but the Democratic Party was the enemy of Blacks (as well as an opponent of women's suffrage).[4] Gompers had led the AFL to support William Jennings Bryant, the populist Democratic Party candidate in 1896 and 1904, but after those failures, Gompers sought a more serious, long-term relationship to the national Democratic Party.[5] By 1906 the AFL had definitively linked its fate to the Democratic Party, centralising those operations in the hands of Gompers and his lieutenants. At the same time then Gompers and the AFL became bitter opponents of Eugene Debs and the Socialist Party, since the Democratic Party and the SP were rivals for the workers' votes.[6]

2   The AFL Views of Foreign Policy

The late nineteenth and early twentieth century represented the apex of the old imperial powers – Spain, France, and Great Britain, Russia, and the Ottoman Empire – and the arrival on the scene of new ones: the United States, Japan, and Germany that threatened to disrupt the global order, a threat that would later be realised in two world wars. The Berlin Conference of 1884–85 peacefully divided Africa among the European Powers who then used their military power to invade, occupy, and incorporate their African colonies, though by the end of the century there would also be conflicts among the European nations over Africa. In Oceania, Asia, and Latin America greater conflict existed because of the rivalry of Great Britain, the United States, Russia and Japan in those continents. Imperialism affected national economies and world trade and also threatened war. Where did Gompers and the AFL stand on these questions before Mexico became an important issue?

Gompers and other AFL leaders and the various affiliated unions' members tended to be quite cognisant of international politics because so many union members were immigrants from Europe, particularly from Great Britain, Ireland, Germany, and Russia. At the same time, Gompers himself, as a

---

4   Buhle 1999, p. 49.
5   Buhle 1999, p. 53.
6   Buhle 1999, p. 27; Greenstone 1969, p. 27.

cigar maker – an industry that employed many Cubans – was especially well informed about issues in Cuba, the Caribbean, and Latin America. While Gompers and most AFL leaders were American patriots and nationalists, and even racists, they could also be motivated by a sense of solidarity with working people in other countries, compassion for those oppressed by tyrants, and a particular sympathy with the people of their own homeland, ethnic group, or language. All of these things meant that until the twentieth century, the AFL tended to be anti-imperialist, that is, opposed to what we might call Old World imperialism with its colonies. At the same time, Gompers and AFL leaders were concerned about competition from both workers in other countries and from new immigrant workers in the United States. While Gompers thought of himself as a reformer uplifting the working class, including black workers, he was convinced that it was northern and western European white workers who were the vanguard of the workers movement. As he said on one occasion in 1906, 'I have stood as a champion of the coloured man and have sacrificed self and much of the movement that the coloured man should get a chance. But the Caucasians are not going to let their standard of living be destroyed by negroes, Chinamen, Japs, or any others'.[7]

Gompers was not only concerned about low-wage competition in the United States but was also particularly sensitive to foreign competition with American workers, especially as he came from an industry that had facilities in both the United States and in Cuba. So, while a believer in the superiority of white workers, from early in his career Gompers undertook work in solidarity with workers in Cuba, Puerto Rico, and Mexico in order to help them organise unions and raise their wages, and thus to protect American workers from low-wage competition. His business union partnership with US companies, however, meant that he also supported American capitalists' investments abroad, since the economic health of American corporations, he thought, would ultimately be good for American workers. He wanted workers in Latin America to accept the AFL model of unionisation and wanted those workers as political allies in an international labour movement that accepted capitalism and US investment, as well as the dominant political role of the US government in Latin America. This programme, of course, made him an opponent of anarchists, syndicalists, Socialists, and later Communists, and he saw it as his organisation's job to block their advance.

At the turn of the last century three international crises tested the AFL's anti-imperialist foreign policy: first, the Venezuela boundary dispute; second, the

---

7   Gompers 1906, pp. 1–2.

proposal that the United States annex Hawaii; and third, and most important, the Spanish-American War. The Venezuela boundary dispute had its roots in Great Britain's acquisition of British Guiana (today Guyana) from the Netherlands in 1815, a British survey in 1835, and a boundary dispute with Venezuela in 1841. The discovery of gold in the disputed area led Great Britain to expand it claim and Venezuela to break off relations with Great Britain in 1876. For nineteen years Venezuela petitioned the United States for support, but it was not until 1895 that US Secretary of State Richard Olney invoked the Monroe Doctrine in a strongly worded note to the British government. The British argued that the Monroe Doctrine had no legal standing, leading President Grover Cleveland to call upon Congress to create a boundary commission and enforce its findings 'by every means'. American newspaper began to talk of the United States going to war with Great Britain.[8]

Gompers, as leader of the AFL, spoke out strongly condemning the warmongers in language much like that used by the Socialists of the time:

> Labour is never for war. It is always for peace. It is on the side of liberty, justice and humanity. These three are always for peace .... Who would be compelled to bear the burden of a war? The working people. They would pay the taxes, and their blood would flow like water. The interests of the working people of England and the United States are common. They are fighting the same enemy. They are battling to emancipate themselves from conditions common to both countries. The working people know no country. They are citizens f he world, and their religion is to do what is right, what is just, what is grand and glorious and valorous and chivalrous. The battle for the cause of labour, from times of remotest antiquity, has been for peace and good-will among men.[9]

The internationalist spirit was no doubt made easier by the fact that the United States and Great Britain, despite a series of minor dust-ups in Central America, shared a common political culture and language and more important significant common economic interests; and also, because many AFL members either came from the British Isles or were descendants of British immigrants. Finally, though Britain did call into question the Monroe Doctrine, the loss or gain of territory in Venezuela would have no direct impact on the United States, its economy, or on jobs. The issue was in the end settled amicably when the American

---

8   Office of the Historian, n.d.
9   Gompers 1986, pp. 80–101.

boundary commission found in favour of the British 1835 boundary line, dis-
appointing Venezuela, but the commission also rejecting Great Britain's more
recent attempts to expand its territory in Guiana at Venezuela's expense.

The second issue to test the AFL was Hawaii. On 16 July 1897, President
William McKinley submitted to the Senate for approval a treaty that would
annex Hawaii to the United States. Many local and regional AFL and Knights
of Labor unions rejected the annexation as a jingoist scheme of millionaires.
They were particularly concerned that it would encourage systems of contract
labour opposed by the unions. The 1897 AFL convention passed a resolution
opposing the annexation of Hawaii and calling upon the Senate to reject the
treaty.[10] There can be little doubt that the AFL leadership saw the United States
expansion across the Pacific toward Asia as raising the danger of what was
known at the time as the 'Yellow Peril', that is, the xenophobic notion that the
Asian peoples represented a particular danger to the United States, the American people, and especially the well-being of the working class. For labour this
was summed up in the often-repeated comment that the 'Orientals could live
off a bowl of rice a day, as no white man can or will'.[11] Hawaii's annexation then
was rejected out of opposition to imperialism and territorial annexation, but
also out of racism and fear of low-wage workers gaining access to the American labour market.

3   The Spanish-American War of 1898

The US declaration of war against Spain, leading to the Spanish-American War
in 1898, was the most complicated, most significant, and most decisive of the
three late nineteenth-century trials of AFL foreign policy. After the American
Civil War, US investments in Spanish Cuba had grown significantly, while the
Cuban independence struggles against Spain between 1868 and 1898 created
the kind of political instability that investors deplore. At the same time, the
Cuban people's struggle for independence won the sympathy of many Americans who had no financial interests in Cuba. Throughout the years of the Cuban
independence movement, many labour organisations passed resolutions of
support for the Cuban people in their struggle against the Spanish empire.
The 1897 AFL convention passed a resolution too in sympathy with the Cuban

---

10   Foner 1955, pp. 407–8.
11   I myself more than once have heard American workers say this, among them my step-
       father Kenneth Hornke, a union house painter in the San Diego, California area from the
       1940s to the 1970s.

people but rejected a stronger version that called for US intervention, which might have led to war. Gompers personally supported the non-militaristic resolution.[12]

Pro-war groups among American businessmen, in government, and in the press continued to press for war. The explosion on the *uss Maine* in the Havana harbour on 15 February 1898 – the cause of which was unknown but which much of the US press blamed on Spain – provided the pro-war movement with the incident needed to incite much of the public to support the call for war. Most AFL and other unions, however, continued to oppose military involvement until war was declared, whereupon most unions either came out in support for the war or remained silent.[13] Gompers and other labour leaders defended their position, arguing that if the unions opposed the war, the government would persecute them. A number of unions also supported the war because it meant more work for their members.

While he and the AFL had initially opposed the war, once it was declared, Gompers extolled it as 'a glorious and righteous one as far as the United States is concerned'.[14] As Foner writes, 'Gompers was then primarily concerned that labour should receive full credit for its contribution to the war effort', pointing proudly to some 250,000 trade union members who he claimed had volunteered to fight.[15]

Following the war, President McKinley proposed to the Senate a peace treaty that would incorporate the Philippines and Puerto Rico as US colonies and give the United States tutelage over Cuba. This led to a national debate over the question of imperialism and colonialism, including in the labour unions. Gompers and the AFL came out strongly against the treaty. The 1898 AFL convention passed a resolution condemning the peace treaty and committing the organisation to work for its defeat. The resolution read in part:

> Whereas, As a result of the war with Spain a new and far-reaching policy, commonly known as 'imperialism' or 'expansion' is now receiving the attention of the National Government, and if ratified by the United States Senate will seriously burden the wage-workers of our country, thrust upon us a large standing army and an aristocratic navy, and seriously threaten the perpetuity of our Republic, therefore be it

---

12   Foner 1988, vol. 1, pp. 14–15.
13   Foner 1955, vol. 2, p. 415.
14   Foner 1988, vol. 1, p. 21.
15   Foner 1988, vol. 1, p. 21.

> Resolved, That this convention offers its protest against any such innova-
> tion in our system of government and instructs our officers to use every
> honorable means to secure its defeat.[16]

With this resolution the AFL became part of the anti-imperialist movement. The Anti-Imperialist League, founded on 15 June 1898 in Boston, elected Samuel Gompers as a vice-president. The AFL participated in the movement through-out the country, particularly opposed to the annexation of the Philippines and Puerto Rico, their opposition inflamed by the US military imposing bans on strikes in the Philippines, Puerto Rico, Cuba, and Hawaii. They compared US troops firing on Filipino independence fighters with Federal troops suppres-sion of the miners strike in Coeur d'Alene, Idaho. There can be little doubt that there was also among many in the rank and file of the AFL opposition to the incorporation of territories whose populations were people of colour.

As the presidential election of 1900 drew near, with both the Republican McKinley and the Democrat Bryan supporting some sort of incorporation of the Philippines, sentiment grew for the creation of an anti-imperialist third party. Gompers – though he had been a tireless activist in the anti-imperialist movement following the war – would not support the call for a new party. Within a few years, however, the AFL's forceful and outspoken opposition to imperialism and colonialism began to diminish. For example, in 1904 the AFL declined to become involved in supporting the organisation of cigar makers in the Philippines, a US colony, because such skilled workers had been involved in the independence movement there and support for them would antagonise business and government.[17] Nevertheless, one has to conclude that until the twentieth century Gompers and the AFL remained fundamentally opposed to what might be called Old World imperialism and colonialism. Yet within a few years, both Gompers and the AFL would come to support a New World ver-sion of economic imperialism without colonisation, of which the United States' relationship with Mexico was the prime example.

4   Gompers' Solidarity with Mexican Workers

Gompers, who headed the AFL from 1886 to 1924 (except for one year), first became interested in Mexico in 1883 when working alongside Mexican cigar

---

16   Foner 1955, vol. 2, p. 421.
17   Foner 1955, vol. 2, pp. 426–39.

makers who opposed the dictatorship of Porfirio Díaz. Gompers later wrote in his autobiography, *Seventy Years of Life and Labor*:

> They introduced me to a number of Mexicans who were interested in the movement to secure relief from the tyranny and corruption of the Díaz regime .... In the course of the years, we were shopmates, many of the Mexican revolutionaries came to New York, so that I was pretty well informed as to Mexican revolutionary thought and activity.[18]

After 1886, when Gompers founded and went to work full-time for the AFL, his Mexican friends continued to send visiting Mexican revolutionaries to his office. Gompers recorded that after 1897 when the AFL moved to Washington, 'conferences with Mexican revolutionists became more frequent'.[19]

In his autobiography, Gompers mentions that, 'For a number of years I had been in touch with the leaders of the Liberal Party in Los Angeles, the two Magón brothers, Ricardo and Enrique, Lázaro Gutiérrez de Lara, Antonio I. Villareal, and Librado Rivera'.[20] In this way, Gompers followed the PLM's activities and was aware of the campaign of harassment against them organised by the Mexican and US governments of Porfirio Díaz and William Howard Taft. Gompers was sharply critical of the role of the US government. As he put it, 'our government was used to help Mexico hunt down and punish political refugees'.[21] He offered in his memoir a vivid description of how the Mexican government's nefarious agents reached across the border and into the United States.

> Under that machinery Mexico suborned local police, detective and immigration authorities so that these men were receiving pay both from the American and Mexican government and were taking orders from Mexico to arrest and return political refugees. These refugees were harassed by all manner of efforts to arrest and imprison them on illegal grounds and not a few of them were kidnapped and taken across the border. In most cases, when the charges could be brought before a court, it was easy to show that the evidence submitted against them was manufactured.[22]

---

18   Gompers 1925, vol. 2, p. 303.
19   Gompers 1925, vol. 2, pp. 304–5.
20   Gompers 1925, vol. 2, p. 306.
21   Gompers 1925, vol. 2, p. 304.
22   Gompers 1925, vol. 2, p. 307.

So, when in 1907 three leaders of the Mexican Liberal Party – Ricardo Flores Magón, Antonio I. Villarreal and Librado Rivera – were jailed in the United States on charges of violating a US neutrality act, Gompers decided that the AFL should work for their release. Gompers got the 1908 AFL Convention to pass a resolution supporting the Mexican revolutionaries and calling for a campaign to raise money for their legal defence. Union organiser Mary Harris Jones, better known as 'Mother Jones', worked with the United Mine Workers, the Western Federation of Mine Workers, and the AFL to raise funds for the jailed PLM leaders.

Union activist, John Murray, a member of the International Typographical Union and a Socialist from California, also became involved in the defence campaign, though initially not through Gompers and the AFL. Murray, the scion of a wealthy Quaker family from New York, read Leo Tolstoy while a student and became convinced that he should dedicate his life to uplifting the downtrodden. Murray went to work in California organising Mexican farm workers and became a member of the Socialist Party. Murray, who had earlier organised a Political Refugee Defence League to support Russian refugees, expanded his group's efforts to support the Mexican revolutionaries as well. But Murray hesitated to work with the more conservative Gompers. As Gompers put it, 'He then identified with the Socialist Party and was suspicious of me because he knew my attitude toward the Socialist Party'.[23]

Murray had met PLM leaders through Socialist attorney Job Harriman, and Murray wrote many articles in their defence for the labour and socialist press. But Murray's interest went beyond mere journalism. In 1908 he travelled to Mexico City, possibly on a political errand for Ricardo Flores Magón and the PLM. The US government arrested Murray when he returned on the preposterous trumped-up charge of attempting to murder US President William Howard Taft as he was meeting with Mexican President Porfirio Díaz in El Paso in October 1909.

Once out of jail, Murray contacted Democratic Party congressman William B. Wilson, a former UMW officer from Pennsylvania, and convinced him to push for a Congressional investigation of the US persecution of Mexican exiles in the US When the Congressional hearings were held Murray testified, as did PLM leader Lázaro Gutiérrez de Lara, Socialist Party of America member John Kenneth Turner, author of *Barbarous Mexico*, and union organiser Mother Jones. Gompers also submitted a letter condemning both the Díaz government and the US government officials for their repression of the Mexican exiles in the

---

23   Gompers 1925, vol. 2, p. 308.

United States. Gompers later wrote, 'It is not in any way an exaggeration to say that the American labour movement was the most potent single agency in inducing President Roosevelt and President Taft to refuse to permit the United States government to hunt Mexican refugees'.[24] Though, in fact, the US government continued to hunt them.

When the Mexican Revolution broke out, Gompers opposed 'the big interests', that is, US corporations with large investments in the neighbouring nation that wanted military intervention in Mexico. As Gompers later explained:

> The labor movement of the United States was endeavoring to establish guarantees for political justice as well as opportunities of freedom which were necessary for the development of a Mexican labor movement.[25]

Gompers came to believe that Madero and the leaders of the Mexican Revolutionary movement should and would establish a democracy and carry out land reform.[26]

5   The AFL Breaks with the PLM, Supports Madero

After the victory of Francisco I. Madero and his revolutionary forces over President Porfirio Díaz, Mexican and US radicals split over the question of the future of the Mexican Revolution. The Socialists and the AFL supported Madero as representing the first stage of a democratic revolution that would make it possible for unions to organise. And as we have seen, Ricardo Flores Magón and the Mexican Liberal Party on the other hand opposed Madero's bourgeois revolution and issued an anarchist manifesto calling for direct action to carry out agrarian reform and social revolution. The Industrial Workers of the World as well as Emma Goldman and the American anarchists sided with Flores Magón.

Madero, seeking support from the US labour movement, invited Mother Jones and the United Mine Workers union to come to Mexico, ostensibly to help organise mine workers. In addition to Jones, Frank Hayes, vice president of the UMW, and Joe Cannon, a leader of the Western Federation of Miners, also met with Madero who told them that he supported the right to union organisa-

---

24   Gompers 1925, vol. 2, p. 309.
25   Gompers 1925, vol. 2, pp. 309–10.
26   Gompers 1925, vol. 2, p. 310.

tion in Mexico. Madero, however, had other interests in inviting the American unionists. Manuel Calero, who had been Secretary of Justice in the interim government after the revolution, asked the union leaders to try to persuade Ricardo Flores Magón and the PLM to give up their armed movement.

Jones did speak to Magón and subsequently wrote a report to Calero regarding her talk with him and other PLM leaders. Jones said she had tried to persuade the Magonistas to return to Mexico and to work through legal channels. But she told Calero, 'they believed only in direct action, the taking over of the lands'. The PLM leaders, she wrote, also predicted 'that it was only a question of time until Madero would be overthrown'. Unable to win over the leaders of the PLM, Jones threatened them, telling the Magonistas in no uncertain terms, 'If you are again arrested the labour movement will take no hand in your defence'. She then went around to the Los Angeles unions and, as she wrote, 'I exacted a promise from them that they would not in the future by any means permit the qualified labour unions of Los Angeles to render any aid to those men'.[27] Flores Magón berated Jones and the other AFL leaders for doing the Mexican government's dirty work, and attacked Jones in the PLM newspaper *Regeneración*.

6   The House of the World Worker

In 1910 Mexico City, with a population of one and a half million, was home to hundreds of thousands of workers, most of them artisans, service workers, or labourers. Most manufacturing workers still laboured in small shops, though those shops had been undergoing some mechanisation leading to deskilling of artisanal workers. The city had 10,000 factory workers, mostly textile workers employed in large mills. There were also 7,000 streetcar workers, 1,200 railroad repair workers, and 13,000 agricultural workers in the metropolitan area. Most women worked as domestic servants, over 30,000 of them, but thousands of other women were employed as cigarette makers, seamstresses, laundresses, and tortilla makers. Women made up 35 percent of the paid workforce in Mexico City, far above the national average of 12 percent.[28]

The most common form of worker organisation was the mutual aid society that provided for members and their families in times of poor health, injury, unemployment or death. Workers paid monthly dues in return for support in those times of need through the society, which was a kind of workers' insurance

---

27   Fabela 1976, vol. 10, pp. 371–3.

28   Lear 2001, pp. 49–85.

organisation. Though workers generally organised their own mutual societies, employers or politicians also organised some of them, in which case the
society and its members then became dependent upon them. Men were more
likely to have mutual aid societies than women, but there were several women's
organisations as well. These societies often promoted cooperation between
employers and workers while stressing the moral improvement of their members through abstaining from drink. Mutual aid societies were not unions and
did not usually negotiate contracts or carry out strikes, but at moments of conflict they often took on that role. Workers' chief concern was job security in a
city where cheap labour existed in abundance.[29] Mutual aid societies, like the
anarchist movement, eschewed politics.

     While some workers did organise unions, those unions had had no clear legal
status during the Porfiriate. At times Díaz, state governors and local politicians,
while crushing militant or anarchist unions, had tolerated and promoted moderate labour organisations. Workers who attempted to organise radical or confrontational unions might be imprisoned, conscripted, or be forced to do a stint
of forced labour on plantations in the Yucatan or the Valle Nacional – a punishment which was often fatal. Díaz permitted the moderate unions and mutual
societies to come together in the Congreso Obrero (Workers Congress) led by
Pedro Ordóñez. Those unions often participated in Díaz's political machine,
negotiating slates that often included workers for lower-level offices such as city
council. Such relations between the political machines and the labour organisations tended to corrupt the latter with their 'antidemocratic practices'.[30] In
any case neither the Congreso Obrero nor its political slates were intended to
represent workers' interests.

     The new century opened an era of union organisation and what the pro-
government newspaper *El Imparcial* called '*huelgamanía*' (strike mania). The
Mexican strike wave opened around 1900 reaching its climax in 1907 when
the depression of that year brought fear of unemployment and an end to the
walkouts. In response to the strike wave, and with the collapse of the Congreso Obrero after the death of Ordóñez in 1903, Governor Guillermo Landa
y Escandón created the Mutualist and Moralising Society of Workers of the
Federal District. Landa y Escandn's organisation brought together government
officials, factory managers, and workers in a 'loosely corporatist' structure. The
paternalistic society emphasised the moral reform of workers through sobri-
ety and commitment to family. With the coming of the election of 1910, the

---

29   Ibid.
30   Lear 2001, pp. 106–23.

Society, which was linked to the campaign of Porfirio Díaz, was swept away by the Revolution.[31]

The victory of the revolution led by Madero and his election to the presidency in 1911 brought a new wave of genuine union organising and strikes as workers, awakened and excited by the overthrow of the dictator and the triumph of the revolution, sought to exert more power in the workplace, as well as creating new social and political movements. Unlike the industrial unions and strikes of miners and textile workers, most of the new unions in the Madero era were developed in the cities and were made up of artisans.[32]

Workers became interested in politics and first attempted to influence the presidential election of October 1911, then the city council elections of December 1911, and finally the congressional elections of April 1912 through workers political clubs. Many were workers affiliated with Madero's newly formed Progressive Constitutional Party (PCP), though some were supporters of the candidates of the old regime. Workers joined other citizens in enthusiastically electing Madero to the presidency, though many were critical of the way his political organisation had marginalised working people. Then, in the Mexico City Council elections, workers clubs succeeded in electing several progressives, among them Serapio Rendón, Felipe Gutiérrez de Lara, and Antonio Villareal, the latter two former Mexican Liberal Party (PLM) members. While Villareal had given up the PLM and abandoned his enthusiasm for its labour program, Gutiérrez de Lara, who had come from the socialist wing of the PLM, remained on the labour left and would go on to join the House of the World Worker. Still the candidates of the old regime maintained a majority on the Mexico City council, which then elected a Porfirista council president.[33]

Two workers parties participated in the congressional elections of June 1912, the small Socialist Workers Party (PSO), founded in 1911 by the German-born piano turner Paul Zierold, and the Popular Workers Party (PPO), dominated by Jesús Flores Magón, who had broken with his brother Ricardo and the PLM to become Madero's Minister of the Interior. More important on the left than either of those was the Liberal Party (PL), founded by former PLM leaders Juan Sarabia, Antonio Díaz Soto y Gama, and also Jesús Flores Magón. The new Liberal Party had its roots in the Mexican Liberal Party and its 1906 programme, but though socialists, were critical supporters of the Madero government that had wavered in their support of workers, for example during the street workers'

31   Lear 2001, pp. 119–23.
32   Carr 1976, p. 45.
33   Lear 2001, pp. 143–53.

strike of September 1911.[34] The workers and left parties, however, did poorly and the elections, so workers had only a few congressional representatives, among the former PLM member Juan Sarabia and Heriberto Jara, a man of middle class origins who had been a bookkeeper in Rio Blanco and who had participated in the strikes there in 1908. (Jara would later become the leftist governor of the state of Veracruz.) The left's poor showing was due in large measure to the low turnout among voters; while skilled workers and some factory workers voted, the great mass of the poor, the *pelados*, did not participate in the elections. Disillusionment with the elections led to splits in the PL, PSO, and PPO parties, with many workers now giving up on electoral politics and turning to organisation in the workplace. Among them was the group Luz (Light), which published a newspaper of the same name, an anarchist split from the PSO.

Workers now transformed many of their mutual societies into 'resistance societies', a step on the road to becoming craft or industrial unions. The Confederation of Graphic Arts led the way in creating these 'resistance societies' and was joined by others organised by tailors, stonecutters, and many other trades. With the creation of the resistance societies, the rhetoric of the labour movement became more class conscious, with society newspaper articles and speakers now criticising 'the bourgeoisie'.[35] Many of those societies soon joined the House of the World Worker.

The PLM, while strongest among Mexicans in the United States and in the northern states of Mexico, also had some influence in Mexico City. There the PLM's anarchism converged with that of Spanish anarchist immigrants in the city's emerging labour movement. A variety of mutual aid societies, resistance societies, and unions, from bakers and typographer to tailors and stone masons, as well as many other trades, both men and women workers, had begun to organise in their own trade unions as well as to meet together to create what would become at first a city-wide and then later a national labour organisation: La Casa del Obrero Mundial or The House of the World Worker (Casa).[36]

The House of the World Worker was founded on 22 September 1912 in Mexico City by an 'amalgamation of tendencies', writes historian Luis Araiza,

---

34   Lear 2001, pp. 156–8.
35   Lear 2001, pp. 169–70.
36   Araiza 1963, pp. 14–29. The trades involved included: typographers, stone workers, office workers, textile workers, carpenters, public employees, metal workers, coach drivers, painters, bakers, electricians, factory assembly workers, construction workers, saddlers, waiters, brewery workers, musicians, commission workers, and coal workers. Also included were a dozen intellectuals and seven Federal Deputies, that is members of Congress.

an amalgamation that included simple trade unionists, anarchists, anarcho-syndicalists, communists, Christian Socialists, Masons and political activists. Some were working-class, others middle-class intellectuals. Several had been members of the PLM or the more moderate PL. Another writer calls the Casa 'pluralist' noting that some of the members were supporters of President Francisco Madero.[37] While the federation may have been an amalgamation of political tendencies, among the most popular was anarchism as indicated by the many pamphlets the Casa published by authors like Proudhon, Bakunin, Kropotkin, Malatesta, and Reclus. The Casa had no statement of principles, no statutes, and was not organised like a federation; there was no agreed upon project. It was founded simply as 'a centre for the propagation of advanced ideas'.[38] 'Advanced ideas' included the anarchist opposition to God and state. Traditional Mexican liberalism joined with anarchism in a fierce opposition to organised religion, the anti-clericalism that became the glue of Mexico's revolutionary nationalist movement for decades. The establishment of the Casa represented both the workers' response to their economic and social conditions and their hopes that they could play a larger role in society thanks to the revolutionary political process through which Mexico City and the entire country were passing, though as anarchists, as a matter of principle they opposed all politics and government, so they took no side in the revolution at that point.

While the Casa's dominant philosophy may have been anarchism, urban historian John Lear cautions that this should not be taken too literally. He writes that, 'anarchism was at best a prominent component among a variety of orienting ideologies that included popular liberalism and even social democracy (the latter through the Socialist Workers Party)'. Spain may have served as the source for much of this anarchism, but it had been, 'Mexicanised to fit national traditions and contexts'. Anarchism provided the Casa's members 'a vocabulary for articulating class differences and an imperative for independent organization, free of many of the constraints of mutualism. Anarchism also provided a timely explanation for the limits of Maderista democracy', writes Lear.[39] Labour and left historian Barry Carr writes that while nominally anarchist, the Casa had no very clear and well-articulated ideology and that the group's anarchism was largely rhetorical and not very deep among the members.[40]

---

37   Morales Jiménez 1982, p. 53.
38   Arraiza 1963, p. 24.
39   Lear 2001, p. 173.
40   Carr 1976, pp. 55 and 61.

The Casa's affiliates, the organisations and the individuals, were not by-and-large interested in organising unions, carrying out strikes, and winning better wages and conditions; they were, rather, a group of men and women, mostly artisans and workers as well as many mutual society and union members, committed to bringing about a better society for all. These anarchist workers and intellectuals had already begun in July to publish their newspaper *Luz* (*Light*) and at about the same time opened their Rationalist School inspired by the Spanish anarchist educator Francisco Ferrer Guardia.[41] It was they who gave the initial impulse to the founding of the Casa. The Casa offered a wide variety of courses in practical skills and foreign languages and insisted upon the equality of the sexes in all spheres of its activities, with women both teaching and taking courses together with men, something rare in Mexico at the time.[42] What would this group do as a new government came to power?

Francisco Madero, who became president on 6 November 1911, had at the beginning no labour policy whatsoever. His manifesto, the Plan de San Luis, had never mentioned the labour question, and after taking office he made many contradictory statements. Given his experience of conflict with the Mexican Liberal Party in the North, it is not surprising that he now attempted to smother in the crib the infant anarchist labour movement in Mexico City. Madero closed the Rationalist School, arrested the anarchists involved in publishing *Luz*, and expelled them from the country on 10 September 1912 as an undesirable immigrant one of the leading Spanish anarchists of the Casa, Juan Francisco Moncaleano, just days before the inauguration of the Casa. Madero's repression of the anarchists, however, only brought greater notoriety and prestige to the infant labour movement, which despite repression continued to expand its influence.[43]

On the other hand, the Madero's administration did not send out troops or police to put down strikers; and he frequently met with strikers and even sometimes took their side against repressive employers. With the Casa closed, Madero, following in the footsteps of Porfirio Díaz sponsored his own government-controlled labour federation, The Great Worker League, as an alternative to the anarchists. And, under pressure from the rising union movement, Madero's administration created a Labour Department and negotiated a nationwide pattern agreement for the textile industry, though neither of these came near to meeting the workers' demands for more rights, more power,

---

41   Salazar 1972, vol. 1, pp. 36–41; Araiza 1963, pp. 19–33.
42   Lear 2001, p. 174.
43   Salazar 1972, vol. 1, p. 45.

and for better wages and better conditions. Meanwhile the government officials continued to publish in the Madero party's paper attacks on the Casa.[44] Madero's government, extremely cautious and legalistic, unable to resolve the problems of the peasants or the workers and facing opposition from both the old Díaz crowd and from the Zapatistas, found that it had a shrinking base of support. His legalism, indecisiveness, and vacillation only encouraged the opposition.

Just three months later, General Victoriano Huerta colluded with other right-wing rebels, Félix Díaz, the nephew of Porfirio Díaz, and Bernardo Reyes, and, in a coup coordinated by US Ambassador Henry Lane Wilson, overthrew and assassinated Madero and his vice-president, Pino Suárez on 18 February 1913.[45] Ironically Huerta's right-wing coup ended the Madero government's harassment of the Casa, which was now able to reopen and return to its work. Taking advantage of its newfound liberty, the Casa organised a mass meeting in the Lírico Theater on 15 May, which was attended by members of all of the unions in the city in support of the Casa. Speaking at the meeting, the era's great populist orator Antonio Díaz y Soto declared that the Mexican people would rise in revolution and coming from the North and the South drive the usurper Huerta from the presidential throne. Just hours after the meeting, several labour activists were arrested and five Spaniards among them expelled from the country under Constitutional Article 33, which forbid foreigners from involving themselves in Mexican politics.[46] Serapio Rendón, an attorney who defended workers, a member of the Casa, and a member of the Mexican House of Deputies, spoke out in the National Legislature in defence of those who had been arrested and deported, though not long after these events, on 22 August, Huerta had Rendón arrested and then assassinated.

The Casa workers also put forward a petition on behalf of their comrades demonstrating their internationalist principles. Demanding that the legislators do their duty of defending the Mexican people, the Casa petition also spoke out on behalf of the immigrant activists:

> We want respect for the so-called foreigners by reason of their birth who have collaborated in the work for the universal welfare of man and shared with us the bitter penalties of the fight for human needs; they have a perfect right to reside in our Territory.

44   Carr 1976, pp. 48–52.
45   Knight 1986, vol. 1, pp. 485–90.
46   Salazar 1972, vol. 1, pp. 54–5.

The barbarous Article 33, which has been used against them, is a disgrace against which we energetically protest with anguished hearts having witnessed how they have been brutally ripped from their homes, leaving their families completely unprotected.

We also protest with all of our energy, before you, representatives of the people, for the attacks and jailings which our coworkers, members of the House of the World Worker, have suffered, being unjustly held since Sunday in the Belén jail.[47]

The petitions demanded justice and freedom for those who had been imprisoned.

What is most notable in this statement is the anarchists' rejection of a narrow nationalism – at a moment when nationalism was at its height – in defence of the principle of internationalism. The anarchists held that the Spaniards like the Mexicans had been engaged in the common work of improving life for all of humanity, and therefore the idea of expelling them from the country was repugnant. A position they took at a time when most Mexican working people, who hated the arrogant Spanish owners, supervisors, and foremen, whom they referred to contemptuously as *gabachos*, were demanding that Spaniards be expelled from the country.

Despite the attack on its members, the House of the World Worker continued to organise, sponsoring the first May Day or International Labour Day celebration in Mexico on 1 May 1913. By the second decade of the twentieth century, 1 May had become recognised around the world as the day of commemoration of the 'Martyrs of Chicago', the five anarchist leaders of the labour movement condemned to death for their role in the Haymarket affair of 1886. Throughout Europe and in the United States, 1 May was recognised among anarchists, socialists, and labour unionists as an international day of working-class protest and celebration. In 1913, 25,000 workers participated in the parade in Mexico City on 1 May, marching behind the newly adopted red-and-black banner of the labour movement shouting, 'We demand the eight-hour day!' and 'We want Sunday for a day of rest'. The May Day protest left many shops and factories abandoned as workers poured into the *zócalo*, Mexico's national plaza, and filled the surrounding streets.[48]

The May Day demonstration of 1913 made it clear that the House of the World Worker was not only a leftist educational centre, but that it had also become the

---

47   Salazar 1972, vol. 1, pp. 55–7.
48   Araiza 1963, pp. 50–6; Salazar 1972, vol. 1, pp. 50–1.

centre of a movement of great potential power, and therefore a danger to the Huerta regime. Newspapers aligned with the Huerta regime now began a campaign against the Casa, accusing its members of being not only anarchists, but also Maderistas engaged in revolutionary activity against the Huerta government. At that point, in part as a result of developments in the labour movement and in part because of its fear of repression from the Huerta regime, the Casa reaffirmed its political neutrality. In June of 1913, the Casa adopted a statement affirming that, as an organisation committed to direct action it would not engage in politics, it would not permit political speeches on its premises, and that it would only work to organise workers into trade unions.[49] This was, of course, in keeping with its anarchist philosophy but also reflected failures of the Madero administration to respond to workers' needs.[50] At the same time, this posture suggests that, despite its anarchist roots, it was, in reality, since Victoriano Huerta's overthrow of Madero, seeking a modus vivendi with the Mexican state. But the Casa's June 1913 statement repudiating politics and adopting trade unionism as the focus of its activities was not simply an opportunistic measure intended to calm Huerta; it was also a reflection changes in the international labour movement and the continuing influence of Spanish leftists. We are present at the birth of anarcho-syndicalism in Mexico.

'The New Unionism' as it was called in the English-speaking countries, was developing throughout the industrialised world in the late 1890s and early 1900s, in France, Germany, Italy, Spain and the United States. In some countries it was called syndicalism, revolutionary syndicalism or anarcho-syndicalism from the French word *syndicat* (union). The confrontational French Confédération Générale du Travail (General Workers Confederation – CGT), led the way, inspiring workers in other countries to adopt its principles, strategies, and tactics. In the United States the new unionism took the form of the Industrial Workers of the World (IWW). A new, militant, mass movement of workers was sweeping the industrial world, and, via Spain, Cuba, and the United States, its message was arriving in Mexico.

Syndicalism arose in Europe out of a frustration with, on the one hand, the failure of craft unions to confront the corporations and their great industrial plants, and, on the other hand, the failure of the Socialist Parties to carry out a militant fight for workers. The new unionists everywhere were moving from craft unionism to industrialism unionism in order to challenge the corpora-

---

49   Salazar 1972, vol. 1, pp. 56–7.
50   Lear 2001, p. 181.

tions. The syndicalists called for 'direct action' as opposed to the old European (and especially German) socialist formula of labour unions plus labour parties known as 'multiple action'. They also rejected politics, including the Socialist parties, arguing that Social Democracy was not fighting capitalism, but that direct action, union organisation, especially industrial union organisation, and the general strike, could bring down capitalism and put workers in power. The new union movement activists often called themselves 'revolutionary unionists'.[51]

The Casa had debated these issues in 1912 inviting advocates of various views to speak before their assembly. Pedro Juno Rojo, a leader of a rival organisation, the Confederation of Workers Unions of the Mexican Republic (Confederación de Sindicatos Obreros de la República Mexicana) based in Veracruz, and French leftist, Alberto Frisson, advocates of 'multiple action' (unions and politics), were invited to speak to the Casa. Jacinto Huitrón, one of the leaders of the Casa wrote in his history of the Mexican unions in this period, 'we rejected this system and we declared ourselves frankly and loyally advocates of Revolutionary Syndicalism, based on the books we had received from Spain by authors such as Luis Fabri [Luigi Fabbri], Anselmo Lorenzo, Ricardo Mella, José Prat and other great writers'.[52]

Throughout the period from 1912 to 1914, faced with both rising prices and the interruption of work because of the revolution, the working class changed its tactics. The mutual societies, resistance societies, and trade unions became more syndicalist, more confrontational toward the employers, and made more demands on the government. Labour organisations now talked openly about 'defending themselves from the bosses' and about 'class struggle and direct action'. More workers societies and unions joined the Casa, and more of those who joined were unskilled workers and women. The Casa became more centralised and it helped to establish the city unions and the General Workers Confederation of Mexico.[53] Workers became more militant in their demands, pushing for the ten-hour day or in some cases the eight-hour day; skilled workers demanded workers' control in the workplace; everyone wanted higher wages and better working conditions. Workers demanded equal pay for Mex-

---

51   André Tridon 1913; Dubofsky 1969; Foner 1971; Dreyfus 1995.

52   Huitrón 1978. Luigi Fabbri (1877–1935) was an Italian-born anarchist active in Europe and South America; Anselmo Lorenzo (1842–1914) was a Spanish anarchist sometimes called the 'grandfather of Spanish anarchism'; Ricardo Mella (1861–1925) was a Spanish anarchist particularly active in Galicia and Asturias; José Prat (1867–1932), born in Spain, was an anarchist journalist active in Spain and Argentina.

53   Lear 2001, pp. 175–8.

ican and foreign workers, that is, to bring Mexicans' pay up to the level of the foreigners.[54] Mexican railway workers also carried out a national campaign to 'Mexicanise' the railroads by driving out US or other foreign-born workers who monopolised the skilled positions from which Mexicans were excluded.[55]

The Madero government had, before it was overthrown, created a Labour Department, and in response to strikes in the textile industry, had put forward a *Ley Obrero* (Worker Law) that would reduce taxes on textile companies that adhered to government guidelines, which suggested a 10-hour day, a complex uniform minimum wage system, and limitations on factory fines. Madero's government, however, never went beyond voluntary employer participation, never recognised the workers' rights to self-organisation in labour unions, to strike, or to collective bargaining.[56] Congress had debated Madero's *Ley Obero* and the 'worker question' for two months, but virtually no one in the legislature made concrete proposals to improve workers' rights and enhance their power. Only the Catholic deputy Salvador Moreno Arriaga, reflecting the influence of Pope Leo XIII's 1891 encyclical *Rerum Novarum* with its acknowledgement of workers' issues, suggested that the legislature should recognise workers' right to organise unions and make contracts with employers. The weak *Ley Obrero* was passed, but no genuine and comprehensive labour law was passed during the Madero administration. Many union activists were predisposed by their anarchism to reject political leaders and parties, as well as governments, but the failure of Madero's administration to respond to their needs also seemed to show the limits of political reformism and turned some workers against politics altogether. The Casa, in adopting its June 1913 statement rejecting politics, was thus responding to the Mexican situation, but also to the new radical European ideas combining anarchism and unionism.

Proclaiming its political neutrality, the Casa was in the short run attempting to avoid repression by the Huerta government, but the attempt failed. On 27 May 1914, Huerta's police closed the Casa, destroyed its archives and its library, and beat, arrested, and jailed several of its members.[57] Some Casa leaders fled to Veracruz where they encountered new problems.

---

54   Lear 2001, pp. 195–200.
55   Alzati 1946, *passim*.
56   Lear 2001, p. 184.
57   Salazar 1972, pp. 63–5; Araiza 1963, pp. 66–7.

7   Gompers, the AFL, and Wilson's Invasion of Veracruz

After Victoriano Huerta's coup, Gompers and the AFL – who had supported Madero – took no immediate position in support of any of the various rival leaders (Zapata, Villa, or Carranza) who now rose up against the usurper. Gompers did, however, see that the AFL passed a resolution in November 1913 opposing any US government armed intervention in Mexico.[58] The Revolution continued in 1914, now as a civil war between rival leaders, alternative political programmes, and opposing armies.

Huerta's dictatorship posed a very serious problem for the Woodrow Wilson administration. The US president feared that Huerta would be dominated by the British or Germans, but in any case, by European banks; at the same time, Wilson did not see any revolutionary force that he could support outright, though he was coming to feel that Venustiano Carranza's Constitutionalists represented the best option. Wilson wanted above all a transition that would preserve the Mexican Army – that is, leave the old Porifiran state intact as a protector of US investments – an option that was out of the question for Carranza. Then Wilson proposed to Carranza that the United States occupy much of Mexico, presumably the northern states and the Gulf coast, to aid Carranza and his revolutionary allies in their war against Huerta, a suggestion that Carranza emphatically refused. Seeing no other option, Wilson finally decided that he would provide arms to Carranza's forces, hoping in that way to bring them under his paternalistic control.[59] Carranza accepted the armaments but, defending Mexico's sovereignty, still would not defer to Wilson.

Believing he needed more leverage in order to be able to break Carranza's will and force him to obey American dictates, Wilson therefore decided to invade Mexico, choosing the historic strategy – dating back to Hernán Cortez – of a landing at Veracruz and then a march on Mexico City. All he needed was a pretext and that was soon provided.[60] When several American sailors were arrested in the port city of Veracruz on 9 April 1914, Wilson succeeded in turning the issue into a major international incident. The United States demanded an apology accompanied by a 21-gun salute of the American flag, which Huerta, seeing an opportunity to turn himself into a national hero, refused to give. Meanwhile, Wilson learned that a German ship, the *Ypiranga* was on its way to Veracruz with arms for Huerta. So, on 21 April US Marines landed in the port,

---

58   Leverstein 1971, p. 15.
59   Katz 1983, pp. 195–202.
60   Ibid.

and while Huerta ordered the army to withdraw, cadets and citizens resisted until suppressed by a US naval bombardment.[61]

Carranza condemned the US invasion and called for the immediate withdrawal of troops from Veracruz, warning of the possibility of Mexico going to war against the United States. When US troops continued their advance in the state of Veracruz, Carranza called for the Americans to withdraw, implicitly threatening a general Mexican-American war. Pancho Villa, however, expressing a view shared by many lower-class Mexicans, declined to condemn the invasion, fearing that a war between the US and Mexico would only serve upper class interests.[62] At the same time, in the United States, there was a tremendous reaction against Wilson's invasion of Mexico by unions, churches, and peace organisation, though some American corporations with interests in Mexico, especially in the oil fields of the Gulf coast, supported Wilson. Nevertheless, the combined opposition of Carranza and other Mexican leaders, including Emiliano Zapata, and the outpouring of opposition in the United States stopped Wilson from pursuing his initial plan of sending the American forces on to Mexico City.[63]

Unlike the AFL's earlier positions on Venezuela, Hawaii, and the Spanish American War, and despite significant opposition to the war among many unions and their members, this time the AFL, led by Gompers, came down strongly on the side of President Wilson. At the 1913 AFL convention, before Wilson's invasion of Veracruz, Gompers won the removal from a resolution on Mexico a clause condemning, 'American and foreign corporations, and certain jingo newspapers, to force intervention by the United States government in Mexico'. Now, however, Gompers argued that it would be a mistake 'to denounce intervention', invoking the Monroe Doctrine and the necessity of keeping foreign powers out of the Americas.[64] Gompers' position was entirely motivated by geopolitical concerns, invoking neither the interests of American workers nor those of the Mexican people.[65] Later in his autobiography Gompers wrote, 'It was due to extreme self-control and wisdom of the President in dealing with Vera Cruz and Tampico that general bloodshed was avoided',[66] though in fact there had been quite a lot of blood shed by both Americans and Mexicans. In December 1914, Wilson ordered US troops out of Veracruz, turning it over to

---

61   Quirk 1962, *passim*.
62   Katz 1998, pp. 336–8.
63   Katz 1983, pp. 195–202.
64   Foner 1987, pp. 102–3.
65   Andrews 1991, pp. 29–31.
66   Gompers 1925, vol. 2, p. 311.

Carranza's forces and ending the brief intervention. His invasion had failed to break the will of Carranza.

The US occupation of Veracruz, which lasted six months, had drawn the AFL into a new foreign policy. The invasion represented a key turning point in US labour-government relations. Wilson and Gompers were moving together toward a new conception of foreign policy, opposed to Old World imperialism and colonialism, but strongly supportive of US intervention to defend American economic interests abroad. Within this framework, Gompers soon developed a vision of the AFL also expanding abroad under the shield of the US government: labour imperialism.

8   The Revolution Divided

Huerta's ascendancy and his authoritarian regime were short lived. The forces that had risen up against Díaz – Francisco 'Pancho' Villa and Venustiano Carranza in the North and Emiliano Zapata in the South – rose up again in revolution against Huerta. The vice was soon closing on Huerta as the revolutionary forces of Zapata in the south joined by those of Villa, Álvaro Obregón, and Carranza in the north began to converge on Mexico City leading the usurper to resign and flee the country in mid-July 1914. The Casa del Obrero Mundial, which had by then become the centre of a national labour network with an estimated 52,000 members was able once again to open its doors on 21 August 1914.

Huerta having been defeated, the successful revolutionaries met in the Convention of Aguascalientes in October 1914, some 150 delegates, most of them officers of the military forces, though few of the leading generals themselves attended. Dominated politically by the Zapatistas and Villistas the delegates declared the Convention sovereign – over the objections of Carranza – and endorsed Zapata's Plan de Ayala calling for the redistribution of land to the peasants. The Convention removed Villa from his military command, while also demanding that Carranza step down. When he refused, the Convention appointed Villa to be General-in-Chief and ordered him to subdue Carranza who was declared to be in open rebellion. Álvaro Obregón, who had come to the Convention with great hopes for reconciliation among the revolutionaries, found his desires frustrated and returned to the Carranza fold. The revolutionary forces thus divided between a plebeian left wing led by Villa and Zapata, known as the Conventionists, and a capitalist, state-building right wing led by Venustiano Carranza and Álvaro Obregón, the Constitutionalists. The civil war began once again, this time between the revolution's left and right wings. The violent revolution would go on for another five years.

Where did the Casa stand? Many members of the Casa were initially attracted to Emiliano Zapata and his Liberating Army of the South and some anarchists went off to Morelos to join Zapata's movement. And when the Convention took place, the Casa collaborated closely with it, embracing its labour resolutions. Yet already by 1914 it was clear that the Casa leadership had begun to orient toward the Carranza and his Constitutionalists.[67] While the Casa generally admired Zapata as a military leader and supported his Plan de Ayala with its call for 'the land to he who works it', many of the anarcho-syndicalists tended to share the view of many urban middle-class and working-class Mexicans that Zapata and his troops represented the most backward and ignorant elements of Mexican society. In particular, the anarchists were appalled by the Zapatista peasants' fervent Catholic faith. Jacinto Huitrón, for example, ridiculed the Zapatistas for 'their ignorance', pointing out that 'they wear scapulars and of course pictures of the Virgin of Guadalupe pinned to their hats'.[68] A particular point of contention between the Zapatistas and the Casa was the fact that General Obregón had given the Casa several Catholic building for use as meeting places or housing. The Zapatistas believed that the buildings were sacred and therefore should not be given over to secular organisations.[69] For the anarchists, nothing was more reactionary than the Church, and if the Zapatistas were religious, then they were in some fundamental way reactionary.

But it is also the case, as Alan Knight has argued, that the Convention's military leaders, that is, Villa and Zapata, had taken no action to support the labour movement. Labour issues simply did not appear on their horizon.[70] The Constitutionalist leaders, 'Obregón, Calles, Alvarado, Múgica, had a better grasp of political options, a broader, national vision and a greater awareness of the potential of organised labour ...'.[71] This outlook would make all the difference in terms of the ultimate outcome of the Mexican Revolution.

Obregón recognised the importance of industrial and transport workers in controlling the future course of the revolution; after all it was workers who ran the railroads, worked in the armaments factories, produced the textiles and boots used for uniforms, mined the ore and drilled the oil that constituted some of the country's most important exports, and workers had tremendous

---

67 Carr 1976, pp. 62–3.
68 Huitrón 1976, p. 275; Carr 1976, pp. 63–4.
69 Huitrón 1976, p. 275.
70 Knight 1986, vol. 2, pp. 315–21.
71 Knight 1986, vol. 2, p. 318.

social weight in the cities. So Obregón on behalf of Carranza's Constitutionalists began to make overtures to the Casa and other union groups in order to win their support. Operating through his agent the painter Gerardo Murillo, better known by his pseudonym Dr. Atl, the Constitutionalists began negotiations with the Casa, offering to the unionists, as already mentioned, the use of religious buildings which had been seized – the Church of Saint Brígida and the College of Josephine – as well as the print shop of *La Tribuna* newspaper. In addition, Obregón offered to give the unions a large sum of money to support workers who had lost their employment because of the disruption of the revolution. The Carranza wing of the revolution was not only tolerating unions, but also supporting and encouraging them. Under pressure from Obregón, on 12 December 1914 Carranza published a decree recognising the rights of the labour movement as represented by the Casa.[72]

Soon after, Carranza and Obregón, in recognition of the strike in support of the revolution by the newly formed Mexican Electrical Workers Union (SME), turned the operation of the Mexican Telephone and Telegraph Company over to the SME, with union leader Luis N. Morones becoming the manager of the company. Jacinto Huitrón, secretary of the Mechanics Union, rose repeatedly in the Casa assembly to declare that having been given the *Tribuna* print shop, the Catholic church and school, and financial support from Obregón, 'We now have a country to defend. Viva la Revolución!'[73] Several of the anarchists' leaders, throwing aside years of anarchist study groups and schools, debates and resolutions became overnight supporters of a capitalist government.

The Casa leadership, which had earlier been inclined toward Zapata, now held a debate on the question of allying their labour organisation with the Carranza forces, but, with their long anarchist history, the workers at a meeting of more than 1,000 refused to support Carranza or any other faction in the Mexican Revolution. From the workers' anarchist point of view, it was not the revolution that they wanted and they would not take sides. But a group of 67 leaders of the Casa, impressed by the promise of government support for union organisation, ignoring the members' wishes, met in Veracruz and on 17 February 1915 signed a pact with the Carranza government, a decision that represented one of the most significant developments of the Mexican Revolution, establishing a bond between the new capitalist state and a large section of the labour movement.[74]

---

72   La Botz 1988, p. 23.
73   Salazar 1972, vol. 1, p. 75.
74   Gilly 2005, pp. 187–91.

Not all of the anarchists accepted the alliance with the Carranza government. When Huerta outlawed the Casa, a group of anarchists and socialists had gone down to Morelos to join Zapata, becoming advisors to the peasant revolutionary; with the Casa-Carranza pact others now joined them, but they were only a handful.[75]

The Casa leaders who backed Carranza now created the Red Battalions made up of approximately 5,000 workers who joined the Constitutionalist army.[76] It is hard to overstate the importance of the agreement between Carranza and the House of the World Worker. It would aid Carranza in both winning the war in the field and in controlling the cities and establishing what became the modern Mexican government, while at the same time throughout Mexico union organisers took advantage of the government's support to establish new unions. Most important, the relationship between Carranza's party and the Casa established the precedent for the subordination of the unions to that state and its ruling group, a relationship that proved to be decisive for the future of Mexican unions, which would exist principally under the domination and tutelage of the state for decades to come.[77]

The immediate impact of the pact was tremendous. Everywhere that Carranza's army marched, the Casa and other unions organised workers; tens of thousands flooded into the unions. During 1916 and 1917 there was an enormous strike wave as large groups of all sorts from artisans in small shops to industrial workers in plants of thousands struck for shorter work weeks, for higher pay – sometimes 30 or 50 percent higher – and over a variety of other issues. Constitutionalist governors and legislatures passed pro-labour laws in many areas, including the right to unions and collective bargaining, as well as protective legislation. The strike led to the organisation of the Federation of Union of Workers of the Federal District (FSODF) in Mexico City as well as of the Confederación de Trabajadores de la Región Mexicana – Confederation of Workers in the Region of Mexico (CTRM), the first attempt at a united front of all of the country's labour unions. All of this culminated in the unions' call for a general strike in Mexico City on 31 July 1916.[78] Let us return to the 1916 general strike after turning to look at what was happening in the United States with Gompers and the AFL.

---

75   Womack, 1968, p. 193.
76   Carr 1976, p. 68.
77   I have argued this point in my earlier books: La Botz 1988; 1992; 1995.
78   Matute 1983, pp. 283–324.

9   The AFL and Carranza

Samuel Gompers and the AFL, it will be remembered, after having at first supported the Magonistas of the Mexican Liberal Party, changed their allegiance
to Francisco Madero and his Anti-Reelectionist or Democratic Party. With the
overthrow of Madero, the AFL once again had to make a decision about which
leader and party it was backing in Mexico and on what political basis: Zapata?
Villa? Carranza? Gompers and the AFL decided in November of 1914 that they
supported Carranza and went on record as officially endorsing him.

Carranza was now anxious to get the AFL to influence the Wilson administration and win its official recognition. On 5 August 1915 Colonel Edmundo
Martínez, Carranza's representative, who also carried credentials from the Federación de Sindicatos Obreros de la República Mexicana (Federation of Unions
of Workers of the Mexican Republic), a labour organisation based in Veracruz,
sent a letter to Gompers. He explained that the Federación had chosen him 'to
come to the United States to present before the American workingmen our side
of the Mexican case'. He went on to state that, 'The Mexican working people
have chosen Mr. Venustiano Carranza as the leader of the people in its struggle
for freedom and have appointed him the First Chief of its armies on the field'.
He argued that, 'Owing to the desertion from the ranks of Generals Villa and
Zapata, the struggle has been prolonged more than any Mexican desires'. He
claimed that Carranza was the voluntary choice of the Mexican people: 'We
Mexicans are not ruled by Carranza against our will'. He ended his letter with
a plea: 'If General Carranza's Government is recognised, it will be a triumph of
the people. Will you help us do it?' He signed his letter omitting his military
rank.[79]

The formal letter to Gompers represented only one element of what were
various meetings and discussions between Gompers and Martínez and other
representatives of both the Carranza government and the Mexican unions. The
letter was the formal document that Gompers could share with members of the
AFL executive council and with President Wilson. On 22 September 1915, Gompers wrote to Wilson explaining how he saw the Mexico situation:

> Under the Madero government there were the beginnings of a labor
> movement and an effort of the workers to organize for the realization of
> their ideals and for the betterment of themselves and their fellow work-
> ers. This hope was overshadowed by the barbarism of Huerta but again

---

79   Gompers 2003, pp. 305–7.

grew strong and steady when Carranza asserted himself as the leader of the people.

> General Carranza is recognized as the friend of the working people and the real leader of the people generally of Mexico. He has granted to the wage-earners the right of organization and has secured them opportunities for carrying out the legitimate purposes of organization. He has been thoroughly in sympathy with the ideals of greater opportunity and freedom of the masses of the people. The working people have been supporting him. They have adjourned as lodges and trade unions to enlist in the Carranza army with their union officials serving as officers of their regiments.[80]

Gompers stated that, 'The sympathies of the workers of the United States have been very deeply touched by the struggles of our fellow workers of Mexico'. And so, he wrote Wilson:

> It is with the desire that we Americans who have so much liberty and so much opportunity should use our influence to aid those who are less fortunate, that as representatives of the labor movement of America we urge upon you recognition of General Carranza as the head of the Mexican government.[81]

Gompers enclosed in his letter to Wilson the letter that has been sent to him by Martínez.

Wilson did go on to recognise the Carranza government later in October 1915, but probably more as a result of Pancho Villa's raid on Columbus, New Mexico than of Gompers' suggestion.[82] Nevertheless Gompers claimed in a letter to Martínez that the AFL had successfully pressured Wilson, preventing both an invasion of Mexico and winning US recognition.[83] Gompers' support for Carranza put the American union movement on the side of the new Mexican state just as it launched its war against plebeian armies of Zapata and Villa. It also laid the basis for the future collaboration between the AFL and Mexico's state-sponsored unions.

---

80   Gompers 2003, p. 325.
81   Ibid.
82   Knight 1986, vol. 2, pp. 343–4.
83   Gompers 2003, pp. 360–7.

At about the same time that those events were transpiring in Washington, Gompers had succeeded in getting the socialist John Murray to become his ambassador to the Mexican labour movement. In 1915 Murray left for Mexico as a correspondent for *The Call*, the Socialist Party's daily newspaper in New York City. Some accounts say that it was Gompers who actually sent Murray as his emissary to the Mexican labour movement. In any case, Murray had moved to the right, and once in Mexico he conducted himself as a representative of the American Federation of Labor. He met with leaders of the House of the World Worker, who had just signed their agreement with the Carranza government, and tried to convince them to also ally themselves with the American Federation of Labor.

Murray must have been a wonderful talker, for he succeeded in winning over the former anarchists and anarcho-syndicalists to join an alliance with Gompers and the AFL. But, of course, it was not simply that Murray had a great spiel. Murray's meeting with the leaders of the House of the World Worker occurred at a propitious moment. The House of the World Worker had just broken with their own anarcho-syndicalist past and principles, which rejected politics, in order to enter into a political alliance with Carranza's Constitutionalist government. Having broken with their former syndicalism, they now also decided that they would explore an alliance with the much more conservative American Federation of Labor. In both cases, the Casa seems to have been motivated principally by the belief that labour was too weak to fight its own battles and needed the patronage of more powerful allies, first the new Mexican state and second the US unions. The Casa might have affiliated with the Industrial Workers of the World, but presumably rejected such an affiliation because the IWW could not help the Mexican labour movement politically.[84]

Murray was so successful in selling the AFL that the House of the World Worker voted to make him a member of its Revolutionary Committee. One Mexican historian later wrote with some exaggeration, 'John Murray was without a doubt the first international worker ambassador, and consequently a pioneer of continental worker unity'.[85] Hyperbole aside, Murray succeeded in making the first link between the conservative American Federation of Labor and the rightward moving former anarchists of the Mexican House of the World Worker.

When Murray returned to the United States he reported immediately and directly to Gompers at AFL headquarters. Gompers also invited Santiago Igle-

---

84   Leverstein 1971, p. 21.
85   Leverstein 1971, pp. 20–1.

sias who would come to be a key figure in AFL relations to the Mexican unions. Iglesias was the founder of the Free Federation of Workers of Puerto Rico in 1899, and a leader of the Socialist Party of Puerto Rico. He had established ties with the AFL in 1900 and had become a close associate of Gompers.[86] Gompers' two nominally Socialist subordinates, Murray and Iglesias, would help him develop his strategy toward the Mexican labour federation and toward other Latin American unions. Gompers also invited James Lord, head of the AFL Mining Department to join them in planning the AFL strategy for winning over the Mexican labour movement.

10   Gompers Looks toward Mexico and Latin America

Developments encouraged Gompers, Iglesias, Murray and Lord to believe that the AFL should work with Mexican unions and the unions of Caribbean and Latin American nations to launch a continental labour movement, which would later be named the Pan-American Federation of Labor. Gompers had already engaged in what might be called labour imperialism in Canada in the early years of the twentieth centuries, organising craft unions inspired by his business union philosophy.[87] The AFL unions in Canada fought, as they did in the United States, against industrial unionists and labour radicals in a series of battles which were partial successes for the AFL but detrimental to the Canadian union movement overall. Now Gompers had his eyes on Latin America.

Murray's successful meeting with the House of the World Worker laid the basis for US-Mexican union cooperation and also raised the possibility of greater involvement in Latin America. It was Murray who had introduced Gompers to Santiago Iglesias, a Puerto Rican socialist who would later become Gompers' agent in that American colony. Iglesias had been attending the First Pan-American Financial Congress, a meeting of the bankers of the hemisphere held in 1915. He was disturbed that the financiers were organising the to carry out the exploitation of Latin America at the expense of working people and he believed that labour also needed to organise on a pan-American basis in order to resist capital. Gompers found this idea attractive for a number of reasons, not least of which as his desire to extend the American craft union and business union model to Latin America. But Gompers was also disturbed by press

---

86   Whittaker 1968, pp. 378–93; Ojeda Reyes 1987, pp. 311–46.
87   Babcock 1974, *passim*.

reports that the House of the World Worker might be a revolutionary syndicalist organisation like the Industrial Workers of the World, an interpretation shared by the Wobblies themselves. Therefore, Gompers wanted to prevent an alliance between the IWW and Mexican unions, which could potentially threaten his back. And so, Gompers, Murray, Iglesias, and Lord began to conceive of a continental labour organisation to expand the AFL's influence to Latin America and to block the IWW.[88]

Several problems erupted that threatened to disrupt their plans: Catholic opposition, a war threat in Mexico, and Carranza's break with the unions. First was the fact that Frank Duffy, an Irish Catholic and head of the Carpenter's Union, opposed AFL support for the Carranza government, which he accused of attacking the Catholic Church and martyring priests and nuns. This also included a refusal to support the Casa, which was explicitly anti-clerical. The Catholic Church in Rome and in the United States was a fierce opponent of the Mexican Revolution, which was attacking its privileges. In fact, the Mexican Revolutionaries, with the exception of Zapata and his Liberating Army of the South, were very hostile to the Church and often did persecute Catholic priests and nuns. Gompers wrote to Carranza to ask his understanding and opinion of events, but to the best of our knowledge never received a reply. Edmundo Martínez sent a letter in which he said he had been in touch with Carranza and quoted him as saying that he would dismiss anyone accused of persecuting the Church and that under his government there would be complete religious tolerance, with Catholics, Protestants and Jews enjoying equal rights.[89] While this reply appears to have been fabricated to placate the AFL, Gompers was happy to receive it, share it with the AFL Council, and reduce the damage being done by Duffy and the Catholic element.

Second, in January of 1916 Pancho Villa had raided Columbus, New Mexico and executed a number of Americans. In response, President Wilson sent General John 'Back Jack' Pershing into Mexico to punish Villa.

In the United States, Secretary of the Interior Franklin K. Lane, aware of Gompers connections to the Mexican unions and to Carranza, invited Gompers to help him persuade Mexican negotiators, Secretary of the Treasury Luis Cabrera, Ignacio Bonillas and Alberto Pani, to adopt a more conciliatory stand on the issue of the government's nationalist economic policy. Gompers duly met with Mexicans, but they refused to discuss economic policy until Pershing's troops evacuated Mexico. Gompers raised with the Mexican negotiators

88   Sinclair 1960, pp. 7–12.
89   Leverstein 1971, pp. 33–4; Snow 1960, pp. 19–20.

Carranza's actions in the Mexico City strike. 'I added', wrote Gompers later, 'that if that attitude of Carranza was maintained the assistance and cooperation which American Labour gave and was willing to give would be withdrawn'.[90] Gompers failed in his attempt to help negotiate a solution to that conflict, but once again Gompers and the AFL had drawn closer to the US government in an attempt to shape developments in Mexico.

A US anti-war movement opposing this new military intervention in Mexico quickly organised the American Union Against Militarism (AUAM) led by Socialists, anarchists, pacifists and some religious leaders. Gompers himself, however, never opposed Wilson's second invasion of Mexico, and while some AFL leaders met with the AUAM, Gompers worked to keep AFL unions off the streets and out of the Socialist demonstrations and attempted to use his influence to negotiate some settlement.[91]

After Mexican troops and citizens at El Carrizal took US soldiers prisoner in June of 1919, it once again looked like a full-scale war was eminent. Some American soldiers were arrested and at the suggestion of Judge Charles A. Douglas, Carranza's representative in Washington, Gompers sent a telegram to Carranza suggesting that he work to release the US soldiers. Carranza sent a reply to Gompers saying that the prisoners had already been freed.[92] Gompers could once again claim that he and the AFL had helped to save the Mexican government and put it back in the good graces of the United States.[93] Gompers, however, 'refused to criticise the Pershing expedition or repudiate the right of the United States to intervene in Mexico's internal affairs', writes historian Gregg Andrews, adding that, 'Gompers theoretical position can hardly be called "anti-imperialist"'.[94] In any case, all of this led to fear that the United States might invade an initiate a full-scale war with Mexico, which would put all plans on hold.

Yet, to take up the third issue, relations between Carranza and the unions had begun to go sour already in early 1915 and by early 1916 had nearly broken down completely. In January 1916 Carranza ordered the disbanding of the Red Battalions. In some areas the process took place very amicably, though by the end of the month Carranza was also ordering the arrest of some Casa leaders. Constitutionalist General Pablo González dismissed the labour troops with a

---

90   Gompers 1925, vol. 2, pp. 312 and 316; Andrews 1991, p. 66.
91   Andrews 1991, pp. 51–2.
92   Snow 1960, p. 23.
93   Snow 1960, p. 22.
94   Andrews 1991, pp. 45 and 57.

diatribe in which he declared that, 'While the revolution has combatted capitalist tyranny, it cannot now sanction the proletarian tyranny that the workers
especially those in the House of the Worker, intend to impose'.[95]

When finally, after weeks of petitions and appeals to the government to do
something about the problem of inflation and the worthless currency, in Mexico City on 1 August 1916 the unions declared a general strike and 90,000 workers walked out in a movement that affected both private employers and the
government, paralysing the city. Carranza met with the leaders of the unions
and not only refused to negotiate with them, but, using an old law of the Benito
Juárez era of the 1850s, had them arrested for vagrancy and promoting social
rebellion. He also declared martial law and had other union officials arrested as
well, claiming that the strike was unpatriotic and organised by foreign organisations, mentioning the Industrial Workers of the World. He militarised the
railroads, turning workers into soldiers. His decree imposed the death penalty
on those who organised strikes affecting public services, and at least one leader,
Ernesto Velasco of the Electrical Workers, was so charged, arrested and convicted, though his sentence was later commuted to twenty years in prison.[96]
The House of the World Worker closed down voluntarily in order to avoid the
repression, but in doing so it ended forever its role as the centre of the Mexican labour movement. When the strike was over, Carranza approved a wage
increase for the workers, a crass case of repression and concession.[97]

News of this event came to Gompers at the AFL's 1916 Convention meeting
in Baltimore, pouring cold water on his plan for a Pan-American Federation
of Labor. Carranza, the man that Gompers had called 'a friend of the working
people', was at war with the unions.

11   Gompers Goes Ahead with US-Mexico Labour Meeting

Despite his Catholic union members' protests, the Carrizal incident, and Carranza's betrayal of the labour movement, Gompers determined to go ahead
with his attempt to build ties between US and Mexican labour. As one historian suggests, though Gompers plans to cooperate with Carranza may have
been frustrated, he could still salvage a relationship to the Mexican unions.[98]

---

95   Carr 1976, pp. 72–3.
96   Carr 1976, pp. 72–3; Matute 1983, vol. 16, pp. 304–24; Lear 2001, pp. 331–9.
97   González Casanova 1980, vol. 6, p. 21.
98   Leverstein 1971, pp. 33–4; Snow 1960, p. 35.

Without initially consulting the AFL Executive Council, Gompers called for a joint US-Mexican labour conference to be held in El Paso, Texas. Dr. Atl, a Casa intellectual and editor of *Acción Mundial*, a labour newspaper, accepted Gompers invitation, writing that he saw it as an opportunity for the two labour movements to prevent war.[99]

Gompers publicised the event widely, writing a major article in the *American Federationist* in which he discussed both the coming US-Mexico labour meeting and plans for a broader Pan-American Federation of Labor. He wrote:

> Those who know and understand the force of the industrial ties that unite Mexico and the United States know that there is no boundary line between the industrial problems of the workers of the two countries. This is not only because of the overlapping of the interests of the employers of the two countries but because of the intermingling and blending of the workers of the two countries.[100]

Taking up an issue that worried AFL members, Gompers pointed out that two million Mexicans lived and worked in the United States, and he expressed his concern that some had been used during recent strikes as strike-breakers. To end this problem, he wrote, 'There must be understanding and cooperation between the workers of Mexico and the United States in order that neither may permit themselves to be used for the undoing of all'.

In his article Gompers also laid out his vision of the Pan-American Federation of Labor, which would 'help in the establishment of a broad international labour movement of the whole world, and that international parliament of which philosophers have dreamed and poets have sung, and which it is the mission of the workers to establish [and realise]'.[101] The grandiosity of the language should not obscure the fact that Gompers hoped to create a kind of labour international based in the United States, inspired by the AFL, committed to the craft union model and to a philosophy of business unionism.

The Mexican unions agreed to a meeting, but suggested the meeting be held at Eagle Pass. Meanwhile the Eagle Pass meeting to take place in June had at the suggestion of the Mexicans been transformed into an international meeting of labour representatives to discuss how to avoid a US-Mexico War.[102] Then,

---

99   Leverstein 1971, p. 38.
100   Leverstein 1971, pp. 36–7.
101   Leverstein 1971, p. 36.
102   Leverstein 1971, pp. 38–40; Snow 1960, pp. 23–4.

surprisingly, the next initiative in US-Mexican labour relations came not from the Casa or some other union but from General Salvador Alvarado, a northern Constitutionalist general sent by Carranza to become governor of Yucatan. Alvarado, who had been influenced by American progressivism (as discussed in Chapter 1) also championed feminism, labour unionism, and created one of the first models for post-revolutionary labour legislation. Alvarado sent two men who were supposedly labour representatives to the meeting with Gompers and other leaders of the American Federation of Labor. The Yucatan representatives, Carlos Loveira y Chirinos, a Cuban novelist, and Baltazar Pages, a Spanish anarchist and editor of *La Voz de la Revolución* (The Voice of the Revolution) in Yucatan, met with Gompers and expressed their support for a joint US-Mexican labour conference.[103]

Meanwhile the actual union representatives from Mexico City had gone to Eagle Pass for a meeting with the AFL, but when they found no AFL representatives there, they contacted Gompers who suggested that they proceed on to Washington. So, no labour meeting ever took place in Eagle Pass, but Luis N. Morones, a key leader in the Mexican labour movement representing the country's most powerful labour group, the Federación de Sindicatos Obreros del Distrito Federal (FSODF), and his companion Salvador González García, a minor figure representing unions of the Yucatan, arrived in Washington in June of 1916. A conference was then held involving Gompers, Murray, the AFL Council from the United States and Morones, González García, Edmundo Martínez, Carlos Loveira and Baltazar Pages from Mexico to discuss the creation of a Pan-American Federation of Labor.

When Loveira, the novelist, apparently naively asked if the Industrial Workers of the World would be permitted to participate in such a Pan-American Federation, Gompers replied forcefully that the IWW would certainly not be welcome. Gompers insisted that the basis for the Pan-American Federation of Labor (PAFL) would be the American Federation of Labor's philosophy and structure. The AFL was the model for unionism throughout the Americas, asserted Gompers, and the Mexicans acquiesced agreeing to join in a common venture.[104]

The US and Mexican unionists came to an agreement and announced on 3 July 1916 that they were calling for another larger and more representative conference, which would create a Pan-American Federation of Labor, but because of the current political situation they would have to postpone the

---

103   Snow 1960, pp. 35–6.
104   Andrews 1991, p. 62.

meeting for a year. The unionists from both countries urged the labour movements to provide a way for the masses of the US and Mexican people to express themselves in international affairs and called upon the US and Mexican government to create a citizens' commission to help resolve problems between the two governments.[105]

There was a most serious problem, however. The Casa had ceased to exist, so that there was in Mexico no national organisation of labour. The so-called labour representatives who had met with the AFL, with the exception of Morones, either really represented Mexican political leaders or small and ephemeral organisations. And, of course, the tensions between the United States and Mexico continued, as did Mexico's civil war. Nevertheless, Gompers, Murray, Iglesias, and Lord pushed on, determined to create a pan-American labour organisation.

12   In Pursuit of the Pan-American Federation of Labor

The term 'Pan-American' had a history going back a quarter of a century. Pan-Americanism was a term associated with a series of conferences beginning in 1890 initiated by former US Secretary of State James G. Blaine in an attempt to establish greater US domination over the political and economic life of the Americas. While couched in terms of international cooperation, the term might be called the popular name for American imperialism in Latin America in that era. Gompers now intended to extend Pan-Americanism to the labour movement of the Western hemisphere, what I have called labour imperialism. Gompers' Pan-American Federation of Labor (PAFL) would serve several purposes. First, it would align the AFL foreign policy with that of Wilson and served to enhance the AFL's reputation in the White House. Second, it would block the Industrial Workers of the World in Mexico and in other countries of Latin America. Third, it would enhance Gompers' reputation with American corporations, such as those he worked with in the National Civic Federation that had investments in Latin America. Finally, and above all, it would provide Gompers with a vehicle with which to expand his business union model to all of Latin America.

The November 1916 AFL convention gave Gompers authority to create the Pan-American Federation of Labor Conference Committee. A conference committee made up of Gompers, Murray, Iglesias, and Loveira, met in January 1917

---

105   Snow 1960, pp. 33–4.

and then issued a manifesto in February calling upon unions in other Latin American countries to join in creating the new continental labour federation. 'If the employers, the capitalists, of Pan-America thus united for the protection of their common advantage', read the manifesto, 'it becomes all the more evident that the wage earners of these countries must also unite for their common protection and betterment'.[106] The Manifesto called for workers of the Americas to join together to fight for higher wages, shorter workdays, and healthier and safer workplaces. The committee's Manifesto opposed child labour and argued for the rights of free association and assembly, free speech and press, and the right to strike. Few Latin American unions responded to the AFL's call, though Antonio Correa of Cuba and Cardenio González of Chile did join the Conference Committee.[107]

Under the tutelage of Gompers, the Yucatan representatives, Loveira and Pages, wrote a pamphlet called *El movimiento obrero de los Estados Unidos* (The Labour Movement of the United States), which laid out the philosophy, purposes, and structure of the American Federation of Labor as a model for Latin American unionists. The AFL distributed the pamphlet to Latin American unions in March of 1917. Gompers and his allies intended to provide Latin union leaders and workers with an alternative to both anarcho-syndicalism and socialism.[108] Still, though there was now a manifesto and a pamphlet, the AFL had no real partner in Mexico and virtually no takers in Latin America.

Developments in Mexico, however, began to create the conditions for a new Mexican labour movement. The general strike of 1916 had been a turning point in Mexico and it was out of that defeat that General Álvaro Obregón, leader of what has been called the Jacobin wing of the Constitutionalists, came to the conclusion that a new sort of state was necessary.[109] Carranza remained at heart a landlord and a bourgeois politician, but Obregón and his allies who had emerged from the revolution, more petty-bourgeois and populist in origin and character, recognised the need for a different sort of government and a new labour movement. They wanted a regulatory state but one that could enter into a long-term social pact with a new and more pragmatic labour movement. They would have to create both.

---

106   Snow 1960, pp. 41–4.
107   Ibid.
108   Snow 1960, p. 48.
109   Gilly 2005, p. 236.

13   The New Constitution and Article 123

Under pressure from the leaders of the army, Carranza called a Constitutional Convention in which 151 delegates, many of them officers in the Constitution-alist Army as well as political leaders and intellectuals participated in deliber-ations that lasted from 1 December 1916 to 31 January 1917. The Constitution of 1917 did many things, among the most important eliminating the role of the Church in education and establishing national, lay, public education, claim-ing the subsoil (that is, mineral and oil wealth) for the nation, and establishing rights and protections for labour.[110] Article 123 not only legitimised the exist-ence and activities of unions, including strikes, but also created protective legislation – the eight-hour day, a minimum wage commission, banned child labour, and protected pregnant women, among others – fulfilling the earlier agreements between the Constitutionalists and the House of the World Worker. At the heart of Article 123 were the Boards of Conciliation and Arbitration (*Juntas de Conciliación y Arbitraje*) to mediate labour disputes. The employ-ers denounced it as a 'Bolshevik' law while the anarchists refused to accept the right of the government to control in any way the workers' movement. Never-theless, it was now the law of the land, though it would take a while to work out what the new law meant in practice.

The Mexican Constitution's Article 123 has often been described as the most progressive labour law anywhere in the world at that time, but at the same time – reflecting the influence of both American Progressivism and European Socialism – its purpose was to impose state regulation on both capital and labour. Strikes, for example, were legal only when they contributed to balancing the power of capital and labour.[111] At first the capitalists did not understand all that they had won, and, as Pablo González Casanova writes, 'the anarchists who had achieved great influence in the culture and workers' consciousness, refused to recognise their defeat. They would continue striving for the project of a soci-ety without a state and a state without politics, subjected to new defeats that would convert them into a mere chorus raising its laments and protests against the constitutional evils and the renascent bourgeoisie'.[112] Obregón and the Jac-obin wing of the Constitutionalist, however, shared a growing sense of their

---

110   Constitución Federal.
111   Article 123, §XVIII reads in the original: 'Las huelgas serán lícitas cuando tengan por objeto conseguir el equilibrio entre los diversos factores de la producción, armonizando los derechos del trabajo con los del capital'.
112   González Casanova 1980, vol. 6, p. 11.

own power and of its possibilities, and they would in the process of channelling workers' struggles into the new legal structures create both the new state and the new labour movement.[113]

The Constitutional Convention's adoption of the Constitution and Article 123 guaranteeing the right to union organisation and to strike led to a wave of strikes of unprecedented proportions involving tens of thousands of factory workers and other labourers throughout 1917 and 1918. Workers in Mexico City, Puebla, and Tlaxcala, but in other states as well, struck for shorter hours, higher pay, and a variety of other issues and demanded that the government use its new power as mediator to resolve the issues of the strike in their favour. Governors and state legislators created boards of conciliation and arbitration or political leaders simply intervened and mediated the disputes themselves. While the outcomes proved to be highly diverse, some victorious and some defeated, repression alternating with concessions, still gradually more and more the state intervened granting concessions to the unions. Through this process the Mexican governing class learned to use its new power, workers learned to accommodate to the new Constitution and to the emerging state laws, and the employers gradually accepted that their powers were no longer unlimited but that they too could protect and even advance their interests through the new labour institutions. Soon the government was intervening to oversee the negotiation of contracts in a variety of industries.[114]

Not long after the adoption of this Constitution and its remarkable labour article, an effort was made to organise a new Mexican labour movement. Since Carranza's smashing of the 1916 strike and repression of the House of the World Worker, Mexico had had no national labour union. But in 1918 Governor Gustavo Espinosa Mireles of Coahuila, a Constitutionalist leader and part of the Jacobin wing allied with Obregón, called for a labour conference to be held in Saltillo on 1 May 1918. The conference was attended by 120 delegates of 113 labour organisations and represented most of the important industrial workers in the country: miners, railroad workers, textile workers, metal workers, electrical workers, dock workers, and streetcar workers as well as construction workers, such as carpenters and painters, and there were also unions of shoemakers and agricultural workers as well as members of cooperatives. 'Really the conference represented the great majority of the organised industrial proletariat and of the urban artisans of the of centre, the north, and the gulf; of the Federal District, Guadalajara, Puebla and Veracruz'.

---

113   González Casanova 1980, vol. 6, p. 23.
114   González Casanova 1980, vol. 6, pp. 24–85.

There were anarchists, former members of the Casa, and members of the Industrial Workers of the World.[115]

Governor Mireles, his Secretary of Labour Juan Lozano and Luis N. Morones had organised the meeting, and Morones was elected to chair it; not surprisingly at the end he emerged as the general secretary of the Regional Confederation of Mexican Workers (CROM). During several days of deliberation, the conference organisers and the authors of the various resolutions took great care to avoid differences with the anarchists, to sidestep language that would threaten the capitalists, and to prevent criticism of politicians or government officials. Nor was there any mention of expropriating the means of production. While maintaining some anarcho-syndicalist symbolism and rhetoric, the CROM stood for a political alliance with the Mexican government and a reformist approach to the employers.[116] The founding of the CROM represented a turning point for the Mexican workers' movement, a turn away from anarchism and toward pragmatism; it also provided Gompers with what he had been seeking, a genuine Mexican labour organisation, national in scope, moderate in its views, and interested in a partnership with the US labour movement.

14 A New Set of Circumstances: World War and the Russian Revolution

Since Gompers had first begun thinking about creating a hemispheric labour federation two really world-shaking events intervened, forcing Gompers both to re-think his project and to take action to realise it. First, World War I had broken out in August 1914, and this became a new motive for organising the Pan-American Federation of Labor. Since the outbreak of World War I, Gompers had ignored or opposed attempts by the United Mine Workers and other unions to organise a labour-based anti-war movement, and instead, helped along by the National Civic Federation, Gompers moved in the direction of munitions manufacturers and the British Embassy which sought materiel from the United States for their war with the Central Powers made up of Germany, Austria-Hungary, and the Ottoman Empire. By 1916 Gompers had become an advisor to President Wilson's Council of National Defence, joining the president in the policy of national preparedness and ready to follow him to war. Working with Wilson, Gompers became involved in efforts to prevent a Mex-

---

115   González Casanova 1980, vol. 6, pp. 72–3.
116   González Casanova 1980, vol. 6, pp. 61–85.

ican alliance with Germany.[117] The creation of a Pan-American Federation of Labor, both Wilson and Gompers realised, could help cement the labour organisations of the two countries and could also pressure the Mexican government to drop its stance of neutrality and pro-German attitude.

Second, the Bolshevik or Soviet Revolution of October 1917 had taken place, and it soon became clear that Bolshevism, that is, Communism, would become a new force in the world's labour movements and in politics. The Socialist or Second International had broken up at the outbreak of the First World War when most of its members violated the organisation's earlier resolutions against militarism and war and rallied to their own national governments. But working-class internationalists found a new inspiration, symbol, and model in the Russian Revolution of October 1917. The Bolshevik Revolution attracted the support of working-class militants around the world, socialists, syndicalists, and anarchists, as well as, some middle-class intellectuals, colonial nationalists, and some members of the civilian and military elites of various nations.[118]

The Communist International, founded in 1919, appeared as a new centre of proletarian internationalism and political power. Given the ten years of violence and the anarcho-syndicalist rhetoric of the Mexican Revolution, Mexico appeared to many in the American government and business groups as a dangerous breeding ground for Bolshevism. Gompers viewed the new Bolshevik or Communist movement as a dangerous threat and as a blood enemy of the US and Mexican labour movements. He was determined to isolate and destroy Bolshevism – and the Pan-American Federation of Labor would be one of the principal tools he would use.

15   The Founding of the Pan-American Federation of Labor

Finally, after many months, acting on the suggestion of Carranza's representative Judge Douglas, who felt it was necessary to combat Mexican neutrality in World War I, Gompers decided to call for the initial conference of the Pan-American Federation of Labor. In May of 1918 Gompers sent an AFL delegation made up of Murray, Lord and Iglesias to visit Morones and the CROM in Mexico City. The delegation's secret mission was to win Carranza's support for the Allied war effort. The three unionists met with the US embassy, Carranza, and then with the CROM leaders. While attacked by pro-German newspapers and

---

117   Andrews 1991, p. 37.
118   Ferro 1967, *passim*.

Mexican leftists and criticised by some CROM leaders for their position on the IWW, Murray, Lord and Iglesias succeeded in getting the CROM to agree to a labour conference to be held in Laredo, Texas on 3 November 1918. A Mexican delegation, consisting of Morones of the CROM and Salvador Álvarez of the Federal District Unions, visited Washington in June of 1918 and met with Murray, Iglesias, and the AFL Executive Council to make final arrangements.

Gompers hoped to get the US government to finance the Pan-American Federation of Labor, but initially met with rejection from President Wilson. Wilson, however, soon overcame his reluctance and decided to provide covert funding for the PAFL through George Creel's Committee on Public Information (CPI), Wilson's wartime propaganda machine, and through its labour arm, the American Alliance for Labour and Democracy (AALD), an organisation created by Gompers to fight pacifism and socialism. The CPI and AALD would provide funds for organisation and for the publications of the Pan-American Labor Press, some 50,000 copies a week. Chester Wright, the former editorialist for the Socialist Party's newspaper *The Call*, worked in press and public relations for both the AALD and the CPI, and he now also became involved in establishing the Pan-American Labor Press.[119] The AFL set up headquarters for the Pan-American Labor Press in San Antonio, Texas, and Murray, Iglesias and Lord took responsibility for editing and publishing the weekly, bilingual newspaper to promote the conference. Wilson's role in footing the bill for the conference was not known at the time, but only the most naïve could believe that Gompers movement was independent of the US government. Thus, began what would become a decades long history of US funding for American unions operating abroad, a practice that continues today.

US and Mexican labour unionists met in Laredo, Texas from 13–16 November 1918, just two days after the end of World War I to found the PAFL. Some 72 delegates were present at the PAFL Founding Congress: the AFL was represented by 46 delegates, the Mexicans by 21, while Guatemala, El Salvador, Costa Rica and Colombia each had one. President Wilson dispatched Secretary of Labour William B. Wilson to attend, and President Carranza sent General Pablo de la Garza.[120] Samuel Gompers served as chairman, and Luis N. Morones as vice-chairman. In addition to founding the PAFL as a permanent international labour alliance, the convention faced three key questions: Woodrow Wilson's peace proposals, Mexican labour migrants and their treatment in the United States, and the Industrial Workers of the World.

---

119   Andrews 1991, pp. 81–6.
120   'Pan-American' 1918, pp. 601–5.

Gompers wanted the Mexican labour unionists to join him in supporting Woodrow Wilson's proposals to be carried to the Paris peace conference, but the Mexican were reluctant to do so, perhaps both out of their own convictions and for fear of being criticised by Mexican leftists. Gompers also asked the Mexicans to support the proposals of the Inter-Allied Labour and Socialist Conference held in 1918, proposals that were virtually identical to Wilson's Fourteen Points presented in Paris. The Mexicans opposed the proposal's call for a League of Nations and disliked the proposal's opposition to economic nationalism, but fundamentally the Mexicans wanted to avoid voting on issues of US foreign policy for fear of being seen as pawns of the US State Department. Gompers demanded that the Mexicans vote in favour of the proposals, but Morones, saying they disagreed refused. Gompers became infuriated and shouted, 'Yes, sir; you will'.[121] Eventually a compromise was reached. The Mexicans agreed to sign as individuals but said that they would take the motions back to their union members for approval.

The second issue was the question of Mexican migrant labourers in the United States. CROM leader Morones raised the issue of racial discrimination in the United States against Mexican workers. The AFL and the CROM agreed to investigate the issue of discrimination in the United States and to establish AFL-CROM offices in border cities to deal with problems. The AFL also agreed that Mexican workers in the United States should be allowed to join AFL unions on an equal basis with US union members.

Third, there was the question of discrimination within the US labour movement. Morones union, the FSODF, put forward a resolution charging the AFL with discrimination against Mexican workers and calling for an end to it. H.S. McCluskey of the Mine, Mill and Smelters Union responded by accusing the Mexican workers of failing to join and support the AFL unions. Then, too, Mexican unions wanted their members' union cards to be honoured in the United States without having to pay AFL initiation fees. William Green of the AFL claimed preposterously that the American federation did not discriminate against Mexicans when it came to union membership. In the end these matters were papered over with promises.[122]

The fourth and final big issue was the question of the members of the Industrial Workers of the World who had been imprisoned for their labour or anti-war activities. The Mexican delegates put forward a resolution: 'That an agreement be reached as to the best way for finding honorable means to exert

121   Leverstein 1971, p. 89.
122   Snow 1960, pp. 82–90.

influence so that justice and protection be imparted to those working men who for various reasons, are deprived of their liberty in the jails of the United States'.[123] When Gompers asked to whom this resolution referred, Mexican delegate Rafael Quintero informed him that it referred to the jailed members of the IWW. The Mexicans even suggested that the AFL had cooperated with the US government in the violent suppression of the IWW during the war, and in the jailing of the IWW leaders. Gompers responded by violently attacking the IWW and the Soviet Bolsheviks:

> The I.W.W.'s in the United States are exactly what the Bolsheviki are in Russia, and we have seen what the I.W.W. Bolsheviki in Russia have done for the working people of Russia, where the people have no peace, no security, no land and no bread.[124,125]

Charles H. Moyers, a famous former Wobbly who had accompanied Gompers and the AFL to the convention, also warned the Mexicans against the IWW. With Gompers clearly opposed to any concessions on the IWW issue, the resolution was defeated. The Mexicans, who had lost on the issues they had raised, nevertheless went along with the conference majority. Gompers and the AFL delegates left the Laredo meeting leading the CROM by a leash. Gompers had succeeded in subordinating the Mexican unions, just as the United States had politically subjugated Mexico, as US banks and corporations had for many years dominated the Mexican economy.

The Mexican government also paid its respects to the AFL. In April of 1918, General Álvaro Obregón, a major figure in Carranza's Constitutionalist army, visited the United States, met with important figures in the US government, and also conferred with Gompers. Obregón, the Mexican leader closest to the labour movement at the time, provided Gompers with letters of introduction to help further the organisation of the PAFL.[126] A few years later Obregón would call upon Gompers again for more serious help.

The Second Congress of the PAFL took place in New York City on 7 July 1919, with 25 delegates from the US, Mexico, Guatemala, El Salvador, Honduras, Peru, Ecuador, the Dominican Republic, Costa Rica, Chile and Argentina. Again, Gompers presided over this convention, which authorised him to represent various Latin American unions at the International Federation of Trade

---

123   Snow 1960, p. 84.
124   Andrews 1991, p. 90.
125   Snow 1960, p. 55.
126   Snow 1960, p. 55.

Unions (or Amsterdam International). In this way, Gompers parlayed his success in Mexico and Latin America into a larger role in Europe and the world labour movement. In Paris in 1919, while heads of state met to discuss the peace, international labour organisations also met. Gompers, his authority enhanced by the creation of the PAFL, chaired that conference which created the International Labour Organisation (ILO).[127]

In Mexico, the most violent decade of the revolution was nearly over. Carranza had had General Pablo González assassinate Emiliano Zapata. Pancho Villa's army had been defeated and the revolution's greatest general was reduced to fighting small rear-guard guerrilla actions with no hope of victory. General Felipe Ángeles' attempt to create an alternative military force around a moderate political programme had failed completely. The country was nearly at peace. But then 1919 brought a new crisis.

Elections for president were to be held in 1920. Since the revolution had been fought over opposition to presidential succession in office, Carranza could not be a candidate – but he did want to choose his successor. He chose his friend, Ignacio Bonillas, an engineer who Carranza had made the Mexican ambassador to the United States in 1917. Bonillas had had virtually nothing to do with the Mexican Revolution, neither with its military struggles, nor with its peasant and worker upheavals, and one suspects that Carranza thought that once Bonillas was elected he would be no more than Carranza's puppet. Pablo González, one of Carranza's generals – the organiser of the murder of Zapata – also pretended to the presidency but had little following. General Álvaro Obregón, on the other hand, had been a central military figure in the revolution and had supported both peasant and labour movements. He too announced his candidacy for president in 1919. While Obregón's programme appeared moderate, only calling for a more democratic government and not touching on social issues or explicitly differing with the Carranza's Constitutionalist administration, he was understood to be a candidate of the popular movements, as demonstrated by his alliance with the Zapatistas.[128]

When in March of 1920 Carranza attempted to have Obregón arrested, the general fled and began to organise his supporters first in Sonora and then throughout the country. Again, the revolution was divided, though this time, there would be no civil war. When in April Obregón issued his *Plan de Agua Prieta* calling for the removal of Carranza and the appointment of Adolfo de la Huerta as provisional president, the army rallied behind the Sonoran general,

127   Snow 1960, pp. 95–101.
128   Gilly 2005, pp. 298–315.

as did worker and peasant organisations. Carranza, militarily and politically isolated, fled Mexico City toward Veracruz, pursued by the forces of Obregón and the Zapatistas. Carranza's entourage of military and civilian aids gradually deserted him as he fled until his former bodyguards murdered Carranza in his sleep in the town of Tlaxcalantongo. He was killed on 21 May 1920. Congress, which had already backed Obregón, chose Adolfo de la Huerta as interim president and when elections were held in 1920, if the official count is to be believed, Obregón won 95 percent of the approximately 1,180,000 votes cast, becoming the elected president of Mexico.[129]

Even before he became president, Obregón had established an alliance with Morones and the CROM. Obregón and the CROM had signed a secret pact on 6 August 1919 that only became known years later, an agreement in which the presidential candidate promised to appoint a Secretary of Labour acceptable to the CROM and to deal directly with the CROM about labour issues. As historian Pablo González Casanova makes clear, this was a key development in modern Mexican history, writing that, 'With their "secret pact" the labour leaders and the Sonoran *caudillos* [de la Huerta, Obregón, and Calles] laid the foundation of the new state'.[130] The first step in the creation of the Mexican corporate state had been the pact of Veracruz between Carranza's forces (a pact arranged by Obregón through Dr. Atl) back in 1914, and the second step was the secret pact between Obregón and the CROM. Mexico would be a corporate state in which the ruling political elite held sway over the unions and would continue to do so throughout the twentieth century.

At about the same time, the CROM, under Morones' leadership, had formed its own political party, the Partido Laborista Mexicano (Mexican Labour Party or PLM) in May of 1919. Morones and the other PLM leaders had met with Bonillas, González, and Obregón and chosen to support the latter because of his full acceptance of the PLM's goals, which we now know were later agreed to in the secret pact. While this party claimed to be the completely independent representative of the workers, it would in reality become an organisation, like the CROM, that mediated between the Sonoran dynasty and the working class. The CROM and the PLM became the crucial social supports of the new Obregón government, and the government became the defender of the CROM and its unions.

While Morones was forming the alliance with Obregón, he was also firming up his relationship with Gompers. In the United States, since 1918, Albert

---

129   Ibid.
130   González Casanova 1980, vol. 6, p. 105.

Bacon Fall, the Senator from New Mexico who fought for the interests of his friend the oilman Edward L. Doheny and other Mexican oil investors and mining interests, had taken advantage of the anti-Bolshevik hysteria in the United States to pressure the Wilson administration to break off relations with Carranza with the goal of a US military attack on Mexico to protect US investments there.[131] Morones sought Gompers' support in opposing a US military intervention, travelling to attend the AFL convention in June 1919 as a fraternal delegate and following up afterwards with more pleas for the federation's assistance. At the same time, Morones, now an Obregón supporter, told Gompers and the AFL leadership that Carranza intended to restrict the right to strike. Gompers and Morones mobilised the PAFL officers to protest against the Carranza government. When Carranza was overthrown and assassinated, Gompers, like Morones, quickly moved to support the new Obregón government.[132]

Obregón, understanding the value of the CROM-AFL relationship, sent Morones to ask Gompers to arrange a meeting between the Mexican government's attorney Myron M. Parker and the Wilson administration. The US government feared that the Constitution's Article 27 would be used to seize the American-owned oil wells in Mexico. At Gompers' urging, Parker met with the State Department's Mexican Affairs Office and assured them his government would not jeopardise US investments in Mexico. Gompers also set up a meeting of himself, Morones, and Canuto Vargas, the PAFL secretary, with Wilson's private secretary Joseph Tumulty and Secretary of State Bainbridge Colby. Morones assured the State Department that the Obregón government could be trusted to respect American property. Nevertheless, a strike wave during de la Huerta's brief interim presidency troubled American investors and led the US government to send several diplomatic notes protesting the Mexican government's decisions favouring labour over capital.

With tensions rising, Gompers sent his emissaries Lord and Wright to Mexico City to personally deliver a note expressing his support to de la Huerta and Obregón. Gompers and Morones arranged to hold the PAFL Convention in Mexico City in 1921. While in Mexico for the convention, with Morones' help, Gompers delivered letters from Wilson and the State Department to Obregón and discussed with the Mexican president the American concerns about Article 27. Obregón promised that he would have it declared unconstitutional.[133] But that never happened, and 17 years later it would be used by President Láz-

---

131   La Botz 1991, pp. 92–4.
132   Andrews 1991, pp. 99–100.
133   Andrews 1991, pp. 100–1.

aro Cárdenas to expropriate the British and American oil companies in Mexico, just as the oil companies and the US government had feared.

While Gompers succeeded in winning over the CROM, the left wing of the Mexican labour movement nevertheless remained critical and opposed to the project. As Rosendo Salazar, a veteran of the Casa later wrote, 'at bottom, the fraternity invoked by [Gompers] the head of the American Federation of Labor ... was rather a certain imperialist proposal for the absorption of the organised working class in Mexico'.[134] The Mexican labour left, the anarchists and the Communists, would in reaction organise their own labour organisation, the *Confederación General de Trabajo* (CGT – General Confederation of Workers), still calling for a workers' revolution in Mexico. With the government's backing the CROM succeeded in driving the CGT from the field. The government-sponsored unions proved victorious. The CROM continued to work with the AFL, while the AFL continued to dominate the PAFL throughout its brief history, until the international federation became non-functional by 1928 and finally formally dissolved in 1934.

In his autobiography Gompers wrote:

> Our labor movement has never been associated with any efforts to secure economic concessions or struggle for world markets; hence, we are not handicapped by having to explain or defend our motives. It is accepted that our motive is always to advance human welfare and what better principle is there upon which to square international policies?[135]

But in reality, the phenomenal growth of capitalism in the United States in the late nineteenth century and America's rise to political power and financial dominance throughout the hemisphere had also lifted the AFL to a prominent role in the labour movement of the Americas where, as the junior partner of the State Department, it worked to stop leftist unions in Mexico and other Latin American countries and to prevent them from opposing US political and economic interests. In the end, Gompers proved successful in building his PAFL as a bulwark against the IWW, the anarchists, and later the Communists. The business union model, the partnership between labour and capital, however, did not become dominant in Mexico. While in the United States the partnership was between the bosses and the unions, in Mexico there was a different model, that of a partnership between the state and the unions. In both coun-

---

134   Salazar 1972, vol. 1, p. 157.
135   Gompers 1925, vol. 2, p. 320.

tries with their distinct forms of unionism, capitalist interests were defended and enhanced, but the mechanisms were different. In fact, there was not much of a market for business unionism anywhere in Latin America where under-development, lack of democracy, and the history of anarchism and socialism made such unionism marginal. Nevertheless, Gompers' PAFL, an instrument of US labour imperialism, served to advance American economic and political interests.

PART 2

Americans Organise on the Ground in Mexico

∵

Introduction to Part 2

The American labour and left movement had become deeply involved in organising solidarity with the Mexican Revolutionary movements of the period of 1900 to 1917, first with Ricardo Flores Magón and the Mexican Liberal Party (PLM), then with Francisco Madero and his Anti-Reelectionist Party (later the Progressive Constitutionalist Party), and then with Venustiano Carranza and the Constitutionalists (Liberal Constitutionalist Party), but it had done so mostly from the American side of the US-Mexico border. There were magazine articles and books about Porfirio Díaz and the evils of his regime: its lack of democracy, its violence, its exploitation of labour. The American Federation of Labor and the Socialist Party had passed resolutions condemning Díaz and supporting his opponents. Labour and the left organised meetings and protest demonstrations against the Mexican government and in support of the democratic and left movements opposing it. The Industrial Workers of the World and the anarchists in the Southwest had gone further, crossing the border to support the Mexican Liberal Party with disastrous results for the far left of the Mexican movement.

By 1917, however, everything had changed. After a year of debate, on 5 February 1917, Mexico's Constitutionalists led by Venustiano Carranza – by then winning the civil war against the Conventionists of Pancho Villa and Emiliano Zapata – had held a convention and adopted the Constitution of 1917. A new Mexican capitalist state was born. Then, in April of 1917, the United States entered World War I on the side of the Triple Entente Alliance of Britain, France, and Russia. Next, in October of 1917 the Bolsheviks overthrew the Kerensky government in Russia and thrust power into the hands of the *soviets* or workers' councils, creating the new government of Soviet Russia. These developments changed completely the political landscape in which relations between the American and the Mexican labour and left movements took place. In the United States the Woodrow Wilson government engaged in the severe repression of the Socialist Party and the Industrial Workers of the World and of all who opposed the US role in the World War. In Mexico, the Carranza government welcomed American war resisters and leftists who seemed to be useful allies in resisting the pressures of the United States. And in Soviet Russia, the Bolsheviks, now called the Communists, convened the Communist International and began to organise a worldwide revolutionary movement, soon recruiting representatives of the Mexican Socialist Party and then sending Communist organisers to Mexico.

In this new period, American leftists no longer simply supported the Mexican Revolution from the United States, sometimes engaging in small, armed

incursions along the US-Mexico border, rather a group of leftists became political exiles in Mexico and took up organising with their Mexican counterparts.
In 1917, the group known as the 'slackers', that is, American anti-war activists,
draft resisters and draft evaders, fled to Mexico in 1917 and soon became active in the Mexican left and in the unions and helped to found the Mexican
Communist Party. These men and women also collaborated with leaders of
the Mexican peasant leagues and organised other radical organisations, among
them the Mexican Administration of the Industrial Workers of the World and
the Feminist Council of Mexico. While the word 'slacker' had derogatory connotations in the United States, in Mexico it came to mean both an anti-war
activist and working-class internationalist. Some slackers adopted the word as
a badge of honour: it meant they opposed the war and continued the fight for
socialism. Under the impact of the Russian Revolution, and the opportunities
created by the Mexican Revolution, a few of the American slackers came to
form part of an international radical elite of professional revolutionaries and
Communist cadres.

   During World War I and shortly after, Americans took the floor in the Mexico City union halls, led picket lines at the oil refineries and shipping docks in
Tampico, helped organise a socialist feminist group in Mexico City, and carried the Industrial Workers of the World and the Communist Party to workers
in cities and factory towns, and even to peasant groups in the countryside
in various parts of Mexico. Throughout the war and into the early 1920s, the
slackers' opposition to the war and their escape from the draft made them
objects of the scorn of angry American patriots, and subjects of surveillance
by the US government intelligence agencies. They were, in the eyes of politicians, the press, and much of the public, turncoats and traitors. Newspapers in
the United States reported on the American reds in Mexico – such as Roberto
Haberman, Linn A.E. Gale, Charles Francis Phillips, Irwin Granich, Hendrik
Glintenkamp, Herman Levine, and José Allen – as alleged dangerous conspirat-
ors who, supposedly working with the Mexican revolutionary government, the
Kaiser's military, and the Russian Bolsheviks, threatened subversion or perhaps
even revolution from the dark underbelly of America.

   While there was a kernel of truth in all of these fantastic claims, the danger
from the slackers in Mexico was never exactly what the American press and
politicians imagined or suggested. The real threat to American business and
government was their vision of working-class internationalism and their attempt to create a revolutionary party linking the Mexican and US labour movements to the revolutionary labour movement in Soviet Russia and Europe.
This was a project only adumbrated, and which never became a reality during
that period. In 1921 Mexican President Álvaro Obregón expelled several of the

leading slacker activists as part of the political settlement ending the conflicts between revolutionary Mexico and the United States.

But, just as the Mexican government was expelling the first group of war resisters as 'pernicious foreigners', other American radical activists arrived in Mexico. The members of this second group – Louis Fraina, and Bertram D. Wolfe, and the Japanese Sen Katayama, who had lived in the United States – had also been socialist anti-war activists, but only found their way to Mexico after the war ended, taking up the work of labour and socialist organising where the earlier war-time exile group had left off. Fraina and Katayama went voluntarily to organise for the Communist International, while Wolfe was a refugee from the United States government's persecution of the Communist Party in the early 1920s. Though the Communist organisers are not usually included under the rubric of the famous slackers of World War I, their social and political origin was nearly identical: they came out of the left wing of the Socialist Party, they had similar experiences as socialist conscientious objectors, and they had engaged in common activities as American radical activists in the socialist and labour movement. As American socialist opponents of war who also became Communists and organised in Mexico, they form part of the same saga.

As the Socialist Party, the Industrial Workers of the World, and other radical organisations were being suppressed in the United States, the slackers attempted to keep those movements alive in Mexico. Consequently, the story of the slackers in Mexico represents the transportation to foreign soil of America's Progressive Era radical and social movements. But in Mexico, those movements immediately fell under the influence of and became subordinated to the Mexican revolutionary process and the rise of the new nationalist state. Moreover, that process of political transmigration took place under the profound impact of the Russian Bolshevik or Soviet Revolution, which transformed both the American and the Mexican radical movements and their ideologies and created a new kind of revolutionary: the Communist.

The slackers' Communist activities grew out of their unique experience as political exiles. World War I was the first time in American history that a group of radicals felt they had to flee abroad not only to escape the draft, but also to continue their left-wing political activities. The slackers were political refugees, and their exile represented a particularly wrenching – and in some cases exhilarating – psychological, social, and political experience. As exiles the Americans became aliens, strangers in a roiling, revolutionary land. Banished from their own country, without economic resources, without jobs or incomes, without political contacts, without a knowledge of the language and culture, like immigrants and refugees everywhere, they had first to find a way to survive. Survival in Mexico meant that the socialist slackers had to invent a new

personal and political identity. For most of those we discuss, the role they chose
was that of the international socialist, the Bolshevik, the Communist. How did
these American Socialists come to believe that they should continue their activities as Communists?

The Revolution in Russia in 1917 (the October Revolution) was followed
almost immediately by the Soviet government's announcement that it was
withdrawing from the war. To anti-war activists it seemed like a whole nation
behaving like a socialist conscientious objector. An entire people simply refused to serve, refused to fight. The American slackers and other socialists and
pacifists around the world became convinced by that experience of a simple
but enormously powerful idea: peace by revolution. If socialist revolution had
brought peace to Russia, it could bring peace to other countries as well. If
revolutions like the one that had taken place in Russia were carried out in other
countries, the socialist anti-war activists reasoned, a new, global, socialist society would bring peace to the entire world. The slackers thus moved from being
at first supporters of the Russian Revolution to being supporters of Soviet Russia, and then of the Bolshevik Party (soon to be called the Communist Party).
But in 1917, the year of the founding of the Communist International, 'Communist' was itself an identity still in the making. As the French-Russian Victor
Serge wrote about the years 1919 and 1920, 'To tell the truth, outside Russia and
perhaps Bulgaria, there were no real Communists anywhere in the world'.[1]

While Serge was writing about Europe, his claim would be even truer of
Latin America and particularly Mexico. In Mexico to be a Communist was not
so much an identity to be adopted as a role that had to be created, defined,
and defended. As they created their new identity, the slackers became far more
important in Mexico than they had ever been in the United States. Most of the
radical slackers had been rank-and-file, Socialist Party anti-war activists in the
United States, sometimes at most local leaders or spokespersons for the anti-
war movement. But in Mexico they began to put themselves at the centre of
movements and organisations that made their activities of interest and concern to the governments of the United States, Mexico, and Soviet Russia. The US
government spied on the slackers and infiltrated their organisations because
it feared that their activities could have a significant impact on the war, on
Mexico, or on the United States. Similarly, the Mexican government first protected and then patronised them because it believed that the slackers might
be politically useful. The Russian Communists and their Communist International expected the slackers and their Mexican and foreign allies who became

---

1   Serge 1984, p. 104.

Communists to create not only a Mexican Communist Party, but also a Latin American Communist organisation.[2] The shoulders of the handful of American leftists in Mexico were asked to carry a tremendous burden, the revolutionary aspirations of a hemisphere.

Why should these rank-and-file American activists have been elevated into important political leaders in Mexico? First and most important, the slackers' flight to Mexico coincided with a new era in inter-imperialist confrontations that made their activities of particular interest to a number of governments. World War I had created a new kind of international competition and skulduggery. As Friedrich Katz writes, 'The new strategy of exploiting social conflicts and anticolonial struggles was not adopted by the European powers until World War I, when each side tried to aid revolutionary movements that were directed at its rivals'.[3] This new period of imperialism meant that each rival government attempted to identify, to ally with, and to shape the activities of the revolutionary groups that threatened its opponents. During World War I Mexico became the scene of rivalry and intrigue involving the United States, Great Britain, and Germany as each competed for influence not only with the Mexican government but also with the various revolutionary factions.

The Bolshevik Revolution also contributed to the complexity of this new stage of inter-imperialist struggle. Both the Soviet Russian government and the Communist International became players in the global contest. Soviet Russia sought diplomatic recognition, international political alliances, and economic relationships.[4] At the same time the Communist International sought to create a world party of revolution. As Eric Hobsbawm writes, 'The October revolution produced by far the most formidable organised revolutionary movement in modern history'.[5] While it did not produce it everywhere or all at once, the Bolshevik Revolution and then the Communist International created 'a corps of utterly committed and disciplined activists, a sort of global striking force for revolutionary conquest'.[6] And, as Hobsbawm writes, 'though their numbers were small, the twentieth century cannot be understood without them'.[7] Strangely enough one of the first countries outside of Russia to establish a Communist Party was Mexico, and the people who founded it were the American slackers, other foreigners and their Mexican collaborators.

---

2 Spenser 2011, pp. 63–88.
3 Katz 1983, pp. x and 11.
4 Spenser 1998, *passim*.
5 Hobsbawm 1996, p. 55.
6 Hobsbawm 1996, p. 69.
7 Hobsbawm 1996, p. 73.

Upon arrival in Mexico the American slackers received the protection of the government of President Venustiano Carranza who believed that the radicals could prove useful in his country's fight against the United States. Engaged in a difficult struggle against US economic interests – particularly the oil companies – and against the US government itself, Carranza welcomed the slackers and the radicals in particular as potential allies. The war-resisters, Carranza knew, were not only fervent critics of US policy toward Mexico but could also provide important contacts to the US peace movement, largely led by the Socialist Party. For those reasons, President Carranza welcomed the slackers. The protection of the Carranza government enhanced the slackers' prestige and their influence in Mexican political circles, even in the leftist opposition to the conservative Carranza. While the Mexican Constitution's Article 33 prohibited foreigners from engaging in politics in Mexico, Carranza not only permitted but even encouraged their political activism, but of course he also attempted to shape it to conform to his government's interests.

Carranza's Minister of the Interior, Manuel Aguirre Berlanga, became the first principal political protector of the American war resisters. He became the patron of slacker Linn Gale, and the sponsor of the Indian nationalist M.N. Roy who worked closely with the American slacker Charles Francis Phillips. Carranza's government, which criticised US and British imperialism, and which attempted to organise an alliance of Latin American states against the US government's Pan-American imperialism, found it useful to have its arguments buttressed by American radical critics of the United States and by Indian critics of the British empire. Other Mexican revolutionary leaders, political factions, and social movements found it useful to have ties to the American and other foreign radicals as well. Americans Roberto Haberman and Charles Francis Phillips found Mexican patrons among generals and politicians, as did the Pole Joseph Retinger and the Indian M.N. Roy.

During this period of social upheaval – the Mexican Revolution of 1919–1920, the US invasions of Mexico in 1914 and 1916, the World War from 1914 to 1918 – economic and political relations and institutions were transformed both internationally and domestically. In Mexico during this time rival governments rose and fell; labour organisations surged up, declined, and were replaced by others; peasant movements organised, dissolved and reorganised. In such a period, political and military figures, labour union and peasant leaders, and feminist activists found it important to understand both the national and the international context in which things were changing so rapidly, as well as to establish contacts with emerging political forces. The American slackers and other radical foreigners in Mexico provided links to the US, British, and European labour organisations, to other colonial revolutionary movements, and to the Socialist and the new Russian Communist international organisations that appeared as potential counterweights to the imperial powers.

In Mexico during the revolutionary and post-revolutionary periods, every political leader and faction wanted to strengthen its own local, regional or national organisation, and to do so it needed political intelligence and desired international ties. Yet Mexico's revolutionary generals, political leaders and labour union or peasant leaders had only a small pool of intellectuals and political activists on which to draw for those services. In 1910 only 28 percent of the Mexican population was literate, only a small percentage had finished primary school, and only a handful had any secondary, much less university education. The revolution had destroyed the old Mexican state, its bureaucracy, and its army. Much of the Mexican political and economic elite, the better educated classes, had fled abroad to Europe or the United States, or had retired to safe areas in the countryside. Many Mexican intellectuals stayed abroad during the revolution and did not return home until the mid-1920s. As educated men and women, and in some cases as university-trained professionals or intellectuals, most of whom quickly became functionally bilingual, the slackers and other foreign radicals would in any case have been potentially useful allies. But as experienced anti-war activists, union militants, and Socialist Party members with ties to organisations in the United States, Europe, and then Soviet Russia they represented very useful allies indeed. They became important figures in the attempt by various Mexican political organisations to strengthen their particular faction within the larger chess game that the was struggle for hegemony within the Mexican Revolution. Consequently, Mexican revolutionary leaders sought out American radicals in Mexico, and attempted to incorporate them into their various political projects.

Leaders of Mexican labour and peasant organisations, inspired by an anarchist or socialist ethic of internationalism, also welcomed the American slackers, no doubt impressed by their struggle against the draft and the war in the United States and by their commitment to continued political activism in labour unions in Mexico. Thus, Felipe Carrillo Puerto, head of the peasant Leagues of Resistance and of the Socialist Party of the Southeast in Yucatan hired the American Socialist Roberto Haberman to head his cooperative organisations. Later the powerful Labour leader Luis N. Morones, head of the Regional Confederation of Mexican Workers (CROM), would make Haberman his liaison to the Socialist Party of America and more important to Samuel Gompers of the American Federation of Labor, and Minister of Education José Vasconcelos would have Haberman head his foreign language department. Vasconcelos also later hired Bertram and Ella Wolfe, and other American slackers.

General Salvador Alvarado, the former governor of the Yucatan and presidential hopeful, hired Charles Phillips to be the editor of the English language page of his Mexico City newspaper *El Heraldo de Mexico*.

The left also welcomed the slackers. Adolfo Santibañez, the head of the Socialist Party of Mexico, welcomed Phillips, Gale, and Roy into his small political group. Mexican Labour activist Manuel Díaz Ramírez and radical youth leader José C. Valadés were also attracted to the slacker activists and joined the slackers in the newly founded Communist Party. Once that party was organised, peasant leaders Primo Tapia and Úrsulo Galván – both of whom had lived and worked in the United States – also joined the Communist Party and worked with the slackers. Pedro Coria, a Mexican industrial worker who had lived in the United States, also joined. Úrsulo Galván, Pnmo Tapia, Manuel Díaz Ramírez, and Pedro Coria – all of whom joined the Mexican Communist Party organised by the slacker Charles Francis Phillip – had all lived and worked in the United States, and the last three had all been members of the IWW, while Tapia may also have been a member of the Communist Party of the United States. The Mexican and American radicals shared commitments to agrarian reform, to union organising, to feminism and to the construction of a revolutionary socialist party. The Mexican leftists saw the Americans as comrades, but as comrades with important links to the United States and later to Soviet Russia. At the same time, the newly organised Communist International in Moscow found the American slackers and other foreigners in Mexico useful in the attempt to extend Communism from Europe to the countries of Latin America.

In addition to the initiatives to organise a Communist Party in Mexico by Mexicans, Americans, and foreigners, beginning in 1917, the Russian Bolsheviks or Communists also sought to organise the anti-war socialists, anarchists and syndicalists into new national Communist Parties that would form part of the Communist or Third International. The Communist International was indeed founded in March of 1919, but at the time there were only three Communist Parties in existence outside of Russia (German, Austrian and Hungarian). The CI's leaders wanted to extend the Communist International to the Americas, particularly to the United States, but also to Latin America. As early as 1918 the Communists dispatched Mikhail Borodin, a Russian who had lived in the United States, as an organiser to Latin America, and there he discovered the slackers in Mexico and recruited several of them to the new Third International. The CI subsequently sent organisers to Mexico who founded and periodically reorganised the Mexican Communist Party (PCM) and the Red International of Labour Unions (RILU), the Red Peasant International (the KRESINTERN), the All-American Anti-Imperialist League (AAAIL) and a

Communist Latin American Bureau. Several of the slackers became intimately involved in the Communist International and its political and union work.

In Mexico, the Communist International's agent, Borodin, who had for several years been a member of the Socialist Party of America, helped the slackers and their other foreign associates organise the first Communist Party in Mexico, which was also the first in Latin America. This proved to have collateral benefits as Borodin and Phillips also organised the Communist Party of Spain almost in passing, and M.N. Roy, became the head of the Communist Party of India. Later in 1921 the CI sent Louis Fraina (Lewis Corey) and Sen Katayama to Mexico. When Bertram Wolfe arrived, he took up the work on behalf of the Communist International. Both the first group of slackers of the 1917 to 1921 period and the second group of the 1921 to 1927 period played key roles in organising the Mexican Communist Party, and later the All-American Anti-Imperialist League, which established important political contacts throughout Latin America.

While politically active in Mexico, and working with the Moscow-based Communist International, the slackers also maintained ties to the left in the United States, principally to the Socialist Party, the new Communist Party, and the Industrial Workers of the World. While they had all been anti-war activist in the United States, none of the slackers found any way to remain connected to the American anti-war movement, which had been largely suppressed by the US government. A few of the slackers maintained ties to the Socialist Party headquartered in New York, writing occasionally for its newspaper *The Call*. But the Socialist Party was in disarray and decline following the split which led to the formation of the Communist Party and the Communist Labour Party in the United States in 1919, and those parties soon went underground both as a proof of their revolutionary character, and to avoid the post-war repression of the Palmer Raids. During the period from 1918 to the early 1920s it was therefore extremely difficult for the slackers to maintain contact with the American Socialist or Communist parties, but the slackers did keep up their ties to the Chicago-based Industrial Workers of the World.

On the eve of World War I, the Industrial Workers of the World had concentrated its efforts on the organisation of metal miners, oil workers, lumberjacks, and agricultural workers, particularly in the wheat fields. All of these were industries crucial to the US war effort. The IWW's organising efforts among miners and oil workers both in the United States and Mexico particularly seemed to jeopardise the US government's military preparedness and later wartime industrial production. US government prosecutors understandably saw the IWW as a threat to the strategic economic, political and military interests of

the government. The Wobblies organising activities in crucial wartime industries helps to explain the ferocity with which the US government repressed the
IWW.[8]

Nearly destroyed by government repression during World War I in the United
States, the Wobblies welcomed news about the organisation of the Mexican
Administration of the IWW. During World War I and the early 1920s, the success
of IWW organisers in Scandinavia, Australia, Mexico, Argentina, and especially
in Chile kept alive the hope for the survival and vindication of revolutionary industrial unionism.[9] The existence of IWW locals in Mexico, particularly
in the petroleum and maritime industries in Tampico held out the hope that
with the end of the war the IWW would also revive and recoup its losses in the
United States. Thus, the slackers successfully defied Woodrow Wilson's attempt
to crush Industrial Workers of the World, for they kept the revolutionary union
alive and kicking in Mexico.

As this survey of their activities makes clear, the slackers operated not only
in social movements, but also within the powerful force fields exerted by the
government of the United States, the newly formed revolutionary nationalist government of Mexico, and the revolutionary Communist government in
Soviet Russia. The threat of repression in the United States, the attraction of
Communism in Russia, and the various factions in revolutionary Mexico and
its government affected every action of the American radicals. A most immediate and important influence was the developing Mexican state. The longer
they stayed in Mexico, the more deeply the American slackers became involved
not only in union, peasant and women's organisations, but also indirectly and
sometimes inadvertently and contrary to their own best intentions in a web of
relations tied to the Mexican government. The labour and peasant leaders with
whom the slackers worked almost inevitably turned out to be linked in one way
or another to governors, generals, or cabinet ministers.

While attempting to organise an independent and internationalist movement, the American war resisters constantly found themselves being drawn
into the powerful orbit of the Mexican government. The slackers helped bring
the American feminist tradition into contact with the Mexican feminist counterpart. They proselytised among railroad and petroleum workers, women activists and mestizo and Indian peasants. They organised union, led strikes, and
armed workers' detachments that participated in rebellions. Their Communist
comrade Primo Tapia had close ties to Governor Francisco Múgica, while fellow

---

8   Dubofsky 1969, pp. 291–444.
9   Cole 2017, *passim*.

Communist Úrsulo Galván was connected to Governor Adalberto Tejeda. Thus, the American slackers tended to become linked either directly or indirectly not only to the social movements, but also to Mexican political leaders and parties. The culmination of this process came when Bertram Wolfe, as a leader of the PCM, worked with Galván's organisation to defend the government of president Obregón against the coup of Adolfo de la Huerta. The American leftists in Mexico found they could not avoid being drawn into the wake of Mexico's nationalist government.

The significance of the slackers lies not only in their organisational accomplishments in Mexico, but also in their moral-political stand *vis-à-vis* the United States government. When Woodrow Wilson and the US government had crushed the Socialist Party, the Industrial Workers of the World in the United States, and the People's Council of America for Democracy and Peace, the slackers determined to keep dissent, pacifism and socialism alive in Mexico. At the same time, with nationalism driving the world to war, and their own nation joining wholeheartedly in the imperial struggle to divide the planet, they attempted to create international solidarity between the world's workers through the Communist International. The slackers did many things, but perhaps the most important thing they did on the moral plane was to take a stand for peace and internationalism, peace by revolution.

CHAPTER 8

Conscription, Repression and Flight: America's First Revolutionaries in Exile

The US entry into World War I in May of 1917 and the beginning of conscription in June of that year, led to the development of a significant anti-war movement. Many sectors of American society were opposed to the war and millions of men sought and found ways to evade the draft and military service. During the war, US President Woodrow Wilson created the most repressive administration in American history, jailing hundreds of members of the Socialist Party and the Industrial Workers of the World and suppressing many newspapers and magazines, while local police, the American Legion, and vigilantes beat, tortured, and in a few cases killed anti-war and anti-draft activists. All of this would create the conditions that led thousands of men to seek refuge elsewhere. Since flight by ship was virtually impossible and Canada had already entered the war did not welcome American draft evaders, many fled to Mexico. Several of the war resisters and draft evaders who were denigrated as 'slackers' came from New York City's left-wing circles around Columbia University and Greenwich Village. These socialists were anti-war, internationalist, and feminist and they would take those values with them to Mexico.

During the Spring and Summer of 1917, a small stream of Americans began to cross the border into Mexico, clandestinely and illegally. They were American wetbacks, fleeing the war and the draft and wading over the Rio Grande in search of asylum. Many of those refugees were radicals who fled political persecution in the United States. As socialist, anarchist, or syndicalist opponents of militarism, war, and the draft, they had no legal claim to conscientious objector status however sincere their convictions might be. At that time only religious claims to conscientious objection were honoured in the United States. To escape the authorities' 'slacker' raids, government prosecutors, military conscription, or prison – and the beatings, torture and murder which were meted out to a number of conscientious objectors – the leftists joined thousands of other draft evaders in choosing flight and seeking refuge in Mexico. While it was not initially part of their plan, some would soon become political activists in Mexico.

What began as a trickle became a steady stream, and soon, some would claim, a flood. *The New York Times* reported in June of 1920 – a year and a half after the end of the war – that an estimated 10,000 draft evaders still remained in Mexico.[1] Senator Albert Bacon Fall told the Associated Press that an estimated thirty thousand Americans had crossed into Mexico to evade the draft law.[2] Linn A.E. Gale, himself a draft dodger in Mexico, agreed with that figure.[3] We will never know exactly how many Americans went to Mexico during World War I because those who went had successfully evaded the authorities in the United States and revolutionary Mexico could not and did not keep accurate records at its borders and ports of entry. But certainly, comparing the various estimates and contemporary accounts, the number must have been in the thousands.

What led the American exiles to go to Mexico? Most went simply to avoid the draft. Others fled the Woodrow Wilson administration's severe political repression during World War I. For many socialist, anarchist, and syndicalist opponents of war, life in the United States became impossible during World War I. Under the conscription act of 1917, all male US citizens between the ages of 21 and 30 were eligible for the draft and had to register with the Selective Service. While foreign-born immigrants who were not citizens were not eligible for the draft, they too had to register. The president established a system of local draft boards made up of civilians to oversee the Selective Service system. The first registration day was 5 June 1917 when 9.6 million men registered. The failure to comply with the law by registering for the draft was a misdemeanour, punishable by up to one year in a federal prison. No provisions whatsoever had been made for conscientious objectors, and only gradually were procedures for conscientious objectors established mainly for religious objectors. Humanitarian and political objectors, internationalist and socialist opponents of war had no exemption under the system's rules and regulations.

The entry of the US into the war and the adoption of conscription were not universally accepted. On the contrary, the war was opposed by large segments of American society, particularly recent immigrants, at least up until the spring of 1917. Two of America's largest immigrant groups, the Germans and the Irish, generally opposed the war. The German-Americans would rather not have to fight their former countrymen in Germany and Austria. Many Irish did not want to enter the war as allies of England, a country they saw as their oppressor. Many Russians, Poles, and Eastern European Jews who had escaped from Russia, tended to oppose joining a war on the side of the Czarist autocracy. Most American Socialists, about 100,000 party members and nearly one mil-

---

1 'Ask Mexico' 1920, p. 9.
2 Gale, March 1920, p. 1.
3 Gale, March 1920, p. 7.

lion voters, also opposed the war, at least initially, as too did many US labour unionists both in the left-wing of the American Federation of Labor and in the Industrial Workers of the World. Traditional peace churches, such as the Quakers and the Church of the Brethren, opposed all war and the Great War was no exception. Most American Indian groups opposed the war in which they felt they had no stake, since they didn't feel themselves to be part of the American nation. That was also true of many African Americans. Many progressives, especially professionals such as social workers, teachers, and doctors were also against the war, at least at first.

Many Americans who accepted the war nevertheless opposed conscription. The United States had not had a conscription law for over fifty years, since the end of the Civil War, and even that had been a limited draft law. The country had never had a universal military service law for males such as the conscription law that was passed in 1917. To many who held traditional American views on military service, that is, who believed in the raising of a volunteer citizen army, the draft law seemed an expression of tyranny. Only European imperialist states had previously adopted such universal military training and service laws, and so Americans identified conscription with monarchy, militarism, and empire, which many and perhaps most abhorred. Populists and Socialists opposed conscription, arguing that it represented a violation of the Thirteenth Amendment to the Constitution, which prohibited involuntary servitude. Conscription, they argued, was slavery, an unthinkable law in a land of free men. This view inspired many who opposed the draft, and some who later evaded it. What had been an anti-militarist sentiment soon became a social movement.

A vocal and quite militant anti-war and anti-draft movement exploded into existence on the eve of the war made up of socialists, labour unionists, feminists, populists, and progressives. Led by the Women's Peace Party, the Emergency Peace Federation, and the Socialist Party, men and women in major cities and many small towns and rural areas across the United States demonstrated or in other ways opposed US entry into the war and the draft. Even after 6 April 1917 when President Woodrow Wilson asked for and the Congress approved a declaration of war on Germany, populists frequently joined Socialists and feminists in opposing conscription, particularly in the South and in the far West.

On 31 May, the Emergency Peace Federation convened its supporters and went on to form the People's Council of America for Democracy and the Terms of Peace. Perhaps influenced by the Russian Revolution – the organisation took its name from the *soviets* or councils which had formed in Russia – the People's Council opposed US entry into the war, demanded democratic rights at home, called for a just peace without annexations in a new democratic international order. Woodrow Wilson's government, undeterred by the anti-war movement and determined to crush it, unleashed the greatest suppression of civil rights in US history.

During World War I, the United States carried out a repression of dissent greater than that during the Civil War and more severe than in Britain, France or Germany.[4] The state's force was particularly directed against labour and leftist opponents of war. The US government arrested some 165 leaders of the radical labour union the Industrial Workers of the World, and several hundred, perhaps as many as 2,000, other IWW activists throughout the country on a variety of largely fabricated charges from vagrancy to murder. The Wilson administration also waged a campaign of harassment against the anarchist and socialist anti-war movement, eventually jailing Eugene Debs and Katherine Richards O'Hare for anti-war speeches and expelling foreign-born anarchist anti-war leaders such as Emma Goldman and Alexander Berkman. Protected by the government and the military, groups such as the American Legion busted up labour union, socialist, and anti-war offices, beat up and in a few instances murdered anti-war activists or other radicals.[5] The US government also created what one historian has called a 'surveillance state' to spy on its people.[6] Government action against the left also often had an anti-Semitic character, especially in New York.[7]

How many resisters and evaders were there? Millions. During the US involvement in World War I (1917–18), 24 million men registered for the draft, and 4,791,172 men served in the war, but 'an additional 2.4 to 3.6 million may have successfully avoided draft registration'.[8] In addition, the US Provost Marshal General reported that 337,649 men who had registered either failed to report for induction when called by the draft boards, or deserted after arrival at the military camp. Beside those evaders, 64,700 men filed claims for conscientious objector status before their local selective service boards. The number of war resisters and draft evaders may thus have reached nearly four million. Many of the draft evaders never fell into the government's grasp. But for those who did, the repression could be severe. Hundreds of war resisters were held on military bases, while other hundreds of pacifists who refused to cooperate in any way

---

4 Mowat 1968, p. 563.
5 See: Peterson 1957; Goldstein 1978; Blanchard 1992.
6 Polenberg 1987, pp. 154–6; Katz 1983, p. 433. In Chapter 5, 'The Surveillance State', Polenberg discusses how the government kept track of dissidents. The slackers would find out that the 'surveillance state' also extended to Mexico, where several different US intelligence agencies spied on US citizens and others.
7 Michels 2005, pp. 219–22.
8 Chambers II 1987, p. 211.

were jailed. At best estimate 17 conscientious objectors died from beatings or were simply murdered, several while in the custody of Federal authorities.[9]

In an attempt to nab draft evaders, the Justice Department, working with local police and civilian deputies, organised round-ups of young men on the streets, the so-called 'slacker raids'. Five percent of those detained proved to be draft evaders. In the first week of September 1918, the government organised the biggest 'slacker raid' of the war. Some 2,000 soldiers, federal agents, local police and the American Protective League rounded up hundreds of thousands, eventually detained over 50,000, and turned 15,000 over to local draft boards for various sorts of violations.[10]

American political leaders, military officials, the pulpit and the press adopted the word 'slacker' as a derogatory epithet to characterise war resisters, draft evaders, and all others who refused to fight or in other ways support the war. The press complained of 'industrial slackerism' among those in the factories. Those who didn't buy liberty stamps or bonds were also sometimes labelled slackers as well. Women who were insufficiently patriotic were labelled slackers, as were foreign-born immigrants who were less than enthusiastic about war, though under the draft law, women and foreign-born residents were under no obligation to serve in the US military during World War I. There were plays and epic poems written to deride the slacker.[11] Moreover, the use of the word 'slacker' was an implied threat of physical abuse, beating, or even murder. Bruno Grunzig, a conscientious objector at Camp Dix, New Jersey reported that, 'The guards took keen delight in telling all willing to listen, that we were slackers, deserters, coward, etc., etc .... [We were marched] all through camp again, with the whole camp shouting "slacker", now will you be good, you will run will yez, you'll like it alright, just like we do'.[12]

---

9   Chambers II 1987, pp. 211–17. The boards certified 56,000 of the 64,700 who claimed c.o. status. Of those 30,000 passed their physical examinations and 20,873 were indeed inducted into the army. After a time in the military camps, 16,000 abandoned their conscientious objections, took up arms, and went to war. Still 3,989 continued to refuse to participate in the military. Some 1,300 served in the Medical Corps or other non-combatant branches. Another 1,300 were furloughed for civilian work. Some 940 stayed in the training camps but were segregated there. The 450 so-called 'absolutists', those who refused any cooperation with the military machine, were tried before courts martial and then jailed in military prisons.

10   Chambers II 1987, p. 216.

11   'slacker' 1978; Rawson 1989, p. 358. For an anti-slacker song: Dattilo 1917; (lyrics) and Minnie May Bauer (music), 'Don't Marry a Slacker, Girls', 1917; an anti-slacker play: Tull 1917; and an anti-slacker epic poem: Parker 1918.

12   Letter of Bruno Grunzig to Frances M. Witherspoon, 23 June 1918, box 2, New York Bureau of Legal Advice Papers, Swarthmore College Peace Collection, cited in Early 1997, p. 103.

With the Socialist, syndicalist, and anti-war movement on the defensive and the US government using its power to suppress dissent, some peace activists undertook the defence of civil rights through organisations such as the Civil Liberties Bureau and the Bureau of Legal Advice. Among other work, these organisations attempted to protect the rights of war resisters and conscientious objectors. But the civil liberties organisations could only help a small number of the tens of thousands caught in the maw of the state.[13] Not surprisingly, some US pacifists and conscientious objectors concluded that if they stayed in the United States, they would very likely be conscripted and sent to kill or die in Europe. Or if they continued to resist and protest, they might be beaten or killed by vigilantes, or imprisoned by the government and tortured or murdered in the stockade or penitentiary. So, thousands of Americans fled to Mexico.

1   The Slacker's Ideology

What was the intellectual, ideological and cultural baggage that the slackers carried to Mexico? We don't know much about most of the thousands of young men who crossed the Mexican border in 1917 or 1918 to avoid the draft, but several of the radical slackers belonged to the Socialist Party of America (SPA) or its periphery. Charles Francis Phillips, Herman Levine, Roberto Haberman, Carleton Beals, and Irwin Granich had all been members of the SPA. Hendrik Glintenkamp and Maurice Becker had probably been socialists too. Even the Russian Mikhail Borodin who later joined them had lived in the United States and been a member of the SPA. Of the small group of prominent American slacker activists, only Linn Gale had not been a socialist activist in the United States, and he converted to socialism just before he left for Mexico. For this small group of radical slackers, we have a variety of sources, ranging from their own writings to government intelligence agencies' reports.

The socialist-pacifist men and women who went to Mexico tended to share not only a common socialist organisational affiliation and ideology, but several of them also shared a common culture, the culture of New York's largely Jewish socialist community. Several of the future slackers, Charles Francis Phillips, Herman Levine, and Bertram D. Wolfe, came from this Jewish socialist milieu. The Jewish immigrants from Eastern Europe's shtetls gave a particular character to New York's Socialist Party in the 1910s as they later would to the New

---

13   Early 1997 gives a brief account of the struggle for the rights of some working-class and political conscientious objectors.

York Communist Party in the 1930s. Jewish boys studied not only in the Hebrew heders and the New York public schools, but also gathered in literary clubs to read the English poets and in socialist circles that studied Marx's *Capital*. The radical Jewish, mostly male youth read the socialist newspapers first in Yiddish and German and later, as they became more acculturated, studied socialist papers and pamphlets in English. Jewish attorney Morris Hillquit headed the New York Socialist Party, and the Jewish garment workers made up much of the party's rank and file. Unlike the moralistic Christian Socialists of the Midwest or Milwaukee's stodgy Socialists shaped by German Social Democracy, the New Yorker Socialists tended to be urban and urbane, sophisticated and intellectually iconoclastic.[14]

Columbia University provided many of the dominant ideas, values, and early political experiences of these young radicals. Future slackers Charles Francis Phillips, Eleanor Parker, and Herman Levine all studied there, where professor Charles Beard was one of the dominant intellectual figures. The historian Beard, strongly influenced by his colleagues James Harvey Robinson and E.R.A. Seligman, had helped lay the foundations for social and economic history, which challenged the conservative character of the American Constitution and the state. Beard's economic history coincided at points with the Socialist Party's ideology and served to reinforce the socialist college students' internationalism and anti-imperialism. Charles Francis Phillips remembered fondly walks and talks with Charles Beard while Phillips was a student at Columbia in the period when he became an anti-draft activist.[15]

But the impact of Columbia was not simply intellectual; it was also political. Columbia's Socialist Club, the local chapter of the Intercollegiate Socialist Society, brought together undergraduates from Columbia, Barnard 'girls', and some graduate students. Arriving at Columbia in 1914, Phillips, who studied journalism, was elected secretary of the club and was soon joined by other journalism students like Eleanor Parker and Morris Ryskind, and together they brought anti-war speakers to campus. Dr Leon Fraser, who coached the debating team and opposed the war, organised debates on the question of war or peace. Psychology professor James M. Cattell and English professor Henry Wadsworth Longfellow Dana also formed part of the anti-war faculty. Dana joined with students in Columbia's Anti-Militarism League and in the People's Council for Peace and Democracy. When Columbia's president Nicholas Mur-

---

14   On the New York Jewish left milieu of New York in the 1910s, see: Michels 2005; Ackerman 2016; Wolfe 1981; and Freeman 1936.

15   Shipman 1993, pp. 13–14.

ray Butler fired Dana and Cattell, for their political activities, history professor Charles Beard, who supported the US entry into the war, resigned his position in protest.

The idealism of Columbia's students and professors helped to shape the ideals and politics of some of the slackers. From Beard, Seligman, and Robinson they took an interest in Marx and the role of economics in history; from the Columbia Socialist Club they took their Socialist politics; and from the Anti-Militarism League and the People's Council they took their radical activist approach to building a socialist anti-war movement. The slackers would take Marxism, socialism, and activism to Mexico with them.

Greenwich Village, at the other end of Manhattan, represented the other great intellectual and cultural influence on the slackers. The Village in the pre-war years brought together avant-garde art, radical politics, and experimental lifestyles to create America's most famous bohemian quarter. *The Masses*, edited by Max Eastman and Floyd Dell, became the voice of the Village radicals and of the Socialist Party's left wing that espoused the politics of revolutionary socialism, the direct-action syndicalism of the IWW, and socialist feminism. *The Masses* magazine, as Joseph Freeman wrote, was the real university of young radicals in the pre-war period. In its articles and drawing, the magazine celebrated the workingwomen and the immigrants of the industrial working class, while raising radical views that challenged the political shibboleths of both mainstream politics and the reformist leadership of the Socialist Party.

Those who read *The Masses* not only imbibed its left-wing socialism but also its socialist feminism. Editor Max Eastman, the guiding spirit of *The Masses*, gave the magazine a feminist thrust, supporting both suffrage and the struggles of working women. Influenced by his suffragist mother and his sister Crystal Eastman, Max had organised the Men's League for Woman Suffrage in 1909. 'To me it seemed the big fight for freedom in my time', he later wrote in his autobiography.[16] Max's and Crystal's socialist feminism meant not only winning women's right to vote, but also supporting women's strikes for higher wages. That pro-working class, socialist feminism also became part of the ideology of the slackers who when they fled to Mexico later helped to organise a Mexican Feminist Council.

The Masses became directly involved in the anti-war movement, leading to its persecution and prosecution. The US Postal authorities barred the magazine from the mails, and the US Justice Department indicted its editors and staff for conspiring to obstruct enlistment. After a mistrial the second jury split and the

---

16   Eastman 1948, p. 306.

defendants went free. But in the meantime, the magazine had ceased publication, and *Masses* illustrators Hendrik Glintenkamp and Maurice Becker had both become slackers and gone to Mexico.

One other essential element should be added to the slackers' ideology, and that is internationalism. Several of the slacker Socialists in Mexico had been steeped in a romantic, revolutionary internationalism, a sentiment that became even stronger on the eve of the outbreak of the First World War. Socialists in general, and the left wing in particular, considered themselves to be internationalists, that is, part of one worldwide socialist movement for the liberation of humanity. Before his apostasy, Jack London, perhaps the most popular American socialist writer of the period, produced an essay called 'Revolution' (originally written in 1905 and subsequently collected and published in a book with the same title in 1912) which captured the radical and romantic spirit of this internationalism. The socialist revolution, he wrote, was 'unique, colossal'. 'It is alone of its kind, the first world revolution … the first organised movement of men to become a world movement, limited only by the limits of the planet'. London told his readers that, 'The comradeship of the revolutionists is alive and warm. It passes over geographical lines, transcends race prejudice'.[17] While Jack London later became a right-wing Socialist and a racist, his 1905 essay captured the idealistic internationalism of the Socialist left wing of the pre-war period. To imperialism and world war, socialists counterpoised internationalism and the world revolutionary movement as the way to achieve world peace.

In the years just before the war, Randolph Bourne, who worked closely with some of the future slackers, developed another, more complex vision of internationalism. In essays in which he developed the idea of 'transnationalism', Bourne declared, 'I am almost fanatically against the current programs of Americanism, with their preparedness, conscription, imperialism, integration issues, their slavish imitation of the European nationalisms which are slaying each other before our eyes'. Americanism had to be replaced by a new internationalist vision which accepted ethnic and national differences, what he called 'transnationalism'. Bourne saw the cosmopolitan immigrant cities like New York, the university, and the Jewish ideal of Zionism (this is Zionism before Israel) as models for internationalism and a new humanism. Bourne argued, 'It is for the American of the younger generation to accept this cosmopolitanism, and carry it along with self-conscious and fruitful purpose'.[18] Of course in addition to his internationalist writings, Bourne was an outspoken critic and

---

17   London 1912, pp. 4–5.
18   Bourne 1964, pp. 117 and 126.

opponent of militarism, war and conscription, famous for his line, 'War is the health of the State'. When the US entered the war and adopted conscription, Bourne directly supported the activities of the New York City anti-war student activists and future slackers such as Charles Francis Phillips and Eleanor Parker.

So, many of the slackers went off to Mexico carrying in their heads the experience of the Jewish immigrant study circles and the Socialist Party, Columbia University and Charles Beard, Greenwich Village and *The Masses* – all of it to be unpacked and reorganised once they reached Mexico. The ideas of America's Progressive era, or rather the most radical version of those ideas in the form of revolutionary socialism, syndicalism, and feminism, were shipped off to Mexico in the slackers' heads and hearts. But once in Mexico, when they became activists, they would find that their socialist vision and strategy could not simply be transplanted but would have to be grafted on to pre-existing Mexican ideas and social movements. While Mexico had socialist, syndicalist, and feminist organisations and ideologies, they had somewhat different roots and branches, and existed in an altogether different political climate, one shaped by years of revolution and the rise of a new state. The slackers would find that their ideas would be influenced and altered by the Mexican experience, and even more by the distant Russian Revolution of October 1917.

2   The Slacker Exodus

The slacker exodus began shortly before 5 June 1917, the national draft registration day in the United States. Four days before registration day, US government agents began to refuse to allow male citizens between the ages of 21 and 31 to cross the border into Mexico. New York's daily Socialist Party newspaper, *The Call*, reported that on 1 June, two American youths were arrested at Laredo, Texas and charged with 'seeking to leave the United States to avoid military registration'.[19] While those two failed to get across, many others succeeded, for the US-Mexico border was a sieve.

Why did these slackers choose Mexico? First, because after the US government instituted registration and conscription in mid-1917, it was difficult to get out of the United States by ship. Men desiring to leave the country and to go overseas had to show a draft card, and the card had to show an exemption. Draft evaders and resisters often did not have draft cards, and those who did

---

19   'Draft' 1917.

had no exemption, and so they could not get visas, passports, or steamer tickets. Consequently, slackers avoided the harbours and the docks, especially the more notorious draft resisters whose names and faces had been in the newspapers.

With overseas travel ruled out in this era before the passenger plane, the only alternative was to travel by land to the northern or southern national border. Canada was not a desirable refuge because as part of the British Empire, Canada had joined the war in 1914, and in 1915 sent its first contingent of troops to a battle with a poison gas attack at Ypres where many met their deaths. Canada had instituted national registration in 1916, and a draft in early 1918.[20] Moreover, border guards in both countries would have questioned anyone crossing, demanding proof of draft registration or military service. While some war resisters and draft evaders must have succeeded in hiding out in Canada, most would have feared that the British, Canadian and US governments would have cooperated to repatriate them and force them into the army or put them into prison.

During 1917 and 1918 it was still possible to travel to the Mexican border by train or highway and then slip by the US army troops patrolling the border and enter Mexico. The US-Mexico border was 1,950 miles long and border patrols were spread thin. Slackers could most easily wade across the Rio Grande River in Texas, or walk over the hills south of San Diego, California. The Mexican Constitutionalist government of President Carranza made no attempt to exclude the draft evaders and welcomed some of the more political ones as potential allies in its struggle against the pressures of the United States government. In addition to its accessibility, Mexico was warm and cheap, which were not negligible factors in the minds of the thousands of gandydancers, bindlestiffs and barnstormers, draft dodgers all, who were making their way south.

There were few precedents for American political exile in Mexico. During the US-Mexican War of 1847, a group of about 300 mostly Irish-American US soldiers deserted and went over to the Mexican side, taking the name the Saint Patrick's Battalion. Political opportunism of their leaders, a spirit of adventure among some of the followers, and a history of anti-Irish and anti-Catholic discrimination led them to desert the US Army and join the forces of Catholic Mexico. The grateful Mexicans later raised a plaque in Mexico City to honour those American expatriates, but that was another sort of anti-war movement in an altogether different era.[21] Another migration of political refugees or exiles

---

20   Rothwell 1987, pp. 122–47; Allen 1961, pp. 71–84 and 146–7.
21   Hogan 1997, *passim*; Miller 1989, *passim*.

was that of hundreds of Confederate government officials, army officers and soldiers, and many white Southerners of all sorts who after the end of the Civil War headed south to Mexico, fleeing defeat and humiliation, and attempting to preserve their slave society and its values. The Emperor Maximilian's government welcomed them as experts in plantation agriculture, and some found jobs working on haciendas. But this too was a rather isolated experience, and certainly one that created no tradition or continuity of US political exiles in Mexico.[22]

While there were few former experiences of exile or political asylum in Mexico, the slackers' experience as Americans in Mexico was not unique. As discussed earlier, beginning in the 1870s Americans began a small but steady stream of migration to Mexico made up of missionaries, businessmen, and industrial workers. Through those migrations American political, economic, social and cultural influence began to spread into Mexico. Protestant missionaries established a network of churches, schools, and teachers' colleges in Mexico. Mormon missionaries created prosperous economic colonies in the northern states. Some black Americans also fled the United States and its pervasive racism and sought a new future in Mexico.[23]

Most important US finance capital invested hundreds of millions of dollars in industry – especially railways, mining and petroleum, making the United States corporations the dominant foreign investors in Mexico.[24] US businessmen established ranches, farms, and plantations in various parts of Mexico. US multinational corporations' investments in Mexico were the economic force that drove the migration of US workers to Mexico. Every plantation, railroad, mine, and oil well required managers, supervisors, technicians, foremen, skilled workers, and clerks, and they were mostly American, though some were Canadian or British. In December 1910, shortly after the outbreak of the Mexican Revolution, US President William Howard Taft stated that there were 40,000 Americans in Mexico.[25] While some were diplomats, businessmen, and missionaries, and a number of others colonists, most must have been workers. In the years before the Mexican Revolution, American railroad workers, miners and oil workers were frequent migrants to Mexico. They dominated the administrative positions and the skilled trades and received higher pay and better treatment than their Mexican co-workers.

---

22 Rolle 1992, *passim*.
23 On various US immigrant groups that migrated to Mexico see: González Navarro 1994; Rolle 1992; Reynolds 1952; Redkey 1969; La Botz 1991.
24 On US corporate investment in Mexico see: Hart 2002; Cecena 1991; Brown 1993.
25 Ampudia 1996, p. 198.

As we have seen in Part I of this book, American workers took their labour unions with them to Mexico, the racist craft unions of the Railroad Brotherhoods, the militant Western Federation of Miners (WFM), and the radical Industrial Workers of the World (IWW). American workers and their labour organisations had influenced Mexican workers in various industries and regions of Mexico.[26] In short, the presence of US workers and labour unions in Mexico in the period from the 1880s to the 1910s had made both the gringo workers and their unions familiar to at least a small group of Mexican workers. Many Mexicans had also migrated to work in the United States where they had become familiar with US labour unions there. Significant numbers of Mexican workers knew about the Industrial Workers of the World, the one union in the United States that published Spanish language union newspapers, actively recruited Mexican immigrant workers, and not only deigned to organise them but also led strikes to fight for them.[27] Those experiences no doubt later helped to make Mexicans receptive to the American war resisters and draft evaders, some of whom became IWW organisers in the oil fields and on the docks.

The slacker migration to Mexico also represented a continuation of American solidarity with the Mexican Revolution from 1900 to 1916. The American Socialist slackers who went to Mexico after June 1917 would very likely have read essays or books on Mexico by John Kenneth Turner and John Reed. A decade of Socialist involvement in support of the Mexican Revolution and in opposition to US military intervention made it seem to the young American Socialists as if Americans and Mexicans were comrades in a common fight against the moguls of mining, the lords of petroleum, and against the US government's military intervention. This historic connection between the United States and

---

26   Concerning US workers in Mexico in the period of the Mexican Revolution and World War I, see: Alzati 1946, pp. 305–7; Miller 1974, pp. 239–60; Sariego 1988, p. 113; Reyna Munoz, Manuel, ed. 1969; Brown 1993, p. 319; Caulfield 1987; Caulfield 1995; de Shazo 1974.

27   Many IWW Spanish language newspapers circulated in the United States and Mexico. In Phoenix, Arizona, Local 272 published the first Spanish language IWW newspaper, *La Union Industrial* (The Industrial Union). Los Angeles IWW published La *Huelga General* (The General Strike) and *El Rebelde*. San Francisco IWW Local 173 published *Brazo Latino* (The Latin Hired Hand). In Ybor City, near Tampa, Florida, the IWW published *El Obrero Industrial* (The Industrial Worker). The IWW's Marine Transport Workers International Union in New York City published a weekly newspaper *Cultura Obrera* (Workers' Culture). Finally, the IWW later published national Spanish language newspapers *Nueva Solidaridad* (New Solidarity) and *Solidaridad* (Solidarity). In addition, there existed IWW newspapers published in Mexico such as *El Obrero Industrial*. Most of these newspapers probably also circulated in Mexico, carrying the IWW ideal of the international unity of the industrial workers in One Big Union.

Mexico helped to make possible the American slackers' choice of Mexico as a place of refuge, and later their decision to become actively involved in the Mexican left and labour movements.

3   The Press Vilifies the Slackers

The US press vilified the American slackers in Mexico as traitors, criminals and cowards. 'Unfortunately for the United States', wrote George E. Hyde, a reporter for *The New York Times* in 1920,

> A large part of the small group which makes up Bolshevism in Mexico is composed of renegade Americans who took refuge in Mexico during the war to escape military service. To this is added a few forgers, refugees under the Mann Act and other petty offenders whose communistic principles induced them to dispose of other men's money and other men's wives with apparent justification to themselves. This group appears variously as the Mexican Soldiers and Workmen's Council, the executive committee of the Mexican Communist Party or the representatives of the Industrial Workers of the World in Mexico.[28]

Linn Gale wrote what was probably the best characterisation of the slackers by a slacker. 'In Mexico the word [slacker] has become a part of both the English and Spanish languages, meaning simply a man who was conscripted for military service – probably in the United States, altho [*sic*] the same word is used referring to men from other countries – and fled from his own land to Mexico to avoid being compelled to fight', wrote Gale. 'Unquestionably "we slackers" are a bad bunch. We are desperate, unpatriotic, decidedly nervy and usually shamefully irreligious, or if we have religion, it is not the kind officially recognised by orthodox Christian diplomacy'.[29] But, above all, wrote Gale, the slackers were opponents of war:

> Like many other criminals, 'we slackers' laboured under a hallucination. We were obsessed with an idea. The idea was that there was no good

---

28   Hyde 1920, p. 19. The White Slave Traffic Act of 1910 – also known as the Mann Act for its author, Illinois congressman James Robert Mann – made it a crime to transport women across state lines 'for the purpose of prostitution or debauchery, or for any other immoral purpose'.

29   Gale 1918, pp. 8–9.

reason why we should go to Europe, and fight for the Allies. We insisted with irritating obstinacy that the war was simply a disgusting wrangle between two gangs of robbers, one headed by the late lamented kaiser, the Krupps and the Junkers of Potsdam, and the other headed by the monied men of Lombard Street, London and Wall Street in the United States.[30]

So, said Gale, we thought 'we might better get out of the country and go to a spot where we could obey these peculiar promptings of our conscience without being punished'.[31] We see in this essay by Gale one of the slackers' attempts to define themselves, to construct an identity in Mexico. The starting point of that identity was that they were internationalist and opponents of war.

The slackers in Mexico with whom we are concerned here, that is the political radicals, were mostly idealists, people of deeply held principles. Their own socialist anti-war principles led them to refuse to register for the draft, or, if drafted, to resist participation in the military and the war. In several cases they were drafted anyway and carried off to military camps, some were tried for various crimes, jailed, or imprisoned. Their principled stand interrupted their education or cost them their jobs or careers. The choices they made about the draft and the war suddenly altered their lives and their prospects. They had intended to be workers, teachers, writers, and political activists in their own country. While as Socialists they held an internationalist outlook, they would not necessarily have chosen the life of an international revolutionary. If someone had asked them in 1916, they would not have said that they planned to spend the next five or ten years of their lives in revolutionary Mexico organising the Industrial Workers of the World or the Communist Party.

The choices they made about the war and the draft, because of political principle, transformed them. The war appeared simultaneously as both a cataclysmic worldwide, world-historical event, and as a profound personal challenge and commitment. The war became both the most intimate and the most universal of experiences. These young men of socialist convictions were suddenly confronted with the question: What will *you* do about the war? What is the relationship between your principles and your practice? Will you practice what you preach? Will you stand up to the system or will you participate in what you have denounced as a capitalist, imperialist war? Will you organise a movement to oppose the draft and the war? Or will you go off to kill other workers and even other Socialists from other countries? Are you willing to go to jail for your beliefs?

---

30   Ibid.
31   Ibid.

Many resisted. The experience of opposing the war and resisting the draft transformed a few of these young men and women from rank-and-file Social-ist Party members into political activists, spokespersons and leaders. Charles Francis Phillips, Eleanor Parker and Owen Cattell, arrested on 1 June 1917, may have been the first case, but in any case, it was certainly among the very first, brought against anti-draft activists. What they said and did then suddenly took on enormous importance because these three young people had suddenly become representatives and spokespersons for the anti-draft movement. Her-man Levine, the Brooklyn schoolteacher who refused to register for the draft, had to testify in court, was asked to speak to the press and wrote letters to the newspapers from jail. He became a spokesperson for the Socialist Party, for the anti-war movement, and for his generation. The experience of resisting made these young people into resisters. They chose through their actions to become who they thought they should be, who they thought they were: socialists, inter-nationalists, revolutionaries.

In doing so, these young people made a serious, even dangerous choice. We have to remember that American society suddenly had become threatening to the political opposition, to dissidents, and especially to anarchist, syndicalist, and socialist opponents of war. Hundreds of members of the Industrial Workers of the World, the Socialist Party, and anarchist organisations were arrested and jailed. Military officers or soldiers, police and prison guards, patriots and vigil-antes beat, tortured and even murdered some radical anti-war activists. At least 17 conscientious objectors or other opponents of war were killed in the United States during World War I. The socialist war and draft resisters now had to ask themselves another question: What made more sense? To be carried off to a military camp and beaten into submission? To be imprisoned for the next sev-eral years in Leavenworth? Or to evade the draft by going to Mexico? The threat of death often hung over the choice: After Charles Francis Phillips received notes threatening to kill him, and was threatened with being re-conscripted, he decided to go to Mexico.

For the first time in modern American history, Woodrow Wilson's repression of the pacifist, socialist, and labour union movement had produced a group of American leftist revolutionaries in exile. By the time the war resisters went off to Mexico, they were different people than they had been just a few months before. The war and the draft had transformed them into political activists and local leaders and then in some cases into national figures. In a few cases they had become full-time, Socialist anti-war activists, one might almost say, professional revolutionaries. As such activists and revolutionaries, they left for Mexico. The question must have arisen in their minds: What would they do in Mexico? Would they continue to be Socialist political activists? Would they fight the war and the draft from down there?

4   Into Mexico

Crossing the border into Mexico, the slackers became in fact what they had considered themselves to be in theory: international socialists. The refusal to be drafted and go to war had itself represented a rejection of nationalism for internationalism. But that internationalism had been rather abstract: they could not actually reach out and take the hand of the German worker. But crossing the border into Mexico became a concrete expression of their internationalism. If they could not hold out their hand to the distant German, they could embrace the Mexican worker. They could create an international socialist movement, a movement of Americans and Mexicans. Several of them would try to do so.

The Mexico they entered was in the final stages of a violent revolution that lasted 10 years (1910–20), took nearly one million lives out of a population of 15 million, and propelled hundreds of thousands of refugees to the United States. If some of the war resisters had been theoretical revolutionaries before, they now found themselves in the middle of a practical revolution. To these socialist anti-war activists, the time in which they lived appeared not only as an era of war, but also as a revolutionary epoch. Revolution had shaken China, Persia and Turkey. Russia had just undergone two revolutions. American Socialists greeted the Russian Revolution of February 1917 with enthusiasm and the November 1917 Revolution with near ecstasy. As Phillips later wrote, it seemed that, 'The liberation of the world had begun!'[32]

The Russian Revolution of November 1917, that is the Bolshevik or Soviet Revolution, became a catalytic event that profoundly affected the left, the labour movement, and many millions of people around the world. To the slackers heading for Mexico – though this was still rather hazy at the time – Bolshevism or Communism offered an alternative political and personal identity. Politically, in the global panorama, Communism presented a revolutionary alternative to Social Democracy and labour reformism, which had collapsed at the outbreak of World War I in August 1914. To some of the slackers as individuals – and this would only become clear over time – Communism held out an alternative self-conception, the identity and the career of a professional, international revolutionary in the Bolshevik of Communist movement.

---

32   Shipman 1993, p. 44.

CHAPTER 9

Socialists and Internationalists: Four American War Resisters Who Chose Mexico

Conscription began on 5 June 1917, and almost immediately the state's screws began to tighten on pacifists, anti-war activists, draft resisters and the men who now became draft evaders. The government adopted the posture that young men who refused to register for the draft or who didn't report when called – especially if they did so publicly, for political reasons or as part of an anti-draft and anti-war movement – had to be made into examples. The US District Attorneys and the Federal Courts clamped down; they arrested, tried, often convicted, and jailed many of these men. At first the judges tended to mete out short and symbolic jail terms, later they handed down longer prison sentences.

The experience of resistance and repression, combined with the flight into exile, tended to strengthen the Socialists' ideological commitment, but also to transform it. The Socialist Party of the 1910s had been a big tent held together by the party's electoral political activity. But fighting the war and the draft and fleeing to preserve their freedom and their very lives tended to transform these Socialists into deeply committed radical activists. They would take to Mexico their socialist politics, virtually unknown in that neighbouring nation, but there they would discover other equally committed revolutionaries of various sorts: nationalist, anarchist, and syndicalist.

1 Charles Francis Phillips

In the spring of 1917 in cities throughout the United States, Socialists and other leftists organised anti-war activities, increasingly focusing their work on opposition to the draft as the national registration day, 5 June 1917, drew near. Charles Francis Phillips, a Socialist and journalism student at Columbia University, threw himself into an intense campaign against conscription, creating organisations, holding meetings, writing and distributing leaflets. He soon found himself to be virtually the first draft-resister in the country locked in a confrontation with the state, a conflict that would drive him to Mexico.

Phillips was born on 10 August 1895 in New York City, the son of Harry and Eva Phillips. His father Harry was a Jewish immigrant from Russia who became a small clothing manufacturer. His mother was the daughter of another Jewish immigrant, a wealthy footwear manufacturer named Hyman Jacob. Charles grew up in a non-religious, but conservative Republican family.[1] At the age of eight, Charles was sent to study at the Mt. Pleasant Military Academy in Ossining, New York, a boarding school, staying there until he was 14. His parents later transferred him to eighth grade at New York's Public School 10, and from there he went to the High School of Commerce but left before finishing. Charles then worked at odd jobs, first as a salesman for a piece-goods firm and then as a stock boy for a publishing house. Neither job pleased him.

While still a child Charles had already rebelled against his conservative family's values. When a group of workers from his father's shop came to the family's house to protest against their poor working conditions, the young Charles took their side against his father. His angry father silenced Charles. 'But from then on, my sympathies were on the side of striking workers', wrote Phillips in his autobiography *It Had to Be Revolution*.[2] In 1912 when Theodore Roosevelt ran for president on the Progressive ticket, Charles Phillips wore Roosevelt campaign buttons and distributed Bull Moose Party leaflets. But Phillips and his friends also listened to socialist soapbox orators such as August Claessens and Jacob Panken. By the age of 17 Phillips had developed a political identity; he had become a radical. Phillips had begun to write, and his father encouraged him to return to school. At the father's urging, Walter Lippmann, a distant relative of the Phillips family, agreed to talk to young Charles. Lippmann, a protégé of the famous muckraker Lincoln Steffens, had once been a Fabian socialist and he was rapidly becoming famous as the author of *A Preface to Politics*. He persuaded Charles to enrol at Columbia University's Pulitzer School of Journalism.[3]

In September 1914, just a month after the outbreak of the war in Europe, the 19-year-old Phillips entered the university. At Columbia he took a course in European history with James Harvey Robinson, the man who introduced the work of Karl Marx into the History Departments of American universities. He also took courses from Charles Beard, whose books he admired and with whom he became friendly. Phillips joined the Columbia Socialist Club, which formed part of the Intercollegiate Socialist Society (ISS), and he was elected the club's secretary. At the same time, he began to frequent Greenwich Village, hanging out around the office of *The Masses*, the socialist magazine edited by Max Eastman and Floyd Dell, the attractive, radical magazine that expressed the views

1   Shipman 1993, pp. 1–7.
2   Shipman 1993, p. 8.
3   Steel 1981, pp. 24–5.

of the literary left wing of the Socialist Party and that favoured the Industrial Workers of the World, feminism and the working woman. *The Masses*, the literary intersection of radical politics, artistic modernism, and socialist feminism, exuded a romantic, rebellious, and libertarian vision of socialism that Phillips found exhilarating. At *The Masses* office, he had an opportunity to meet not only Eastman and Dell, but also other writers and artists including John Reed, Clement Wood, Boardman Robinson, Robert Minor, Lydia Gibson, Ida Rauh, Mary Heaton Vorse, Susan Glaspell, Louis Untermeyer, and Art Young.

'The Masses inspired me to promote a radical student magazine at Columbia', wrote Phillips in his memoir. Money for the publication of Phillips's magazine came from Professor James McKeen Cattell of the Department Psychology, Anthropology, and Philosophy at Columbia. Phillips called the magazine *Challenge* after poet Louis Untermeyer's magazine of the same name. Phillips later wrote:

> Inevitably the war in Europe dominated our pages. Both the Entente allies and the Central Powers had apologists in this country. We supported neither. Socialist and internationalist, we reiterated the timeworn adage that whichever side won, the people would lose. We advocated two things: end the fighting, and prevent our country from being drawn into it.[4]

While anti-war, the magazine was not pacifist. 'I was not a pacifist (and never have been)', Phillips wrote. 'I was ready to concede that some wars could be justified with all the suffering. But not this one'.[5] Phillips expresses here several of the key ideas that characterised the leftist ant-war movement of the period. First, the leftist anti-war movement stood for socialism, the organisation of the world's economy on a collective or social basis. Second, the movement opposed both the Entente and the Central Powers, and saw itself as internationalist, that is, the proponent of an alliance between the working people of the world. Third, the leftists were not absolute pacifists necessarily opposed to all wars, but as socialists were opposed to this particular capitalist and imperialist war. The heart of these socialist anti-war views was the idea of internationalism, based on the common humanity of all people and on proletarian internationalism, a belief in the central role of the international working class in the liberation humanity.

On 7 May 1915, a German submarine sank the *Lusitania* without warning, taking over a thousand lives, including those of 128 Americans. President Woodrow

---

4   Phillips 1993, p. 21.
5   Ibid.

Wilson immediately moved from neutrality to preparedness, and American pacifists, anti-militarists, and anti-war activists became more concerned with keeping the US out of the conflict. Rosika Schwimmer, a Hungarian feminist and pacifist, convinced the American industrialist Henry Ford, who was anti-war at that time, to sponsor a 'Peace Ship', which would tour Europe with leading anti-war spokespersons and students and seek to persuade the European powers to make peace. The Schwimmer-Ford peace mission involved 163 persons, of whom 55 were considered delegates. A number of others, socialists and feminists, 40 reporters, and 25 students also sailed. The latter were 'all interested in internationalism, though only two or three called themselves pacifists'.[6]

At the last minute, Charles Francis Phillips joined the passengers on the Oscar II, the Peace Ship that sailed for Europe on 4 December 1915. 'I had no faith in the pilgrimage', wrote Phillips, 'it seemed quixotic'. But the trip gave Phillips 'an opportunity to get to know anti-war students from all over the country. And that was exciting'. The Peace Ship voyage also gave Phillips a chance to meet 'veterans of the international struggle against militarism, campaigners of proved effectiveness'.[7] The voyage took Phillips to Christiana (Oslo), Stockholm, Copenhagen, and Holland, the first of what would be many trips abroad.

Phillips returned to the United States in January 1916, and threw himself into anti-war activities. He worked on his magazine *Challenge* and joined the Collegiate Anti-Militarism League, taking over the editorship of its magazine *War?* Phillips was joined in the League by Eleanor Parker and by Owen Cattell, son of the Columbia professor. They began a campaign against Reserve Officers Training programs, and Phillips took on the role of organising secretary for the New England region. At the same time, Phillips's interest in the Socialist movement became more serious. On 7 November 1916, he cast his first vote, opting for Socialist presidential candidate Allen L. Benson, and shortly after the election he joined the Socialist Party. The war, which had first made Phillips an anti-war activist, now made him a committed Socialist, not only a Socialist voter, but a party membe, a militant.[8]

On 3 February 1917, Germany sank a US ship in the war zone, and Wilson broke off diplomatic relations. Shortly thereafter Russian revolutionaries overthrew the Czar and established a new government under Paul Miliukov and

---

6 Kraft 1978, p. 116. In 'Appendix 1' Kraft provides a list of the 25 students, and Charles Francis Phillips's name appears there, though he is not mentioned in her narrative.
7 Phillips 1993, p. 25.
8 Phillips 1993, p. 33.

Alexander Kerensky. The overthrow of the Czar in Russia, which was allied with England and France, ended the autocracy, created a parliamentary democracy, and made it possible for Wilson to lead the United States into the war on the side of the allies – all of which now with the overthrow of the Czar were democratic nations – in order 'to make the world safe for democracy'. As Wilson moved the nation toward war, Charles Phillips prepared to organise resistance to both war and draft.

On 30 March 1917 Phillips wrote a letter to Randolph S. Bourne, a friend of the anti-war professors and students at Columbia, asking him if he could write something for a special 'War Number' of the Collegiate Anti-Militarism League magazine *War?* 'We have a pamphlet already prepared for the presses, and we want to be prepared to send it out immediately in the event of a declaration by Congress .... There is, however, no reason why the work of our organisation must cease following a declaration. There will still be enlistment, conscription, mental intolerance, compulsory military training, censorship, military government, national hate and the whole military system to combat'.[9] Phillips clearly understood the seriousness of the task he was undertaking, even if he did not foresee the kind of repression that the anti-war movement would almost immediately experience.

The United States Congress voted war on 6 April 1917, and the next day the US Socialist Party issued a proclamation reaffirming its internationalism, its opposition to the war, and calling for 'continuous active, and public opposition to the war, through demonstrations, mass petitions ...'. Phillips recalled, 'I knew little, as yet, of the internal ideological rivalries, but I was proud of my party's St. Louis proclamation'. Inspired by the Socialist Party's stand, Phillips called a meeting of some of 60 anti-war activists at Columbia to decide what they should do in the event that Congress passed a universal conscription law. The group of young people decided 'to assail the proposed conscription measure' and 'to urge men twenty-one to thirty to defy it by not registering'. Phillips, Parker and Owen Cattell were then chosen to put out a leaflet titled 'Will You Be Drafted?' Phillips had it printed and mailed it to everyone in their files. They also organised the distribution of copies on street corners near Columbia University, New York University, City College, Brooklyn College, and Fordham University.[10]

While the Socialist Party had called for collective opposition to the war, and supported draft resistance, neither the party nor its youth organisations had a

---

9   Letter of Charles F. Phillips to Randolph Bourne, 30 March 1917, Bourne Collection. Special
     Collections, Columbian University Libraries.
10   Phillips 1993, pp. 35–6.

clearly worked out plan. The Socialist Party members who decided to resist did so largely on their own initiative out of both political principle and personal conviction. Like other conscientious objectors to war whether Christian pacifists or liberal humanitarians, the socialists also recoiled at killing men they did not know, or being killed themselves for a cause in which they did not believe. When individual Socialists began to refuse to register for the draft or to report for duty, the Socialist Party press took up their cases, and the publicity no doubt encouraged others to follow their example.

Meanwhile the Wilson administration had begun a severe repression of all opponents of the war, and Phillips's leaflet was not overlooked. On 1 June 1917 Phillips, Parker and Cattell were arrested for conspiring to interfere with the draft.[11] The crime was a felony carrying a maximum sentence of two years in federal prison, a $10,000 fine, and loss of citizenship rights. 'Our case was the first one involving defiance of registration and the papers were full of it', Phillips wrote in his memoir.[12]

While in jail awaiting trial, Phillips had been involuntarily registered for the draft. But when 5 June 1917, the national registration day arrived, Phillips once again refused to register voluntarily.[13] Consequently he was arrested again on the night of 5 June 1917 and indicted by the Grand Jury on a charge of refusing to register. Phillips pleaded not guilty and was charged by Judge Mayer and held with bail set at $10,000. Later, however, he appeared again before the court, pleading guilty this time and, saying he was willing to register, but only to test the constitutionality of the conscription act.[14] Phillips read the following statement:

> Believing that the so-called conscription law is in direct violation of our constitutionally guaranteed liberty of conscience and freedom from involuntary servitude, and that conscription is a menace to the democratic institutions of our country, and believing, furthermore, that registration is an integral part of the draft, I refused to present myself before the registration board on June 5, and I now make the plea of guilty, withholding the right to test the constitutionality of this law upon the charge of conspiracy for which I stand indicted.[15]

---

11   '3 Students' 1917.
12   Phillips 1993, p. 37.
13   'Phillips' 6 June 1917.
14   'Draft Slackers' 7 June 1917; 'Objector' 1917.
15   'Objector' 1917.

Phillips's argument that conscription violated the Thirteenth Amendment to the Constitution, which prohibits involuntary servitude, was invoked throughout this period by Populists and Socialists. Tom Watson, famous leader of the Southern Populists used that argument, as did Seattle Socialist Hulet M. Wells.[16] Clearly the argument was popular because conscription was obviously both involuntary and a form of servitude, though no court ever upheld the argument. In any case, the judge accepted Phillips' willingness to sign-up, whatever the motive, and reduced his bail to $500.

Phillips's second arrest and indictment for failure to register on 5 June became a factor in the trial of the leaflet case involving Phillips, Parker and Cattell. The prosecution attempted to use the second indictment to prove Phillips's culpability in the matter of the leaflet, and, though Judge Julius M. Mayer ruled it out of order, it probably influenced the jury.

Owen's father, Professor Cattell, helped his son and the other two young people organise their defence. He suggested they get in touch with Roger Baldwin of the National Civil Liberties Bureau (later the American Civil Liberties Union). Baldwin in turn suggested that the group contact the Socialist Party attorney Morris Hillquit and ask him to represent them. Hillquit, one of the principal local and national leaders of the Socialist Party and the co-author of the Socialist Party's strong statement against the war, was busy organising the People's Council for Peace and Democracy, a coalition of socialist, pacifist, and liberal opponents of the war.[17] Still, he agreed to take the students' case, which was largely handled by as his assistant Winter Russell.

The case came to trial almost immediately. Eleanor Parker was acquitted of all charges for lack of evidence, so she was not tried.[18] Government prosecutors dropped the case against Parker, no doubt believing that it would be easier to convict the two young men as 'slackers' if they were tried alone. The government's witnesses against Phillips and Cattell were two Justice Department agents, the socialist printer Max Siegel (or Moses Spiegel), who had printed their leaflet but had then adopted a pro-war position, and – to Phillips's shock and dismay – his own father. Hillquit and Russell tried to get the charges dismissed on the ground that the draft was unconstitutional and that in any case the law carried no legal penalty. But Judge Mayer would hear none of it.[19]

Phillips, Parker, and Cattell all testified that they had intended to make sure that the pamphlet was within the law, but that the Federal Secret Ser-

---

16   Woodward 1979, p. 456. Peterson 1946, p. 22.
17   Pratt 1979. See: Chapter 11, 'Hillquit and the War, 1914–1917'.
18   'Columbia Girl' 21 June 1917.
19   'Draft Illegal' 19 June 1917.

vice had seized the proofs of the pamphlet before they could make the necessary changes.[20] The jury did not believe them and found the two men guilty. Judge Mayer subsequently sentenced them: Owen Cattell was given one day in prison and a fine of $500; Phillips was given five days in jail and a fine of $500. Phillips's father paid the fine but would not speak to his son. Because the sentences were so short, Phillips and Cattell were allowed to serve their time in the Toombs jail in New York City.[21] Eleanor Parker, whose charges had been dismissed, read a statement to the press on behalf of her friends: 'We do not understand how it can be illegal to join in a protest against a conscription law which had at the time not been enacted, when the constitution guarantees freedom of speech and assembly'.[22]

The students were not only prosecuted by the state, but their university also penalised them. Columbia University President Nicolas Murray Butler expelled the activists from the university, stating that 'what was wrongheadedness and folly is now sedition and treason'. Butler declared, 'There is, and will be, no place in Columbia University, either on the rolls of its faculties or on the rolls of its students for any person who opposes or who counsels opposition to the effective enforcement of the laws of the United States, or who acts speaks or writes treason'.[23] But one of Columbia's most famous alumni came to the defence of the students. Randolph Bourne, then a writer for *The New Republic* and a friend of the student anti-war activists, told the press, 'As a Columbia alumnus, I am proud that the name of my university is connected with students willing to take so uncompromising a stand against our real enemy, militarism. As students of a university whose president and many of whose professors were workers in the peace propaganda when peace was popular, they are carrying along in their idealistic resistance to the war the best traditions of Columbia radicalism'.[24] Convicted of a crime, expelled from Columbia University, written up almost daily in *The New York Times* and other newspapers, Phillips became briefly, but notoriously, one of the most prominent war resisters in the country.

In addition to expelling Phillips and Owen Cattell, Columbia president Butler also fired Professors Cattell and Dana for their anti-war statements. Some of his critics argued that Butler was motivated by political ambitions, aspiring to be a vice-presidential candidate in the next national election. In protest against the firing of his colleagues, even though he was pro-war, Prof. Charles

---

20   'Boys' 20 June 1917; 'Anti-Draft' 23 June 1917.
21   'Two Students' 13 July 1917.
22   'Two Students Fined $500 and Day in Custody', *The Call*, 13 July 1917.
23   'Objector to Draft Agrees to Register', *The Call*, 7 June 1917.
24   'Patriotism Convicted Two Students, Says Writer', *The Call*, 23 June 1917.

Beard, the nationally famous historian and very popular teacher, resigned his position at Columbia and left the academy forever to become an independent scholar. Phillips' anti-war activities thus became even more widely known for their connection to this academic and political storm centre.

As soon as he was out of jail, Phillips, together with Cattell and Parker, returned to the offices of the Collegiate Anti-Militarism League. Phillips, now completely alienated from his father and having decided to marry Eleanor Parker, needed a way to support himself. Hillquit found Phillips a job as a copyreader at *The Call*, the New York City Socialist Party daily newspaper. He worked at *The Call*'s copy desk with Irwin Granich, a young writer who would later adopt the pen name Mike Gold and become famous as a novelist. Meanwhile Phillips and Parker were married at City Hall on 31 October 1917.

The Socialist and anti-war movements in which Charles Phillips was now deeply involved were transformed by world events in late 1917. On 7 November 1917 there was a second Russian Revolution – called the October Revolution because of the use of the Georgian calendar in Russia – led by the Bolshevik faction of the Russian Social Democratic Labour Party. The Bolsheviks dispersed parliament and declared that the '*soviets*' or councils of workers, soldiers and peasants would form the new government. Two men virtually unknown outside of Russia, Vladimir Lenin and Leon Trotsky, headed the new state. Phillips attended an enormous mass meeting at Madison Square Garden organised by the Socialist Party to celebrate the victory of the second Russian Revolution. He later wrote that he felt that, 'The liberation of the world had begun'.[25]

Like many in the Socialist Party and like many anti-war activists, Phillips sympathised and identified with the Russian Soviet government and the Bolshevik Party (soon to be renamed the Communist Party). Phillips remembered that, 'The first act of the regime was an appeal for immediate peace'. The Bolsheviks, who had apparently led the workers and peasants to power, now promised to withdraw Russia from the war. In effect the Russian nation had become a socialist conscientious objector. Phillips cheered himself hoarse for 'Our socialist fatherland', a view held at that time 'by practically the entire American socialist movement'.[26]

Phillips's new orientation toward Soviet Russia and its Bolshevik Party represented a significant transformation of his politics, as of the politics of many Socialist Party members. In the past their internationalism, their support for the international working class and socialist movement had expressed itself

25   Phillips 1993, p. 44.
26   Phillips 1993, p. 45.

as support for the Socialist or Second International. But the collapse of the Second International in August 1914 with the outbreak of the war had left many deeply disappointed and disillusioned. Now the October Revolution, the new Soviet government of Russia, and the Bolshevik Party of Lenin and Trotsky, gave new them new hope in internationalism and a new centre – a workers' government – with which to identify.

In February of 1918 Phillips received a notice to report for military duty but decided to ignore it. The Draft Board notified the press, and Phillips explained to the newspapers his intention to defy the order. Within a few days the police arrested Phillips and delivered him to Camp Upton at Yaphank, Long Island. He was forced through a physical examination, forcibly dressed in a uniform, and when he refused to participate in military drill was punched and kicked by the drill sergeant. Such treatment of pacifists or resisters was not uncommon. Julius Eichel recounted that when because of his beliefs as a conscientious objector to military service he refused to stand guard duty, an officer ordered another man to tie him to a bench and keep him awake all night by making him stare at a fire.[27]

After a second day of mistreatment and beatings, Phillips was transferred to a conscientious objector barracks with several Quakers, religious fundamentalists, and two other socialists. Phillips spent a few weeks on the base, until 3 March 1918 when, seeing that he was intransigent, the camp commandant, General Johnston, had Phillips dishonourably discharged from the military as a convicted felon, based on Phillips's conviction of conspiracy for his anti-draft activities. Eichel remembered that 'a great stir was caused by the arrival of a young man, Francis Phillips, who had achieved fame on the Columbia University campus with another young man whose last name was Catall [Cattell], because they had engaged in anti-war activity'. Eichel recalled, 'We found him a very intelligent and interesting fellow, but unfortunately, he stayed with us for only three days, at the expiration of which the government freed him on the pretext that he was mentally unfit. No doubt the authorities considered him too dangerous for the camp'.[28]

Phillips' discharge became headlines in the New York City papers that very afternoon, for Phillips seemed to have found a way to successfully dodge the

---

27   Eichel 1981, p. 23.
28   Eichel 1981, pp. 31–2. Eichel continues erroneously, 'He [Phillips] later went to Mexico where, I have been told, he achieved fame and distinction as president of the Yucatan Republic' (p. 32). Eichel had confused Phillips with Roberto Haberman, another American socialist, who went to the Yucatan and worked with future governor Felipe Carrillo Puerto.

draft. Defying conscription, he became a felon, and being a felon, he was then ineligible for the draft. Clearly this would be unacceptable to the government and to the right-wing pro-war groups.

While he had apparently escaped both the army and prison, Phillips could not escape the notoriety, the poison pen letters, the critical newspaper articles and condemnatory editorials. On 4 March 1918 Phillips received a letter signed 'J.R. King' that called him 'a FELON, A CRIMINAL, A LOAFER, A SLACKER, A PACI-FIST and everything else that could make a MISERABLE DIRTY CUR'. The writer went on, 'You are one of the VILEST, most DEGENERATE CREATURES on the face of the Earth, and are not fit for DOGS TO ASSOCIATE WITH. Damn your Rotten Soul'. One day Phillips came home to find a note on his door that read: 'You dirty looking cur at this very corner before many months is [*sic*] gone you will get a damned good bullet put through your rotten heart you are a danger to the country you rotten anarchists [*sic*]'.[29] At the time war resisters were being beaten, tarred-and-feathered, and in several instances murdered, so Phillips could not regard these notes as idle threats.

The New York Times in an editorial published on 9 March 1918 and titled 'Martyrdom Won Far Too Easily', expressed its indignation that Phillips had not only 'defied the Government and escaped the draft, but he has revealed to all of like mind the way to do the same thing and attain the same distinction among their fellows'.[30] The editorial suggested the US government authorities were planning to draft Phillips again, and send him back to the camp, and this time, if he refused to cooperate, to subject him to military trial and punishment.

Nevertheless, Phillips continued to organise resistance to the war and the draft. The Collegiate Anti-Militarism League having died, Phillips, with the help of the pacifist leader Rebecca Shelly, put together a new organisation called Young Democracy. The Socialist Party's Rand School provided him with a national mailing list, and Phillips was back in business. The new organisation planned an anti-war convention to be held on 4 and 5 May at the Mountain House in Valhalla, New York, but the Post Office Department declared the notices of the convention 'unmailable', and the Justice Department kept the movement under surveillance. Again *The New York Times* took up the issue, in a 12 April editorial titled 'His Triumph Gives Him Courage', noting Phillips's return to anti-war activism, suggesting that he had made a mockery of the authorities and insisting that something should be done about it.[31]

---

29   Phillips 1993, pp. 50–1.
30   Cited in Phillips 1993, p. 52.
31   Cited in Phillips 1993, p. 53.

Fearing that he would be redrafted and sent to a military camp, or perhaps that some overzealous patriot would attempt to kill him, Phillips decided he had to make a plan. Phillips and his new wife Eleanor deliberated with their confidants, Owen Cattell, his father Professor Cattell, and a few other friends. At the suggestion of Professor Cattell, Charles and Eleanor decided that if it seemed as if Charles would be re-drafted, then they would flee to Mexico. Owen Cattell also decided to go to Mexico, though separately. The couple did not have to wait long. A few days later, on 15 April, the newspapers reported that the War Department had criticised General Johnston's discharge of Phillips. At the beginning of May Secretary of War Ray Stannard Baker announced that Phillips would be re-drafted.

Charles Phillips and Eleanor Parker left at once for Mexico.

2   Herman Levine

Meanwhile, over the bridge in Brooklyn, another New York anti-draft activist found himself caught up in a similar drama, though being Brooklyn and not Manhattan it took place without the luminaries and literati. Herman Levine, a public school teacher was also an anti-war activist, and on 5 June 1917, his personal and political convictions led him to refuse to register for the draft – and he said so publicly. The result was a conflict with the draft board, the school board, and the courts, conflicts that would propel him too to Mexico.

Born in 1893, Levine had grown up in New York City. He attended Public School 84 in Brooklyn, graduated with honours, and then went on to Brooklyn Boys' High School and later took courses at City College of New York where he was an outstanding student. In 1913 he won the college's first annual oration contest with a speech titled: 'War – What For?'[32] Like many Jewish immigrant children, Levine aspired to become a professional, in his case an educator. In 1914 Levine became a schoolteacher, taking a job at Public School 160 at Rivington and Suffolk streets on the Lower East Side of Manhattan, and became active in his profession. 'He originated a series of departmental conferences in which he wrote and lectured extensively', wrote a newspaper reporter. 'This system was made the subject of a special borough teachers' conference in September 1916'.[33] While teaching, the intellectually ambitious Levine also took courses in history and government at Columbia University, though he doesn't seem to

---

32   'Draft Opponent' 13 June 1917; 'Draft Slackers' 7 June 1916.
33   'Draft Opponent May Be Jailed', *The Call*, 13 June 1917.

have moved in the same circles as Phillips and Parker and we don't know if they ever met at that time.

In addition to his teaching and studies, Levine was an active Socialist Party member, affiliated with the Addison Socialist Club in Brooklyn. One of the Socialist Party's principal activities was anti-war work, and Levine was also an anti-war activist. In early April of 1917 he participated in a lobbying effort as part of a peace delegation to the US Congress in Washington, D.C. He also served as a delegate from the Addison Socialist Club to the First American Conference for Democracy and Terms of Peace, which had been organised by the newly formed People's Council.

Twenty-three years old when the US began conscription on 5 June 1917, Levine was required to register. 'He surrendered himself to authorities after registration day, declaring that he was opposed to war and therefore was compelled by his principle to refuse to register, as to do so would mean acquiescence in the war', reported the Socialist newspaper *The Call*.[34] Levine reported voluntarily on 6 June to United States Marshal James M. Power, announcing that he had not registered and did not intend to. Not having $1,000 bail, he spent the night in the Raymond Street jail. On 7 June he appeared for arraignment in federal court in Brooklyn with his attorney Winter Russell.[35] In short order Levine was tried and found guilty of violating the conscription law.

On 18 June Levine appeared in court again, this time for sentencing. United States Judge Chatfield offered him one more chance to register. His parents and sisters begged him to take it. 'Levine replied that he believed the war to be unjust, and that as his principles forbade him to fight, he would not register'.[36] The Judge then sentenced Levine to serve 11 months and 29 days – the maximum penalty less one day. The judge stipulated that the sentence had to be served in jail with no time off for good behaviour. Before leaving the courtroom, Levine was involuntarily registered for the draft by the authorities.

Apparently, a prison term was not enough punishment, for Levine was also fired from his job. The state commissioner of education deprived Levine of his license to teach, and the school board at a meeting on 11 July 1917 dismissed him from his teaching position at Public School 160.[37] The state and the school board made it impossible for Levine to practise his profession in his native state, and no doubt this became another factor in driving him into exile.[38]

---

34   'Draft Opponent' 13 June 1917.
35   'Kramer Trial' 8 June 1917.
36   'Limit of Law' 14 June 1917; 'Get's Law's Limit' 14 June 1917.
37   'Levine Dismissed' 13 July 1917; 'Board Dismisses' 12 July 1917.
38   Such actions were not uncommon at the time. In Minneapolis, Minnesota on 21 Septem-

While in jail, Levine was duly notified that he would still have to appear for his mandatory physical examination. Standing on his principles, he wrote from jail to *The Call*, rather sententiously, 'I shall ... not raise any technicality, but offer myself as a sacrifice, if need be, to the greedy, exploiting and devastating system of capitalism'.[39] As Levine's statement makes clear, he was a conscientious objector to the war because he was a socialist opposed to capitalist wars. He asserted, 'My life will affirm what my mind and heart dictate. I have refused to do their bidding by refusing to register. I will refuse to do their bidding in the future'.[40] Levine's statements published in *The Call*, thus also served, as he surely realised, as anti-draft and anti-war propaganda. His own intransigence might serve as an inspiration to other young men to resist.

Levine also wrote a letter from jail to a friend who then passed it on to be published in *The Call*:

> My fate is by no means sad. What can be higher than to oppose that barbaric and inhuman process of killing our fellow men whom we have never seen and against whom we bear no hatred. I cannot be really sad, and if gloomy moments do appear, they are hurried off by the gleam of the coming day.[41]

'The coming day', as his friend and the readers of *The Call* would have understood, was an allusion to the coming socialist revolution. Levine advised his correspondent, apparently, another socialist conscientious objector, to stick to his principles.

Having been registered against his will in prison, when Levine finished his prison sentence, he was still subject to the draft, and, if he refused, to imprisonment. Evidently preferring his freedom, he must have left for Mexico immediately upon release in June 1918. Levine reached Mexico City shortly thereafter, and adopted two aliases and identities: Mischa Poltiolevsky, claiming to be a Russian immigrant, and Martin Paley, an American schoolteacher. Much as in the case of Phillips, Levine's experience in jail and prison must have hardened his radical convictions, for when he left and fled to Mexico, he continued his

---

ber 1919 the board of education dismissed D.J. Amoss from his teaching job at Central high school because of his alleged membership in the Industrial Workers of the World. 'Minneapolis Teacher' 22 September 1917, p. 9.

39   'Levine Refuses Physical Test', *The Call*, 9 August 1917.

40   'Levine Dismissed by School Board', *The Call*, 40; 'Teacher Who Resisted Draft Content in Jail', *The Call*, 3 September 1917.

41   'Teacher Who' 3 September 1917.

political activity, though now as a leftist labour organiser rather than as an anti-war activist.

3   Carleton Beals

As sons of Jewish immigrants, students at Columbia University, Socialist Party activists, and committed anti-war activists, Phillips and Levine fairly epitom-ise the student New York anti-war movement of 1917. Carleton Beals, on the other hand, represented another stronghold of American socialism and anti-war activity, the Southwest and Far West of the United States. Beals too resisted the draft and went to jail and military prison for his convictions, but he had come to his political principles by a different route.

Beals was born on 13 November 1893 in Medicine Lodge, Barber County, Kan-sas to Leon Eli Beals and Elvina Blickensderfer Beals. Leon was a lawyer and the publisher of the local newspaper *The Barber County Index* and Elvina was a schoolteacher.[42] Both parents were radicals, active first in the Populist Party and the labour movement, and later in the Socialist Party.[43] The family library contained Karl Marx's *Capital*, and the family once hosted Socialist Party leader Eugene V. Debs in their home when he was on a speaking tour. Carleton thus grew up in a socialist culture, and Marxism and the socialist movement were everyday topics of conversation in the Beals home.

When Carleton was still a boy the family moved to Pasadena, California where his father Leon failed in two businesses, first in a poultry farm and then in a general store. The former attorney and publisher took up clerical work, while continuing his activities with the labour unions and the Socialist Party. Carleton Beals went to Pasadena High School, played sports, and even worked on the floats for the Tournament of Roses Parade. He may also have had some familiarity with Mexican-Americans because his father Leon worked with a union that organised Mexican-American workers in the sugar-beet industry.

When Carleton Beals entered the University of California in 1911, the entire family moved to Berkeley to help support him both financially and emotion-ally. At first Beals studied mine engineering, apparently thinking that would offer him an economically secure future, but he soon changed his major to Eng-lish with a minor in economics. Beals took a course from leftist economist Paul

42   Britton 1987, *passim* and Beals 1938, *passim*.
43   The movement of former Populists into the Socialist Party was fairly common in the Southwest. See: Green 1978.

Blissen called 'heretical' economics, studying Ricardo as well as Marx and Engels. While studying Marx at Berkeley, Beals also worked with the Socialist Party to help arrange a visit by Debs. At the same time, Beals developed his journalistic skills by writing for the campus newspaper, *Student Opinion*.

In June of 1916 Beals graduated from Berkeley and enrolled at Columbia University Teachers College in New York City. We have no record of his being involved in political activity while at Columbia, nor of his having any involvement in the New York Socialist Party. He does not appear to have known either Phillips or Levine at Columbia, though he would later get to know both in Mexico. While working part time, Beals received his Master's degree in just nine months and then took a student teaching job in New Jersey. When the term ended, Beals returned to California, taking another teaching job in the San Francisco Bay area. Beals's plan for a teaching career was interrupted when on 8 August 1917 he was ordered to report for a pre-induction physical examination by Selective Service Local Board No. 135 of New York City. Beals chose, however, to report to Berkeley Exemption Board No. 2, which was his right. He informed the Berkeley board that he was a conscientious objector and refused to register for the draft, so the Berkeley board had him arrested. Beals told the press that he believed conscription to be 'un-American and undemocratic' and explained that he planned to challenge the constitutionality of conscription in the courts. In explaining his views, Beals claimed that his religion was 'Positivism', a religion that forbid him from taking a life.[44] The 'Positivism' argument, however, was simply a ruse. Beals's real religion may be said to have been socialism, and it was that which prevented him from taking a life, at least in a capitalist war.

After a few days in jail, the Berkeley police released Beals, but soon he was arrested again, this time on a charge of desertion. Six days later Beals was once again released. On 13 December Beals received an order from the New York Board to report to the Berkeley Board, which he ignored. Consequently, on 17 December he was arrested by a US Marshal and jailed at the Presidio military prison in San Francisco. At that point the New York board ordered Beals to be inducted at the nearest military base, but for some reason the Berkeley Board preferred to keep him in the Presidio prison. Beals had become snared in a web of bureaucracy, which at least for the moment saved him from the war.

Beals never wrote about his experience in the Presidio, but certainly it must have been unpleasant at best. As Eichel wrote from his own experience, 'The military prisoner is the most abject, cringing, and helpless person imaginable'.

---

44   Britton 1987, pp. 10–11.

Writes Eichel, 'Some of the objectors died in meeting the full onslaught of this system which punished the body as well as the spirit, but those who survived, retained their spirit and the militarists were frustrated'.[45] Beals would be among the latter.

Carleton's mother Elvina, meanwhile, had contacted Roger Baldwin of the National Civil Liberties Bureau, which appealed to Secretary of War Newton Baker for Beals's release, though the appeal was unsuccessful. Nevertheless, Beals won his freedom apparently because the Presidio company commander considered the presence of a conscientious objector on the base to be a nuisance. The commander supposedly told the base physician to find some problem with Beals's health, and consequently Beals was 'diagnosed' as having both a serious heart problem and a hearing disability. Beals was discharged on 11 February 1918 with the Selective Service classification 5-G as totally and permanently unfit for military service.[46] Like Phillips and Levine, Beals had his convictions tested, in his case by both jail and military prison. He had made his own the socialist principle in which he had been raised. If before he had been a theoretical opponent of the capitalist state, now he was its enemy in practice.

Returning to Berkeley, Beals took a job briefly with Standard Oil Company, probably because, as a conscientious objector, school teaching was out of the question. But he found his job with the Standard Oil boring, and moreover he must have felt far from secure. Carleton Beals had narrowly escaped the draft, but neither he nor his family could have felt completely confident that the US government would not try to draft or imprison him again. Furthermore, Carleton's brother Ralph Beals remained eligible for the draft. Apparently with their parents' blessing, in July 1918 the two brothers left Berkeley and headed for Mexico in a second-hand Ford. The men crossed the border without incident and headed south. When they got to Culiacán, Sinaloa, Ralph took a job with a German-American businessman, while Carleton continued on to Mexico City first by burro and then by railroad.[47]

Carleton Beals may have been the best prepared to enter Mexico. He was not yet wanted by the police. He had the comfort, at least at first, of travelling with his brother. Having grown up in the Far West, he had some familiarity with Mexicans and could well have known a few words of Spanish. After leaving

---

45   Eichel 1981, pp. 41–3.
46   Britton 1987, p. 11.
47   Beals R 1977, pp. 13–32. Unfortunately, Ralph Beals does not expatiate much on his anti-war views, nor on his experience in Mexico. In November 1918, Ralph Beals returned to the United States, spent a couple of weeks in jail in Tucson, Arizona, and then with his mother's help returned to Berkeley.

his brother, however, Carleton Beals's trip to Mexico City, at points travelling by burro through arid land, proved difficult and led to a tormenting series of adventures, illnesses, and accidents before he eventually reached Mexico City. He arrived completely broke.[48]

4   Linn A.E. Gale

Unlike the other slackers described here, all of whom had spent time in and around the Socialist Party and anti-war movements, Linn A.E. Gale came out of the Democratic Party, and had no history of anti-war or anti-draft activities. Gale only turned to socialism after he became a draft evader, and even then, never broke with his long-held belief in spiritualism. In 1909 at the age of 17, Gale compiled, edited and published the *Genealogy of the Descendants of David Gale of Sutton. Mass*, an account of his own forbearers. The family history ended or, perhaps better, culminated in himself: 'Linn A.E. Gale was born in McDonough, May 31, 1892', read the genealogical entry. 'He is a student of Oxford High School in his junior year and his displayed remarkable literary talent and intellectual genius'. Among his other accomplishments the entry noted that Gale had organised 'the Mystic Order of the Esoteric Shrine', complete with a secret ritual that he himself had devised. Gale described himself as a debater 'with few equals among young men of his age' and noted that he served twice as president of the Calliope High School debating society and as an officer or member of several other societies, including Grand Secretary of the Future Men of America.[49]

Already at just 17, he claimed, he was 'a correspondent for several newspapers, occasionally contributed to magazines, and held the position of reporter with the *Norwich Sun* daily at Norwich in the summer of 1908'. Gale also described his intellectual interests and political views. 'He is an ardent student of political science and a Democrat of the radical Bryan type. In religion he is not connected with any church and is an adherent of the New Thought Philosophy'. In sum: 'Mr. Gale is a brilliant young man of superior attainments, clean upright character and unusual determination'.[50] Gale appears never to have lost this inordinate sense of self-importance, which he first developed as a teenager and maintained throughout his adult life.

---

48   Beals 1927, p. 294.
49   Gale 1909, p. 54.
50   Ibid.

After leaving high school, Gale pursued a career in journalism and in Democratic Party politics. 'In the little city of Norwich, containing 10,000 people, more or less, I got my experience as a "cub" in the newspaper game', Gale wrote later in Mexico. 'Subsequently migrating to Oneonta, Albany, New York, Worcester, etc., becoming an editor of a daily and later publisher of my own magazine', he claimed. Then Gale 'landed political jobs under Governors Sulzer and Glynn'.[51] Martin H. Glynn was both a newspaper publisher and the Governor of New York, and Gale worked as one of his publicists. While working for the Democratic Party machine in Albany, Gale also met his future wife Magdalena, who worked in a government office as a stenographer.[52] Using his literary skill in the service of Governor Glynn, Gale claimed he was 'fiercely denounced' by Glynn's Republican opponent Charles S. Whitman.

It was when Republican Whitman defeated Democrat Glynn for the governorship, Gale claimed, that all of his problems began. Governor Whitman, wrote Gale, 'secured his revenge by having the American News Company boycott my magazine, by persecuting me in various ways and finally by having his own bodyguard arrest me on a false and ridiculous charge'.[53] It is always difficult in reading Gale's account of events to separate fact from fiction and to distinguish actual political vendettas from paranoid fears of persecution, and then too there is always the self-aggrandisement. According to Gale's own account he first got in trouble with the law for using the mail for illegal purposes. He was apparently charged with obscenity for sending birth control information through the US mail. Later Gale was charged with overdrawing his bank account, and finally arrested on a complaint of Saks & Co. for writing bad cheques.

Still, wrote Gale, his enemies were not satisfied. Gale had heard that, 'Governor Whitman said, "Get that man Gale. I don't care how you do it, but get him, somehow! Send him to the army or anywhere else so he cannot continue that damned magazine"'. Gale suggests that Governor Whitman used the draft board to persecute him. Gale had registered for the draft, but had been excused in November 1917, pending an operation on his nose. But in December 1917 he was reclassified as 1-A, that is fit for duty, and ordered to report for a new physical exam on January 1918. He was then inducted in absentia on 4 April 1918.[54] So, wrote Gale, 'As a culmination of all this persecution [by Republican Gov-

---

51   Gale, March 1919a, p. 12.
52   Gale, March 1919b, p. 21.
53   Gale, March 1919c.
54   Christopulos 1980, p. 379.

ernor Whitman], I was conscripted for military service'.[55] To avoid the draft, Gale, travelling with his wife Magdalena, left Oxford, New York in April of 1918.[56] In what was their first involvement with the socialist movement in any form, the couple moved to a utopian socialist community in Sables, Louisiana where they resided for a short time.[57] From Louisiana they went to Texas and 'waded the Rio Grande in a shallow place near Laredo'.[58] Wrote Gale, 'I outwitted them in this, as in everything else, for I left the United States and came to Mexico, where I resumed publishing my magazine'.[59]

Unlike most of the other slackers, the Gales crossed the border to Mexico with over $5,000 in cash from Magdalena's savings, a very large sum in those days.[60] That sort of money must have made it possible for the Gales to take the train from Laredo south to Mexico City. His wife's savings also made it possible for Gale to look for a printer and begin publishing his magazine, *Gale's*, dedicated, as it proclaimed on its masthead, to international communism and spiritualism.

5   American Socialists in Mexico

All of the men discussed here had in common their resistance to conscription and their conflicts with the US government. Three of the prominent slackers discussed here – Phillips, Levine, and Beals – had a serious commitment to socialism and anti-militarism, as demonstrated by their membership in the Socialist Party, their participation in the anti-war or anti-draft movements, and their public statements, as well as their publications. Levine had written an anti-war essay on the theme '*Why War?*', while Phillips had published an anti-war magazine and later anti-conscription leaflets. Beals, Levine, and Phillips had all been Socialist Party members and all three became draft resisters. Socialism, anti-militarism and internationalism formed the core of their political commitment as well as of their personal philosophy Though we know less about her, with her participation in the anti-war movement clearly Eleanor Parker also shared these values and beliefs.

---

55   Gale, March 1919c, p. 3.
56   Gale, May 1920, p. 10.
57   Christopulos 1980, p. 379.
58   Gale, March 1919b, p. 9.
59   Gale, March 1919c, p. 3.
60   Letter of 16 June 1920 from Linn A.E. Gale to José Allen, p. 3, RG 165, Box 2290, USMID.

The Socialists' strongly held internationalist convictions led them to defy the government and to refuse the draft, as well as to face jail or prison terms. In choosing this course, the political activists interrupted their education and careers, and some broke their ties with their families. The experience of the courts and jail hardened their convictions and gradually turned them from radicals into revolutionaries.

Gale, however, represents another kind of person with a different psychology and different principles. He turned to political opposition to the war and the draft only after the United States entered the conflict, and only when he was personally threatened with conscription. Gale subsequently became a socialist only after he had become a draft evader. Gale's behaviour seems opportunistic and self-serving; a last-minute conversion to socialism and anti-militarism as a justification for dodging the draft and stiffing his creditors. Who knows? We do know that later Gale would change his political views again, moving to the far right in the early 1920s, in order to save his skin. But who can say what was in his mind when he went to Mexico? Perhaps for a time he shared the idealism of the others, as his personal predicament coincided briefly with a shift in world opinion and working-class politics. We know little of Magdalena Gale except her stubborn loyalty and devotion to her husband, but perhaps she also shared his newfound socialist convictions.

When these war resisters entered Mexico, the country was in the last stages of a violent decade-long revolution. Certainly, it is clear from these accounts that until sometime in early 1917 none of these men and women had any plan to go to Mexico, and while they were international socialists, they certainly didn't foresee becoming active in the left and labour movement of another country with a different language and culture. In a certain sense, their flight to Mexico appears as an accident, the only door left open by which they might escape the military or prison. But their pacifist, socialist and internationalist politics made it possible for them to consider refuge in Mexico as a new opportunity to continue their struggle against war and in favour of the socialist movement. At least for the three long-time Socialists, their socialist and internationalist politics made it possible for them to turn their accidental fate into an opportunity to participate in the labour movement in a new international framework. They were following in the wake of other socialists, such as John Kenneth Turner, John Murray and John Reed, who had also gone to Mexico – if only briefly – in the pursuit of socialism and internationalism.

The socialist slackers' internationalist convictions allowed these men to recast their identities and political roles in Mexico as international revolutionaries. But the role of the Russian Revolution in all of this can hardly be exaggerated. The two Russian Revolutions of February and November 1917, occurring in the very midst of their fight against the war and the draft, had an enormous impact on young people like these. The October Revolution, followed by the announcement of Russia's withdrawal from the war, must have seemed like an entire nation doing what they had done, objecting conscientiously to participation in the war. In their experience, the revolution, the Soviet Revolution, brought – if only briefly – the peace for which they had been striving. At the same time, as Socialists, they saw the Bolshevik Party, as the leader of that first successful workers' socialist revolution. Virtually every radical in America rallied to the Russian Revolution, the great symbol of the coming world socialist transformation.[61] In Phillips's words, it seemed that 'the liberation of the world had begun'. Now they would join that struggle for world liberation as international revolutionaries in Mexico.

---

61   'Until the formation of the Third (Communist) International in 1919 there was hardly a radical in America who did not support the Bolshevik Revolution, though some had already begun to dissociate themselves from one or another Bolshevik theory. Particularly among the intellectuals, who saw in the leaders of the new Russia not merely men of will but also men of ideas, there occurred a renewal of political hope'. Howe 1962, p. 25.

CHAPTER 10

Political Refugees in Revolutionary Mexico: Socialists and Spies

The American war resisters and draft evaders who fled the United States for Mexico in 1917 and 1918, or who came later in the early or mid-1920s, were entering another world: an arid, technologically backward, agricultural country with an utterly alien Spanish and indigenous cultural heritage, a nation then in the midst of a great revolutionary upheaval. While American radicals might have followed political developments in Mexico in the pages of Socialist Party papers *The Call* or the *Appeal to Reason*, or could well have read John Kenneth Turner's *Barbarous Mexico* or John Reed's *Insurgent Mexico*, that could hardly have prepared them to be suddenly thrust into revolutionary Mexico.

Most of the radical draft evaders were young men and their women companions in their early twenties, with little worldly experience. Few had ever travelled abroad. With the exception of a few Mexican-American workers, like Pedro Coria, none of the American radicals spoke any Spanish when they first arrived. Almost none had ever lived in or visited Mexico or any other place in Latin America. They had no jobs, most had no money, and their prospects were unclear. As political activists – anti-militarists, socialists, labour union activists, and feminists – they had no comrades and no contacts. They were starting from scratch.

Politically, they understood little or nothing about Mexico or its revolution. As Charles Francis Phillips, the student anti-draft activist from Columbia University, later explained in his autobiography, upon arrival in Mexico, the American war resisters knew only that the United States had recognised the government of Venustiano Carranza, and that General John J. Pershing had failed to catch the revolutionary leader Francisco Villa after his raid on Columbus, New Mexico.[1] The rest was terra incognita.

The danger of revolutionary Mexico was quickly conveyed to most of them. They learned, for example, that, because of the possibility of attack, trains travelled only during daylight hours, and then only with a military escort. Some American war resisters witnessed the violence or its results themselves. The slackers could see the revolution's wanton destruction of human life as they

---

1 Shipman 1993, p. 57.

travelled along the nation's highways and railroads. Journalist Carleton Beals remembered visiting with Federal troops the Desierto de los Leones in the mountains outside of Mexico City, an area held by Zapata's troops. 'Elongated wind-dried human cadavers, hung from trees or telegraph poles, turned slowly in the breeze', he wrote. Later he went on the old road to Cuernavaca, 'Many more cadavers dangled by the roadside – macabre weather-vanes of civil war'.[2] M.N. Roy, the Indian nationalist revolutionary, engaged in a secret mission attempting to buy guns for the revolution in India, took a train across the Isthmus of Tehuantepec. Bandits ambushed the train's military escort, 'a minor affair, which did not last more than half an hour'. Roy recalled that, 'Our train moved on and presently we were regaled with the gruesome spectacle of nine freshly killed human bodies dangling from trees and telephone poles'.[3] The public display of the corpses of rival revolutionary factions could be seen in many parts of the countryside, a shocking and horrifying token of the tens of thousands killed in the civil wars.[4]

If the slackers sometimes felt afraid, it was not unreasonable, for the Mexican Revolution had taken many human lives. At the beginning of the Revolution in 1910, Mexico's population was 15.1 million; in 1921 the population was only 14.3 million.[5] The ten most violent revolutionary years from 1910 to 1920 resulted in one million deaths through combat, starvation, and disease.[6] Among those deaths, the victims of the Spanish influenza in 1918 reached 500,000.[7] In addition to death, there was also great dislocation of populations and huge refugee movements. At least 300,000, but some estimate as many as one million Mexicans, fled to the United States.[8] Later the Cristero Rebellion of 1926 to 1929 resulted in thousands more deaths and another 400,000 refugees fleeing Mexico across the US border.[9]

In 1917 and 1918 when the American slackers arrived, the Mexican Revolution remained in process, a complex and frequently confusing struggle between social classes, political factions, revolutionary armies, and regional caudillos. Certainly, the revolution had not brought democracy to Mexico. The Spaniard

2   Beals 1938, p. 19.
3   Roy 1964, p. 103.
4   Langston Hughes, the African American poet, happened to live in Mexico during the Revolution, and he too remembered the bodies hanging in the trees. Hughes 1986, p. 59.
5   Instituto 1994, vol. 1, p. 13.
6   Meyer 1973, p. 109.
7   Matute 1994, p. 226.
8   Cardoso 1980, pp. 38 and 91.
9   Jean Meyer 1973, p. 109.

Vicente Blasco-Ibañez, who criticised and condemned the Mexican Revolution and the government of Carranza in his popular book *El Militarismo Mejicano* [*Mexican Militarism*] published in 1920, wrote, 'In Mexico, he who votes knows that he engages in a useless act'.[10] While accompanied by an enormous amount of electoral propaganda, elections tended to be rigged by the state or federal government. The government of President Carranza was notoriously corrupt, his Constitutionalistas became known as the *Consusuñaslistas* – that is those with their claws ready to rip out the wealth of the country. The word Carrancear (to behave like Carranza) came to mean 'to steal'. President Obregón told jokes about himself, ridiculing the avarice of the new political elite. He often recounted how when he lost his arm in a battle of the revolution, the soldiers went searching for it but could not locate it. Then one of his officers drew a bag of coins from his pocket and threw an Azteca, a ten-dollar gold piece, into the carnage of the battlefield, and a out of the tangle of corpses came a hand that seized the coin and came out dragging the arm behind it. That was of course the hand and arm of Obregón. The Obregón story might serve as a metaphor for his government and for the new political class who became the nouveau riche.

With a little time, the American socialist slackers came to understand the revolution as a class struggle between peasants and workers on the one hand, and landowners, industrialists, the church and the old Porfirian state on the others. The slackers tended to see the revolution as an incomplete process which, having overthrown Díaz and then Huerta, had brought to power a nationalist government which represented on the one hand the partial achievements of the revolutionary movement, and on the other stood as an obstacle to the rule of the peasants and workers. As socialists who had fallen under the influence of the Russian Bolshevik or Soviet Revolution, they came to see their task as completing the Mexican revolution, or carrying out a new socialist or soviet revolution which would put the economy and political power in the hands of Mexico's workers and peasants. But it would be sometime before all of that would become clear to them.

At first the slackers focused on their own survival. When they arrived in Mexico most had little or no money. Many must have found themselves destitute within a short period of time. Destitution could lead to desperation, and to moral compromises. In his autobiography, Charles Francis Phillips intimates that with his tacit approval his young wife Eleanor Parker may have traded personal attentions and perhaps sexual favours for money and housing for the two slackers for the six months they stayed in Mazatlán. Observing the young

---

10   Blasco-Ibañez 1979, p. 57.

American couple's plight – almost starving and sleeping on the benches – a wealthy Mexican businessman named Jesús Escobar offered to hire Eleanor Parker at three pesos a day plus a modestly furnished, one-room adobe hut rent-free. Escobar paid the three pesos per day, but never found any work for Parker. Instead, Escobar became a frequent visitor to the young couple's house and occasionally brought them 'small presents'. 'In the meantime, we pondered his intentions concerning Eleanor', wrote Phillips.[11]

Phillips described how Escobar, as a man who frequently bragged about his sexual exploits, 'had tricked, cheated, betrayed, despoiled, abused, and out-raged so many people that he had made a multitude of enemies and no friends. He was in fact the most hated man around'. Phillips writes that he and Eleanor concluded that Escobar had befriend them because he 'probably needed to feel he had done at least some good'. But Phillips' surmise is not convincing, and the reader is left with Phillips's own doubts and suspicions about Escobar and Eleanor.[12]

Others too compromised their morals to survive. Carleton Beals arrived in Mexico City almost broke and 'lived for quite a while on five centavos' worth of peanuts and five centavos' worth of bananas a day'. But poverty soon gave rise to pilfering. 'Once my money was gone, I stole a roll of bread out of the basket of a sleeping vender. I am not ashamed to confess this, except that I stole it from someone nearly as poor as myself'.[13] Greater moral challenges would arise in the future when political patrons would offer some of the slackers protection and money in exchange for political support for the Carranza government.

To deal with their poverty, loneliness, and alienation the slackers formed friendships and established social ties, usually first among other American war resisters. Almost as soon as they crossed the border and arrived in some town or city, the draft evaders began to meet each other and to form a network of Amer-ican contacts. In Mazatlán on Mexico's north Pacific coast, in his first few days in Mexico, Charles Francis Phillips ran in to Herbert Calvert. 'We discovered we were both socialists, both pro-Soviet, both readers of *The Masses*, both inter-ested in literature', wrote Phillips. Calvert introduced Phillips to his wife Mellie Calvert and to their friend Harold Herrick. The Calverts and Herrick had all been students together at the University of California at Berkeley.

But not all slackers were university students or intellectuals. All sorts of American men became slackers. Phillips recalled in his memoir meeting some

---

11   Shipman 1993, p. 69.
12   Ibid.
13   Beals 1938, p. 15.

war resisters in Mazatlán in 1918 who were professional athletes, and one who was gay. 'Leslie Gam was a pansy, and a prizefighter, and a slacker', wrote Phillips. 'Quite a nice guy. You'd never take him for a prise fighter, he was delicately built, I guess a featherweight, but he was a very sweet fellow'.[14] Also in Mazatlán was Walt Carman, a semi-professional baseball player, a pitcher and a pacifist. The slackers in Mazatlán hung out in Nick's Cantina, owned by a Greek cook who had previously lived in New York and spoke English.[15] Thus the slackers created for a while an American expatriate community and a little Greenwich Village in Mazatlán.

The largest American exile community by far grew up in Mexico City. When Carleton Beals, finally reached the capital after a long series of adventures and calamities, he immediately met a number of other slackers. By chance he happened to run into Linn A.E. Gale, 'the editor of a maverick English [language] magazine'. Beals described Gale as: 'A pallid, red-bearded man, a queer refugee from the United States, he made a living giving spiritualist séances and curing by the laying on of hypnotic hands'. Beals slept in Gale's apartment for a week while looking for work. 'For a few days I tried soliciting advertising for his magazine, but what with it not being an important medium – perhaps because of its advocacy of everything from the Socialist commonwealth to eating raw carrots – and the drawback of my poor Spanish, I got no results except sore feet'. Then Beals ran into a man who called himself Martin Paley, actually the Brooklyn schoolteacher Herman Levine, with whom he started a language school called the 'English Institute'.[16] The experience of Phillips and Beals as they met other American war resisters and formed friendships, political networks, and small businesses must have been repeated many times over.

Within a few months, American socialist war resisters seem to have constructed a network that extended to Americans living in different cities in Mexico. While living in Mazatlán on the Pacific coast, Phillips had somehow managed to correspond with Irwin Granich (who later took the name Mike Gold). Granich was living in Tampico, a port on the coast of the Gulf of Mexico, and 'a popular wartime refugee haven'. Apparently through Granich, he also learned that Maurice Becker, the illustrator from *The Masses*, and Owen Cattell, his fellow anti-draft activist from Columbia University, were also living in Tampico. Phillips and Eleanor meanwhile moved to Guadalajara and

---

14   Charles Francis Phillips, 'Autobiography', manuscript, 8/5, Jafifee papers, Archives, Emory University, p. 16; Shipman 1993 p. 59.
15   Shipman 1993, p. 59.
16   Beals 1938, pp. 15–16. Beals gives Gale a pseudonym, but the identity is quite clear from the description of the man and his activities.

found jobs there and then contacted Granich and convinced him to join them.[17] American war resisters in Mexico, much like other immigrants, refugees, and exiles everywhere, formed networks for economic survival, for their own psychological needs, social support, and for political purposes.

Most of the American war resisters decided for their personal security as well as for economic and political reasons to head for Mexico City. American draft evaders did not want to remain too close to the border where they might be seized – legally or illegally – by US authorities, detective agencies, or vigilantes, and dragged back across the international frontier to be tried for draft evasion or other crimes. Moreover, at that time, all the border towns had very small, even tiny populations, few economic opportunities, and could have held little attraction for the American radicals. For that matter, most other cities were not very large or cosmopolitan: Guadalajara, Mexico's second largest city, had about 120,000 inhabitants, and Monterrey, the third largest, only about 65,000.[18]

1   Exiles in La Capital

The war resisters soon learned that Mexico City, the nation's capital, was the most cosmopolitan of the country's urban centres, that it held the greatest economic opportunities, and that it represented the centre of the nation's political life. If there was a socialist and labour movement, they conjectured, it would most likely be found in Mexico City. Most of the war resisters therefore went directly from the border to the capital, though for a variety of reasons some took weeks or even months to get there. Life in Mexico City, the nation's capital, despite seven years of revolution, remained busy and bustling. In 1917 as today, it was the country's largest city, a centre of government, finance, commerce, transportation, and industry, with a population then probably close to 800,000.[19] After the outbreak of the revolution in 1910, various revolutionary armies had taken turns occupying the capital, though that phase of the revolution had concluded by 1917 with the military and political victory of Carranza. While large-scale revolutionary violence continued in the provinces, in such states as Morelos, Chihuahua and Durango, the city was relatively safe and

---

17   Shipman 1993, p. 70.
18   INEGI 1994, pp. 34–5, gives Guadalajara's population in 1910 as 119,468 and in 1921 as 143,376; it gives Monterrey's population in 1910 as 78,528 and in 1921 as 88,479.
19   INEGI 1994, p. 17, gives Mexico City's 1910 population as 720,753 and 1921 population as 906,063.

secure. But even in the cities there was violence, though of a different sort. 'Generals, drunk with sudden power, splattered their ill-gotten wealth around recklessly, shot up cafes, even looted homes', wrote Beals. He recalled that, 'Trouble those days might start unexpectedly even in the most respectable restaurants. Several times bullets spattered around when I was present'.[20]

'The capital of Mexico is a sad city', wrote Blasco-Ibañez.[21] The combination of revolution, civil war, and economic disruption meant that for seven years there had been no construction and little maintenance. The revolutionary wars had destroyed a few sections of Mexico City, though most areas had not been seriously damaged. The oldest quarters in the centre of the city retained their early Spanish colonial character combined with the French Empire style favoured during the Porfirian dictatorship. The section between the *zócalo* (the principal plaza) and the Alameda Central (the central park) constructed in the Porfirian era and modelled on Paris, made up of somewhat taller buildings with mansard roofs and elaborate wrought-iron ornaments, held a particular continental charm. Mexico City appeared somewhat dilapidated, but still vibrant. The post-revolutionary reconstruction period and its residential and commercial building boom would not take off until the late 1920s.

Mexico City was in many respects a modern metropolis. Blasco-Ibañez called it 'one of the best illuminated cities of the world', because 'electricity is very cheap'.[22] The Light and Power Company, whose employees were organised by the important Electrical Workers Union (SME), provided the electric power for the lighting system and the streetcars. The extensive streetcar system served the city centre and its neighbourhoods, and its workers had joined the militant anarchist General Confederation of Workers (CGT).[23] The Ericsson Telephone Company provided telephone service to a small proportion of the city's political and economic elite. The capital boasted several daily newspapers, some of which in an attempt to reach the large Anglo-American community had English language pages or columns.

With the return of political stability beginning in 1917, some wealthy upper- and middle-class Mexicans, many of whom had fled during the violent years for the provinces, Europe or the United States, had returned and began to reestablish themselves in Mexico City. Upper-class Mexicans, usually educated in Europe, spoke not only Spanish, but sometimes French as well, and some spoke English. By 1920 a new revolutionary political class had cohered, linked to a new

20   Beals 1938, p. 21.
21   Blasco-Ibañez 1979, p. 177.
22   Blasco-Ibañez 1978, p. 178.
23   Rodríguez 1980, *passim*.

state and the financial and industrial bourgeoisie. Their motorcars became the symbols of the new economic and political elite.

Before the revolution, the Francophile upper classes had dominated Mexican culture. In the late teens and early 1920s a young generation of revolutionary intellectuals and artists began to lay the foundations for a new Mexican nationalist cultural. Under the Álvaro Obregón government, which came to power in 1920, and particularly under the impetus of Obregón's minister of culture, the philosopher José Vasconcelos, cultural and intellectual nationalism became dominant. Vasconcelos hired Diego Rivera, the great muralist, to paint the walls of the Ministry of Education in the style and symbols that established the dominance of Mexican nationalism in art.

The Mexican Revolution had brought hard times to the city's workers and poor people. As wealthy businesspeople fled the country, some important businesses had been closed, at least temporarily. The revolution had frequently disrupted the normal activities of life, sometimes keeping people from their jobs and denying them an income. The interruption of rail service occasionally closed textile mills and paper plants in the Mexico City suburbs. In 1910 only half of Mexico City's population was literate, but by about 1920 things may have been worse because half the public schools had closed and there was a great deficit of teachers.[24] Revolutionary troops sometimes entered the city, completely disorganising urban services. The rival revolutionary governments issued various inflated currencies, usually only honoured by one regime or one general, contributing to the great economic instability, insecurity, and hardship among the lower classes.[25]

Carleton Beals remembered the life of workers and the poor in Mexico in those years, and particularly the effects of the revolution on the women. 'Mexico City itself was wild, with a murderous night-life. Prostitutes – unfortunate women washed up by the disorder – swarmed everywhere', wrote Beals in his memoir. 'Sometimes women came to bachelor doors and for small sums offered their twelve- or thirteen-year-old daughters "to work" for a week or so'.[26]

But Mexico City workers had also participated in the labour radicalisation, an upsurge in labour union organising and strikes that established collective bargaining agreements in some industries and services and raised workers' wages. Unions, often under the leadership of Spanish anarchists, organised not

---

24   Pani 1936, p. 31; Matute 1995, p. 7.
25   Kandell 1988, pp. 432–3.
26   Beals 1938, p. 20.

only electrical and streetcar workers, but also bakers, shop clerks, and even waiters. Textile workers in the Mexico City suburbs and neighbouring towns formed important labour unions with strong unions and contracts. Women workers in the cigar factories sometimes also participated in strikes. Anarchists like the streetcar workers, fought not only for unions and contracts, but also for workers' control of production and ultimately for the 'social revolution', which they hoped would liberate them from the bosses.[27]

Despite the revolution, many foreigners and immigrants continued to live and work in Mexico, and especially in Mexico City, among them small numbers of Spaniards, French, German, Syrian-Lebanese (often called Turks because they came from the Ottoman Empire), Chinese, Jews, and a large English-speaking community made up of Americans, Canadians, and English. Thousands of Americans lived in Mexico, and probably most of them in Mexico City. Since the outbreak of World War I in 1914, Mexico City had also been a centre of international intrigue as the Germans, British, and Americans attempted to shape the revolution to serve their military and political interests. Among the foreigners in Mexico City, one could find ambassadors and other diplomats, spies and secret agents all of whom attempted to win over politicians in the government, revolutionary insurgents, or counter-revolutionaries.[28]

The wealthy Americans and English population lived in social isolation from the Mexican population, or as the East Indian M.N. Roy put it, 'it kept its boarders away from the native dirt and smell'. Roy found that 'the arrogant exclusiveness of the small Anglo-American colony was very objectionable'. English and American hotel guests 'behaved as if they were living not only in a beleaguered fortress, but must also protect themselves from infectious maladies'. Roy notes that the Anglo-American colony was 'immune to the virus of revolution'. 'They all bemoaned the good old days of the Díaz dictatorship, and wished that the Golden Age would return'.[29]

The better-off Americans living in Mexico also disgusted slacker Carleton Beals when he arrived. 'The American who comes to Mexico is too frequently a colourless nobody whom race prejudices have filled with strutting pretensions; or he is a barbarian or an adventurer trying to forget his origins', wrote Beals. He too found the Americans ignorant and bigoted:

---

27   See: Ruíz 1978; Bortz 1997; Salazar 1962; Salazar 1972; Araiza 1963; Rodriguez 1980.
28   Katz 1983, *passim*.
29   Roy 1984, p. 56.

By and large the Americans I have met in Mexico (with some remarkable exceptions) when speaking Spanish will ask you to sit down in the past subjunctive tense or commit some worse faux pas: will call the Mexicans, from whom they should be learning something, 'yellow-bellies', and do their travelling in the Hotel Regis in Mexico City, and are quite unfamiliar with the country and its ways, with Spanish-Mexican history, and traditions. These people who believe in race superiority, who are decades behind in politics, fully convinced that everything in the United States and elsewhere in the world should be run as it was back in Podunk, Arkansas, twenty years before – these people will never learn the heart, the spirit, the soul of the Mexican people.[30]

Beals youthful indignation at American racism and provincialism was also an expression of the slackers' own internationalist ethic.

Rosa E. King, a wealthy and politically connected English landowner from the state of Morelos, was an exception to the rule. Surprisingly she came to sympathise with Emiliano Zapata and his peasant revolution in that state. In her memoir she painted a fascinating picture of the social life of the Anglo-American and European colonies in Mexico City at about the time of the arrival of the American war resisters. She wrote:

> Curious as it seems, those of us living in the foreign colonies were more excited about what was going on in France, where the World War was drawing to its close, than about the latest developments around us. We could not afford to think too much about what was going on in Mexico; it was too close to us. After all, we were foreigners and there was nothing we could do to help stabilise the situation; and meanwhile the effects of the long-drawn-out struggle on our personal fortunes were too important and painful to dwell on. Since there was no pushing serious affair, Mexico City was very gay: a constant round of parties, and wartime balls and benefits of all kinds.[31]

Roy, with German money and connections, could afford to move in those elite circles when he chose, but most of the American slackers with their scant economic resources and their radical politics would never have much to do with the Anglo-American businessmen and diplomats. The world of the American war resisters and draft evaders was altogether different.

---

30   Beals 1927, pp. 326–7.
31   King 1935, p. 307.

Harry L. Foster, an American adventurer, reporter and writer who visited Mexico in about 1919 described in his book *A Gringo in Mañana-Land* the many American expatriates he found loitering in the parks and plazas of Mexico City. 'Some were draft-evaders that had come to Mexico during the War and had been unable to return. Others were professional vagabonds who had gravitated southward to enjoy the privileges of a country that recognised vagrancy as a legitimate profession'.[32] Some of the thousands of American slackers there during the war had no doubt been to Mexico before where they had worked on the railroads, and in the mines and oilfields. Perhaps some of them hung out in Mexico City while waiting for word of a job in those industries, though others may simply have been passing time waiting for the end of the war. In any case, when slackers arrived in the capital, they had no trouble finding one of their own, and perhaps joining a 'slackers club'.

These young men and some few women, once settled in Mexico City, found themselves in an exotic land, in exhilarating times, encountering a new culture for the first time. For some of the American war resisters, living in Mexico became a personally liberating experience. Carleton Beals felt that his exile in Mexico had saved him from a life of middleclass conformity. When he had tried to be a writer while living in the United States, Beals believed that he had become trapped in 'the staid, middle-class milieu that strangled this urge'.

> I became caught up in the American herd gospel: success, college friends, a conventional engagement, everything led me to a job in a shipping-office instead of to a garret of books and cobwebs and poetry. But here in Mexico there was no herd. I was outside the herd, looking aloof at its queer, unreasoning antics. Now I found myself freed by all my experience in Mexico from a 'compulsion for success', for position, moneymaking, respectability, pose. I had touched the bottom and the elemental realities of life. I had in fact, at last chosen life instead of success .... My experience had been like a sweeping fire that had burnt away the clutter of dead growth that is falsely planted by society in every young heart.[33]

Not only had Mexico helped to free Beals from conventional middleclass existence, but it also led him to appreciate courage and respect tradition. He wrote that,

---

32   Foster 1925, pp. 120–1.
33   Beals 1927, p. 317.

> Mexico taught me my first true lessons in aesthetics; it stimulated and awakened in me as never before the keen pleasurable life of the senses: form, colour, rhythm – things omnipresent in Mexico, part of the handicraft heritage, part of the Spanish heritage, quiveringly alive in the very air one breathes. And these impressions I began to put on paper.[34]

Living as a war resister and draft evader and in Mexico, Beals chose to become the writer he had always wished to be.

Bertram Wolfe also remembered Mexico as having a great impact on him and his wife Ella when they arrived in the mid-1920s. 'To one born and brought up in the United States, to live in Mexico is like doubling one's personality', wrote Wolfe. Mexico offered a completely different politics, culture, and language, which enriched the experience of the immigrant. Wolfe was fascinated by the village fiestas, the cantinas, the churches, the markets. 'To us it seemed that almost everything this folk created had its touch of beauty'.[35] Certainly other American war resisters and draft evaders in Mexico must also have felt something of the same sense of liberation, as well as an awakening of their aesthetic sense.

2   American Slackers in the Mexican Labour Movement

While fascinated by Mexican culture, and particularly by its handicrafts and arts, the radical slackers were above all political people. As socialists, they saw their role as working with the unions and the working class. 'I wanted to work in the labour movement', wrote Phillips later in his memoir.[36]

The revolutionary years in Mexico from 1910 to 1920, and especially the post-revolutionary 1920s, were a time of tremendous labour upheaval as workers organised labour unions, conducted strikes, entered into alliances with various revolutionary factions, and participated as armed detachments in the national revolutionary movement. The slacker's arrival in Mexico in 1917 and 1918, coincided with an important split in the Mexican labour movement which had become polarised between the government-supported reformists of the Regional Confederation of Mexican Workers (CROM) and the anarchist revolutionaries who organised the General Confederation of Workers (CGT). At the

---

34   Beals 1927, p. 318.
35   Wolfe 1981, p. 293.
36   Shipman 1993, p. 73.

same time both federations were being affected by the pull of the Russian Bolshevik or Soviet Revolution and the call to organise a new Communist International. While still getting settled and politically oriented, the slackers plunged into the political storm of the Mexican revolution and began to organise labour unions, form political parties, make alliances with peasants, and even create a feminist organisation.

One has to wonder: how did Mexican worker activists and union leaders react to the presence of American radicals in their midst? While revolutionary Mexico exhibited certain xenophobic tendencies, sometimes even violent anti-foreign riots and pogroms, especially against the Spanish and the Chinese, in the left and labour movements where the radical slackers were active, the anarcho-syndicalist or socialist ideology of proletarian internationalism meant that the slackers were generally extended a fraternal hand both by Mexican workers and by Spanish and South American anarchists active in the Mexican left and labour unions. As anarchists, labour unionists, Socialists or Communists they could participate in union activities, and as well-educated and literate men and women, who soon spoke Spanish, they frequently played important roles.

The anarchists among the Mexican union leaders had read such writers as Mikhail Bakunin, Peter Kropotkin, Enrico Malatesta, and Elisée Réclus, all of whom were advocates of revolutionary internationalism. Bakunin for example had written in 1869 in his 'Program of the International Brotherhood' about the need for moving beyond a national revolution to a 'universal revolution', a revolution 'embracing all the rebel countries in the name of the same principles, irrespective of old frontiers and national differences, [which] will have as its chief objective the administration of public services, not the governing of peoples'.[37] Mexican anarchist workers were familiar with this anarchist internationalist creed, and this helped shape their positive attitude toward the slackers.

Another internationalist influence came from the American syndicalist union, the Industrial Workers of the World, the Wobblies, with which many Mexican migrant workers had experience in the United States. After 1911, the Industrial Workers of the World's many Spanish language newspapers circulated widely in Mexico, coming in across the northern border on the railroads, and entering the ports of Tampico and Veracruz on the Gulf Coast. The philosophy of the Wobblies was also internationalist. As a delegate to the 1905 founding convention had told his fellow-workers: 'all the boundary lines that were

---

37   Bakunin 1971, p. 154.

ever established have always been established by men who were a bunch of robbers, thieves, exploiters, and we want to combine ourselves as humanity, as one lot of people, those that are producing the wealth of our oppressors, and we want to have under that banner our brothers and sisters of the world'.[38] This strong internationalist sentiment found expression in Wobbly newspapers, which spoke of one international workers' movement irrespective of race, religion, or nationality. Unlike the American Federation of Labor, the IWW organised Mexican workers, joined with them in strikes, and welcomed them into their organisation.

The importance of the idea of internationalism among Mexican workers can be seen in the opposition by the House of the World Worker (*Casa del Obrero Mundial*) to the extradition of foreign labour activists by Victoriano Huerta. In May 1913, following a large May Day march and protest demonstrations, the counter-revolutionary president Huerta had shut down the Casa and expelled from the country a number of radical labour activists. In response, as we have already discussed, the Casa's anarcho-syndicalist activists organised a protest on 29 May, at the House of Deputies, the lower house of the Mexican legislature, at which they demanded that the repression of their labour organisation be ended and insisted that foreign workers not be expelled from Mexico.

> We want those so-called foreigners by reason of their birth – who with perfect right reside in our Territory, collaborating with our work for the universal good of man and sharing with us the bitter penalties of the struggle for human needs – to be treated with respect. The barbarous Article 33, applied against them, is an ignominious law against which we energetically protest with an anguished heart on seeing them brutally taken from their homes, leaving their families completely distraught.[39]

This internationalist conception stood in sharp contrast to the dominant nationalist ideology of the Mexican Revolution. Such attitudes among anarchist union leaders and activists helped make possible the American slackers' participation in the Mexican left and labour movement.

While the bonds of solidarity were strongest between Mexican, Spanish and Latin American anarcho-syndicalists, such solidarity also extended to labour activists from the United States. John Kenneth Turner, the author of *Barbarous Mexico*, worked closely with the anarchists of the Mexican Liberal Party,

---

38   Industrial Workers of the World 1905, cited in De Shazo 1974, p. 2.
39   Salazar 1972, vol. 1, p. 56.

serving not only as journalist and propagandist, but also as messenger and gun-runner. When John Murray went to Mexico either for the Socialist Party or for the American Federation of Labor, he was welcomed by the House of the World Worker, and even made a member of its revolutionary committee. Mexico's rad-ical labour activists generally did not see foreign nationality or alien race as an obstacle to full participation in their labour movement.

Mexican labour union activists accepted the American slackers as part of their movement. José C. Valadés, a Mexican labour and political activist and later an important historian, remembered how the meaning of the word 'slack-ers' was explained to him at that time:

> The slacker was a person from the United States who, for his ideas, or out of fear, had fled from the United States so as not to have to go to the World War. There were hundreds, if not thousands of slackers in Mexico. The national government protected them, because president Carranza sym-pathised with the central imperial powers.[40]

The gathering place for Mexico's foreign political activists on the left, Valadés recalled, was the Bakery Workers Union in Mexico City. Genaro Gómez, one of Mexico's few socialists, headed the union, and allowed the Bakers' 'Netza-hualcoyotl Hall' (named after the great Aztec leader, rebel, and sage) to be used by a variety of radical organisations. One of those radical groups was the anarchist Egalitarian Youth, which had been organised by Valadés and his friend Enrique Delhumeau. Valadés later described in his *Memoirs of a Rebel-lious Youth* the founding meetings of this group, probably in 1919, at which he first encountered some of the American slackers. His account captures the international character of the radical slacker community in Mexico City at the time:

> Here was Linn A.E. Gale, general secretary (so he said) of the Commun-ist Party of Mexico [PC de M], With him were two or three others from the United States, who muttered their names between clenched teeth. Beside Gale there was Roberto Haberman. Behind Haberman, Calogero Speziale, the Italian anarchist. After him, Leopoldo Urmachea, the Per-uvian anarchist. Followed by José Allen, general secretary of the Mexican Communist Party [PCM], Accompanying Allen, Frank Seaman [Charles Francis Phillips], a Communist from the United States. Afterwards came

---

40   Valadés 1986, vol. 2, p. 76.

Martin Paley [Herman Levine] a Jew, representing the Industrial Workers
of the World in Mexico, as well as Joseph Ellsworth, delegate of the Socialist Party of the United States. Finally, I greeted Pablo Pablos, a bearded
Russian with a beautiful profile who held the hand of his lovely daughter
Helen. With Pablo was Alfred Stimer [Edgard Woog].[41]

Valadés' memoir describes the slackers as a group of American war resisters
and radicals whose activities overlapped those of South American and Spanish anarchists, all radicals and revolutionaries who sought support among their
co-religionists in Mexico. Valadés' recollection makes clear that Mexicans and
other foreigners accepted and welcomed American revolutionaries as comrades in the struggle against capitalism.

This internationalist attitude continued through the teens and on into the
1920s. On a number of occasions, for example, Mexico's labour organisations
solidarized themselves with American unions and workers. The Union of Port
Workers of Tampico sent a statement in 1918 supporting Tom Mooney, the
labour activist on trial for a bombing in California, and distributed a statement
protesting persecution of the anarchists Nicolas Sacco and Bartolome Vanzetti, two Italian immigrants on trial for murder in the United States in 1921.[42]
Similarly in the early 1920s the Regional Confederation of Mexican Workers
(CROM) backed the United Mine Workers Union of West Virginia and supported Sacco and Vanzetti.[43] Employers were horrified by the idea of working class
internationalism. The employers associations expressed alarm at the foreign
agitators active among the port workers of Tampico.[44] *The Bulletin of the Confederation of Chambers of Industry*, referring to the workers' strike of 1916 in
Mexico City, declared that the unions had 'not only ... attacked national security, but in some cases they have even attacked the legitimate interests of the
Fatherland.'[45] Employers complained that 'the workers movements which have
been developing in our country try to erase borders; as many of the agitators are
renegades who have abjured the love that is due to the mother, their country'.[46]

---

41   Valadés 1986, vol. 2, p. 76.
42   'A1 H. Consul United States of America, Tampico, Tamps., Meéxico. Los Trabajadores del
      Puerto Tampico, Estado de Tamaulipas, en sesión ...', 9 December 1918, in Record Group
      84, Tampico, vol. 387, no. 800, and 'De Pie, Junto al Dolor, Aquí Nos Teneis, Asesinos del
      Pueblo!' November 1921, Record Group 84, vol. 438, no. 800. Both documents thanks to
      Robert J. Halstead of Portage, Wisconsin.
43   Salazar 1972, vol. 1, p. 321.
44   'Las Últimas Huelgas' 1920, pp. 10–11.
45   Retana 1920, p. 62.
46   Collado Herrera 1966, pp. 259–60, citing 'Una lección' 1922, pp. 145–6.

Indeed, the Mexican anarchists did want to erase borders, as did the American socialist slackers.

Another factor in the Mexicans' attitude toward foreigners, and especially toward Americans, was the entrance of the United States into World War I. When Charles Francis Phillips and Eleanor Parker crossed into Mexico in 1917 so that Phillips could escape conscription or prison, they found that because of the political situation they were accepted in Mexico. 'Gringos were resented and hated in Mexico', Phillips later wrote.

> But we were gringos with a difference. As refugees from the American war power, we were enemies of the American establishment, and consequently Mexico's friends.[47]

Since American slackers were known to be radical political activists, they generally did not face the same hostility as other foreigners. On other occasions, when they were simply gringos, they could run into problems. Carleton Beals remembered that,

> Ill-feeling against Americans was particularly strong – a hold-over from the Pershing and Vera Cruz expeditions and Mexico's resultant pro-German attitude during the World War. Once I fought my way out of a central business bar, a wooden stool in hand.[48]

Still, in the several autobiographies of foreigners in Mexico during the 1910s and 20s – by Carleton Beals, Bertram Wolfe, Charles Francis Phillips, and Manabendra Nath Roy – there are few mentions of xenophobic feelings or hostile acts. Moreover, in the labour movement the slackers seem to have been accepted much like the Spaniards and South Americans who were also active in those circles. Whether at the Bakers' Union's Netzahualcoyotl Hall, in the small Socialist Party, among the petroleum workers of the Industrial Workers of the World in Tampico, with the railroad workers in their confederation, or in dealing with the peasant leagues or the feminist organisations the slackers appear to have been accepted as comrades. The primary reason for this acceptance was the common belief of the Mexicans, the Spanish and South Americans, and the Americans that they formed part of an international revolutionary working-class movement. The employers' association had it right: they wanted to erase

---

47   Phillips 1993, p. 67.
48   Beals 1938, p. 21.

borders. The revolutionary internationalist ideology held by anarchists, socialists, and syndicalists in Mexico, and for that matter throughout the Americas
and around the world, helped make it possible for the slackers to become activists and even leaders in Mexico.

3   Secret Agents: José Allen and Roberto Haberman

The American war resisters in Mexico found themselves not only in the midst
of a tremendous national revolution, but also in a world of geopolitical rivalry,
international intrigue, and espionage at least initially far beyond their compre-
hension. Revolutionary Mexico fairly swarmed with foreign agents, as spies of
various nations carried out surveillance on the important political movements
in Mexico, including those of the American radicals. Working in the Mexican
left and labour movement, the slackers' activities were closely observed both
by the Mexican and the US government.

Two men who played significant roles in the business of intelligence and
political manipulation in Mexico and particularly in the slacker milieu were
José Allen and Roberto Haberman. Because Allen had an Anglo-Saxon name
and Haberman, a Romanian immigrant, spoke English like an American, and
because both moved among the radical labour and left activists, many believed
that they were simply two more American slackers. But in fact, neither was a
draft evader. Allen was born a Mexican citizen while Haberman had become
one after immigrating to Mexico. Both Haberman and Allen were government
agents, but not for the same government.

Allen reported on the American slackers to the US Military Intelligence Division (USMID), while Haberman reported on the labour movement and the
left to his friend, the Mexican Minister of the Interior, Plutarco Elías Calles,
the future president of Mexico. Both men acted as intelligence agents, Allen
for money, and Haberman, at least at the beginning, out of a sense of loyalty
to what he considered a socialist government. While Haberman was a self-
acknowledged and altogether public agent of the Mexican government and the
CROM, Allen was a secret agent whose espionage activities were unknown to
the American war resisters and radicals with whom he worked. While it is difficult to judge the impact these men had on the American slackers' activities,
certainly both worked in different ways to keep the radicals under surveillance
and under control.

Haberman was an American socialist who had come to Mexico on the eve of
World War I. Born to Jewish parents in Romania, as a boy Haberman had immigrated to the United States with his family. He served in the Spanish-American

War, and then had become a pharmacist and a lawyer. He first went to Mexico in 1917 before the outbreak of the war as a reporter for the Socialist Party newspaper *The Call*. He developed a close political relationship to Felipe Carrillo Puerto, head of the Socialist Party of the Southeast in the Yucatan. Haberman helped write the party's constitution, taught courses in Marxism, and became head of the party's cooperative program, until Carranza suppressed the party.

Haberman fled the Yucatan, seeking refuge in Mexico City where he became an assistant to Luís N. Morones, head of the Regional Confederation of Mexican Workers (CROM). Through Morones, Haberman became a protégé of Minister of the Interior Calles and of president Álvaro Obregón. Eventually Morones made Haberman his liaison to Samuel Gompers, head of the American Federation of Labor, and also commissioned him as his emissary to the Socialist Party of America. Among his other activities, Haberman kept Morones, Calles, and Obregón informed about the activities of the American slackers. Haberman also attempted to shape those activities through fear and favours, sometimes with success.[49]

The other important spy in the Mexican labour movement was José Allen. Allen was first identified as a USMID agent in 1981 by historian Barry Carr, based on documents in the US National Archives.[50] A Mexican citizen who had been raised in a bi-lingual and bi-cultural Anglo-American family, Allen's perfect English and Spanish, made him the ideal agent for operating in the slacker milieu. An electrical engineer, he had been working in a Mexican government munitions plant when he was recruited by Major R.M. Campbell to work as a spy for the US Military Intelligence Division. At first Allen's job was simply to provide information on the operation of Mexican military factories. Later USMID asked Allen to join the Great Central Body of Workers (*Gran Cuerpo Central de Trabajadores*), which was then becoming an important labour organisation. Allen did so and subsequently became a liaison between that labour federation and the Socialist Party of Mexico. In that capacity, he was present at the founding of the Mexican Communist Party. Ironically the delegates to the Communist Party's founding convention chose him to be the

---

49   This account of Haberman's life is based primarily on: John M. Murphy, 'Robert Haberman Suspected German Agent', FBI New Orleans Office, July 9, 1917. This report is part of approximately 300 pages of FBI reports obtained under the Freedom of Information Act (FOIA). See too the obituary in the *New York Times*, 5 March 1962. Also: Gregg Andrews 1990, pp. 189–211; Andrews 1988; Andrews 1991, pp. 140–68; and La Botz 1991, pp. 7–21. The archives of the Fideicomiso Calles Torreblanca also contain many letters from Roberto Haberman to Calles.

50   Carr 1981, pp. 37–47. Carr based his article on B.S. 330 202600-1913 and Record Group 165, Bureau of Investigation, USNA; and Carr 1992, p. 20.

first general secretary, the organisation's top officer, thus placing him in a position where he not only participated in all the important meetings and saw all the party's most significant correspondence, but actually wrote much of it himself.[51]

José C. Valadés, one of the early leaders of the Mexican Communist Party, who never knew of Allen's role as US military spy, recalled that he lived modestly with his wife María Cruz in the Tacubaya neighbourhood in central Mexico City. His wife was the daughter of Roberto Cruz, a general in the Mexican Army. Allen had typographical equipment and small, manual printing presses in his home that also served as the Communist Party office. 'The home of Allen was the centre of Communism in Mexico', Valadés remembered. 'All of the leaders of Mexican radicalism could be found there at one time or another: the Russian Borodin; Francisco Múgica, governor of Michoacán; Felipe Carrillo Puerto, head of the party of the Southeast and governor of Yucatan; Roberto Haberman, the American socialist; Manuel Díaz Ramírez, IWW organiser and Communist party leader, and many others.' Valadés recollected Allen as having a real 'devotion to communism'.[52]

When the slacker radicals arrived in Mexico, Roberto Haberman was likely to be one of the first people they ran into. Always on the lookout for talent, Haberman helped to find jobs for American radicals with the Mexican government or at the national university. He also attempted to draw American leftists into working with him on projects to promote Mexico's government and the pro-government labour federation the CROM. And if the American radicals moved in Communist circles, they were sure to meet José Allen. Whether attracted to nationalism and reform or internationalism and revolution, someone was always keeping an eye on the slackers. Whatever one thinks of their activities, the correspondence of Haberman and the reports of Allen helped make it possible to write this account of the slackers.

---

51   Allen's remarkable role as simultaneously head of the Mexican Communist Party and chief US military spy in Mexico was not without precedent. Other spies had succeeded in playing leading roles in other Communist parties. In Russia, Roman Malinovsky served as a member of the Bolshevik central committee, chairman of the editorial board of the party's newspaper *Pravda* in 1912, and as the head of the Bolshevik parliamentary group in the Russian Duma of 1913. Malinovsky was Lenin's personal spokesman in the Russian parliament. But after the revolution when the government's files were opened, it was revealed that he had been a secret agent for the Okhrana, the Russian secret police. Allen may have been the first and perhaps the only police agent to actually head a Communist Party organisation. See: Serge 1972, pp. 24–6 and Cliff 1975, vol. 1, p. 324.

52   Valadés 1986, vol. 2, p. 91.

CHAPTER 11

American Slackers and the Organisation of the Mexican Communist Party

Several of the American war resisters and draft evaders in Mexico quickly found and joined the small Mexican Socialist Party, and, with the help of other foreign radicals in Mexico, within a year they had transformed it into a Communist Party. The American slackers' activities seem to have taken place with the knowledge and tacit approval of the Mexican government of President Venustiano Carranza, if not precisely with its endorsement and support. Presumably the Carranza believed the Americans were potential allies in the struggle against the United States, and perhaps he saw a new Communist Party as yet another small radical labour party that he could keep under control.

The first tentative steps of the slackers and their Mexican and foreign allies involved nearly all the important political tendencies of the Mexican labour left, but a sorting out soon took place. The founding of a Communist Party meant a break both with the reformist labour movement, principally the Regional Confederation of Mexican Workers (CROM), and, though not at first, eventually too with the anarchists who founded the General Confederation of Workers (CGT). This would later have important implications for the new Communist Party and the slackers. Since Carranza's successor as Mexican President, Álvaro Obregón and his Interior Minister Plutarco Elías Calles supported the CROM, it saw the Communists as antagonists. The new government soon came to consider the slackers to be enemies of the regime and *personae non gratae*.

At the beginning, however, the radical slackers had the backing of the Carranza government and of important political figures with in it and they took advantage of the opportunity to organise. At the end of 1918, the Americans would in fact found two rival Communist parties, one led by Charles Francis Phillips and M.N. Roy and the other led by Linn A.E. Gale. Slackers propagandised for the new Communist ideology through their newspapers. While Phillips had found a job and a role for himself as the editor of the English language page of *El Heraldo de Mexico*, Gale had established himself as newspaper publisher and editor of his own publication: *Gale's Magazine*. At about the same, time Herman Levine in Tampico, who also eventually became a Communist, had begun working on the IWW paper *El Obrero Industrial* (The Industrial Worker). The publishing and editing of political magazines gave the slackers important tools for organising.

1   Linn A.E. Gale and His Magazine

Somewhere between Albany and Mexico City, perhaps among the utopian socialists in Sables, Louisiana, Gale, while not giving up his belief in New Thought, spiritualism, and his commitment to scientific birth control, became converted to the industrial unionism of the Industrial Workers of the World (IWW), to socialism, and then to Bolshevism. Unlike most of the slackers who arrived in Mexico with very little money, Linn and Magdalena Gale were relatively well off. In a letter to José Allen in 1920, Gale wrote, 'I arrived in this city [Mexico City] in August of 1918, with plenty of money, that I used to reestablish my magazine here, which I knew could not be profitable. In addition to my own money, my wife furnished $5,000.00 (dollars) of money that she had earned during many years of working as a stenographer in Albany, New York'.[1] Once they arrived in Mexico City, Linn and Magdalena decided that she should work until he could make his magazine into a paying proposition. As Gale wrote to José Allen, 'Because I want to give all my energies to the cause, Mrs. Gale who is just as revolutionary as I, has worked disinterestedly practically all the time we have been here'.

When she first arrived in Mexico, Magdalena used her stenographic skills to find a job working for Samuel W. Rider, President of the American Chamber of Commerce in Mexico. But when Rider found out that she was married to Gale, he fired her. She sued in the Mexican labour courts, and won $75 in wages, but did not get her job back. She then went to work for G. Amsinck Company, a firm that represented Westinghouse in Mexico. But she was fired again, and again sued, this time settling for $375. Next, she worked for Carr Bros., an American importing house, but was fired supposedly at the instigation of the American Embassy. She sued again and got $325. Finally, she was hired by Walter C. Taylor of the Young Men's Christian Association (YMCA), but Taylor too fired her, and again she was forced to sue.[2] Devoted to her husband, and apparently sharing his commitment to New Thought and socialism, Magdalena Gale apparently never tired of working as a business stenographer or English teacher by day and as her husband's secretary at night.[3]

---

1   Letter of 16 June 1920 from Linn A.E. Gale to José Allen, page 3, RG 165, Box 2290, USMID, USNA.

2   Gale 1919b, p. 21; 'We Slackers in Mexico', *Gale's Magazine*, March 1919, 21; Gale 1920, p. 23.

3   Letter of 16 June 1920 from Linn A.E. Gale to José Allen, page 3, RG 165, Box 2290, USMID, USNA. Gale March 1919b, p. 21; Gale, August 1920b, p. 23. Magdalena Gale found it easy to get jobs but quickly lost them when employers learned the identity of her husband. Probably because her husband had the support of the Mexican government, she won the labour board cases that provided her with compensation.

After staying in a series of hotels and apartments, the Gales eventually found a place to live and work in a three-story house at Calle López. On the ground floor was Chávez and Son printers, which printed *Gale's Magazine* and the IWW newspaper, *El Obrero Industrial* (The Industrial Worker). On the second floor were an Austrian social club and the Gale's apartment. The third floor contained a French restaurant, and later the offices of Gale's Communist Party and the Industrial Workers of the World. The meetings of Gale's branch of the Mexican IWW convened on Sunday mornings on the roof of the building.[4] So in this internationalist, bohemian, radical and gastronomic roost, Linn Gale set to work. Like Phillips, who worked for Gen. Salvador Alvarado, the owner of *El Heraldo de Mexico*, Gale also found a patron, Manuel Aguirre Berlanga, Carranza's Minister of the Interior. With Berlanga's support, Gale was not only permitted to publish his magazine, but also to take an active part in Mexican political and labour union life. Berlanga also financially subsidised Gale's activities.[5] Gale in turn offered his political support to the Mexican government of Carranza, and from time to time made favourable mention of Berlanga in *Gale's*.

Gale supported the Carranza government because, he wrote, 'The greatest danger faced by the Mexican working class today, is the danger of intervention'. He criticised other Mexican leftists (and US leftists in Mexico) who failed to do so, arguing that, 'If the Carranza government were overthrown today, American and British capital would come into this country and rule it with a rod of iron'. He claimed that, 'There is today a good prospect of liberation for the Mexican working class. If Mexico is permitted to retain a government of its own, that government which is already liberal, can be made Socialist'.[6] Gale's position was that leftists should support the Mexican Constitutionalist government of Carranza and attempt to push it to the left. Were it not for the threat of US intervention, He even suggested that Mexico might soon become socialist. 'Carranza is not a Socialist', he wrote, 'but there is good reason to believe that a moderate policy of state Socialism would have been put into practice if he had not been constantly menaced by the Damocles' sword of intervention'.[7]

Gale's Magazine, though published in Mexico, was written entirely in English and distributed in Mexico, the United States, and several other countries. Gale

---

4 Gale, August 1920a, p. 2.
5 Letter from Linn A.E. Gale to Plutarco Elías Calles, October 30, 1924, File 'The Gale News Service', Gav. 73, Exp. 12, Inv. 5594, Archivo Plutarco Elías Calles, Fideicomiso Calles Torreblanca.
6 Gale, August 1919a, p. 8.
7 Gale, January 1920, p. 6.

himself wrote most of the articles, either under his own name or under pseudonyms, such as *El Viejo Luchador* (The Old Fighter), though his associates also
wrote some pieces. *Gale's* also reprinted articles from the Communist press by
the Russians Vladimir Lenin, Grigory Zinoviev, and Alexandra Kollontai, as well
as by other revolutionaries such as the British Communist Sylvia Pankhurst, the
Hungarian Communist Béla Kun, and the Japanese Communist Sen Katayama.
In addition, Gale published reports and documents of the Communist International and offered updates on development of the Communist movement
around the world. Both as advertising and to vouch for the magazine's radical
credentials, Gale's frequently included letters of support garnered from labour
and leftist leaders, including Theodore Debs, the brother of Eugene V. Debs, and
William D. 'Big Bill' Haywood, the head of the Industrial Workers of the World.
Gale also wrote for all sorts of left-wing newspapers and magazines around the
world, thus creating a reputation for himself as the expert on Mexico's politics,
its left, and its labour movement.

At the same time, Gale never gave up his interest in New Thought, a spiritualist sect with its origins in New England religious currents that had also
given rise to Unitarianism and Christian Science. He reviewed many spiritualist
titles, carried spiritualist advertising, and occasionally dedicated a long piece to
the subject, such as his article on 'Occultism and Socialism' in which he wrote
that, 'Socialism needs Occultism and Occultism needs Socialism'.[8] Socialism
would solve the social evils of capitalism and warfare, and occultism would
help men and women understand the divine powers within themselves. Such
spiritualism was common in the socialist movement worldwide in the 1910s but
disappeared almost completely by the end of the 1920s.

In addition to his advocacy of socialism and spiritualism, Gale like some
American socialists also championed healthy attitudes toward sexuality, promoted contraception, and advocated working-class feminism. He called for
public education about sex and reproduction and in addition translated, sold,
and published information in English and Spanish about birth control and
abortion. On one occasion this got him into trouble with the Mexican authorities. In 1919 he was arrested after being charged by Dr. José María Rodríguez,
head of the Mexico City Health Department, with illegally publishing a book
giving birth control information. 'In this particular instance', Gale wrote, 'I had
published a Spanish translation of Margaret Sanger's book *Family Limitation*,
which tells how to prevent conception by scientific methods used and officially
approved in several European countries'. He explains why:

---

8   Gale, August 1919b, p. 14.

I believed – as I still believe and shall always believe – that no woman, particularly no woman who works and whose husband works, should ever bear an accidental child. I believed she should possess the knowledge which would enable her to prevent children that would be unwelcome or that could not be properly cared for. I believed Mexico would be a greater and happier country if its poorer class raised less children and gave each one more food, clothing and education.[9]

The rich had this information, wrote Gale. 'I wanted the poor, who needed the knowledge most of all, to have it too'. He was arrested, fined $55, which he refused to pay, and spent a few days in jail.

Gale's articles were wide-ranging, commenting on both Mexican and American political events. Gale supported the left wing of the Socialist Party and later the Communist Party in the United States and promoted the Industrial Workers of the World. He advocated and supported union strikes, such as the great steel strike of 1919. He defended Mexico against attacks by the United States, and in general backed the revolutionary Mexican governments of Carranza and later Obregón. In his articles about Communism, it is clear that Gale shared all the idealism, all the enthusiasm, and all the illusions and confusions of the early Communist movement, particularly of the 'left Communists'. Like them, he was an advocate of Soviets and an enemy of parliamentary democracy. He stood for the IWW, industrial unionism and direct action, and was an opponent of Samuel Gompers and the American Federation of Labor (AFL) in the United States.

Gale put himself forward as the leader of the revolutionary movement in Mexico, as its Lenin. As Mexico's self-appointed revolutionary leader, Gale attacked the reformists. While he still had the support of Carranza and his Minister of the Interior Berlanga, he was an outspoken critic of Luis N. Morones, the head of the recently organised Regional Confederation of Mexican Labour (CROM). As a self-proclaimed Communist, Gale ridiculed the Mexican labour leader, whom he described as, 'Luis N. Morones, sleek, well-groomed, pot-bellied agent of Samuel Gompers'.[10] He railed against Morones, the CROM, and the CROMs political organisation, the Labour Party, while calling upon Mexican workers to join the IWW or to form soviets.

A caricature drawing of Gale published in his own magazine in 1921 shows him in profile. He is a thin, youthful looking man in his late twenties, dressed

---

9   Gale, July 1919, p. 8.

10   Gale, September 1919, p. 7.

in a shirt and tie, wearing a sports coat. He sports a full head of hair, combed out from his forehead in an exaggerated pompadour, and tucked behind his ear is a pencil. His straight, sharp nose stands out above his moustache and over a very long, pointed and neatly groomed Van Dyke. In the picture he is intently reading a newspaper, *Labor* something or other, with the headline, 'Soviet Russia Gaining in Poland'. The caption reads: 'Linn A.E. Gale: Member of the Executive Committee of the Communist Party; in charge of the Department of Public Service of the I.W.W'. The drawing presents Gale: the journalist and editor: the revolutionary intellectual.

One of the agents of the US Military Intelligence Division in Mexico, probably José Allen, wrote a report titled 'Who's Who Material – Mexican Radical Elements' on 15 October 1920. Among those sketched was Linn A.E. Gale:

> Gale is not a leader of men. He is powerful in the seclusion of his office, weak in the open before men. He is energetic and enthusiastic, but he has not the presence necessary to the nature of the Communist type. In the office Gale is only partially dominant. He is a forceful, convincing writer, but he is an inefficient organiser, a lax administrator. He is important, then, only insofar as his writings provide arguments to the Mexican Communists. Provide arguments his writings do, for they are widely read and quoted by Mexican labour.[11]

While he may not have been a leader of men, Gale did have his following. He headed up a small group of American slackers in Mexico City made up of Charles F. Tabler, a German-American; Fulgencio C. Luna, a Filipino; and F. Snyder, a native-born American. In addition, Gale had slacker supporters in his circle that lived in other cities: J.C. Parker in Tamaulipas, Frederick (Federico) Sommer in Tlaxcala, and John Jutt in Tampico. Gale's circle also included George Barreda, a Mexican railroad worker who had been a member of the IWW in the United States. This group was later joined by Albert Fodor, editor and publisher of the *Arizona Labor Review*, and, according to Gale, a long-time defender of Mexican workers in the United States and critic of the Texas rangers. Fodor had fled criminal charges in the United States and sought refuge in Mexico. Gale soon drew these men into his plan to organise the Communist Party of Mexico.

---

11   'Who's Who Material – Mexican Radical Elements', 15 October 1920, Box 2290, Record Group 165, USMID, USNA.

2   Charles Francis Phillips and *El Heraldo de México*

Phillips too found his patron, in his case General Salvador Alvarado. Alvarado, who was from Sonora, had been an important military leader in northern Mexico. Carranza had made Alvardo governor of Yucatan in 1915 and he served there until 1918, implementing progressive programs for peasants, workers, and women. After the assassination of Carranza, Alvarado appears to have aspired to become president, and so he founded the Mexico City newspaper *El Heraldo de México* to raise his public profile. The paper was aimed at both the Mexican and foreign public, most of the latter Americans, and so Alvarado established an English language page and hired Phillips to edit it, a position he held from June to December 1919.

Phillips edited and wrote most of the copy for *El Heraldo* himself, though his comrades M.N. Roy and Alexander Borodin (both of whom we discuss below) no doubt helped him.[12] As a sophisticated young New Yorker, Phillips's articles in the English language page of *El Heraldo* show the influence not only of New York's socialist newspaper, *The Call* but also of the radical and artistically avant-garde magazine *The Masses*. Phillips wrote not only about politics but also reviewed books and wrote poetry. Phillips took advantage of his position to study both domestic and international questions and to clarify his own views. During the six months he edited *El Heraldo*'s English page, he wrote dozens of articles. His views came to coincide virtually completely with those of the Bolshevik Party and the Communist International.

Phillips was, of course, a harsh critic of the World War, but also of the Great Power imperialism that had brought it about.[13] He advocated self-determination for colonial nations such as India and Egypt, as well as the virtual colony Cuba.[14] Like Lenin, who called the League of Nations 'a thieves' kitchen',[15] Phillips argued that the organisation, as developed by the diplomats in Paris, was 'nothing but a shrewd consolidation of the economic and political rulers of the world, a masters' international set up as a bulwark against the threatening international of the masses'. He concluded that, 'Mexico too would find all hope gone if such a League is created'.[16]

---

12   For the sake of simplicity in the bibliography and notes, I am attributing all of the English language articles from *El Heraldo* that are cited here to *Phillips*.
13   Phillips, 4 January 1919; 7 August 1919.
14   Phillips, 19 September 1919; 15 January 1920a; 31 October 1919; 19 September 1919; 31 October 1919; 13 January 1920a; 15 January 1920.
15   Lenin 1968, vol. 25, p. 97.
16   Phillips, 10 September 1919.

Phillips published a great many articles and editorials in the English language page of *El Heraldo* opposing US military intervention. In all of these
pieces, Phillips blamed the United States for its aggression and defended Mexico. He constantly criticised the US government and those individuals and corporations who promoted US military intervention in Mexico. He also encouraged his readers, and particularly his American readers, to support Mexico's
struggle to maintain its sovereignty.[17] While Phillips defended Mexico from US
intervention, he was also critical of the Mexican government. He lamented the
direction taken by the Mexican Revolution and noted that until now, 'there
have been no Bolsheviks in Mexico'.

> Mexico's feeble attempts at nationalization, tendencies springing out of
> the Revolution, have nothing to do with Bolshevism. The Mexican Revolu-
> tion is not a Bolshevik revolution. It was in reality an effort on the part of
> an emerging middle class of small farmers and businessmen to shake off
> the feudal trust established on land and industry by [former President
> Porfirio] Díaz. The workers were used for the fighting, but they have no
> control now as [as they do] in Russia.[18]

In his coverage of Mexican politics, Phillips made it clear that he was on the
side of the Mexican working class in its fight both against US imperialists
and against the Mexican government. Phillips reported sympathetically on the
Tampico oil workers' strike against the US-owned Pierce Oil Company.[19] He
may have received information from his friend Herman Levine, who, using the
name M. Paley, was involved in organising the oil workers into the Industrial
Workers of the World. In an article titled 'Red Rule Grips Tampico as Strikers
Riot', Phillips declared, 'Bolshevism has fired the striking workmen of Tampico
and they seem to have stopped all traffic there for some time yesterday, killing
a federal major who tried to interfere and wounding his aid[e]'.[20] He argued
that while public attention was focused on Pancho Villa and the battles on
the northern border, that the really interesting and important fight was taking
place in Tampico. There revolutionary socialists were at work: 'They are spread-

---

17   Phillips, 6 August 1919; 8 August 1919; 13 August 1919; August 1919; 21 August 1919; 23 Novem-
      ber 1919; 29 November 1919; 7 December 1919; 18 December 1919; 28 August 1919; 23 Septem-
      ber 1919; 24 August 1919b; 22 August 1919; 30 August 1919; 4 November 1919; 17 December
      1919; September 1919.
18   Phillips, 18 November 1919.
19   Phillips, 16 June 1919.
20   Phillips, 17 June 1919.

ing their propaganda, they are inflaming the men, they are actually and openly agitating for Bolshevism. And they are having success too'.[21]

Writing in English for a mostly American readership, Phillips also covered US labour and political developments, often in great detail, from actors' and streetcar workers' strikes to labour action on the railroads and in the steel industry.[22] Unlike John Reed and the Left Communists who only supported the IWW and rejected political action, Phillips also supported work in the AFL labour unions and believed in the necessity of a Labour Party. He was particularly concerned during the 'Red Summer of 1919' with black workers and their fights against racism and lynching.[23] He also published W.E.B. Du Bois's essay 'On Being Black', which had appeared in *The New Republic*. These articles on and by Black Americans are remarkable for the time, even among those on the Socialist and Communist left. They suggest that Phillips not only carefully followed developments among African Americans and sympathised with their struggles, but that he also supported black Americans in their use of armed self-defence.

His job as editor of *El Heraldo* not only gave Phillips a job and money, but also provided him an opportunity to expand his knowledge of world affairs, work out his opinions, and proselytise among the American left in Mexico. Phillips became an accomplished political journalist. He had learned to write simply and clearly and might well have been capable of rousing masses to action. The irony, of course, is that because he was in exile in Mexico, and because he was the editor of an English language paper in a largely illiterate Spanish speaking country, he could only reach a few thousand of his own compatriots, and most of them were businesspeople and diplomats. Still, as long as the job lasted, the paper provided him with a vehicle to organise among the American expatriates, and he made the most of it.

Phillips found himself in substantial agreement with the left Socialists who had joined the Communist Party, though he was even closer to Lenin than they were. He coincided with Lenin on the national question and the right to national self-determination, on the need for American leftists to work in the AFL, as well as on other issues. The few months he spent as the editor of *El Heraldo*, in which he analysed world events from a socialist perspective, had a crucial impact on his political development and made it possible for him to later play a role as a leader in both the Mexican and the US Communist Parties

---

21 Phillips, 19 June 1919.

22 Phillips, 7 September 1919; 24 September1919; 31 August 1919; 5 November 1919; 11 September 1919; 2 September 1919.

23 Phillips, 30 September 1919a; 30 September 1919b; 4 October 1919; 1 November 1919.

and as a delegate to the Communist International. As editor of *El Heraldo* Phillips developed what would be many of the key ideas of the future Mexican Communist Party, which he would go on to found, a revolutionary, internationalist socialism politically virtually identical to Russian Bolshevism. When in January 1920 Carranza first arrested and then drove Alvarado into exile in the United States, Phillips's work as editor of *El Heraldo* ended.

Both Gale and Phillips had surveyed the Mexican left and located the small Socialist Party led by Adolfo Santibañez. Gale and his principal partner, Fulgencio Luna, cultivated a relationship with Santibañez and invited him and his collaborators to write for *Gale's Magazine*. Gale succeeded in becoming particularly close to one of the Mexican Socialist Party members, Enrique Arce. The American war resisters in Mexico City had split into two rival groups. Phillips, editor of the English language page of *El Heraldo de Mexico*, became the centre of one group of American slackers, and Linn A.E. Gale, editor of *Gale's Magazine*, became the leader of the other. While both Phillips and Gale identified with the left wing of the Socialist Party of the United States, admired the Industrial Workers of the World, supported the Russian Revolution and looked for leadership to the Bolshevik Party and the Communist International, the two men could not cooperate. Probably the principal reason was Gale's eccentricity, vanity and need to *épater le bourgeois*. Phillips, who was a much more serious political activist, thought Gale a fool and a charlatan.

3   Enter M.N. Roy, Indian Nationalist

At about that time another foreigner entered the little Mexican Socialist Party, an Indian named Manabendra Nath Roy. At the age of 31, Roy already had a 15-year career as a revolutionary. Born in Arbalia, Bengal state in 1887 with the name Manabendra Nath Bhattachaijee, he had been an activist in the Indian nationalist movement since the age of 14. When World War I broke out, he went in search of German arms to fight the British, travelling from India to Java, to China, to the United States, and finally to Mexico. Roy planned to make contact with German diplomats and military officers in Mexico who might help him purchase arms for a revolution against the British government in India. The Mexican revolutionary government of Venustiano Carranza, while officially neutral in the war, sympathised with the Germans, and Roy could operate more freely there than in the United States.

Arriving in Mexico around the end of 1917, Roy quickly established contacts with both the German Embassy and the Mexican government, and both eventually provided him with money. He later remembered that Carranza's Minister of War informed him, 'I only wanted to reassure you that you are in a country which has fought for freedom ever since the days of Hidalgo and Juárez. You are free and safe here'.[24] Subsequently Roy was directed by government officials to a Mexican newspaper editor who asked him to write a series of articles about British Rule in India. The paper's editor assigned him a private secretary and translator, and had the bank pay him 10,000 pesos, or about 5,000 dollars. Roy understood that the Mexican government had arranged a financial subsidy to support his activities against Great Britain in the form of the payments for his newspaper articles.[25] At the same time, the Germans gave Roy money to arrange the purchase of guns for India, so that Roy soon accumulated another 50,000 pesos or about 25,000 dollars.[26] This was a great deal of money at the time and especially in Mexico. Roy would eventually use the money to finance the founding of Mexico's first Communist Party and to send its delegates, himself among them, to the Communist International in Soviet Russia.

While in the United States a short time before, Roy had been exposed to the idea of socialism. He had met the socialist, pacifist, and feminist crowd at Stanford University. He had apparently begun to read Marx and had probably come into contact with the Socialist Party of America. 'Culturally, I was still a nationalist: and cultural nationalism is a prejudice that dies very hard', Roy wrote later in his *Memoirs*. 'Socialism appealed to me because of its anti-imperialist connotations'.[27] So, when Roy arrived in Mexico, he scanned the horizon, looking for the Socialists.

Roy soon found the office of the small Socialist Party of Mexico headed by Adolfo Santibañez and introduced himself. Santibañez had read Roy's newspaper articles about British Rule in India and had been favourably impressed. So Santibañez invited Roy to attend the meetings of the small Mexican Socialist Party. Roy had the same impression as Phillips, that while the group professed to be Socialists, most were actually anarchists. He was appalled to find that the Socialists held that in the event of a US invasion of Mexico, they would be neutral, viewing it as a war between two bourgeois governments. Roy spent the next several months meeting with the Mexican socialists and arguing his own

---

24   Roy 1984, p. 61. Roy's *Memoirs* are not entirely reliable and have to be used with caution. Internal evidence and comparison with other records indicate that Roy sometimes forgot, confused, or exaggerated various elements of his experience in Mexico between 1918 and 1920. This remark, however, is very likely true.

25   Roy 1964, pp. 61 and 71.

26   Roy 1964, pp. 90–1.

27   Roy 1964, p. 59.

newly acquired Marxist views against their anarchism and his socialist anti-imperialism against their anarchist neutrality.

During one of his visits with Santibañez and the Socialist Party members, Roy met 'a couple of young American radicals'. Roy had already run into American slackers in Mexico and remembered them later in his *Memoirs*:

> Hundreds of pacifists, anarcho-syndicalists, socialists of all shades, had escaped to Mexico in order to evade compulsory military service, which was introduced soon after America joined the war. They were derogatorily called the slackers. According to their respective persuasion and predisposition, some wanted to join the Zapatistas, others to go to the El Dorado of Yucatan, and the rest to try their luck anywhere. Most of the Radical refugees, however, ultimately drifted toward the capital and congregated there.[28]

Roy became friends with Charles Francis Phillips, and Phillips introduced Roy to what was practically *The Masses* staff in exile: Maurice Becker, Hendrik Glintenkamp and Irwin Granich (Mike Gold). For Roy, an English speaker and a socialist, it was no doubt comfortable to become part of the slackers' milieu.

4   The Slackers Reorganise the Socialist Party

Roy, Phillips, and the other Americans all joined the Socialist Party of Santibañez and became some of its most dynamic members. Roy discretely used the money he had acquired from the German and Mexican governments to finance the Socialist Party's newspaper *El Socialista*. With Roy's money, the paper expanded from eight to 32 pages and began to carry articles about the revolutionary labour movement in Europe. Roy also financed Socialist Party organising trips to the towns of Pachuca, Hidalgo, in the mining region and to Orizaba, Veracruz, the centre of the textile industry. In this way the Socialists made contract with the most militant centres of industrial workers.

M.N. Roy's *Memoirs* provides a detailed account of the reorganisation of the Socialist Party and the role of himself and the slackers. Unfortunately, his account cannot be relied upon, both because it exaggerates his own role at the expense of the other protagonists and because he sometimes appears to confuse and conflate events. His version of the reorganisation of the little Socialist

---

28   Roy 1964, p, 109.

Party puts him at the centre, and also makes the entire process dependent upon the tolerance and support of President Carranza. His account does not agree with that of Phillips, who makes the venture appear to be politically independent. In his *Memoirs* Roy claimed that soon after giving up his nationalist views and becoming a socialist, he devised a broad strategy for his activities that involved: first, a defence of the Mexican revolutionary government of Carranza against US aggression; second, the creation of a socialist movement to both support and pressure the Mexican government for social reforms; and third, the creation of a Latin American league against US imperialism. To accomplish this programme, Roy believed that he would have to establish a relationship to the Mexican president and, with the resulting support from the Mexican government, build a Communist Party, which would appear as a supporter of the government rather than as a threat to it. Roy suggests that he convinced both the American slackers and Santibañez and the Socialists to adopt his programme.[29]

President Carranza, Roy says, eventually granted the interview he had been seeking for some time, though it is not clear that this took place.[30] In his *Memoirs* Roy explained that he first met with 'Don Manuel' (this would be Manuel Aguirre Berlanga, Carranza's Minister of the Interior), and outlined a plan of action calling for the Socialist Party to organise a demonstration against US intervention in the capital, followed by a strike of petroleum workers against foreign owned oil companies. In exchange, the Mexican government would support the workers' economic demands. Berlanga, according to Roy, approved this program. Berlanga then presented Roy to Carranza. When Roy met with Carranza, he later claimed, 'the President congratulated me on my success in reminding the Socialists that they were also Mexicans, and must do their duty to the *patria* (fatherland)'.[31] Roy says he also discussed 'the plan of the Latin American League'.[32] He would have known that Carranza and his protégée, Hermila Galindo, whom Roy had already met, had called for an alliance of Latin American states against US imperialism. Roy's plan for a Latin American

---

29   Roy 1964, pp. 94–5 and 118–21.

30   There is no record of this interview or of any other meeting with Roy in the Carranza papers in the Condumex Archive in Mexico City. However, many of Carranza's papers were lost when he fled Mexico City in 1919 carrying with him the national archives, so the absence of any reference to Roy in the papers does not prove that the two did not meet. I believe that a meeting between Carranza and Roy would be thoroughly consistent with Carranza's policies and Roy's plans, still it may not have happened.

31   Roy 1964, p. 139.

32   Roy 1964, p. 149.

coalition, perhaps influenced by Carranza and Galindo, could be considered the first prototype of what would later become the Communists' All American Anti-Imperialist League.

While the documents do not confirm that a meeting between Carranza and Roy ever actually took place, it is altogether possible and even likely, for such a contact would have been completely consistent with Carranza's politics both internationally and domestically. Carranza and Galindo were already engaged in promoting an alliance of Latin American states against the United States.[33] They would have found Roy, an opponent of British imperialism (when Britain was the ally of the United States), to be a useful person, and would have found his ideas about an international anti-imperialist alliance to be close to their own. Carranza would have been willing to accept the organisation of a Communist Party in Mexico, if he believed that he could control or influence its leaders, such as Roy or Gale, and keep its activities aimed at foreign capitalists, particularly the oil companies, rather than at the Mexican government.

For Roy, the most important task of the moment was the reorganisation of the Socialist Party. With characteristic vanity, he claims that he called for a conference of the Socialist Party 'with the object of forming a mass party of the working class'.[34] It seems more likely that Roy and Phillips worked with Adolfo Santibañez, the leader of the Mexican Socialist Party to call such a meeting. The leaflet calling for the meeting recounted that there had been four workers' congresses in recent years, but that this was the first socialist congress. The conveners invited all labour union and socialist organisations to attend and promised to take up 'the future of the labour movement, now that socialist ideas were being carried out in practice by Russian Bolsheviks, Hungarian Communists and German Spartacists. The leaflet ended with the usual anarcho-syndicalist salutation, 'Health and Social Revolution', and was signed by the Organising Committee: Adolfo Santibañez, Francisco Cervantes López, Felipe Dávalos, and Timoteo García.[35]

Roy recalled in his *Memoirs* that a Socialist Party congress meeting took place in December 1918, though it actually occurred in August and September 1919.[36] He has left this colourful description of the event:

---

33   Galindo 1919, *passim*.

34   Roy 1964, p. 131.

35   'El Primer Congreso Nacional Socialista de Mexico', Papers of the Partido Comunista (PC), Box 1, Folder 1, CEMOS.

36   Spenser 2011, p. 49.

Among the delegates, there were workers from the oil fields, some of them highly skilled mechanics, men and women employed in textile mills, miners, dockers, railwaymen, motor drivers; there were artisans as well as a few small traders; and many came from the land; not ordinary labourers, but overseers in large modern farms. Intellectuals and professional men, such as teachers, writers, artists, physicians, lawyers, who mostly belonged to the capital. Provincial delegate included a good many schoolmasters.[37]

He remembered that 'the industrial workers were mostly anarcho-syndicalists', but 'all were fervent Utopians – passionate believers in social revolution'. In addition, there were a number of 'bourgeois' delegates, members of the Mexican Senate or House of Deputies, and government or university officials.[38]

The hall was adorned with portraits of Mikhail Bakunin, Peter Kropotkin and Karl Marx, and one of the American slackers had received a photograph of Vladimir Lenin from the American Communist Party founder John Reed, which was hung in the place of honour. Reed had also written a message of greetings to the Mexican Socialist conference. Charles Francis Phillips and Irwin Granich led a demonstration with a portrait of Lenin and banners reading: 'Petroleum Belongs to the Mexican People', 'Long Live the Revolutionary Alliance of Latin American Republics', 'Long Live the Bolsheviks', and also 'Long Live the Soviet Republic of Mexico'. The demonstration marched to the *zócalo*. the national plaza, where Phillips gave a speech and cried, 'Down with Yankee Imperialism!' Carranza appeared on the balcony of the National Palace to greet the people and declared that 'the voice of the people being the Voice of God, he would obey it'.[39] Or so Roy remembered, although his memory must be questioned.

In fact, fewer than one hundred delegates and observers attended the 25 August 1919 meeting of the First National Conference of the Socialist Party. It included most of the important leftists of the Mexican labour movement and the slackers: Adolfo Santibañez and the old leadership of the Socialist Party; Phillips, Roy and their friends; Linn A.E. Gale and his comrades Fulgencio Luna; Leonardo Hernández, head of the Grain Millers Union, representing the revolutionary syndicalists; Jacinto Huitrón on behalf of the anarchists; José Allen and Eduardo Camacho of the Red Socialist Youth; and the 'Action Group' of Luis N. Morones, head of the Regional Confederation of Mexican Workers (CROM),

37   Roy 1964, pp. 141–8. This account, despite the incorrect date, seems very plausible.
38   Roy 1964, pp. 141–8.
39   Roy 1964, pp. 141–8.

representing the right wing of the Mexican labour movement. Evelyn Trent, Roy's wife, was the delegate of the Radical Women's Centre (Centro Radical Femenino) of Guadalajara.[40] Altogether there were just 60 delegates from labour unions, workers' organisations, and socialist circles.[41] Even so, the Socialist Party Congress was hardly representative of the working class of Mexico City, much less that of Mexico as a whole.[42]

One of the first issues of the conference was a motion to expel Luis N. Morones and the Action Group. Gale supported the motion, but it failed with M.N. Roy in the chair casting the decisive vote against. The Gale-Luna faction and Roy-Phillips faction agreed on joining the Communist International, but on little else. Huitrón continued to argue for his anarchist views. Santibañez, the head of the original Socialist Party, walked out of the Congress shaking his head in disgust, apparently exasperated with the divisive debates. In the end Phillips drafted a resolution, based in part on the founding documents of the Communist International, calling for the socialisation of the means of production, distribution and exchange in the hand of the workers under Communist leadership. Phillips's resolution passed with 22 of the votes, with Santibañez having excluded himself and Huitrón the anarchist and Morones of the Action Group voting against.[43] A national committee was elected, and José Allen of the Red Socialist Youth was chosen for the top office of General Secretary of the reorganised Socialist Party of Mexico.

The choice of José Allen as the general secretary of the reorganised Socialist Party was to prove significant for reasons the members never knew, since he was a spy for the US Military Intelligence Division (USMID). For the next year or two, Allen kept the USMID informed about everything that happened in the party. Though Allen was nominally the organisational head of the party, it appears that Santibañez and the American and Indian exiles Phillips and Roy remained the party's political leaders. Soon, however, another foreigner, this one representing revolutionary Russia, joined them.

5   Mikhail Borodin, Agent of the International

In October of 1919 Mikhail Borodin arrived in Mexico City from the United States accompanied by a man named Rafael Mallén. Borodin took up residence

---

40   Paco Ignacio Taibo II 1986, p. 40.
41   Carr 1992, p. 22.
42   Taibo 1986, p. 40.
43   Taibo 1986, p. 41.

at the Hotel Regis under the name Peter Alexandrescu, posing as a Rumanian-American businessman from Chicago. In reality the man called Alexandrescu was best known for most of his political life as Borodin, had been born and named Mikhail Markovich Gruzenberg in 1884 in Ianovitchi, Vitebsk, Russia. As a young man, he became a member of the Jewish Bund, then of the Bolshevik faction of the Russian Social Democracy. After arrest for his revolutionary activities in Russia he had emigrated to the United States around 1908 and lived in Chicago where he learned to speak English fluently. In the United States he had been a member of the Socialist Party, but he returned to Russia in 1918 after the victory of the Bolshevik revolution. The Bolsheviks recruited him to work for the Commisariat of Foreign Affairs (Narkomindel) and the Communist International. Borodin would later attain great notoriety for his role in the Chinese Revolution of 1927, but his mission in 1919 was to form a Communist revolutionary movement in Mexico.

In April 1919, Borodin left Russia, reportedly using a Mexican diplomatic passport that described him as the Mexican Consul in Soviet Russia. He also carried a Russian passport with the title general consul to Mexico on behalf of the Soviet Federal Socialist Republic, charged with establishing economic relations between the two revolutionary nations. But since he was also working for the Communist International, Borodin carried with him some of the Russian crown jewels, estimated to be worth $500,000 to be used to finance revolutionary activities in the Americas. But along the way the jewels were stolen from him, and his attempt to reclaim the jewels, which will be discussed later, would lead several of his comrades on a wild goose chase. After the theft of the jewels in the Caribbean, Borodin went to the United States where he apparently procured from Ludwig Martens, an agent of the Communist International in New York, $10,000 to carry out propaganda in Mexico and South America. Borodin then arranged for the assistance of a translator through the Socialist Party of America, which provided him with Mallén. Together the two journeyed to Mexico City.[44]

When Borodin arrived in Mexico City, he bought up all the newspapers, and soon found *El Heraldo* and the English language page edited by Phillips. Or perhaps, as the USMID agent reported, he already had their names from the Socialist Party office in New York.[45] In any case, Borodin then went in search

---

44   Memo from the Military Attaché to the Director of Military Intelligence, subject Bolshevist propaganda, May 26, 1920, RG 165, Box 2290, USMID, USNA. See also: Spenser 1998, pp. 55–60.

45   Memo from Military Attaché to Director of Military Intelligence, May 26, 1920, RG 165, Box 2290, USMID, USNA.

of the American slacker socialists. At the offices of *El Heraldo* he met with Charles Francis Phillips and M.N. Roy and soon established a friendship with both, though perhaps particularly with the latter. Roy invited Borodin to live in his house, giving the Indian and the Russian opportunities for long talks. Roy later wrote, 'The discussion of the philosophical aspect of Marxism was confined to Borodin and myself. Beginning after dinner, it usually continued until late in the night. It was the most memorable period of my life. It was during [those months in Mexico] preceding my departure for Moscow that the foundation of my subsequent intellectual development was laid'.[46] Phillips, however, remembered that he too had been part of those conversations, 'we went there [to Roy's place] constantly, and Borodin educated us [the American slackers Phillips, Glintenkamp and Granich] – and Roy – in Marxism'.[47] Borodin began his informal classes in Marxism with the study of the Hegelian dialectic and proceeded through Marx to Lenin.

Roy and Phillips introduced Borodin to the executive committee and other leaders of the Socialist Party, including USMID agent José Allen. The USMID and other US government authorities were thus informed at once of Borodin's presence and activities in Mexico.[48] Through the Socialist Party, Borodin also came into contact with several key leaders of the left wing of the Mexican union movement. In general Borodin was the *éminence grise* of the organisation, instructing Roy and Phillips who in turn made suggestions to the Mexican Socialists. Surprisingly, Linn Gale apparently never even met or talked with Borodin. He later complained that Borodin was 'kept from seeing the real Communists and wined and dined by the aristocrat and fake Bolshevist, Roy'.[49]

In his *Memoirs*, always somewhat suspect, Roy claimed that he arranged for Borodin to meet Mexican President Carranza at a dinner party, though others have challenged the contention that any meeting between Carranza and Borodin ever took place.[50] Roy claimed that Borodin:

---

46   Roy 1964, p. 215.
47   Shipman 1993, p. 84.
48   US Military Intelligence Reports: Surveillance of Radicals in the United States 1917–1941, ed. Randolph Boehm (University Publications of America, Inc., 1984). This microfilm contains reports of surveillance of US radicals in Mexico, with several references to Borodin. See also Record Group 165, USMID, USNA.
49   Gale, June–July 1920, p. 27.
50   Paco Ignacio Taibo II accepts this version (Taibo II 1986). Daniela Spenser, however, believes this interview never took place, there being no record of it in either the Mexican or Russian archives (Spenser 2011).

> ... announced that the new regime in Russia fully sympathised with the struggle of the Latin American peoples against Imperialism and was eager to help [them] in every possible manner. With that purpose, a Latin American Bureau of the Communist International should be established in Mexico, provided that His Excellency the President of the Republic consented ....[51]

Carranza, says Roy, was enthusiastic about the plan to promote Latin American unity against the United States. Roy recorded that Carranza 'requested Borodin to transmit his. good wishes to the head of the new regime in Russia'. Roy argued that this could 'be taken for de facto recognition of the new regime in Russia'.[52] He also claimed that Carranza agreed to let Borodin use the Mexican diplomatic mails. In his autobiography, Phillips denied that any such meeting ever took place: 'Carranza was still glad to see Roy, but the harried old man refused to meet Borodin even informally'.[53] That such a meeting occurred is possible, if unlikely. While the Mexican president did wish to create a Latin American league against US imperialism, it is doubtful that he would have been enthusiastic about the Russian Bolsheviks setting up the base for their international activities in Mexico. The alliance of Latin American states, which the more conservative Carranza and Galindo were attempting to promote, might have been undermined if those other Latin American nations thought that Mexico had embraced the Bolsheviks.

Even if Carranza was not supportive, Borodin, Roy, and Phillips wished to move ahead with the constitution of the Mexican Communist Party (PCM) and the choice of delegates for the Second Congress of the Communist International in Russia. Meanwhile, the Mexican Socialist Party had split into rival factions as a result of difference in personalities, politics, and patrons. Almost immediately after the Socialist Party's National Congress, the Mexico City chapter had expelled Gale for his associations with Carranza's Minister of the Interior Aguirre Berlanga. In response, Gale and Luna then met with their followers on 7 September 1919, and announced the foundation of the Communist Party of Mexico (PC de M). Gale's Communist Party of Mexico viciously attacked Phillips and Roy as agents of Morones and the CROM, principally because Roy had voted against expelling Morones from the earlier Socialist Party conference.

Nevertheless, Borodin, who after all represented the Communist International, urged Phillips and Roy to go ahead with the constitution of their own

---

51 Roy 1964, pp. 295–6.
52 Ibid.
53 Shipman 1993, p. 84.

Communist Party. On 24 November 1919 Roy, Phillips, Allen and four of their followers held a secret meeting at which they changed the name of the Social-ist Party to the Mexican Communist Party (PCM), and chose Roy and Phillips as delegates to the Communist International. Borodin, as the official represent-ative of the Communist International immediately recognised the Roy-Phillips PCM as the genuine and legitimate Communist affiliate in Mexico.[54] Phillips writes in his memoir, 'Ours thus became the first party outside Russia to vote formal affiliation with the International'.[55]

The fact that it was the Mexican Socialist Party, rather than the anarchist labour movement, which gave birth to the Communist Party of Mexico repres-ented a decisive and qualitative break with Mexico's radical past. From the late nineteenth century to the 1920s, the anarchists had been the dominant rad-ical tendency within the Mexican left and labour movement.[56] Beginning in the 1920s the Communists gradually displaced the anarchists, became domin-ant by the mid-1930s, and remained Mexico's most important left organisation until the 1980s.[57] But it was the alliance of the American slackers, other foreign-ers, and Mexicans within the Socialist Party of Mexico that set that long-term process in motion with the founding of the party. At the same time, because they did not come out of the anarchist movement, their base of support among workers was much narrower than it might have been.

6   International Interlude

Once the Communist Party of Mexico had been organised, and affiliated with the Communist International, Borodin asked Phillips to undertake a secret mis-sion for him. Borodin sent Phillips to Cuba to look for his former interpreter Rafael Mallén and a suitcase that supposedly contained important blueprints. Changing his pseudonym from Frank Seaman to Jesús Ramírez, Phillips sailed for Cuba. Since he did not find Mallén in Cuba, Borodin then sent Phillips on to Pétionville, Haiti to look for a Dutchman named Henrik Luders. Phillips found Luders, who it turned out, had the suitcase and the blueprints and turned them over. Phillips returned to Cuba, and there by coincidence found Rafael Mallén's name on the passenger list of the ship he was taking to Mexico. So, with Mallén

----

54   Letter of 29 November 1919 from M. Borodin to José Allen, Record Group 165, Box 2290,
      USMID, USNA.
55   Shipman 1993, p. 85.
56   Hart 1975 and 1978.
57   Carr 1992, *passim*.

and the suitcase full of blueprints, Phillips returned to Veracruz, Mexico, his mission completed and, he thought, a success.

Phillips and Mallén then took the train from Veracruz to Mexico City, and Roy and Borodin met them at the station. But when Phillips handed him the suitcase, Borodin went berserk. 'There's nothing in here but blueprints!' he shouted. 'Where are the diamonds?' Borodin threatened to torture and murder Mallén if he didn't explain what had happened to the diamonds, but when no answer was forthcoming, he let him go. Borodin then explained to Phillips that he had left Russia with the Romanov crown jewels, which were to have been sold in order to finance revolutionary activity in Latin America. He had lost the jewels when he asked the Dutchman Luders to carry the bag through customs for him. Later Borodin had sent Mallén to look for Luders and the bag, but Mallén had then disappeared. So, he sent Phillips to look for both, but despite his remarkable success in locating Luders, Mallén, and the bag, the jewels appeared to have disappeared.[58] US military intelligence, which also learned of the story, estimated the value of the jewels as two and a half million dollars.[59]

Unable to relocate the Romanov crown Jewels, Borodin decided to return to Russia via Europe, and asked Phillips to accompany him. Borodin and Phillips, who travelled again as Jesús Ramírez, correspondent for General Alvarado's newspaper *El Heraldo de Mexico*, left Mexico and sailed for Spain on 1 December 1919. US intelligence reports indicated that Borodin and Phillips entered Spain through Cadiz and Seville and then travelled to Barcelona and Madrid, 'where [Borodin] held conferences with prominent anarchists, socialists and leaders of the Casa del Pueblo [House of the People] in various cities; and furnished them with funds'.[60]

In Madrid, Borodin and Phillips checked into the fashionable Palace Hotel, bought all the newspapers and reading through them began to analyse the different labour and political tendencies in Spain. The impact of the Russian Revolution had already led to the formation of pro-Soviet groups within the Spanish Socialist Party and in its youth group.[61] Phillips read the newspapers, identifying individuals and organisations with leftist views, while Borodin took down the names and made notes. Having identified the people they wanted to meet and talk to, Phillips found them and then, acting as interpreter, intro-

---

58 Manuel Gómez October 64, pp. 37–9 and Shipman 1993, pp. 86–9.

59 Memo from Director of Military Intelligence to Military Observer, Berlin, Germany, subject Jacob Gruzenberg alias Borodin, September 1, 1920, in RG 165, Box 2290, USMID, USNA.

60 Memo from Director of Military Intelligence to Military Observer, Berlin, Germany, subject Jacob Gruzenberg alias Borodin, September 1, 1920, in RG 165, Box 2290, USMID, USNA.

61 Andrade 1979, pp. 19–29.

duced them to Borodin. They met Daniel Anguiano, a union leader, as well as Ángel Pesataña, one of the foremost leaders of the anarcho-syndicalist labour unions in Spain who would later attend the Second Congress of the Communist International.

Phillips and Borodin also went to the literary-political club, El Ateneo, which had the reputation of being the centre of Spain's intellectual life. There Phillips noticed a young man reading English books and introduced himself. The man turned out to be the American writer John Dos Passos, and Dos Passos introduced them to two important Spanish intellectuals, Professor Fernando de Los Ríos and Mariano García Cortés. García Cortés turned out to be a prominent figure in the socialist movement, and sympathetic to Soviet Russia. Later Phillips returned to García Cortés' *tertulia*, an evening dinner and discussion, and there he met Ramón Merino García, a former medical student who had been expelled from the university and was working as a waiter. Merino Garcia expressed interest in the Soviet Union and the Communist International, so Phillips introduced him too to Borodin. Both Phillips and Borodin found Merino Garcia intelligent as well as political, and moreover, he claimed to have a following in the Spanish Socialist Party (PSE) and was willing to lead a fight to affiliate the PSE with the Communist International. 'In short, he was our man', Phillips later wrote in his memoir.[62]

Phillips found that 'Ramón worked fast and effectively. Before long we were meeting with a cohesive group pledged to achieve Socialist endorsement of the Third International in defiance of the party leadership'.[63] In addition to Merino García, Phillips also had the support of political activists Juan Andrade, Virginia González, and union leader Anguiano. With the organisation of a Spanish Communist organisation apparently well underway, Borodin left for Amsterdam, Berlin and Moscow, leaving Phillips in charge of organising a Spanish Communist Party before the coming Second Congress of the International. Phillips, living in the home of a shoemaker, stayed in Spain organising the new Communist movement until February, when he ran out of funds. Needing money, he travelled to Paris where he hoped he could find someone who would give him the fare so he could get to Berlin and find Borodin to obtain more money for the Spanish organising campaign.

In Paris Phillips connected with French socialists at Jean Longuet's newspaper *Le Populaire*. Longuet, who was Karl Marx's grandson, advised Phillips to see Pierre Loriot, the head of the Committee for the Third International. Phil-

---

62   Shipman 1993, p. 93.
63   Shipman 1993, pp. 92–3; Manuel Gómez, October 1964, pp. 37–9.

lips found that Loriot and his chief lieutenant Boris Souvarine were in jail and visited them there. They arranged his railroad fare to Zurich. Phillips knew that M.N. Roy and Evelyn Trent were staying in Zurich and he located them. Roy, who always had money, provided Phillips with $200 to return to Madrid, and wired money to a bank in Madrid so that he would have the necessary organising funds.

Once back in Madrid, Phillips and Merino García continued their work, concentrating on organising within the Socialist Party youth organisation. They created a Spanish Committee for the Third International and built branches as far away as Bilbao and Málaga. Phillips, Merino and their Committee also published a newspaper called *El Obrero* [The Worker], When the Socialist Party expelled Juan Andrade and Merino García, they used their expulsion as the pretext for splitting the party. Phillips later wrote, 'Although our group was tiny and made up almost entirely of youth, it was the basis for the Communist Party of Spain'.[64] US Military Intelligence agreed, their report indicating that Borodin was 'held responsible for the split in the Socialist Party which occurred in April 1920'.[65]

Anxious to make his way to the Second Congress of the Communist International, Phillips travelled to Genoa in June of 1920, finding the city in the midst of the Italian general strikes and factory occupations known as the *Biennio Rosso*, the two red years. From Italy he went north to Berlin, and from there to Stockholm, and with the help of the Mexican Ambassador, he journeyed from Stockholm to Estonia. Without an exit visa from Estonia, Phillips arrived at the Russian border where he jumped on a train, left Estonia illegally and entered the Soviet Union.

Phillips spent a few weeks exploring Petrograd and meeting the arriving delegates to the Second Congress of the Communist International. He passed most of his time with the English-speaking delegates, particularly the Americans: John Reed, Louis C. Fraina, Jimmy Gilday, and the Japanese Sen Katayama who had lived in the United States and spoke fluent English. He also met some of the Communist leaders, he wrote later, and 'got to know them, fairly well, especially N.I. Bukharin and Karl Radek'.[66]

The Second Congress opened on 17 July 1920 in Petrograd, but later moved its sessions to Moscow. Mexico was for the first time represented there, by the Indian Roy and the American Phillips. Phillips spoke from the floor only once

---

64   Shipman 1993, p. 97.
65   Memo from Director of Military Intelligence to Military Observer, Berlin, Germany, subject Jacob Gruzenberg alias Borodin, September 1, 1920, in RG 165, Box 2290, USMID, USNA.
66   Shipman 1993, p. 115.

during the entire Congress. Roy, who had been sent as a delegate from Mexico became upon his arrival the delegate from India. As the only delegate from a colonial country Roy spoke at length on the Communist International's policy toward the colonial peoples. He challenged Lenin on the question of movements for independence in the colonial world, with Lenin presenting a position supporting the national bourgeoisie's leadership of them, while Roy argued that the national bourgeoisie would capitulate to imperialism. In the end, the Congress surprisingly adopted both resolutions.[67]

Though critical of certain aspects of it, Phillips found the Second Congress exhilarating. 'I felt confirmed in my Communist faith, ready for my assignment'.[68]

While in Moscow, Phillips asked for and was granted a meeting with Lenin. The Russian leader told Phillips he was seeing him only because he came from the Mexican Party and confessed that his knowledge of Mexico was fragmentary. He asked Phillips about the role the Mexican Communist Party was playing among the peasants. Phillips then explained that much of the peasant population was indigenous, a fact about which Lenin had been ignorant. Lenin then asked him if they had publications in the indigenous languages. When Phillips explained that the Indians were illiterate, Lenin told him that they should have Indian speakers. 'Those Indians, he [Lenin] said, should be your number-one objective in the countryside'.[69]

Having first organised the fledgling Communist Parties of Mexico and Spain, Phillips had now visited the Soviet Union, attended a Congress of the Communist International, and had met and talked with Lenin. His travels through Europe and his meetings and discussions with revolutionary leaders had given him a wider view of the revolutionary movement throughout the world. He had become one of the Comintern's cadres, what Lenin and the Bolsheviks called a 'professional revolutionary'. He was now completely committed to the building of the Communist International, the world party of revolution. He would dedicate the next decade of his life to that project.

In addition to that substantial political education, Phillips also had two quite moving personal experiences while in Moscow. When in Russia, Phillips had

---

67   La Botz 2017, pp. 67–106.
68   Shipman 1993, p. 25.
69   Shipman 1993, p. 118; Gómez, October 1964, pp. 42–3. Interestingly José Carlos Mariátegui had come to the same conclusion as Lenin, arguing that revolutionary socialist propagandists in the indigenous peoples' own languages were essential to building a revolutionary movement in Peru and other regions in Latin America. See his essay 'El problema de las razas en America Latina', in Mariátegui 1982, vol. 2, pp. 181–6.

grown friendly with John Reed, who, while attending the Congress of the Oriental Nations at Baku, had fallen quite ill and had to be hospitalised. Phillips, together with Reed's lover Louise Bryant and their friend Louis Fraina, visited John Reed every day at his sick bed in the Kremlin, until he died in mid-October. At the same time, Phillips fell in love with one of the young women working in the hotel where he stayed in Moscow, an apolitical 18-year-old named Natalia Alexandrovna Mikhailova. Though he was still married to Eleanor Parker – the woman who had accompanied him to Mexico, and who had then left him for the artist Hendrik Glintenkamp – Phillips now became a bigamist by marrying Natalia, who became Señora de Ramírez. With legal passports in the name of Mr and Mrs Ramírez, Phillips and Natalia returned to Mexico via Estonia, Berlin, Antwerp, New York and Laredo.

When Phillips arrived back in Mexico City, he was greeted by Roberto Haberman who arranged a dinner for him at the home of the artist Diego Rivera. Haberman also invited Felipe Carrillo Puerto, the governor of the Yucatan and the leader of the Socialist Party of the Southeast. All were anxious to hear about Phillips's travels to Russia, the Congress of the Communist International, and his meeting with Lenin. Phillips had not only grown in self-confidence after his travels, but also, because of his association with Soviet Russia and the Comintern, he had assumed a new stature and importance in the eyes of others in Mexico.[70] Phillips found that in his absence the small Mexican Communist Party had expanded, and its prospects seemed to be looking up. A talented young man named José C. Valadés had joined the organisation, and Phillips began to work closely with him. The young Communist Party probably had about 200 members.[71] That small group of American slackers and Mexican Communists now set out to organise the Mexican working class into the Industrial Workers of the World.

---

70   Gómez, April 1965, p. 116.
71   Valadés 1988, vol. 1, pp. 81–90.

CHAPTER 12

American Slackers and the Industrial Workers of the World

The Americans and Mexicans who organised the two Communist parties in Mexico also attempted to shape the Mexican branch of the Industrial Workers of the World (IWW). While the US-based IWW had been active in Mexico for years, Linn A.E. Gale attempted to establish the first Mexican Administration of the IWW organisation in September 1919, with a three-person committee headed by himself. Gale's IWW was clearly an extension of Gale's Communist Party of Mexico (PCdeM). To add to the confusion between the IWW and the PCdeM, Gale created a new magazine, *El Comunista de Mexico: Órgano del Partido Comunista de Mexico y de la 'I.w.w'. de Mexico* (The Communist of Mexico: Organ of the Communist Party of Mexico and of the 'I.W.W'. of Mexico), the journal serving as the official publication of both groups.[1]

The US-based IWW, however, did not approve of Gale's first attempt to form an organisation of the IWW controlled by his Communist Party of Mexico (PCdeM). In late 1919, the principal IWW newspaper in the United States, *The Industrial Worker*, attacked Gale's IWW arguing that it was paternalistic and constructed from above by the PCdeM. The US-based IWW particularly attacked a clause in Gale's Mexican IWW rules, which said that three members of the Communist Party of Mexico and three members of IWW would each participate in the executive committee of the other.[2] Gale, nevertheless, went ahead with his project, while attempting to convince the IWW leadership in the US that he was building a genuine IWW organisation.

A few months later, in February 1920, *Gale's Magazine* carried an article signed by John A. Jutt, announcing that, 'The Mexican Administration of the Industrial Workers of the World has been organised and is now functioning'. Ángel Bernal had been chosen chairman, José Villalobos and John A Jutt, served as members of the executive committee. The IWW had begun organising industrial unions 'thruout [*sic*] Mexico', the article claimed, and would

---

1 A copy of *El Comunista de México* June 1920 is available in the archives of the Centro de Estudios de la Historia del Movimiento Obrero y Socialista (CEHMOS), Coyoácán, Mexico City. With issue Number 4 in October 1920, *El Comunista* was simply the organ of the Communist Party of Mexico (PCdeM) and no longer also of the IWW.
2 'Mexican Communists', October 1919, cited in Taibo II 1986, p. 48.

soon hold a national convention.[3] 'The job delegate system will be utilised, of course, as the proper one for organising workers on the job, and several of these delegates are already busy in different parts of the country', wrote Jutt. The job delegates were: J.C. Parker in Tamaulipas; Charles F. Tabler among miners in Guanajuato; Enrique and José Rodríguez among typographical workers; John A. Jutt and F.H. Guerrero among oil workers in Tampico. The delegates represented Gale's circle of slackers and Mexican radical friends and associates.[4]

Jutt argued that Mexican workers had suffered from wage slavery, craft unionism, and treacherous union officials who had sold out their strikes. The Mexican Wobblies, he wrote, had another programme. 'We propose to build up a powerful nation-wide One Big Union of Mexican workers who will not compromise with their masters, who will not tolerate divisions in the same industry and who constantly recognise that all our struggles with the masters are but the prelude to the final struggle that shall wrest industry, land and resources from those masters for ever'.[5]

The same issue of *Gale's* carried a letter from William D. 'Big Bill' Haywood, apparently now convinced that Gale was on the right track, congratulating Mexican workers on the creation of a Mexican Administration of the IWW. 'It is good indeed to learn that you have held a convention of the Mexican workers and made some permanent steps towards organising a Mexican Administration of the Industrial Workers of the World', Haywood wrote on 18 December 1919. 'Your country has been so cruelly torn and battered with many long years of revolution and counter-revolution that it is full time that the workers had adopted the only kind of organisation that means for them in the ultimate a life of peace and comfort'.[6]

Gale's IWW executive committee was composed mostly of Mexicans. He described his executive board in an article published in *Gale's* in August 1920, and signed 'El Luchador Viejo' (The Old Battler), one of Gale's pseudonyms. In the new setup José Refugio Rodríguez, a printer, held the position of secretary-treasurer; Hipólito Flores, a policeman, headed the Department of Agriculture, Fisheries, and Aquatic Products; and Charles F. Tabler, the German-American miner in Guanajuato, directed the Department of Mining. Vicente Ortega, 'a Mexican fellow worker who lived in the United States several years, being active in the I.W.W. there', oversaw the Department of Transportation and Commu-

---

3   Jutt 1920, p. 20.
4   Ibid.
5   Jutt 1920, p. 6.
6   Haywood 1920, p. 20.

nication. Maclovio Pacheco became chief of the Department of Construction. 'Wretched wages he gets and ragged clothes he wears', Gale wrote of Pacheco. 'He is a hobo from head to feet in appearance but he cares nothing for that. He wants to stay just where he is until his class can rise with him'. Francisco Cervantes López of the Mexican Socialist Party, the owner of a small print shop, served as head of the Department of Manufacturing. Finally, there was Gale himself, in charge of the Department of Public Works. 'Gale is the eternal storm-centre yet nobody is more constructive and practical in suggestions', El Luchador Viejo wrote of himself. 'He is a perfect electric battery of energy and supplies that executive ability and genius for organisation that we Mexicans so seldom have'.[7]

With a certain political perspicacity, Gale attempted to situate his Mexican Administration of the Industrial Workers of the World at the centre of the upsurge of workers' and union movements then taking place in Mexico. An article on 'Industrial Unionism in Mexico', in *Gale's Magazine* of April 1920, reported on the activities of the Federation of Unions of Puebla, the Union of Industrial Wage Workers of Cananea, the Chamber of Industrial Workers of Orizaba, and the Marine Transport Workers' Union and Oil Workers' Union of Tampico, as well as various railroad workers' unions and Mexico City unions of streetcar workers, linotypists, and bakers. He suggested that all of those important industrial unions and his Mexican Administration of the IWW were part of the same movement.[8] In fact, a great wave of industrial union organising and strikes was getting underway led by Mexican revolutionary syndicalists, but Gale's IWW had only a tangential relationship to the industrial unions and the strike-wave.

1   Organising Orizaba

Gale attempted to organise IWW chapters in some of the important industrial centres. For example, Gale authorised the establishment of a Communist-IWW group in Santa Rosa, near Orizaba, Veracruz. Orizaba, together with the surrounding towns such as Santa Rosa, was at the time a great centre of the Mexican textile industry, and a hotbed of militant labour unionism. Workers had carried out an important strike at nearby Río Blanco in 1907, and in 1914 the anarcho-syndicalist House of the World Worker had sent organisers to Orizaba.

---

7   Gale, August 1920a, p. 2.
8   Gale, April 1920, p. 7.

The first local unions were formed in 1915, the same year that General Cándido Aguilar, governor of the state of Veracruz promulgated the state's first labour law.

The state of Veracruz had a remarkable radical labour movement in those years. Inspired by the revolution, workers in Orizaba and towns like Santa Rosa not only organised unions but also took power on the shop floor, elected union activists as mayors of the towns and cities, and carried out a series of general strikes. The worker-mayors supported union strikes and sometimes used the police to jail employers or managers. Eventually most of those radical workers affiliated with the government-sponsored Regional Confederation of Mexican Workers (CROM), but they maintained an independent, democratic, and extremely militant unionism often at odds with the bureaucratic, corrupt, and conservative leadership of the CROM, Luis N. Morones and his caucus, the Action Group.

The Orizaba textile unions, including Santa Rosa's, as historian Bernardo García Díaz writes, engaged in 'permanent struggle'.[9] Between the foundation of the union in 1915 and the end of the radical period in 1925 there was hardly a year without a strike and several with general strikes. In 1919, the year of the Great General Strike, the textile, electrical, railroad, and streetcar workers all struck simultaneously. Some of the strikes and demonstrations led to gun battles. Workers also engaged in strikes on the job, demonstrations and meetings in the plants, as well as direct confrontations to drive imperious managers out of the factories, while taking control of many aspects of production from management.

Some workers in the Orizaba area also formed anarchist or Communist clubs. At the centre of these groups were Aurelio Medrano, a skilled workman from Orizaba, and Anicleto Arroyo, a textile worker from Río Blanco, who organised anarchist study circles where workers read authors such as Kropotkin and Marx. Linn Gale somehow learned about this anarcho-communist group in the Orizaba area, and began to write to one of its leaders, Cutberto H. Arroyo. Or perhaps it was the other way around. In any case, between March and September 1920, Gale and his associates wrote at least eight letters to the Orizaba group His correspondence is significant because it gives us some idea of Gale as an organiser and administrator, as well as of the politics of the IWW as he conceived it.

In March 1920 Gale wrote to Cutberto Arroyo to welcome him and a group of his friends into the IWW, promising to send them membership cards and

9   García Díaz 1990. See in particular the essay 'Acción Directa y Poder Obrero (1915–1924)', pp. 203–47.

other materials as soon as possible. He concluded, 'our emancipation has to be the work of ourselves, the workers, since only we, for the most part, suffer the social injustices'.[10] A month later Gale wrote again to say that he still did not have the membership cards or other materials, but was 'sending them a picture of Eugene Debs to hang in their house'.[11] Gale wrote once more on 27 April 1920, explaining that he still didn't have the IWW membership cards, but congratulating them for their 'adhesion to the Third International', that is, the Communist International.[12]

Gale told Arroyo that as IWW members, they should not participate in the struggle between Carranza and Obregón for president in 1920:

> We the workers should separate ourselves from the political campaign. because, in the end, the only beneficiaries are the shameless capitalists, and the workers are only cannon fodder. We must dedicate ourselves to the Industrial Labour, the Union Labour, and leave the politicians alone, whether they be Carranza or Obregón, – for us they are all the same. It is necessary to struggle for the clearly working-class Social Revolution.

He advocated struggling for economic improvements through 'sabotage' or 'the strike on the job'. He closed, not with an IWW slogan, but with a Mexican Communist salute: 'Long Live the Social Revolution and the Dictatorship of the Proletariat'.[13]

Finally, on 14 May 1920 Gale sent Arroyo ten membership cards – but not for membership in the IWW, but rather in Gale's Communist Party of Mexico (PCdeM). Gale explained that the Communist Party of Mexico was actually supervising and organising the work of the IWW. The Communist Party existed to carry out 'propaganda and education, while the I.W.W. is the real organ of the struggle in the industrial camp; of strikes and similar things'. Gale went on

---

10   Letter of 23 March 1920 from Linn A.E. Gale to Cutberto H. Arroyo, from the private archive
      of Francisco Olivares, copies given to me by Benedikt Behrens, historian of the University
      of Hamburg.
11   Letter of 16 April 1920 from Linn A.E. Gale to Cutberto H. Arroyo, from the private archive
      of Francisco Olivares, copies given to me by Benedikt Behrens, historian of the University
      of Hamburg.
12   Letter of 27 April 1920 from Linn A.E. Gale to Cutberto H. Arroyo, from the private archive
      of Francisco Olivares, copies given to me by Benedikt Behrens, historian of the University
      of Hamburg.
13   Letter of 27 April 1920 from Linn A.E. Gale to Cutberto H. Arroyo, from the private archive
      of Francisco Olivares, copies given to me by Benedikt Behrens, historian of the University
      of Hamburg.

to explain that it was impossible to tell when the social revolution would come, but that, 'We should prepare ourselves with care, so that we can take advantage of the opportunity when it arrives'. He announced that when the social revolution did come, 'all the workers in each factory should then form a Factory Committee or "Soviet", that could take control of that factory, of course'. Each factory committee would elect a delegate to the Central Soviet of the industry; eventually all industries would participate in the Great Central Soviet to administer the economy of the entire country. Gale told Arroyo that the function of the IWW was not only to fight for higher wages and shorter hours, but also 'to acquire enough power experience to govern the industries when the opportune moment came'.[14]

Gale related to Arroyo the story of William D. Haywood and the Industrial Workers of the World in the United States during the World War. He explained that when the World War broke out, IWW leader Haywood had been sentenced to 20 years and that, as Haywood himself wrote later, 'thousands' of IWW members had been sent to prison for five, ten, or 15 years simply because they opposed the war.[15] He closed his letter with the prophecy that only the Industrial Unions could avert a social catastrophe and create a 'New Social Order'. Gale wrote again in June to invite Arroyo and his fellow-workers to attend a Radical Workers' Congress to take place at some time in the future.[16]

José Refugio Rodríguez, the secretary-treasurer of Gale's branch of the IWW wrote in July 1920, thanking Cutberto Arroyo for a letter sent to Gale. Rodríguez explained that Gale's IWW had changed the name of its newspaper *El Comunista* (The Communist) to *El Obrero Industrial* (the Industrial Worker), and he invited the Orizaba IWW chapter members to write articles for the paper 'on the form in which industry in general should be administered once it was in the power of the workers, as well as on the special constitution which should govern us, given the conditions, ethnic groups, and psychology of our Region'.[17] Evidently the Orizaba radicals eventually decided to join Gale's Communist-

---

14   Letter of 14 May 1920 from Linn A.E. Gale to Cutberto H. Arroyo, from the private archive of Francisco Olivares, copies given to me by Benedikt Behrens, historian of the University of Hamburg.
15   Haywood 1929, p. 303.
16   Letter of 12 June 1920 from Linn A.E. Gale to Cutberto H. Arroyo, from the private archive of Francisco Olivares, copies given to me by Benedikt Behrens, historian of the University of Hamburg.
17   Letter of 10 July 1920 from José Refugio Rodríguez to Cutberto H. Arroyo, from the private archive of Francisco Olivares, copies given to me by Benedikt Behrens, historian of the University of Hamburg.

IWW organisation. Aurelio Medrano wrote to the Santa Rosa group in September that they would need to choose 'delegates of the 'Soviets' of the region of Orizaba', as soon as delegates were named from the other factories.[18]

These letters to Arroyo in Orizaba, reflect Gale's view that the Wobblies, the Communist Party, and the creation of a Soviet government of workers' factory councils formed part of the same process and even seem to give the impression that they were all fundamentally the same thing. Such a perception was common among radicals in the first few years after the Russian Revolution, not only in Mexico but in other countries as well, since most radicals had little actual knowledge about the experience of the Russian Bolsheviks or Communists and the Soviets, it was all the same to them.

As awkward, tentative, and confused as Gale's organising efforts were, he had succeeded in establishing ties to one of the most important and militant groups of workers in a key industrial region of Mexico. The Mexican administration of the IWW could now claim a handful of members in Mexico City and the Federal District, in Tampico harbour, and in the Orizaba textile area, all of which were among the most important industrial centres of Mexico. Unfortunately, since Gale was primarily a writer and not an organiser, once he had established such contacts with workers, he had no idea what to do with them. Neither a labour union organiser nor a real political party leader, he simply wrote letters and distributed membership cards, newspapers, and photographs. It was this inability to turn contacts into union organisation and to engage in building a powerful labour movement that led to differences with other activists in the IWW.

2   A Brooklyn School Teacher in Tampico

In October of 1920, a struggle broke out within Gale's IWW supposedly over 'the admission or non-admission of non-wage-workers as members'. But this was actually a fight for control of the IWW between Gale, on the one hand, and Herman Levine on the other, a contest over whether or not the IWW would be led by the radicals in Mexico City or by the industrial workers in cities like Tampico.

Levine, the Brooklyn schoolteacher who had resisted the draft and fled to Mexico, eventually found work as a clerk in Tampico, where he set about reorganising the local chapter of the Industrial Workers of the World. Tampico,

---

18   Letter of 11 September 1920 from Aurelio Medrano to the General Secretary of the Communist Group of Santa Rosa, from the private archive of Francisco Olivares, copies given to me by Benedikt Behrens, historian of the University of Hamburg.

the port for the Mexican oil industry, had developed rapidly beginning with the outbreak of the war in Europe in 1914. With the expansion of industry there was also a rapid growth in the number of oil workers, stevedores and seamen. These workers, often led by Spanish anarchists or sometimes American Wobblies, formed unions which grew rapidly in size, strength, and militancy.

Labour unionism in Tampico had begun during the first years of the twentieth century when workers had established a variety of unions, such as the Moralising Union of Carpenters (Unión Moralizadora de Carpinteros). By 1915, the major anarcho-syndicalist labour federation, the House of the World Worker, had reached Tampico, and began organising both trades and industrial workers. The practice of striking to improve wages and working conditions became widespread and frequent among workers in Tampico.[19]

The Industrial Workers of the World already had a foothold in Tampico before Levine arrived. While it remains unclear if the IWW had any specific strategic plan for Tampico, in general the IWW organised unions of workers in a particular industry with the goal of affiliating them eventually into a national and then a worldwide industrial union, the One Big Union, as they sometimes called it.[20] In the United States, the IWWs strategy led it to organise oil workers, copper miners, lumberjacks in the spruce forests, and agricultural workers in the wheat fields: all strategic wartime industries. Following capital and heavy industry over the border to the south, Wobblies found themselves working in Mexican mines and oil fields, as well as on Mexican docks and on ships of various nations. There they would employ the same strategy of industrial unionism.

One group of the Industrial Workers of the World arrived in Tampico in force in 1916 when the *C.A. Canfield* arrived in port. The crew of the *Canfield* belonged to the IWWs Marine Transport Workers (IWW-MTW), and many were Spanish speaking. They recruited Mexican seamen to their union, which probably also gained a foothold among the stevedores. Pedro Coria, a Mexican IWW organiser from Arizona arrived in Tampico in January 1917 and organised Local #100 of IWW-MTW.[21] Workers in Tampico had many grievances, but one of their major complaints was that they were paid in worthless currencies; they demanded pay in gold or silver. In 1917 there was a series of strikes that began over this issue, culminating in a great general strike in the Tampico area involving petroleum workers and stevedores from both the House of the World Worker and

19   Adelson Gruber 1982, pp. 424–70.
20   Cole 2017, pp. 124–39.
21   Caulfield 1995, p. 57.

the IWW.[22] The US Embassy sent a note to the Mexican Secretary of Foreign Affairs in October of 1917 on 'The Tampico Situation', which gives an impression of the US government's concerns. The note reads:

> Reports from Tampico indicate that that place is quiet but that labour leaders are agitating for a general strike to which the Germans and Industrial Workers of the World are disposed to lend support. It is reported that the National Socialist Congress to which delegates from the United States and Cuba have been invited is now in session. A great many of the delegates are said to be anarchists, and the situation seems charged with danger.[23]

On 8 January 1919, *Excelsior*, a Mexico City newspaper, repeated a story that had apparently originated in New York that there were 'secret soviets' in Tampico, organised by the IWW.[24]

By the time Levine arrived in Tampico in 1919 or 1920, the IWW was an established organisation among industrial workers with a legendary militancy. Levine joined in the work of the IWW as editor of the group's newspaper. In 1920, US intelligence agents reported that Mischa Poltiolevsky – they apparently believed this was Levine's real name – 'is working in Tampico under the name of M. Paley. He is a very active agent'.[25] They were correct. Levine had become one of the most dynamic leaders of the Tampico IWW organising among stevedores and oil industry workers.

The former socialist Levine had undergone a conversion experience: he had given up his membership in the Socialist Party and had joined the IWW. During the period between 1917 and 1919, he rethought his political ideals, rejecting his belief in socialism and espousing revolutionary syndicalism. In a letter to the Industrial Workers of the World headquarters in Chicago, he explained his personal situation and his political views:

> I have never learned a trade, nor am I a manual worker, and this I regret, for I recognise that the workers on the job must prepare themselves to

---

22   Cole 2017, pp. 124–39.
23   US Embassy to Mexican Secretary of Foreign Relations, unsigned, 'Memorandum: The Tampico Situation', 13 October 1917, Expediente 18-1-146, SRE.
24   Taibo II 1986, p. 32.
25   Memo of 26 May 1920 from the military attaché of the American Embassy to the Director of Military Intelligence, G.S., Washington, D.C. on the subject of Bolshivist [*sic*] propaganda, Record Group 165, Box 2290, USMID, USNA.

run industry, and the workers on the job must determine radical tactics during the struggle to attain their aim, because they alone are surrounded by that environment from which real radical measures surge. I am opposed to political action. An industrial administration must be prepared for industrially. Political action wastes energy that could be used in the class struggle – on the job. I intend to learn a trade as soon as possible, so that my views may arise in the proper environment. Until then, I shall suggest nothing – but shall affirm that radicals on the job, in the factory, on the farm, in the mine – theirs is the final voice.

Levine concluded his letter, 'I was a member of the Socialist party, Local Kings [County], N.Y., but sent in my resignation last May [1919]'. In a hand-written postscript he added, 'As soon as I become a worker on the job, I intend to join the IWW. But for the present as an office worker, I cannot do so'.[26]

Why did Levine leave the Socialist Party? Perhaps because so many prominent figures in the party had supported the war and even gone to work for the Wilson administration. Or maybe Levine had fallen under the influence of American or Mexican Wobblies who had convinced him of their revolutionary syndicalist principles and strategy. Or perhaps his own experience as a slacker had simply driven him to the left, and, at the time, the far left was the IWW. In any case, though he did not have an industrial job – or perhaps precisely because he did not have such a job – Levine, using the name M. Paley, became the editor of the Tampico IWW newspaper, *El Obrero Industrial* (The Industrial Worker). The newspaper was just one or two tabloid size sheets of paper folded into four or at most eight pages, written in Spanish it was aimed at the Tampico oil workers and stevedores. Its articles advocated direct action and industrial unionism and called for the use of the general strike to create a workers' government.[27] (To add to our confusion, Gale had adopted the same name for his newspaper.)

Levine's newspaper and his organising activities became a serious concern to the US Military Intelligence Division (USMID). The USMID officer in Laredo, Texas wrote to his superiors in July 1920:

---

26   Letter (unsigned) by Levine to Whitehead, November (date scratched out), 1919, Record Group 165, Box 2290, USMID, USNA.

27   A number of copies of *El Obrero Industrial* can be found in Record Group 165, USMID, US National Archives. The newspaper reported on local activities in Tampico, but its main political ideas were identical to those of the IWW of the United States: direct action, industrial unionism the general strike.

The [US] Government is receiving copies of 'The Industrial Worker' [El Obrero Industrial] paper being printed in Tampico, which in its editorials is spreading the doctrine of Lenine and Trotzky. The paper says the strikers will not cease until they have accomplished their purpose. Reports also state that at their meetings the strikers have red flags and that the cry 'Vive la Russia' [sic] can be heard. The oil companies told the labourers that the pay will not be increased one cent, as they claim they are paying the best salary in the country.[28]

At the time many IWWs were supporters of the Russian Revolution and the Soviet government, and some were attracted to the Bolsheviks, who were in the process of organising the Communist International. As editor of *El Obrero Industrial* Levine, like other Wobblies, followed the Russian Revolution with sympathy and offered it his support from afar. Later he would join in the foundation of the Mexican Communist Party (PCM).

The writer B. Traven, whose real name was Ret Marut and who was a German revolutionary refugee of the post-war conflicts in that country, lived in Tampico in the early 1920s. Traven spent some time with members of the Industrial Workers of the World and left a picture of the American radicals in his novels *Die Baumwollpflücker* (The Cottonpicker) and *Der Wobbly* (The Wobbly). Traven even named the protagonist of his fiction 'Gale', though Linn Gale never lived in Tampico, and his fictional character less resembles Gale than Levine. In his fictional account of a strike Traven gives us some idea of Levine's Tampico:

in this country [they] do not suffer from a clumsy, bureaucratic apparatus. The union secretaries do not regard themselves as civil servants. They are all young and roaring revolutionaries. The trade unions here have only been founded during the last ten years, and they have started in the most modern direction. They absorbed the experience of the Russian Revolution, and they embody the explosive power of a young radical force and the elasticity of an organization which is still searching for its form and changes it tactics daily.[29]

Traven's stories and novels caught the spirit of Tampico's Wobblies and other radical unionists.

---

28   Report from Intelligence Officer, Laredo, Texas, to department Intelligence Officer, Fort Sam Houston, Texas, 23 July 1920, Record Groups 165, in Box 2291, USMID, USNA.
29   Zogbaum 1992, p. 14, citing Traven 1962, p. 72.

The employers took the matter of what they saw as the foreign-inspired labour unions in Tampico quite seriously. R.D. Hutchinson, of the British 'El Águila' Oil Company told the *Bulletin of the National Chambers of Industry* that the Tampico general strike of 1920 represented a 'giant step toward the dictatorship of the proletariat'. He went on:

> Mexican workers have unionised with the goal of imposing themselves on capital in Tampico and they have done it at the insistence of two different kinds of agitators: some foreigners, who, preaching Bolshevik ideas, have done a profound job, a deep job among the proletarians of the oil zones; and the others, Mexican politicians, who pursuing, if not identical goals, disrupt the peace by attacking the established interests at this crucial moment.[30]

As both Traven's novel and this company manager's remarks suggest, Levine, Coria and other slackers together with the Mexican workers had constructed a powerful, radical industrial union movement in Tampico that threatened the existing order.

The British government was also alarmed at the growth of the IWW in Tampico and other cities. The British Ambassador, H.A.C. Cummins reported to Lord Curzon at the Foreign Office in London in April of 1921, 'The I.W.W. organization obtained some influence here during the war, an influence which has not lessened, and it is known that the confederated labour unions [CROM] are being directed by these dangerous extremists, and that they are laying plans with a view to establishing a Soviet administration in Mexico'.[31] As Cummins's communication indicates, in Tampico both the IWW and the more moderate state-sponsored CROM unions carried out militant campaigns against the employers. While both foreign employers and foreign consuls sometimes exaggerated the threat from the IWW, their exaggerations were based on the very real, and quite formidable Wobbly movement.

3   Levine's View of Gale

While Levine worked in Tampico organising petroleum workers into the IWW, Linn A.E. Gale, back in Mexico City, wrote letters, distributed membership

---

30   'Las Últimas Huelgas' 1920, p. 10.
31   Bourne n.d., p. 307.

cards and photographs of Debs, and claimed to be the leader of the Mexican organisation. We know Levine's opinion of Gale and his IWW group from a long letter (eight single-spaced pages) in which Levine wrote to Fellow Worker Whitehead, that is, Thomas Whitehead, the secretary-treasurer of the IWW in the United States. Whether or not a copy ever reached Whitehead is unclear, because the letter was intercepted by USMID. Levine portrayed Gale as the antithesis of a genuine labour organiser. Thus, the letter gives us a great deal of insight into Levine's political principles and his notion of the proper role as an American revolutionary and labour organiser in Mexico and it is worth reviewing in some detail.[32]

Levine wrote, 'He [Gale] is a businessman seeking political preferment and social position', while *Gale's Magazine* is 'not a radical nor socialist organ'. He went on:

> The name characterizes it admirably. It is *Gale's magazine* – to boost Gale, first, last and all the time. No sincere radical ever did nor ever will launch a magazine with his name in the title.

Levine claimed that Gale had had little contact with Mexican workers, but that those few Gale had met had been disgusted by him.[33]

Levine was particularly critical of Gale's praise of Mexican President Venustiano Carranza's Minister of the Interior, Manuel Aguirre Berlanga. 'The Mexican government is a government of the government, by the government and for the government', wrote Levine. 'They are not frank in their statements – but they are brutally frank in their acts; force, brute force being the rule and Berlanga is the official in charge of such proceedings'. Levine pointed out to Whitehead that it was Berlanga who had quashed the teachers' strike of 1919.

In general, Levine was critical of Gale's notion that the Mexican government was a radical government moving toward socialism. What had the peasants and workers gained? asked Levine. 'The worker's reward? The right to have the military forces used against him when he goes on strike, printing presses seized,

---

32   Letter (unsigned) to Whitehead from Levine, date November (date scratched out) 1919. Box 2290, Record Group 165, US National Archives. The following several citations come from this letter.

33   Letter (unsigned) to Whitehead from Levine, date November (scratched out) 1919. Box 2290, Record Group 165, US National Archives. The following several citations come from this letter.

union halls closed'. Levine gave the examples of the suppression of the Mexico City teachers strike in May and of the Tampico oil workers strike in November of 1919.

'What is the essence of the Mexican Government?' asked Levine rhetorically. 'It is an incipient capitalist state'. Carranza, Levine argued, had 'tried to establish industry on a firm capitalist basis', inviting the Chambers of Commerce of Dallas, Chicago and other US cities to come to Mexico to help:

> Carranza invited them to invest capital in Mexico, but denied them any special privilege. He wants Mexico to develop on a capitalist basis, without intervention of foreign capitalist governments. 'Mexico for the Mexican Capitalists, for the Mexican Government' is his slogan.

Most modern historians would agree with Levine's assessment of the Carranza regime. Levine argued that Gale's call for support of Mexico against foreign intervention missed the point that the Mexican government actually supported foreign economic investment and protected foreign investors.

> Tampico oil is in the hands of foreign exploiters. But when workers go on strike, the union halls are closed down, printing presses seized despite specific constitutional provisions to the contrary, right of assembly denied – by whom? Not by foreigners, but by the military officials of that very government which we are asked to defend.

Levine lumped Gale together with Gompers as foreigners meddling in Mexican workers' affairs.

> Mexican radical policy will be determined by Mexicans. The Mexican working class is fighting its fight where it ought to be fought – on the job. It [the Mexican working class] is not revolutionary – but it becomes aroused over the right to organize – as is proved by the Orizaba [textile] strike now before the public eye. Mexican Labor is too conservative, its leaders and organizations being bound up with the American Federation of Labor. But there are radical elements, and it is to them that we must look for action.

Interestingly, while he and other American slackers participated in the Mexican labour movement, Levine clearly believed that Mexican workers should ultimately determine its policies.

Levine concluded his critique by arguing that:

Radicals should fight intervention, not by praising and supporting the
Mexican Capitalist Government – but by denouncing the war as capitalist
in its origin, by refusing to fight for the American Capitalist and his Mexican counterpart, and by demonstrating that the only sane solution for
Intervention is Workingclass Revolution. American radicals should fight
against American Capitalism; Mexican Comrades should fight their own
exploiters. The class struggle – cannot – will not – be sidetracked.

The letter ended: 'cooperation with [Gale] by the ɪww is dangerous to the
Wobbly movement'. Levine clearly believed that genuine labour organisers
would work not with Mexico's capitalist government, but with the 'radical elements' among the industrial workers in the organisation of the class struggle.
Levine, as this letter makes clear, held Gale in utter contempt.[34]

4   The Fight for the Backing of the US ɪww

The battle between the American slackers for control of the Mexican Industrial Workers of the World was fought both in Mexico and in the pages of the
ɪww magazine and newspapers in the United States. Both slacker groups in
Mexico wanted the endorsement of the Chicago headquarters of the ɪww, and
each wrote long articles arguing its point of view and attacking the opposition.
The imprimatur of the Chicago office of the ɪww was just as important for the
slacker unionists as the endorsement of the Moscow headquarters of the Communist International was for the slacker Communists.

  As usual, Linn Gale struck the first blow with an article titled 'The War
Against Gompersism in Mexico' published in November 1919 in *The One Big
Union Monthly*, the magazine of the ɪww executive committee in the United
States. He recounted the first national congress of the Mexican Socialist Party
and attacked M.N. Roy for voting to admit Gompers. He also attempted to discredit Roy. Gale wrote that the 'Hindu' (M.N. Roy) is 'said by some to be a spy
for the American government. As to the truth of this I do not know'. He claimed
that during the congress Roy had been 'working hand-in-hand with Morones'.
Gale explained that 'Roy voted in favor of seating Morones, casting the deciding vote!!!' Consequently, Gale explained, he and others had withdrawn from

---

34   Letter (unsigned) to Whitehead from Levine, date November (date scratched out) 1919.
      Box 2290, Record Group 165, US National Archives. The following several citations come
      from this letter.

the Socialist Party and formed the [Gale's] Communist Party of Mexico, which was 'in favor of Industrial Unionism'.

The editor of *The One Big Union Monthly* observed that, 'Not knowing the condition in Mexico, we publish the above with some mental reservation, insofar as we believe that the i.w.w. men of Mexico may take a different view of cooperation with the new Communist party'.[35] In the same issue there appeared an excerpt from Gale's Communist Party of Mexico manifesto, obviously sent to the paper by Gale, endorsing the iww, denouncing the afl, calling for the use of strikes, boycotts and sabotage, and looking forward to the eventual establishment of the 'Dictatorship of the Proletariat'. The manifesto also called for a 'Constant and intelligent co-operation between the Communist Party and the industrial unions of Mexico and the Communist Parties and industrial unions of other countries'.[36]

The other slacker faction was not long in responding in the American Wobbly press. Irwin Granich [Mike Gold] wrote a long article, 'Sowing Seeds of One Big Union in Mexico', in which he described political, economic, and social conditions, and rebutted Gale's attack. Granich gave his own report on the first national congress of the Socialist Party, and his own interpretation of events. First, he argued that the Socialist Party congress really functioned as a kind of iww convention. As he put it:

> The Socialist party, dominated by i.w.w. elements, had called the congress because there was no union able to call it. It was called for the purpose of bringing to the workers the message of One Big Union and to help them create a national body based on industrial lines.

The Socialist Party congress, said Granich, succeeded in doing so despite the sabotage of Luis Morones and Linn Gale. He described Gale as 'an American adventurer and labour provocateur who has a shady past and has just organised a so-called Communist party of six or seven members for some sinister ends'. Gale 'is really a nonentity, dangerous only because he is trying to bleed the movement for money, and because he is of the type that will ultimately sell out and turn spy – if he has not already achieved this profitable end, as the Soviet Bureau in New York believes'. Granich asserted that despite Morones and Gale, the congress had been a success and the delegates had launched two new magazines, *El Soviet* in Mexico City and *El Obrero Industrial* in Veracruz.[37]

---

35   Gale, November 1919, pp. 23–5.
36   'I.W.W. in Mexico', November 1919, p. 50.
37   Granich 1920, pp. 36–7.

In the March 1920 issue of *The One Big Union Monthly*, the editor felt obliged to explain why he was continuing to print letters from the rival slacker factions in Mexico, and his explanation bears citation because it shows the US IWW's interest in establishing continental industrial unionism. 'First', wrote the editor, 'it is just as important for us to be familiar with conditions down in Mexico as it is for us to know conditions in Canada. The question of direct cooperation between the One Big Union of Canada, of United States and of Mexico is bound to come up in the near future, and for that reason it is necessary that we should be somewhat conversant with men and condition[s] in Mexico as well as in Canada'.

'Second', wrote the OBU editor, 'we want our members to know the state of affairs down in Mexico City when they get down there, so they do not act blindly'.

Finally, said the editor, the IWW rejected political parties, whether Socialist or Communist. 'We enjoy to see the politicians destroy one another before an audience of wage workers', because 'it fills the workers with disgust for the political game and makes them turn to industrial organization'. So, he let the debate in the pages of his magazine continue.[38] The editor asked that future articles respond to a number of specific questions, namely a history and survey of the Mexican labour movement, a discussion of the experiments in the Yucatan, a discussion of the roles of Emiliano Zapata and Pancho Villa, and a survey of Mexican industry with statistics.

José Refugio Rodríguez, Secretary of Gale's IWW organisation, took up the offer and wrote an article on 'The Working Class Movement in Mexico' which avoided the recriminations of the earlier articles and described the general conditions of Mexican labour. Rodriguez's article characterised the various leaders and tendencies in the Mexican Revolution. He rejected support for Obregón, who was 'seeking the support of the American and Mexican financial interests', and also repudiated Carranza who was 'at best only a Liberal'. Rodríguez also characterised Villa and Zapata. He wrote, falsely, that the former 'is no more and no less than a despicable murderer who once served in the American Army and there learned completely the science of killing his fellow human beings'. He expressed admiration for Zapata as an 'honest man', but noted that 'the tales published in foreign periodicals about the wonders of "Zapataland" make us laugh and also make us shed bitter tears'.

His 'Zapataland' only existed over a few hectares of land in the days of its greatest success. It was very crude, undeveloped, unorganised, and could

---

38   'The Mexican', March 1920, p. 44.

not therefore, last long. In the great land over which Lenin is the guiding figure and where Industrial democracy has come to remain forever, there is much of science, order, skill, wisdom and shrewdness, to match that of the capitalist empires without. But there was none of this in 'Zapata-land' – only honest intentions, high ideals, bad organizations, big blunders and inevitable failure.[39]

What is striking in Rodríguez's essay is the nearly complete rejection of all of the Mexican revolutionary factions, including the plebeian movements of Zapata and Villa, and his absolute confidence in Lenin and the Russian model. Gale and his comrades, it seemed, having rejected the Mexican revolution entirely, intended to implant the models of the Chicago-based IWW and the Moscow-centred Communist International.

5   Levine Leads the IWW into the United Front

Whatever appeared in the papers in Chicago, the fight to control the Mexican IWW would be settled in Mexico and Mexican workers would play a central role. Levine had found two allies in his struggle against Gale. Both Charles King and Pedro Coria had been active in the Industrial Workers of the World in the United States, as well as in Mexico. A USMID report, probably written by José Allen, simultaneously head of the Roy-Phillips Mexican Communist Party and a US spy, described Levine's new supporters. The description of King was brief.

> King claims to be an American Communist. He has been in Mexico approximately eighteen months. He is five feet eight inches tall; weight about one hundred and sixty pounds; dark hair; dark eyes; swarthy complexion. He is very sarcastic and cynical. He appears to be very well educated; he speaks Spanish and English equally well. Trade unknown.

The spy's account of Coria went into more detail, painting a picture of a sophisticated political activist. 'Corea [sic] is a Mexican of the railroad man type; age about forty; about five feet eight inches tall; weight about one hundred and eighty pounds; thick, black hair; black eyes; slightly florid complexion', wrote the spy. 'He has travelled very widely in the United States and South America; he speaks English very well. He is said to speak Portuguese fluently. For many

---

39   Rodríguez, June 1920, pp. 26–7.

years he has been a political leader. He is said to have been imprisoned in South America. He is not a very well-educated man, but an active mind and great personality make him a leader'.[40]

Coria told his own story in an autobiography written in the 1960s. Raised in a military orphanage, Coria eventually became a foundry worker and after working in several Mexican cities travelled to the United States. While living in Chicago, Coria learned to speak English fluently and also became acquainted with the American labour movement. He apparently attended an early convention of the Industrial Workers of the World and became a Wobbly. As a Wobbly organiser in various parts of the West, Coria had participated in numerous organising campaigns, strikes, and protest demonstrations. At various times he was beaten, jailed, and had his life threatened. As a working-class pacifist, he opposed both the violence of the revolution in Mexico and the war in the United States. When the US government suppressed the IWW, Coria fled to Tampico, no doubt because he knew there was an active IWW group there.[41]

As soon as he arrived in Tampico, Coria made contact with the IWW and joined other Wobblies in organising Petroleum Workers Industrial Union 230 and Marine Transport Workers union 510. He quickly became one of the most prominent IWW leaders in Tampico and was sent by the local IWW as delegate to the important labour convention in Saltillo, Coahuila held on 1 May 1918, the meeting that produced the Regional Confederation of Mexican Workers (CROM). It must have been not long after returning from Saltillo that Coria met Herman P. Levine.

Coria's experience made him a highly valuable IWW organiser. His knowledge of English and Spanish, his familiarity with the labour union and political movements in both countries, and his courage and dedication made him particularly useful in the attempt to organise the IWW in Mexico. So, it was natural that in Tampico, Coria became one of the closest allies of Levine.

Levine – now backed up by Coria and King – proposed at the 17 October 1920 IWW meetings in Mexico City, which involved both factions, that the IWW's US rule excluding non-wage-workers be enforced. The observation of that rule would have meant the expulsion from membership in the Mexican IWW of Gale, the newspaper publisher; Cervantes López, the printer; Hipólito Flores, the policeman, and other non-worker members of Gale's committee.

---

40   'Who's Who Material – Mexican Radical Elements', 15 October 1920. RG 165, Box 2290.
41   Coria, March 1971. Thanks to Robert J. Halstead for calling this series to my attention and providing a photocopy.

Gale responded evasively that the IWW had to organise soldiers and sailors, and should not, for example, exclude a woman fired from her factory who became a fruit vendor.[42]

There was another important element in this debate, in addition to the question of a member's social class. Levine and Coria also proposed to take the Mexican IWW into an alliance with the anarchists, anarcho-syndicalists, and the Roy-Phillips Communist Party in order to form a united front among all the labour radicals in Mexico. It was this issue that accounted for the presence at the Mexico City meeting of Jacinto Huitrón, a leader of the anarcho-syndicalist labour movement, and Manuel D. Ramírez, the future head of the Mexican Communist Party. It was this group which would later establish the important though short-lived labour organisation the Communist Federation of the Mexican Proletariat.[43]

The debate over the rules was postponed, but Gale refused to call another meeting, so the other faction, Levine, Coria and King, now joined by Gale's former allies Rodríguez, Pacheco and Ortega, called their own meeting of the executive board, revised the rules to exclude non-workers, and elected their own executive committee. Gale was out.

The Gale-Levine faction fight ended in the pages of the IWWs magazine in the United States at the end of 1920. In December, an article apparently written by Herman Levine, announced the victory of the 'wage workers' over the 'petit-bourgeois' faction led by Linn Gale. 'The wage workers faction, the most numerous and the strongest, with the general secretary-treasurer and the majority of the G.E.B. [General Executive Board] with them, are continuing in charge of the organisation, and hope for better progress now that they have rid themselves of the political and petit bourgeois element', stated the author. The IWW, now firmly in proletarian hands, the author reported, was organising oil workers in Tampico, metal mine workers in Guanajuato, and industrial workers in Mexico City.[44]

After Levine, Coria, and King took charge of the IWW, it immediately entered into a united front with the other factions of the revolutionary labour move-

---

42   Gale 1920, p. 6; 'Memorandum to the A.C. of S. for Military Intelligence', 15 October 1920, in Box 2290, Record Group 165, USMID, USNA, an account of these differences within the IWW, probably written by José Allen, says that Pedro Coria was disputing the leadership of the union with Gale and Charles King. This is probably the same struggle. See also Taibo II 1986, p. 101.

43   'Memorandum to the A.C. of S. for Military Intelligence: Notes on Radical Activities', 15 October 1920, USMID, Record Group 165, Box 2290, USMID, USNA.

44   Levine, December 1920, p. 57.

ment. The anarcho-syndicalists, the IWW, the Roy-Phillips Mexican Communist Party, and some independent unions formed first the 'Revolutionary Bloc', in August 1920, which subsequently became the Communist Federation of the Mexican Proletariat (FCPM). The FCPM was meant to be an alternative to the CROM. It stood for revolutionary labour unionism, the fight for workers' control, the overthrow of capitalism, and, passing through a brief dictatorship of the proletariat, for Social Revolution. While most of its members were anarchists or anarcho-syndicalists, the FCPM sympathised with the Soviet Union. Later the FCPM would become the anarchist General Confederation of Workers or CGT.

In addition to Levine's wing of the IWW, the Mexican Communist Party (PCM) (that is the party founded by Roy and Phillips) also joined the new federation. Within a few months the PCM Communists were involved in the leadership of a genuine working-class upheaval in Mexico City, Veracruz, Orizaba and Tampico. Two of the PCM's new young leaders, Manuel Díaz Ramírez and José C. Valadés were elected secretaries of the executive board of the FCPM.[45] The Communist Federation and its activists such as Levine, Valadés and Díaz Ramírez were far more serious about organising than Gale had been. For example, Díaz Ramírez, who was himself from Veracruz, contacted Aurelio Medrano and other leaders of the Orizaba textile workers' anarcho-communist group, the group with which Gale had been corresponding. Díaz not only wrote them and sent the Communist magazine *Vida Nueva* and the *Boletín Comunista*, but he also went to Orizaba gave a public lecture on 'Unionism and Communism'. He met privately with local activists and attempted to win the group over to the Communist Federation of the Mexican Proletariat, and to the Mexican Communist Party (PCM).[46] Díaz urged the local anarcho-communists and CROM activists to join the Communist Federation and later its successor the General Confederation of Workers (CGT). The Orizaba group decided to stay in the CROM, though they remained in its left wing.[47] Nevertheless, Díaz and the Communists demonstrated a new commitment to building the IWW and the Communist Party among workers.

The US-based IWW sent one of its members to Mexico to get a first-hand view of the situation. In February of 1921, IWW member W.J. Lemon visited Mexico and subsequently wrote a long and well-informed article on the conditions there for the new IWW magazine *The Industrial Pioneer*. Gale, meanwhile,

---

45   Taibo II 1986, Los Bolshevikis, p. 103.
46   García Díaz 1990, pp. 240–1.
47   García Díaz 1990, pp. 270–1.

had opportunistically moved dramatically to the right, becoming a supporter of Morones and the Obregón government. Lemon criticised Gale for his claims that 'Soviet Mexico is near'. Lemon argued that Mexico did not have a workers' government and pointed out that the Obregón government had used troops to smash the 1920 railroad workers' strike, including jailing and killing workers. The railroad workers had been 'betrayed by the leaders of the unions'. Lemon recognised that there were Socialists and labour unionists in the government, but argued that 'it does not mean anything to the workers to be represented in a coalition government. Many countries have passed thru the same experience to the sorrow of the workers'.

Differing from both Gale and the Levine factions, Lemon wrote, 'Mexico has no such thing as a red movement, i.e., a well-organised, disciplined body that knows what it wants and how to get it. There may be a few scattered groups here and there but they are of no importance at the present moment. The real Mexican movement is unfortunately, still in embryo'. An attempt was being made 'to organise a left-wing movement, but it is still too early to predict what success it will have'. The attempt was the new General Confederation of Workers (CGT), founded at a convention of 53 delegates from 12 states representing 40,000 workers. Lemon pointed out that Gale – who had by then broken with the radicals – had joined with Morones in condemning the founding convention of the CGT. From the article it is not clear that the America Wobbly ever talked to either Gale or Levine, and remarkably Lemon did not even mention the IWW as a factor in Mexico.[48]

During the next year or so, Phillips and the PCM and Levine and the IWW drew closer together. In 1921 the Mexican Communist Party (PCM) in Mexico City called for a conference of labour activists to launch a united front organisation. Phillips invited Levine to attend representing the IWWs in Mexico City and Tampico. A USMID agent in Mexico, probably José Allen, reported to his superiors on 12 May 1921:

> The Syndicates [*sindicatos* or labour unions] have decided to send José Rubio [a Spanish revolutionary] and M. Paley [Levine] to Tampico and other oil regions for purposes of 'agitation' amongst the workmen of these regions.

The agent went on:

---

48   Lemon, May 1921, pp. 23–7.

Paley [Levine], it appears, is in agreement with Seaman [Phillips], to spread propaganda amongst the IWWs of Tampico for the purpose of converting them into out and out Communists, abandoning entirely the 'industrialist' principles of the IWW organization.[49]

The money for this operation apparently came from Sen Katayama, the Japanese-American Communist sent by the Communist International to organise in Mexico and Latin America (about whom we write more below). This letter implies that Levine moved to a position close to the Mexican Communist Party and may have joined.[50]

Levine (also known as Paley) came to Mexico City for the 1921 May Day labour march, which 'passed without incident of special importance'. The only notable exceptions, according to a USMID agent (probably Allen), were the speeches of four radicals, one of whom was Herman Levine. When the May Day march passed the US Consulate on Francisco Madero Street, the Spanish revolutionary José Rubio and the American slacker known as Martin Paley (Levine) addressed the assembled workers and radicals. Levine and Rubio reportedly made 'bitter attacks against the US government which they declared cruel on account of its persecution and imprisonment of working men'. Levine also spoke out against the Mexican Government, which he accused of taking orders from the White House. The agent reported that, 'Both of these speakers incited the Mexican workmen to follow the example of the Spaniards who do not permit themselves to be intimidated, the orators declared, by the police, nor by government troops, nor by government ministers, but actually attack them, as is proved by the dead bodies of policemen, soldiers, and lastly of Cabinet Minister Dato himself'. While attributed by the agent to both Paley (Levine) and Rubio, it seems likely that the Spaniard delivered this speech.[51]

While May Day in Mexico had been fairly tame, the situation in Tampico was altogether different. On the evening of Thursday 2 June 1921, a 'radical labour demonstration' was violently dispersed by General Arnulfo Gómez. The US Consul in Tampico, Claude Dawson, reported: 'Headed by I.W.W. agitators, the mob took possession of the public square on which the municipal building faces, and began tirades against organised governments generally, and

---

49   Report from Mexico to USMID dated 21 April 1921, in Box 2291, Record Group 165, USMID, USNA.

50   USMID General *Intelligence Bulletin*, 4 June 1921, p. 30, in Boehm (ed.) 1984.

51   Monograph report from Mexico to USMID regarding May Day Demonstrations, 5 May 1921. Box 2292, Record Group 165, USMID, USNA.

the United States and Mexican governments in particular'. When the speakers 'vehemently attacked president Obregón', General Gómez and his troops stepped in, firing shots in the air, dispersed the demonstration but failed to capture the leaders, among whom presumably was Levine. Dawson suggested that the presence of US warships would discourage such radicalism.[52]

In 1921 a detailed report in the USMID *General Intelligence Bulletin*, again probably written by Allen, discussed all aspects of the political situation in Mexico, but with special emphasis on labour and the left.

> I.W.W. meets at Calle de Academia No. 12, Mexico City, and while very small in Mexico City has an active group of organisers in Tampico among them being a man known as King, an American who fled from the US for some trouble occurring during the war. King is probably not a deserter being apparently a little too old. Other I.W.W. members are mainly or entirely Mexicans ... In Tampico ... the I.W.W. is strong and violently active and makes savage attacks against the American and the Mexican governments. It is bitter against [Luis N.] Morones [head of the CROM] calling him a 'Trimmer' who compromises with Obregón and enemies of the radicals in order to keep his job.

The spy-author characterised Levine, whom it described as the editor of *El Obrero Industrial*, as 'a leading spirit in the organization'.

The author speculates that 'Extradition of Levine might not be difficult due to his attack against Obregón'. The IWW's repeated attacks on Morones, the CROM, and especially on President Obregón made Levine a target for deportation. By that time, however, Obregón had just about decided to deport the whole bunch of 'pernicious foreigners'.[53]

6   Conclusion: Internationalist Ideal

The American slackers became central figures in the Mexican Industrial Workers of the World between 1917 and the early 1920s, a union with real power in the oil fields, on the docks, and on the ships in Tampico. While many of the

---

52   Letter regarding 'Soviet demonstration in Tampico' from American Consul Claude Dawson to US Secretary of State, 6 June 1921, Record Group 165, USMID, USNA.

53   'Report Covering Attitude of Prominent Mexican Government Officials Toward the American Government, Bolshevist Activities in Mexico and Other Matters of Importance to the American Government', 10, in Boehm (ed.) 1984.

details remain obscure, it is clear that the Americans like Gale and Levine and Mexican Americans like Coria played an inordinately large part in the Mexican IWW. Why should this have been the case?

Many workers in Tampico were Americans or other foreigners including Canadians, English, mostly experienced and often skilled workers who spoke English. American radicals would have had a natural following among some of their own countrymen and other English-speaking foreigners. The IWW's principles and strategy also attracted the Mexican workers, many of them common labourers, who came to make up the majority of the IWW membership in Tampico. What attracted all of these workers was the union's effective use of the strike to raise wages, improve conditions, and put the employers and their managers and foremen on the defensive. While Mexicans joined the IWW in Mexico, politically sophisticated Americans, such as Levine, Gale, and Coria, found it easier than Mexicans would have to establish and maintain contacts with the leadership at IWW headquarters in Chicago, as their letters and articles suggest. The history of the period suggests that Mexican workers were prepared to welcome American radicals like Levine not only as members but as leaders.

The cooperation among American, Spanish, South American, and the Mexican majority of labour activists was possible because from 1918 to about 1920, they tended to converge ideologically around industrial unionism and revolutionary syndicalism, support for Soviet Russia, and the idea of a dictatorship of the proletariat, that is the rule of the working class. The ideals of the labour movement in that period in Mexico had a strong internationalist element. While most Mexican political and military leaders (and perhaps most Mexicans) may have been nationalists, in the teens and twenties Mexican working-class activists, particularly its most radical elements like those in Tampico, tended without any sense of contradiction to be simultaneously both nationalists and internationalists and their ideals permitted the choice of union and political leaders not only from Mexico, but also from Spain, South America or the United States. Given the anarchist and socialist traditions in which they placed themselves, it would not be such a stretch to follow the American Big Bill Haywood. Some of those Mexican workers also read and admired foreign intellectuals such as the Russian Kropotkin and the German Marx. And soon some were also prepared to follow the Russians Lenin and Trotsky.

The American slackers and their friends played a role not just in the Mexican unions but in the peasant organisations and the feminist movement as well, as we will see in the next chapter.

CHAPTER 13

The Slackers, the Feminist Council, and the Revolutionary Peasant Leagues

While the American slacker radicals concentrated their efforts on the organisation of workers into the Communist Party and the Industrial Workers of the World, they also undertook two other important areas of political work: the organisation of women and of peasants. In both cases, their efforts coincided with already existing movements of Mexican activists and organisations. American slackers' ideas about feminism and organising agricultural workers, which they had brought with them from the United States, tended to meld with or were grafted onto the existing Mexican movements and organisations and their ideologies.

The American slacker Communists who organised women and peasants found that they were working with Mexican activists – Elena Torres Cuéllar, Primo Tapia, and Úrsulo Galván – who also had strong ties to major Mexican political leaders, respectively to Governor Felipe Carrillo Puerto of the Yucatan, Governor Francisco Múgica of Michoacán, and Governor Aldalberto Tejeda of Veracruz. Neither Torres, nor Tapia, nor Galván could ever act completely independently of the political leaders with whom they were associated. Thus, as the slackers attempted to build the Mexican Communist Party, they found themselves sometimes cooperating with the very leaders who were building the new Mexican national state. Only a few documents comment on this problem, but the ambiguity of their position must have been evident to the slackers. The slackers found their internationalist project becoming circumscribed by the ideology and the political reality of nationalism.

The slackers had limited success with feminist organising, though they did help to establish one of the few Mexican feminist organisations of the 1920s. Their involvement with peasants was more substantial and put them in contact with and eventually established strong ties to two of the most important peasant leaders and organisations in Mexico. Their experiences in these two areas complete the picture of their activities and their impact on the Mexican social movements.

1   Slackers, Feminism, and Women's Organising

In tandem with organising the Communist Party, the slackers and their other
foreign and Mexican comrades undertook the organisation of a socialist feminist movement in Mexico. In 1919 and 1920 they played a role in bringing
American and Mexican feminist traditions together and helped to create a feminist organisation oriented to the working class. It was to be expected that they
should do so. Socialists had a long history of support for women's equality and
for women's political and economic rights dating back to Karl Marx, Friedrich
Engels, and August Bebel, the author of *Women Under Socialism*.[1] In Germany,
socialism and feminism converged in the late nineteenth and early twentieth centuries, albeit not without tensions, into a common movement for the
emancipation of the working class, of women, and all of humanity.[2] Socialist
feminism became an international movement throughout Europe and also in
the United States and Latin America.[3] The Russian Bolsheviks or Communists
took up and continued the socialist feminist tradition, with Alexandra Kollontai as the leading Russian Communist advocate of women's liberation.[4] And
after the formation of the German Communist Party, Clara Zetkin became the
leading spokesperson for women's equality in Germany. European anarchists
and especially anarchist women also brought their feminism – uninterested
in political equality but concerned with economic and social equality – from
Italy and Spain, Cuba, and Argentina.[5] So, it is not at all surprising that the Mexican Communists of the late 1910s and early 1920s in Mexico would also have
seen the liberation of women as part of their programme and as one of their
tasks.

American feminism, which dated back to the early demands for economic
and political equality of the Seneca Falls Declaration of 1848, reached its peak
on the eve of the US's entry into the First World War. In that era feminism meant
above all the fight for the right to vote, but it also included the struggle for
working women's rights and new ideas about women's rights to greater social
and sexual freedom.[6] As war loomed, feminists also became involved with the
emerging anti-war movement where they formed relationships with the socialist movements. Women such as Crystal Eastman, who led the American Union

---

1   Draper 1970, pp. 20–9; Bebel 1971, *passim*.
2   Thönnessen 1973, *passim*; Quataert 1979, *passim*.
3   Boxer 1978, *passim*; Lloyd 1971, *passim*.
4   Kollontai 1971, *passim*; Kollontai 1977, *passim*.
5   See, for example, Molyneux 1986, pp. 119–45.
6   Evans 1986, pp. 145–74; Rosenberg 1992, pp. 63–101.

Against Militarism, and Frances Witherspoon, who headed up the Bureau of Legal Advice, saw themselves simultaneously as socialists, pacifists, and feminists.[7] Some of the men involved in the pacifist or socialist movement also supported women's suffrage and other feminist goals. Since New York was the centre of this reciprocal interaction between the movements for peace, socialism, and women's rights, it was natural that several of the 'slackers' who came from New York shared those values. Both the men and the women radicals who fled to Mexico to avoid the draft and the war saw the fight for feminism and the organisation of women as part of their socialist politics. They also made it part of their activity in exile joining with Mexican feminists already engaged in the task.

Certainly, Mexican women had an interest in their own liberation. Mexican women enjoyed few rights and the condition of working women and peasant women was abysmal. Hermila Galindo, an educated, upper-class feminist who worked closely with Mexican President Venustiano Carranza on issues of foreign policy, described the condition of Mexican women under the Civil Code of 1884:

> The wife has no rights whatsoever in the home. [She is] excluded from participating in any public matter [and] she lacks authority to draw up any contract. She cannot dispose of her personal property, or even administer it, and she is legally disqualified to defend herself against her husband's mismanagement of her estate .... [A wife] lacks all authority over her children, and she has no right to intervene in their education .... She must, as a widow, consult persons designated by her husband before his death, otherwise she can lose her rights to her children.[8]

Mexico finally passed a divorce law over the objections of the Catholic Church in 1904.

The social conditions of women were poor. A.J. Pani produced a report in 1919 in which he described Mexico City as 'crowded and unsanitary, poorly fed, poorly housed, poorly governed, and subject to epidemics'.[9] It was women as mothers and homemakers who bore the brunt of these conditions. Public education expanded during the late nineteenth century but it was highly discrim-

---

7   Early 1997, pp. 5–26.
8   Galindo 1916, p. 14.
9   Ellsworth Huntington, 'The Relation of Health to Racial Capacity: The Example of Mexico', *Geographical Review*, 11, no. 2 (April 1921), pp. 243–64. Huntington's article provides an excellent example of the profound racism of some American professionals of the time.

inatory in practice; the state educated children at a rate of four boys to every girl. By 1910 illiteracy had been reduced to 78.4 percent; that is less than one in four Mexicans could read, but for women the rate of illiteracy must have been much higher. Women entered the workforce in significant numbers toward the turn of the century. Prostitution provided work for many. In 1905 one physician gave the extraordinary estimate that 22 percent of the women in Mexico between the ages of 15 and 30 worked as prostitutes. Mexico had many textile factories and by 1900 women made up 13 percent of the workforce, meaning long hours in miserable conditions for low wages. At the turn of the century a woman textile worker might earn 80 centavos a day and her girl child 30 to 50, but many women earned only 25 centavos a day.[10] It would be an understatement to call these poverty wages. During the Porfiriate, the government and large landowners took most of the peasants' land, forcing them to work as day labourers, and in some states and crops a significant percentage of them were women, generally working for half the wages of the men.[11] Life expectancy for both men and women was approximately 30 years, with many women dying in childbirth, and with high rates of infant mortality. The Spanish flue of 1918 carried off 4,749, mostly young adults in Mexico City, some .7 percent of the population.[12] Life was hard for all working people, but hardest for women.

When the slackers and their female companions arrived in Mexico, some of them undertook the organisation of a women's or feminist movement in Mexico, but they did not do so alone, nor were they the first. Mexico had its own feminist movement that had begun in the late nineteenth and early twentieth centuries, smaller but similar in many respects to those in Europe, the United States, and some other parts of Latin America. In those years upper- and middle-class Mexican women concerned about politics, property rights, civil rights, and economic equality had formed a variety of feminist clubs and published a number of feminist newspapers.[13] The movement may be said to have taken off with the struggle against the dictatorship of Porfirio Díaz that began at the turn of the century.

---

10   Soto 1990, pp. 7–17.
11   On the condition of rural women, see several of the essays in Salamini 1994.
12   Gerard Chowel et al 2010, p. 573.
13   Macías 1982, pp. 3–24. See also Lau 1993.

2 The Mexican Women's Movement

Women played an important part in the Mexican Revolution and in the post-revolutionary period as well. The Revolution brought violence and hunger, but it also created new roles for women. Women became involved in the pre-revolutionary struggle against the Porfirian dictatorship, joining the clubs calling for political reform. Some women joined the Mexican Liberal Party's clandestine organisations and participated in the insurrections in 1906, while others formed part of Francisco Madero's No Reelection Party. Ricardo Flores Magón had written a famous essay in 1910 titled '*A La Mujer*' (To Woman), blaming both the state and the Church for women's lowly position.

> Humiliated, degraded, bound by the chains of tradition to an irrational inferiority, indoctrinated in the affairs of heaven by clerics, but totally ignorant of world problems, [the woman] is suddenly caught in the whirlwind of industrial production which above all requires cheap labour to sustain the competition created by the voracious 'princes of capital' who exploit her circumstances. She is not prepared as men for the industrial struggle, nor is she organised with the women of her class to fight alongside her brother workers against the rapacity of capitalism.[14]

As anarchists who eschewed political parties and the state, Flores Magón and the PLM did not, however, support women's right to vote. Nor were they later supportive of the Feminist Congresses held in Mérida, Yucatan in January 1916, disdaining them altogether. 'What good the lovely and talented Yucatecans would have done for humanity, if in a moment of sane inspiration, they would have set democracy aside, and in its place adopted the Anarchist principles ...' wrote Magón.[15] When Ricardo Flores Magón got into an argument with feminist Juana Gutiérrez, he called her a 'lesbian – a degenerate'.[16] The PLM was in effect and opponent of the women's political movement and their sexual liberation.

Women themselves valued their political rights. Dolores Jiménez y Muro, a former PLM member, joined the *Liga Femenina Anti-releectionista 'Josefa Ortiz de Dominguez'* (Women's Anti-Reelectionist League 'Josefa Ortiz de Dominguez') and called for new political leadership. Jiménez y Muro stated: 'equality before the law does not exist in general, since we have ... those who are priv-

---

14   Flores Magón 1974, pp. 4–5, cited in Soto 1990, p. 42.
15   Flores Magón 1923, vol. 2, p. 42. Soto 1990, p. 42.
16   Lomnitz 2014, pp. 202–3,

ileged by fortune, position, or influence, to whom everything is allowed'. She joined with other women to form *Las Hijas to Cuauhtémoc* (The Daughters of Cuauhtémoc. The Aztec Cuauhtémoc was the son of Moctezuma and a national hero). Nationalism and feminism converged.

Some women participated in the initial revolutionary uprising against Porfirio Díaz, and one of them, Carmen Serdán, was wounded in the back, condemned to death but then imprisoned for seven months before being freed by the Revolution of 1910. Lidia Calderón joined the *Club Femenil Revolucionario Lealtad* (Women's Revolutionary Club Loyalty) and distributed Madero's revolutionary Plan de San Luis Potosí. A few women, such as Juana Gutiérrez Mendoza and Dolores Jimémenz de Muro, joined with Madero, working in the area of propaganda. Others, such as Josefina Ranzeta, worked as spies. After Madero was overthrown and murdered, the feminist María Hernández Zarco risked her safety and perhaps her life to distribute the anti-Huerta speech of Senator Belisario Domínguez, who himself had been murdered for making it.[17]

After the Revolution began in 1910, thousands accompanied the revolutionary armies as they fought their way across much of Mexico. Women were essential to the various military forces as they prepared food, including the essential tortillas, washed clothes, and provided companionship for their men. Some women became military combatants, fighting alongside the men, while a few also commanded military units.[18] Women of the middle and upper classes, especially those trained as nurses or teachers, took on more administrative roles. They organised hospitals and hospital trains and other support for the revolutionary armies.[19] Some worked as spies or secret agents during the revolution.

A very few women played political leadership roles. Hermila Galindo became an advisor to Carranza and helped to develop Mexico's nationalist foreign policy and to promote a Latin American alliance against the United States.[20] President Carranza dispatched Galindo as his representative to both domestic and foreign feminist organisations. Carranza's term in office was capped by the Constitution of 1917, which gave women equality before the law and the right to divorce, though in a Roman Catholic country few women took advantage of

---

17   Soto 1990, pp. 31–43.
18   Salas 1995, *passim*.
19   Villegas de Magnón 1994, *passim*. The autobiography of Villegas de Magnon shows the important role of upper- and middle-class women in organising the support networks of Carranza's Constitutionalist forces.
20   Moguel Flores 1994, pp. 43–51.

that right.[21] Women, however, did not have political equality. Galindo, who had helped to organise the Feminist Congress in the Yucatan in 1916, decided in 1917 to run for a seat in the Mexican legislature. She lost and the legislature passed a new law making maleness a prerequisite for running for office.[22] The government's fear that women would be influenced by the Church meant that the revolutionary governments did not extend suffrage to women. In fact, women did not receive the vote until 1953, so the fight for suffrage and the right to stand for public office remained on the agenda of the feminist movement for the first half of the twentieth century.

The Revolution also unleashed a wave of working-class organisation led by both working women and middle-class feminists. From 1915 to 1920 women workers formed labour unions, anarchist and socialist organisations, as well as feminist groups. Schoolteachers María Trinidad Hernández Cambre and Ana Berta Romero in Guadalajara created the Centro Radical Femenino, which published *Iconoclasta* (Iconoclast) carrying the slogan 'For the Liberation of Women'. Textile workers, seamstresses, and telephone operators in Mexico City established a group called *'Alma Roja'* (Red Soul), while women in Zacatecas created the *Centro Femenino de Estudios Sociales* (the Feminine Centre of Social Studies).[23] Women also became leaders of some labour unions in the textile plants.[24]

Feminism in general, which was emerging on the eve of the revolution, combined with the revolutionary rhetoric calling for political democracy and the uplift of the worker, the Indian, and the peasant to produce a revolutionary nationalist feminism, which soon became a kind of official state doctrine. This first feminist upsurge found its clearest ideological expression in the Yucatan where General Salvador Alvarado, then the governor, demanded education and employment for women. Alvarado and the feminist stateswoman Hermila Galindo organised the first feminist congress in Mérida, Yucatan in January 1916, the first such national feminist gathering in Mexico.

The January 1916 Feminist Congress focussed on women's economic and political roles in society, but also took up issues such as the female sex drive, prostitution, and the role of the Church. Anti-feminists at the congress argued that women should find happiness through fulfilment of their traditional roles. Moderates called for an end to laws that discriminated against women and for the opening of schools to women and for careers in teaching. A Second Fem-

---

21   Fisher 1942, pp. 211–28, reprinted in Yeager 1994, pp. 40–54.
22   Cano 2013, pp. 7–20.
23   Taibo II 1986, p. 68.
24   Bortz 2000, pp. 671–703.

inist Congress was held in Yucatan in November and December of 1916, and, after a bitter debate, passed a motion in favour of women's suffrage but rejected a proposition that women should be permitted to stand for office at the municipal level.

Following the two Yucatan meetings, Carranza promulgated the Law of Family Relations of 9 April 1917, which protected the rights of married women. The two feminist congresses of the Yucatan had an impact on both the national and state government. Governor Alvarado used the momentum of the first congress to encourage the establishment of feminist clubs throughout the Yucatan. Both the president and the governor used the state to promote a nationalist feminist agenda that ran counter to Mexican society's traditional, religious, and patriarchal values.

In addition to this state-sponsored nationalist feminism, a socialist-feminist current also developed, linked to labour union and peasant activists. This development too first appeared in Yucatan, as an outgrowth of the state's nationalist feminism. The moving spirit behind this development was Felipe Carrillo Puerto, the head of the peasant Leagues of Resistance, leader of the Socialist Party of the Southeast, and later governor of Yucatan. Carrillo supported economic and political equality for women and also advocated such radical views as 'free love' – meaning women's right to choose their own partners, easy divorce, and birth control. In the early 1920s, Carrillo's sister Elvia organised Feminist Leagues throughout Yucatan, which took up domestic issues such as home economics, hygiene, and childcare but also advocated birth control. During this same period Carrillo Puerto published Margaret Sanger's 'Birth Control or the Compass of the Home', a pamphlet which was still banned in the United States.[25]

Working closely with Carrillo on these projects was schoolteacher Elena Torres. She had been a labour organiser and teacher, active in the House of the World Worker, the most important labour organisation in Mexico between 1912 and 1918. There she had been involved in several significant strikes in Mexico City in 1915 and 1916. Impressed by her, Carrillo Puerto's government hired Torres to establish Montessori schools in Yucatan.[26] Carrillo and Torres linked the struggles of peasants and workers to the fight for feminism. In doing so they created a socialist-feminist movement that sometimes complemented and at other times challenged from the left the revolutionary government's emerging doctrine of revolutionary nationalist feminism.

---

25   Macías 1982, pp. 87–103.
26   Mitchell 2007, p. 25.

3   The Communists and the Women's Movement

When the slackers appeared and began organising the Communist Party and the IWW, they encountered and engaged this existing socialist-feminist movement. The English-speaking socialist group led by Charles Francis Phillips and Manabendra Nath Roy also took on the organisation of a Mexican feminist group. Phillips had been part of the feminist-pacifist-socialist anti-war milieu in the United States, participating, for example, in the founding meeting of the Bureau of Legal Aid on 4 and 5 April 1917 in New York City.[27] When he arrived in Mexico and became the editor of General Alvarado's Mexico City newspaper *El Heraldo de México*, he promoted the US feminist movement in the pages of the newspaper to his English-speaking audience. Phillips published many articles and editorials in *El Heraldo* in support of women's rights in the United States. On 15 June 1919, he lauded the Senate's passage of the women's suffrage amendment to the Constitution. 'Victory has at last crowned the long and untiring efforts of the women who have been working for a national suffrage amendment to the Constitution of the United States'.[28] He followed this up with another editorial in favour of suffrage on 21 June 1919, 'Suffrage is Certain in States', after Illinois passed the suffrage amendment.[29] When Virginia failed to pass the suffrage amendment, he wrote yet another editorial on the issue, arguing that it was no surprise that a conservative, racist Southern state should fail to give women the vote.[30] Phillips' article gives some indication of the radical slackers' deep commitment to support for suffrage. Yet their commitment to feminism went significantly beyond newspaper articles in favour of the right to vote.

When Phillips, M.N. Roy, and Adolfo Santibañez organised the first National Congress of the Socialist Party of Mexico in August and September of 1918, its programme incorporated many feminist demands. The Socialist programme called for universal suffrage for women over 18 years of age, as well as for protective labour legislation and childcare centres for women workers.[31] The Socialists, both the Mexicans and the American slackers, put themselves forward as fighters for women's democratic rights, above all suffrage, but also and in particular for the rights of working women. That position was similar not

---

27   Early 1997, pp. 19–20.
28   Phillips, 15 June 1919, p. 2.
29   Ibid.
30   Phillips, 21 June 1919b, p. 2.
31   'El Primer Congreso Nacional Socialista de Mexico', Partido Comunista Mexicano papers, Box 1, Folder 1, CEMOS.

only to that of *The Masses* magazine but also to the views of American socialist-feminists like Crystal Eastman and Mexican socialist-feminists such as Elena Torres.

But no movement was ever established by a paper programme. It would take women activists to organise a women's feminist movement. It was the American Evelyn Trent Roy who played the leading role in both bringing together the emigrés with the Mexican feminist groups and in propagandising for feminism, especially through her articles in *El Heraldo de México* and in *El Socialista* (The Socialist). Trent Roy had studied at Stanford University, beginning in 1911 and graduating in 1915. After leaving school, Trent remained part of a radical milieu of socialists, pacifists, and feminists loosely associated with Stanford. In 1916 she was living in Palo Alto and was a friend of the Indian poetess Dhangopal Mukeijee. Mukeijee had radical credentials. She was niece of the Irish nationalist De Valera, while her younger brother Jadugopal Mukeijee was an Indian nationalist revolutionary.

The day after M.N. Roy arrived in the United States he went to Palo Alto where he met with Jadugopal and Dhangopal Mukeijee. Dhangopal introduced Roy to Evelyn Trent, and soon thereafter the two became lovers and later married. Dhangopal Mukeijee also introduced Roy to David Starr Jordan, the president of Stanford University, and perhaps the most prominent American pacifist. When Roy decided to leave the United States to avoid arrest and prosecution for his activities, Jordan gave him a letter of introduction to Mexican president Carranza. Roy left for Mexico accompanied by his new wife Evelyn Trent, and the couple arrived in Mexico City in June of 1917. When Roy became a Communist in 1918, Trent did so as well, and both became active in the organisation of the Mexican Communist Party. While M.N. Roy appears to have played no role in feminist organising, for a brief period his wife Evelyn Trent Roy became a central figure in the Mexican women's movement.

In an article written for *El Socialista*, Trent Roy laid out a socialist-feminist critique of Mexican conditions and a programme for their resolution. She argued that the Revolution had transformed Mexican society and industry. Women had taken jobs in industry, and these new economic and social changes altered women's role in society. These changes said Trent Roy, required a transformation of Mexico that could only be brought about by the feminism 'which is the glory and hope of our age'. She emphasised the need for protective legislation for women and children, but also called for a reform of Mexican society for the benefit of all. Workers saw themselves as part of an international socialist movement, and so Trent argued, Mexican women should similarly join the world feminist movement.[32]

---

32   Trent Roy 1919, cited in Taibo II 1986, p. 69.

Trent Roy proved capable of transforming her journalism into activism through her political partnership with Elena Torres, the key figure in Mexican feminism of the era. Fleeing the repression of the left in the Yucatan, Torres arrived in Mexico City just about the time Trent Roy began her feminist organising. By 1919 President Carranza, who had become disgusted with Carrillo Puerto and his socialist experiments in the Yucatan, had sent Colonel Isaias Zamarripa to suppress the Yucatan Socialist Party. Carrillo Puerto, Roberto Haberman, and Elena Torres, among others, were forced to flee for their lives, and, when they arrived in Mexico City, they made contact with the US war resisters. The Communists recruited Elena Torres and made her the only woman member of the Latin American Bureau of the Communist International.[33]

When she became involved with Evelyn Trent Roy in the Communists' feminist organising project. Torres, who had worked with Hermila Galindo on the feminist congresses in the Yucatan, provided a key link to Mexican feminist organisations and individuals. Working together Trent Roy and Torres involved Juana B. Gutiérrez de Mendoza. A former follower of Ricardo Flores Magón and Emiliano Zapata, Gutiérrez had edited various feminist newspapers. Brundig Thorberg, the wife of Roberto Haberman, as well as Estela Carrasco, the companion of Herman Levine also became involved in this feminist organising project.

Probably through Torres, Trent Roy also made contact with several of the Mexican women's organisations that she later succeeded in involving in both the feminist and Communist movements. She established ties to the *Centro Radical Femenino* of Guadalajara, to a radical women's group in Zacatecas, and to various individual feminist leaders. But what made Evelyn Trent Roy's work a success was her collaboration with Torres.

The foreign and Mexican women, Elena Torres, Evelyn Roy, and María del Refugio García,[34] succeeded within a few months in establishing a new feminist organisation.[35] On 3 December 1919, *El Heraldo de Mexico* announced the founding of 'The Mexican Feminist Council'. The author of the article, probably Phillips, wrote: 'Mexico's first national council of women is in the process

---

33 'Manifiesto del Buro Latinoamericano de la III Intemacional a los trabajadores de la America Latina', Partido Comunista Mexicano brochure, Box 1, Folder 2a, CEMOS. The other members of the Latin American Bureau were Leopoldo Urmachea, Martin Brewster, Antonio Ruiz and José Allen, the USMID spy.

34 María del Refugio García is celebrated in the famous feminist work by artist Judy Chicago's 'The Dinner Party' in the Brooklyn Museum, see: https://www.brooklynmuseum.org/eascf a/dinner_party/heritage_floor/maria_del_refugio_garcia

35 Cano 1996, pp. 345–60.

of formation, to be known as THE MEXICAN FEMINIST COUNCIL, with a programme of action which includes most progressive and enlightened measures
for woman's social, economic, and political emancipation and for the regeneration of the society in which she lives'. While the article's author translated the
group's name as the Mexican Feminist Council, its Spanish name was *El Consejo Nacional de Mujeres* or the National Council of Women. An accompanying
news article published by the Mexican Feminist Council's manifesto signed by
the general secretary, Elena Torres. Its demands included 'equal pay for equal
work' and 'equal political rights for men and women'.[36]

In Mexico, radicals – including the left-wing nationalists, anarchists, Socialists and Communists – all tended to see the feminist movement as an integral
part of the struggle for 'social revolution'. Feminism was interpreted by many
on the left in a broad fashion to include suffrage and the right to stand for office,
as well as working women's demands such as equal pay for equal work, social
equality, and sexual reproductive rights such as sex education, contraception,
and abortion. Communists Evelyn Trent and Elena Torres, while no doubt supporting the entire panoply of feminist rights, tended to put more emphasis
on the economic and labour issues. Later, between 1927 and 1935, the Mexican Communists – following the Communist International into its sectarian
and ultraleft 'third period' – would entirely reject what they called the 'bourgeois' women's suffrage movement and would tend to ignore both the fight
for the right to vote as well as the social-sexual-reproductive issues. Instead,
they concentrated their attention entirely on the Communist Party, the unions
it controlled, and its other front groups. However, in the late teens and early
1920s feminism was still thought of as a multi-faceted movement of women
themselves.

The founding of the Council represented a convergence of US and Mexican socialism and feminism which had been running on parallel tracks and
which briefly intersected due to the presence of American and other foreign
exiles in Mexico between 1917 and 1921. The Council's impact probably never
went far beyond a fairly small social layer of educated middle-class, professional women, some organised women workers, and an even smaller number
of peasant women activists. Yet even that was an accomplishment. José Allen,
the general secretary of the Communist Party and at the time and US government spy, thought the organisation of the Mexican Feminist Council important
enough to mention it in his report on the state of the Mexican party prepared

36   Phillips, 3 December 1919a, p. 2; Phillips, 3 December 1919, p. 2. See the discussion of these
      developments in Taibo II 1986, pp. 68–71.

for the Communist International in 1922.[37] There is unfortunately little information about what the group actually did, though it presumably carried out educational and organisational work among women, probably alongside the new Communist Party and the Mexican Administration of the Industrial Workers of the World.

But this socialist feminist movement may have been less than completely independent. Another report by Allen, this one to the US Military Intelligence Division suggested in September 1920 that Elena Torres had broken from the Communists and 'is now paid by Ramírez Garrido (Inspector of Police), Felipe Carrillo and Antonio D. Soto y Gama to dedicate herself exclusively to carrying on Pro-feminist propaganda'. The agent claimed that Torres was provided with enough money to rent an office in the city's centre and to organise 'The Feminist Council'.[38] In his role as general secretary of the Communist Party, Allen reported that Torres used her Feminist organisation as a cover to do political work in favour of General Álvaro Obregón.[39] Whether the spy Allen's reports are to be believed is dubious. Torres had long been associated with Carrillo whose Socialist Party of the Southeast had nearly affiliated with the Communist International. While Torres may have been cooperating with Ramírez Garrido, Carrillo, and Soto y Gama, and carrying out political propaganda for Obregón, she may have seen no contradiction between working with them and her continued involvement with the Communists. In another document to the Communist International, José Allen suggested that the Mexican Communists had broken with Torres because of her self-aggrandisement, but there is no explanation of what he meant by that charge.[40] As a police agent for the USMID, perhaps he had his own reasons to attempt to discredit her.

Historians of Mexican feminism have understood that the organisation of the Council was a Communist Project.[41] But at the same time, the founding of the Mexican Council of Women with socialist-feminist politics grew out of the experiences and ideas of the various US war resisters, American feminists,

---

37   'El Movimiento Comunista en Mexico: Su initiation, sus trabajos, sus errores, su situation actual, y su porvenir', Roll 12, 495/108/25, SASFR.

38   E.O., 'Radical and Labor Activities', 20 September 1920, RG 165, Box 2290, USMID, USNA; and E.O., 'Political, Radical and Labor Activities', 10 November 1920, RG 165, Box 2291, USMID, USNA.

39   'El Movimiento Comunista en Mexico: Su initiation, sus trabajos, sus errores, su situation actual, y su porvenir', Roll 12, 495/108/25, SASFR.

40   Letter from CPM general secretary and the Latin American Bureau [José Allen] to the Communist International, 29 April 1920, Roll 12, 495/108/3 Cap 2, Doc 3, f. 4–10, SASFR.

41   Tuñón Pablos 1992, p. 25.

and the Mexican revolutionaries who established the council. The Communist Party and the Mexican Council of Women certainly overlapped. The Council was not only Communist in inspiration, but also a natural extension of their experiences in the social movements of both the United States and Mexico. Some of the women involved in the Council also became important figures in the small Communist movement in Mexico. As already mentioned, Elena Torres became a member of the Communist International's Latin American Bureau established in December 1919, while Council member María del Refugio García later edited a Communist Party newspaper called *La Mujer* (The Woman).[42] Evelyn Trent Roy might have claimed credit for taking the initiative to organise the Mexican Council of Women, but there her influence ended, for she left for Moscow with M.N. Roy in November 1919, and she never again played any role in Mexican politics or the Mexican women's movement.

The Mexican Council of Women survived at least a few years more. Elena Torres held the position of general secretary, while schoolteachers Elisa Acuña y Rossetti and Luz Vera, who served as journalists and propagandists, also played leading roles. Later the group became established as one of the principal feminist and women's groups of the 1920s. As representatives of the Feminist Council of Mexico, Torres and Vera attended the League of Women Voters meeting held in Baltimore in 1922 where they became the organisers of the Pan-American League for the Elevation of Women, with Torres serving as the vice-president for North America.[43]

None of the men of the movement in that period mentioned the feminist organising in their autobiographies.[44] But Evelyn Trent Roy and Torres working with Mexican school teachers or other feminist activists had succeeded in establishing a feminist group which played a modest role not only in Mexico but internationally as well. The Communists' involvement in organising women should be seen as an integral part of their project. Communism, indus-

---

42   Martínez Verdugo 1985, p. 31.

43   Macías 1982, pp. 106–8.

44   The men involved in the Mexican Communist movement never recognized or even recorded the women's organising projects in their memoirs. M.N. Roy never even mentions the name of his ex-wife Evelyn Trent Roy in his *Memoirs*, and neither Roy nor Charles Francis Phillips discuss the Communist group's involvement in feminist organising in Mexico in their autobiographies. Carleton Beals, who devotes several pages to M.N. Roy, never mentions the name or the role of Evelyn Trent Roy, and, though he was very close to the slackers at the time, he also neglects to mention the Mexican radicals' feminists organising in his memoirs. Roy 1984, *passim*; Phillips 1993, *passim*; Beals 1938, *passim*; Kamik's biography of Roy does not discuss Evelyn Trent Roy (Kamik 1978) and Samaren Roy's biography has only a very brief mention of Evelyn Trent Roy in the text (Roy 1986, pp. 37, 48, and note 15).

trial unionism, peasant and farmer organising, as well as feminism formed part of a unified radical vision in the minds of the Communist organisers.

But Mexican women organisers like Elena Torres apparently believed that they could not cut themselves off from the radical nationalist political leaders like Carrillo Puerto. Though Torres joined the Communist Party and worked with Trent Roy, her allegiance remained divided, though she may have found no contradiction in such a position. To her, fighting for the Yucatan peasants through the league and the local socialist party under Carrillo Puerto, organising women into the feminist movement, and working for Communism may all have been seen as part of one complex radical project.[45]

4   Slacker Communists and the Peasants

The Communists also threw themselves into the peasant movement for agrarian reform. The issue of agrarian reform, that is, the redistribution of land from the great *hacendados* to the landless farmworkers and indigenous peoples from whom the land had been taken, stood at the centre of the Mexican Revolution. Andrés Molina Enríquez had identified the issue before the Revolution in his book *Los grandes problemas nacionales* (The Great National Problems), published in 1909. Later President Venustiano Carranza's leading intellectual Luis Cabrera, had formulated a plan for reform in his 1912 essay '*La Reconstitución de los ejidos de los pueblos como medio de suprimir la esclavitud del jornalero mexicano*' (The Reconstitution of Communal Lands as a Way to Suppress the Enslavement of the Mexican Agricultural Worker).[46] When Álvaro Obregón became president, he formed an alliance with the remnant of Emiliano Zapata's peasant movement (Zapata having been assassinated a year before) and pledged that he would carry out an agrarian reform, which he did on a modest scale where it would benefit him politically. When his successor Elías Plutarco Calles ran for president in 1924, among his first campaign stops was the tomb of Emiliano Zapata where he told the press, 'Let everyone know, and let the conservative element know, Zapata's agrarianism is mine'.[47] Despite these pledges and some significant distribution of land during the Obregón presidency, the government failed to carry out the kind of agrarian reform that would have satisfied the peasants, and it often sided with the landlords both old and

45   Jocelyn Olcott picks up the story of the women's movement in the 1930s (Olcott 2005).
46   Molina Enríquez 1991, *passim* and *Los grandes problemas nacionales* (Mexico: Ediciones Era, 1991) and Cabrera 1994, pp. 124–52.
47   Ramón Puente 1994, p. 82.

new. It certainly had not quelled the peasants' desire for land, a hunger for their own piece of earth that drove a powerful agrarian reform movement, which developed in the early post-revolutionary period.

It was in this context that American slacker Communists began to work with organisers of the peasants. This work overlapped the earlier period of activity by war resisters Charles Phillips and Linn Gale and the later activity of Communist International organiser Louis Fraina and Sen Katayama, whose lives and experience we take up in one of the following chapters. How was it that the American slacker Communists came to be political actors in the peasant movement in Mexico? It seems strange that New Yorkers like Columbia University student Charles Francis Phillips and Brooklyn schoolteacher Herman Levine would ever have ended up in the cornfields and canebrakes of Mexico. They and their American friends were urban men accustomed to the tavern, the book shop, and the political club, the factory, the office and the union hall, men who might have passed their whole lives without ever seeing a farmer in his field, much less a Mexican peasant in his *milpa*. What was it that led them to undertake the organisation of Mexican peasants?

There are three answers to this question. The first has to do with the experience of the IWW in the United States, the second with the impact of the Russian Revolution of October 1917 in Mexico, and the third and most important with the nature of the Mexican Revolution itself. Most of the slacker radicals, as we know, thought of themselves as supporters of the Industrial Workers of the World. The IWW in the years preceding the outbreak of the war, had become the foremost, indeed virtually the only union dedicated to the organisation of agricultural workers in the United States. In 1914, the IWW committed itself to undertaking a major organisational campaign among agricultural workers, a campaign that proved quite successful among workers in the wheat belt in 1915. These efforts were being extended when in 1917 the US entered the war.[48] So this became the slackers' model. For the Wobblies in Mexico, the organisation of industrial workers necessarily included at least the agricultural day labourers and conceivably other peasants who worked on the farms, plantations and haciendas.

A second factor in the Mexican Communists' attitude toward the peasants was the impact of the Russian Revolution. In Mexico from 1917 to the 1940s. There was a tendency among a good many Mexican government officials and revolutionary generals, as well as union officials, peasant leaders, and intellectuals to identify the Mexican Revolution with the Russian revolution and to

---

48   Dubofsky1969, pp. 313–18.

see the parallels between these two contemporaneous events, given that they took place in the same decade in two predominantly agricultural and peasant societies.[49] For Mexican radicals, Russia became not only a symbol of a workers' revolution, but an example of how a peasant society might be uplifted and advanced. After the Russian Revolution, the Russian Bolshevik or Communist Party – historically a working-class party – claimed to be the leader of workers *and peasants*. So Mexican Communists saw their task to organise not only workers but also peasants and agricultural day labourers.

Even more important than IWW strategy or the Russian Revolutionary experience was the experience of the Mexican Revolution itself, a revolution still in process when the slackers arrived in 1917. The Mexican Revolution was a peasant revolution, or, as historian Alan Knight calls it, a 'popular, agrarian movement'.[50] Mexico in the first decades of the twentieth century was a predominantly rural, agricultural land, a land of peasants, farmers and farm labourers of all sorts from small parcellary peasants, to ejidal and cooperative peasants, to day labourers and even virtual peasant slaves. Eighty percent of all Mexicans lived in rural and agricultural areas. Out of a total population of 14 million in 1920, about 12 million Mexicans lived in the countryside. Of those 12 million rural people, three million were Indians who spoke over 100 different indigenous languages.

Mexican Indian peasants often formed a group apart, and stereotypes and caricatures abounded on all sides. Some Mexican revolutionaries such as Enrique Flores Magón, co-founder with his brother Ricardo of the anarchist Mexican Liberal Party, idealised the Indian. Enrique remembered that his father had taught him about the Indians amongst whom they lived as children in Oaxaca:

> All of the land around each one of our villages belongs to the community. Every morning we go out to work the land. All of us, except the sick, the handicapped, the elderly, women and children. Happily, goes everyone who is able. They are encouraged by the thought that the work that they do, he and his companions, is of benefit of all. Comes the time of the harvest. Observe, my sons, how they divide the harvest among the men of the tribe. Each one receives according to his needs ... Among us ... there are no rich nor poor, no thieves nor beggars .... We are all at the same economic level.[51]

49   Spenser 1998, pp. 69–98.
50   Knight 1986, vol. 1, p. xi.
51   Kaplan 1958, cited in Zertuche Muñoz 1995, p. 13.

To revolutionaries like Enrique Flores Magón, and to some of those who joined Emiliano Zapata, the Indian was born an anarcho-communist. To others like Soto y Gama, the Indian was a genuine Christian, but also therefore an anarcho-communist.

Though Mexico's nationalist politicos and intellectuals had begun to define Mexico as a *mestizo* nation, the racial divisions, and the closely related class lines remained clear to the naked eye. Even after the revolution ended, writers like José Vasconcelos could still write about Mexicans as divided into three ethnic-social groups: Mexicans of Spanish descent, *los criollos*, generally lighter complexioned people of the upper classes; people of mixed-race, *los mestizos*, often seen as the urban working classes; and the indigenous people, *los indígenas* (or more commonly and derogatorily, *los indios*).[52] However, it was also Vasconcelos who wrote in a Nietzschean vein about Mexico's ideal of *la raza cósmica*, 'the cosmic race' made up of Europeans and Indians, and Africans and Asians, which represented a stage in the development of a future evolution of humanity.

The American slackers did not share the idealist illusions or the prejudices of the Mexicans, though they certainly may have had their own biases and internationalist misconceptions. Informed by the IWWs strategy, observing the experience of the Russian Revolution, and well aware of the peasant character of the Mexican Revolution taking place around them, the American and Mexican leaders of the new communist movement reached out to make connections to the peasantry. Yet the Communists also argued that the peasant leaders and organisations would have to subordinate themselves to the working class and to its political party, the Communist Party. In a 1921 Manifesto, 'To the Workers and Peasants of the Mexican Region', the Organising Committee of the Communist Party of Mexico proclaimed:

> The working class of Mexico forms a very small percentage of the oppressed masses: alone it cannot continue its struggle. While the peasantry is infinitely larger, neither can it continue its struggle alone. The peasantry forms a mass which cannot control society. It must have leadership, either from the revolutionary proletariat or from the reactionary capitalist class.

---

52   Reading the autobiography of José Vasconcelos, written in the 1930s but mostly about the 1920s, one is struck by his constant use of terms such as *criollo, mestizo,* and *indígena.* While this division of Mexican society into three such groups is simplistic, it was still the dominant view in the 1920s, though that schema disappeared almost completely in the 1930s, along with the word *criollo* (Vasconcelos 1993).

The great and indispensable task of the Communist Party is to combine the industrial and agricultural struggle in order to assure the attraction of peasants and workers and to unite both of them in a struggle for the conquest of power.[53]

This was the view of Lenin, that the peasantry was incapable of leading the society, and would itself have to ally with the working class and follow the revolutionary working-class party, the Communists.

The organisation of the new Communist movement in Mexico coincided with a post-revolutionary upsurge of the peasant movement. The peasants' hunger for land had been one of the forces driving the Mexican revolution, but beginning around 1920, a new agrarian reform movement became one of the central social movements that pressured the new revolutionary government. The peasant agrarian reform movement of the 1920s was the most significant social movement in Mexico in that decade, more significant even than the impressive and important movements of industrial workers.

Sen Katayama, the American-educated Japanese socialist sent to Mexico by the Communist International, and himself a former organiser of farmworkers in California, appears to be the author of a report of 24 August 1921 in which he described the situation.

[The] peasants have been again and again deceived by the revolutionary leaders. It is highly gratifying to know that the Mexican peasants have lately awakened and realised the foolishness of fighting for the selfish revolutionary leaders and in some counties [*sic.*] they are actually confiscating the big landed properties [and distributing them] among themselves. Falling a leaf tells the coming of Autumn! We are very much encouraged by recent application of peasants from the country near the City of Mexico in the effect that they desire to form a Communist section of the Communist Party of Mexico among the peasants themselves.[54]

Another report in August 1921, also probably written by Sen Katayama, stated that 'the peasants [who were] the backbone of the recent revolutions ... are accordingly included in the work of the Organisation Committee [and] the

---

53   'A los Oberos y Campesinos de la Región Mexicana: Manifiesto del Comité de Organización del Partido Comunista de México' (Mexico: Communist Party of Mexico, 1921), p. 7. Partido Mexicano Comunista, Box 1, Folder 14, CEMOS.

54   [Sen Katayama?] to the Executive Committee of the Communist International, 24 August 1921, Roll 6, 521/1/17, SASFR.

formation of Communist local[s] among the farm workers – two have already been organised'.[55] It is unclear what peasant organisations Katayama refers to, but it is likely the organisations of Veracruz and Michoacán, for the Communists had succeeded in making contact with and winning over two of the most important peasant leaders in Mexico: Primo Tapia in Michoacán and Úrsulo Galván in Veracruz. The American slackers and Mexican activists of the Communist Party succeeded in recruiting both peasant leaders to the Communist movement at least briefly. Both Tapia's and Galván's organisations and their mass followings gave the Communist Party an important role in the peasant movement, and therefore in regional politics on both coasts of Mexico at least until 1930. (The Mexican Communist Party also came to lead a mass peasant movement in the 1930s, but in other regions.)

5   Primo Tapia and the League of Agrarian Communities

The first of these movements, the League of Agrarian Communities, was founded by Primo Tapia, an indigenous Mexican who had been an IWW and probably also been a Communist in the United States. Born in Naranja, Michoacán of Tarascan Indian parents in 1885, Tapia was sent to school at a lay seminary at Erongarícuaro, Michoacán.[56] Expelled from school for misconduct and in need of work, Tapia emigrated to Los Angeles, California in 1907. There he met Ricardo and Enrique Flores Magón and joined the Mexican Liberal Party (PLM), which was engaged in attempting to overthrow the dictatorship of Porfirio Díaz. Beginning in 1910 Tapia worked throughout the Southwest and Rocky Mountain regions in the typical Mexican jobs of the era: construction, mining, railroads, and sugar beets. Sometime around 1911he became a member of the Industrial Workers of the World. Nine years later he led an IWW strike in the beet fields of Nebraska, but the strike failed and to avoid reprisals he fled home to Naranja, Michoacán.

Back in his homeland, Tapia joined his uncle in the agrarian reform struggle and soon put himself at the head of the movement among the Purépecha (or Tarascan) Indians. In 1921 Tapia founded the Committee for Material Improvement, which organised against the clergy, the caciques, and the landlords, and

---

55   Report of the American Agency to the Small Bureau of the Executive Committee [of the Communist International], [dated by Daniela Spenser as August 1921], Roll 12, 495/108/8, f. 24–29. SASFR.

56   For this biographical account I rely on Friedrich 1970, pp. 58–130. See also Alicia Castellanos Guerrero 1991 and Martínez Múgica 1976.

petitioned for land under the agrarian reform laws. Successful there, he began to organise throughout the region and on 15–17 December 1923 founded the League of Agrarian Communities. The 1924 League Constitution proclaimed its goal to be 'the defence of the collective interests of the peasants ... [and] to dignify labour, to socialise the land and production in general'. The League also 'recognised that the peasant problem is not one of the states, nor even of the nation, but an international problem, and for that reason, it sees as its brothers the peasants of the whole world'.[57]

Beginning in 1920, Tapia organised the Feminine League (*La Liga Femenil*) to fight against the Church's control over women. 'The organization of the woman is indispensable at this time', Tapia wrote a few years later, 'because the world proletariat is moving ahead. Without organising the women, we will roundly fail, because as long as they are under the influence of the priest, he will wrest the last secret from them'.[58] This view that the Catholic priests could control Mexican women remained widespread in Mexico and dominant in the ruling party through the revolution and for decades after, which, as already mentioned, was the principal reason that women did not win suffrage until 1953.

Throughout the 1920s Michoacán landlords and peasants frequently engaged in armed skirmishes in which both sides suffered casualties. With the League of Agrarian Communities and the Feminine League well established, Tapia and his supporters took over the local militia in the early 1920s. Now fairly well armed, they could defend themselves against the hacienda owners and their *guardias blancas* (white guards).

During this period Tapia entered into a political alliance with Francisco Múgica, the leader of the Socialist Party of Michoacán (PSM) founded in 1917.[59] Tapia's grassroots movement became an important base of support for Múgica, and the governor in turn helped push through the state legislature and the government agencies of the Purépecha communities' demands that local hacienda lands in the Zucapa Valley be turned into ejidos. At the same time Tapia could provide hundreds of armed peasants when necessary to support Múgica's government against the landlords or the hostile Federal government of President Obregón. Tapia's League of Agrarian Communities soon formally became part of Múgica's Socialist Party of Michoacán. Tapia's activities also led him to work closely with governor Mugica's good friend General Lázaro Cárdenas, the future

---

57   Embriz Osario 1982, p. 75.
58   Friedrich 1970, p. 93.
59   On the history of the Partido Socialista Michoacano see: Mijangos Díaz 1997, pp. 110–15 and 131–4 and Sánchez Díaz 1990, pp. 105–24.

president of Mexico. In 1923 Tapia travelled with Cárdenas through a number of Purépecha (Tarascan) communities, and wrote to a friend, 'With General Cárdenas I have been able to get many things', mentioning, for example, that Cárdenas promised to get rid of unacceptable military officers.[60]

The slackers must have learned of Tapia's activities and sought him out. Such contact was no doubt facilitated by Tapia's fluent English and his former involvement in the IWW and perhaps even in the Communist Party of the United States. Friedrich, who has written in most detail about Tapia, believes that he like many other Wobblies, might have joined the US Communist Party in 1918 or 1919.[61] In any case, he would have been capable of bridging the cultural and linguistic gaps between the American slackers and the Mexican peasants.

By 1920 members of both of Mexico's Communist Parties had made contact with the Socialist Party of Michoacán and Múgica. American slackers Charles Francis Phillips (then using the name Frank Seaman), Walter Foertmeyer, and Linn A.E. Gale as well as José Allen reportedly attended meetings of the Socialist Party of Michoacán, presumably with the approval of governor Múgica.[62] It was most likely at this time that the slackers recruited Primo Tapia to the Mexican Communist Party. On 8 May 1920 Charles Phillips, José Allen, and the Spanish revolutionary Sebastián Sanvicente attended a celebration of May Day, or as it is called in Mexico, the Day of the Martyrs of Chicago, in Morelia, Michoacán. The red-and-black strike flag was hung on the Cathedral, scandalising the pious Catholics and conservatives of the city. Four days later the Catholic right exacted its revenge for the blasphemy – and for the peasants' land redistributions – by assassinating Isaac Arriaga, one of the founders of the socialist movement in Michoacán, as well as murdering 15 other radical activists.[63] The slackers escaped the massacre, but their involvement in those events was later used to justify their expulsion from Mexico.

After joining the Mexican Communist Party, Tapia frequently attended party meetings in Mexico City and worked with other Communist peasant organisers such as Úrsulo Galván. In June of 1923, he helped organise the Communist Local of Michoacán, where he took the position of Secretary of Propaganda. In that role, he signed a 'Manifesto to the Workers of Town and Country of Michoacán' calling for the overthrow of the capitalist state and its instruments of oppression and violence, the creation of the institutions of the dictatorship of

---

60   Martínez Múgica 1976, p. 213.
61   Friedrich 1970, p. 69.
62   Martín Sánchez 1994, pp. 180–3 and p. 183, note 358.
63   Embriz Osario 1982, p. 194.

the proletariat, and the communist transformation of the means of production as rapidly as possible. The means to achieve this, the Manifesto said, was 'the armed insurrection of the proletariat'.[64]

Tapia established ties with the PCM leaders, including the American slackers, but he also maintained his close ties to Governor Múgica and General Cárdenas. While the Communists talked about building an independent movement of the proletariat and the peasantry, absolute political independence was a luxury that local leaders such as Tapia could not afford. In this way the slackers found themselves part of a complicated set of political relationships that linked them indirectly to both the Communist movement centred in Moscow and the nationalist movement coalescing in Morelia and Mexico City.

6   Úrsulo Galván

The other peasant organisation with which the slackers established connections, the League of Agrarian Communities of the State of Veracruz (LCAEV), would play a crucial role in the early history of the Mexican Communist Party. Its leader was another impressive grassroots organiser, Úrsulo Galván. He was born in Tlacotepec de Mejía, Veracruz in 1893 the son of Dona Amalia Reyes and Fermín Galván. Deserted by her husband, Úrsulo's mother sold candies and worked in the coffee plantations with her little son working beside her. Later she moved to Veracruz and set up a tortilla business for herself, while Úrsulo was apprenticed to a carpenter.

The master carpenter who trained the apprentice Galván, Manuel Almanza García, also taught Galván radical politics and became his mentor and lifelong companion and comrade. Together Galván and Almanza García joined the Constitutionalist Army and fought in the Mexican Revolution. When Pancho Villa's army defeated the Constitutionalist contingents with which he was fighting, Galvan sought refuge in the United States where he lived and worked until 1917. According to his widow, Galvan's 'experiences in the United States had inspired him to join trade union activities to work for social change'.[65]

Around 1917 Galván met the Spanish activist Junco Rojo and joined the House of the World Worker (Casa del Obrero Mundial), at the time the principal labour union organisation in Mexico. After experiments in electoral politics and the organisation of peasant cooperatives, Galván and Almanza García were

---

64   Castellanos Guerrero 1991, p. 41.
65   Heather Fowler 1970, pp. 90–104, and Falcón 1986, pp. 132–92.

sent by the Casa to the petroleum fields to organise oil workers. Galván came to play an important if rather controversial role in a strike at the Huasteca Petroleum Company owned by the American oilman Edward L. Doheny. When the workers were tempted by an offer to settle the strike, Galván pushed for more militant action, but, after violence broke out, the strike was crushed by the military.

His involvement in the oil workers' organising and strikes brought Galvan into contact with local anarchist and Communist activists. In 1918, he fell under the influence of Manuel Díaz Ramírez, and in 1921 joined his 'English school'. Díaz Ramírez, who had been a member of the Industrial Workers of the World in the United States and spoke fluent English, taught not only that language, but also revolutionary syndicalism. His English School evolved into a Marxist study circle known as Antorcha Libertaria (the Torch of Freedom), and in 1919 it became the Veracruz branch of the Mexican Communist Party. Díaz Ramírez himself became one of the closest collaborators of the slackers and later head of the Communist Party.

Beginning about 1919, Galván and Almanza began to organise peasants. Galván's efforts received the support, encouragement, and sometimes the financial and even military assistance of the radical governor Adalberto Tejeda. In 1923 Tejeda encouraged Galván to establish a statewide peasant organisation. This effort also had the support of the local Communist Party. In March of that year in the state capital of Xalapa, the League of Agrarian Communities of the State of Veracruz (LCAEV) convened, and with the backing of the governor, Galván became the head of the organisation. The League's programme called for agrarian reform, but not for a socialist revolution. With the endorsement and support of the Mexican Communist Party, Úrsulo Galván and his longtime mentors and collaborators Manuel Almanza and Manuel Díaz attended the meeting of the Communist Peasant International (the KRESINTERN) in Moscow in 1924. Much like Tapia, Galvan maintained close ties to both the Communists and to the governor of his state, Tejeda. The slackers' Communist Party, precisely because it attempted to relate to real radical forces for change in Mexico was never very far from the left-wing nationalist establishment, and the new state.

7   Conclusion

What had been the source of the slackers' success in relating to the radical peasant movement? The Communists' ability to recruit Primo Tapia and Ursulo Galván, two of the most important peasant leaders in Mexico, was not surprising, for the Communists, several of them Americans, and the Mexican agrarian movements had several things in common. Both Tapia and Galvan had lived and worked in the United States, and both were familiar with American labour unions. Tapia who had been a member of the IWW in the United States spoke English fluently, and Galván may also have spoken English, but if he did not his friend and former Wobbly Manuel Díaz, who did, could interpret for him. The presence of English-speaking former Wobblies in both states helped the American slacker Communists and IWW organisers recruit the local peasant leaders.

Yet, even though they joined the Mexican Communist Party, both Tapia and Galván remained men of divided loyalties. Both knew that their political existence depended upon the sufferance and support of the state governors. Tapia depended upon Múgica, Galván upon Tejeda. Nevertheless, both Tapia and Galván joined and belonged to the Communist Party, participated in its organisational meetings, and carried out its policies. A few years later when Bertram Wolfe came to Mexico to work with the Mexican Communists, the party still maintained strong ties to both peasant organisations. As will be described in a coming chapter, the peasant organisation of Úrsulo Galván played an important role in the carrying out of the Communist Party policy of supporting the Mexican government and opposing the Adolfo de la Huerta rebellion of 1923, a key event in the party's early history.[66] What was true of the peasant leaders was also true of Mexican feminist leader Elena Torres. Though she joined the Communist Party and worked with Trent Roy in the organisation of the Communist-inspired feminist organisation, the National Council of Women, Torres never cut herself off from Yucatan governor Felipe Carrillo Puerto. She and her feminist associates remained linked to Carrillo Puerto, and through him to other political leaders in the new Mexican state.

Thus, even in their success, the slackers found themselves in an ambivalent situation. They could only further the goals of the Communist International and of the Mexican Communist Party by rooting in local and state social and political movements. But those organisations in turn had established ties to the rising forces of nationalism and the new Mexican state on which they depended for political support, financing, and sometimes for guns for the peasant leagues fighting for their land. Not until 1929 when the Communist Party had entered its so-called 'Third Period' of largely independent armed uprisings against the Mexican government did Galván break with the Communist

---

66   Letter from Bertram Wolfe to the RILU, 10 January 1924, doc. 534/7/393/83, SASFR.

Party. The Communist activists' practical relationships to movements in Mexico would frequently exert a stronger influence than their more distant and more ideological ties to Moscow. At really crucial moments, the Communists were sometimes diverted from their internationalist project, and, as we will see, came down on the side of the Mexican government.

CHAPTER 14

The Expulsion of the 'Pernicious Foreigners'

During Venustiano Carranza's tenure as president (1917–20) the American slackers enjoyed the patronage or at least the tolerance of the highest levels of the Mexican government. Carranza viewed the American radicals as useful allies in his struggles against the United States government. He saw them as valuable critics of United States foreign policy, adversaries of American imperialism, and opponents of a US war with Mexico. Moreover, the slackers were allies who could help create ties to US socialist, labour, and liberal peace organisations. Carranza was therefore prepared to tolerate even such apparently revolutionary activities as the founding of a Communist Party and the creation of a Mexican Administration of the Industrial Workers of the World (IWW). The American radicals were after all a small group, and their organisations had little impact on Mexican society as a whole. Carranza could always expel them whenever it seemed necessary or convenient for him to do so. Unfortunately for the Americans, the foundation of the two rival Mexican Communist Parties and the struggle over the Industrial Workers of the World took place at about he same time that General Álvaro Obregón overthrew President Carranza.

During the election of 1920, Obregón challenged Carranza's handpicked successor, Ignacio Bonillas. Obregón's most important political support came from Luis N. Morones and the organisations he controlled: the Regional Confederation of Mexican Workers (the CROM) and the Labour Party (PL). At least one slacker saw the handwriting on the wall. Gale, although still under the protection of Carranza and Berlanga, proclaimed his party's neutrality, and announced that, 'The Mexican Communists are boycotting the election'.[1]

When Carranza made moves to arrest Obregón and suppress his supporters, in April of 1920, Obregón declared himself in rebellion against the Carranza government. With the support of substantial sections of the army and of Morones and the CROM as well as some other workers' organisations, Obregón soon dominated Mexico. By 21 May Carranza's forces had been defeated and when he fled Mexico City and stopped at the village of Tlaxcalantongo he was assassinated. With Carranza's defeat Obregón, Adolfo de la Huerta and Plutarco Elías Calles, the Sonoran triumvirs, came to power.[2] De la Huerta served as interim

---

1 Gale, March 1920, p. 4.
2 De la Huerta should not be confused with Victoriano Huerta, the rightwing general wo ha overthrown and assassinated President Francisco Madero.

president from May to December 1920, when Obregón was elected president of Mexico with Calles as his Minister of the Interior. Morones, their labour union backer, became one of the most powerful men in Mexico.

With the fall of Carranza, Gale lost his patron, former Minister of the Interior, Berlanga. Moreover, Gale had not supported Obregón in the election and had been a constant critic of his principal supporter, Morones. Attempting to ingratiate himself with the newly elected president, Gale wrote obsequiously to Obregón on 17 March:

> I take this opportunity to give to you and your comrades my most sincere congratulations for your success and the vindication of the right of the Mexican people to govern themselves free from the influence of the tyranny of Carranza and of Wall Street Financiers. I tell you this as my personal thought as well as a member of the Executive Committee of the Communist Party. Even though the party is not involved in political affairs, being dedicated solely to Industrial Unionism, all the Communists hate American capitalism, and naturally take great pleasure in the defeat of that capitalism.[3]

Gale went on to assure Obregón that he understood the president's difficulties and his delicate responsibilities, and that with the danger of American intervention, the new head of state could not do everything that one might have wanted. 'Nevertheless', wrote Gale, 'hopefully you will enact all the Socialist laws and reforms which you believe prudent in these days, and more radical ones when conditions may be more favourable and the new government is stronger'.[4]

A few months later, Gale gave up his grovelling before the Obregón government, and tried another more radical approach. Overestimating his own influence and the radicalism of the Mexican working class, he attempted to instigate a mutiny in the Mexican Army. In August of 1920 a leaflet appeared in army barracks in the Mexico City armory and at the military college addressed to 'Brother Soldiers', and signed by the 'workers', peasants' and soldiers' Soviets'. The leaflet called upon the troops to form soviets in the army, to join with the workers' struggles, and to prepare for the Social Revolution. Gale and comrade Tabler were accused of having written, published and distributed the leaflet,

---

3 Letter from Linn A.E. Gale to Gen. Alvaro Obregón, 17 March 1920, Fondo 11, Serie 030500, Expediente 531, Gav 25, Fondo Obregón, Fideicomiso Calles Torreblanca.
4 Letter from Linn A.E. Gale to Gen. Alvaro Obregón, 17 March 1920, Fondo 11, Serie 030500, Expediente 531, Gav 25, Fondo Obregón, Fideicomiso Calles Torreblanca.

and the police raided Gale's offices. Gale fled to a hacienda in Morelos where he hid out, possibly under the protection of Soto y Gama, the political leader of the Zapatista Agrarian party.[5]

Fearing expulsion and imprisonment in the United States, Gale appealed to Roberto Haberman to get him out of trouble. Haberman arranged for Minister of the Interior Calles to save Gale, at least for the time being, but only at a political price. Gale had to change his line. He had to support the Mexican government, the Labour Party, the CROM, and Morones. Gale's change in political allegiance could be seen almost immediately. The overthrow of Carranza, as already mentioned, was followed by an interim government under Obregón's associate de la Huerta. The September 1920 issue of *Gale's* carried an unsigned article, clearly written by Gale and titled 'Towards Soviets in Mexico', which praised the new Mexican government. 'The [de la Huerta] administration is comparable to one that would result in the United States if the progressive wing of the American Federation of Labor were in control of the government'. Gale even suggested that if the capitalists continued to fight the de la Huerta government, 'It may even result in open espousal of Communism by that government'.[6]

If Gale had been deferential in support of the Carranza government, he was positively cringing before the Sonoran triumvirs. The Mexican regime now appeared in *Gale's* as a labour or socialist government on its way to communism. He praised everything about the new government. In terms of politics, he described the new 'Socialist' majority block in the Mexican Congress, holding 112 out of 185 votes. On the question of agrarian reform, he wrote that, 'The government recently took the initiative in organising a National Agrarian Party whose fundamental principle is the restoration of land to the peasants'. Concerning the economy more generally, Gale reported that, 'The government is quietly encouraging experiments in cooperative production, many of them being conducted by officials themselves'.[7] Mexico now appeared as a social democratic society, or even as a proto-communist utopia. Obregón and Calles found such flattery useful to their image abroad, particularly among American Socialists, English Labourites, and Russian Communists.

Gale's Magazine also found positive things to say about the CROM, portraying its opportunistic and corrupt leader Morones as a Communist. 'One of the

---

5   'Radical and Labor Activities', 29 August 1920, Record Group 165, Box 2290, USMID, USNA. See also: Taibo II 1986, p. 88.

6   Gale, September 1920, p. 2.

7   Gale, September 1920, p. 2.

most striking developments of all in the working class movement here is the shift to the left of the leaders of the ... [CROM]', wrote Gale. 'Today, whipped by the revolutionary impetus of the rank and file in the "Confederation", Luis N. Morones, its moving spirit, and his right-hand men, are out-and-out Bolshevists'.[8] Gale told his readers that the CROM was going to commit itself shortly to the 'overthrow of capitalism', and would apply for admission to the Third International. None of this was true. While Morones sometimes adopted a radical rhetoric, he was certainly no Bolshevik. But after his scare over the 'Brother Soldier' leaflets, Gale found reasons to praise Morones, the CROM, and the Mexican government in virtually every issue of his paper. Gale called himself a Communist and a Wobbly, but he had become an apologist for the capitalist government and the state-supported union federation. Yet his cringing before Obregón's power proved pointless, for the Mexican president had decided to expel the American radicals from Mexico.

Why did Obregón, after only a few months as president, move to oust the slackers? After all, his predecessor Carranza had permitted the radicals to operate in Mexico for three years. What changed the situation and turned Obregón against them? First, Obregón and his Minister of the Interior Calles, and their close associate Morones, were determined to end the decade of revolutionary upheaval that Mexico had endured and to establish a strong state based on stable social institutions. In particular, Obregón and Calles wanted to win the support of the labour unions and peasant leagues for the state, but they faced challenges. The Communist Federation of the Mexican Proletariat (FCPM), which in February 1921 had become the General Confederation of Workers (CGT), was an anarcho-syndicalist labour union based on the principle of 'the separation of the working class and the state'. The CGT represented a major obstacle to the new rulers' plans. The American slackers with their Mexican Communist Party and their Mexican Administration of the Industrial Workers of the World, now played a small but significant role within the syndicalist labour movement. The slackers had ceased to be a mere nuisance and had begun to become a small threat.

Under Carranza, the slackers were useful allies in the struggle against the United States; under Obregón, they appeared as obstacles to the new state's reaching some sort of modus vivendi with the Colossus of the North. Obregón had decided to come to terms with the US government, which had kept almost continual diplomatic and military pressure on Mexico since 1911. He knew that reaching an accommodation with the United States entailed a whole series of

---

8   Gale, November 1920, p. 5.

concessions involving economic and political issues. Expelling the slackers and returning them to the United States for trial and punishment was the simplest and least expensive of the measures, which Obregón had to take to establish some good will the American government.

The complete series of steps by which Obregón tried to reach an accommod-ation with the United States include: 1) the expulsion of the slackers in April and May of 1921; 2) the signing of the de la Huerta-Lamont agreement on the Mexican debt on 16 June 1922; 3) the signing of the Bucareli Accords (Warren-Payne Agreement) on 15 August 1923 dealing with indemnity to be paid to Americans for damages incurred in the course of the Mexican Revolution and also the question of US subsoil property rights in Mexico, that is granting some guarantees to US oil companies.

Obregón basis for action against the American slackers was Article 33 of the Constitution of 1917. That article had a long history: it came almost unaltered from the liberal Constitution of 1857, which copied it from earlier Mexican Con-stitutions.[9] The article simply states that all those not previously defined as Mexican citizens shall be considered foreigners, and that they have the rights guaranteed to Mexican citizens, with the exception that 'the Executive of the Union will have the exclusive power to force to leave the national territory, immediately and without necessity of any previous trial, all foreigners whose continued presence in the country may be deemed inconvenient'. In effect, foreigners could be removed without due process, simply by the president's command. The second and last paragraph of Article 33 defined the principal motive for such expulsions: 'Foreigners shall not, in any way, involve themselves in the political matters of the country'.[10] Although Article 33 was sometimes used to expel criminals, it was not a deportation law; its essential function was political. It was used primarily against foreign-born priests, religious zealots, labour agitators, radicals, anarchists, Communists, or other presumed enemies of the regime. The traditional language used to describe such persons was 'per-nicious foreigners'. Post-revolutionary presidents Francisco I. Madero, Victori-ano Huerta, and Carranza had all used Article 33 to rid themselves of unwanted aliens. So, in 1921 Obregón followed historic precedent when he issued a series of orders for the expulsion of 'pernicious foreigners' under Constitutional Art-icle 33. Among those expelled in this period were Herman Levine and Charles Francis Phillips, but the most famous and celebrated of the deportees was Linn A.E. Gale.

9   Wimer 1996, p. 1.
10   Mexico 1917.

The process of Gale's deportation began on 1 April 1921 when the Inspector General of the Police and the Chief of the Security Commission, carrying out Obregón's order, arrested him in Mexico City. Gale pleaded with the police, telling them, 'I am not an enemy of the Government, or rather only of the ten percent which it lacks to be communist. I combat intervention in my way calling upon the people of the United States, so that by their brotherhood, they may abstain from in any way attacking the people of Mexico'. He showed the policemen letters from former president de la Huerta and the mayor of the Federal District Celestino Gasca, but to no avail. He begged not to be returned to the United States where he was wanted, as he told the policemen, because he was a 'slacker'.[11]

Gale was given his choice of which border of Mexico he chose to be expelled from, and, knowing that criminal charges and jail awaited him in the United States, he picked Guatemala. Obregón obliged and Gale was deported to the town of Ayutla on 2 April. However, the Mexican government informed the Guatemalan government, warning that Gale was 'a dangerous agitator, and that it would be good not to lose sight of him'.[12] Consequently, upon crossing the border, the Guatemalan government had Gale arrested and jailed.

A memorandum to the US Department of State of 7 April 1921, marked 'Secret' and 'Urgent' reported that a reliable source had informed the US government that 'Gale's deportation at Guatemala [was] mere camouflage, engineered by supporters. Gale will be allowed to return to Mexico May 1'. George T. Summerlin, the Chargé d'Affaires of the US Embassy, reported that Mexican Minister of the Interior Calles had helped Gale by advancing him money and giving documents to his friends. But Summerlin's fears proved misplaced. Obregón really did intend to expel Gale, but he was going about it in his own way.

After holding Gale in jail for a week, the Guatemalan government deported him back across the Suchiate River to the Mexican border town of Mariscal, Chiapas. Gale later claimed that it was not the Guatemalan government, which returned him to Mexico, but some 'private parties' perhaps working for the Mexican or US government. In fact, the Guatemalan Foreign Secretary had no record of his deportation, but one account says that he himself secured permission to re-enter Mexico and did so of his own accord.[13]

---

11   Memorandum from A. Arroyo (?), 2 April 1921: in Obregón-Calles, Expediente 421-G-6, AGN.

12   Letter from the office of the Mexican presidency to the government of Guatemala, 4 April 1921, in: Obregón-Calles, Expediente 421-G-2, AGN.

13   Coleman 1921, pp. 86–7.

Upon returning to Mexico, Gale went immediately to see CROM chief Luis N. Morones, the man he had once castigated as the tool of Samuel Gompers. Gale asked Morones to help him by interceding with Obregón. Gale made similar requests to Adolfo de la Huerta, Secretary of the Treasury, to Ezequiel Salcedo, head of the government printing office, to Gen. Antonio Villareal, Minister of Agriculture, and to Celestino Gasca, governor of the Federal District. Supposedly while waiting for those men to intervene with President Obregón, Gale was seized and taken away.[14] His attorney, Walter Holland, claimed that, 'President Obregón ordered the case reopened and was making an investigation when, unknown to him, certain persons kidnapped Mr. and Mrs. Gale and took them to Texas'.[15] Gale claimed that neither Guatemala nor Mexico had deported him, but that in both cases some private party had kidnapped him. But there is no doubt that Obregón had Gale deported to the United States, as many documents testify, including a bill for $180.00 for the shipment of Linn and Magdalena Gale to Laredo, Texas which can be found in the archives of the Secretary of Foreign Relations.[16]

Learning of Gale's probable deportation and transfer to the United States, Secretary of War John W. Weeks sent a letter on 8 April 1921 advising the Secretary of State to have Gale arrested and held at the nearest military base, since the Albany draft board had reported him as a deserter. On 22 April when Mexico deported Gale to the United States at Laredo, Texas, he was immediately arrested and confined at Fort McIntosh.[17] Gale attempted to obtain a writ of habeas corpus while confined in Laredo but failed. Later he was moved to Fort Sam Houston, San Antonio, Texas.

While Gale waited in jail, some of his long-time supporters came to his defence. Elmer Hager, executive secretary of the Socialist Party chapter of Dayton, Ohio wrote to President Álvaro Obregón, criticising the Mexican government for having expelled Gale, since he had opposed US intervention in Mexico.[18] D. Healy of Australia wrote a letter to Obregón that cannot have been very helpful in which he argued that the expulsion of Gale had been 'prompted by the worst enemies of the common people of Mexico'. And, he added,

---

14   Ibid. Though signed by Coleman, this letter was probably written by Gale himself.
15   Letter form Walter Holland to Arthur H. Geissler, US Minister to Guatemala, 6 August 1924, in: RG 59, Box 3764 (1910–1929), 312.1121 – Gale, A. E,, US Dept of State, USNA.
16   'Expulsión de Linn, A.E. Gale y esposa. Gastos', Expediente 27-3-35, SRE.
17   Series of memoranda and letters RG 59 (1910–1929) Box 3764, file 312.11.21 Gale, A.E., US Dept, of State, USNA.
18   Letter from Elmer Hager to Alvaro Obregón in: Galleria Obregón-Calles, Expediente, 707-D-5, AGN.

'It would appear that your government has become the agent of the financiers of New York, who have conspired against the liberty of the Mexican people
almost since Mexico became a nation'.[19] His friends' insults and radical rhetoric
are unlikely to have helped Gale's cause.

The Crusader, the African American socialist magazine in the United States,
also came to Gale's aid. An article by George D. Coleman, announced that, 'Linn
Gale Needs Your Help, Comrade!' However, both the content and the style of the
article suggested that Gale may have written the piece. The author charged that
'the petroleum magnates' and the 'pro-intervention forces' were behind Gale's
arrest. 'Back of the prosecution lurk all the sinister forces that these many years
have tried to annex the southern republic and spend the blood and bodies of
American soldier boys to do it'. The author claimed that, 'The reason for the persecution of Gale may be summed up in one significant word – intervention ....
Gale stood in the way of interventionists and Gale must go'.[20]

From his Texan jail, Gale lashed out at the Mexican government of Obregón,
which had deported him. E.D. Ruíz, the Mexican Consul in San Antonio, Texas,
reported to President Obregón that Gale had attacked the Mexican government and was providing potentially damaging information to the US authorities. Ruíz wrote, 'Gale, against whom Article 33 had recently been applied', had
given detailed information about 'the present government of Mexico and its
men'.

> As was to be expected, he talked in a very derogatory way about the
> highest authorities of our country, because he harbors a deep resentment
> for having been forced to leave Mexico, showing a special anger against
> General Calles [Obregón's Minister of the Interior], and assuring that both
> you [Obregón] and he [Calles] had in your possession red cards issued
> by the Third International of Moscow, identifying you as active members
> of that Bolshevik group. He promised to get a photograph of these cards
> in order to turn them over to the Federal authorities of this country [i.e.,
> the United States]. I can't know how seriously the federal authorities have
> taken the statements of this individual, but I do know that they were for-
> warded to Washington.[21]

---

19   Letter from D. Healy to President Obregón, in: Galleria Obregón-Calles, Expediente 421-
      G-2, AGN.
20   Coleman, July 1921, pp. 86–7.
21   Letter of E.D. Ruíz to President Obregón, 8 May 1921, in Galleria Calles-Obregón, Expedi-
      ente 429-S-l, AGN.

Even if Gale could or did document that there existed some sort of Communist International membership cards in the names of the Mexican president and minister, the claim that Obregón and Calles were members of the Third International was preposterous. Gale must also have known that providing information – whether true or false – that Obregón and Calles had any connection with the Communist International would have strengthened the hand of the most reactionary elements in the US government. But it soon became clear, that he was willing to do anything to save his skin.

The American Civil Liberties Union (ACLU) later made a public statement criticising Gale for giving information on radicals to the government. The ACLU sent a letter to Gale's attorney Samuel M. Castleton of Atlanta complaining that 'when Gale left the United States in 1917 he jumped bond in a criminal case then pending against him in New York City, and although he posed as a radical in Mexico City he has since not only renounced his radical views but offered to give the government incriminating information about others'.[22] In fact Gale had behaved in a manner even more craven and treacherous than the ACLU and other critics realised.

While held at Laredo and San Antonio, and no doubt terrified by the prospect of prison, Gale had caved in completely. He later confessed, 'At Laredo and San Antonio I turned over to the Department of Justice and the Section of Military Intelligence some 30 pages of typewritten matter relating to Mexico – information about radicals and "slackers" there, notes on the characteristics of members of Obregón's cabinet, and other matters I believed would be of some use to the [US] Government'.[23] Later, Gale was taken from Fort Sam Houston in San Antonio, Texas and confined at Governor's Island in New York City to await trial.

Awaiting trial, Gale completely repudiated his Communist credo and appealed to some of the most reactionary figures in the US government – Secretary of the Interior Albert Bacon Fall, Attorney General Harry M. Daugherty, and Postmaster General and Chairman of the Republican Party Will H. Hays – to intervene on his behalf. He also sent a letter to the editor of the *Marion Star*, the hometown newspaper of President Warren G. Harding, in which he wrote, 'I concluded some months ago that radicalism and "revolution" are not the remedies for our social ills'. Rather, wrote Gale, 'a sane, broad-minded Americanism is the key to the problems of the nation. I am today an evolutionist, not a "revolutionist"'. While holding fast to his criticism of Woodrow Wilson, Gale

---

22		ACLU letter cited in article, 'Did Gale Offer to Turn State [*sic*] Evidence?' in: *Industrial Solidarity*, 1 October 1921, p. 3.

23		Letter to Editor, *Marion Star* (Marion, Ohio), from Linn A.E. Gale, 16 September 1921, in: File no. 200655, US Department of Justice, USNA.

embraced the notoriously corrupt and reactionary Harding administration as 'wise, fair, business-like and eminently just'. Via his letter to the editor, Gale proposed, 'Continuing to furnish information about Mexico, radicalism in Mexico, radicalism in the United States, etc. giving such information in fullest and frankest detail'. He also suggested that the government help him re-establish his magazine so that he could urge his readers, friends, and followers to support the Harding administration of which he now so emphatically approved, though, as he wrote, 'I consider myself an independent Democrat'. He would be willing, he said, while publishing his newspaper to live with his wife under constant surveillance in Washington, D.C.

In his lengthy letter to the editor of the *Marion Star*, Gale included an outline of a proposed series of articles on Mexican Bolshevism. The articles would not only attack the Mexican Communists and the Mexican government, but he concluded that an 'American protectorate [is] probably the solution, eventually, but the situation depends on the Mexicans.'[24] As a slacker had prided himself on his opposition to intervention; now he called for the United States to turn Mexico into a virtual colony. More than just a personal surrender to his enemies, his behaviour expressed a complete moral collapse, an ignominious capitulation of all his former beliefs and values.

Gale even went so far as to write a Whitmanesque poem titled 'Our America, Home of the Super-Civilization', in which he repudiated radicalism and embraced Americanism in free verse:

> Wise men with steady hands, clear eyes, great hearts, are at the Nation's
>   head ...
> Let us support and sustain them, comrades.
> Hymns of hate, calls to 'revolution', incitements to the 'class struggle',
>   schemings
> to establish the 'dictatorship of the proletariat', – Away with them.
> Constructive cooperation, earnest effort, steady building of the Super-
>   Civilization of these United States of ours –
> These we conceive, affirm, realise, establish.[25]

Magdalena Gale, who wanted to get her husband out of jail, wrote letters to Attorney General Daugherty pleading for consideration for Gale. She asked

---

24   Suggested Outline for Series of Articles on Mexican Bolshevism, in: File No. 200655, US Department of Justice, USNA.

25   'Our America, Home of the Super-Civilization', in: File No. 200655, US Department of Justice, USNA.

Daugherty, 'why can't he be transferred to the barracks in Washington, where he will be near enough to you officials to prove his sincerity in renouncing radicalism and his usefulness to the government?'[26] In one letter, she wrote, no doubt completely sincerely, 'As I told Sec. Fall, if I were to spend the rest of my days in a hovel with Linn Gale, I should consider myself in Seventh Heaven. With him I can do and stand anything, but without him I simply cannot live'.[27]

But despite the Gales' pleading, the government went ahead with the court martial proceedings which opened on Governor's Island on 17 October 1921 with Col. Louis R. Burgess sitting as president of the court. Captain Joseph Cromwell, Judge Advocate charged Gale with violating Articles of War 58, 62, and 96, accusing him of being a draft evader and a deserter, with encouraging resistance to the draft and of glorifying desertion from the military, as well as with publishing or causing to be published articles attacking President Wilson and members of the Wilson administration during the war. In particular Gale was charged with writing a poem that was 'contemptuous and disrespectful of the president'. The trial, something of a minor political sensation, was covered for several days in *The New York Times*.

Gale was represented by New York attorney Peter P. McElligott as his civilian counsel, and by Major Thomas L. Crystal and Captain Charles F.F. Cooper of the US Army Infantry as his military counsel. The defence concentrated on events surrounding his draft board medical examination. Dr. James F. Rooney of Local Board No. 3 in Albany told the court that he had had Gale examined by examiners for two different local boards and had excused him twice before finally qualifying him for induction. However, Rooney also revealed in direct and cross-examination that Gale had been declared 'pre-tubercular' by Dr. Cudmore, physician for a New York City draft board. The defence called Dr. John Cudmore who appeared to identify the report of the army medical examiner indicating that Gale was pre-tubercular. Dr. George E. Reilby, a medical examiner for the Mutual Life Insurance Company said that he had rejected Gale as an applicant for health insurance in April of 1917. The implication was that Gale had been found unfit, not only by the board examiners but also by a private insurance company and clearly should not have been drafted.

McElligott also read a letter by Gale to the local draft board in which he claimed that because he worked for Democrat Martin Glynn, that his Repub-

---

26   Letter from Magdalena Gale to Attorney General Daugherty, 23 September 1921, in: File No. 200655, US Department of Justice, USNA.

27   Letter of Magdalena Gale to Attorney General Daugherty, 13 August 1921, in: File No. 200655, US Department of Justice, USNA.

lican opponent '[Charles S.] Whitman and some of his friends were out to get him', and that they had worked to see that would be drafted in spite of his pre-tubercular condition. The trial continued behind closed doors. On the fourth day the government introduced into evidence the very information that Gale had provided concerning the activities of radicals in Mexico. His defence attorneys stipulated that Gale had not been informed of his rights, suggesting that the information was not legitimately obtained and was self-incriminating. At the same time, Gale's military defence attorney, Major Crystal, told the court, 'It seems that Gale was pretty nearly an agent of either the military intelligence or the Department of Justice'. While this may have been calculated to save Gale from prison by showing that he had been working in the service of the government, it does not appear to have been true and it also served to destroy whatever remained of Gale's reputation as a radical.

Gale produced several character witnesses. His defence called State Senator Samuel A. Jones who told the court that he had known him since the draft dodger was ten years old. And, he said, Gale had been admired as a newspaperman when Jones served first as an assemblyman and later as a Senator. Jones suggested to the court that 'Mr. Gale's actions may be considered the acts of a man suffering under a misapprehension and guided by wrong advice – that there must have been a screw loose somewhere'. But the Military Court had already decided to exclude any testimony regarding Gale's mental health and therefore the trial president told Senator Jones to step down.

Gale also produced other character witnesses: Sophie Treadwell, a feature writer for a New York daily, and Dr. Horatio M. Polack, a state statistician. Polack, also the editor of the publications of the state hospital commission, testified that he had known Gale, for many years, having first met him in church and later having known him in the Rensselaer Chamber of Commerce, as well as in the Amsterdam Board of Trade and the Albany Civil League. If Gale's witnesses were to be believed, he had always been a church-going, money-grubbing, Democratic Party machine politician, driven half crazy by the Republican Party opposition. He was a sick man unjustly drafted, who to escape his many persecutors fled to Mexico and fell in with a bad crowd. He deserved leniency and possibly even commendation for having recognised the error of his ways, repudiated radicalism, and embraced Republicanism.

Gale's arguments and witnesses were not convincing to the military court. On 28 October, 11 days after the trial had begun, Gale was convicted of all the charges – draft evasion, desertion, encouraging evasion and desertion, and publishing seditious materials – and sentenced to seven years of hard labour at Leavenworth Federal Penitentiary, with the possibility of parole after two years and three months.[28] Gale still hoped that President Harding might include him in a general amnesty for political prisoners, but he did not. Gale went to Leavenworth, where, naturally, he worked in the library and on the prison newspaper.

While Gale was the most notorious of the American radicals who were expelled, he was not alone. The Communists' role in the May Day demonstrations of 1921 in Mexico City and Morelia provided the justification for the government's expulsion of several other foreign agitators. In Mexico City, the Communists had run up the red flag over the Cathedral, while in Morelia they had engaged in similar radical demonstrations that had outraged Michoacán's conservative landlords and religious leaders. On 13 May, President Obregón ordered the deportation of ten more foreign radicals under the Mexican Constitution's Article 33. The list included: José Rubio and Sebastián San Vicente, Spaniards; Natacha Mihailowa, a Polish citizen; José Allen, who supposedly claimed both Mexican and US citizenship, and who unbeknownst to the Mexican government was a spy for the United States Military Intelligence Division; Jorge Sánchez, a Colombian; Karl Limon, a German anarchist; three US citizens, Charles Francis Phillips, Walter Foertmeyer, and A. Sortmary; as well as the supposed Russian agent M. Paley, who in actuality was the US citizen Herman Levine.

Levine was captured and deported two weeks later, on 25 May 1921.[29] He either revealed his citizenship or it was discovered, for the *Washington Post* carried the news of Levine's detention to the public in a story date-lined Laredo, Texas, 27 May 1921:

> Herman M. [*sic*] Levine, of New York City, who fled to Mexico in 1918 and is alleged to have engaged in radical activities there, was deported Wednesday from Monterrey, where he was arrested last week. He was immediately taken in charge by military authorities here and is being held at Fort McIntosh.[30]

---

28   A running account of the trial can be found in *The New York Times*: 'Linn Gale, Writer, Faces Army Court', 18 October 1921; 'Army Court Stops Speech By Senator', 25 October 1921; 'Tilt Over Evidence in Gale Army Trial', 26 October 1921; 'Testify in Gale's Defense', 27 October 1921; 'Gale is Convicted by Military Court', 29 October 1921.

29   Letter from Matthew C. Smith, Col., General Staff, Chief, Negative Branch to W.L. Hurley, Office of the Under-Secretary, Department of State, 28 May 1921; Memorandum for file dated 27 May 1921 regarding phone call from Mr. Hoover to USMID. Both in Box 2292, Record Group 165, USMED, USNA.

30   'Mexico Deports Radicals; Herman M. Levine, of New York Returned to the United States', *Washington Post*, 27 May 1921. Clipping in Box 2291, Record Group 165, USMID, USNA.

The US government's General Intelligence Bulletin No. 53 for 5 June 1921 reported that Levine's 'case will be presented to the Grand Jury for indictment as
a slacker'.[31] After this point, Levine disappears from the records, but what an
experience Levine had had since the day four years before when he decided to
resist the draft. The war and the draft forced him to give up his freedom, his
profession, and his country, and led him to become a political exile in Mexico. While Levine remained a radical, the war also caused him to abandon his
political party, the Socialists, and led him to adopt the revolutionary syndicalist
ideology of the Industrial Workers of the World. As a Wobbly, Levine edited the
union's newspaper in Tampico where he also became one of its leading spir-
its. Of all the American slackers, Levine was perhaps the only one who really
threw himself shoulder-to-shoulder into the organisation of ordinary Mexican
workers in an attempt to bring about a new industrial and economic order.
For a brief period, Levine and his IWW 'fellow workers' had led thousands of
Tampico's oil port workers in a mass movement involving strikes that paralysed
shipping, challenged the employers, and troubled Mexico, the United States,
and Great Britain. Levine had cooperated with Phillips and the other founders
of the Mexican Communist Party and Levine himself appears to have become a
Communist. Like other radicals in Mexico at the time, Levine signed his letters
'Salud y Revolución Social', that is, 'Health and Social Revolution', and he added
in English and with that characteristic Wobbly American accent, 'May it come
damn quick'. Unfortunately for Levine, it did not come.

Whatever happened to Levine? We do not know, but a cross-reference in the
card index of the US Military Intelligence Division files mentions a Herman
Levine who was active in June 1932 in the executive councils of various veterans' organisations and was a bonus marcher. Could that have been the Levine
who led oil workers in Tampico during the years of the World War and the Mexican Revolution? We cannot be sure that this is the same man, but it might well
have been.

Charles Francis Phillips was also supposed to have been deported. The police
arrested him in May of 1921 and took him to Manzanillo to await shipment to
the United States. But Phillips's wife, Natalia, called some friends in the anarchist labour union, the CGT. The CGT union men went to Obregón and pleaded
that their comrade not be returned to the United States where he would be
imprisoned. Obregón relented and had the Spanish revolutionary San Vicente,
Phillips, and Natalia deported to Guatemala.[32]

---

31   Memorandum for file, undated by citing General Intelligence Bulletin No. 53 for 4 June
     1921, Box 2292, Record Group 165, USMID, USNA.
32   Paley/Levine to Seaman/Phillips, undated letter in Box 2292, Record Group 165, USMID,
     USNA.

Phillips decided that he might as well turn his misfortune to good purpose by trying to organise a Communist Party of Guatemala. He and San Vicente attempted to make contact with local radicals, worked on organising a waiters' union, and even attempted to organise some Quiché-speaking Indian teamsters. All of these efforts came to nought, and after about a month they gave up on trying to organise the Guatemalans and decided to return to Mexico. One of the waiters provided Phillips with a birth certificate, and the American slacker changed his name again, this time to Manuel Gómez, a pseudonym he would use for the next ten years. Using that identification Phillips and Natalia married again – Phillips thus became a bigamist again – and with the false birth certificate and the new marriage license they succeeded in getting passports so they could return to Mexico. Back in Mexico City, Phillips could no longer engage in public political activity, so he slipped underground and continued to edit the Communist Party newspaper. As already mentioned, Phillips was the one slacker who had really become a Communist International cadre capable of building a real Communist Party, and he would stay on in Mexico to attempt to do so.

Roberto Haberman claimed that he had been responsible for the expulsion of the American slackers. In 1921, Haberman visited the United States as Luis Morones's representative to Samuel Gompers, head of the American Federation of Labor. Accompanied by E.C. Davison of the International Association of Machinists (IAM), Haberman also paid a visit to J. Edgar Hoover, then number-two man at the Bureau of Investigation.[33] In that meeting, Haberman claimed responsibility for the expulsion of American slackers from Mexico. Haberman told Hoover he wanted help in suppressing the Communists in both Mexico and the United States. As Hoover reported:

> He [Haberman] claims to have been directly responsible for deportation by Obregón of some of the leading Mexican radicals. He stated that GOM-PERS, MORONES, and himself have been subjected for many months to violent verbal assaults by the communists in Mexico, to which they paid little or no attention until direct evidence was obtained that these communists had voted upon a course of action for the purpose of assassinating the leading Pan-American labour leaders.[34]

33　Only later was the name changed to the Federal Bureau of Investigation, of which Hoover became the head.

34　FBI materials obtained under FOIA, Letter of J. Edgar Hoover, 2 August 1921.

There is no evidence that the Mexican Communist Party engaged in political assassination in the 1920s or had made any such plan. Haberman's remarks seem to be a ploy intended to get the US government's domestic intelligence agency to help the CROM and the Mexican government in repressing the Communists. Haberman may have had a hand in Obregón's expulsion of Gale, Levine, Phillips, and the others, but he appears to have been changing the story to appeal to Hoover.

1   A Mexican Reaction to the Expulsion of the Slackers

What was the Mexican reaction to the expulsion of the slackers? One of Mexico's outstanding intellectuals commented on the deportation of the foreign radicals and gave full support to the government of President Obregón. Manuel Gamio, who had studied with Franz Boas at Columbia University at the beginning of the century, had become Mexico's leading archaeologist and anthropologist. His book *Forjando Patria* (Forging a Fatherland) made him one of the principal ideologues of post- revolutionary Mexican nationalism.

The introduction to his famous archaeological study *La Población del valle de Teotihuacán* (The Population of the Valley of Teotihuacán) touched on the question of socialism, and particularly of Bolshevism or Communism and its meaning for Mexico and its peasant majority. Gamio derided the Communists as 'absolutely ignorant' and disdainful of the rural indigenous classes. He opposed any 'attempt to carry out the implantation of the soviet [system] in Mexico, since this, instead of bringing with it the economic and intellectual improvement of the indigenous masses, will only exacerbate their misery and will make their enslavement more difficult to bear'.[35]

Having anathematised the Bolsheviks as enemies of Mexico's Indian peasant majority, Gamio then turned to the matter of Obregón's recent expulsion of the foreign leaders and repression of the domestic activists of the Mexican Communist Party.

> Are there, amongst us, exotic Bolsheviks who endorse and preach the destruction of the foreign capital invested in Mexico, which would bring about instantly not only foreign intervention, but the dismemberment of the Republic and the definitive loss of our nationality? If such persons exist, then they should be eliminated or locked up for their insanity or for

---

35   Gamio 1922, cited in Comas 1975, pp. 40–6.

their treason to the fatherland. When in an unknown future the soviet is established in Washington, in Paris or in London, it will happen in just the same way automatically in Mexico; meanwhile, it is necessary to continue walking sensibly and carefully along the difficult social and international path which is ours.[36]

With this argument, Gamio, one of Mexico's leading intellectuals and advocate of revolutionary nationalism, gave his unhesitating, uncritical, and unconditional approval to President Obregón for his repression of the Communists and his expulsion of the American slackers and other foreign radicals – the 'exotic Bolsheviks'. Yet, Gamio's strident attack on the Communists was unfounded. In fact, the Mexican Bolsheviks had taken an interest in the indigenous peoples and the peasant and had linked up with three of the outstanding peasant leaders of Mexico: Felipe Carrillo Puerto of the Yucatan, Úrsulo Galván of Veracruz and Primo Tapia of Michoacán. Tapia, for example, as we have seen, led a mass movement of Tarascan or Purépecha Indians in a regional struggle for the redistribution of land. Throughout the later 1920s and into the 1930s, Communists would become important leaders of peasant movements.

2   The American Slackers and the Left

What was the significance of the impact of the American slackers of 1917 on the Mexican left and labour movement? What was the importance of the Mexican Communist Party (PCM), the party affiliated with the Communist International, that they organised? Historian Paco Ignacio Taibo II argues that having been chosen in a secret meeting, by a minority of the national committee of the Socialist Party, the new Mexican Communist Party was just a small sect.[37] But, if the PCM was a sect, it was also a remarkably capable little organisation. The new Communist party, the PCM, as historian Barry Carr observes, 'quickly achieved a significant (although sometimes short-lived) presence among several important segments of the urban, and especially peasant, population as well as among vanguard artists and intellectuals'.[38] Between the spring of 1917 when they arrived and the spring of 1921 when several of them were expelled, the slackers organised the Mexican Communist Party and

36   Manuel Gamio 1992, cited in Gamio 1975, pp. 40–6.
37   Taibo 1986, p. 56.
38   Carr 1992, p. 28.

strengthened the Industrial Workers of the World, established contact with important groups of textile workers and miners, formed the Feminist Council, and recruited leaders of the two most important peasant organisations in Mexico, those of the states of Michoacán and Veracruz. While these were small and short-lived, they were significant, though ultimately the slacker failed to create the kind of Communist Party and the mass socialist movement they strove for.

Why did they fail? There were several reasons. The American slackers' attempts to found a Communist Party in Mexico failed to find a mass following in society except in a few areas. Why was this the case? The most important reason, no doubt, was because Mexico was predominantly a rural and agricultural country which had been devastated by a ten-year civil war in which a million people had been killed and hundreds of thousands had fled for refuge into the United States. It was a country with few roads into the thousands of villages isolated in valleys throughout a country that was 80 percent mountainous. The industrial working class of Mexico numbered tens of thousands of mining, railroad, oil, and textile workers as well as urban electrical and streetcar workers in large cities like Mexico, Monterrey, and Guadalajara. But it constituted only about 10 percent of the population. Yet, where the working class existed, the Mexican Communist found various ways to reach and attempted to organise it.

Additionally, the American slackers' strategy of organising a Communist Party by working within the small Socialist Party may have been a mistake. The American exiles own experience in the United States had been in the Socialist Party. Consequently, they attempted to follow the northern European and American model of organising within the Socialist Parties and then either winning them over or splitting off the left wing. The problem was that Mexico's dominant radical labour tradition, like that of southern Europe, was anarchist or anarcho-syndicalist. The Socialist Party of Mexico was tiny – '*los cinco gatos*' (just five cats) as they themselves said – amd at least in 1917 had little following outside of a few workers in Mexico City and Toluca. With a membership of at most a few score, it became even smaller with the divisions between the two American slacker groups. Perhaps the slackers would have been more successful had they initially worked through the anarcho-syndicalist movement with which they later came in contact through the Industrial Workers of the World.

Though they followed events in Europe and Russia closely, and though they had studied the documents of Bolsheviks such as Lenin and Trotsky, the American slackers had little practical understanding of the nature of the Bolshevik Party. Even Borodin's tutelage could not overcome their serious lack of experience. Victor Serge, the famous European revolutionary and author, observed in his autobiography that in 1919 and 1920 in Europe, 'To tell the truth, outside

Russia and perhaps Bulgaria, there were no real Communists anywhere in the world'.[39] If that was true of Europe, it was even truer of the situation in Latin America and particularly in peasant, anarchist Mexico. The attempt to create a Communist movement represented a leap of faith. Communism represented a revolutionary theory, method, and organisation outside the ken of the American and Mexican organisers of the Mexican Communist Party.

Then too, the moment was not propitious. The attempt of the American slackers to found a Mexican Communist Party coincided almost exactly with the fall of Carranza who had been their patron and protector. Carranza had seen the slackers as useful in discrediting the United States' war policy and in creating ties to US socialist, labour, and liberal peace organisations. His policy toward the American war resisters was shared and carried out by his subordinates such as Manuel Aguirre Berlanga and General Salvador Alvarado who also acted as patrons of American slackers.

When Carranza fell in 1919 and General Álvaro Obregón came to power, the American slackers who had established the Mexican Communist Party found that the situation had changed dramatically. The Sonoran triumvirs, Obregón, de la Huerta and Calles, quickly decided that their regime depended on stable and peaceful relations with the United States and therefore on the resolution of a number of outstanding differences with the American government on questions such as reparations to US citizens for damages from the Mexican Revolution, the settlement of Mexico's debts to American and other foreign banks, and a resolution of the rights of foreign companies to Mexican oil. Their decision to reach an agreement with the United States directly precipitated the expulsion of the American slacker radicals.

The Sonorans also decided that their regime's stability depended upon an alliance with politically reliable labour and peasant organisations. In the area of labour, this meant cementing a relationship with the more opportunist wing of the Mexican labour movement, namely, with Luis N. Morones, head of the Regional Confederation of Mexican Workers (CROM), and of the Labour Party (PL). The Mexican state's close relationship with the CROM and the PL necessarily involved a determined effort to crush the left-wing labour movement made up of the anarchists, the Communists, and the Industrial Workers of the World.

Though it does not seem to have been the principal factor, the Mexican Communist Party was also vulnerable because it was under the constant surveillance of the US Military Intelligence Division, and the spy José Allen, who had been chosen as the general secretary of the party. While Allen was not

---

39   Serge 1984, p. 104.

primarily an agent provocateur, he does seem to have exacerbated differences between the PCM and Linn A.E. Gale and his rival Communist Party of Mexico (PC de M), leading to conflicts which only tended to discredit the small Communist movement in the eyes of other radicals, workers and peasants. At the same time, Roberto Haberman kept Morones, Calles and Obregón informed about the activities of the Communists and other leftists.

Another important factor in the failings of the Communist Party was its foreign origin. It was largely foreigners, the American slackers Gale and Phillips, the Indian M.N. Roy, and the Russian Borodin, who had founded the PCM. While the Mexican unions and leftists tended to be accepting of the aliens, their hospitality could not overcome the foreigners' own weaknesses. In their propaganda, the foreign leadership of the Mexican Communist Party tended to emphasise the largest, broadest, and most abstract ideas of the Bolshevik Party and the Communist International – the revolutionary party, the soviets, and later the united front – with less understanding of how to apply those ideas to the particularities of Mexican history, society, and culture.

The American slacker Communists remarkably succeeded in recruiting two of the most important peasant leaders, Primo Tapia in Michoacán and Úrsulo Galván in Veracruz, but the Communists did not seem to fully understand the powerful and sophisticated role being played by the new Mexican revolutionary nationalist government. The slackers and the other Communists did not fully grasp the way in which the leaders of worker and peasant movements with whom they worked often had complicated ties to military generals, government officials, and ultimately to the new state. While trying to weave their own revolutionary movement, they sometimes found themselves ensnared in the net being woven by the new revolutionary nationalist government.

Obregón's expulsions of the American slackers in 1921, together with greater repression of leftists in the Mexican labour movement, ended a brief but important period of the Mexican left. As it happened, Obregón's deportation of the World War I exiles coincided with the arrival of another group, some of them also former war resisters, who had become Communists in the United States and who now arrived in Mexico to continue the organisation of the Mexican Communist Party.

CHAPTER 15

The Communist International Agents in Mexico: Louis Fraina and Sen Katayama

The World War I slackers were the first of two groups of American radicals who became involved in organising the Communist Party in Mexico in the period between 1917 and 1927. Just as the leading figures of the first group – Linn Gale, Herman Levine, and Charles Francis Phillips – were in the process of being expelled from Mexico, a second group arrived. While this later group of leftists – Louis Fraina, Sen Katayama, and Bertram D. Wolfe – had not been exiled in Mexico during the war, they shared many of the characteristics of the slackers. They had also been socialists and anti-war activists and they too had become Communists under the impact of the Russian Revolution. Phillips, who, as discussed in the previous chapter, had succeeded in returning to Mexico following his expulsion, provided the continuity between the two groups. Phillips, who had helped to found the Mexican Communist Party and had become a cadre of the Communist International, had after his deportation, returned to Mexico to collaborate with Fraina and Katayama and later also worked with Wolfe.

These Communists differed considerably from romantic slacker Communists like the young Phillips and Herman Levine. All of these men in both groups shared common political ideals, though it is clear that the Communist International and the Communist Party had begun to change in the period of the mid-1920s, and what was a radical movement of iconoclasts and rebels began to be transformed under the influence of Grigori Zinoviev and his 'Bolshevisation' campaign into an organisation of centrally directed professional political operatives. 'The Fifth Comintern Congress, held in June–July 1924', writes Joel Geier, 'formed the bridge between the four revolutionary congresses of 1919–1922 and the Sixth Congress of 1928, which consolidated Stalin's unchallenged sway'.[1] As Geier writes:

> The purpose of the [Fifth] Congress – which has gone down in history as the 'Bolshevization Congress' – was to change the policies and internal structures of the other [Communist] parties to make them subservient to the Russian [Communist] party. The primary idea, unanimously accep-

---

1 Geier 2014.

ted, was that the Russian party was the only truly Bolshevik (that is, revolutionary) party and therefore all other parties had to be loyal and subordinate to it. The prestige of the Russian Revolution, particularly after the failure of other revolutions, made this easier for leading Communists to accept. Until then, though the Russian leaders had great authority, it was based on political persuasion and the confidence its own ideas and experience inspired in others. Now its authority could not be questioned. In the future every party was expected to carry out instructions from the Russian party, in reality from its Politburo.[2]

The Japanese Communist Sen Katayama was one of those present at the Fifth Congress where, like others, he pledged to follow the Russian Bolsheviks. As he told the Congress, 'I am against the leadership of the world revolution by any other party in the Comintern besides the Russian party'.

Zinoviev drew the conclusion: 'The Comintern must be monolithic ... There can be no question that the right wingers will continue to act as before and actually become a faction. The Communist International will not allow this ... Bolshevization means the formation of a strongly cemented, monolithic, centralized organization which in a friendly and brotherly manner, eradicates all differences in its ranks'. There was no opposition whatsoever to Zinoviev's redefinition of the Comintern as a monolithic international.[3]

Factions had already been banned in the Russian Communist Party and now they would be banned in the Communist International as well.[4]

The fight for succession in the Russian Party following the death of Lenin in 1924, led the Comintern leaders, Zinoviev, Lev Kamenev, and Joseph Stalin (known as the Triumvirate or the Troika) to use the Bolshevisation campaign as a weapon against Leon Trotsky and against the memory of Rosa Luxemburg, who were defined as rightists. Phillips, Katayama, and Fraina, who were the three foreigners designated to lead the Mexican Communist Party, arrived before the Bolshevisation campaign had begun. But already the practice of Russian domination existed in practice.

---

2 Ibid.
3 Ibid.
4 Bolshevisation also affected in the same way the Communist Party of America, which was supposed to look after the Mexican Communist Party. Zumoff 2014, *passim*.

The stories of Fraina, Katayama and Wolfe represent then this second stage of the Comintern and of the American revolutionary socialist presence in Mexico and complete the history of the American revolutionaries in the Mexican labour movement between 1917 and 1927, after which an entirely new period begins, the period of Joseph Stalin's ascendancy and dominance of the Soviet state and the Communist International.

Unlike the slackers who founded the Mexican Communist Party, who had come on their own initiative, the Communist International sent Fraina and Katayama to Mexico. Their assignment was to re-organise the Mexican Communist Party, found a Communist Pan-American Bureau for the entire Latin American region, and to establish in Latin America the Red International of Labour Unions (RILU), the Communists' alternative to the Amsterdam or so-called 'Yellow' or reformist International of trade unions. The plan was to strengthen the Mexican CP and to found new national Communist Parties connected to and led by the Communist International in Moscow. The International would then coordinate the various national Communist parties and their joint efforts in regions such as North America. The US and Mexican Communist Parties might also secondarily have direct connections with each other, but always under the direction of the International through what was called the American Agency responsible for all of the Americas and headed by Karl Jansen who was based in Canada and the United States.[5] The idea of a direct connection between American and Mexican leftists groups, either labour union organisations or individuals outside of the Communist International and the RILU played little, if any, role in their thinking.

Katayama, who had been born in Japan and had lived in the United States and Russia, was an indefatigable worker whose activities produced small but significant results. Fraina's role in Mexico is more difficult to determine, and his brief stay would ultimately prove to be a personal and political disaster. Nevertheless, during the less than a year that they were in Mexico, Fraina and Katayama rebuilt the small Communist Party, although when both suddenly left, that infrastructure was weakened or even collapsed. To appreciate how and why these men came to be in Mexico, it is important to explore their previous roles in the labour and socialist movement.

---

5 Spenser 2007, pp. 151–70.

1   Louis Fraina, Revolutionary Intellectual

Born Luigi Carlo Fraina in Galdo, Salerno, Italy on 7 October 1892, Louis Fraina emigrated to the United States with his family at the age of five. An outstanding student, he won prizes in writing and speaking and graduated class valedictorian of his elementary school at age 13. When his father died in 1908, Louis became the 'head of the family', as his mother put it, and quit school to work for the Edison electric company.

At the age of 17, Fraina joined the Socialist Party of America (SPA), but soon rejected its reformist practice and lack of theoretical rigour. He found both the Marxist theory and the revolutionary perspective he was looking for in Daniel De Leon's Socialist Labour Party (SLP), and soon took a place on the staff of its newspaper *The Daily People*. As a reporter for the paper, between 1910 and 1912 he covered the Pressed Steel Car Company strike in McKees Rocks, Pennsylvania and the textile strike in Lawrence, Massachusetts. Thrilled by the Lawrence strike where immigrants from several nations united, Fraina wrote, 'Would that all the proletariat of America were "foreigners"'.[6]

Though the Lawrence strike collapsed, still socialism seemed to be on the rise. Eugene Debs, the Socialist Party's presidential candidate in 1912, won nearly one million votes and helped to put hundreds of socialists in local elected offices across the country. Impressed by his success, Fraina argued that the Socialist Labour Party should join the growing Socialist Party both to save and to transform it. But the SLP leadership rejected his proposal, and then passed over Fraina in 1913 when they chose Arnold Peterson to succeed the aging and failing De Leon as head of the SLP. A year later Daniel De Leon died, and the *Daily People* folded, but by that time Fraina himself had left the group.

Fraina searched for a political alternative and with his enthusiasm for the recent strike wave, it is not surprising that, as autobiographical notes suggest, he joined the Industrial Workers of the World (IWW). But he only stayed in the syndicalist union for about six months, a leaving because it ultimately proved unsatisfying for him, since the IWW did not share his notion of the importance of revolutionary theory and of politics.[7] In any case, he never played any significant role in the organisation.

---

6   Buhle 1995. See also: Lewis Corey [Louis Fraina] papers, Columbia University, Box 2, Folder 3, 'Outline for Autobiography', 1953; and Esther Corey 1963, pp. 103–31; Klehr 1977, pp. 249–56. Citation from Buhle 1995, p. 12.

7   Lewis Corey papers, Box 2, Folder 3, 'Outline for Autobiography', 1953, Columbia University.

To earn a living, Fraina took a job as the editor of *Modern Dance*, where he became an authority on contemporary music and dance and developed a radical aesthetics. He was also a member of the editorial board of *The New Review*, a leftist magazine founded in 1913 that expressed both the culture of artistic and literary modernism associated with *The Masses* and also the views of 'the new intellectuals' who appeared in the American socialist movement after 1912. *The New Review* quickly became a vehicle for the left wing of the Socialist Party and developed a political programme of revolutionary socialism, anti-imperialism, and militant industrial unionism.

While on the editorial board of *The New Review* Fraina made his first attempts to understand the US role in Latin America and the revolution then taking place in Mexico. He supported Mexico's right to self-determination and from afar critically supported the revolutionary government of Carranza. The nationalism of political or economic colonial peoples, argued Fraina, was different from that of imperialist nations.[8] The positions that Fraina worked out in *The New Review*, which paralleled those of Lenin, formed the basis for his understanding when he went to Mexico in 1921 as a representative of the Communist International.

By early 1917, even before the Bolsheviks had taken power, Fraina had become a supporter of Lenin and the Bolsheviks in Russia. Working with the Socialist Party's Russian language federation, Fraina became the editor of a series of ephemeral but politically important revolutionary publications, among them *The New International*, *Revolutionary Age*, and *Class Struggle*. These publications introduced American socialists to the revolutionary theory of Lenin, Trotsky, and other Bolsheviks. In his own writings, Fraina combined elements of De Leon's conceptions with the Bolsheviks' theory, producing a synthesis of the two that might be called semi-syndicalist revolutionary socialism.

Around this time, Fraina also published *The Proletarian Revolution in Russia*, comprised mostly of articles by Lenin and Trotsky, but edited and with an introduction, notes, and supplementary chapters by Fraina himself.[9] The fat book, over 400 pages, made him the recognised authority in America on the theory of the Bolshevik leaders. Buhle calls it 'the documentary equivalent of John Reed's spectacularly journalistic *Ten Days that Shook the World*'.[10] Fraina's anthology made him an instant candidate for leadership of the left wing of the Socialist Party and the soon-to-emerge Communist Party.

---

8   Fraina, November 1913, p. 95; Fraina, 15 July 1915, p. 121. Louis C. Fraina, 'The Problem of Nationality', December 1915, p. 323. Fraina, April 1916, p. 97.

9   Fraina 1918, *passim*.

10   Buhle 1995, p. 75.

In addition to being a leading socialist intellectual, Fraina was also an anti-war and anti-draft activist. Because he was not a US citizen, he was not liable for the draft, although he was required to register. Since the US had entered the war and passed the Conscription Act in 1917, he had been speaking against both the war and conscription and advocating conscientious objection and other forms of resistance. On 8 June 1917, just after the national draft registration day, he spoke alongside *The New Review* writers Louis B. Boudin, William E. Bohn, and Ludwig Lore at a mass meeting in New York City to some 1,500 people, with 2,000 more being turned away for lack of space in the hall. US Army officers and soldiers interrupted that meeting, like many others at that time.[11]

On 27 September 1917, Fraina spoke again, this time at a meeting of the League of Conscientious Objectors at the Labor Temple in New York City on the theme, 'What About Conscientious Objectors?' He told the audience, 'They cannot conscript a conscientious objector. We will not be conscripted, either, to fight or to do non-combatant service'.[12] US Federal officers and New York police arrested him and another speaker, E. Ralph Cheney, the former president of the Intercollegiate Socialist Society chapter of the University of Pennsylvania, and 'drove the audience into the street'.[13] A few days later, on 3 October, 1917, the Grand Jury indicted Fraina and Cheney 'under [the] criminal section of the espionage act'. They were the first in New York and the third in the United States to be indicted on that charge at that time. The full charges were violation of the criminal section of the espionage law and conspiracy to evade the Conscription Act. The charge brought a possible penalty of 12 years in prison and a fine of $20,000. Judge Shepherd of the US District Court granted a postponement until October 10, and consigned Fraina and Cheney to the Toombs jail with bail set at $2,500 each.

Socialist Party attorneys Morris Hillquit and Louis B. Boudin defended Fraina and Cheney. Hillquit sought a postponement, but Judge Shepherd would grant no more than a day or two. Fraina issued a statement objecting to the government's rush to trial. 'I protest not simply as an individual facing a long term of imprisonment, but as a representative of the conscientious objectors who are, in fact, as much on trial as myself'.[14]

Fraina argued that since this was the first test of a new law, the court should be even more scrupulous in granting the defendant adequate time to prepare. A defence committee of prominent radicals – Anna Strunsky, Edward English

---

11   '1,500', 8 June 1917, p. 1.
12   'Convict Fraina', 19 October 1917.
13   'Two Arrested', 28 September 1917.
14   'Fraina and Cheney', 12 October 1917.

Walling, Algernon Lee, Scott Nearing, Joseph Scholssberg, Elizabeth Freeman, Ludwig Lore, Austin Lewis, Mary E. Marcy and B.J. Rutgers – was quickly organised. The committee argued that, 'Fraina and Cheney are in fact on trial as conscientious objectors, and their conviction would strike a blow at the whole movement for freedom of speech and of conscience'.[15] Louis B. Boudin succeeded in getting trial Judge Robert T. Ervin to dismiss two of the counts, but in the end prosecutor Harold A. Convent won. The District Court jury found the two guilty of conspiring to persuade men of draft age to evade the conscription law.[16]

The maximum penalty possible was two years in Federal prison and a fine of $10,000 each. Judge Ervin sentenced the men to 30 days in the Mercer County Penitentiary in Trenton, New Jersey. Fraina's speeches against the draft and his trial helped to make him a leading public figure in the anti-war movement, as well as the theoretical leader of the left wing of the Socialist Party. During this same period, Frain also met Leon Trotsky, the Russian revolutionary who had escaped persecution in Russia and Europe and come to New York City where he was publishing a Russian language newspaper called *Novy Mir* (New World). Fraina became 'one of Leon Trotsky's closest friends in New York City and the two collaborated in the struggle against the Socialist Party's centre- and right-wing factions.'[17] Working with Trotsky, Fraina fought against Morris Hilquit, a leader of the Socialist Party's right-wing – and Fraina's own attorney.

Fraina spent much of 1918 and 1919 in the bitter factional fights within the Socialist Party and within its foreign language federations. Paul Buhle argues that in the factional fights leading to the formation of the Communist Party, Fraina played a 'mostly negative' role. He attacked his former comrade and attorney Louis B. Boudin, and his comrade Ludwig Lore. Completely involved in the internecine battles, and with his political base in the Russian Federation, Buhle believes that Fraina became cut off from American life. For example, when the great strike wave of 1919 took place, Fraina, who had written such important analyses of the 1910–12 strikes, had virtually nothing to say about the new working-class movement.

These led in September 1919 to the founding of two rival Communist Parties: the Communist Party of America (CPA) led by Charles Ruthenberg, national secretary, with Louis Fraina, international secretary and editor; and the Communist Labor Party (CLP), headed by Alfred Wagenknecht, executive secretary, with John Reed as international delegate. The CPA membership came mostly

---

15   'Fraina Trial', 15 October 1917, p. 5.
16   'Convict Fraina', 19 October 1917.
17   Ackerman 2016, pp. 59 and 160–1.

from the foreign language federations' immigrants, while the CLP had more native- born Americans. By 1922, after a complicated series of splits and fusions, the two original Communist parties and other small groups merged and formed the Communist Party of the United States of America (CPUSA).[18] The new party chose Fraina as one of the delegates to the Second Congress of the Communist International to be held in Moscow in 1921.

After his selection, Fraina made plans to go to Moscow. Driven underground by the New York State Lusk Committee anti-Communist raids, he sought help in making travel arrangements from a fellow Communist, Jacob Nosovitsky, who as it turned out was a US government agent. At the same time another US agent in the leadership of the Finnish Federation of the Communist Party, accused Fraina of being a spy for the US government. Then Santori Nuorteva, a leader of the Finnish Communists in America, formally charged Fraina with spying. So, just two days before he was to leave for Moscow, the Communist Party tried Fraina as a government spy.

In the end, all specific charges were refuted, Fraina was vindicated, and in 1920 the Communist Party even published a 48-page pamphlet, 'The Stenographic Report of the "Trial" of L.C. Fraina' that disproved all the charges. But the pamphlet also presented witnesses' claims that Fraina had been seen in Justice Department Office or with government checks in his possession. The result, as historian Paul Buhle concludes, was that 'Fraina's name had been tarnished, or at least placed under long-term suspicion'.[19]

Fraina finally left for Europe, travelling through Amsterdam, Berlin, and Denmark, before leaving from Germany for Russia disguised as a returning prisoner of war. When he arrived in Moscow, he discovered that the scandal had preceded him, and he was subject to a second hearing on the spying charges by a committee of three officials of the Communist International. This group also confirmed his innocence, and Fraina was admitted as a delegate to the Second Congress of the Communist International in 1921.

In Moscow, Fraina found himself at odds with the new line on labour advocated by Lenin and the Bolshevik leadership. Lenin called upon American Communists to work within the American Federation of Labor (AFL) and to support the formation of a labour party. Most American Communists and their delegates to the Communist International were supporters of the Industrial Workers of the World (IWW) and advocates of the creation of soviets and the construction of a revolutionary Communist party, and they opposed building conservat-

18   Draper 1986, pp. 17–24.
19   Buhle 1995, p. 94.

ive trade unions and a reformist labour party. Though perhaps not convinced, Fraina accepted the Communist International's position – which immediately led the American Communist Party delegation to repudiate him.

John Reed and Louis Fraina found themselves on opposite sides of the fight over the union and labour party questions at the Communist International Congress, but they remained personal friends. Reed, Fraina, and Charles Francis Phillips, three men who eventually all played roles as American revolutionaries in Mexico in different periods, saw each other frequently in Moscow. After John Reed attended the Communist Congress of the Oriental Nations in Baku, as the representative of one of the most powerful of the imperialist countries, he returned sick with typhus and had to be hospitalised. Accompanied by Phillips, Louis Fraina went every day to visit Reed at the hospital, where Reed's companion Louise Bryant also sat watch. When Reed died there in Moscow, Phillips and Fraina were at his bedside.[20]

The time had come for the American Communists to leave Russia, but the American Communist Party and the Communist International had a problem: What to do with Fraina? Before he died, John Reed argued that Fraina would have to play a low-profile role because of the spy charges. Borodin, a leader of the Communist International, shared that view, and suggested Fraina be sent off on some international mission. In the end, the Communist International created a Latin America Bureau, made up of Louis Fraina, the Lettish-American Karl Jansen (or Carl Johnson), and Japanese Communist Sen Katayama. Johnson, who acted as the contact with the International remained in the United States, but Fraina, Katayama and Phillips were sent to Mexico to organise the Communist Party and the Latin American Bureau of the Red International of Labour Unions (RILU or PROFINTERN). Rationalising his exile to Mexico, Fraina later remembered, 'Well, I was designated because I was there [Moscow?] and had a reputation as a theoretician'.[21] He had apparently forgotten or completely suppressed the accusations that led to his banishment from American politics. So, the leading American Communist intellectual left for Mexico posing as a foreign film distributor. According to Theodore Draper, 'Louis C. Fraina was given about $50,000 in Moscow in December 1920 for himself and others to use in Great Britain, Mexico, and the United States'.[22]

---

20   Shipman 1993, pp. 123–6.
21   'Report of the Federal Bureau of Investigation's Investigation of Lewis Corey, 1945–1950', Corey Papers, Box 5, Folder 5, p. 73, Columbia University.
22   Draper 1986, p. 202.

2   Sen Katayama, Japanese-American Communist

The man who was to be Fraina's partner in Mexico, the 63-year-old Sen Katayama, already had a long career in the Socialist movement by 1920. Katayama's
biography is a story of indomitable determination and persistence that makes
clear why the Communist International would have thought an aging Japanese labour organiser capable of establishing the Latin American Communist
revolutionary movement.

Katayama was born in Japan on 8 January 1860 to a peasant family.[23] He
worked on the farm and was mostly educated at home, with only short stints
in school. At the age of 22 he went to Tokyo, found work in a print shop, and
eventually became an assistant typesetter. Driven by a desire for education,
Katayama gave up his job to attend a Chinese university, where he worked as a
janitor while studying.

In 1884 Katayama moved to California where he continued his education.
Working in menial jobs, he first studied English at the Chinese Mission in
Alameda, then at Johns Hopkins Academy in Oakland. While in the Bay Area he
converted to Christianity and eventually became a Congregationalist. He went
on to college, first to Maryville College in Tennessee, and then in 1889 to Grinnell College in Iowa. At Grinnell, Katayama read Richard T. Ely, the progressive
economist, and Ely's writings led Katayama to become a socialist.[24] But at that
time Katayama was a Christian socialist, more influenced by the Social Gospel
than by the idea of class struggle. During that same period, Katayama made
use of the German he had learned in college to read Ferdinand Lassalle, whose
programme of state socialism he found attractive.

After graduating from Grinnell in 1892, Katayama entered Andover Theological Seminary to study for the ministry, but he became more interested
in social work and visited the Andover settlement house in Boston. His new
interest led him to travel to England and Scotland to study social problems
there. He toured slums, visited social work programmes, and observed the
Salvation Army. Returning to the United States, Katayama transferred to Yale
Theological Seminary where he wrote a dissertation titled 'Urban Problems in
Europe in America'.

---

23   Kublin 1964, *passim*; Draper 1957, pp. 7–78. See also: Fraina's 'Introduction' to Katayama
      1918, pp. 11–27.
24   Kublin 1964, pp. 69–71, draws on Katayama's Japanese language autobiography, *Jiden*
      (Katayama 1954). Written before he went to Mexico, *Jiden* does not discuss Katayama's
      experience in Mexico, though the editors mention it.

Having finished his education, the 35-year-old Katayama returned to Japan to teach in a preparatory school and to open one of the first Japanese settlement houses. But he soon became more involved in the workers' movement, founding the first labour unions and socialist organisations, becoming within a few years the central figure of the Japanese labour movement.

At the end of 1903, Katayama travelled to the United States to attend the convention of the Socialist Party of America in Chicago, and later went on the Sixth Congress of the Socialist International in Amsterdam, which met the next year. Speaking in France on the possibility of a Russo-Japanese war, Katayama said, 'Japanese workers have no vital interest in the matter. They do not wish to engage in mutual slaughter with the Russian workers for the possession of Manchuria or even Korea'. He believed, he said, that because of the opposition of peasants and workers the Japanese government would hesitate to make war.[25] Socialist workers, he believed, would prevent war.

But Katayama was wrong. After hostilities between Russia and Japan broke out in February of 1904, he continued to oppose war in principle, but like most socialists, he supported a Japanese victory over feudal and reactionary Russia. In Amsterdam on the Socialist International Congress platform, Georgi Plekhanov, the leader of the Russian Socialist Democratic Labour Party, and Sen Katayama, the founder of Japanese socialism, shook hands in a symbol of international labour solidarity against imperialism and war, bringing the delegates to their feet in an ovation. Even though Katayama had been absent from Japan during the war, he became a world-renowned symbol of the Japanese anti-war movement and of international labour solidarity. Yet rather than returning to join that movement, he sat out the war among Japanese farmers near Houston, Texas, probably fearing he would be imprisoned were he to return to Japan.

After the war ended, Katayama did return to Japan where between 1907 and 1912 he led the more moderate wing of the Japanese labour and socialist movement. In January 1912 he organised the streetcar workers strike in Tokyo, one of the most successful strikes of the Meiji era. For his role, Katayama was arrested, tried, found guilty of violating the Public Peace Preservation Law, and sentenced to five months in Chiba Prison where he began to write his autobiography (*Jiden*). When he came out of prison, Katayama found that the government had been largely successful in suppressing the labour and socialist movement. As one of the most prominent left activists in Japan, he was under constant surveillance. He wrote to the English socialist H.M. Hyndman, 'I am

---

25   Kublin 1964, citing Katayama 1904, p. 304. Katayama's opinion published in that journal originally appeared in *Aurore*, 11 January 1904, before the outbreak of the war.

really driven out of my country because of socialism', adding that he could no longer make a living in Japan.[26] So, in 1914, Katayama emigrated to the United States.

After arriving in California, Katayama settled in San Francisco. He founded the Japanese Day Laborer's Union that attempted, though without much success, to organise the 16,000 Japanese who laboured in California fields. He also started the monthly *Heimin* (Farmer), a labour and socialist journal published in Japanese and English aimed at Japanese-American farmworkers, which had only a small number of subscribers.

Working in the most menial jobs, Katayama might well have fallen into poverty, had he not been saved in 1916 by a telegram from the Dutch socialist S.J. Rutgers, inviting to pay the Japanese socialist's fare to New York City. Katayama moved to New York and lived in a guest room of the Rutgers' home, paying for his room and board by cooking for the family. With Rutgers' help, Katayama wrote the English-language book *The Labor Movement in Japan*, a popular introduction to the Japanese labour and socialist movement, which was published by Charles Kerr Company and included an introduction by Louis Fraina.

Through Rutgers, in December 1916 Katayama met Alexandra Kollontai, Lenin's representative in the United States. She attempted to convince Katayama of the Bolshevik programme to turn the war into revolution, and the necessity of a new Communist International. Gradually coming around to the Bolshevik viewpoint, Katayama participated in the famous meeting in Brooklyn on 15 January 1917, where Ludwig Lore, Louis Fraina, Louis Boudin, Nikolai Bukharin, and Leon Trotsky, among others, founded the left wing of the Socialist Party of America. Katayama later wrote, 'We intended to organise the Left Wing under the direction of Comrade Trotzky, and Mdam Kollontai, who was going to Europe, was to establish a link between the European and American Left-Wing movements'.[27] From then on Katayama worked with Rutgers and Fraina in editing the left-wing journals *Class Struggle, New International*, and *Revolutionary Age*.

Having been convinced by the left-wing socialists of the Bolshevik perspective, Katayama rallied immediately to the victory of the Bolshevik Revolution in Russia in November of 1917. 'Russia is our great hope for the moment', he told *The World* newspaper of Oakland, California in March the next year.[28] With

26   Kublin 1964, p. 166, citing a letter from Katayama to Hyndman, in Hyndman 1919, pp. 190–2.
27   Ackerman 2016, pp. 55–63 and p. 69, citing Katayama, 26 July 1919.
28   Kublin 1964, p. 265, citing McAlpine, 22 March 1918, pp. 1 and 5.

experience in North America, Europe, and Asia, Katayama was in a unique position to grasp the significance of the Russian Revolution for world revolution. Beginning in 1918 he worked to create a Communist Party of the United States, the Communist Party of Japan, and a new revolutionary International. When Lenin and the Bolsheviks made the decision to found the Communist International in December 1919, they sent an invitation to Sen Katayama, who – busy organising the new Communist Party in the United States – could not attend. Nor was he able to appear at the Second Congress of the Communist International in 1920.

With the beginning of the infamous Palmer Raids in January 1920, Katayama, like other Communist leaders, feared arrest and possible deportation for his political activities. The Japanese revolutionary went underground but continued to organise with the Communist Party in the United States, as well as to work indirectly on the establishment of the Communist Party in Japan. When Louis Fraina appeared back in the United States in December 1920 and informed Katayama that he had been assigned to assist the Communist parties in Mexico and other parts of Latin America, Katayama wound up his affairs and packed his bags.

Why did the Communist International send to Mexico the 63-year-old Katayama who had no previous experience in Latin America and spoke no Spanish? Historian Robert J. Alexander speculates that the Communist International sent Katayama because they did not trust Phillips' reports and wanted a more experienced and sophisticated agent there.[29] The Japanese revolutionary certainly had a long involvement in the Socialist movement, he knew what it was to work in foreign countries, and he was devoted to the Bolsheviks and the International. As Katayama's biographer Hyman Kublin writes, Katayama 'was no mere transitory conspirator in the international revolutionary movement, but a member of the tried and tested group of Comintern troublemakers and troubleshooters on call for assignment wherever Communist political capital was to be made'.[30] The Japanese Communist was definitely the senior member of the team, probably sent to Mexico to keep an eye on both the neophyte Phillips and Fraina.

29   Alexander 1957, p. 321.
30   Kublin 1964, p. 275.

3   The Communist International Sets Up Shop in Mexico

Before proceeding to Mexico, Fraina had returned to New York where he briefly visited friends and comrades in the American Communist Party and attempted to patch up factional differences. Katayama apparently left soon after for Mexico, for he had arrived there before Fraina. Calling himself Luis Carlos Fernández, Fraina did not arrive in Mexico until late in the spring of 1921. A native speaker of Italian, Fraina could presumably soon understand and make himself understood in Spanish.

Within a couple of months Fraina, Katayama and Phillips were together in Mexico City where they set to work on their assignments: to organise the Latin American Bureau of the Red Labour International, to reorganise the Mexican Communist Party, and to organise a Latin American Bureau of the Communist International. Phillips, who had been based in Mexico City for several years and spoke Spanish well, introduced Fraina and Katayama to Mexican Communist party leaders José C. Valadés, Genaro Gómez, Manuel Díaz Ramírez and José Allen, though of course they did not know that Allen, was a police agent in the employ of the US Military Intelligence Division (USMID). Through Allen the USMID was kept well informed of the activities of Katayama, Fraina, and Phillips.

Fraina's recollections of his experience in Mexico, as told to an F.B.I. agent around 1950 were extremely vague, probably intentionally so. He remembered that after he arrived in Mexico, he had no contact with the American Communist Party and found only a small Communist group in Mexico City.

> My contacts with whatever Communists there were in Mexico – a man named Valedez [José C. Valadés], I have no recollection of a Communist Party being there when I got there. It is possible that there may have been some small group calling itself the Communist Party of which Valedez [sic] was the representative – or go-between, but if it was, it was insignificant, and actually the Communist Party of Mexico, as a going Party, was organised some years later ....[31]

In another part of the same document, Fraina remembered, that he and Katayama

---

31   'Report of the Federal Bureau of Investigation's Investigation of Lewis Corey, 1945–1950', Corey Papers, Box 5, Folder 5, p. 128, Columbia University.

had direct contact with a group of Mexicans who were syndicalists, with the idea of trying to convince them that in spite of their syndicalism, which calls for no political action ... they ought to affiliate with the Communist International. That's about all we did there. It wasn't very much.[32]

From the 1950 statement to the FBI, one has the sense that Fraina was hiding the identity of Charles Francis Phillips. For example, he kept saying he thought Phillips's name was Hernández. Fraina minimised the significance of the contacts between the US and Mexican Communist Parties, as well as downplaying the importance of his mission. Hyman Kublin, the biographer of Sen Katayama, used Fraina's weak recollections to reconstruct Katayama's experiences in Mexico. With nothing but those notes to go on, he wrote, 'Katayama lived in Mexico City for almost eight months. No other period of his life is so obscure'.[33]

Thanks, however, to the files of the US Military Intelligence Division and documents in the Communist International Archives, as well as several memoirs published in recent decades, a good deal more than what Fraina had wanted to tell the FBI is now apparent. These sources reveal that from the moment they arrived in Mexico, Fraina and Katayama set to work to rebuild the Communist Party and to establish the presence of the Communist International and Red International of Labour Union networks in Latin America. One comes away from the various documents with the impression that it was actually the tireless Katayama, collaborating with the persistent Phillips, who did most of the work, while Fraina did little. Phillips wrote in his autobiography, 'Neither Fraina nor Katayama appeared in public, but I reported to them every day. In a practical sense I was the Latin-American Bureau of the RILU, such as it was'.[34]

José C. Valadés, leader of the Communist youth movement, was one of the few Mexican Communists who actually met Katayama because the Japanese organiser stayed for a time at his parents' house. Valadés described Katayama as a short man who 'carried on his shoulders his age of sixty-two or sixty years'. He goes on:

> he had a face illuminated with a goodness such that it radiated sympathy that grew with a natural, beautiful and sincere smile. He watched listlessly, with little effort. He pronounced English with a marked Asian

32 'Report of the Federal Bureau of Investigation's Investigation of Lewis Corey, 1945–1950', Corey Papers, Box 5, Folder 5, p. 76, Columbia University.
33 Kublin 1964, p. 282.
34 Shipman 1993, p. 130.

accent. Highly educated, he learned a few words of Spanish in order to greet my mother in the respectful manner of an unknown guest.[35]

Valadés' beatific portrait of the old Japanese labour organiser fails to convey his revolutionary commitment, his professionalism, and intense dedication to his work.

In a letter to José Allen, Katayama wrote that he had taken a steamer from New Orleans to Veracruz, and that he had arrived in Mexico City on 31 March. He explained in guarded language, that he was all alone, but that he was 'going to start his business at once'. He intended to issue a 'prospectus' weekly or semi-weekly. Katayama also reported that the 'Amalgamation of two corporations here is now almost an accomplished fact'. This was a reference to his attempt to bring Linn Gale's Communist Party of Mexico (PCdeM) and the Roy-Phillips Mexican Communist Party (PCM) together into one organisation.[36] That proved to be a chimera.

Among Katayama's first tasks in Mexico was to investigate the histories of M.N. Roy and Linn A.E. Gale and others of the original founders of the Mexican Communist parties. He wrote reports in his imperfect English to M. Kobezky in Russia. In one he wrote 'M. Roy abused the credentials of the M.C. Man of his ability and experience, he knew very well, when he carried the M.C. credentials from here, that he was representing neither a Communist Party of real power nor the proletariat of Mexico in a true sense of the word or otherwise'. Roy, Katayama wrote, had simply wanted to get to the Second Congress of the Communist International, and therefore he fought for the credentials.

Regarding Gale, whom he had not met and who had just been deported, Katayama wrote:

> Gale's unpopularity in America and also American colony in Mexico City is especially among comrades well known, but at the same time Gale's unfailing energy and strenuous activities althrough [*sic*] while in Mexico is admitted equally both [by] his enemies as well as his friends. No doubt Gales is a greater worker and fighter with his pen and tongue aided by his faithful almost slavish yet industrious wife, whose financial support out of her own toil has been the very strength in Gale's activities.[37]

---

35   Valadés 1986, vol. 2, p. 107.
36   Letter of 6 April 1921 [from Sen Katayama] to José Allen, Document number 521/1/17, SASRF. Internal evidence indicates this is a letter from Katayama.
37   Letter of 22 April 1921 [from Sen Katayama] to M. Kobezky, Document number 521/1/17, SASRF. Internal evidence indicates Katayama is the author.

Katayama wrote that some said Gale was a 'provocateur', others that he was a 'neurotic' and yet others that he had 'a hyperbolic mania'. 'To me', wrote Katayama, 'Gale is a typical American upstart, able, pushing, aggressive, hasty and careless often compromising to his own sole interest. The type we saw in Wilshire in the '90th [sic] of the last century and you can find today as in Fryn [sic, Flynn?], Morgan, Reed and M. Eastman, the last two come out the best of the same types'. The saddest thing, wrote Katayama, was that Gale had left 'very few followers'. 'As to the Communist Parties – so-called Gale's and Roy's – both are really not a party by any means', Katayama judged. 'Both have a few good comrades. [Díaz] Ramírez counted to me three in his party'.[38]

Katayama was not only delving into the past to better understand the human material he was working with, he was also editing newspapers and producing pamphlets for the Mexican party (writing in English for translation into Spanish). With the money that Fraina had brought, the group had established a newspaper called *El Trabajador* (The Worker). Phillips edited the paper, consulting with Fraina and Katayama. In late June of 1921, he wrote a letter to 'Charles and Cynthea', presumably to Charles Francis Phillips and his wife Natalia, in which he reported that, 'Our little weekly has been becoming a power and influence among the trade union members. We just got [a request for] 1500 copies each week hereafter from one of the strong unions which is affiliated with the Red L.U.I. [Red International of Labour Unions or RILU]'.[39]

In a letter written 29 July 1921 to his Japanese-American comrade Nonaka, Katayama gave a good summary of his organising activities among Mexican unionists. 'Since I came here, I have done quite a bit of propaganda work, among them. I have been publishing a weekly in Spanish'. Katayama noted that so far, he had published 14 numbers of the Spanish language Communist newspaper. 'On the 4th of August I am going [to] issue another weekly called *El Obrero Communiste* [sic] [The Communist Worker] the name signifies the nature of the weekly'. In addition, Katayama established a print shop, where Lenin's book *State and Revolution* and Bukharin's *Communist Party Program*, now translated into Spanish, were being printed in quantities of 5,000 copies each. 'I have to write great deal now a days for those periodicals, beside [which] I have to write some manifestos and official letters to the labour organizations and also look after the work of propaganda'.[40]

---

38   Letter of 22 April 1921 [from Sen Katayama] to M. Kobezky.
39   Letter of 21 June 1921 from Sen Katayama to Charles and Cynthea, document number 521/1/
      17, f. 17, SASRF. Internal evidence indicates this is a letter from Katayama.
40   Letter of 29 July 1921 from [Sen Katayama] to Comrade Nonaka, document number 521/1/
      17, f. 89–90, SASRF. Internal evidence indicates this is a letter from Katayama.

Katayama complained that his endeavours had been made more difficult since the party's principal leaders, who were foreigners, had (as discussed in a previous chapter) all been deported in mid-May. He explained that he had moved three times and 'now I am located quite safe'. He lived alone with a Mexican woman who prepared his food, but with whom he could not converse. For two and a half months he had hardly left the house and only met with one or two comrades, so that the only time he opened his mouth all day was to eat: 'so you see I feel rather lonesome and tired of life. But I have been enjoying with my work, so that releases me my present secluded living'.

Katayama closed his letter to the Japanese comrade asking about the situation of the Japanese on the Pacific Coast of the United States. He then wrote, 'I believe work must be done in the States for Japan, because it is absolutely impossible to do it in Japan .... We must make America our school of Communism and send out our graduate to Japan to preach the gospel of Communism'.[41]

In a report, probably written in August 1921, to the Small Bureau of the Executive Committee of the Communist International, Katayama explained that, 'There was no real Communist Party here, in spite of the existence of two "Communist parties"'. The arrests and deportations of May had revealed the truth of the situation, for when the handful of foreigners were deported, the parties virtually disappeared. 'Roy and Gale left no Communist followers', wrote Katayama. Yet, he said, they 'should not be condemned too severely, since enthusiasm largely get the better of their judgement'.

According to Katayama, the Party's only strength was the Mexican Federation of Communist Youth organised in January 1920, and led by Valadés. The youth group was 'definitely organised, disciplined, of fundamental Communist tendency and had good workers, not being the sport of any one or two leaders'. After consulting with the youth group's leadership, Katayama reported, 'we decided to make the Federation of Communist Youth the starting point for the organization of a Communist Party'. Under his direction the Party had started a school for 'Communist agitators and organisers' taught 'by one of the best Mexican comrades'. Katayama reported that Mexico had been divided into six districts and that comrades would be sent to them to distribute literature and organise communist groups. Special attention would be paid to industrial workers.

Katayama's report also deals with plans for party propaganda and enumerates existing or prospective publication: *El Obrero Comunista* [The Communist

---

41   Letter of 29 July 1921 from [Sen Katayama] to Comrade Nonaka, document number 521/1/
       17, f. 89–90, SASRF. Internal evidence indicates this is a letter from Katayama.

Worker], *La Revista Comunista* [The Communist Magazine], and pamphlets: 1) Zinoviev's 'The Communist Party', 2) Bukharin's 'Communist Program', 3) 'Theses of the Second Congress', 4) Lenin's 'Leftwing Communism: An Infantile Disorder', and 5) Trotsky's 'Terrorism and Communism'. Katayama was also planning on publishing Karl Marx's 'Communist Manifesto'. He also presented an impressive list of pamphlets to be published on Mexican issues: 1) The Agrarian Problem in Mexico; 2) The History of the Development of Private Property in Mexico; 3) From Madero to Carranza (discussing the character and accomplishments of the recent revolutions); 4) The Labour Movement in Mexico (a history).

Katayama explained that he did not intend to make a big splash, but rather to build a sound basis for a future Communist Party in Mexico that would also have an important impact in Cuba, Central America and South America. He pointed out that 'Mexico is directly menaced by American imperialism, and the revolutionary struggle of the Mexican masses already directly inspires the movement of the whole of the Americas'.

In that same report, Katayama surveyed the Mexican political scene putting special emphasis on the anarcho-syndicalist unions. He observed that while 'the radical leaders are almost all Anarcho-Syndicalists, this is not exactly true of the masses; they fall under the Syndicalist influence largely because of their inexperience'. He believed that 'the Anarcho-Syndicalist leaders' influence is waning, since the problem now in Mexico is becoming one of organization and struggle; and the Mexican Anarcho-Syndicalists are woefully incapable of organization and struggle being mostly big mouthed talkers and spinners of fine theory. The best of those leaders are coming over to us'.[42]

Throughout his stay in Mexico, Katayama remained underground, always working through Charles Phillips or other bilingual organisers. A USMID agent (probably José Allen) reported in April 1921 that 'Katayama is remaining in seclusion and receives only Seaman [Charles Francis Phillips] to whom he gives his "orders" and the funds necessary for their work'.[43] A month later the same agent reported that, 'The International Bureau of Red Syndicates [i.e. the Red International of Labour Unions] directed by Katayama, assisted by Seaman [Phillips], is waging active propaganda amongst the labour element of the Federal District in order to bring about a General Strike – using, as a pretext for this

---

42   Report of the American Agency to the Small Bureau of the Executive Committee, from [Sen Katayama], probably August 1921, Document number 495/108/8, f. 24–29, SASRF. Internal evidence indicates this is a letter from Katayama.

43   E.O. 'Political, Radical and Labor Activities', 21 April 1921, RG 165, Box 2291, USMID, USNA.

movement, the present partial strike of the telephone workers of the "Erick-son [*sic*] Company".[44] However, it was in this same month that the Mexican government decided to repress the labour movement, expelling a number of foreign leftists and labour organisers.

Katayama explained to the Executive Committee of the Communist International in a letter of 24 August 1921, that because of the repression in May he had been underground and had 'done everything through comrade Ramírez [Phillips]'. He generally must have first given orders to Phillips who in turn distributed the work to José C. Valadés, leader of the Communist youth organisation, and Manuel Díaz Ramírez, a long-time union activist. In that same August letter to the International, Katayama reported that he had established a Provisional Mexican Bureau of the RILU and begun publishing the newspaper *El Trabajador*. He had also written several letters to Central and South America informing unionists and leftists of the organisation of the Bureau. He had been in touch as well with the Local Congress of the Mexican Federation of Labour at Puebla, and the National Congress of the Regional Confederation of Mexican Workers (CROM) in Orizaba, and too with the Socialist Congress of the Southeast in the Yucatan.

'By the way', mentioned Katayama, 'the Mexican Bureau of the Red International [of Labour Unions] has been just started to organise the oil workers in conjunction with the General Federation of Workers [CGT], Mexico, D.F. and the I.W.W.'.[45] He also noted, 'We are very much encouraged by recent application of peasants from the country near the City of Mexico in the effect that they desire to form a Communist section of the Communist Party of Mexico among the peasants themselves'. This activity among oil workers and peasants would become some of the most important work of the Communist Party throughout the 1920s.

In a report to the US Military Intelligence Division, an agent (again probably José Allen) claimed that Katayama had a complex scheme to combine organisation of the oil workers with attempts to provoke an international war. The agent wrote that Katayama told him

> that he would make an effort to cause trouble at Tampico oil district in order to bring the intervention of the United States, that in case he accom-

---

44   'Political, Radical and Labor Activities', 12 May 1921, RG 165, Box 2219, USMID, USNA.
45   Letter of 24 August 1921 to the E.C. of the Communist International from [Sen Katayama], Document number 521/1/17, State Archival Service of the Russian Federation, Russian Centre for Preservation and Study of Documents of Contemporary History (formerly the Central Party Archive). Internal evidence indicates this is a letter from Katayama.

plished this difficulty [*sic*] it would strengthen the radical work in Mexico, that by the intervention of the United States in Mexico, England would be brought into controversy and also Japan, that he would instruct all those affiliated with the Communist [International] to enlist in the armies of the United States, England and Japan, and in that manner the radicals would be equipped in order to make a fight for their principles.[46]

It seems hard to believe that an experienced organiser like Katayama, who was working modestly but systematically to create a small Communist group, would have presented such a preposterous scheme for causing a foreign intervention and world war. This sounds as if the USMID agent was either utterly confused or intentionally misrepresented Katayma's activities. Police agents, it must be remembered, are paid for providing interesting information, and so sometimes they concoct it. But it confirms that Katayama's efforts were focused on organising the oil workers, who were among the most important industrial workers in Mexico.

Surprisingly none of the reports mentions the General Confederation of Workers (CGT) Congress of September 1921 where the anarchists expelled the Communists in response to news of the persecution of anarchists in Soviet Russia and also repudiated an earlier decision to consider joining the RILU. While the Communists had expected to be rejected by the more conservative Morones and his Regional Confederation of Mexican Workers (CROM), the labour federation linked to the Mexican state, their ejection from the CGT must have come as somewhat surprising and a heavy blow. In that period, Communists, anarchists, and the IWW had all seemed to share the same goals of industrial unionism, anti-capitalist revolution, and even dictatorship of the proletariat. The Communist expulsion must have created a sense of isolation from the revolutionary labour movement. Katayama nevertheless continued to harbour hopes that he might influence the CGT and find a role for the Communists within it, although that did not come to pass.[47]

Fraina, too, must have played some role in all of this organisational work, especially since, as an Italian speaker, he could probably soon communicate in Spanish, though there is little record of his efforts. Valadés, who apparently spent much time with Fraina, mentions many conversations, but has no

---

46   'Report Covering Attitude of Prominent Mexican Government Officials Toward the American Government, Bolshevist Activities in Mexico and Other Matters of Importance to the American Government', Supplement, 11 June 1921, in Boehm 1984, p. 26.

47   Spenser 1998, pp. 65–6.

recollection of the American's efforts. 'Fraina was a unique individual', Valadés recalled. 'What struck one was his elegant head'.

> He exuded talent and social erudition. He cited Marx at every step and wanted to make it known that he was a Marxist theoretician. I learned more Marxism from Fraina than from *Capital*.[48]

Valadés listened to Fraina talk about the history of the United States, about Jacksonian and Wilsonian America, about economics, and about how Fraina and Katayama and the other left-wingers had created the split in the Socialist Party of America and founded the Communist Party of the United States. 'He believed in a soon-to-come capitalist catastrophe', wrote Valadés, 'he had the hope that when it happened, within ten years, it would bring about the fall of the existing regime'.[49]

But Valadés recalled that he was less interested in what Fraina had to say about the United States than in what he had to say about Mexico and Latin America. Valadés' memoirs are particularly important, for they are one of the few recollections we have of a Mexican's impression of the American radicals and their ideas and values. Valadés reported that Fraina, after hearing the glowing reports of Borodin and Roy about the revolutionary possibilities in Mexico, had once he arrived become completely disillusioned. The Russian and Indian revolutionaries had urged Grigori Zinoviev, the head of the Communist International, to send Communists to Mexico to convert the revolutionary generals to Marxism.

> Fraina appeared skeptical about the social value of the Spanish-speaking peoples. Latin America, he said, was everyday further from social revolution. 'Political bossism' [*caudillaje político*] was too powerful to be conquered by the current of ideas.[50]

Fraina's remarks on the Spanish-speaking peoples probably intended no racial or ethnic denigration, as Valadés no doubt well understood. Fraina was simply describing the social and political character of the region. The American simply condemned a system of political corruption so profound that he had little hope that socialist ideas could soon affect it.

By the fall of 1921 Katayama and Fraina were in a position to organise a party congress to refound the Mexican Communist Party. The party Congress took

---

48   Valadés 1985, vol. 2, p. 108.
49   Valadés 1985, vol. 2, pp. 108–9.
50   Valdés 1984, vol. 2, p. 109.

place on 25–30 December in Mexico City with 21 delegates representing 1,000 members. Most of those in attendance were workers, peasants, and teachers. Fraina wrote to the Small Bureau of the Communist International in Moscow a report on the congress:

> The most significant feature of the Congress was its sobriety and steadiness. Mexican congresses as a rule are flamboyant, hysterical, the sonorous phrase and the excited gesture being dominant. This was absent at the Congress. Instead, most of the time of the Congress was used in the work of the various commissions, where every phase of the Mexican problem was earnestly discussed and acted upon.

He reported that the theses and resolutions of the Mexican Party Congress were in accord with those of the Communist International. 'I purposely took no part in the working out of the theses and resolutions, except in general discussion with three of the comrades who met with me regularly during the Congress: feeling that the matter should arise and settle itself spontaneously', writes Fraina rather disingenuously. In fact, he directed the congress from behind the scenes, just as Borodin had directed the original founding convention.[51]

At the end of his report, Fraina evaluated the party leaders. The best and most reliable comrades he felt were the Mexicans José Valadés and Manuel Díaz Ramírez and the Swiss Alfred Stirner. Valadés, wrote Fraina, was young and still excitable. Stirner understood theory but was no leader. Finally, '[Díaz] Ramírez is the best qualified for leader, sober and having the confidence of the workers, a good speaker and organiser'.[52] A US intelligence report confirmed Fraina's judgement when it described Ramírez: 'He is said to be experienced in revolutionary journalism, about 31 years of age, native of Vera Cruz, and to have lived a number of years in the United States where he became an I.W.W.'.[53] Valadés also recalled that Ramírez 'had been a member of the IWW. His long experience in the heart of the IWW gave him authority'.[54] A man with Ramírez's experience in the Wobblies would have been particularly appreciated by Fraina.

---

51 Letter of 2 January 1922 from Louis Fraina to the Small Bureau of the Communist International, Document Number 495-108-22, SASRF. I do not have a complete copy of this document but have relied on Dr. Daniela Spenser's citations and notes.

52 Letter of 2 January 1922 from Louis Fraina to the Small Bureau of the Communist International, Document Number 495-108-22, SASRF.

53 Letter of Mathew C. Smith, Colonel, General Staff, Chief, Negative Branch, to W.L. Hurley, Office of the Under Secretary, Department of State, 26 April 1921, RG 165, Box 2291, USMID, USNA.

54 Valadés 1985, p. 91.

Finally, Fraina's letter provided an overview of the situation. Mexico, as he saw it, was not on the verge of a revolution. The country had a reputation for Bolshevism that it did not deserve. Fraina wrote that there was no social class capable of wielding political power, not even the bourgeoisie, 'who rule because of the weakness of the other classes and through the power of foreign capital'. He concluded, 'Katayama and I somewhat misjudged the situation, imagining that the movement was larger or capable of being made bigger than could be carried through, and expenses were according'. Fraina recommended that a Russian representative be sent to work with the Mexican party, and he complained that the US Communist Party ignored the Mexican Party. On a personal note, Fraina complained that he wrote articles on Mexico for the Communist press, but they were never published because he was the author. He told the Communist International that he was about to go to Argentina to do organisational work.[55] The complaint that his articles were not being published suggests that the accusations of Fraina being a spy still clung to him, however unjustly, and that apparently the American Communist Party and the Communist International were loath to put his name on articles for the party press. But the letter also hints at a new problem, a financial problem, with the remark about big expenses.

So suddenly one day, 'Fraina announced he would go to South America and look things over, and the next day he was gone', Phillips remembered. 'His departure handicapped us in Mexico somewhat, for the bureau's treasury went with him. We were, of course, eager for the first word from him, but nothing came, ever'.[56] Fraina's terse autobiographical notes on this period, written in 1953, say:

> In Moscow I was appointed to a 3-man All-American Bureau of the Communist International and given $50,000 to carry on its work; I go to New York to report to my party, take a strong but unpopular attitude in favor of union among the various communist factions, power-politics and intrigues galore, and to Mexico City where Katayama, a member of the Bureau, awaits me; we carry on educational and organisational activities. Mexico, the Revolution and Obregón fascinate me .... I decide to quit the Communist Party and the International ...[57]

---

55   Letter of 2 January 1922 from Louis Fraina to the Small Bureau of the Communist International, Document Number 495-108-22, SASRF.

56   Shipman 1993, p. 131.

57   Lewis Corey papers, Box 2, Folder 3, 'Outline for Autobiography', 1953, p. 6, Columbia University.

Buhle says that Fraina, having failed in Mexico, 'left for the United States hold-ing the treasury'. Later, writes Buhle, Fraina 'sent the Comintern a letter of resignation and a final financial report, revealing that he had kept $4,200 in funds for a return trip to Mexico'.[58]

The Communists accused Fraina of having embezzled a great deal of money, and in 1922 expelled him from the Communist Party and the Communist Inter-national. Did Fraina really steal the money? Bertram D. Wolfe, also a Commun-ist organiser in Mexico just a little later, did not believe so. In 1952 Wolfe gave a deposition under oath to an investigator of the US Immigration and Naturaliz-ation Service, in which, when asked about Fraina's expulsion from the party for embezzlement, Wolfe stated, 'To the best of my knowledge, those funds were foolishly spent in the Mexican Communist movement rather than embezzled'. Wolfe went on:

> When I arrived in Mexico I made inquiries on this point. I found a pamph-let he [Fraina] had published there on 'American Imperialism' and I got the impression, as a result of my inquiries, that he attempted by the use of Comintern funds to overcome the reluctance of the Mexican Commun-ist Party to participate in electoral campaigns. From a place of hiding, he apparently doled out these funds in response to a hoax. Party leaders gave him receipts for alleged printing of posters, election campaign tours, etc., but the Communist Party did not participate in that election. That I believe is the true secret of the disappearance of his funds.[59]

Wolfe's version of the story, while possible, does not sound very convincing, but, in any case, whatever happened to the funds, Fraina had deserted his post in Mexico. Buhle concludes, 'Fraina's role as a revolutionary agent proved a total fiasco'.[60] The brief Mexican experience ended his career as a Communist.

4   Conclusion

Daniela Spenser has argued that 'The Comintern experiment in Mexico had failed' largely because the Communists did not appreciate the degree to which the Mexican revolutionary state had succeeded in establishing strong ties to the

58   Buhle 1995, p. 96.
59   'Examination of Bertram D. Wolfe ...', 5 March 1952, Wolfe Papers, Box 78, Folder 7, Hoover
       Institution, Stanford University.
60   Buhle 1995, p. 96.

labour unions, thus marginalising the Communists and anarchists. The Communists expected to win over both revolutionary generals and working-class leaders, but largely failed at both. Presidents Obregón and Calles and labour leader Luis Morones had succeeded in subordinating a good part of the organised working class to the state. As Spenser writes, 'the proletariat proved to be less revolutionary and the State more active than the Comintern had expected'.[61] While all of that is true, one might also say that though the Comintern's short-term revolutionary project failed, its long-term party-building project was modestly successful. After all, neither Lenin, nor Trotsky, nor other leaders of the Communist International had expected a socialist revolution in Mexico, believing a revolution in Europe or Asia more likely. Even if the Communists did not succeed in leading a Mexican revolutionary movement, they did create a small party, become active in the unions, and spread their propaganda among the labouring classes.

Fraina and Katayama, principally the latter, did a remarkable job in Mexico in a short time, particularly considering that the Japanese revolutionary had to operate from underground through Phillips. These two laid the intellectual, organisational, and political infrastructure of a Communist Party. Katayama, with Phillips as his intermediary and translator, carried out an extensive correspondence with left and labour organisations in Mexico and Latin America and helped to develop important contacts. Katayama's pamphlets and newspapers represented the first sustained Communist propaganda campaign in Mexico. Working through his translator and organiser Charles Francis Phillips and with José Valadés, Alfred Stirner, and the capable organiser Manuel Díaz Ramírez, Katayama gradually constructed the core of a small party and established important labour work among peasants and oil workers. If the party could bring 21 delegates representing some 1,000 members together, not a negligible achievement, even if the delegates represented half of what they claimed, this was because of Fraina's and Katayama's work. The labour union work would continue through the next few years and become quite important in the mid-1920s when the Communists led movements of tens of thousands in the oil fields and among the peasants. These efforts continued largely thanks to the efforts of another American Communist who arrived in Mexico shortly after Fraina and Katayama left, namely, Bertram D. Wolfe.

---

61   Spenser 1998, p. 67.

CHAPTER 16

Bertram Wolfe, the Communists, and a Right Turn in Mexico

Not very long after Louis Fraina and Sen Katayama left Mexico, the American radical and anti-war activist Bertram D. Wolfe arrived and soon became one of the principal leaders of the Mexican Communist Party. Wolfe would play a far more important role than Fraina and Katayama, partly because he mastered the Spanish language, but largely because he could act openly, even becoming an acknowledged public leader, rather than operating clandestinely. Wolfe's period of leadership coincided with one of the party's greatest tests: Adolfo de la Huerta's rebellion against President Álvaro Obregón. The question arose: Which side would the Communist Party of Mexico support: The Obregón government or the de la Huerta rebels?

Opinion in the party was divided. As Obregón and Calles continued to create the institutions of an increasingly authoritarian order, while making limited concessions to the labouring classes, some party members leaned toward the rebel de la Huerta, who they saw as representing the left. Wolfe persuaded the party to support Obregón, and to take advantage of the moment to arm the Communist affiliated organisations such as Úrsulo Galván's League of Agrarian Communities in Veracruz. Later Wolfe would claim the Communist Party's role in the defence of the Mexican government as a great success, but others would see it a political failure, the beginning of the subordination of the Mexican Communist Party to the Mexican state. In fact, though, the Communist International and the PCM zigzagged back and forth for decades afterward between support for the Mexican government and opposition to it.

While the Communist International had sent Fraina and Katayama to Mexico, Wolfe wandered down south on his own initiative. Without either friends or funds when he arrived, he soon found his feet, and within a year became one of the most important leaders of the Mexican Communist movement. He helped to once again reorganise the Communist Party, became an advisor to labour unions, helped to create a Latin American anti-imperialist movement, and promoted closer contacts between the US and Mexican Communist parties.

1   Bertram Wolfe

Who was Bertram Wolfe? Wolfe was born 19 January 1896 in Brooklyn, New York, the son of a Jewish peddler and his homemaker wife. As a youngster he was a great reader and a brilliant student and entered the City College of New York at the age of 16. At CCNY, Wolfe won a prize for his accomplishments in the German language and would later be recognised as an outstanding student of Spanish.

The outbreak of the war in Europe in 1914 utterly stunned Wolfe, as it did millions around the world. Wolfe later wrote in his autobiography, 'Nothing in my high school and college days, nor my outside reading, nor the utterances of our leaders, had prepared me for war at all in the century that had been rung in with such assurances that it would be "too civilised for war"'.[1] The shocking and horrifying outbreak of the war drove Wolfe to become an anti-war activist, a conscientious objector, and a socialist.

Meanwhile, Wolfe married his high school sweetheart, Ella, and found a job as a teacher in the New York City School system. When the US Congress voted to enter the war and passed the conscription act, the 21-year-old Wolfe registered on 5 June 1917 but claimed an exemption as 'Conscientious objection to murder', as he wrote.[2] Wolfe's draft board, however, ignored the challenge implicit in his registration form and gave him a deferral because he was the sole support of his wife, Ella, who was at the time unemployed. Therefore, unlike many other conscientious objectors, Wolfe was not drafted, arrested, jailed, tried, or imprisoned for his opposition to the war.

Nevertheless, Wolfe faced problems because of his anti-war and anti-draft position. The Mayor of New York sent an order to all New York City school principals, directing them to get all teachers to sign a 'loyalty pledge' supporting President Wilson in whatever decisions he might make. Wolfe was the only teacher in his school who refused to sign the pledge. The principal decided that rather than firing Wolfe, he would drive him out of the profession by making his life miserable. He transferred him from teaching English to maths, and then to Latin, until finally Wolfe resigned.

---

1   Wolfe 1981, p. 115.
2   Wolfe 1981, p. 140.

2   Into the Anti-war Movement and Socialist Party

No longer able to work as a teacher, Wolfe landed a job as the editor of the trade paper of the Jewish Master Bakers' Federation, *The Mediator*, and entered the anti-war movement.

> I cooperated with the People's Council, as the Emergency Peace Founda-
> tion was now called ... I founded and edited an antiwar newspaper; and,
> although I was not a convinced socialist, I joined the Socialist Party and
> became active in its ranks because its whole activity was concentrated
> during the war on opposition thereto, and it seemed to me the most stable
> and firmest of bodies in its antiwar activities.[3]

As a conscientious objector and a Socialist, Wolfe gravitated towards the party's left wing.

Wolfe raised money among City College students for his anti-war newspaper, *Facts: The People's Peace Paper*, the first issue of which appeared on 31 May 1917, selling for five cents a copy. Several artists from *The Masses* and other leftwing-ers, such as Robert Minor, Art Young, Maurice Becker, Boardman Robinson, William Gropper, Hugo Gellert, H.J. Glintenkamp, and Louis Lozowick illustrated the paper. After the first issue the pacifist paper was declared 'unmailable' by the US Post Office, so Wolfe killed the magazine rather than submit its youthful vendors to prosecution under the Espionage Act of 15 June 1917. Only six issues of the paper ever appeared, but it helped Wolfe establish ties to leaders and activists in the anti-war movement.

As he later explained, Wolfe joined the Socialist Party principally because he saw it as an anti-war organisation. He was quickly recognised for his gifts as a speaker, writer, and teacher. He began a party career as a street-corner orator, speaking twice a week, for which he was paid three dollars a night. He gradually took up more important tasks in the Socialist Party. He served as publicity dir-ector of the Party's Rand School and worked on Morris Hillquit's Socialist Party campaign for mayor. He also undertook a serious study of the socialist classics, including, of course, Karl Marx.

Under the combined influence of the war, the draft, and the anti-war move-ment, Wolfe quickly radicalised, and soon became a member of the National Council of the Left Wing of the Socialist Party. Talented and ambitious, he quickly became a leader. He participated in the left wing's famous founding

---

3   Wolfe 1981, p. 146.

meeting held in Brooklyn together with Ludwig Lore, Louis B. Boudin, Louis Fraina, John D. Williams, the Japanese socialist Sen Katayama, Sebald Justius Rutger from Holland, the Russian Gregory Chudnovsky, and four recent Russian arrivals in the US: Nikolai Bukharin, Alexandra Kollontai, V. Voldorsky, and Leon Trotsky.[4] Together with John Reed and Louis Fraina, Wolfe wrote the group's 'Manifesto', for which he was soon secretly indicted by the State of New York on charges of 'criminal anarchy'. He was never arrested, apparently because the police never found him.[5] Wolfe became the editor of one of the left wing's newspaper, *The Communist World*. When police agents appeared at Wolfe's house to arrest him, probably on the criminal anarchy charge, he evaded them and went underground in New York state.

3   Labour Activist in San Francisco

Finding the situation in New York untenable because of the warrant for his arrest, Wolfe decided to move to San Francisco without informing the party leadership. He feared that his request to move would either be denied or intercepted by government spies in the party who would have him arrested. Once in San Francisco, he quickly established contact with the Communist Party there. Taking the name Alfred Albrecht or later Arthur Albright, he worked as an accountant and taught courses at the San Francisco Workers School in the history of socialism and the labour movement.

Wolfe's teaching at the Workers School brought him to the attention of the leaders of a coalition of some 30 left-wing labour unions who asked him to become the editor of their newspaper *Rank and File*. He changed the paper's name to *Labor Unity* and during his editorship another ten or 20 unions joined the coalition that published the paper. His successful work as teacher and editor then brought a proposal from the Cooks' Union, part of the progressive bloc, that he become its representative to the Central Trades and Labor Council. So, on 22 February 1922 Wolfe fried two eggs in the Paradise Coffee Shop before a union committee and was inducted into Cooks' Union, Local 44. He soon became one of the principal spokesmen for the progressive bloc of the Labor Council.

Wolfe also remained active in the California Communist Party, and in August 1922 he was sent as its delegate to the clandestine convention of the Communist

---

4 Wolfe 1981, p. 183.
5 Wolfe 1981, pp. 48–9.

Party of the United States held in Bridgeman, Michigan. The US Federal Bureau of Investigation and Michigan police raided the convention, but Wolfe somehow managed to escape the dragnet. The Federal government, nevertheless, indicted him under his aliases of Albrecht and Albright, so Wolfe could not return to his Communist and labour union activities in California.

Once again, he moved across the continent, this time to Boston. From Boston, Wolfe travelled frequently to New York to see friends and family, and to attend labour and Communist meetings. While in New York on one of these visits, he heard the English labour leader Albert Purcell, a member of the British Trade Union Commission to Russia, speak at the Civic Club on the topic 'What I Saw in Russia'. At that meeting, Wolfe was introduced to Roberto Haberman, a former American Socialist then living in Mexico, and the head of the Department of Foreign Languages of the Federal District. Though Wolfe did not know so at the time, Haberman was the principal contact between Luis N. Morones, the head of the Regional Confederation of Mexican Workers (CROM), and Samuel Gompers, leader of the American Federation of Labor (AFL). Haberman asked Wolfe if he would like a teaching job in Mexico. Not taking Haberman's offer too seriously, Wolfe gave it no more thought and returned to Boston. A couple of weeks later, however, Haberman sent a telegram to the two Wolfes, Bertram and Ella, appointing them teachers of English in Mexico City effective 1 January, their duties to begin 5 February 1923. Since Wolfe was still wanted for arrest under two indictments, the young couple decided to take up the offer and to move to Mexico.

4   Communist in Mexico

Without consulting the US Communist Party, in 1923 Bertram and Ella Wolfe took a Ward Line steamship from New York to Veracruz and then the train to Mexico City. Haberman had arranged for Bertram and Ella Wolfe to teach two one-hour classes five days a week at the Miguel Lerdo de Tejada Girls' High School for the equivalent of 150 US dollars. This provided them a very comfortable income. Yet Haberman's ulterior motive in bringing Wolfe to Mexico was to use the latter's writing talent. Soon after they had begun teaching, Haberman called Wolfe to his office and told him that Carleton Beals had refused to collaborate with him in writing any more articles for *The Nation*, *The New Republic*, or *The Call*. 'I should like you to collaborate with me on articles on Mexico', Haberman told Wolfe. 'Well, you and Carleton have been picturing Mexico as a socialist paradise', said Wolfe, 'I can hardly think of Mexico as either socialist or a paradise'. His offer rejected, Haberman dismissed Wolfe from his office and fired the couple from their jobs.[6]

The Wolfes had no labour union, so they decided to appeal their case to their school principal, who in turn appealed directly to José Vasconcelos, the Minister of Education and an enemy of both Haberman and his patrons Morones and Minister of the Interior Plutarco Elías Calles. Vasconcelos agreed to reinstate the Wolfes in their teaching jobs. This gave Bertram Wolfe the financial independence to pursue his political activities in the Mexican Communist Party.

Wolfe, a real linguist, soon mastered Spanish and began to write for the Mexican Communist Party newspaper *El Machete*. He also taught at the Mexican Union of Railway Carpenters, at that time the most radical group among the railroad workers.[7] 'My course was a mixture of history, sociology, and political thought, called "The Class Struggle Through the Ages"', wrote Wolfe. 'Gradually, railway workers and workers from other crafts began to attend, and I came to be considered the educational director of the railwaymen's unions. When in 1925 sixteen of the seventeen railway crafts set up a strike committee, they insisted that I should serve on it in an advisory capacity'.[8]

Wolfe spent the next year as one of the Mexican Communist Party's principal political leaders. Part of Wolfe's work was to try to persuade the famous Mexican muralist Diego Rivera, to resign from the Communist Party. Rivera, David Alfaro Siqueiros and Xavier Guerrero had founded *El Machete* in 1924 as the newspaper of the Union of Technical Workers, Painters and Sculptors, but the artists soon joined the Communist Party, and *El Machete* then became the party's newspaper.[9] The participation of these famous and popular artists brought great prestige to the small Communist Party, but also created problems. 'After the entry of these artists into the Party, they tended to dominate it completely', according to one historian.[10] Rivera, by virtue of his reputation as a painter and his powerful personality, inevitably played an important and not always a very beneficial role in the small party. Preoccupied with his painting, Rivera would miss party committee meetings and even public speaking dates.

---

6   Wolfe 1981, pp. 280–1.
7   Barrios 1978, p. 48. Barrios was an activist in the railroad workers' union in the 1920s and he concurs that: 'La Unión de Carpinteros y Similares, [fue el] grupo de vanguardia de entonces ...' (The Carpenters Union was the vanguard of that time ...), that is, in the early 1920s. But he does not mention Wolfe, perhaps because Barrios continued in the Stalinist PCM of the 1930s while Wolfe became a Bukharinite, which in the US was a Lovestoneite, that is, part of the Communist International's rightwing.
8   Wolfe 1981, p. 302.
9   Martínez Verdugo 1983, pp. 75–8.
10   Alexander 1957, p. 322.

But the real issue may have been Rivera's mercurial and volatile personality; in a disciplined organisation he was a political maverick. Wolfe wanted Rivera to resign from the party because 'it had become increasingly clear to me that the best service he could give was with his brush'.[11] Wolfe suggests that he convinced Rivera to resign, but that in 1926 Rivera was readmitted to the party until expelled in 1929 for 'rightist' tendencies.[12] But Rivera was no rightist and later, after leaving the Communist Party, he became for a while a supporter of the dissident Communist left opposition leader, Leon Trotsky.[13]

It was also in 1924 that Stanislav Pestkovsky, an old Bolshevik, became the Soviet Union's ambassador to Mexico. Pestkovsky like other Communist ambassadors saw his role as both representing the interests of the Soviet Union publicly while privately assisting the Communist International and the local Communist Party. He provided money for the printing of *El Machete* and other Communist publications, helped fund Communist activities, and also facilitated financial support for the Mexican railroad workers strikes that later developed. He invited Latin American revolutionaries opposing the dictatorial regimes backed by the United States in their countries to look to him, the Communist International, and the Soviet Union for assistance. His support for the Communists and other leftists in the struggle against the government-backed CROM may have been the reason that President Calles asked Pestovsky to leave before he was expelled.[14] In 1926 Pestovsky returned to the Soviet Union,[15] but while in Mexico his political orientation and his munificence aided Wolfe in his work, especially his work with the unions.

Wolfe's role with the railway unions reflected not only his own talent, but also the Communist Party's growing influence among those unions. As an educated man in a country of vast illiteracy, Wolfe quickly gained influence within the labour movement and the Communist Party. He became a leader of the Mexican Communist Party at a crucial juncture in its history, and his intervention in the party would have an important impact upon its organisation and its politics. The Mexican government's ruling 'Sonoran Dynasty', the triumvirs Adolfo de la Huerta, Álvaro Obregón and Plutarco Elías Calles had a political

---

11   Wolfe 1981, p. 305.
12   Wolfe 1981, pp. 304–5; Alexander 1961, pp. 193–4.
13   Gall 1991, *passim*.
14   Spenser 2018, pp. 77–98.
15   After leaving Mexico, Pestovsky held many other diplomatic posts. Though he had sent a personal letter to Trotsky after the latter's deportation to Turkey expressing his sympathy, Pestovsky continued to serve Stalin's Communist International, decorated for his service by both Mexico and the Soviet Union, and remarkably for an Old Bolshevik survived the entire Stalin period, dying in Moscow in March of 1954 (de Pablo 2014).

falling out. Obregón chose to support Calles as his successor to the presidency, and de la Huerta then broke with them, deciding to mount his own political campaign. Both sides understood that the fight might end in another revolution and perhaps a civil war.

The two factions had similar characters. Both were led by Sonoran military *caudillos*, both were multiclass coalitions, and both made similar claims to having progressive programmes. Obregón and Calles had the support of the government's reformist unions of the Regional Confederation of Mexican Workers (CROM), which in turn had the backing of Gompers and the AFL. De la Huerta sought an alliance with the railroad unions, the anarchist General Confederation of Workers (CGT), and with the Communist Party, and, according to Wolfe, even offered a 'huge bribe to Manuel [Díaz] Ramírez [General] Secretary of the Communist Party'.[16]

Wolfe was convinced that siding with de la Huerta would be disastrous. 'I led the opposition to the acceptance of the subsidy', that is, of government support, he later wrote in his autobiography, 'and urged that Obregón and Calles, and the larger of the two trade union bodies [CROM] and the Labourista Party [of Morones], represented the lesser evil'. Wolfe remembered that he told the Mexican Communists:

> I have been fighting to make the unions and labour organizations independent of subsidy. Since Obregón lost the generals, we can get him to arm the workers and peasants in states like Michoacán and Veracruz, the Comunidades Agrarias [Agrarian Communities] are under our leadership. This is our chance to make the Communist Party independent of all subsidies and a power in its own right.[17]

Wolfe and his ally Rafael Carrillo, leader of the Communist youth movement, succeeded in convincing the Central Committee.

The Communists not only supported the government on paper, but also put troops in the field to defend the Obregón-Calles faction in states such as Veracruz. The most important Communist detachments were those of Úrsulo Galván, leader of the 20,000-member League of Agrarian Communities in Veracruz. 'Comrade Galvan rose up and assumed leadership of the irregular troops of the State thus winning the confidence of all of the peasants', wrote Wolfe in a report to the Red International of Labour Unions in Moscow.[18]

---

16   Wolfe 1981, p. 329.
17   Wolfe 1981, p. 303.
18   Letter from Bertram Wolfe to the RILU, 10 January 1924, doc. 534/7/393/83 in SASRF.

When the Obregón-Calles government won the brief civil war, and de la Huerta was defeated, Wolfe's policy was apparently vindicated by the role of Communists as an independent military fighting force in the field in Veracruz.[19] But their opposition to the de la Huerta rebellion had thrown the Communists into the arms of Calles. The new executive committee, of which Wolfe formed a part, pushed the Communist Party to campaign 'actively for Calles, presenting him as a popular figure, a labour candidate, and even a socialist who was supported by the overwhelming majority of workers and peasants'.[20] The Communists, including Wolfe, would have been hard pressed to explain and justify their support for Calles whose regime was laying the foundations of capitalist development in Mexico, especially while Calles, Morones, and the CROM remained the sworn enemies of the Communists and anarchists.

5   Representing Mexican Communism in Moscow

Wolfe was elected the party's delegate to the Fifth Congress of the Communist International. His preparations to leave for Moscow reveal much about the strange and fascinating relationship between the Mexican government and the Mexican Communist Party. In getting ready for his trip to Moscow, Wolfe, who was after all a lowly, part-time foreign language teacher, requested and received an interview with the Minister of Education, José Vasconcelos. Wolfe informed Vasconcelos that he had been chosen as delegate of the Mexican Communist Party to the Congress of the Communist International. He requested a leave of absence. When Vasconcelos granted his leave, Wolfe said Vasconcelos told him, 'You can tell them that as far as their plans involve a struggle against American Imperialism, I am with them'.[21]

Wolfe also paid a visit to Mexican Undersecretary of Foreign Affairs Genaro Estrada to ask for a Mexican passport, to which as a US citizen he was certainly not entitled. Estrada immediately arranged for the passport, though it is not clear whether he knew that Wolfe was not a Mexican. Finally, Wolfe arranged to write a series of articles for the newspaper *El Demócrata* later titled 'La Unión Soviética en 1924'. Wolfe borrowed money for the trip to New York, and then stowed away on a Polish-American ship, the ss Polonia. Once the ship was out at sea, he revealed himself and arranged to do menial work for his fare. He landed

---

19   Wolfe 1981, p. 303; Alexander 1957, pp. 322–3.
20   Carr 1992, p. 41.
21   Wolfe 1981, p. 306.

at Copenhagen, and then went to Berlin where he met his Communist International contacts. From Berlin he travelled to Hamburg and then to Leningrad (Petrograd) by ship. Since the Congress's official language was German, Wolfe, who spoke that language fluently, functioned as an interpreter into Spanish and English, as well as being a Mexican delegate.

As the Mexican representative to the Communist International, Wolfe spoke only twice. Once he explained the Mexican Communist Party's position in supporting the Obregón-Calles government against the de la Huerta rebellion. He argued that the strategy had been justified since they had succeeded in getting the government to arm the peasants, who had subsequently refused to return the guns.[22] Wolfe also spoke on his party's attempt to form independent labour unions that were not subsidised by the Mexican government.[23]

The Comintern Archives contain a short (four-page, double-spaced) memo that Wolfe wrote to leaders about the difficulties of organising workers in Mexico. Titled 'Memorandum on Financial Situation in the Communist Party of Mexico', Wolfe noted that Mexico was a big country geographically speaking, 'three times the size of Germany', which could only be organised by 'slow and costly railroad trips, often even without direct rail connections'. He pointed out that, 'The workers and peasants of Mexico are often extremely poor', earning only 30 to 50 centavos per day, so that even those who wanted to 'cannot buy party papers'. Workers would come to party demonstrations and 'freely endanger their lives', but they did not pay dues. Consequently, the party had no paid secretary, and party workers had to quit their party jobs to support their families, and in one case a party functionary had collapsed from 'malnutrition'.

Wolfe pointed out that the party's poverty made it susceptible to being suborned. 'Our conventions have hitherto been possible only because the reformist government in its fights with the reactionary landowners desires our aid and without making conditions has given our delegates railroads passes'. But he noted that, 'this is a very unhealthy condition for a Communist Party'. He insisted that the Communist Party needed 'a weekly party organ, a printing press and a paid secretary'.

In the same memo, Wolfe suggested that Mexico could play a special role in North America. 'There also exist possibilities for the Mexican party to serve as a connecting link between the American [US] and Latin American labour movements and parties'. He pointed out that Mexico already served 'as a means of

---

22   Wolfe 1981, p. 325.
23   Wolfe 1981, p. 336.

aiding in the organization of movements in Cuba, Central America, and Peru'. After several years of involvement of Americans in the Mexican Communist Party, this is one of the few suggestions for actual cooperation between US and Mexican unions and workers.

Finally, Wolfe concluded his memo arguing that,

> The growth of American Imperialism and the opposition to it necessitate the establishing of an open continental propaganda against imperialism and illegal organization to investigate the next moves of American imperialism, to gather facts, to relate and coordinate the various revolutionary movements against it such as those of Central America, Peru, Venezuela, Bolivia, etc.

In this regard he wrote that any discussion of such an organisation would be incomplete without an evaluation of 'the unfortunate experience of the International, its "Agency", and the Fraina affair'.[24] He suggested that in the future there would have to be strict financial accounting in any such venture. Wolfe returned to Mexico via the Communist Party's headquarters in Chicago. While there he spoke to Communist party committees and public meetings on US investments in Latin America, on the Mexican labour union movement, and on the Mexican artistic renaissance. No doubt William Z. Foster and other Communist labour leaders in Chicago must have received private, first-hand accounts of the state of the Mexican labour unions. At the same time Wolfe apprised himself of the state of the Communist Party of the United States and its work in the unions.

Meanwhile, in Mexico, *El Demócrata* had been publishing Wolfe's articles on Soviet Russia, the first serious discussions of the new Soviet Union to appear in Mexican newspapers. Daniela Spenser argues that those articles constitute what is perhaps Wolfe's most important contribution to Mexican Communism, because for the first time they provided a picture of the nature of Soviet Russia and the Soviet Communist Party, as well as a view of Russian society since the revolution.[25]

---

24   Bertram D. Wolfe, 'Memorandum on Financial Situation in the Communist Party of Mexico', Document 495/108/210, SASRF.

25   Personal communication from Daniela Spenser, April 1997.

6   Wolfe, the Communists and Labour Organisation

When he returned to Mexico, Wolfe wrote a report in January of 1925 to the Red International of Labour Unions in which he explained his work with the party's unionists. 'The entire year', he wrote, 'was dedicated to overcoming [the Communist Party's] reputation as splitters (*divisionistas*) and making our members join the unions, to destroying the splitter mentality (*psicología divisionista*) which is still dominant in our own ranks and to prove it in fact by means of a campaign for working class unity'. During the course of the year, the majority of Communists had either joined the CROM or independent unions. 'We took on a struggle for the affiliation of the autonomous unions with the CROM, and succeeded in affiliating the Carpenters, and electing as general secretary of that group Comrade Bernal of our Party, who later attended the Congress of the Regional Confederation of Mexican Workers as a delegate'. Wolfe himself joined the Editors Union and became a delegate to the Federation of Graphic Arts. In Michoacán, the Communists encouraged several independent unions to join, and Alfonso Soria became the delegate to the CROM. Ironically, Wolfe wrote, 'our forces within the CROM are growing now in such a way that a new campaign of expulsions against us has been undertaken'. Communist members or sympathisers in the Iron Workers Union and others in the Factory Workers Union and Wolfe himself in the Editors Union were all under attack.[26]

Wolfe reported that despite this new anti-Communist campaign, 'Our organization in Tampico dominates the port and has held a local congress of the organizations (CROM, CGT, and independent unions)'. That same congress agreed to a local united front. 'In Tampico, Gregorio Turrubiates, an active member of the party, assumed leadership of the great strike of the workers of the El Águila Petroleum Company, and despite the treason of Morones, won a partial victory'. That strike was followed by others at La Corona, Mexican Gulf, la Huasteca, Pierce Oil, and other companies. 'Our national Senator, Luis G. Monzón, has carried out a very effective agitation in the Senate'.[27]

In addition to the oil workers, the party had two other important areas of work. Wolfe noted that, 'The President of the Railroad Workers Alliance [Elías] Barrios has joined the Party and three more of the most active members'.[28] The

---

26   Letter of 10 January 1925, from Bertram D. Wolfe to Bureau Ejecutivo de las ISR [RILU], Document #534/7/393, f. 83, SASRF.

27   Ibid.

28   Ibid.

recruitment of Barrios, an important asset to the Communist Party for many more years, would prove to be very important for Wolfe's own future. Finally, he noted that, 'The most important progress has been among the campesinos', and he mentioned the role of Úrsulo Galván, 'our leader' of the League of Agrarian Communities in Veracruz with 20,000 members.[29] At the end of 1922 the Communist Party local of Veracruz had formed a special commission of Úrsulo Gálvan and Manuel Almanza to organise peasants, and the result had been the very successful Liga de Comunidades Agrarias. The League also affiliated with the Communist Peasant International (KRESINTERN).[30] The party intended to help Galván form a national peasant federation. Wolfe's report to the Red International of Labour Unions suggested that the party was on the verge of a real breakthrough in labour organising, with important work among railroad workers, petroleum workers, and peasants.

7   The Third Congress of the Communist Party

The work of the earlier slackers like Phillips, the Communist International envoys Louis Fraina and Sen Katayama, as well as that of the itinerant radical Bertram Wolfe all came to fruition in Mexico in the mid-1920s in the development of the small Communist Party's growing strength and influence. Moscow, it should be remembered, had assigned the Communist Party of the United States to be responsible for Mexico. Jack Johnstone, a leader of the Communist Party in Illinois was sent to evaluate the Mexican Communist Party in 1924. Perhaps under-informed and overly optimistic, he wrote a long report in which, while pointing out the weaknesses of the PCM, wrote that 'the revolutionary movement in Mexico and Latin America is now crystallising and our party should play a leadership role in these developments, with the pivot in Mexico'.[31]

The Mexican Communist Party's Third Congress was held in Mexico City in April of 1925. Wolfe, writing in the Communist *International Press Correspondence* on 18 June 1925, considered it the 'small beginning of a real Communist Party in Mexico', as the local chapters had revived, begun to pay dues, carry out

---

29   Ibid.

30   Domínguez Pérez 1986, pp. 34 and 70.

31   Jack Johnstone, '*Informe del movimiento revolucionario panamericano y del Congreso del PanAmerican Federation of Labor*', Relación de documentos sobre México en el Centro Ruso, Biblioteca Manuel Orozco y Berra Instituto-Instituto Nacional de Antropología, Mexico, Rollo núm 17,515–539, cited in Kersffeld 2012, p. 48.

political tasks, and follow party discipline.[32] For the first time since its founding in 1919, the Mexican Communist Party seemed to have some organisational
stability, even if minimal.

Charles Francis Phillips, using the name Manuel Gómez, returned to Mexico on 5 April 1925 to attend the Mexican Communist Party Convention as the
delegate of the Workers Party (the legal name at that time of the Communist Party) of the United States. Phillips, having been a founder of the Mexican
Communist Party, had a good deal of authority, and he appears to have super-
vised the Mexican Communist Party convention. After the Congress, he wrote
a 19-page, single-spaced report in which he analysed the Mexican convention
and the party in some detail. The report gives a picture of Bertram Wolfe as the
principal intellectual leader of the Mexican Communist Party and of the party's
successes and failures under his leadership. Phillips observed that although he
arrived only two days before the convention, 'only the vaguest preparations had
been made'. This reflected, the 'indefiniteness about the entire organizational
side of the Party'. For example, 'No one knew how many delegates would come
to the Congress'. Phillips observed that, 'The Congress was essentially an organization congress', that is a meeting to – once again – found the party.[33]

The central conflict on the eve of the congress revolved around the plan of
Wolfe and Rafael Carrillo to oust Manuel Díaz Ramírez from the post of general
secretary of the party. Wolfe and Carrillo accused Díaz Ramírez of 'open and
flagrant violation of party discipline, *chambismo* [government job-seeking], an
un-Communistic attitude during the street car workers' strike and persistent
opportunism'.[34] Phillips presented a motion to the national committee calling upon Wolfe, Díaz Ramírez and one other person to come up with a way
of dealing with the issues without jeopardising the organisation. The Mexican
Communist Party's national committee named Phillips as the third party. He
succeeded in getting Wolfe and Díaz Ramírez to work together despite their
differences. Thus, the controversy between its three most important leaders
(Carrillo, Díaz Ramírez and Wolfe) did not prevent the Congress from carrying
out its work.

Evaluating the Congress itself, Phillips reported, 'The Party is still young, dis-
organised, woefully weak, and ideologically unsteady, but in spite of all this, it is
slowly taking on the impress of a Communist movement and is becoming, bit
by bit, a real party'. The party's membership, generously estimated, said Phil-

---

32   Alexander 1957, p. 323.
33   Manuel Gómez [Charles Francis Phillips], 'Report on CP of Mexico and its Third Annual
       Congress, April 7–13, 1925', Document 495/108/48, pp. 5–8, SASRF.
34   Ibid.

lips, was 191 members, in addition to 20 or 25 Young Workers League members. The Congress delegates came from Tampico, Veracruz, Morelia, Orizaba, Río Blanco, Mérida, Guanajuato, and Mexico City. In addition, there were fraternal delegates from the Workers (Communist) Party of the United States and from the Communist Party of Central America. There were also present important figures, such as the peasant leader Úrsulo Galván.[35]

The Congress agenda was to deal with five points of discussion:

1) The alliance between the Calles government and the CROM and their joint attack upon the working class.
2) 'The unity of the trade union movement and means of united struggle against the bosses, CROM leaders and government'.
3) 'Bolshevization of the Communist Party'.
4) 'Establishing mass contacts with the poor peasants and winning leadership in the agrarian movement'.
5) 'The struggle against American imperialism'.[36]

Phillips reported that while the Mexican Communist Party had stressed activity in the trade unions, there were many serious problems. 'Owing to the campaign of expulsions initiated by Morones and the other Mexican allies of the A.F. of L. bureaucracy, our Mexican comrades find themselves in very much the same situation of isolation in the trade unions that we are experiencing here [i.e., the United States] and in other countries'. The Mexican Communists had turned to the rank-and-file workers. 'However, this is not developing as fast as it might and is not being crystallised into a definite left wing alignment, because of complete absence of a coordinated minority movement in Mexico'.

Phillips believed that, 'The [Mexican] C.P. is handicapped in its trade union work because it has not been able to develop the nuclei system of boring from within'. This 'nuclei system of boring from within' meant the creation of small Communist Party groupings within each of the unions, whether CROM, CGT, or independent that would organise rank-and-file workers and crystalise them into an active oppositional organisation. Nevertheless, wrote Phillips, the party did have some influence. 'Among local unions of masons, carpenters, bakers, etc., the party has sympathisers'. Many CROM members, wrote Phillips, formed part of a 'mute and fearful opposition' with which the Communists had to make better contact.

There was, however, one highlight on the labour scene, reported Phillips. 'It is in the oil fields in the Tampico district that the C.P. has accomplished some

---

35   Ibid.
36   Ibid.

of its best work. Under the leadership of Comrade Turrubiates the Communists have been making great gains among the oil workers and have directed
them in a number of successful struggles against the oil companies'.[37] Phillips explained that the Tampico region had 72,000 organised workers, 50,000
of them oil workers. He noted that, 'The American IWW once had some organisation among the Tampico oil workers but this has been dissipated'.[38] In 1925,
there were about 80 local unions divided among several federations. The CROM
had two; and the CGT three. Twenty-three belong to the local Federation de Sindicatos and 44 to another federation called 'Pacto Solidario'. 'The Communists',
reported Phillips, 'have organised a good many of the local unions, and have
led the workers to several victories against the bosses'. Wolfe told the Congress,
'Tampico is the point of departure for all of our work in Mexico and one of
the first tasks of the new executive committee is to build up a more effective
movement there'.[39]

Another important industry in Mexico was the railroads. Phillips reported
that, 'The Communists are not without strength among the railroad workers.
Their influence is perhaps small but it is exerted at strategic points. Carlos
Rendón, chairman of the trade union committee of the Party, is an active rail-
roader, who understands the problems of railroaders and who is doing good
work for the Party among them'. Since President Calles had declared that the
railroads would be returned to private ownership, and the unions and workers
feared that they would then lose higher wages and conditions, the Communists
were proposing the 'immediate formation of councils of action' to fight privat-
isaton.[40]

The issue of privatisation formed an important point of the party's six-point
program, paraphrased here:
1) No restoration of the railroads to private ownership.
2) Preservation of the railroad unions at all costs.
3) Transformation of the craft unions into industrial unions.
4) The creation of a national federation of independent unions.
5) Immediate formation of councils of action for the coming railroad strike.
6) Refusal to let the railroad situation benefit either politicians or military
   coups.[41]

---

37   Ibid.
38   Ibid, p. 8.
39   Ibid.
40   Ibid, pp. 8–9.
41   Ibid, p. 9.

If, with the exception of the oil workers, the party's labour work was rather weak, the Mexican Communists had 'important triumphs' in the 'developing peasant movement of Mexico'. But in the countryside, Communist success had an ambivalent character, since the peasant leaders retained ties to generals and governors linked to factions in the national state. Mexican Communists or sympathisers, such as Primo Tapia in Michoacán and Úrsulo Galván in Veracruz, were leading a mass movement of tens of thousands of peasants. This might suggest considerable CP influence among the peasants but as Phillips noted, 'The actual fact is that these peasants do not follow the C.P. and most of them do not know of the existence of the C.P.'.[42] Only the peasant leaders like Galván had any real connection to the party.

Galván, though not then a party member, reported on the peasant work. He told the Congress that there were three million organised peasants in Mexico. He called for the creation of a 'national league of peasant communes'.[43] And in fact, a Liga National Campesina (LNC), the National Peasant League, held a founding congress in November 1926 with 158 delegates representing ten states and the Federal District, and claiming to represent 300,000 peasants. The LNC also affiliated with the Communist led Peasant International, the KRESIN-TERN.[44]

In addition to its work among peasants and workers, the Communist Party had also recruited a senator, Luis G. Monzón who joined the party in 1925. Monzón played an active role in defence of the petroleum workers and the peasant organisations in Veracruz, and a pamphlet of his writing on Communism had been published in 1924.[45] The recruitment of a Mexican leftist politician was not without its problems. 'He desires with all his might to be a Communist', wrote Phillips, 'but his age, training and background are against him'. The Party also published its newspaper *El Machete* with a circulation of between four and five thousand, larger than any other labour paper in Mexico.

'The Congress showed that a long and extensive campaign of education is one of the most urgent requirements of the Mexican Party', wrote Phillips and he reported a telling anecdote: 'For instance the delegate from Río Blanco, in his report announced that his local has lost all prestige before the workers because at a recent meeting someone had asked the leader of the local: "What is Communism?" – and nobody in the local was able to answer'.

42   Ibid, p. 5.
43   Ibid, p. 10.
44   Domínguez Pérez, *Política y Movimientos Sociales en el Tejedismo*, p. 71; José Rivera Castro, 'Vera Cruz: Organización y Radicalismo Campesino', in Reyna Muñoz 1996, p. 214.
45   Monzón 1924.

Surely when the Communists did not know what Communism was, there was some educating to be done.[46]

Phillips's pet project was the creation of the All American Anti-Imperialist League (AAAIL). On behalf of the Workers (Communist) Party of the United States, Phillips made the speech on the AAAIL. He later explained, 'In my speech to the convention I called attention to the unity of the struggle of the Mexican and American workers'. But Phillips also called for 'drawing into the struggle against Wall Street all sorts of anti-imperialistic elements of Latin America, including workers organizations, peasant leagues, student groups, patriotic societies, political parties, etc.'. 'I emphasised the role which could be played by the [All] American Anti-Imperialist League, as a united front organization under Communist leadership'.[47]

Both Phillips and Wolfe understood the importance of the anti-imperialist and internationalist sentiment that had spread throughout Latin America under the influence of thinkers such as the Mexican José Vasconcelos, the Peruvians Victor Raúl Haya de la Torre and Carlos Mariátegui, and the Argentinians Manuel Ugarte and José Ingenieros. Latin Americans, or Indo-Americans as they often called themselves, wanted a political vehicle to unite the Latin people of the American continents against the Anglo-Saxon, Protestant, capitalist power to the North.

Phillips laid out a series of proposals for the new Anti-Imperialist League. He called for:

1) The creation of a Mexican section of the AIL;
2) The holding of a Congress of the League either in Argentina or Mexico on 1 November 1925;
3) The holding of a Latin American Peasant Congress immediately before or after the AIL Congress;
4) That the Mexican CP condemn US President Coolidge's interference in the Tacna-Arica controversy and call for the solidarity of the people of Chile and Peru.[48]

To launch the League, Phillips proposed making 4 July the beginning of an anti-imperialist week throughout the Americas. He noted that the Anti-Imperialist League already had support from Vasconcelos, Ingenieros, and from Dr Carlos León of Venezuela, all well-known intellectual and political figures identified with the struggle both against Latin American dictators and US imperialism.

46   Manuel Gómez [Charles Francis Phillips], 'Report on CP of Mexico and its Third Annual Congress, April 7–13, 1925', Document 495/108/48, pp. 10–12, SASRF.
47   Ibid, pp. 10–13.
48   Ibid, pp. 15–16, SASRF.

With some differences of opinion amongst the delegates, the Mexican Communist Party voted that the Anti-Imperialist League headquarters should be in the United States. Thus Phillips, not Wolfe, would become the AAAIL organiser.[49]

Phillips ended his report with a caveat that reflected the ambivalent situation in which the Communist Party found itself. He warned that the Mexican Communist Party had never conducted a genuinely Communist political campaign. 'Today parliamentary opportunism constitutes the greatest danger before the Mexican party', he wrote. He indicated that if he were in charge, he would forbid the party from carrying on any parliamentary campaigns for an indefinite period, except under its own name. Perhaps it was the party's dependence on political leaders such as Galván with close ties to the leading political figures and the state which made Phillips fear the danger of parliamentary reformism. In an appendix, Phillips evaluated the characters and qualities of the Mexican Communist Party leaders. Wolfe, Carrillo and [Díaz] Ramírez, he suggested, were 'the only ones in the convention who had a clear understanding of the duties of Communist leadership'. Phillips also noted that all party members admitted that 'whatever his [Wolfe's] faults may be, he is the undoubted intellectual leader of the Party'.[50]

One of the striking things about the Mexican Communist Party Congress of 1925 was that two Americans, Bertram Wolfe and Charles Francis Phillips played key roles in the proceedings. Of the three leaders of the Mexican Communist Party in 1925, the one who functioned as its intellectual and political leader was the American Wolfe. The American leftists could take a good deal of credit for the party's work among unions of peasants, oil workers and railroad workers, although they worked in close conjunction with Mexican Communist leaders such as Carrillo and Díaz Ramírez. What was taking place in the late 1920s and would be complete in the 1930s was the transfer of leadership to the Mexicans.

8   The All American Anti-Imperialist League

Phillips's report emphasised that one of the major accomplishments of the Congress was the organisation of the Anti-Imperialist League. Wolfe claimed

---

49   Kersffeld 2012, pp. 55–66, using different documents also gives an overview of this PCM congress and the League at that time, painting a similar picture.

50   Manuel Gómez [Charles Francis Phillips], 'Report on CP of Mexico and its Third Annual Congress, April 7–13, 1925', Document 495/108/48, pp. 4, 11, 13, 16, SASRF.

that the League was his brainchild. He remembered that after reading Lenin's *Imperialism*, he had undertaken a study of US investment in Latin America. Then he studied a number of Latin American authors who wrote on the question. His investigation led him, he recalled, to propose that the Communists establish an anti-imperialist magazine and organisation. 'I knew the Latin-American refugees [that José] Vasconcelos [Mexican Minister of Education] had invited to teach in his schools and universities, and they all confirmed my feeling', wrote Wolfe. Haya de la Torre, leader of the University reform movement in Peru, then in exile in Mexico, also promised to support the project. The Soviet ambassador Stanislaw Pestovsky, who already provided funds to the Mexican Communist Party and its publications,[51] agreed to help finance the AIL project.

Phillips wrote later in his autobiography that, 'Although the weak Mexican Communist Party did not provide much of a nucleus for a broad front organisation, the general population's hatred of sticky-fingered *Yanquilandia* provided a strong base for our All-American Anti-Imperialist League'.[52] Phillips was responsible not only for the overall operation of the League, but also for organising the US chapters. 'Though I'd been named secretary at the United States section of the All American Anti-Imperialist League, that section in fact still had to be created'. He recalled that, 'The organised labour movement [of the United States] was not interested; indeed, the speakers we sent to meetings of trade union locals usually failed even to be admitted'. He found, however, that the idea appealed to the radical Federated Press; its Chicago Bureau made up of Carl Haessler, Leland Olds and Art Shields, were all willing to help with publicity. A wealthy Chicagoan, William H. Holly provided the League with money. Phillips also succeeded in interesting William Pickens of the National Association for the Advancement of Coloured People (NAACP), Roger Baldwin of the Civil Liberties Union, as well liberals such as Robert Morse Lovett, Paxton Hibben, Lewis Gannett, Freda Kirchwey, Arthur Garfield Hays, and Scott Nearing, all of whom lent their names to the masthead. So, of course, did Communists William Z. Foster, William F. Dunne, and Manuel Gómez, the latter name being one of Phillips's aliases.[53]

Meanwhile, in Mexico, Wolfe named the League's magazine *El Libertador: Órgano de la Liga Anti-Imperialista Panamericana* [The Liberator: Organ of the Pan-American Anti-Imperialist League]. *El Libertador* carried articles on the labour unions and peasant movements of Mexico, Central America, and South

---

51   Spenser 2018, pp. 77–98.
52   Shipman 1993, p. 155.
53   Shipman 1993, pp. 156–7.

America, as well as a letter of support from the Communist Party of the United States. The Mexican artists provided the illustrations. José Vasconcelos, the Argentine Manuel Ugarte, and the young Cuban revolutionary Julio Antonio Mella all contributed to *El Libertador*, as did Americans, among them Samuel Guy Inman, Scott Nearing, Ernest Gruening, and Jay Lovestone. By creating the All American Anti-Imperialist League and its magazine *El Libertador*.[54] Wolfe and the Communist Party had created a publication, an example of the united front approach of the period, that gave voice to the anti-imperialist sentiments of Latin Americans and North Americans of many different political views.

9   The Deportation as a Pernicious Foreigner

Wolfe continued to work with the Mexican railroad workers. As they prepared for a strike in the summer of 1925 their unions invited him to join the strike committee. Wolfe thought it inappropriate to become a member but agreed to participate as an advisor. But, just before the strike began, he was arrested and deported from Mexico under Constitutional Article 33, just as the slackers had been a few years before. He was deported from Mexico 'in perpetuity', with the warning that, if he returned, he would be jailed for five years and then deported again. As soon as Wolfe had been expelled, the Mexican Minister of the Interior put out the story first that Wolfe had been a drug dealer, but the minister also claimed that Wolfe had smuggled 50,000 US dollars in Russian gold to foment a railroad strike. Wolfe denied that he had ever brought any money back from the Soviet Union to Mexico, though he may have.[55] Wolfe's deportation from Mexico in the summer of 1925 was a significant loss to the Mexican Communist Party, for he had proven a capable political leader, a superior journalist, an asset to the party's labour union work, as well as its leading intellectual.

Wolfe's rise to influence in the Mexican Communist Party had come about as a result of his successful struggle to get the party to support the Obregón-Calles government over the de la Huerta rebellion. He would later describe this tactic as the beginning of the strategy of the united front in Mexico and imply that it was a great victory for the Mexican Communist party.[56] Yet others disagree. For example, the Mexican writer and historian Paco Ignacio Taibo II, writes quite correctly:

54   Melgar Bao 2006.
55   Wolfe 1981, pp. 337, 366–7.
56   Wolfe 1981, p. 325.

Although Bertram Wolfe would characterise this as the birth of the 'united front' in Mexico, it was really the consummation of the great rightward turn of the party in the first years of its life.[57]

Similarly, Manuel Márquez Fuente and Octavio Rodríguez Araujo in their history of the Mexican Communist Party state that Wolfe's policy of alliance with the government had a terrible impact on the party and which entered into a *decadencia total*, that is, a 'complete decline'.[58]

The Mexican Communist party had allied itself with the state and identified with the government. Wolfe's policy made the Mexican Communist party, rather than an independent workers' party, a party dependent upon two states: The Soviet Union and Mexico.

Barry Carr, the author of the definitive history of the Mexican Communist Party, observes:

> In practice the party oscillated violently between two extreme positions – an uncritical acceptance of the anticapitalist potential of the Mexican Revolution and of its associated governments ('pushing the revolution to the left') and a blunt, undifferentiated condemnation of these governments as 'despotic', 'bourgeois', 'capitulating to imperialism', etc.[59]

Wolfe's policy of support for the government during the de la Huerta rebellion contributed to the party's confusion regarding the character of the Mexican state. The party had risen to defend the revolutionary state against de la Huerta, but it succumbed to the seduction of the rhetoric of Calles, who called himself a socialist, even a Bolshevik, but who was in fact the nationalist builder of the new capitalist state. If there had been confusion before, Wolfe's right turn had deepened it.

Yet, despite that rightward turn toward the new Mexican state, Wolfe retained a radical internationalist vision that inspired imaginative projects such as the All-American Anti-Imperialist League. The League, even if it failed to accomplish its goals, represented a daring initiative. Theodore Draper pointed out that, 'In the United States, the Ant-Imperialist League never amounted to much more than a letterhead front with a small membership'.[60] But outside the United States, in some countries of Latin America, the League had a significant

---

57   Taibo II 1986, p. 228.
58   Márquez Fuente 1973, pp. 99–100.
59   Carr 1992, p. 39.
60   Draper 1986, p. 178.

impact and in a few became a movement. Ironically the League contributed to the building of both the Communist Party in some countries and of its competitor, Haya de la Torre's American Revolutionary People's Alliance (APRA) in others.

Even though Wolfe had once raised the idea of cooperation between US and Mexican Communists in the labour union movement, he seems never to have succeeded in establishing such joint cross-border collaboration. US and Mexican railroad workers might have coordinated their efforts, supporting each other's job actions and strikes particularly in northern Mexico and the southwest of the United States. Joseph 'José' W. Kelley, an organiser for the International Association of Machinists (IAM), arrived in Mexico in 1921, almost at the same time as Wolfe, and undertook just such a program. With the aid of the IAM and the AFL, Kelley had a good deal of success. Why didn't Wolfe ever develop such a transnational organising strategy? Probably because the US and Mexican Communist parties were both too small, too weak, too unstable, and altogether lacking in a clear political direction until the victory of Joseph Stalin in the succession struggle in the Soviet Union late 1920s provided the Communist Interntonal with a clear program, albeit a disastrous one, that of the 'third period'. And at just that moment, Lovestone and Wolfe were expelled from the Communist Party for being followers of Nikolai Bukharin and part of the so-called 'rightwing' of the International.

10   Conclusion

Wolfe's period as a Communist Party organiser in Mexico proved modestly successful on several fronts. He re-organised the Communist Party, built up the party's union work, and created the All-American Anti-Imperialist League. Wolfe, Carrillo and Díaz Ramírez laid the foundations for a pathetically under-funded and under-staffed Communist Party organisation. At the same time, with few resources they led the party to become involved in important labour organising among a wide variety of craft unions from bakers and carpenters to iron workers. Most impressive, however, the Communists became leaders of significant movements of industrial workers: railroad workers and oil workers. And they continued to work with the peasant leagues. It is not an exaggeration to say that under Wolfe's leadership, the Communist in 1925 were capable of leading union struggles involving tens of thousands of Mexican workers.

The establishment of the All-American Anti-Imperialist League no doubt represented Wolfe's most significant contribution to international labour solidarity, although it functioned mostly among Latin Americans. While the Anti-Imperialist League had little impact in the United States except among a small group of journalists, radicals and liberals, in Latin America the League brought together major intellectual and political figures, some with real followings in the respective countries. These included Victor Raúl Haya de la Torre and José Carlos Mariátegui both of Peru; Manuel Ugarte and José Ingenieros of Argentina; Julio Antonio Mella of Cuba; and José Vasconcelos of Mexico. Each of those men, whether as writers or organisers, had thousands of followers in their own countries and throughout Latin America. Thus, a handful of American and Mexican Communists, under the leadership of Bertram D. Wolfe and Charles Francis Phillips, working with their Latin American allies, created a continent-wide intellectual and political centre for the liberation of Latin America. Unfortunately, in 1929 Stalin decided to turn the League into a Communist front-group, and thereby destroyed the broad alliance and potential international force that it represented.

Under Wolfe's leadership, the Mexican Communist Party made one particularly lamentable political decision, which was its support of Obregón and Calles against the de la Huerta rebellion. There was little to choose politically or socially between the two sides – though most of the left labour movement went with de la Huerta – and opting for Obregón and Calles put the Communists in the position of supporting a capitalist regime that was in the process of subordinating the labour and peasant movements to their government while using the state to crush those they could not subordinate. Backing Obregón and Calles only deepened the confusion about the nature of the Mexican state and undermined the political independence of the small Mexican Communist Party.

We should stop here and make a general evaluation of the Communist experience in Mexico, one that includes both the slackers of 1917 and the Communist International agents and Wolfe in the 1920s. The Communists' theory and practice in the period under consideration here focused on organising the working class, whether in Russia, Europe, or in Latin America. (Only after the disaster of the Communist uprising in Shanghai in 1927 did Mao Tse-tung and other Chinese Communists, breaking with Marxism, turn to a concentration on the peasantry, and that experience did not have much of an impact on other Communists at that time.) Communists in Mexico wanted above all to build a working-class revolutionary party, but the working class was relatively small. As mentioned earlier, estimates of the size of the Mexican industrial working-class range between 8 and 15 percent of the population; historians using the census of 1910 and other materials have counted 107,000 mine workers and 624,000 manufacturing workers. Some eighty percent of the Mexican population depended upon agricultural income and 96 percent of rural households had no land at all.[61] As a result of ten years of revolution that affected the railroads, mines, and other industries, the population declined by 7%, and the working class probably declined by even more, though the economy picked up a little in the 1920s.

Adolfo Gilly in his history of the revolution writes:

> There were a number of reasons why the working class played only a secondary role in the Mexican Revolution – it's previous history, its relatively small numerical weight, and the very disposition of the central conflict. Some of its struggles were important, and its class organization moved forward, but its policy and leadership did not attain independence of the state and the leading bourgeois tendencies of the revolution.[62]

Throughout the revolutionary period, the working class failed to create its own political party, much less a revolutionary party. Contrary to the claims of some,[63] neither the Mexican Liberal Party nor the Zapatistas ever constituted a vanguard organisation of the working class, neither having a substantial base in the class as a whole.

The Communist organisers between 1917 and 1927, both foreigners and Mexicans, had only a small nucleus of revolutionary cadres, a handful in 1919, a few score by the 1920s, and no more than 1,500 rank-and-file members by the end of the period. While they had important relations with leaders of the railroad unions, the petroleum workers unions, and peasant organisations, they proved to be incapable of having the galvanising effect on the working class that they hoped would lead to the creation of an independent, revolutionary, working-class party. Throughout this period as Gilly, Spenser, and other historians have argued, the power of the Mexican nationalist state, the ruling party, its subordinate workers unions and peasant leagues and the ideology of nationalism held both the working class and the majority of the peasantry in their grip, a violent and iron grip when necessary. So, the American agents of international Communism failed in their ultimate goal, though in the early and mid-1920s, they contributed to founding and expanding the small Communist Party. The power of Mexican nationalism and the factionalism in the Soviet Union would make further advances impossible until the 1930s, but then Stalinism raised a variety of other problems.

---

61   Cockcroft 1983, pp. 86–96.
62   Gilly 2005, p. 332.
63   Cockcroft 1983, p. 113.

Joseph 'José' W. Kelley: The Farmer Labor Party in Mexico

In 1921 Joseph W. Kelley, a labour organiser from the United States, arrived in Mexico to carry out a programme of cross-border labour organising aimed at strengthening both Mexican and US unions, increasing the solidarity between the unions of the two countries, and building progressive forces in the United States, while at the same time working for recognition of the new revolutionary government in Mexico. His three-year experience shows us how American Federation of Labor's foreign policy got carried out on the ground in Mexico in the midst of the Mexican Revolution. At the same time, it also shows how a progressive Farmer Labor Party activist could see in the Mexican government the expression of the politics of the state-labour alliance in which he fervently believed.

Kelley's conviction that the Mexican government represented the Farmer Labor Party in power was so great that while still working for the International Association of Machinists (IAM) and the AFL, he actually became a paid agent of Mexico and its lobbyist in the United States. But for Kelley there was no contradiction between working for the American unions and for Mexico, because they were all more or less the same to him, part of a workers' movement. His ideas and activities at that time thus reveal all the contradictions, both the real strengths and the profound weaknesses, of those progressive politics in the context of international cross-border organising between Mexico and the United States.

As a Farmer-Laborite, Kelley was not simply working within the limits set by Samuel Gompers and the AFL. He was trying to push the envelope and create a rather more radical version of international labour solidarity. When Kelley saw the Obregón government, he thought he recognised something like the US Farmer Labor Party in power, a utopian view of the Mexican government that informed and justified his activities both in Mexico and the United States. Thus, inspired by the politics of the Farmer-Labor movement, Kelley worked to create better relations between US and Mexican labour organisations and among the workers and farmers of both countries. He sought to involve rank-and-file workers, to organise labour, social and political demonstrations, and to encourage strategic strikes. In the United States he challenged and fought racism against Mexican workers and insisted on Mexico's right to national sovereignty. Yet, Kelley was no radical, no socialist, and certainly no friend of the Mexican anarchists, the Industrial Workers of the World (IWW), or the new Mexican Communist Party. He was a progressive American labour bureaucrat, part of the IAM and AFL labour bureaucracy, allied with an emerging Mexican capitalist state. The combination of his ability to speak Spanish, a sense of adventure, and his progressive politics made him a labour diplomat. His programme was social democracy, not socialist revolution and that, in fact, made him an opponent of Mexican anarchists, syndicalists, Wobblies, and Communists.

Joseph W. Kelley, also sometimes known as John Kelley or José Kelley, was the son of Protestant missionaries who proselytised in China, and he was raised there. After returning to the United States, he fought in the Spanish-American War, and afterwards became a labour activist and organiser in California, working for the International Association of Machinists (IAM) between 1916–19 on the campaign to free Thomas Mooney, the man accused of the San Francisco Preparedness Day bombings. His experience in the Mooney campaign apparently brought him to the attention of IAM leader William Johnston who chose Kelley to work as the IAM organiser in Mexico.

Sent by the IAM to Mexico, José W. Kelley, as he then called himself, organised Mexican railroad workers into the IAM and advised officers of the Federation of Mexican Railroad Societies of the Mexican Republic.[1] If his experience was extraordinary, it was not unique, because as we have seen other men and women engaged in similar activities throughout the 1910s and 20s, though working for other organisations and with different goals. Kelley's experience

---

1   The Fideicomiso Archivos Plutarco Elías Calles y Fernando Torreblanca preserves several hundred documents related to Kelley's activities. The documents include many letters of Kelley himself, scores of letters of US labour unionists, telegrams of Interior Minister Plutarco Elías Calles, and other Mexican government officials, letters from the Mexican Embassy and Consular officials, US Bureau of Investigation reports, and clippings of newspaper articles. Taken together these documents provide a detailed record of many of Kelley's activities in the early 1920s as he attempted to promote ties between Mexican and US union members and campaigned for the recognition of Mexico (Fideicomiso Archivos Plutarco Elías Calles y Fernando Torreblanca, Archivo Plutarco Elías Calles, Kelley José W. Exp. 3, Leg. 1–17/17). Some papers concerning Kelley's activities can also be found in the Archivo General de la Nación in Galería 3, Fondo Calles-Obregón, Dirección General de Gobierno. There are also records of Kelley's activities in the American Federation of Labor papers, Reel 122; and in the US State Department Record dealing with the Internal Affairs of Mexico. The papers dealing with Kelley's activities in those collections confirm the information in the Fiedicomiso papers, though they are not nearly so complete and do not reveal his ties to high officials in the Mexican government, including the Mexican president. This chapter is based primarily on the papers in the Archivo Plutarco Elías Calles (PEC).

was only one of the wide variety of US-Mexican cross-border organising activities in the era of the Mexican Revolution including those described earlier in this book, such as Ricardo Flores Magón's Mexican Liberal Party (PLM), Emma Goldman and other US-based anarchists, the IWW, the US Socialist Party, the AFL, and finally the Communist International and US and Mexican Communist parties. Each labour federation or socialist tendency brought its own vision of internationalism, often different than and sometimes diametrically opposed to the others. The claim of engaging in the work of building international labour solidarity often obscured other national political agendas, class interests, and the objectives of particular labour organisations and their leaders. Then, just as today, there could be no such thing as a neutral cross-border organising strategy; every strategy represented an expression of a particular organisation and its ideology.

Kelley was a sincere advocate of international labour solidarity – but of a very specific sort worked out over the previous decade by Samuel Gompers and the leadership of the AFL. Gompers and the AFL developed an international policy in Mexico subordinated to the foreign policy of the United States – though never merely an extension of it.[2] Gompers called for international labour solidarity and an alliance with Mexican workers. As he himself said,

> There is an ideal that has been the scope of liberty-loving men and women of all ages and the labour movements of all countries – internationalism ....
>
> One of the most important features therefore of the declaration signed by members of the Mexican-United States labour conferences was that which called attention to the necessity for international relations between the labour movements of all these countries.[3]

But for Gompers any such alliance had to be led by the AFL. Just as he had moved into Canada to reorganise unions there, and had established the AFL in Puerto Rico, so Gompers intended to extend the sway of the federation not only over Mexico but also throughout the Americas. Paralleling the movement of US gunboats into the Caribbean and Central America, and of US corporations into Mexico and other parts of Latin America, so, in Gompers's vision, the AFL

2 Andrews 1991, p. 197.
3 Walling 1927, p. 89.

would expand southward transforming and dominating the labour federations of Latin America. We can call this, labour imperialism.

Just as he had in the United States, Gompers believed in establishing officially chartered organisations and rejected the idea of any competing unionism, what he called 'dual unionism'. Gompers would only support unions that emphasised bread and butter issues, practical matters, and business-like methods, and he fiercely opposed anarchist, syndicalist, Socialist, or Communist ideologies and organisations. While the United States became the gendarme of the 'American Lake' – that is, the Caribbean – Gompers used 'AFL socialists as point men' in Mexico and Puerto Rico while he worked to restrain those within the AFL who would have outright opposed American imperialism.[4]

As discussed above, with this goal in view then, in Mexico toward the end of the First World War and the Mexican Revolution, the AFL helped to found and then developed a close alliance with the *Confederación Regional de Obreros Mexicanos* (Regional Confederation of Mexican Workers or CROM). Gompers had played midwife to the CROM, easing its birth and supporting the infant organisation. In doing so, he consciously built an alternative to the IWW, which had chapters in various parts of Mexico, and to what soon became the anarchist Confederación General de Trabajo (CGT), as well as to the new Mexican Communist Party. The CROM, led by electrician Luis N. Morones, became closely allied with the government of President Álvaro Obregón and in particular with the political faction of Plutarco Elías Calles, then head of the Mexican Ministry of the Interior (*Secretaría de Gobernación*), and later president of Mexico.[5] Thus the CROM came to be something like a state-sponsored version of Gompers-style business unionism, simultaneously supported by both the AFL and Mexican government.

Calles worked closely with Morones to promote an image of the Mexican labour movement and of the Mexican government as pro-labour, progressive or even social democratic – depending on the audience. Coming to birth in the midst of the Mexican Revolution, the CROM of Morones frequently used a much more radical rhetoric than Gompers and the AFL could have ever tolerated in the United States. But for Obregón and Calles, and for Gompers and Morones, the CROM stood as a barrier against the IWW and the CGT's anarchism, and in the next few years would come to be the government's and the

---

4 Andrews 1991, p. 197.
5 On the role of the CROM and the PLM see: Carr 1981; Guadarrama 1981; and Barbosa Cano 1980. The relationship of the CROM and other Mexican unions to the state is explored in Middlebrook 1995; La Botz 1988; 1992; Meyer 1971, pp. 1–27; Salazar 1962, pp. 124–44; Basurto 1981, pp. 153–208; Araiza 1963, *passim*; La Botz 1988, pp. 15–48.

employers' enforcer of labour peace against radical activists and discontented workers. But in 1921 the nationalist CROM and the anarchist CGT were struggling over the soul of the Mexican railroad workers' unions. So, when the AFL's Machinist union, one of the most important railroad workers' unions in the United States, sent John Kelley to Mexico in 1921, both the Mexican government and the CROM welcomed him with open arms.

Shortly after, when Calles, the powerful Minister of the Interior, decided to launch a public relations campaign in conjunction with the AFL to win recognition of Mexico by the United States, he chose Kelley to head up the campaign. Calles's choice was astute, for Kelley proved to be an inspired and indefatigable campaigner. Kelley's energy and activity derived from his faith in the project, for he was not simply a member of the AFL, he was one of the cadres of the Machinists union. Kelley worked directly under William H. Johnston, president of the IAM and founder of the Conference for Progressive Political Action (CPPA). Kelley's work was guided by Johnston's Farmer-Labor ideology, a social democratic worldview that Kelley shared.

Farmer-Labor politics had emerged as a result of domestic policies during World War I. President Woodrow Wilson, after crushing the Industrial Workers of the World, had established a partnership with the American Federation of Labor. Under Wilson's tutelage, the AFL's membership grew, it negotiated more union contracts, and workers' wages and conditions improved. Nowhere was this partnership more important than in the railroad industry, where the AFL's Railway Employees Division (RED), including the Machinists, 'became grateful partners with the Wilsonian state'.[6] The Wilson administration actually took over management of the railroads for the duration of the war. AM leader Johnson told the 1920 AFL convention, 'We accomplished more, fellow delegates in the three years of government control than we did in twenty-give years of private control'.[7]

After the war, the railroads – which had always remained privately owned – were returned to private management, and then came the post-war depression. The Pennsylvania Railroad led the attack on the unions, and defeated their great shop crafts strike of 1922, in which US President Warren Harding's Secretary of Justice Harry M. Daugherty used a barrage of lawsuits in the courts to break the union's power.[8] After that experience, the Machinists and other union officials and union members looked back upon the alliance with the

---

6   Davis 1997, p. 46.
7   Davis 1997, p. 48.
8   Davis 1997, pp. 101–15.

Wilson government as a kind of paradise lost. They were anxious to find a way to use the federal government to support labour.

Inspiration for the Farmer-Labor movement also came from the British Labour Party's post-war Reconstruction Programme which called for a 'new social order'. Throughout the teens and early twenties labour parties or farmer-labour parties appeared in various cities and state across the United States and were championed by the leaders of the Chicago union movement, John Fitzpatrick and Edward N. Nockels. The two brought together some 124 labour and farmer leaders around the country to form the Conference for Progressive Political Action (CPPA) in Chicago in February of 1922. Later the railroad brotherhoods became involved, including the International Association of Machinists led by Johnston. The Communist Party of America boycotted that original conference, but in 1923 the Communists moved into the CPPA and succeeded in capturing it, while simultaneously driving out many other labour groups.[9] Nevertheless, the Farmer-Labor movement survived that crisis and Johnston and other railroad union leaders continued to support it, hoping to return to the halcyon days of government administration of the railroads. The union officials of the IAM and other unions in the CPPA advocated this vision of a government-labour alliance, what they saw as a kind of state-socialism, as the best way forward for workers in the United States.

Within the AFL and the broader world of American labour, these union officers represented an officially tolerated left wing. Samuel Gompers found them preferable to William Z. Foster and other labour radicals who had gone off to organise the Communist Party and the Trade Union Education League (TUEL). Compared to the Communists' call for revolution and a soviet America, the CPPA represented a moderate alternative.[10] It was as a servant of this Farmer-Labor movement with its notion of state-union cooperation that Kelley went to work in Mexico.

Kelley was involved in Mexico between 1921 and 1924, key years in the country's history of and in the history of the Mexican labour movement, which was then divided between the state-supported CROM and its rival the anarcho-syndicalist CGT.[11] Each of those federations attempted to win the powerful Mexican railroad unions to its side. Kelley's role then was clear. He would never in his career in Mexico express the slightest support for the anarchists of the

---

9   Draper 1986, pp. 29–51.
10   Lens 1969, pp. 293–5; Weinstein 1962, pp. 224–33 and 272–339; Howe 1957, pp. 108–43; Draper 1986, pp. 37–97; and Shannon 1955, pp. 156–63 and 170–1.
11   There had also been a Catholic trade union movement that flourished briefly at the opening of the Mexican Revolution in 1910 but was soon surpassed in size and influence by the anarchists.

CGT or its affiliated unions. In fact, his work among streetcar and railroad workers coincided with the efforts of the Mexican state and the CROM, to suppress
the revolutionary alternative that the CGT represented in that industry. Kelley's
notion of international labour solidarity meant solidarity with the unions supported by the AFL, the American railroad brotherhoods, and the Mexican government, and definitely not with anarchist workers and their vision of revolution and libertarian communism.

1   An American Labour Organiser in Revolutionary Mexico

Kelley arrived in Mexico about the time that Álvaro Obregón became president,
signalling the end of ten years of violent revolutionary upheaval, beginning a
period of social and economic reconstruction, of populist peasant and worker
movements, and initiating the gradual creation of the modern Mexican state.
Obregón, and his allies Plutarco Elías Calles and Adolfo de la Huerta, the leaders of the so-called 'Sonoran Dynasty', the group of northern military leaders
committed to the construction of a modern state and a capitalist economy in
Mexico, found themselves politically obliged by circumstance to offer of concessions to emerging movements of both the peasantry and the working class.
    The social base of the Sonorans was not only in their armies, but also in
the remnants of the Zapatista peasant organisations and some of the formerly
anarchist unions, and this helped determine the populist character of their
politics. As readers will remember, the Supreme Chief of the Constitutionalist
forces, Venustiano Carranza, had entered into an alliance with some leaders of
the anarchist House of the World Worker (COM) as early as 1914, granting union
recognition and rights in exchange for troops to fight the plebian rebels Francisco Villa and Emiliano Zapata. Because the Sonorans came to depend on this
relationship with the unions, generals Obregón, Calles, and de la Huerta cultivated and deepened these relationships with the labour movement. As interim
president of Mexico between June and November of 1920, de la Huerta established close ties with the railroad unions, while Calles worked with the newly
established Confederation Regional de Obreros Mexicanos (CROM) headed
by Luis N. Morones. Under Calles the CROM became the 'official' or state-
sponsored and largely state-controlled federation.
    At the end of February 1919, the railroad workers' unions struck for union
recognition as well as specific economic demands of job security and higher
wages.[12] President Obregón refused to recognise the union, sent the army

---

12   Ortíz Hernán 1988, vol. 2, p. 155.

to seize the railway terminals and facilities, and offered protection to strike-breakers. Three craft unions, the conductors, the brakemen and the machinists refused to support the strike or honour its picket lines. Some Mexicans who had been working in the United States returned to Mexico, taking jobs as strike-breakers. But most of the railroad unions and workers remained on strike.

Both the anarcho-syndicalist CGT and the CROM nominally supported the railroad strike. However, when the CGT attempted to organise a general strike in defence of the railroad workers, the CROM – loyal to the government – declined to call out its members. By mid-March Obregón indicated that he was pre-pared to recognise the railroad workers' Federation but would not do so if it appeared that he was capitulating in the face of the workers' pressure. Mor-ones and leaders of the CROM therefore arranged a secret pact by which the strike would be lifted and the government would then recognise the union and meet other demands. So, the strike ended with the Federation's unilateral lift-ing of the strike followed by government recognition of the Federation. But in the end, the CROM's tactics discredited it in the eyes of many railroad unions, some of whom moved closer to the anarchist CGT.[13]

Throughout the 1920s both Obregón and Calles were hostile to the Mex-ican railroad workers' unions, first because they remained independent of the CROM, and second because strikes on the railroads threatened foreign capital, particularly US capital invested not only in railroads, but also in mining, thus jeopardising Obregón's attempt to win US recognition of Mexico. The railroad workers unions' independence and militancy also represented a threat to the symbiotic arrangement between the state and the official CROM unions. The government's support for Kelley's work was no doubt influenced by these con-siderations.

When John Kelley arrived in Mexico in 1921 as representative of the Inter-national Association of Machinists of the United States, he approached the unions through President Obregón's Minister of the Interior, Plutarco Elías Calles. Between 1921 and 1925, Kelley kept in regular contact with Calles who, as the new revolutionary government's first Minister of the Interior, defined that office as not only head of the secret police but also as the nation's top political fixer, dealing with the peasant and labour organisations, especially the latter. If this was international labour solidarity, it was solidarity from above, through the Mexican state.

One of Kelley's principal activities in 1921 was the organisation of Mexican railroad workers directly into the IAM and the establishment of closer ties

---

13   Basurto 1981, pp. 226–31.

between Mexican and US railway unions.[14] Kelley became involved in working with the railway unions just after the establishment of a national organisation of Mexican railroad workers and a large and important railroad strike. In 1921, Adolfo de la Huerta, who had just ended his term as interim president of Mexico, convened and financed the Railroad Workers Congress of the Mexican Republic (*Congreso Ferrocarrilero de la República Mexicana*). Fourteen railroad craft unions (modelled on the US Labour unions' craft structure) attended the congress and on 17 January 1921 they signed a 'Pact of Confederation' giving birth to the Federation of Railroad Societies of the Mexican Republic (*Confederación de Sociedades Ferrocarrileras de la República Mexicana*).[15] The Federation with 28,000 members did not create an industrial union, but it could be seen as representing something like the first step toward the creation of one, though the individual craft unions were still far from unified.

Kelley set to work, organising some Mexican railroad workers directly into locals of the Machinists. The IAM had had members in Mexico before, but that was in the late nineteenth and first years of the twentieth century, and they were virtually all Americans, along with some English and Canadians. Organising Mexicans directly into a US-based union in this period was something quite novel. In 1921 Kelley wrote to W.C. Myers, the Secretary of the Central Labor Council at the Labor Temple in San Diego, California that 'the I.A. of M. has begun to establish lodges in the Republic [of Mexico], the First one in Mexico City is named after the Director General of the Railroads, "Ramon Negri", who incidentally is also a dues-paying member of the Machinists Union and so is President Obregón'.[16]

Apparently, Kelley thought it both appropriate and politic to have the government-owned national railroad's top bosses – Obregón and Negri – become members of the workers' union. The letter reveals that Kelley's union organising efforts in Mexico on behalf of the IAM had the support both of the management of Mexico's nationalised railroads and of the very highest levels

---

14   To the best of my knowledge, José W. Kelley's activities and the work of the IAM in Mexico
      as an organizer of railroad workers has never been discussed in any of the histories of the
      Mexican railroad workers unions, though the earlier phase of US union involvement in
      the unions in the late 1800s and early 1900s is well known. The standard histories of the
      railroads and railroad unions include: Ortíz Hernán 1988; Ortega Aguirre 1979; Gill 1971;
      Rodea 1944; Lombardo Toledano 1994, pp. 102–7.
15   Ortega Aguiree 1979, pp. 10–12; Rodea 1944, pp. 211–24; Lombardo Toledano 1994, pp. 106–7.
16   Archivo PEC, Kelley papers, Exp. 3 Leg. 2/17. I have throughout this chapter changed
      the spelling, punctuation, and capitalisation in Kelley's letters to conform to standard
      usage.

of the government itself. As chief IAM representative in Mexico, Kelley himself probably chose the lodge's name in an attempt to ingratiate the union with the director. He no doubt saw Negri as not only the company director, but also as a union brother, even as a comrade in the Farmer-Labor movement of his imaginaton.

The IAM also carried out strikes in Mexico. Kelley recounted in a speech before the Texas State Federation of Labor convention in El Paso, Texas, in April of 1922 that he had organised an IAM local on the Mexico City Tramway System. When George R. Conway, general manager of the company, fired the IAM Shop Committee Chairman, Fernando León, Kelley's IAM lodge organised a sit-down strike. The strike, Kelley recalled, was finally settled through the intervention of Celestino Gasca, a top leader of the CROM and the Governor of the Federal District. The strikers were returned to work with back pay, a cash indemnity of 2,500 pesos, and a written apology for the firing of Leon.[17] The Obregón government understood that it had at times to placate the workers if it was to maintain their support.

2   Assisting the Railway Federation of Mexico

In addition to organising IAM locals, Kelley worked with the Federation of Railroad Societies of the Republic of Mexico, then made up of 13 Mexican railroad unions, in an attempt to help strengthen their fledgling organisation.[18] Kelley was critical of the way the Federation had been organised by de la Huerta, writing that 'the real ground of objection is that the movement was attempted from the top down instead of starting from the Rank and File of the Unions'. As a result, said Kelley, the organisation was 'a debating club where the leaders, jealous of each other had a chance to air their personal grievances'.[19] Nevertheless,

---

17   Archivo PEC, Kelley papers, Exp. 3 Leg 5/17.

18   The Mexican unions involved were: Alianza de Ferrocarrileros Mexicanos, S.C.L.; Asociación Nacional de Moldeadores y Aprendices; Orden de Maquinistas y Fogoneros de Locomotoras; Sociedad Mutualistas de Despachadores y Telegrafistas; Sociedad Ferrocarrilera Departamento de Vía; Unión de Auditores de Trenes Ferrocarrileros; Unión de Caldereros y Aprendices Mexicanos; Unión de Cobreros, Rojalateros y Ayudantes; Union de Mecanicos Mexicanos; Unión International de Forjadores y Ayudantes; Unión de Pintores Mexicanos; Unión de Carpinteros y Similares; Unión de Modelistas de los Estados Unidos Mexicanos. Letter from A. Vargas, 19 November 1921, Archivo PEC, Kelley papers, Exp. 3, Leg. 1/17.

19   'Memorandum of Survey/Alianza Ferrocarrileros', (undated) in Archivo PEC, Kelley papers, Exp. 3, Leg. 2/17. See also Kelley's long letter to Ramon De Negri where he dis-

whatever his objections to its top-down origins and its leaders' lack of real commitment to unity, Kelley worked to strengthen the federation. Kelley assisted the Federation in negotiating contracts with the major Mexican railway lines in 1921.[20] One of the benefits of Kelley's assistance was the negotiation of a clause that provided that the employers must use a union-controlled hiring hall for all new employees in whatever craft.[21]

In a lengthy memorandum, Kelley laid out, presumably for other officials of the IAM, the AFL, and for Calles, his long-term plan of work with the Mexican railway workers unions. Kelley's plan is striking for its audacity, or, perhaps better, its presumption and arrogance, its sense of the superiority of US labour organisations, but also for its commitment to a certain ideal of democratic unionism and local union autonomy.

'My plan', wrote Kelley, 'is to first of all endeavor to strengthen the workers that so far have indicated they have an idea of Solidarity (I mean the Railroad men), by strengthening the weak organizations, i.e., the machinists and office men. I propose to go to the Rank and File of these organizations and by a series of lectures point out the faults of the system of organization and offer a better one'. Having reorganised the railroad workers, Kelley proposed that he would then go on to organise the mechanics working in other shops with which he had had contact. 'After starting the Organization campaign', Kelley wrote, 'I would go to the Rank and File of the various unions and point out to them the necessity for Solidarity and urge them to affiliate with the General Labour movement'. Presumably Kelley refers here to the CROM.

Perhaps because he was accustomed to the IAM traditions of local union autonomy and committed to rank-and-file participation, Kelley was disgusted by the authoritarian leaders' domination of Mexican unions. 'From the talks I have had with the Mexican workers', Kelley continued, 'the ideal would appeal to them. But at present they are dominated by the leaders. For example, the Machinists: their Executive Board assumes dictatorial powers and instead of the various local unions telling them what to do, they tell the Locals'.[22]

---

cussed his views of specific Mexican railroad union leaders. Letter to Negri (3 November 1921), Archivo PEC, Exp. 3, Leg. 2/17.

20   See Kelley's letters to J.W. Kline (7 November 1921) and to J.A. Franklin (7 November 1921), in Archivo PEC, Kelley papers, Exp. 3, Leg. 1/17.

21   Letter from A. Vargas (9 November 1921) Archivo PEC, Kelley papers, Exp. 3, Leg. 1/17.

22   'Memorandum of Survey/Alianza Ferrocarrileros', (undated) Archivo PEC, Kelley papers, Exp. 3, Leg. 1/17.

3   Establishing Ties between Mexican and US Unions

While attempting to strengthen the Mexican railroad Federation, Kelley also worked to establish direct ties between railroad workers' unions in Mexico and the United States. In a letter to B.M. Jewell, president of the Railway Employees Department of the American Federation of Labor, Kelley explained his project and expressed his view of Mexican workers and unionists in a passage worth quoting at length:

> I believe that all of the Internationals should get in touch with the respect-ive unions here. These men have splendid organizations for the short time they have been in existence, and they appreciate what we have done in the States and are trying to copy from us. No International need fear to make arrangements with them. All of these organizations pay higher dues than any in the United States and there would not have to be any reduction. Neither do they need to fear an influx of men to the United States. All of the Railway workers are determined to build up the conditions in their own country and there is no danger of migration. I have found as a general rule that the native-born Mexican is a pretty solid Union man, and from my investigation 90% of the so-called Mexican Scabs are those born in the US where they imbibed a good dose of 100% Americanism and Open Shopism, and quite a number of our own country member have imbibed the same thing.[23]

No doubt Kelley's sincere appreciation of the Mexican workers' capabilities, even with all of its condescension, together with the apparent absence of racism in Kelley's discussions of the Mexican people were qualities that made him an effective organiser in Mexico. At the same time, he attempts to allay his American union brothers' fear of mass migration and economic competition from Mexican workers.

Kelley's project evidently appealed to A. Carrillo Vargas, head of the Railway Federation of Mexico, who wrote a letter to the Federation's member unions explaining that Kelley had proposed a 'Friendship Treaty' between the railroad workers unions of both countries. Carrillo Vargas spoke highly of Kelley and the US unions and urged the federation's affiliates to discuss the proposal for a Friendship Treaty and to get in touch with the US unions.

---

23   Letter to B.M. Jewell, Archivo PEC, Kelley papers, Exp. 3, Leg. 1/17.

Kelley himself wrote many letters to US railroad union leaders explaining his project and collected from them their union constitutions and by-laws which Mexican labour officials were anxious to see.[24] Kelley told two US leaders, one head of the Blacksmiths and the other leader of the Boilermakers, that some railroad workers, at least in northern Mexico, held union cards in those crafts in both the Mexican and the US labour organisations.[25] Several national leaders of the US railway unions wrote to Kelley and expressed a willingness to cooperate with his efforts to establish international links between railroad workers' organisations.[26] Kelley claimed to have succeeded in getting three organisations, his own Machinists, the Engineers and the Boilermakers to enter into formal pacts with the Mexican Railway Federation.[27]

4   Mexican Support for the Shop Crafts Strike

The ties Kelley established between Mexican and US railroad unions were to prove valuable to US workers during the great shop crafts strike of 1922–23. When the strike broke out in 1922, the International Association of Machinists assigned Kelley to work on 'South Western lines', with responsibility for the strike in the states of Texas, New Mexico, and Arizona.[28] Kelley wrote to Calles in mid-July 1922:

---

24   Kelley worked to put the Mexican unions in touch with the following US labour unions: Brotherhood of Boilermakers, Brotherhood of Blacksmiths, Railway Carmen, Pipe Fitters, Sheet Metal Workers, Maintenance of Way, Stationary Firemen, Railway Clerks, Brotherhood of Locomotive Engineers, Brotherhood of Locomotive Firemen, Order Railway Conductors, Brotherhood of Railway Trainmen, Switchmen's Union, and Order of Sleeping Car Conductors. Letter from A. Vargas, 9 November 1921, Archivo PEC, Kelley papers, Exp. 3, Leg. 1/17.

25   Archivo Calles Torreblanca, Archivo PEC, Kelley papers, Exp. 3, Leg. 1/17, Letter to J.W. Kline, 7 November 1921 and letter to J.A. Franklin, 7 November 1921. Interestingly, two US union leaders – of the Switchmen and Blacksmiths – wrote to Kelley that their unions had once had locals or members in Mexico, while the head of the Electrical Workers indicated that they had been in touch with the 'Electrical Workers of Mexico' (the Sindicato Mexicano de Electricistas, SME). Archivo Calles Torreblanca, Archivo PEC, Kelley papers, letters to Kelley from Cashen of Switchmen, 15 November 1921, from Kline of Blacksmiths, 17 November 1921, and from Noonan of IBEW, 17 November 1921.

26   See several letters from railroad workers' union officials in Archivo PEC, Kelley papers, Exp. 3, Leg 1/17.

27   'Memorandum/Alianza Ferrocarrilero', (undated) in Archivo PEC, Kelley papers, Exp. 3, Leg. 2/17.

28   Letters to Calles (1 July 1922 and 18 July 1922) Archivo PEC, Kelley papers, Exp. 3, Leg 8/17.

The [US railroad] men are standing splendidly and are well pleased with the spirit of solidarity shown by their Mexican brothers. On the border the American workers have discovered real qualities in the Mexicans, and when the strike is over, there will be an entirely different feeling among the two people, a feeling that I believe will result in a closer co-operation and the spirit of solidarity.[29]

More than talk was involved. Mexican railway workers in Nuevo Laredo declared a sympathy strike in support of US workers.[30]

Kelley continued throughout the strike to praise the solidarity of Mexican workers with their US brothers. 'The Solidarity of the Mexicans during this strike is the wonder of the country and you may be sure I am getting that information into every union in the United States', Kelley wrote to Calles on 1 August 1922. He pointed out in particular that the US railroad men refused to allow anyone to use racist language against Mexican brothers. 'Right in these border states, Americans have fought outsiders who dared to use the term Greaser against the Mexicans who are standing shoulder to shoulder in this struggle'. Kelley reported, for example that, 'At Needles, California two men were badly injured for calling a couple of striking Mexicans "Greasers". We are going to abolish that and every other term of reproach'.[31]

Kelley helped to organise a demonstration on 1 August 1922 by Mexican railroad unions and the CROM in support of US strikers, which was covered by newspapers in the United States.[32] Always attentive to the possibilities of publicity and organisation, Kelley wrote to Calles that, 'The secretaries of all the unions where we have many Mexicans are going to give me a statement and a letter commending the Mexican strikers for their Solidarity during the strike and the cheerfulness they displayed. These I will use wherever I go'.[33]

Kelley sent out a press release on 15 September 1922 claiming that the Mexican railway unions were sending $87,500 each month to help the US strikers, and he noted that $500 had been turned over to C.N. Idar, general organiser of the AFL.[34] The $87,500 per month contribution seems so large that it may be an exaggeration, but Mexican railway workers probably made some financial

---

29   Letter to Calles (18 July 1922) Archivo PEC, Kelley papers, Exp. 3, Leg. 8/17.
30   Andrews 1991, p. 118.
31   Letter to Calles (1 August 1922), Archivo PEC, Kelley papers, Exp. 3, Leg. 8/17.
32   Letter to Calles (16 August 1922), Exp. 3, Leg. 9/17.
33   Letter to Calles (18 August 1922), Archivo PEC, Kelley papers, Exp. 3, Leg. 8/17.
34   Letter to Organised Labor (15 September 1922), Archivo PEC, Kelley papers, Exp. 3, Leg. 9/17.

contributions to US strikers. Or the Mexican government might have provided the funds, perhaps funnelling them through the unions.

As part of his attempt to foster better relations between US, Mexican, and Mexican-American workers, Kelley got them to march together on Mexican Independence Day, 16 September 1922, in the Mexican community's parade in El Paso, Texas. 'For the first time in the history of the day in this country', Kelley wrote to Calles, 'Americans paraded with their Mexican brothers'. Marching in the Mexican parade were 1,200 union members from the Carpenters, the Bricklayers, the Electricians Union and the Machinists. 'It was a fine, beautiful demonstration of International Solidarity on the part of the two people', Kelley wrote.[35] The parade expressed symbolically Kelley's own aspirations for international worker unity.

Mexican government officials, with whom Kelley cultivated good relations, also provided support for the striking US railroad workers. According to Kelley (and probably at his urging), Ramon de Negri, Director General of the National Railways, spoke out in support of US unionists on strike and criticised the privately owned US railroad companies.[36] Other officials helped as well. Kelley wrote to Calles to praise Mr. Valdez, the Consul at El Paso, Texas for his support. Valdez had asked Mexicans not to 'scab' on the US workers' strike.[37] 'From the very beginning of the strike he has been a source of strength, not only to the Mexican citizens that are out [on strike], but [to] the Americans [who are on strike] as well'. Kelley lauded Valdez's 'sympathy and encouragement' and that of other Mexican officials as well.[38] Kelley told an audience in Fort Worth, Texas, Minister of the Interior Calles himself had 'sent $500 to the striking shopmen in El Paso as soon as the strike began'.[39] (Could this have been the same $500 Kelley presented to the strikers, claiming it was from Mexican workers?)

While US Attorney General Daugherty eventually smashed the US shop crafts strike in a flurry of repression involving redbaiting, arrests, lawsuits, and numerous trials,[40] Kelley had certainly done everything he could to help win the strike. He had brought to the strike a new element of international labour solidarity through the Mexican Railway Federation, the CROM, the IAM, and the AFL.

---

35   Letter to Calles (17 September 1922), Archivo PEC, Kelley papers, Exp. 3, Leg. 9/17.
36   Letter to John Horn (12 November 1921), Archivo PEC, Kelley papers, Exp. 3, Leg. 1/17.
37   Andrews 1991, p. 118.
38   Letter to Calles (20 September 1922), Archivo PEC, Kelley papers, Exp. 3, Leg. 10/17.
39   'Farmer Labor Party Plans Complete Ticket', *Fort Worth Star Telegram*, 18 January 1923, in Archivo PEC, Kelley papers, Exp. 3, Leg. 11/17.
40   Davis 1997, *passim*.

5   Campaign for the Recognition of Mexico

By far Kelley's most important political work at this time was his national campaign in the United States for the recognition of Mexico. The campaign involved the organisation of mass meetings, the production of literature, public speaking tours and political lobbying. Within three years Kelley set up a national headquarters, created the semblance of a national organisation, produced a regular bulletin, and spoke before tens of thousands of workers from one end of the country to the other.

Kelley was no novice at this sort of thing. Just a few years before he had worked on the defence campaign of Thomas Mooney, a labour radical convicted of the famous 1916 San Francisco Preparedness Day bombing. The Mooney campaign from 1916 to 1919 was supposed to culminate in a 4 July 1919 general strike to free Mooney, but the American Federation of Labor voted at its Atlantic City convention in June 1919 not to support the movement.[41] Kelley's involvement in that defence campaign must have given him useful experience, if also some doubt about the reliability of the AFL. 'My plan is to work along the same lines as I did in the Tom Mooney case', Kelley wrote to Calles. 'It would be better to hold big mass meetings, in that way we can reach thousands, whereby appearing before the Labor Councils the crowd will naturally be smaller – however I will do my best whether the crowd is large or small'.[42]

In addition to the Mooney campaign, Kelley was also influenced by the organisations on behalf of independence for Ireland and the Philippines and for recognition of the government of the Soviet Union.[43] 'While in Washington', Kelley wrote to Calles, 'I saw the Friends of Irish Freedom, the Friends of Soviet Russia and others working, and it made me feel bad because the claims of Mexico were being kept hid under a bushel'.[44] Certainly a progressive like Kelley would have been particularly aware of the campaign for the recognition of the Soviet Union which involved not only the Communist Party and the Trade Union Education League, but also many Socialists, Farmer-Labor activists, and

---

41   Murray 1964, pp. 109–17.
42   Letter to Plutarco Elías Calles, 14 December 1921, Archivo PEC, Exp. 3, Leg. 2/17.
43   Letter to Calles, 18 April 1922, mentioning Ireland and Russia; Exp. 3, Leg. 8/17, Letter to Calles, 5 August 1922, mentioning the Press Bulletin of the Philippine Commission of Independence; and Exp. 3, Leg. 10/17, Letter to Calles, 16 December 1922, mentioning the friends of Irish Freedom and the Friends of Soviet Russia, all in: Archivo PEC, Kelley papers, Exp. 3, Leg. 4/17.
44   Archivo Calles-Torreblanca, Archivo PEC, Kelley papers Exp. 3, Leg. 10/17, Letter to Calles 16 December 1922.

trade unionists. The pro-Soviet campaign may have been the model for his own crusade for the recognition of Mexico.

Kelley began his campaign as a one-man, Los Angeles-based effort, concentrating on the US Southwest, no doubt because he was born, raised, and lived in Southern California, and most of his contacts were in that region. Soon, he moved his headquarters to El Paso, Texas on the Mexican border, apparently because that location permitted him to make forays into the Midwest.

Kelley had a class-based vision of the campaign for the recognition of Mexico. He felt that Obregón and Calles should not emphasise appeals to US corporations and businesspeople, but rather reach out to US workers and farmers. 'Your government has spent thousands of dollars to bring Businessmen to Mexico, a number of which have accepted your hospitality and then gone home and lied about Mexico', Kelley wrote to Calles. 'Not one labour man that has ever been to Mexico has done that, and yet he [Obregón] holds back from getting his message to the real people of the United States, the common people'.[45] Kelley's approach was to concentrate on unionised workers and politicised farmers, though he too would sometimes make appeals to businesspeople and politicians.

Kelley presented himself as an independent and unbiased advocate of Mexican recognition. 'I have no official connection with the Mexican government and I did not go to Washington as its representative', Kelley frequently told his audiences and the press.[46] But this was not true. The Mexican government paid for Kelley's campaign. While the Machinists paid Kelley's salary, Mexican Minister of the Interior Calles paid for his entire publicity campaign, his train fares, hotel bills, and printing costs. Kelley was forever writing to Calles asking for more money for expenses for his next trip, apparently because Calles was reluctant to authorise more than a few hundred dollars at a time.[47]

When he spoke to American audiences, Kelley often claimed to be not only an organiser for the International Association of Machinists, but also a vice-president of both the Mexican Federation of Railroad Unions of the Mexican Republic and the Mexican Federation of Labour (a common popular transla-

---

45 Archivo Calles-Torreblanca, Archivo PEC, Kelley papers, Exp. 3, Leg. 4/17, Letter to Calles, 20 April 1922.

46 Archivo Calles-Torreblanca, Archivo PEC, Kelley papers, Exp. 3, Leg. 14/17, newsclip, 'Mexico Farms, Labor Control, Kelley Shows', *Orleans Item*, 5 May 1923.

47 Many of the letters in the Kelley papers deal with his expenses, such as: Exp. 3, Leg. 10/17, Letter to Calles, 5 October 1922. See also: Archivo General de la Nacion, Direccion General de Gobierno, Exo 121-R-E-3, letter July 1920 from Consulate General of San Francisco to President.

tion in the period for the CROM). To the best of my knowledge, his claims to be an official of the Mexican unions were not true, though he may have been an honorary official or may have made these claims with the approval of Vargas and Morones. He also might simply have fabricated them. Such titles certainly would have added to his credibility and would have made him the personal embodiment of the international solidarity he fought to create.

Kelley must have realised, however, that nothing could be as effective in creating a sense of international labour solidarity as the presence of a real Mexican labour unionist. So, on his earlier speaking tour in the southwest, Kelley brought along a Mexican worker: Consuelo González, the former private secretary of Rosendo Salazar, a leader of the CROM and the Director of the Mexican government's Department of Printing and Engraving. 'She is an 18-year-old girl who, out of her interest in the cause of the labouring class of her country, gave up her splendid place at a salary of 225 pesos a month in order to study the labour movement of this country and carry back to Mexico the results of her observations', wrote one newspaper reporter.[48]

Kelley, no doubt fearing some criticism of his morals, told his audiences that he 'and his wife' had brought González to the United States, and that while only 18 she had been active in the labour movement for three years.[49] Sometimes González was introduced as a member of the Mexican Welfare Commission, as, for example, when she spoke with women involved in the Women's Minimum Wage Law movement, but the title may have been a convenient fiction, like Kelley's Mexican union vice-presidencies. González also spoke to the women of the Waist and Dressmaking Union, Local 103 in Los Angeles. González appears to have spent only a few weeks working with Kelley in California. No doubt he could not afford the added expenses of a companion on his tour.[50]

His speaking tours in the Southwest having proven a modest success, in 1922 Kelley created the 'American Friends of the Republic of Mexico'. At least at first, the organisation was little more than a letterhead and a mailing address at the Labour Temple in El Paso, Texas. To produce the organisation's first publication, Kelley took a speech he had given before the Texas State Federation of Labor (discussed in detail below) and turned it into a pamphlet titled 'The Truth About Mexico' by Joseph W. Kelley, General Organiser of the Interna-

---

48   Archivo Calles-Torreblanca, Archivo PEC, Kelley papers, Exp. 3, Leg. 3/17, newspaper clipping: 'Kelley Speaks About Mexico', *San Bernardino Sun*, 11 January 1922.

49   Archivo Calles-Torreblanca, Archivo PEC, Kelley papers, Exp. 3, Leg. 5/17, undated and unidentified newspaper clipping, 'Reception and Dinner Was Complete Success'.

50   Archivo Calles-Torreblanca, Archivo PEC, Kelley papers, Exp. 3, Leg. 5/17, 'Handbill'.

tional Association of Machinists, with an initial press run of 10,000 copies.[51] Kelley mailed copies of the tract to union halls throughout the country.

Kelley also initiated a letter-writing campaign. In the spring of 1922, Kelley sent a memorandum to AFL state federations, councils, and local unions throughout the country, urging them to send letters to President Harding, their senators, and congressmen endorsing the AFL Convention resolution calling for the recognition of the Mexican government.[52]

To spread the word about his activities, Kelley relied on the left and labour press, such as *The Call* in New York, *The Federated Press*, and the AFL *Federationist*. Kelley also cultivated a relationship to the Hearst newspapers, which, partly through his efforts, had after years of hostility, become more friendly toward Mexico. But Kelley wanted to create his own publication as a way to reach farmers, workers and the broader public in the United States. As he wrote to Calles:

> I would start a weekly paper. This paper would be of vast assistance and I am sure that I could get the labour movement including the Railroad Brotherhoods back of it. This paper would not be local, it would have a national character, devoting its efforts to the upbuilding of the labor Movement, the Farm Labor alliance and the Recognition of Mexico, and creating a better understanding between the workers of both nations.[53]

As is clear from this passage, Kelley's activities were informed by his own Farmer Labor Party politics, and his vision of the government of Mexico as his party in power. However, without adequate financial resources, Kelley had to give up the newspaper idea; instead, he published a more modest bulletin with an initial press run of 1,500, later raised to as many as 6,000 copies per issue.[54]

Kelley seems to have been effective at most work he undertook, but perhaps the most impressive thing about Kelley's campaign was his tireless touring and talking. Like so many labour organisers of his day, Kelley proved a relentless traveller and an inspired public speaker, a combination which permitted him

---

51   Archivo Calles Torreblanca, Archivo PEC, Kelley papers, Exp. 3, Leg. 6/17, several letters discuss this material.

52   Archivo Calles-Torreblanca, Archivo PEC, Kelley papers, Exp. 3, Leg. 7/17, Letter to Organised Labor, 15 June 1922.

53   Archivo Calles-Torreblanca, Archivo PEC, Exp. 3, Leg. 9/17, Letter to Calles, 16 August 1922.

54   Archivo Calles-Torreblanca, Archivo PEC, Kelley papers, Exp. 3, Leg. 9/17, Letter to Calles, 10 September 1922 and 12 September 1922. Also Kelley papers, Exp. 3, Leg. 10/17, Letter to Calles, 27 October 1922.

to reach thousands of workers, farmers, union leaders and ordinary citizens with his message. Just one of the scores of letters sent by union officials may give some understanding of Kelley's activities and impact. Mary M. Wise, Business Representative of Local 31 of the United Garment Workers of America, AFL, wrote to Calles that she had heard Kelley speak at the Houston Labor and Trades Council meeting held in the Labor Temple there.

> I feel strongly impelled to write to you and say that Mr. Kelley's address was like a search-light turned into a dark place. My impressions of Mexico having been gathered solely from newspapers. I had but the most vague and contradictory ideas about conditions there; but after hearing Mr. Kelley tell about how the long-suffering people had at last come into their own, had taken over their government and were striving so hard to uplift themselves, I feel that the truth should be shouted from the housetops. I wish that every labor organization in this country, and every working man and woman in this country, could hear the truth as Mr. Kelley told it.[55]

Even if Kelley had asked Wise to write and to send the letter to Calles, as seems probable, that is simply another indication of Kelley's resourcefulness.

6   Kelley's Story of Mexican History and His Vision of Mexico

What was it that Kelley said that could have so moved his audiences? In advocating the recognition of Mexico, Kelley, like most public speakers, developed a standard speech, his was titled, like his pamphlet, 'The Truth About Mexico'. Kelley's standard speech shows both how he saw the Mexican government and labour movement, and how he attempted to convince his listeners of his vision, often with great success.

Kelley usually began his speech with an overview of Mexican history told in language taken from the old Protestant black legend of the Spanish Catholic conquest and from the rhetoric of the US populist and labour movements. Speaking before the Texas State Federation of Labor Convention in El Paso, Texas on 20 April 1922, Kelley told his 'fellow workers':

---

55   Archivo Calles-Torreblanca, Archivo PEC, Kelley papers, Exp. 3, Leg. 7/17, Letter to Calles from Mary Wise, no date.

Cortez found a wonderfully advanced civilization, a Nation skilled in the arts, in architecture – a nation that had reached the highest stage for that time, standing on a par with the then existing civilizations of Europe. But the Spanish conquerors proceeded to enslave these people. They were the forerunners of the misnamed American Plan and of the labor hating Merchants and Manufacturers Associations of America. They were the forerunners of the super-patriotic 100% Americans who establish or are trying to establish the beneficent 'Open Shop' in the State of Texas. Cortez gave the Mexicans the Open Shop 400 years ago, and after giving it the fairest kind of a trial for all that time, the Mexican people want no more of it.

Cortez, said Kelley, established the same system 'that your bosses are trying to put over' on you today.

Kelley continued his history lesson. 'About 100 years ago these people revolted, resulting in the overthrow of the Viceroy of Spain. But it was only a change in masters'. Kelley told his listeners, 'a Republic in name only. They had their own flag, their own song, but they still had the same old holes in the walls, the same old hovels, same scant cotton clothes and they still lacked shoes and decent food'.

Porfirio Díaz, said Kelley, came to power with promises of liberty and freedom. But Díaz invited in foreign investors, some from the United States, who participated 'in further exploiting the Mexican workers'. Inspired by John Kenneth Turner's *Barbarous Mexico*, Kelley described the conditions on the haciendas during the Porfiriate. 'In the States of Morelos, Puebla and other states of the Mexican Republic the workers had been kept in virtual slavery all of their lives. We have the same system of slavery and peonage in the States of Louisiana and part of East Texas, and other sections. And the Open Shoppers would like to see it established all over as a national policy'.

Out of that experience of peonage, Kelley suggested, came the revolution. 'The workers had no rights that anyone was bound to respect, so they decided to throw off the yoke of oppression and they used the only means at their command, the rifle and the bullet'.

Kelley continued:

and after ten years of fighting in the Republic South of the Rio Grande conditions have been brought about where men have the right to go to the ballot box and right their wrongs. The men of Mexico now hold up their heads as real free men. They have adopted a constitution that is the most modern document in the world.

At the centre of the Constitution of 1917, Kelley explained, were Articles 123 and 27. Kelley called Article 123 'Labor's Bill of Rights' and summarised it for his usually working-class, union audience:

> It is provided that eight hours will be the limit for a day's work, it does not say for Government employees or for workers in the arsenals and navy yards [as was the case in the United States], but for the Mexican worker no matter where he is employed. For night work the hours shall be seven. Unhealthy and dangerous occupations are forbidden to women and children, night work in industrial occupations is forbidden to women. For three months preceding child birth women shall be free and following child birth they shall enjoy an extraordinary period of one hour for the purpose of nursing the child. The time preceding child birth and for the month after shall be paid by the employer. The same wage shall be paid regardless of sex or nationality. All over-time shall be paid at an increase of 100 % more than the rate fixed for straight time, in no case shall overtime exceed three hours daily or for more than six consecutive days, [and] no woman shall be allowed to work overtime.

Kelley also explained Article 27 that stipulated that Mexico's people owned the rights to the subsoil, including minerals and petroleum.

In his standard speech, Kelley emphasised the material improvements in workers' lives, especially improved wages. 'Wages have been increased from 12 1/2 cents for a 12-hour day to four pesos for eight hours'. Kelley explained to his audiences that Mexico had established 12,000 schools within the last three years, and that with the help of 5,000 volunteer teachers 'illiteracy is being wiped out rapidly'. Kelley told his listeners about the government's $15,000,000 irrigation project in the Yaqui Valley of Sonora, and $20,000,000 being spent on renovating the Mexican railroad lines. 'The Agriculture Department', Kelley told his worker and farmer meetings, 'is dividing up the big estates that for decades had held a large percentage of the population as peons, and is supplying land, seed, agricultural implements and even burros to men'.[56]

Perhaps most important, in his speeches, Kelley argued that Mexico was a Farmer-Labor government. While there was not exactly a Farmer Labor Party, Kelley explained, the workers and peasants had united to create a kind of workers' government in Mexico. Kelley frequently told his audiences that Presid-

---

56   Newsclip, 'Mexico to Open Market for Atlanta', *Atlanta Georgian*, 1 May 1923, in Archivo PEC, Kelley papers, Exp. 3, Leg. 14/17.

ent Obregón, Minister of the Interior Calles, and other leaders of the Mexican government were card-carrying IAM members.[57] In reality, Kelley himself had bestowed the honorary membership cards on the Mexican leaders, who were in fact nearly all businessmen, professionals and generals in the revolutionary army. Kelley told his audience that labour has 'adopted the most powerful weapon the workers of a free republic have, the ballot, and in the last elections elected 206 congressmen out of a total of 260, 24 senators out of a total of 60, and 12 governors out of a total of 29 states'.[58] Kelley evidently sincerely believed that Obregón, Calles and the other cabinet members and legislators represented the working class.

Kelley frequently concluded his overview of Mexico with an idyllic picture:

> Mexico is at peace with the world and is asking nothing more than a square deal from other nations ... A constitutional government is functioning. The army has been reduced from 150,000 to 38,000. Courts are dealing justice to all the people ... Swords have been turned to plowshares and the people are happy and prosperous as never before.[59]

Mexico was fast becoming an Eden, if only the US would leave it unmolested.

Kelley usually explained that the forces who opposed the Mexican government were the same economic interests who opposed unions in the United States. The same American industrialists who opposed unions at home also opposed the revolution in Mexico. Workers in the United States, he concluded, should not support the periodic calls for military intervention in Mexico and should urge their representatives to support the recognition of Mexico.

Finally, near the conclusion of his talk, Kelley appealed to the US patriotism of his listeners.

> My forefathers fought to establish this Republic, they fought in the Civil War and I went into the Spanish War, and I hold that I have the right as

---

57 'Mexican Labor Representative is Heard by Large Audience in the Local City Hall Last Night', *Daily Paragraph*, Dennison, Ohio, 21 May 1923, Archivo PEC, Kelley papers, Exp. 3, Leg. 14/17.

58 Newsclip, 'Mexico of Today', *The Labor Record: Official Organ – New Orleans Building Trades Council* (New Orleans, LA), 30 March 1923, in Archivo PEC, Kelley papers, Exp. 3, Leg. 12/17.

59 'Central Trades Asks Boycott of Ward Bakery' [article about Central Trades and Labor Council Meeting of New York and Vicinity at which Kelley spoke], *The New York Call*, 18 May 1923, in Archivo PEC, Kelley papers, Exp. 3, Leg. 15/17.

an American Citizen to tell the truth and show up any group of exploiters who are trying to use my Government to pull their chestnuts out of the fire. I shall continue to fight against American capital imposing Open Shop conditions on the Mexican people as well as on my own.[60]

Telling the story of the Mexican Revolution in terms that resonated with his listeners' own experiences and aspirations, appealing both to their sense of working-class consciousness and to their American patriotism, it is not surprising that Kelley's speeches were frequently interrupted by applause and often concluded in ovations. US labour leaders wrote to Mexican officials to tell them Kelley's talk was a 'revelation'.[61]

But Kelley's talks often went beyond the appeal to labour. Speaking to university students, churches, business groups, civic organisations, and to the press Kelley broadened his arguments. Sometimes Kelley added to his talk claims that recognition of Mexico would mean millions of dollars of business for companies in the United States. At other times, Kelley suggested opportunities not only for investment, but also for farming, prospecting and colonisation in Mexico. For example, in a speech in New York, Kelley told his audience:

The Government and people of Mexico are most friendly to Americans, thousands of whom are going into fertile fields and productive mines of the west coast country. The Mexican Government and the Mexican people want to do business with the United States and American businessmen, but must await recognition by this country. There is an immediate need down there for millions of dollars worth of mining machinery, sugar and coffee machinery, oil tanks, pipe lines, etc. It is a golden opportunity for the business interests of the United States.[62]

60   'Address of J.W. Kelley' (20 April 1922) Archivo PEC, Kelley papers, Exp. 3, Leg. 5/17.

61   Letter of Frank Burch, Secretary-Treasurer of the Central Labor Union of Philadelphia and Vicinity to Arturo M. Elías (brother of Plutarco Elías Calles), Consul General of Mexico in New Orleans, 14 May 1923, in PEC, Kelley papers, Exp. 3, Leg. 14/17. There is also a virtually identical letter from Burch to Manuel Téllez at the Mexican Embassy.

62   'Rejuvenation of Mexico Told by Labor Man', *New York Evening Journal*, 19 May 1923, in PEC, Kelley papers, Exp. 3, Leg. 15/17. Similarly, in a speech in Atlanta, GA in April 1923, the local newspaper reported, 'A market for millions of dollars worth of badly needed machinery will be opened in Atlanta and other industrial cities of the South if the United States government gives official recognition to Mexico, according to J.W. Kelley, vice president of the Mexican Federation of Labor' ... – 'Mexico to Open Market for Atlanta', *Atlanta Georgian*, 1 May 1923, in Archivo PEC, Kelley papers, Exp. 3, Leg. 14/17.

The argument that recognition of Mexico would mean markets in Mexico appealed not only to his worker and farmer audiences, but also to business-people, chambers of commerce and government officials, whom Kelley also certainly had in mind. In those remarks one can see Kelley projecting a convergence of interest between, on the one hand, the Mexican government and Mexico's state-controlled unions such as the CROM, and, on the other, US labour unions and US corporations which in the early 1920s hoped to establish greater trade with Mexico.

Occasionally in these speeches, though not usually, Kelley attacked the role of the Catholic Church in Mexico. Kelley, who described himself as the son of missionaries who had grown up in China, assailed the church as a reactionary, anti-labour, force. Because of its reactionary role, said Kelley, 'Protestant churches are springing up all over the country [Mexico]'.[63] Such attacks on the Catholic Church, however, were not typical of Kelley's speeches and might well have gotten him in trouble with Catholic leaders of the AFL had he pushed that issue.[64]

7   Political Lobbyist

Kelley's union chief, Johnston, was apparently pleased with Kelley's campaign, for by August of 1922 Kelley could write to Calles:

> It has been proposed to us that we move to Washington and make that our headquarters. We have this from Johnston of the Machinists, Noonan of the Electrical Workers, Franklin of the Boilermakers, Doak of the Trainmen and others, including some Senators, such as La Follette, Walsh and Shortbridge ... [If the headquarters is moved there] we could make use of the various associations such as the League of Women Workers, the Farmers National Council, the Private Soldiers and Sailors Legion, and the Political Amnesty League, all of which have been successful in whatever they undertook in the past.[65]

---

63   Archivo Calles-Torreblanca, Archivo PEC, Kelley papers, newsclip, 'Labor Making Mexico Over, Kelley Asserts', *Houston Press*, 20 June 1922. The reference to Kelley being the son of a missionary is found in Kelley papers, 'El Trabajo en México sobre base firme', translation of an article from *The Citizen* of Los Angeles, 2 March 1923.

64   Andrews 1991, pp. 43–69.

65   Archivo Calles-Torreblanca, Archivo PEC, Kelley papers, Exp. 3, Leg. 8/17, Letter to Calles, 5 August 1922.

About a month later, on 18 September 1922, Kelley wrote to Calles, 'Mr. Gompers believes that the work I am doing is good and he suggested some time ago that I transfer my activities to Washington'.[66] Kelley regretted that he could not move at the time because of his involvement in the shop crafts strike. Six weeks later Kelley wrote again to Calles:

> On several occasions I have received communications from Gompers, Johnston, Congressman Keating, Congressman Casey, and others urging me to transfer my activities to Washington and set up a regular headquarters there ... We have the assurance of assistance from the labour movement and other groups but it is going to take finances and hard work. Senator Ashurst of Arizona, Senator Jones of New Mexico, Senator Shortridge of California and Senator Johnston of California have all promised assistance. I have talked with all of these gentlemen personally and each of them urged me to go to Washington together with a group of trained speakers and start a drive.[67]

Kelley was pressing Calles for financial support for the headquarters, which Calles evidently declined to provide. But by the end of January 1923, Kelley had things all set up, he reported. 'After March 1st my headquarters will be in the Machinists Bldg in Washington, D.C.', he wrote to Calles. 'They will rent us desk room or an office very cheap and all the internationals located there will assist'.[68]

Being in Washington was important, because Kelley was not only carrying out a public relations campaign; he was also engaged in a political lobbying effort. Kelley's job, in part was to talk with Congressional Representatives and Senators and convince them to come out for the recognition of Mexico. In December 1922, for example, Kelley wrote to Calles (via Mexican Consul F.A. Pesqueira), that on 13 December at the Machinists building he had been introduced to Senators La Follette, Borah, Johnston, Walsh; senator-elect Copeland of New York, Edwards of New Jersey, Wheeler of Montana, Frazier of North Dakota, and Fess of Ohio; as well as congressmen Morrow of New Mexico, Casey of Pennsylvania, and Linaweaver of California. Almost all of these formed part

---

66   Archivo Calles-Torreblanca, Archivo PEC, Kelley papers, Exp. 3, Leg. 9/17, letter to Calles, 3 September 1922.

67   Archivo Calles-Torreblanca, Archivo PEC, Kelley papers, Exp. 3, Leg. 10/17, Letter to Calles, 27 October 1922.

68   Archivo Calles-Torreblanca, Archivo PEC, Exp. 3, Leg. 11/17, Letter to Calles, 26 January 1923.

of the Progressive bloc in the US Congress. For four hours, wrote Kelley to Calles, he had talked about Mexico's political, social, educational, religious, and labour situation. Kelley had explained the Mexican Constitution, especially the land and mineral article 27 and the labour article 123. Similarly in April 1923 Kelley met with Senators LaFollette, Ladd and Brookhart.[69] Then in June 1923 he met with Colorado's Governor Sweet and Senator Adams. Kelley bent the ears of legislators and other public officials from one end of the country to the other, arguing that the United States should recognise Mexico.

8　　Recognition: Victory for Farmers and Labour?

On 31 August 1923, the administration of US President Calvin Coolidge recognised the government of Mexico and named Charles B. Warren as ambassador. While there would be future tensions in US-Mexican relations, particularly in 1926–27 and again in 1938, Coolidge's recognition of Obregón's government represented the end of an era in US-Mexican relations. The United States declared, in effect, that Mexico was no longer a political and economic pariah. Kelley's campaign was over, and he could claim victory.

What role had Kelley's campaign had in winning recognition for Mexico? Probably very little. While Kelley, the labour movement, and the progressives cried out for recognition of Mexico, neither the Harding nor the Coolidge administrations paid much attention to labour. In the end, the United States decided to recognise Mexico because the Obregón and Calles governments reached an agreement with the US banks on their debts, indicated that they would not expropriate US petroleum companies and conceded that agrarian reform would not impinge on US landowners in Mexico. On 29 September 1922, the Mexican government and US bankers signed the de la Huerta-Lamont agreement in which Mexico agreed to pay its foreign loans, including the railroad loans not previously guaranteed by the government. Then on 15 August 1923, the Mexican and US government had signed the Bucareli Accords dealing with US citizens' claims and US property in Mexico. In these various agreements and actions, Mexico capitulated to the bankers and oilmen, making diplomatic recognition possible.

69　　Archivo Calles-Torreblanca, Archivo PEC, Kelley papers, Exp. 3, Leg. 13/17, Letter to Arturo M. Elías, 11 April 1923.

9   Conclusion: Radical Reformers, Labour Bureaucrats, and the State

While he may not have been responsible for winning recognition from Mexico, between 1921 and 1925 José W. Kelley carried out a remarkable political campaign with that goal. In hundreds of letters and publications, in scores of meetings before thousands of workers and farmers, Kelley advocated not only the recognition of Mexico, but also his brand of working-class solidarity and internationalism. At the heart of this work was Kelley's understanding of Mexico as the Farmer Labor Party in power.

Kelley's standard speech, for example, was informed by the US tradition of labour republicanism and imbued with working-class radicalism. Kelley always described Mexico as a 'Republic', a word that in the United States in the 1920s implied a political democracy with representative institutions, political parties, and a civic consciousness. Yet Mexico in the 1920s was hardly what most US citizens would have considered a Republic. Kelley's main contact, Plutarco Elías Calles, an admirer of Mussolini, was the central figure of the emerging authoritarian regime, the future strongman of Mexico in whom the lineaments of dictatorship could already be seen. Calles and his ally Morones were busily engaged in the destruction of both the Catholic rebels' army on the one hand and the anarchist and Communist opposition on the other.[70] At the time, many Mexicans and some foreigner visitors criticised Mexico for its authoritarian military regime. Modern historians and political scientists often describe Mexico of the 1920s as Caesarist or Bonapartist, not republican.

Today, historians recognise that the ruling Generals such as Carranza, Obregón, and Calles managed to capture and subordinate the workers' unions and peasant leagues.[71] While Mexico's government was more interventionist than that of the United States, capitalists and landlords were the ultimate beneficiaries of government regulation in the era of Obregón and Calles, not workers or peasants.

Though he usually called his talk 'The Truth About Mexico', Kelley gave his audiences a picture of Mexico that was far from complete. Kelley neglected to mention the important struggle taking place in Mexico between the left-wing unions of the CGT and the government-sponsored labour confederation the CROM. He never mentioned the government's violent crushing of railroad strikes, or the assassination of the anarchist leaders of the streetcar workers.

---

70   The story of Calles's war against the Christian peasants of Mexico is told in Meyer 1994.
71   Carr 1976, pp. 111–26.

At the same time that Kelley was travelling the United States supporting Obregón's new government and the CROM, some other US labour unionists, Socialists, Communists, and the Industrial Workers of the World were supporting the Confederacion General de Trabajo (CGT) in Mexico. Founded by Mexican anarchists, Communists and IWWs, the CGT represented a significant current in the Mexican working class with a large following among many workers in a variety of industries. While Kelley provided glowing pictures of the political, social, and economic achievements of Mexico, the CGT was locked in bitter struggle with the CROM and the Mexican state. With the protection of the Obregón and Calles governments, the CROM provided strikebreakers, union goons, and even engaged in assassination of rival union leaders.[72] By about 1923 it became clear that the CROM was winning the fight against the CGT largely because it enjoyed the support of the Mexican state. By 1924, the state had won.

Yet Kelley never even mentioned in his letter, reports, and talks the existence of other union movements and organisations, nor did he discuss the important differences in the various Mexican labour movements. How could Kelley so loyally support the CROM and ignore the other Mexican unions? Certainly, at least at the beginning, the nature of the CROM and its relationship to the Mexican state may not have always been completely clear. The CROM retained the radical, class struggle, and internationalist anarchist rhetoric of its predecessor the House of the World Worker (COM). The CROM, at least at the beginning, had many left-wing locals in various parts of the country that sometimes cooperated with anarchists, Communists, and IWWs. In 1921, the year Kelley got involved, the CROM also had contacts with the Red International of Labour Unions organised out of the Soviet Union by the Communists, though those contacts soon broke down and turned hostile.[73] In the early 1920s, the CROM leadership was not yet the completely bureaucratised, conservative and corrupt organisation, which it would become a few years later. Morones and the 'Action Group' of the CROM were still developing the strategies that would eventually make them the dominant trade union federation. So, one could argue that Kelley might not have understood exactly what he was dealing with when he first got involved with Calles and Morones.

Yet many of the key fights between, on the one hand, Calles, Morones, and the CROM and, on the other, the left, the independent unions, and the CGT took place precisely in the areas in which Kelley was working, such as the railroads

---

72   Reyna 1972, pp. 785–813; Taibo II 1986, pp. 200–65; Carr 1976, pp. 155, 163, 184, 190, 224, 264.
73   Rivera Castro 1981, *passim*.

and the streetcar lines.[74] Kelley, who had constant contact with government officials, with the executives of the national railroads and the streetcar company, with union officials and with workers, could not have been unaware of the struggle of the government and the CROM against the anarchists. It seems possible that Kelley's organisation of the IAM on the streetcar lines may have been encouraged by the government precisely to rid itself of the anarchist presence there. Likewise, Kelley's work on the railroads may have been intended to break the power of the independent unions and draw them closer to the CROM.

Kelley was no political innocent. We know, for example, that in 1921 when Felipe Carrillo Puerto's Socialist Party of the Yucatan considered affiliation with the Communist Third International that Kelley, probably at the urging of Roberto Haberman, sent a telegram urging the Yucatan socialists not to affiliate with the Communists.[75] As that letter indicates, Kelley was a conscious opponent of revolution and an advocate of reform from the state, from above.

José W. Kelley's work for unions, international solidarity, and political recognition for Mexico represented a social democratic programme for North America, one in which capital would rule but unions and farmers' organisations would be respected and would have a voice, the governments would regulate business, and social programmes would assist working people. The programme proved undoable in the conservative 1920s but later found expression in a very limited way in the United States in Franklin Delano Roosevelt's New Deal and in Mexico in Lázaro Cárdenas's leftist nationalism and in the solidarity that existed in the 1930s between the CIO and the CTM, though that was more influenced by Stalinist Communism.

---

74   Rogelio Vizcaíno 1984, *passim* and Rodriguez 1980, *passim*.
75   Andrews 1991, p. 156.

CHAPTER 18

Failed Movements and Varied Fates: The Slackers and Communists after Their Mexican Adventure

By 1925 American leftists' adventures in Mexico were over at least for a while. Most of that generation's activists had returned home to the United States or gone elsewhere and had begun to make new lives for themselves. The revolutionary hope of the period immediately after the Great War when it seemed to some as if workers and peasants might swiftly overturn capitalism on a world scale had faded. The socialism and syndicalism of the late 1910s and the early 1920s, of which the slackers had formed a part, hardly existed any longer. The period of idealism which brought together socialists, internationalists, conscientious objectors, feminists, and union organisers in an attempt to create a new world of human possibilities had vanished. The revolutionary, often romantic, creative, and iconoclastic Communism of the immediate postwar period had been replaced by Stalin's harder, narrower, and more dogmatic politics, ultimately a counter-revolutionary development.

For those who had lived through exile in Mexico, the world had changed. While they had been slackers and then radical activists together in Mexico, their individual lives thereafter had little in common. Of course, they all experienced or observed over the next few decades the same political developments: the decline of the revolutionary socialist movement, the rise of Stalinism in Russia and Fascism and Nazism in Europe, World War II, the Cold War and then, in the United States, McCarthyism. People changed: a few ascetic idealists became money-grubbing realists; some former Communists were transformed into vehement and virulent reactionary anti-Communists; some former revolutionaries evolved into reactionaries. The fate of the founders and early organisers of the Mexican Communist Party varied widely. One would eventually rise to socialise with industrialists and financiers, another would stand and beg on the corners of Washington, D.C.; one became a leading anti-Communist; while another died in a Stalinist concentration camp. Their common or overlapping experiences in Mexico had taken place during a brief moment of radical optimism; the fragmentation of the movement in which they had once participated would be an enduring reality for decades.

1   Linn A.E. Gale

There was no one typical post-war, post-Mexican exile experience. Each of the slackers had a unique story. While Gale served his time at Leavenworth in the early 1920s, working in the library and on the prison newspaper, his devoted wife Magdalena waged a continuous campaign for his release, and finally with the help of US Senators William Borah, Royal S. Copeland, and Robert M. LaFollette succeeded in having his sentence commuted, so that Gale was released after spending three years in the penitentiary. Though he had been one of the founders of the Mexican Communist Party and the head of the Mexican Administration of the IWW, Gale played little role later in the American left or labour movement. Sometimes he figured as the eccentric author of rather odd occasional articles in radical publications. No doubt after it became public that he had repudiated his Communist views and had provided information to the government on other radicals in Mexico, he must have been a pariah on the left.

After Gale left prison on 18 June 1924, he moved to Washington, D.C. and established the Gale News Service. Learning that the new Mexican president, Plutarco Elías Calles was planning a visit to the United States, he wrote asking for a meeting. In his letter to Calles, Gale described himself as a 'political prisoner', and he denied having betrayed his principles or having informed on his fellow radicals. He attributed his expulsion from Mexico to 'the liar Ole Hansen', governor of Washington State who, he claimed, had shown Obregón the only article he had ever written criticising the Mexican president. Perhaps most interesting, Gale explained to Calles that he should be trusted because he had previously received political and financial support from several Mexican governments.

> Of course, I had accepted assistance from Berlanga, as well as from Adolfo de la Huerta (when he was president) and from various labourites in the cabinet of President Obregón. This doesn't mean that I was a supporter of Berlanga or of any other individual. I accepted the protection of any Mexican government with gratitude.[1]

Gale probably could never have understood that this remarkable confession of political subornation and economic dependence implied that he operated

---

1   Letter from Linn A.E. Gale to Plutarco Elías Calles, 30 October 1924. File name: The Gale News Service, Gav. 73, Exp. 12, Fideicomiso Calles Torreblanca.

within limits set by the state and, in the minds of many leftists, that would have utterly discredited any leftist political work he had done. Gale closed his letter in his usual obsequious style: 'I give you thanks and salute you in the spirit of comraderie, as the First Worker Chief of a government in America'.[2] Calles never granted him an interview.

In addition to running his news service, during the 1920s Gale wrote almost a dozen pamphlets, an odd collection of anti-imperialist and anti-Catholic tracts. He must surely have authored, under the name Porfirio R. Herrera, the pamphlet titled 'The Double Kidnapping of Linn A.E. Gale'. This promised to be the first in a series of pamphlets dealing with Gale's arrest and prison experiences, though no other pamphlets in that series were ever published.[3] Gale also wrote two political pamphlets in 1927 in defence of Mexico, 'The Threat of a New War', and 'Prepare to go to the Slaughter in Defence of Oil and Holy Water'.[4] He authored three virulently anti-Roman Catholic diatribes, all published by the proudly bigoted Rail Splitter Press of Milan, Illinois. These crude tracts, 'The Altar of the Prostitutes', 'Romanism, Mexico's Cancer', and 'If the Pope Comes to Washington! Or Catholicism in the National Capital', accused the Catholic Church of everything from running brothels to fomenting counter-revolution in Mexico and planning to overthrow the US government.[5] Finally, Gale wrote another brochure against Protestant attempts to promote Sunday closing laws titled, 'The Bigotry Trust in the USA', published by the old socialist press Haldeman-Julius Publications of Girard, Kansas.[6] And in this same period, he wrote a 32-page pamphlet entitled 'Evolution of Mankind: Some Observations on Anthropology' published by the Bender-Baker press in 1926.[7]

While still running his news service, around 1930 Gale had opened 'The Gale Book Shop' in the Annapolis Hotel, featuring 'Unusual and Unconventional Books'. He had evidently returned to the radical views that he had repudiated

---

2 Ibid.
3 Herrera 1925.
4 File 'Rail Splitter', Fondo 12, Series 010702, Exp. 70, Legajo 1, Fondo Elías Plutarco Calles, Fideicomiso Calles Torreblanca. The file contains translations into Spanish of pamphlets by Linn A.E. Gale. I give here the dates and the Spanish translation of the titles: 'La Amenaza de una Nueva Guerra' [The Threat of a New War] The Rail-Splitter, February 1927 and 'Preparense para ir al Matadero en Defensa del Petróleo y del Agua Bendita' [Prepare to go to the Slaughter in Defence of Oil and Holy Water] The Rail-Splitter, February 1927.
5 Linn A.E. Gale n.d. 1; Gale n.d. 2, Gale, n.d. 3.
6 Gale 1928.
7 Gale 1926.

when he was arrested, for he now expressed his support for the Soviet Union, where Joseph Stalin had come to power. He wrote to the feminist Mary Ware Dennett in that year, to explain why he had not yet paid her for some books, and in passing he observed:

> Marx's words are coming true. The most inspiring thing of the time is the splendid progress being made by the Soviet Union. Perhaps it is also encouraging that the imperialist, bigoted, puritanical United States is hell-bent for the crash, which will mark the end of the old system. Let us hope that the militant minority is ready to seize power when the time comes and establish its proletarian dictatorship instead of allowing a Fascist dictatorship to be set up instead.[8]

Gale continued to be an eccentric and cantankerous character. In January of 1931, he was forced to remove his bookstore from the Annapolis Hotel. He was also banned from working as a reporter in the US Treasury Building for having violated the rules and looked at private documents without permission. He mailed out a rather desperate two-page, legal size leaflet, enumerating the trials and tribulations he had been through and asking for financial assistance from the public.[9] The Great Depression and his own personal problems had reduced him to begging on street corners in the national capital.

Although Gale dropped out of sight for a while, eight years later he was still in Washington running the 'Gale News Service: Day and Nite Service to Newspapers in All Parts of the Country, Linn A.E. Gale, Proprietor'. He wrote again to Dennett on 19 November 1938, this time about nudism and about his work to repeal the Comstock Law. But he mentioned in passing that he was thinking of going to New York to arrange for the publication of his book, '"War Resister in Mexico", describing my hectic experiences of two decades ago when I ran Gale's International Monthly in Mexico and defied the militarists'. Gale went on:

> As you may surmise, I distinguish in the book between the situation in 1918 and that in 1938. I am not a pacifist and while I sincerely hope we keep out of the European hell, I feel that there might be justification for war-

---

8   Letter of Linn A.E. Gale to Mary Ware Dennett, 5 August 1930, in: Box 24, File 437, Mary Ware Dennett MC 397, Schlesinger Library, Radcliffe College, Harvard University.

9   Leaflet: 'A Cruel Christmas: Do You Care? If so, How Much?' in: Letter of Linn A.E. Gale to Mary Ware Dennett, 2 January 1931, in: Box 24, File 437, Mary Ware Dennett MC 397, Schlesinger Library, Radcliffe College, Harvard University

ring against Nazi-ism, altho I still see no excuse for participation in the war against the Central Powers.[10]

Whether or not he ever actually wrote his book on the slackers is unknown; no manuscript of the book has been found.

Gale died on 15 August 1940, and his obituary published in the *New York Times* described him as the national secretary of the 'Islands for War Debts Committee, formerly the Make Europe Pay War Debts Committee'. The obituary gave no cause of death but noted that, 'His widow survives him'.[11] As the Second World War expanded in Europe and Asia, and the United States hesitated on the threshold of the conflict, few then would have remembered Gale's notoriety as a draft-evader in the First World War, a slacker in Mexico, a Wobbly, and a Communist.

2   Charles Francis Phillips

While Gale never had any important impact on the American left, Charles Phillips became one of the leading cadres of the Communist Party of the United States and of the Communist International, and he later went on to a successful career in high finance and the railroad business. In mid-1922, Phillips left Mexico under the pseudonym Manuel Gómez, stopping briefly in New Orleans before settling with his Russian wife Natalia in Chicago. Phillips joined the above ground Workers Party and the underground Communist Party (two faces of the same group) as Manuel Gómez, and his fellow party members took him to be a Mexican immigrant. Wanting to be accepted as a rank-and-file party member, Phillips told his comrades nothing of his international work for Borodin, the Red International of Labour Unions, or his participation in the work of the Communist International.

A man of Phillips's talent and commitment was not likely to stay for long in the rank and file. The North Side Branch of the Chicago Communist Party elected him a member of the City Central Committee. Phillips took on organisational tasks for the party but also interested himself in cultural activities. In the mid-1920s he produced 'The Last Revolution', the play that he and Irwin Granich – who now used the name Mike Gold – had written in Mexico.

---

10   Letter of Linn A.E. Gale to Mary Ware Dennett, 19 November 1938, in: Box 44, File 712, Mary Ware Dennett paper, MC 392, Schlesinger Library, Radcliffe College, Harvard University.

11   'Lynn [*sic*] A.E. Gale' 15 August 1940.

Phillips later also edited a 50-page collection of poetry titled *Poems for Workers: An Anthology*, published by the party's Daily Worker Publishing Company in Chicago.[12]

To earn a living, Phillips worked briefly at Sears Roebuck but then found a position as a reporter at the *Chicago Economist* newspaper and later at the *Investment News*. At the same time, he worked as the 'Agitprop' (Agitation and Propaganda) director for his Communist Party branch and then for the party's District 8. He travelled throughout the Midwest teaching classes on the 'Rudiments of Marxism-Leninism', 'Revolutionary Marxism', and the 'American Labour Movement'. He also continued to be the party's expert on Latin America and the head of the All-American Anti-Imperialist League. From Chicago he published the League's newsletter *The Liberator*. Harry Haywood, a young member of the African Blood Brotherhood in Chicago who joined the Young Communist League in 1923, remembered working with Manny Gómez – that is Phillips – when the League attempted to organise opposition to prevent a US invasion of Nicaragua.[13]

In 1923 and 1924 Phillips participated in the organisation of the Farmer Labor Party, which had been founded by John Fitzpatrick, head of the Chicago Federation of Labor. An attempt by the Communists to take control of the Farmer Labor Party led to a rupture between the Communists and the labour leaders who had organised it, which proved a disaster for both the CP and the FLP. The unions and farmers' organisations withdrew, leaving the Communists to capture themselves. Phillips must surely have felt heartsick to see the effort collapse.

At about that time, Phillips joined a group within the Communist Party led by William Z. Foster. When the latter's group won control of the party in 1924, Foster moved the headquarters to Chicago and began publication of the *Daily Worker* newspaper. Phillips, writing under the name Manuel Gómez, became one of the regular contributors. He also became the acting editor of the party magazine *The Workers Monthly*.[14]

Under Foster's leadership, Phillips also headed the Anti-Imperialist Department of the Communist Party. Among his other assignments were continuing to maintain relations with the Communist Party of Mexico and organ-

12   Gómez 1925.
13   Haywood 1978, pp. 133–4.
14   Letters from Manuel Gómez [Charles Francis Phillips] to Joseph Freeman, in February 1925, Joseph Freeman Papers, Box 25, Folder 7, Hoover Institution, Stanford University. These letters indicate that Phillips was 'acting editor' of the *Workers' Monthly*.

ising the All-American Anti-Imperialist League in Latin America. As previously described, he travelled to Mexico in 1925 and worked with Bertram Wolfe on the organisation of the Mexican Communist Party convention. Back in the United States, Phillips also helped the Communist Party organise backing for General Augusto C. Sandino in Nicaragua, though Sandino refused the support.[15] In 1927 Phillips represented the Anti-Imperialist League at the Congress Against Colonial Oppression and Imperialism in Brussels,[16] where Stalin's call to transform the League into a Communist front-group led to the withdrawal of the Latin American intellectuals.[17]

When Jay Lovestone took over the leadership of the Communist Party in 1927, the party headquarters moved to New York, and Phillips was brought along. For a wage of $30 per month he continued to write for the *Daily Worker*, to head the anti-imperialist department, and help to organise the fight to save Sacco and Vanzetti and the Scottsboro boys. Ironically when the Anti-Imperialist Department endorsed the slogan 'Enlist with Sandino', Phillips, the notorious World War I slacker, war resister, and agent of the Communist International, had to defend himself within the party against the charge of 'pacifism'.

The mid- to late 1920s were marked by the factional struggle in Soviet Russia between Bukharin, Trotsky, and Stalin. 'We in the American party accepted the decisions from Russia unanimously', wrote Phillips in his autobiography. 'On the basis of the information available to us, no one doubted that Trotsky and his followers had been wrong'. But, said Phillips, he and others in the Foster group 'deplored the machine-like process employed in the affair'.[18]

In 1928, Phillips travelled to the Sixth World Congress of the Communist International in Moscow, the first he had attended since the Second Congress in 1920 when he had used the name Jesús Ramírez, then a delegate from Mexico. He supported Stalin's proposals at the convention, contributed to the struggle against Nikolai Bukharin and Jay Lovestone in a meeting with Molotov and was shocked and dismayed when a fellow delegate and a member of the Foster group, James P. Cannon, became a supporter of Trotsky. At the Sixth Congress, Phillips was given highest recognition by the new Stalinist leadership of the Communist International with his appointment as a full member of the new

15   La Botz 2018, p. 62.
16   Record Group 59, Box 7148, contains a collection of documents of the US Department of State, USNA, deals with Phillips central role in the organisation of the All-American Anti-Imperialist League and the Congress held in Brussels.
17   Riddell 2018.
18   Shipman 1993, p. 167.

Executive Committee.[19] Phillips later claimed that after reading Lenin's 'Testament', which charged Stalin with attempting to concentrate power in his own hands, he had become critical of Stalin. 'Stalin, I now believed, was the nemesis of Communist freedom', he wrote. 'To work in support of him was degrading, but to work against him impossible – if you raised your voice, you were out'. But, Phillips stated, 'I was not a Trotskyite, and never became one'.[20] Disillusioned with Stalin, he quit attending party meetings and was dropped from the party payroll.

Phillips's explanation of his break with Stalinism remains unsatisfying. As a leader of the American party and member of the Communist International Executive Committee, he had access to much information and many points of view, and yet he never explains his thinking about the nature of the Russian Revolution, the revolutionary regime, or the Communist International.

To support himself Phillips got a job for the *Wall Street News*, a small financial paper that was subsequently absorbed by the *Wall Street Journal*. He worked as investment editor for the *Journal* and gained an education in financial matters. Later he moved on to become financial editor at the *New York Post*. At the same time, he continued to work with the party, more as a sympathiser than a member, teaching classes on Leninism, for example. But finally, he found he could no longer abide the Stalinist Communist Party, and in 1930 he left for good. Two years later, the party officially expelled him 'for petty bourgeois tendencies'. Still, he continued to work with Communist Party groups, such as the John Reed Club, a group for writers, and he wrote articles from time to time for the party's magazine the *New Masses*.

Phillips became involved with an independent theatre group close to the Communist Party called the Theater Union and began producing plays. The group's first attempt was an anti-war play called 'Peace on Earth', followed by a play about a stevedore called 'Wharf Nigger'. Later Phillips worked with the German playwright Bertolt Brecht to produce 'The Mother', based on Maxim Gorky's novel of the same title.

Stalin's show trials of 1934 to 1937 shocked Phillips, and he believed that some other leftists must have felt as disturbed as he did. He decided to probe the Communist Party and see if there was any opposition group within it with which he might work. But his attempts only led to his denunciation as a Trotskyist – then the Communist Party's most vicious epithet – by his former friend and slacker comrade in Mexico, Mike Gold (the former Irwin Granich). Com-

---

19   Draper 1986, pp. 312–13.
20   Shipman 1993, p. 176.

munist Party leader William Dunne also wrote a letter severing all relations with Phillips. By 1938, Phillips found, 'The Party was now definitively closed to me'.[21]

While his attempt to find an opposition group to join in order to reform the Communist Party was aborted, his career as a journalist and economist proved quite successful, particularly in the midst of a national depression. By 1935, now using the name Charles Shipman, he had landed a job with Standard and Poor as a financial analyst. The company management made Phillips the railroad editor and he gradually became an authority on railroads and railroad securities.

His years in the Communist Party receded into the past. Tiring of his position at Standard and Poor, after 13 years Phillips quit in 1948 and took a position with Robert R. Young, head of the Allegheny Corporation. Young was a brilliant entrepreneur who was in the midst of reorganising the railroads. In 1946 he had become famous when he dramatized his demand for a reorganisation of the country's passenger service with the advertising slogan, 'A hog can cross the country without changing trains, but you can't'.[22] Phillips became one of the principal advisors to Young in organising the takeover of railroads worth billions of dollars.

Working for Young, Phillips received high salaries, stock options in various corporations, and was appointed to serve on corporate boards. He came to hobnob with such powerful industrialists as petroleum magnate Clint Murchison and the financier Cyrus S. Eaton. He continued to work with Young until the railroad tycoon killed himself in 1958 by blowing off his head with a shotgun.[23] By that time Phillips had his own business and a substantial income and no longer had to worry about his future. Though visited by the FBI in the 1940s and 1950s, Phillips escaped the repression of the McCarthy era, which devastated so many other lives. He died in 1989 at the age of 94.[24]

Unlike the eccentric and unstable Gale, Phillips's experiences in the antiwar movement and later in exile in Mexico transformed him into a professional revolutionary who, for a dozen years from 1918 to 1930, worked for the Communist International or one of the Communist Parties. He had founded the Mexican and Spanish Communist parties, had attempted to start a Communist Party in Guatemala, and had worked with the US Communist Party for eight years in positions of responsibility. He also attended two congresses of the Communist

---

21   Shipman 1993, p. 204.
22   'Young, Robert Ralph', p. 696.
23   Egan 1958, p. 46.
24   'Charles Shipman' 1989, p. 14.

International, the Second and the Sixth, and at the latter was appointed to the International's Executive Committee. Few men or women in the Communist movement had his kind of experience in and commitment to the revolutionary movement. But, dissatisfied with Stalin's leadership of the movement, Phillips first left the Communist Party and eventually left radical politics. Talented and ambitious, the former Communist came to work very successfully and lucratively in the heart of the capitalist system that he and his comrades had failed to overthrow.

3   Mikhail Borodin

Mikhail Borodin, who had been the principal person behind the founding of the Mexican Communist Party in 1918, had, as the reader will remember, left Mexico with Phillips to attend the Second Congress of the Communist International. But Borodin's adventures were only beginning. Afterwards the Communist International assigned him to work in Turkey, Persia, and then China where in October 1923 he became one of the chief political advisors to Sun Yat-sen and the National Revolutionary government of China. 'His job was to reorganise and pump new life into the Kuomintang', wrote historian Harold Isaacs. Under Borodin's tutelage, 'The Kuomintang was transformed into a rough copy of the Russian Bolshevik Party'.[25]

As Comintern agent in China, Borodin bore responsibility for carrying out Stalin's disastrous policy in China based on subordinating the Chinese Communist Party to the nationalist revolutionary party, the Kuomintang. When Chiang Kai-Shek and other reactionary military leaders of the Kuomintang turned on the Communist Party in 1927, massacring thousands of its members, the Chinese Communist Party was devastated. Stalin's policy, and Borodin's work in carrying it out, brought about the rule for the next 20 years of Chiang Kai-Shek's reactionary government, while Mao Tse-Tung went off with the remnants of the party to form an altogether different sort of Communist Party: the party as peasant army.

Borodin later figured as a fictional character in Andre Malraux's novel about revolutionary China, *Les Conquerants* (*The Conquerers*), published in 1928. Leon Trotsky, who had led the fight against Stalin's and Borodin's policies in China, reviewed the novel and took up both the fictional character and career of the real Borodin:

---

25   Isaacs 1961, pp. 63–4.

Borodin, who remains in the background all the time, is characterised in the novel as a 'man of action', as a 'professional revolutionist', as a living incarnation of Bolshevism on the soil of China. Nothing is further from the truth! ... Having quit Russia before the first revolution and having returned after the third, Borodin appeared as the consummate representative of the state and party bureaucracy that recognised the revolution only after its victory.[26]

For Trotsky, Borodin's policy in China had represented only the interests of Stalin and the Soviet Communist bureaucracy, not the interests of the Chinese workers or the international working class.

For ten years, from 1917 to 1927, Borodin had been one of the most important agents of the Communist International. From the time that he went off to Mexico with the Romanov crown jewels to finance revolution in Latin America until the coup of 1927 in Shang-Hai, he was one of a handful of Comintern agents who attempted to lead revolutions that they hoped would turn the tide and lead to the overthrow of capitalism on a world scale. The experiment ended in failure. The waning of revolutionary developments abroad led to reaction in Russia, and finally to the overthrow of the socialist experiment in the Soviet Union and its replacement by Stalinism, that is, bureaucratic collectivism, accompanied by the rise of Nazism in Germany, leading to World War II.

After returning to Moscow in 1927, Borodin 'lapsed into obscurity'.[27] Somehow, he managed to survive the Stalin purges of the 1930s and the vast destruction of World War II in the Soviet Union. After the end of the war, he became a journalist, the editor-in-chief of the English-language *Moscow Daily News* and then head of the Communist Information Bureau. Suddenly in 1949 Stalin had him and other members of the editorial staff, including the American Anna Louise Strong, arrested and accused of espionage. Borodin died in a concentration camp in the Soviet Union in 1951, though the charges against him were voided posthumously in 1955.[28] His last years in the Communist movement were as dismal and depressing as his first years had been romantic and exhilarating.

---

26   Trotsky 1976. Trotsky's review was originally published in the April 1931 issue of *Nouvelle Revue Français* (Paris).
27   Isaacs 1961, 276n.
28   Medvedev 1971, pp. 484–5.

4   M.N. Roy

Another major foreign figure in the organisation of the Mexican Communist Party, M.N. Roy, became famous as a theoretician of third world revolutions, organised a led a variety of political organisations in India, and played a significant if decidedly subordinate role in the struggle for Indian independence. In the end his loyalty to the Soviet Union and his support for the allies in World War II cut him off from the independence movement and alienated him from the Indian people.[29]

Roy had gone with Phillips to the Second Congress of the Communist International as a representative of the Mexican Communist Party. Once he arrived, however, he became the representative for India. In a famous private discussion with Lenin, Roy criticised the Bolshevik leader's theses on the question of national and colonial policy, and differed with his position that Communists should support revolutionary movements in the colonial countries led by the national bourgeoisie. Roy believed that Lenin failed to understand that national liberation movements in colonial countries were led not by a revolutionary democratic bourgeoisie, but rather by a feudal and reactionary capitalist class. Their debate revolved around the figure of Mohandas K. 'Mahatma' Gandhi, the leader of the Indian struggle against British colonialism. Where Lenin saw Gandhi advancing the cause of the liberation of the Indian masses from colonial oppression, Roy saw the Mahatma as an expression of Indian's feudal past. In the end Lenin invited Roy to submit his theses together with his own to the Communist World Congress. Lenin's theses on the national and colonial question were adopted by the Second Congress, but incongruously accompanied by Roy's supplementary theses.

With the support first of Lenin and later of Stalin, Roy advanced rapidly in the hierarchy of the Communist movement. He served as a candidate member of the Executive Committee of the Communist International in 1922 and a full member in 1924. By 1926 he had served on all four of the leading bodies of the Comintern: the Presidium, the Political Secretariat, the Executive Committee, and the World Congress.

Working as a leader of the Communist International, Roy took on the task of attempting to organise from abroad a revolutionary movement in India. In 1920 he attempted to organise an army of Indians in Tashkent to invade India by way of Afghanistan. The plan was aborted before any invasion could be organised. Roy then moved to Berlin where he edited the journal *Vanguard of Indian Inde-*

---

29   Kamik 1984, pp. 565–604; Alexander 1981, pp. 231–52.

pendence, a revolutionary newspaper carried to India by sympathetic seamen. He wrote three books in this period – *One Year of Non-Cooperation*, *Aftermath of Non-Cooperation*, and *The Future of Indian Politics* – all of which were Marxist critiques of Gandhi and the Indian Congress Party. In addition, he sent Indian emissaries from Germany to India, so that eventually local Communist centres were established in Bombay, Calcutta, Kanpur, Lahore, and Madras. The British colonial government retaliated by indicting Roy in the Communist conspiracy cases of 1924 and 1929 in Kanpur and Meerut respectively and issued warrants for his arrest.

In the late 1920s, Roy separated from his wife and political partner Evelyn Trent Roy, who had been involved in organising the Feminist Council in Mexico.[30]

Meanwhile, the faction fight between Joseph Stalin and Leon Trotsky had come to head in the Communist Party of the Soviet Union and in the Communist International. Roy supported Stalin against Trotsky and backed the former's disastrous policy in China. At the Sixth World Congress of the Communist International, Stalin and his faction began an attack upon Roy. With that, Roy moved closer to the so-called Right Communists or Communist Party Opposition led in Russia by Nikolai Bukharin, in Germany by Heinrich Brandler and in the United States by Jay Lovestone and Bertram Wolfe. After he published a series of articles in an opposition Communist newspaper in Germany, the Communist International expelled Roy in 1929. After being ousted from the Communist International, he was, of course, also repudiated by the Indian Communist Party. Roy later wrote *Revolution and Counter-Revolution in China* to vindicate himself and distinguish his position from that of Stalin and Borodin.[31]

Still living in Germany, Roy established the Oppositionist Indian Communists and began to orient toward the Indian National Congress. For the Congress convention at Lahore in 1929, he wrote a pamphlet in which he endorsed the Congress's call for independence and expounded a political and economic programme for achieving it. At the same time, he and his supporters formed the League of Indian Independence within the Congress to push it toward the left.

In 1930, still facing warrants for his arrest in the Kanpur and Meerut conspiracy cases, Roy returned to India with his new wife Ellen Gottshalk, a German Jewish ex-Communist. Disguised as Dr Mahmud, he travelled through

---

30   Letter from Evelyn Trent Roy to Henk Sneevliet, 13 March 1927, available at: https://www
      .marxists.org/archive/roy-evelyn/1927/march/13.htm
31   Roy n.d.

the country, organising students and peasants, and soon became one of the principal forces in the Central Peasants League. He also attended the Karachi session of the Indian National Congress in February 1931 where he met with Jawaharlal Nehru and Subhas Chandra Bose. But Roy's involvement with the Congress proved to be short lived. The British government of India arrested Roy on 21 July 1931, and he was brought to trial for the Kanpur Communist conspiracy case, charged with attempting to separate India from Great Britain. The court found him guilty and sentenced him to 12 years transportation; he was imprisoned at Bareilly in Uttar Pradesh. From there he led his political organisation, commonly known as the Roy Group, wrote scores of articles and pamphlets, and authored three more books. After spending five years and four months in jail, he was released on 20 November 1936.

Once free, Roy joined the Indian National Congress at the invitation of Jawaharal Nehru, one of its most important leaders. Roy and his followers joined the Congress Socialist Party and succeeded in winning several leading positions. Through his new newspaper *Independent India* published in Calcutta, he pushed to make the Congress Party more democratic and more activist. Throughout this period Roy counterposed his radicalism to the politics of Gandhi who dominated the Congress.

Following the outbreak of World War II, in August 1942 Gandhi had started the Quit India movement, calling for the complete withdrawal of the British. Roy, however, coming to a position close to that of Stalin and the Communists, supported the Allied Powers war effort as a people's anti-fascist struggle. As a sympathiser of the Soviet Union, he also feared that Nazi Germany might invade and destroy the Communist government in Russia. His views, unpopular among Indian fighters for independence, caused him to be denounced as an agent of British imperialism, and finally led to his expulsion from the Congress.

Though expelled from the Congress Party, Roy was elected the general secretary of the All-India Trade Union Congress, later known as the Indian Federation of Labour. He turned his efforts to labour organising, while still continuing to try to whip up support for the war against Nazi Germany. He also established the Radical Democratic Party, though his ideas and organisations remained marginal.

Toward the end of the war Roy broke with Marxism and began to call himself a 'humanist'. Roy wrote a 'Humanist Manifesto', later published as the booklet titled *The New Humanism*, in which he concluded that political parties were an obstacle to the people's exercise of their sovereignty. In his last big book, *Reason, Romanticism, and Revolution*, published in two volumes in 1952 and 1955, Roy wrote, 'New Humanism advocates a social reconstruction of the world as a commonwealth and fraternity of free men, by the cooperative endeavour of spiritually emancipated moral men'. He continued:

> New Humanism is cosmopolitan. A cosmopolitan commonwealth of spiritually free men will not be limited by the boundaries of national States – capitalist, fascist, socialist, communist, or of any other kind – which will gradually disappear under the impact of the twentieth-century Renaissance of Man.[32]

So, Roy came to reject the Communist movement he had helped to found in Mexico and India. Interestingly, his views in the 1950s sounded rather like those of the romantic radical socialist slackers of the teens and twenties whom he had met in Mexico.

In 1953 Roy suffered a cerebral thrombosis and on 25 January 1954 he died in Dehra Dun, India, survived by his second wife Ellen. Of all the figures mentioned in this story of the slackers in Mexico, Roy was one of the few who had really played a major role in his own country as well as in the international arena.

5   Carleton Beals

After the slacker years, Carleton Beals continued to be an interpreter of developments in Latin America to US liberal, labour, and leftist readers. Between 1923 and 1970 he wrote 40 books and hundreds of newspaper and magazine articles, most of them dealing with Latin America. He continued to be a critic of US imperialism in Latin America and a supporter of leftist causes.

It was as an apparently independent leftist that in 1937 Beals agreed to serve as a member of the Trotsky Commission headed by John Dewey. The Commission was intended to give the famous Russian revolutionary then in exile in Mexico an opportunity to respond to Stalin's charges that Trotsky was a counter-revolutionary and a Nazi collaborator by conducting an international inquiry. Under the chairmanship of the renowned American progressive and pragmatist philosopher John Dewey, the trial began on 10 April and lasted a full week, with Trotsky himself as the principal witness in his own defence.

When Beals's turn came to question Trotsky he pursued an odd line of inquiry. Surprisingly, he asked about Trotsky's relationship to the Russian Revo-

---

32   Roy, *Memoirs*, p. 603.

lutionary Mikhail Borodin who had been sent by the Communist International to Mexico in 1919. Had it been Trotsky who sent Borodin to Mexico, as an informant claimed, asked Beals. Trotsky replied that he had not sent Borodin and asked Beals for the source of his information. Beals replied that his informant was Borodin himself, still alive then in Stalin's Russia. When Trotsky asked how Borodin had communicated this information to him, Beals refused to say.

Beals's questions appeared to have little to do with the supposed purpose of the inquiry, which was to challenge the show trials in Moscow that had smeared Trotsky. Rather Beals's questions seemed calculated only to embarrass Trotsky and to create political difficulties for Mexican President Lázaro Cárdenas who had offered asylum to the Russian revolutionary. Beals attempted to portray Trotsky as the organiser of a revolutionary movement in the very country that later provided him a haven. Trotsky's supporters feared that allegations that he had tried to stir up revolution in Mexico might lead to his extradition and make him once more a man without a country. Moreover, although Beals provided no explanation of how he could have communicated with Borodin, he must certainly have reached him through Soviet government or Communist Party channels. Infuriated at what seemed an attempt to jeopardise his asylum, Trotsky accused Beals of being a Stalinist agent sent to disrupt the very hearing intended to vindicate Trotsky. The mostly Trotskyist sympathisers on the Commission made things difficult for Beals who subsequently resigned.[33]

Was Beals a Stalinist agent? Beals had been friends with American, Mexican and Cuban Communists, and he may have served briefly as the treasurer of the Mexican Communist Party in the early 1920s, though there is no proof that he was a member of the Communist Party at the time of the trial, nor that he was an agent of Stalin. At one point in the late 1920s the Mexican Communists rather disliked Beals because they found him too unreliable. In December of 1929 Hernán Labourde, the general secretary of the Mexican Communist Party, wrote on behalf of the Mexican Communist Party's central committee to the US radical Joseph Freeman asking him to help in having Beals removed as the correspondent for TASS, the Soviet news agency. Labourde wrote to Freeman:

> It is obvious that the government tries to isolate our party by preventing the news of repression to be known abroad. Carlton [sic] Beals, the correspondent of the TASS has shown very little or no interests [sic] at all in transmitting this information, which is natural considering the fact that he has never been very near to us, and to-day less than ever.

---

33   Dewey 1969, pp. 425–8. Deutscher 1963, pp. 74–376; Britton 1987, pp. 166–86.

In consequence the C.C. [Central Committee] desires to ask you, that you take, if it is possible to you, the necessary steps towards substituting Beals by a correspondent who would comply with his duty as correspondent of a news agency, whose purpose is principally, as we understand it, to counteract the work of the bourgeois news agencie[s], by transmitting true and timely information on the international revolutionary movement.[34]

While this letter was written almost a decade before the Trotsky commission's work in Mexico, it suggests that Beals sometimes had difficult relationships with some leaders of the Mexican Communist Party. At least in December 1929 Beals – even if he still sympathised with or was even a secret member of the Communist Party – remained somewhat independent in his views, independent enough to get him in trouble with the Mexican Communist Party's general secretary.

Yet Beals's resignation from the Trotsky Commission and his press statements denouncing it suggest that indeed he was a Communist agent sent to disrupt and discredit the hearings. 'Thus far', Beals told reporters in an evident attempt to discredit Trotsky's damning testimony against Stalin, 'no investigation has been conducted, but merely a pink tea party – with everyone but myself uttering sweet platitudes. Trotsky had wings sprouting from his shoulders'. He went on: 'By its Czarist methods', he told the press, 'the Commission prevented me from clarifying matters'. He alone, he suggested, could question Trotsky effectively and reveal the truth about his acts, but only if the commission were disbanded. Beals concluded: 'Until Trotsky is willing to disavow the stupidities of the Commission, he can twiddle his thumbs so far as I am concerned'. If Stalin had not sent him, Beals appeared to have volunteered for Stalin.[35]

Decades later Beals was still active on the left. When the Cuban Revolution occurred in 1959, Beals defended it, although as a more traditional Marxist he initially criticised Castro and his movement for lacking working-class support and the absence of a leftist political programme. Beals remained a lifetime defender of Latin America, a critic of US foreign policy, and an enemy of American imperialism.

---

34   Letter of 25 December 1929 from Heman Labourde, general secretary of the Mexican Communist Party, to Joseph Freeman, Joseph Freeman Papers, Box 175, Folder 8, Archives, Hoover Institution, Stanford University, has both the Spanish language original and the English translation, possibly by Freeman, which is cited here.

35   Martin 2002, pp. 415–16.

6   Louis Fraina

Louis Fraina, who had such an unfortunate career in the Communist revolutionary movement, including the accusations that he was a police agent in the United States and an embezzler of Communist funds in Mexico, went on to become a famous economic historian, sociologist, and political commentator – at least until he was investigated by the FBI in the 1950s.

Fraina, whose career as a Communist in Mexico had been tainted by accusations of corruption, returned to New York in 1926 and began to publish articles on economics for the *New Republic* under the name Lewis Corey. In 1929 he won a grant from the Brookings Institution, which allowed him to complete his book *The House of Morgan*, published in 1931, a work which established his reputation as one of the leading economic historians in the United States.

From 1931 to 1934 Fraina-Corey worked as an associate editor of the *Encyclopedia of Social Sciences*, while at the same time he also wrote *The Decline of American Capitalism* published in 1934, a leftist work on the Great Depression and its significance for American life, which became a bestseller. He followed it with *The Crisis of the Middle Class* in 1935, which helped to solidify standing as a sociologist and social critic.

Gradually, based on the reputation he won with his publications, Fraina-Corey began to return to leftist politics and to the labour movement. He served as editor of the independent *Marxist Quarterly*, and then worked for several months as an economist for the Works Progress Administration (WPA) in Washington. From 1937 to 1939, he was education director for the International Ladies Garment Workers Union Local 22 in New York. In 1940 Fraina-Corey was one of the founders of the Union for Democratic Action, later Americans for Democratic Action (ADA). His role as a founder of ADA marked Fraina-Corey's transition from radicalism to liberalism and anti-Communism. Finally, in 1942 he became professor of economics at Antioch College, perhaps the only person in the United States with such a position who had not finished high school.

In 1950, working with the Amalgamated Butcher Workmen's Union, Corey published *Meat and Man* and then took an appointment with that union as its educational director. Even though Corey was no longer a Communist and had opposed Stalin and the Soviet Union, and had even called for US victory in Korea over the Communists, he was still on the FBI's enemies list. Around 1950 the FBI began to persecute him and threatened to deport him under the McCarran Act. The deportation order arrived on Christmas Eve 1952. Ironically the US Justice Department had decided to deport a leading liberal anti-Communist intellectual because of his former role as a Communist revolutionary. Before the order could be carried out, Fraina-Corey suffered a cerebral haemorrhage and died in New York City on 17 September 1953.[36]

Paul Buhle, Fraina's biographer, argues that in the fight of the left wing of the Socialist Party to construct a new Communist Party, Fraina showed an 'irresponsible indifference' to the party's base of workers and poor farmers in the West. Buhle contends that Fraina accelerated the 'destructive factional approaches that exiled the Left from American life'.[37] Buhle's assessment is harsh, but certainly it is true that, although Fraina was a brilliant intellectual, he sometimes proved to be a poor political leader. He was never cut out to be a mass leader, a political maneuverer, or an international adventurer. The combination of the spying charges and trials, followed by the sudden moves to Moscow and Mexico, and then the questions of how he had spent the Comintern's money left Fraina utterly alienated from the party and personally disoriented, and in 1921 he suffered a kind of failure of the will. Fraina spent the next ten years rebuilding his confidence and proved remarkably successful, going on to become one of the country's leading academics and political commentators.

7   Sen Katayama

Sen Katayama, the old Japanese socialist who had briefly led the Mexican Communist Party from underground, left Mexico on 12 November 1921. He travelled first to Paris, then to Berlin, and on to Soviet Russia where he was greeted by an honour guard of the Red Army. Leon Trotsky, military commander-in-chief, whom Katayama had known in New York when they joined with other socialists to organise the left wing of the Socialist Party of America, gave the official greeting. Also among the welcoming delegation were several top Soviet Communist leaders: Kalinin, Zinoviev, Radek and Lunacharsky. For the next 11 years, Katayama dedicated himself to the organisation of the Communist International and its parties in Asia, giving particular attention to his own homeland, Japan. He participated in the First Congress of the Toilers of the East held in Russia in January 1922. Not long thereafter at the Fourth Congress of the Communist International, he saw the Japanese Communist Party seated as a member in good standing, the fulfilment of a project he had started several years before.

---

36   'Lewis Corey Dies', 1953.
37   Buhle 1995, pp. 172–80 and Gabriel Kolko 1995, p. 89.

The Japanese Communists early successes in organising were soon dealt a defeat by the September 1923 police attacks in which all-important Communists were arrested and ten union organisers were executed. The fierce police repression led the leaders of the Communist Party of Japan to dissolve the organisation in 1924, an extraordinary and until that time unprecedented event in the history of the Communist International. The dissolution of the party was considered so disastrous and depressing, that at the Fifth Congress of the Communist International, the news was suppressed, and Katayama even reported that the movement was proceeding satisfactorily.

In 1926, Katayama made a trip to Shanghai and then conducted a long trip through China to survey the revolutionary situation. In the debates between Stalin and Trotsky over China, he surprisingly played no important part, although he ultimately sided with Stalin. From that point forward, Katayama became identified with the Stalin forces in the factional fight in the Soviet Communist Party and in the Communist International. His vote was important, since he served on the Executive Committee of the Communist International and on the Presidium.

Meanwhile, working from Moscow, Katayama focussed his attention on rebuilding a Communist Party in Japan, directing the reorganisation of the party and its participation in elections. On 15 May 1928, Japanese police unleashed a fierce repression arresting thousands of Japanese citizens considered to be 'dangerous elements', shutting down political parties and union organisations, and the Communist Party in particular. Despite Katayama's efforts, once again the Japanese Communists were in retreat.

The Communist International, now led by Stalin, held its Sixth Congress in 1928, opening the so-called 'Third Period' of 'class against class warfare'. Speaking on the question of Japan, Katayama said, 'the time has come to prepare ourselves for the fight against world imperialism which threatens our fatherland, the Soviet Union'.[38] The Comintern, Katayama, and other Japanese party leaders called upon the Japanese Communists to rebuild their party and the mass organisations and to lead an assault on the Japanese employers and the state. This was a sectarian and suicidal policy utterly unlike the practice by which Katayama had built the first Japanese labour unions.

After about 1929 Katayama yielded leadership of the Japanese Communist movement to new, younger Japanese leaders. During the depression years, he continued act a spokesman for the Communist International at anti-war and anti-imperialist meetings in Western Europe as a kind of senior statesman of

---

38   Kublin 1964, p. 329.

Communism, a living symbol of internationalism and revolution. Perhaps he failed to understand the significance of the changes taking place around him as Stalin and the bureaucracy of the party carried out a counter-revolution that buried the workers' revolution of 1917. No doubt he remained faithful after his fashion to the project he had begun when he first read Richard T. Ely and became a convert to Christian socialism, then later to social democracy, and finally to Communism. In his mind, no doubt, Katayama still stood with the workers, but he failed to recognise that the Communist Party of the Soviet Union and the Communist International no longer did.

On 5 November 1933, Sen Katayama died in a Moscow Hospital at the age of 73 years. The Soviet Union held a special ceremony to honour him, and, led by Joseph Stalin, 150,000 people passed by his bier to pay their last respects. Perhaps some of them remembered the famous moment, when Katayama and Plekhanov shook hands before the Socialist International, a gesture of peace and internationalism defying the Russo-Japanese War of 1904. Probably only a handful knew that among his other many responsibilities, Sen Katayama had once led the Mexican Communist Party.

8   Bertram Wolfe

Returning to the US after being expelled from Mexico, Bertram Wolfe spent another four years as a member of the Communist Party of the United States before being expelled from the party in 1929 as part of the Right Opposition led by Jay Lovestone.[39] He went with Lovestone into the Communist Party of the USA (Opposition), but in the early 1930s he gradually gave up political activism for a career as a writer. Wolfe and his old friend from the Mexican Communist Party, the artist Diego Rivera, produced two books, *Portrait of Mexico* and *Portrait of America*, which combined Wolfe's brilliant popular historical writing with Rivera's magnificent paintings and drawings in beautiful editions produced by the leftist publishing house Covici Friede.[40]

Wolfe, like his mentor Lovestone, evolved into a Cold Warrior and an ardent anti- Communist. During much of the 1950s he was 'the chief ideological advisor of the International Broadcasting Office of the State Department'.[41] Later he became a senior researcher with the Hoover Institution, one of the

---

39   Draper 1960, p. 430.
40   Rivera 1934 and Rivera 1937.
41   Alexander 1981, p. 134.

leading centres of academic anti-Communism at the time. Wolfe also wrote the best-selling *Three Who Made a Revolution: Lenin. Trotsky. Stalin*, the book which was for 20 years the standard text in many modern Russian history courses. On the basis of this work, he was appointed Distinguished Professor of Russian History at the University of California, as well as visiting professor at Columbia University.

Somewhat like Phillips, Wolfe, who had been a professional revolutionary from 1918 into the early 1930s, eventually left politics. Less an organiser and more an intellectual than Phillips, Wolfe had played an important role in the Communist Parties of Mexico and the United States and also served as delegate to the Fifth Congress of the Communist International. Unlike Phillips who left politics for the world of business and moneymaking, Wolfe turned to a new political career with the State Department and with anti-Communist organisations such as the Hoover Institution. Once an intellectual at the service of Communism, he became one of the principal ideologues of American anti-Communism.

9   Roberto Haberman: In Exile in the United States

Roberto Haberman, who, while not a slacker, had been the first of the American radicals to arrive in Mexico during World War I, was also one of the last to leave. Unlike slackers who opted for Communism and the Industrial Workers of the World, Haberman had been a man of the Mexican state. He had worked closely with Luis N. Morones, leader of the CROM, and with presidents Álvaro Obregón and Plutarco Elías Calles. Beginning in 1928 Haberman gradually fell from the heights of power in the Mexican establishment. In that year Obregón decided to violate the revolutionary slogan of 'no re-election' and ran for president again. A Catholic militant assassinated Obregón on the eve of the election, though many Mexicans believed that Luis N. Morones, who had been a rival of Obregón and had aspired to be president himself, had actually been responsible for the former president's assassination. Calles, who was still president and who would remain the power behind the throne until 1934, withdrew the government's support from his old ally Morones and the CROM which almost immediately began to fall apart. (The Mexican pun is the '*desmoronamiento del CROM*' or 'the crumbling of the CROM'.) Haberman, who had been one of Morones' closest associates and friend of presidents, now began a long slide downwards. Though still protected by Calles, Haberman's long association with Morones now placed him on the margins of Mexican political life.

Six years later, Lázaro Cárdenas became president and not long after drove former president Calles out of Mexico. With Morones and Calles both out of the picture, Haberman was not only without support, but liable to persecution. Reading the writing on the wall, he left Mexico for the United States.

Haberman set up a law office first in Washington and later in New York and dedicated himself to divorce law. He even wrote a book: *The Divorce Laws of Mexico, with Appendices Including Decisions of Local Jurisdictions in the United States with respect to Foreign Decrees*.[42] From dealing with important affairs of state, Haberman was reduced to dealing with the details of separation and divorce. Ironically, Roberto Haberman – the naturalised American who had become a Mexican citizen in 1924 at the insistence of President Obregón – was forced to become an exile in his former adopted homeland, the United States. After World War II, when Mexico's government turned in a more conservative direction, Haberman returned and under President Miguel Alemán Valdez helped to organise the newly established Mexican Institute of Social Security, the country's public health and retirement system. In the 1960s Haberman, now old and sick, returned for the last time to the United States. A US military veteran of the Spanish-American War, he died in the Veterans Administration Hospital in Lebanon, Pennsylvania in 1962.[43]

Just as the anti-war movement, the Socialist Party, and then the Communist Party had once united several of these men, the movement's failure divided them and sent them off in various directions. Looked at from today's perspective of the end of the century, the days in which they organised workers, peasants, and women into the Industrial Workers of the World, the Feminist Council of Mexico, and the Mexican Communist Party might appear to be almost insignificant. In the context of their later lives, the moments of idealistic aspirations and revolutionary intrigue in Mexico seem almost like an accident. The famous slackers of 1917 and the 1920s are all dead now, and their movement is all but forgotten. Yet it was not without its impact and its importance. Each of the men and women in this era participated in the great social experiment in internationalism, each with a different vision and strategy, and with distinct results. Some, however, succumbed to either US or Mexican nationalism, while others became Stalinists, none proved capable of maintaining an independent internationalist socialist position.

---

42   Haberman 1930.
43   'Roberto Haberman Dead', 5 March 1962, *New York Times*, p. 23.

Epilogue

The American left and its relations to the Mexican revolutionary movement during period from 1900 to 1925 provide us with a fascinating social laboratory in which to see the role of different left tendencies: the social gospel, progressivism, craft unionism, social democracy, anarchism, revolutionary syndicalism, and the revolutionary socialism of the early Communist Party. Each of the major left political tendencies and organisations of the United States manifested in their relationships with the Mexican Revolution's various forces their fundamental politics and demonstrated their capability or their incapacity to implement those politics in their work in Mexico. At the same time, the Mexican, the American, and the Soviet governments all worked to shape the left and the labour movements in Mexico.

All of this took place during an era of world war and revolution during which 20 million died in World War I, principally in Europe, one million died in the Mexican Revolution, and eight million in the Russian Civil War. Within this horrifying context of slaughter, disease, and starvation on a world scale, labour and the left attempted to create some sort of humane alternative, though the left itself was deeply divided, first between those who sought to reform capitalism and those who sought to overthrow it, and then among the revolutionaries between the syndicalists, the anarchists, and the Communists each of which sought a different sort of new society. The left's experience in the laboratory of the Mexican Revolution cannot be compared to the experiences of the left in Germany and Central Europe in the same era, where the working class was so much larger, the parties so much more developed, and the contest for power between the workers and the capitalist class had become palpable and real. Still Mexico offers lessons to be learned.

Initially, the American left seemed to be unified in its support for the Mexican Revolution. The Mexican Liberal Party, an anarchist organisation led by Ricardo Flores Magón, initiated the period of the Mexican Revolution with its first calls for a national uprising in 1906. Forced to flee Mexico even before that date, Flores Magón and other PLM leaders fled to the United States and made contact with Emma Goldman and her anarchist comrades in St Louis, Missouri. The Mexican and American anarchists – both influenced by Mikhail Bakunin – recognised each other as sharing the same political philosophy and ideals and pledged their solidarity to one another. Later, other American anarchists such as Voltairine de Cleyre and British-American William C. Owen would argue that Emiliano Zapata's 'Commune of Morelos' represented the anarchist ideal of the self-organised community of the producers, though in fact the peasants of Morelos did not look forward to anarchism but rather looked back to a profoundly religious and traditional communal peasant society. Throughout the period from 1906 until World War I American anarchists – as well as the Socialist Party, the AFL, and the IWW – all supported the Mexican revolutionary cause. The anarchists did so morally and materially, that is, through education and modest financial contributions, and a few also crossed the border to ride with the revolution there. The brief moments of unity of the American left in support of the PLM was largely based on ignorance or misunderstanding of the PLM's politics.

The PLM's anarchism proved to be disastrous for the movement it led. The Mexican anarchists' strategy of repeated calls for insurrection, together with an insecure clandestine organisation, led to the arrest of the leaders and the crushing of the movement. Then the PLM's 1911 invasion from Southern California into Baja California together with its allies in the Industrial Workers of the World, some anarchists, and a number of soldiers of fortune, proved to be a fiasco from which the group never recovered. Opponents argued that the PLM and its American allies represented American *filibusterismo*, that is, political piracy, an attempt to rip off a part of Mexico for the United States. The PLM then split, with its socialist faction leaving to join Francisco I. Madero's liberal capitalist revolution. But it was the combined repression of the Mexican and American governments that finally killed the Mexican anarchist movement. The US government tried and convicted Ricardo Flores Magón of sedition under the Espionage Act of 1917 and he was sentenced to twenty years in prison for obstructing the war effort, dying in the Leavenworth Penitentiary, Kansas in 1922 at the age of 48. Meanwhile, the victory of the Bolsheviks in the Russian Revolution, accompanied by repression of the anarchists there, as well as in the United States and Mexico led to enmity between anarchist and Communists.

The AFL's business unionism proved more successful, but then it had allies in the governments of two nations and very different goals. Samuel Gompers, future head of the American Federation of Labor, first learned of Mexican conditions from fellow workers while still working at the bench in a cigar manufacturing shop. As he rose to union leadership, Mexican visitors kept him apprised of events, including the rise of the Mexican Liberal Party, which he initially supported. With the appearance of Madero, however, Gompers became a supporter of his liberal capitalist revolution. During these same years, the AFL gradually sought a closer relationship with the Democratic Party and with the US government, a relationship that prospered under President Woodrow Wilson and especially during World War I when the AFL appeared as the patriotic alternative to the revolutionary Industrial Workers of the World.

Gompers' goal was the extension of the AFL model of business unionism to the entire American continent. The AFL, advocate of business unionism and the labour lieutenant of American capitalism and US imperialism, worked with the US government and with the Mexican government, as well as with reformist union leaders in an attempt to shape the emerging labour movement in Mexico. The AFL cooperated with the Mexican government and its state-controlled Regional Confederation of Mexican Workers (CROM) and then joined with the CROM to create the Pan-American Federation of Labor (PAFL) as a capitalist, reformist bulwark against anarchism, syndicalism, and Communism. While Gompers succeeded in establishing a beachhead for his business union model in Canada, Puerto Rico, and Mexico, and won a few converts in other countries, he was never able to extend his form of unionism to all of Latin America before he died in 1924.

The Socialist Party of America, while it too had initially supported the Mexican Liberal Party in the opening years of the twentieth century, also turned to support the liberal capitalist government of Francisco Madero after 1911. Socialist John Kenneth Turner's book *Barbarous Mexico*, a project he undertook on behalf of the PLM, would be the most important piece of socialist propaganda on an international issue in that era before World War I, turning many Americans against the dictatorship of Porfirio Díaz, leading to much sympathy first with the Magonistas and later with Francisco Madero's liberal revolution. A few years later, John Reed literally rode with the Mexican revolution, saddling up and setting off to accompany Francisco 'Pancho' Villa, whom he came to appreciate and even admire. Reed's book *Insurgent Mexico* left us with sensitive and moving descriptions of the life of the men and women of the vast spaces of arid northern Mexico as he rode alongside Villa's soldiers. He also conveyed how Villa established, to the extent possible, a social democratic government in Chihuahua. Socialist authors like Turner and Reed contributed to a sympathy in the United States for the Mexican people and their revolution.

Eugene V. Debs, America's most famous labour leader and socialist, initially sympathised with the PLM, but once Madero appeared on the scene, Debs too led the Socialist Party to back Madero's project of a capitalist revolution and a republic, which Debs, working in the tradition of the Socialist International, saw as the next and only possible stage for Mexico and her people. When revolution turned into civil war in 1914, Debs and other SP leaders subsequently embraced the Constitutionalists of Venustiano Carranza against the plebeian and radical Conventionists led by Pancho Villa and Emiliano Zapata. The US entry into World War I in April 1917 led Woodrow Wilson to suppress the Socialist Party, jailing leader Debs and other members, and ending any significant organised Socialist Party support for Mexico. After the war ended, the combination of Attorney General Palmer's raids on leftists, accompanied by arrests and deportations, and at the same time the split between Socialist and Communists, led to the decline of the American left in the 1920s, while Debs himself died in 1926.

Young, left-wing Socialist Party members, draft resisters like Charles Francis Phillips, Herman Levine, and Carleton Beals, together with their left-wing women companions such as Eleanor Parker, fled to Mexico in 1917, and for the first time the American left became directly involved in that country's revolution on the ground. They first joined the Socialist Party of Mexico and then under the influence of the Communist International's agent Mikhail Borodin, founded the Communist Party and became organisers of the Industrial Workers of the World, allied with the most radical peasant movement leders, and established the Feminist Council. The Communist International's first intervention in Mexico made a very small impression on that country's labour movement and the left, though later the International would make a more systematic attempt with somewhat more significant results.

The Industrial Workers of the World (IWW), despite its involvement in the fiasco of the invasion of Baja California, proved to be relatively successful for a time in leading a mass workers' movement in Mexico, principally in the port of Tampico. Unlike the other organisations discussed here, the IWW had existed since the beginning of the twentieth century in a practical sense as a transnational organisation. Mexican workers who came to work in the United States, generally finding themselves excluded from the AFL unions, joined the IWW, participated in its organisation, and joined its strikes. And at the same time, American workers who went to Mexico often brought their IWW union with them, so that the IWW became a truly international organisation. IWW organisers like Pedro Coria and Charles King had experience as IWW members on both sides of the border. With the extraordinary expansion of the Mexican oil industry on the Gulf Coast in the 1910s and 1920s, the IWW became for a while the leading labour organisation in Tampico, Mexico. The IWW organised and led strikes that sometimes paralysed the oil industry and proved capable of winning improved conditions and wages for workers. And very briefly Wobblies, anarchists, syndicalists, and Communists joined together to create an alliance of impressive economic power. The IWW eschewed politics, but in any case, the Wobblies would have found it hard to accommodate to the new Mexican state. In the post-war and post-revolutionary period, the Mexican government and the American companies proved capable of breaking or taming the unions. The IWW's revolutionary syndicalism showed workers their tremendous economic power but left them without a way to challenge the political system.

In 1921 the Communist International made a second intervention in Mexico, this time sending three organisers to rebuild the Mexican Communist Party:

the Italian-American Louis Fraina, the Japanese Sen Katayama, and slacker Charles Francis Phillips who had been one of the original founders of the party. While Fraina's role is rather obscure, Katayama's assiduous clandestine work together with Phillips' contacts in the labour unions and the left, brought this second effort more success: the construction of a Communist youth group under José Valadés, the beginning of a Communist labour organisation under Manuel Díaz Ramírez, and the important relationship with peasant leader Úrsulo Galván. Yet, by 1922, this second Communist International intervention ended with Katayama leaving Mexico for Moscow and Fraina leaving the Communist movement altogether. Phillips too left Mexico for a while but would return a few years later to make one final attempt at building a real Communist Party in the mid-1920s.

Bertram D. Wolfe, though his involvement in Mexico was initially fortuitous, would play the central role in the Communist International's third attempt to build a Communist Party in Mexico. Wolfe played a leading role in the party's work and, remarkably, he became the most important intellectual leader of the party. As its dominant political figure, he persuaded the party to support the Obregón government against the de la Huerta rebellion, with the argument that the government would have to arm the workers. The result, however, was the strengthening of the Obregón-Calles regime that went on in the next year to defeat the remaining radical forces in the labour movement, and to subordinate the unions and peasant leagues to the state, and, despite his support for the government, expel Wolfe as a 'pernicious foreigner'.

A little later Joseph 'José' W. Kelley of the International Association of Machinists and the Farmer Labor Party arrived in Mexico to work with the railroad unions there. He saw the Álvaro Obregón government as a kind of Farmer-Labor government in power and he collaborated closely with Minister of the Interior Plutarco Elías Calles, who helped to finance his work in the unions and to whom he reported on a regular basis. He evidently viewed the relationship between the revolutionary government and the CROM unions as progressive and as a reformist alternative to the capitalist dominated United States government, then in the process of crushing the US railroad shopcraft unions.

During the 1920s the Mexican state achieved relative stability that was based on having reached a modus vivendi with the United States. Beginning with Álvaro Obregón's coming to power as president of Mexico in 1920, the Mexican government carried out a series of reforms and implemented a severe repression that together suppressed or co-opted much of the class conflict that had existed in Mexico since 1906. The Obregón administration succeeded in gaining control over the majority of the labour movement organised in the CROM, led by Luis N. Morones, while virtually destroying the IWW and the General Confederation of Workers (CGT) led by the anarchists and Communists.

Peasants, after their leaders like Zapata had been assassinated, were pacified by rather modest land distributions. Plutarco Elías Calles continued the same policies from 1924 until Obregón decided to run for president and was assassinated by a Catholic militant in 1928. At that point Calles brought together the country's military and political leaders to create the National Revolutionary Party (PNR), the organisation that would rule Mexico (by different names) until 2000. To Americans, by the mid-1920s, Mexico no longer looked like a dictatorship, and in fact to many it appeared to be a kind of progressive democracy. Solidarity with a people yearning for freedom no longer seemed to be needed in the same way as it had been during the years of the struggle against the Díaz dictatorship. Consequently, interest in and sympathy for Mexican working people declined, interest in Mexico's politics diminished, and when Americans turned to Mexico again in the 1930s, the interest would be mainly in the country's culture and art.

At the same time, in the United States by 1924 nearly all of the political tendencies we have discussed in this book had gone into crisis and by 1930 they had all virtually ceased to exist as major players in international solidarity. Samuel Gompers, the head of the American Federation of Labor and the driving force in the creation of the Pan-American Federation of Labor, died in 1924. While his successor William B. Green shared Gompers' business union philosophy, he seems to have lost interest in international affairs when Woodrow Wilson left the White House in 1921, to be followed by the corrupt, anti-union administration of Republican President Warren G. Harding. Green did not share his predecessor's obsession with imposing the American model of trade unionism on Latin America and so the PAFL languished, virtually collapsing with the beginning of the Great Depression in 1930.

The Socialist Party of America suffered tremendous repression during the presidency of Woodrow Wilson whose administration imprisoned SPA leaders such as Eugene V. Debs, Kate Richards O'Hare, and many others, while American Legionnaires and other such patriots broke up SPA offices and beat the organisation's members. And then, when the war ended, the Socialist Party experienced a bitter faction fight between its right and left wings, with the latter leaving and, after various vicissitudes, eventually forming the Communist Party. All attention in the immediate post-war period was focused on Europe, first the rise of Communism in Russia and then of Fascism in Italy, while there was much less interest in the Socialist Party of America in the political affairs of the Americas. In any case, faced with its own crisis, the Socialist Party had little time or energy to examine the Mexican situation or to offer solidarity to any group there.

Like the Socialist Party, the Industrial Workers of the World and the anarchists had also suffered the severe repression of the Wilson administration, the jailings during the war, and then in the 1920s the Palmer Raids and the deportations. The IWW would continue to be active in some parts of the United States throughout the 1920s, but it was no longer the force it had been from 1905 to 1917. Some of its members continued their labour activism in the new Communist Party, but others simply drifted away from the One Big Union. At the same time anarchism, which had been in its heyday in the period from the 1870s to the 1910s, had also been virtually obliterated, likewise a victim of Wilson's repression and the Palmer Raids. A few anarchists remained active in the working class, others became Communists, yet others, now less likely to be part of the working-class movement, became denizens of the underworld of American bohemianism to be found in Greenwich Village or San Francisco, producing pamphlets and giving talks to small audiences. And, as with other left groups, the anarchists' interest in Mexico declined.

The experience of Joseph Kelley of the International Association of Machinists and the Farmer Labor Party had really been largely a fluke. Kelley's own experience in the Southwest, his knowledge of the Spanish language, and his enthusiasm for the Mexican revolutionary government made him useful to the IAM's ambition of extending its influence in the North American railroad industry and to the AFL's desire to create stronger ties with Mexican labour and influence both Mexican and US government policy. With the exception of Kelley's experience in the mid-1920s, the IAM and the Farmer Labor Party seemed to have little interest in Mexico. And the Farmer Labor Party largely declined in the later 1920s, becoming gradually aligned with the Democratic Party of Franklin D. Roosevelt in the 1930s.

The Communist Parties of the United States and Mexico, affiliated with the Communist International and aiming to build a revolutionary socialist movement through North America, survived the period of the 1920s, though just barely, and subsequently began to grow. The Communist Party of the United States had only a few thousand members in the 1920s, while the Mexican Communist Party had only a few hundred. At the time, the Communist International and its affiliated parties were being transformed by developments in Russia. Lenin died in 1924, leading to a battle for succession between Zinoviev, Kamenev, Bukharin, Rykov, Trotsky, and Stalin. In that period Zinoviev carried out the 'Bolshevisation' of the Communists Parties, that is bringing them under the control of the Communist Party of the Soviet Union. Then in the 1930s, Stalin emerged victorious and became the absolute dictator. Stalin carried out a counter-revolution, exterminating thousands of the Old Bolsheviks of the era of the Russian Revolution, he fused the party and the state, and pressed ahead to build 'socialism in one country' with the forced collectivisation of agriculture (in which six million perished) and a frantically rapid programme of industrialisation through intense exploitation of the working class. Stalin at the same time transformed the Communist International from a coordinating centre for revolutionary workers' parties into an arm of Soviet foreign policy.

In fact, between 1927 and 1937, Stalin carried out a counter-revolution that overturned whatever remained of workers' power or socialist politics in Soviet Russia, creating a new kind of bureaucratic collectivist society. The Soviet Union under Stalin and afterwards until its fall in 1991, represented a new – if temporary – form of class society, neither socialist nor capitalist, and hostile to both, if often willing to compromise with the latter. Soviet Communism – though it was imposed upon, or spread, or was imitated in the nations of Eastern Europe, North Korea, North Vietnam, and Cuba – proved to be a historical side-track, a road to nowhere that proved incredibly expensive in terms of human progress. Yet, beginning in the 1930s and through the 1980s – that is until the Hungarian Revolution, the Prague Spring, and Polish Solidarność, and finally the fall of the Soviet Union in 1991 – Communism seemed to be a way forward, especially for the economically developing world.

In the 1930s, for the first time, the International had the resources to build Communist Parties in Latin America, parties that by and large adhered loyally to Stalin's line. In 1928, the Communist International entered its 'Third Period', a period of sectarian ultra-leftism based on the notion that the Social Democratic Parties were really 'social fascists'. Communists were to take the initiative to launch revolutionary insurrections where they could, a policy that was devastating everywhere, including in Mexico. With the turn to the 'Popular Front' period in 1935, based on alliance with non-fascist capitalist parties and governments, the Mexican Communist Party became an ally of the government of President Lázaro Cárdenas, and it grew and prospered in his shadow and that of his successors until the Cold War began in the late 1940s.

But, returning to our central argument, the American left of the 1910s and 1920s was divided into two currents on the question of Mexico, one interested in reforming Mexican capitalism and the other interested in a workers' revolution and a socialist Mexico. The Protestant churches and the Progressives, Eugene Debs of the Socialist Party and Samuel Gompers of the AFL, and later John Kelley of the Farmer Labor Party supported the forces in Mexico that they believed could build a progressive capitalist society, perhaps even a pro-labour, social democratic society. They supported first Madero, then Carranza, and finally Álvaro Obregón and Plutarco Elías Calles, and while the society began to modernise and capitalism flourished in some sectors – agriculture, mining and oil in particular – capitalism did not lead to democratisation. The

Obregón and Calles regime carried out some reforms intended to solidify its labour base, but it was not fundamentally progressive and certainly it was not democratic. Whether or not they had intended to, the American reformists contributed to an authoritarian capitalist state. Reformism did not lead to reform; it ultimately led to reaction.

The American idealists of the 1910s and 1920s in the left wing of the Socialist Party, in the Industrial Workers of the World, and in the young Communist Party affiliated with the new Communist International had attempted to create a revolutionary socialist party within the broader context of constructing a militant workers' movement. They found that they could not rival in power or influence the rising nationalist movement and the new Mexican government with which they attempted to compete. While they failed, for the most part, they did not contribute to the building of that new authoritarian capitalist state; on the contrary, their efforts largely contributed for a decade to the development of a militant labour movement as they attempted despite the difficulties to create an independent left. In retrospect, we can admire their ideals and their effort, even if their project failed, overcome by the powerful forces of American reformism, Mexican nationalism, and Soviet Communism becoming Stalinism. As conservative forces became dominant worldwide, so ended the 25 extraordinary years of Americans riding with the Mexican Revolution.

Bibliography and Works Consulted

Archival Sources

Archivo General de la Nación (Mexico City) – AGN – Dirección General de Gobiemo Presidentes Calles and Obregón Archives and Manuscripts, Bancroft Library, University of California at Berkeley

Centro del Estudio del Movimiento Obrero y Socialista (Mexico City) – CEMOS

Columbia University Libraries (New York), Special Collections Bourne collection. Lewis Corey papers.

Condumex Archive (Mexico City)

Emma Goldman Archives, University of California (Berkeley, California)

Fideicomiso Calles-Torreblanca (Mexico City)

Hoover Institution, Stanford University. Joseph Freeman Papers (Palo Alto, California)

Jaffee Papers, Archives, Emory University (Atlanta, Georgia)

Lewis Corey [Louis Fraina] papers, Columbia University (New York, New York)

Oral History Collection, University of California (Berkeley, California)

Schlesinger Library, Radcliffe College, Harvard University Mary Ware Dennett papers, MC 397. (Cambridge, Massachusetts)

Secretaría de Relaciones Exteriores – SRE – (Mexico City, Mexico)

Socialist Collection in the Tamiment Library, New York University Collections, Collection IX (New York, New York)

State Archival Service of the Russian Federation, Russian Center for the Preservation and Study of Documents of Contemporary History (formerly the Central Party Archive) SASRF (Moscow, Russia)

USNA – US National Archives – USNA Department of State Record Group 59, Box 3764 Record Group 59, Box 7148 Department of Justice File No. 200655 (Microfilm) (Washington, D.C.)

US Military Intelligence Division – USMID Record Group 165, Boxes 2290, 2291, 2292 430 Reproduced with permission of the copyright owner. Further reproduction prohibited without permission. Government Documents Randolph Boehn, ed., *US Military Intelligence Reports: Surveillance of Radicals in the United States. 1917–1941* (Microfilm) (University Publications of America, 1984).

Newspapers and Periodicals

Boletín de la Confederación de Cámaras Industriales (Mexico)

El Comunista de Mexico: Órgano del Partido Comunista de Mexico y de la 'I. W. W' de Mexico

El Heraldo de México
El Obrero Industrial
El Socialista
Gale's Magazine
Industrial Worker
International Socialist Review
Mother Earth
The Call
The Industrial Pioneer
The International Socialist Review
The New York Times
The One Big Union Monthly

References

'3 Students Seized on Anti-Draft Charge', 1 June 1917, *The Call.*

'62 Congress, 1st Session. J.J. Res. 29. Joint Resolution Relative to the Mexican Situation', introduced in the House of Representative 5 April 1911.

'1,500 Voice Cry for Repeal of Conscription', 8 June 1917, *The Call.*

Abbott, Leonard D. May 1914, 'Let us Make War Against War!' *Mother Earth*, vol. IX, no. 3, 82.

Ackerman, Kenneth D. 2016, *Trotsky in New York 1917: A Radical on the Eve of Revolution.* Berkeley: Counterpoint.

Adelson Gruber, Steven Lief 1982, 'Historia Social de los Obreros Industriales de Tampico, 1906–1919', Doctoral dissertation, Colegio de México.

Adler, William M. 2012, *The Man Who Never Died: The Life, Times, and Legacy of Joe Hill, American Labor Icon.* New York: Bloomsbury.

Aguilar Camín, Hector 1995, 'Los Jefes Sonorenses de la Revolución Mexicana', in D.A. Brading, *Caudillos y campesinos de la Revolución Mexicana.* Mexico: Fondo de la Cultura Económica.

Aguilar Mora, Manuel 1982, *El Bonapartismo Mexicano.* Mexico: Juan Pablos Editor.

Akers Chacón, Justin 2018, *Radicals in the Barrio: Magonistas, Socialists, Wobblies, and Communists in the Mexican-American Working Class.* Chicago: Haymarket Books.

Alexander, Robert J. 1957, *Communism in Latin America.* New Brunswick, NJ: Rutgers University Press.

Alexander, Robert J. 1981, *The Right Opposition: The Lovestoneites and the International Communist Opposition of the 1930s.* Westport, CT: Greenwood Press.

Alexander, Robert J. 1961, *Trotskyism in Latin America.* Stanford, CA: Stanford University, Hoover Institution Press.

Allen, Ralph 1961, *Ordeal by Fire: Canada. 1910–1945*. Garden City, NY: Doubleday & Company, Inc.

Alonso, Harriet 1993, *Peace as a Women's Issue: A History of the US Movement for World Peace and Women's Rights*. Syracuse, NY: Syracuse University Press.

Alvarado, Salvador 1985, *La Reconstrucción de México*. Mexico: Comisón Nacional para las Celebraciones del 175 Aniversario de la Independencia Nacional y el 75 anniversario de la Revolución Mexicana, vols. I and II.

Alzati, Servando A. 1946, *Historia de la Mexicanización de los Ferrocarriles Nacionales de México*. Mexico: no publisher.

Ampudia, Ricardo 1996, *México en los informes presidenciales de los Estados Unidos de América*. Mexico: Fondo de Cultura Económica.

Anderson, Perry 2013, 'American Foreign Policy and Its Thinkers', *New Left Review* September–October.

Andrade, Juan 1979, *Apuntes para la historia del PCE*. Barcelona: Editorial Fontamara.

Andrews, Gregg 1988, 'American Labor and the Mexican Revolution, 1910–1924', PhD dissertation, Northern Illinois University.

Andrews, Gregg 1990, 'Robert Haberman, Socialist Ideology, and the Politics of National Reconstruction in Mexico, 1920–25', *Mexican Studies/Estudios Mexicanos* 6, 189–211.

Andrews, Gregg 1991, *Shoulder to Shoulder: The American Federation of Labor, the United States, and the Mexican Revolution: 1910–1924*. Berkeley: University of California.

'Anti-Draft Case Goes to Jury Today', 23 June 1917, *New York Times*.

'Appeal of the Rangel-Cline Defense Fund', December 1913, *Mother Earth*, vol. VIII, no. 10, 304–7.

Araiza, Luis 1963, *Historia de la Casa del Obrero Mundial*. Mexico: Sindicato de Obreros y Artesanos de la Ind. Cervecera y Conexas.

Arshinov, Peter 1974, *History of the Makhnovist Movement (1918–1921)*. Detroit: Red and Black.

'Ask Mexico to Send Draft Dodgers Back', 7 June 1920, *New York Times*, 9.

Avrich, Paul 1971, *The Anarchists in the Russian Revolution*. Ithaca, NY: Cornell University Press.

Avrich, Paul 1978, *An American Anarchist: The Life of Voltairine de Cleyre*. Princeton: Princeton University Press.

Avrich, Paul 1995, *Anarchist Voices: An Oral History of Anarchism in America*. Princeton: Princeton University Press.

Babcock, Robert H. 1974, *Gompers in Canada: A Study in American Continentalism Before the First World War*. Toronto: University of Toronto Press.

Baena Paz, Guillermina 1982, *La Confederación General de Trabqjadores: Antología*. Mexico, D.F.: Centro de Estudios Historicos del Movimiento Obrero Mexicano-CEHSMO.

Baginski, M. 1913, 'The Significance of the Mexican Revolution', *Mother Earth*, vol. VIII, no. 10 (December), 300–4.

Bakunin, Mikhail 1971, *Bakunin on Anarchy: Selected Works by the Activist-Founder of World Anarchism*, ed. by Sam Dolgoff, Preface by Paul Avrich. New York: Random House.

Balanbanoff, Angelica 1968, *My Life as a Rebel*. New York: Greenwood Press.

Baldwin, Deborah J. 1990, *Protestants and the Mexican Revolution*. Urbana: University of Illinois Press.

Barbosa Cano, Fabio 1980, *La CROM: De Luis N. Morones a Antonio J. Hernández*. Puebla: ICUAP/Editorial Universidad Autonoma de Puebla.

Baron, Samuel H. 1963, *Plekhanov: The Father of Russian Marxism*. Stanford, CA: Stanford University Press.

Barrios, Elías 1978, *El Escuadrón de hierro*. Mexico: Ediciones de Cultura Popular, S.A.

Bastian, Jean-Pierre 1993, *Los Disidentes: Sociedades protestantes y revolución en México. 1872–1911*. Mexico: Colegio de México and Fondo de Cultura Económica.

Basurto, Jorge 1981, *El Proletariado Industrial en México (1850–1930)*. Mexico: UNAM.

Beals, Carleton 1927, *Brimstone and Chili: A Book of Personal Experiences in the Southwest and in Mexico*. New York: Alfred A. Knopf.

Beals, Carleton 1938, *Glass Houses: Ten Years of Free-Lancing*. New York: J.B. Lippincott Company.

Beals, Carleton 1931, *Mexican Maze*. With Illustrations by Diego Rivera. Philadelphia: J.B. Lippincott Company.

Beals, Ralph L., and Diane L. Dillon 1977, 'Anthropologist and Educator: Ralph L. Beals', interviewed by Diane L. Dillon, Oral History Program, manuscript copy in Bancroft Library, University of California at Berkeley.

Berkman, Alexander 1914, *Selected Workers of Voltarine de Cleyre*. New York: Mother Earth Publishing Association, available at: https://www.gutenberg.org/files/43098/43098-h/43098-h.htm#The-Mexican-Revolution

Blaisdell, Lowell L. 1962, *The Desert Revolution: Baja California. 1911*. Madison: University of Wisconsin.

Blanchard, Margaret A. 1992, *Revolutionary Sparks: Freedom of Expression in Modern America*. New York: Oxford University Press.

Blasco-Ibañez, V. 1979 [1920], *El Militarismo Mejicano*. Bacelona: Plaza & Janes Editores.

Bortz, Jeffrey 1997, '"Without Any More Law Than Their Own Caprice", Cotton Textile Workers and the Challenge to Factory Authority During the Mexican Revolution', *International Review of Social History* 42, 253–88.

Bortz, Jeffrey 2000, 'The Revolution, the Labor Regime and Conditions of Work in the Cotton Textile Industry in Mexico, 1910–1927', *Journal of Latin American Studies* 32, no. 3, 671–703.

Bottomore, Tom, and Patrick Goode, trans. and eds. 1978, *Austro-Marxism*. Oxford: Clarendon Press.

Bourne, Kenneth, and D. Cameron Watt, eds. n.d., *British Documents on Foreign Affairs: Reports and Papers from the Foreign Office Confidential Print*, general editors Kenneth Bourne and D. Cameron Watt, Part II, From the First to the Second World War. Series D, Latin America. 1914–1939, editor George Philip, Volume 2, *Central America and Mexico. 1914–1922*. n.p.: University Publications of America.

Boxer, Marilyn J., and Jean H. Quataert, eds. 1978, *Socialist Women: European Socialist Feminism in the Nineteenth and Early Twentieth Centuries*. New York: Elsevier.

Brechin, Gray 1999, *Imperial San Francisco: Urban Power, Earthly Ruin*. Berkeley: University of California.

Bricianer, Serge 1978, *Pannekoek and the Workers' Councils*. St. Louis, MO: Telos Press Ltd.

Britton, John A. 1987, *Carleton A. Beals: A Radical Journalist in Latin America*. New Mexico: University of New Mexico Press.

'Board Dismisses Levine', 12 July 1917, *The New York Times*.

Boudin, Louis 1972, *Socialism and War*. New York: Garland Publishing, Inc.

Bourne, Randolph 1964, *War and the Intellectuals: Essays by Randolph Bourne*. New York: Harper & Row.

'Boys, Accused of Conspiracy, Give Testimony', 20 June 1917, *The Call*.

Brissenden, Paul 1919, *The I.W.W.: A Study of American Syndicalism*. New York: Columbia University Press.

Brown, Jonathan C. 1993, *Oil and Revolution in Mexico*. Berkeley: University of California.

Bruce, David 2016, 'Bleeding Mexico', *International Socialist Review* XVI, no. 10, 581–5.

Buhle, Paul M. 1995, *A Dreamer's Paradise Lost: Louis C. Fraina/Lewis Corey and the Decline of Radicalism in the United States*. New Jersey: Humanities Press.

Buhle, Paul M. 1999, *Taking Care of Business: Samuel Gompers, George Meany, Lane Kirkland, and the Tragedy of American Labor*. New York: Monthly Review Press.

Bukharin, Nikolai 1973, *Imperialism and World Economy*. New York: Monthly Review Press.

Bustillo Oro, Juan 1973, *Vientos de los veintes: crónicas testimonial*. Mexico: Secretaría de Educación Pública.

Bustos Carrillo, Antonio 1949, *Yucatán al servicio de la patria v la Revolución*. Mexico City.

Cabrera, Luis 1994, *Revolución e historia en la obra de Luis Cabrera (Antologia)*, ed. Eugenia Meyer. Mexico: Fondo de la Cultura Económica.

Cano, Gabriela 1996, 'Más de un siglo de feminismo en México', *Debate Feminista* 14, 345–60.

Cano, Gabriela 2013, 'Debates en torno al sufragio y la ciudadanía de las mujeres en México', *Estudios Sociológicos* 31, número extraordinario, 7–20.

Cárdenas, Hector 1974, *Las Relaciones Mexicano-Soviéticas: antecedentes y primeros contactos diplomáticos 1789–1927*. Mexico: Secretaría de Relaciones Exteriores.

Cardoso, Lawrence A. 1980, *Mexican Emigration to the United States: 1897–1931. Socio Economic Patterns*. Tucson: University of Arizona Press.

Carey, James C. 1984, *The Mexican Revolution in Yucatan. 1915–1924*. Boulder, CO: Westview Press.

Carr, Barry 1976, *El movimiento obrero y la política en México, 1910–1929*. Mexico: Ediciones Era.

Carr, Barry 1981, 'Radical Trip: Los orígenes del PCM', *Nexos* 40, 37–47.

Carr, Barry 1992, *Marxism and Communism in Twentieth-Century Mexico*. Lincoln: University of Nebraska.

Carr, E.H. 1961, *The Romantic Exiles: A Nineteenth-Century Portrait Gallery*. Boston: Beacon Press.

Castellanos Guerrero, Alicia, and Gilberto López Rivas 1991, *Primo Tapia de la Cruz, un hijo del pueblo*. n.p.: Centro de Estudios del Agrarismo en México and Confederación National Campesino.

Caulfield, Norman 1987, 'The Industrial Workers of the World and Mexican Labor, 1905–1925', Master's Thesis, Department of History, University of Houston.

Caulfield, Norman 1995, 'Wobblies and Mexican Workers in Mining and Petroleum, 1905–1924', *International Review of Social History* 40.

Cecena, José Luis 1991, *México en la órbita imperial: Las empresas transnacionales*. Mexico: Ediciones El Caballito.

Chambers II, John Whiteclay 1987, *To Raise an Army: The Draft Comes to Modern America*. New York: The Free Press.

Chambers II, John Whiteclay 1991, *The Eagle and the Dove: The American Peace Movement and United States Foreign Policy. 1900–1922*. Syracuse, NY: Syracuse University Press.

'Charles Shipman, A Securities Analyst and Writer, 94, Dies', 22 November 1989, *New York Times*, 14.

Chassen de Lopez, Francie R. 1977, *Lombardo Toledano y el Movimiento Obrero Mexicano: (1917–1940)*, Mexico: Extemporaneos.

Chatfield, Charles 1971, *For Peace and Justice: Pacifism in America. 1914–1941*. Knoxville: University of Tennessee Press.

Chowel, Gerard et al, 2010, "Mortality patterns associated with the 1918 influenza pandemic in Mexico: evidence for a spring herald wave and lack of preexisting immunity in older populations," J Infect Dis. 2010 Aug 15;202(4):567–75

Christopulos, Diana K. 1980, 'American Radicals and the Mexican Revolution, 1900–1925', PhD Dissertation, State University of New York at Binghamton.

Cliff, Tony 1975–79, *Lenin*. 4 vols. London: Pluto Press.

Cline, Howard F. 1963, *The United States and Mexico*. Revised edition. New York: Atheneum.

Cockcroft, James D. 1968, *The Intellectual Precursors of the Mexican Revolution, 1910–1913*. Austin: University of Texas.

Cockcroft, James D. 1983, *Mexico: Class Formation, Capital Accumulation, and the State*. New York: Monthly Review Press.

Cohen, Morris R. 1949, *A Dreamer's Journal: The Autobiography of Morris Rafael Cohen*. New York: Farrar, Straus.

Cole, Peter, David Stuthers, and Kenyon Zimmer 2017, *Wobblies of the World: A Global History of the IWW*. London: Pluto Press.

Coleman, George D. 1921, 'Linn Gale Needs Your Help, Comrade!' *The Crusader*, July, 186–7.

Collado Herrera, María del Carmen 1966, *Empresarios v políticos*. Mexico: Instituto Nacional de Estudios Históricos de la Revolución Mexicana.

'Columbia Girl Is Acquitted in No-Draft Case', 21 June 1917, *The Call*.

'Conditions in Mexico' 1905, *International Socialist Review* v, no. 11, 675–7.

Constitución Federal de 1917, at: http://www.bicentenario.gob.mx/PDF/MemoriaPolitica /1917COF.pdf

'Convict Fraina and E.R. Cheney', 19 October 1917, *The Call*.

Córdova, Amaldo 1975, *La ideología de la Revolución Mexicana*. Mexico: Ediciones Era.

Corey, Esther 1963, 'Lewis Corey (Louis C. Fraina), 1892–1953: A Bibliography with Autobiographical Notes', *Labor History* 4, 103–31.

Coria, Pedro 1971, 'Adventures of an Indian Mestizo', *Industrial Worker* (Chicago), January, February, March, April, and May.

Croly, Herbert 1963 [1909], *The Promise of American Life*. New York: E. Dutton & Co., Inc.

Cuban anarchists 1908, 'Mexico', *Mother Earth* III, no. 3, 172.

Curti, Merle 1936, *Peace or War: The American Struggle, 1636–1936*. New York: W.W. Norton & Company.

Dattilo, Gus (lyrics), and Minnie May Bauer (music) 1917, 'Don't Marry a Slacker, Girls'.

Davis, Colin J. 1997, *Power at Odds: The 1922 National Railroad Shopmen's Strike*. Chicago: University of Illinois Press.

DeBenedetti, Charles 1980, *The Peace Reform in American History*. Bloomington: Indiana University Press.

Debs, Eugene V. 1911, 'The Crisis in Mexico', *International Socialist Review* XII, no. 1, 23.

Debs, Eugene V. 1990, *Letters of Eugene V. Debs*. 3 vols. Chicago: University of Illinois Press.

de Cleyre, Voltairine August 1911, 'The Mexican Revolt', *Mother Earth* VI, no. 6, 167.

de Cleyre, Voltairine August December 1911, 'The Mexican Revolution', *Mother Earth* VI, no. 10, 302–3.

de Cleyre, Voltairine August December February 1912, 'The Mexican Revolution', *Mother Earth* VI, no. 12, 376.

de Cleyre, Voltairine August December February March 1912, 'The Commune Is Risen', *Mother Earth* VII, no. 1, 14.

de Cleyre, Voltairine August December February March April 1912, 'Report of the Work of the Chicago Mexican Liberal Defense League', *Mother Earth* VII, no. 2, 60–2.

de Pablo, Óscar 2014, sv 'Stanislav Pestovsky'. *La rojería: Esbozos biográficos de comunistas mexicanos*. Mexico: Penguin Random House Grupo Editorial México.

Degler, Carl N. 1970, *Out of Our Past: The Forces that Shaped Modern America*. New York: Harper & Row Publishers.

De Leon, Daniel 1900, 'Labor Lieutenants at Work', *Daily People*, 19 November, available at: http://www.slp.org/pdf/de_leon/eds1900/nov19_1900.pdf

De Shazo, Peter, and Robert J. Halstead October 1974, 'Los Wobblies del Sur: The Industrial Workers of the World in Chile and Mexico', Unpublished paper. University of Wisconsin.

Deutscher, Isaac 1963, *The Prophet Outcast: Trotsky: 1929–1940*. New York: Vintage Books.

Dewey, John et al. 1969 [1937], *The Case of Leon Trotsky*. New York: Merit Publishers.

Domínguez Pérez, Olivia 1986, *Política y movimientos sociales en el Tejedismo*. Xalapa: Universidad Veracruzana.

'Doings of the Month' August 1916, *International Socialist Review* XVII, no. 2, 69–73.

'Draft Illegal, Hillquit Tell Federal Judge' 1917, *The Call*, 19 June.

'Draft Opponent May Be Jailed' 1917, *The Call*, 13 June.

'Draft Slackers Must Face Trial' 1917, *The New York Times*, 7 June.

'Draft Subjects Unable to Leave United States' 1917, *The Call*, 2 June.

Draper, Hal 1970, 'Marx and Engels on Women's Liberation', *International Socialism* (1st series), 44, July/August, 20–9, available at: https://www.marxists.org/archive/draper/1970/07/women.htm;

Draper, Hal 1990, *Karl Marx's Theory of Revolution*, Vol. IV, *Critique of Other Socialisms*. New York: Monthly Review.

Draper, Theodore 1957, *The Roots of American Communism*. New York: The Viking Press.

Draper, Theodore 1986 [1960], *American Communism and Soviet Russia*. New York: Vintage.

Drees, Ada M.C. 1913, *Mexico: From Letters of Charles W. Drees*. New York: The Abdingdon Press.

Dreyfus, Michael 1995, *Historie de la CGT: Cents ans de syndicalisme en France*. Paris: Editions Complexe.

Dubofsky, Melvin 1969, *We Shall be All: A History of the Industrial Workers of the World*. New York: Quadrangle/New York Times.

Duval, George June 1915, 'Educational Value of the Mexican Revolution', *Mother Earth* X, no. 4, 142–3.

Early, Frances H. 1997, *A World Without War: How US Feminists and Pacifists Resisted World War I*. Syracuse, NY: Syracuse University Press.

Eastman, Max 1948, *The Enjoyment of Living*. New York: Harper & Brothers Publishers.

Egan, Leo 1958, 'Robert Young, Financier, Ends Life in Palm Beach', *New York Times*, 26 January, Section 1, 46.

Eichel, Julius 1981, *The Judge said '20 Years': The Story of a Conscientious Objector in World War I*. Yonkers, NY: AMP&R.

'Editorial' July 1911, *International Socialist Review* XII, no. 1, 47.

Embriz Osario, Arnulfo, and Ricardo León García (eds) 1982, *Documentos para la historia del agrarismo en Michoacán*. n.p.: Centro de Estudios Históricos del Agrarismo en México.

Evans, Sara M. 1989, *Born for Liberty: A History of Women in America*. New York: The Free Press.

Fabela, Josefina E. (ed.) 1976, *Documentos Históricos de la Revolución Mexicana*. Vol. X. Mexico: Comision de Investigaciones Historicas de la Revolucion Mexicana.

Falcón, Romana, and Soledad García 1986, *La semilla en el surco: Adalberto Tejeda y el radicalismo en Veracruz: 1883–1960*. Mexico: El Colegio de Mexico.

Ferro, Mar et al. 1967, *La Revolution d'Octobre et le Mouvement ouvrier européen*. Paris: Études et Documentation Internationales.

Fisher, Lillian Estelle 1942, 'The Influence of the Present Mexican Revolution Upon the Status of Mexican Women', *Hispanic American Historical Review* 22: 211–28.

Flores Magón, Ricardo 1989, *Correspondencia de Ricardo Flores Magón (1904–1912)*, Recopilación e introducción de Jacinto Barrera Bassols. Puebla: Universidad Autónoma de Puebla.

Flores Magón, Ricardo 1974, *A la mujer*. Oakland: Prensa Sembradora.

Flores Magón, Ricardo 1923, *Semilla libertaria*. 2 vols. Mexico: Ediciones del Grupo Cultural 'Ricardo Flores Magón'.

Flores Magón, Ricardo et al. February 1908, 'Manifesto to the American People', *Mother Earth* II, no. 12, 546–54.

Flores Magón, Ricardo et al. April 1915, 'The Organizing Junta of the Mexican Liberal Party, To the Workers of the United States', *Mother Earth* X, no. 2, 85–8.

Flores Magón, Ricardo et al. 1991, *Regeneración, 1900–1918*. Mexico: Ediciones Era.

Foner, Philip S. 1955, *The History of the Labor Movement in the United States*, vol. 2, *From the Founding of the A.F. of L. to the Emergence of American Imperialism*. New York: International Publishers.

Foner, Philip S. 1967, *The Bolshevik Revolution: Its Impact on American Radicals, Liberals, and Labor: A Documentary Study*. New York: International Publishers.

Foner, Philip S. 1971, *The Industrial Workers of the World, 1905–1917*, vol. IV of *History of the Labor Movement of the United States*. New York: International Publishers.

Foner, Philip S. 1988, *US Labor Movement and Latin America: A History of Workers'*

Response to Intervention, vol. 1, 1846–1919. South Hadley, MA: Bergin & Garvey Publishers, Inc.

Foster, Harry L. 1925, *A Gringo in Manana-Land*. New York: Dodd, Mead and Company.

Fowler, Heather 1970, 'The Agrarian Revolution in the State of Veracruz, 1920–1940: The Role of Peasant Organizations', PhD dissertation, American University, Washington, D.C.

Fowler Salamini, Heather, and Mary Kay Vaughn 1994, *Women of the Mexcian Countryside, 1850–1990*. Tucson: University of Arizona Press.

Fraina, Louis C. November 1913, 'The Monroe Doctrine', *The New Review*.

Fraina, Louis C. July 1915, 'Mexico and Foreign Capital', *The New Review*.

Fraina, Louis C. December 1915, 'The Problem of Nationality', *The New Review*.

Fraina, Louis C. April 1916, 'The Assault Upon Mexico', *The New Review*.

Fraina, Louis C. April 1918, 'Introduction' to Sen Katayama, *The Labor Movement in Japan*. Chicago: Charles H. Kerr & Company Cooperative.

Fraina, Louis C. April (ed.) 1918, *The Proletarian Revolution in Russia*. New York: The Communist Press.

'Fraina and Cheney Get Hillquit's Aid' 12 October 1917, *The Call*.

'Fraina Trial Starts Today' 15 October 1917, *The Call*, 5.

Freeman, Joseph 1936, *An American Testament: A Narrative of Rebels and Romantics*. New York: Farrar & Rhinehart Incorporated.

Friedrich, Paul 1970, *Agrarian Revolt in a Mexican Village*. Englewood Cliffs, NJ: Prentice-Hall, Inc.

Gale, Linn A.E. 1909, *Genealogy of the Descendants of David Dale of Sutton. Mass.* Oxford: The Times Publishing Company.

Gale, Linn A.E. March 1919a, 'Economic Determinism and the "Norwich Sun"', *Gale's Magazine*, 12.

Gale, Linn A.E. March 1919b, 'We Slackers in Mexico', *Gale's Magazine*, 21.

Gale, Linn A.E. March 1919c, 'Who is This Man Gale?' *Gale's Magazine*, 3.

Gale, Linn A.E. July 1919, 'In the Penitentiary', *Gale's Magazine*, 8.

Gale, Linn A.E. August 1919a, 'The Duty of the Mexican Socialists', *Gale's Magazine*, 8.

Gale, Linn A.E. August 1919b, 'Occultism and Socialism', *Gale's Magazine*, 14.

Gale, Linn A.E. September 1919, 'Gompers Dominates Mexican Socialist Congress; Communist Party Organized', *Gale's Magazine*, 7.

Gale, Linn A.E. November 1919, 'The War Against Gompersism in Mexico', *The One Big Union Monthly*, 23–5.

Gale, Linn A.E. January 1920, 'The Reason for Intervention in Mexico and the Result', *Gale's Magazine*, 7.

Gale, Linn A.E. March 1920, 'They Were Willing', *Gale's Magazine*.

Gale, Linn A.E. April 1920, 'Industrial Unionism in Mexico', *Gale's Magazine*, 7.

Gale, Linn A.E. May 1920, 'Two Years Ago I Became a Slacker', *Gale's Magazine.*

Gale, Linn A.E. June–July 1920, '"Bolsheviki Gold" in Mexico', *Gale's Magazine*, 27.

Gale, Linn A.E. August 1920a [byline El Luchador Viejo, pseud. of Linn A.E. Gale], 'Mexican Wobblies Convene on the Roof', *Gale's Magazine*, 2.

Gale, Linn A.E. August 1920b, 'Mrs. Linn A.E. Gale Fired Again', *Gale's Magazine*, 23.

Gale, Linn A.E. January 1920, 'The Reason for Intervention in Mexico – and the Result', *Gale's Magazine*, 6–7.

Gale, Linn A.E. March 1920, 'The Mexican Presidential Election', *Gale's Magazine*, 4

Gale, Linn A.E. September 1920, 'Towards Soviets in Mexico', *Gale's Magazine*, 2.

Gale, Linn A.E. October 1920, 'Mexican I.W.W. in Fight Over Rules', *Gale's Magazine*, 6.

Gale, Linn A.E. November 1920, 'Workers Wax Stronger in Mexico', *Gale's Magazine*, 5.

Gale, Linn A.E. n.d. 1, *The Altar of the Prostitutes*. Milan, IL: The Rail Splitter Press.

Gale, Linn A.E. n.d. 2, *Romanism, Mexico's Cancer*. Milan, IL: The Rail Splitter Press.

Gale, Linn A.E. n.d. 3, *If the Pope Comes to Washington!* Milan, IL: The Rail Splitter Press.

Gale, Linn A.E. 1926, *Evolution of Mankind: Some Observations on Anthropology*. New York: Bender-Baker Press.

Gale, Linn A.E. 1928, *The Bigotry Trust in the USA*. Girard, KS: Haldeman-Julius Publications. Little Blue Book No. 1314.

Galindo, Hermila 1916, *Estudio de la Srita. Hermaila Galindo con motivo de los temas que han de absolverse en el Segundo Congreso Feminista de Yucatán*. Mérida: Imprenta del Goberierno Constitutionalista.

Galindo, Hermila 1919, *La doctrina Carranza y el acercamiento indolatino*. Mexico: Imprenta Franco-Mexicana, S.A.

Gall, Olivia 1991, *Trotsky en México y la vida política en el period de Cárdenas, 1937–1940*. Mexico: Ediciones Era.

Gamio, Manuel 1922, *La Poblacóon del valle de Teotihuaca*. Mexico.

Gamio, Manuel 1975, *Antología*, edited by Juan Comas. Mexico: Universidad Nacional Autónoma de Mexico.

García Cantú, Gastón 1969, *El Socialismo en México: Siglo XIX*. Mexico: Édiciones Era.

García Díaz, Bernardo 1990, *Textiles del Valle de Orizaba (1880–1925)*. Xalapa, Veracruz: Universidad Veracruzana, Centro de Investigaciones Historicas.

Geier, Joel 2014, 'Zinovievism and the Degeneration of World Communism', *International Socialism* 93, available at: https://isreview.org/issue/93/zinovievism-and-degeneration-world-communism

'Get's Law's Limit for Defying Draft' 1917, *The New York Times*, 14 June.

Gill, Mario 1971, *Los Ferrocarrileros*. Mexico: Editorial Extemporáneos.

Gill, Mario 1978, *Mexico y la Revolución de Octubre*. Mexico: Ediciones de Cultura Popular.

Gilly, Adolfo 1994, *El Cardenismo: una utopía mexicana*. Mexico: Cal y Arena.

Gilly, Adolfo 1971, *La Revolucion interrumpida: México, 1910–1920: una guerra campesina por la tierra y el poder*. Mexico: Ediciones El Caballito.

Gilly, Adolfo 2005 [1971], *The Mexican Revolution*. New York: The New Press.

Ginger, Ray 1970 [1949], *Eugene V. Debs: The Making of an American Radical*. New York: Collier Books.

Gladden, Washington 1908, *The Church and Modern Life*. Boston: Houghton Mifflin, available at gutenberg.org.

Goldman, Emma 1970 [1934], *Living My Life*. 2 vols. New York: AMS Press.

Goldstein, Robert Justin 1978, *Political Repression in Modem America*. Cambridge, MA: Schenkman Publishing Company.

Gómez, Manuel 1925 [pseud. of Charles Francis Phillips], *Poems for Workers: An Anthology* (No. 5 of the Little Red Library). Chicago: Daily Worker Publishing Co.

Gómez, Manuel 1964 [pseud. of Charles Francis Phillips], 'From Mexico to Moscow', *Survey: A Journal of Soviet and East European Studies* 53 (October 1964) 37–9; 55 (April 1965) 116–21.

Gómez Morin, Manuel 1927, *1915*. Mexico: Editorial 'Cultura'.

Gómez-Quiñones, Juan 1977 [1973], *Las ideas políticas de Ricardo Flores Magón*. Mexico: Édiciones Era.

Gómez-Quiñones, Juan 1994, *Mexican American Labor 1790–1990*. Albuquerque, NM: University of New Mexico.

Gompers, Samuel 1893, 'Address', 28 August, *Papers*. Urbana: University of Illinois Press, 1989, Vol. 3: available at: http://www.gompers.umd.edu/1893%20more%20speech.htm

Gompers, Samuel 1986, 'Speech given at New York Central Labor Union meeting on Dec. 29, 1895', *Papers*, 1986, Vol. 4. Urbana: University of Illinois Press, 80–101.

Gompers, Samuel September 1906, 'Samuel Gompers: Addresses at St. Paul and Minneapolis', *American Federationist*, 1–2.

Gompers, Samuel September 1925, *Seventy Years of Life and Labor: An Autobiography*. 2 vols. New York: E. Dutton & Company.

González, Gilbert G. 2004, *Culture of Empire: American Writers, Mexico, and Mexican Immigrants (1880–1930)*. Austin: University of Texas Press.

González Casanova, Pablo 1980, *En el Primer Gobierno Constitucional (1917–1920)*, Vol. 6 of *La Clase obrera en la historia de México*. Mexico: Siglo Veintiuno Editores.

González Navarro, Moises 1994, *Los Extranjeros en México v los Mexicanos en el extranjero: 1821–1970*. 3 vols. Mexico: Colegio de Mexico.

González Ramírez, Manuel (ed.) 1954, *Planes políticos y otros documentos*. Mexico: Fondo de la Cultura Económica.

Granich, Irwin January 1920 [pseud. of Michael Gold], 'Sowing the Seeds of One Big Union in Mexico', *The One Big Union Monthly* II, no. 1, 36–7.

Green, James R. 1978, *Grass-Roots Socialism: Radical Movements in the Southwest, 1895–1943*. Baton Rouge: Louisiana State University Press.

Greenstone, J. David 1969, *Labor in American Politics*. New York: Vintage Books.

Guadarrama, Rocío 1981, *Los sindicatos y la politica en Mexico: la CROM (1918–1928)*. Mexico: Édiciones Era.

Guerra, François-Xavier 1992, *México: del Antinguo Régimen a la Revolución*. 2 vols. Mexico: Fondo de la Cultura Económica.

Gutiérrez de Lara, L., and Edgcumb Pinchon 1914, *The Mexican People: Their Struggle for Freedom*. New York: Doubleday, Page & Co.

Haber, Samuel 1964, *Efficiency and Uplift: Scientific Management in the Progressive Era: 1890–1920*. Chicago: University of Chicago Press.

Haberman, Roberto 1930, *The Divorce Laws of Mexico*. New York: R. Haberman.

Harris, Rev. W. S 1908, *Hell Before Death*. No place: no date.

Hart, John Mason 1978, *Anarchism and the Mexican Working Class. 1860–1933*. Austin: University of Texas.

Hart, John Mason 1975, *Los anarquistas mexicanos: 1860–1900*. Mexico City: Secretaria de Educación Publica.

Hart, John Mason 1987, *Revolutionary Mexico: The Coming and Process of the Mexican Revolution*. Berkeley: University of California Press.

Hart, John Mason 1988, *El anarquismo y la clase obrera mexicana*. Mexico: Siglo XXI.

Hart, John Mason 1989, *Revolutionary Mexico: The Coming and Process of the Mexican Revolution*. Berkeley: University of California Press.

Hart, John Mason 2002, *Empire and Revolution: The Americans in Mexico since the Civil War*. Berkeley: University of California Press.

Hassell, James E. 1991, 'Russian Refugees in France and the United States Between the World Wars', *Transactions of the American Philosophical Society* 81, no. 7.

Haywood, Harry 1978, *Black Bolshevik: Autobiography of an Afro-American Communist*. Chicago: Liberator Press.

Haywood, William D. February 1920, 'Letter ...', *Gale's Magazine*, 20.

Haywood, William D. February 1929, *Bill Haywood's Book: The Autobiography of William D. Haywood*. New York: International Publishers.

Heatherton, Christina 2022m *Arise! Global Radicalism in the Era of the Mexican Revolution*. Oakland: University of California Press, 2022.

Herrera, Porfirio R. [Linn Gale?] 1925, 'The Double Kidnapping of Linn A.E. Gale'. Milan, Illinois: The Rail Splitter Press.

Hilferding, Rudolf 1985, *Finance Capital: A Study of the Latest Phase of Capitalist Development*. Boston: Routledge & Kegan Paul.

Hobsbawm, Eric 1996, *The Age of Extremes: A History of the World, 1914–1991*. New York: Vintage Books.

Hobsbawm, Eric 2010, *Primitive Rebels*. New York: Norton.

Hobson, J.A., 1967, *Imperialism: A Study*. Ann Arbor: University of Michigan.

Hofstadter, Richard 1955, *The Age of Reform*. New York: Vintage.

Hogan, Michael 1997, *The Irish Soldiers of Mexico*. Guadalajara: Fonda Editorial Universitaria.

Hollinger, David A. 1975, *Morris R. Cohen and the Scientific Ideal*. Cambridge, MA: MIT Press.

Homberger, Eric, and John Biggart 1986, *John Reed and the Russian Revolution: Uncollected Articles, Letters and Speeches on Russia, 1917–1920*. New York: St. Martin's Press.

Howard Hopkins, Charles 1940, *The Rise of the Social Gospel in American Protestantism, 1865–1915*. New York: AMS Press.

Howe, Irving, and Lewis Coser 1962, *The American Communist Party: A Critical History*. New York: Frederick A. Praeger.

Hughes, Langston 1986 [1940], *The Big Sea: An Autobiography*. London: Pluto Press.

Huitrón, Jacinto 1978 [1974], *Orígenes e historia del movimiento obrero en México*. Mexico: Editores Mexicanos Unidos.

Hyde, George E. 1920, 'Renegade Americans Promoting Bolshevik Movement in Mexico', *New York Times*, 5 September.

Hyndman, H.H. 1919, *The Awakening of Asia*. London: Cassell.

I.D. (initials only) 1914, 'More Murdered Children! A Letter from the Front in Mexico', *International Socialist Review* XIV, no. 12, 731.

Inman, Samuel Guy 1919, *Intervention in Mexico*. New York: Association Press.

Industrial Workers of the World 1969 [1905], *Proceedings of the First Convention of the Industrial Workers of the World*. New York: Merit.

Instituto Nacional de Estadística, Geografía y Informática 1994, *– Estadísticas Históricas de México*. 2 vols. Mexico: INEGI.

Isaacs, Harold 1961, *The Tragedy of the Chinese Revolution*, second revised edition. Stanford: Stanford University Press.

'I.W.W. in Mexico' November 1919, *The One Big Union Monthly*, 50, 208.

Jeifets, Victor, and Lazar Jeifets 2015, *América Latina en la Internacional Comunista 1919–1943*. Ariadna Ediciones. Ebook edition.

'John Kenneth Turner' 1994, *Diccionario Histórico y Biográfico de la Revolución Mexicana*, Tomo VIII, vol. 8, entry, 8220. México, D.F. Instituto Nacional de Estudios Históricos de la revolución Mexicana.

Johnson, Benjamin Heber 2003, *Revolution in Texas: How a Forgotten Rebellion and Its Bloody Suppression Turned Mexicans into Americans*. New Haven: Yale University Press.

Joseph, G.M. 1982, *Revolution from Without: Yucatan. Mexico, and the United States: 1880–1924*. New York: Cambridge University Press.

'Joseph Steffens Dead' 1 February 1912, *Sacramento Union* 163, no. 32, available at: https://cdnc.ucr.edu/cgi-bin/cdnc?a=d&d=SU19120201.2.8&e=-------en--20--1--txt-txIN-------1

Jutt, John A. February 1920, 'The Mexican Administration of the i.w.w.', *Gale's Magazine*, 20.

Kandell, Jonathan 1988, *La Capital: The Biography of Mexico City*. New York: Random House.

Kamik, V.B. 1978, *M.N. Roy: Political Biography*. Bombay: Nav Jagriti Samaj.

Kaplan, Samuel 1958, *Combatimos la tiranía, Conversaciones con Enrique Flores Magón*. Mexico: Biblioteca del Instituto Nacional de Estudios Históricos de la Revolución Mexicana.

Katayama, Sen 15 March 1904, 'La guerre russo-japonaise et le socialisme international', *Mouvement Socialiste*.

Katayama, Sen 1931, *Jiden*. Tokyo: Kaizōsha, Shōwa.

Katayama, Sen 1918, *The Labor Movement in Japan*. Chicago: Charles H. Kerr & Company Cooperative.

Katayama, Sen 26 July 1919, 'Morris Hillquit and the Left Wing', *Revolutionary Age*.

Katz, Friedrich 1998, *The Life and Times of Pancho Villa*. Stanford: Stanford University Press.

Katz, Friedrich 1983, *The Secret War in Mexico: Europe, the United States, and the Mexican Revolution*. Chicago: University of Chicago Press.

Kautsky, Karl 2015 [1909], *The Road to Power*. no place: Forgotten Books, or online at: http://www.marxists.org/archive/kautsky/1909/power/index.htm.

Kautsky, Karl 1964 [1918], *The Dictatorship of the Proletariat*. Ann Arbor: University of Michigan Press.

Kautsky, Karl 1971 [1908], *The Class Struggle*. New York: Norton.

Kersffeld, Daniel 2012, *Contra El Imperio: Historia de la Liga Antiimperialista de las Américas*. Mexico City: Siglo Veintiuno Editores.

King, Rosa E. 1935, *Tempest Over Mexico: A Personal Chronicle*. Boston: Little, Brown, and Company.

Klehr, Harvey 1977, 'Leninism, Lewis Corey, and the Failure of American Socialism', *Labor History* 18, no. 2: 249–56.

Knight, Alan 1986, *The Mexican Revolution*. 2 vols. Lincoln: University of Nebraska Press.

Kolko, Gabriel 1963, *The Triumph of Conservatism: A Reinterpretation of American History: 1900–1916*. Chicago: Quadrangle Books.

Kolko, Gabriel 1995, *The Decline of Radicalism in the United States*. New Jersey: Humanities Press.

Kollontai, Alexandra 1971, *The Autobiography of a Sexually Emancipated Communist Woman*. New York: Herder and Herder.

Kollontai, Alexandra 1977, *Selected Writings*, ed. by Alix Holt. New York: W.W. Norton & Company.

Kazin, Alfred 31 March 1974, 'Lincoln Steffens', *The New York Times Book Review*.

Kraft, Barbara S. 1978, *The Peace Ship: Henry Ford's Pacifist Adventure in the First World War*. New York: Macmillan Publishing Co., Inc.

'Kramer Trial June 11; May Free Students: H. Levine, School Teacher, Arraigned for Not Registering, Spent Night in Jail', 8 June 1917, *The Call*.

Krauze, Enrique 1985, *Caudillos culturales en la Revolución Mexicana*. Mexico: Secretaría de la Educación Pública.

Kropotkin, Peter 1899, *Memoirs of a Revolutionist*. New York: Houghton Mifflin Company.

Kropotkin, Peter 1909, *The Great French Revolution, 1789–1793, translation by N.F. Dryhurst*. 2 vols. New York: Vanguard Press.

Kropotkin, Peter November 1914, 'Kropotkin on the Present War', *Mother Earth* IX, no. 9.

Kublin, Hyman 1964, *Asian Revolutionary: The Life of Sen Katavama*. Princeton: Princeton University Pres.

Kučera, Josef, 1911, *Revoluce y Mexiku*. New York: Volnych Listu.

Labadie, Charles Joseph Antoine August 1914 'The Public Forum', *Land and Liberty* 1, no. 4, 10.

Labor, Earle 2013, *Jack London: An American Life*. New York: Macmillan.

La Botz, Dan 1988, *The Crisis of Mexican Labor*. New York: Praeger.

La Botz, Dan Spring/Summer 1991, 'Roberto Haberman and the Origins of Modern Mexico's Jewish Community', *American Jewish Archives* 43, 7–21.

La Botz, Dan 1991, *Edward L. Doheny: Petroleum, Power, and Politics in the United States and Mexico*. New York: Praeger.

La Botz, Dan 1992, *Mask of Democracy: Labor Suppression in Mexico Today*. Boston: South End Press.

La Botz, Dan 1995, *Democracy in Mexico*. Boston: South End Press.

La Botz, Dan 2016, *The Nicaraguan Revolution: What Went Wrong?* Leiden: Brill.

La Botz, Dan 2018, 'The Communist International, the Soviet Union, and their impact on the Latin American Workers' Movement', *Tensões Mundiais* 13, no. 24, January–June, available at: file: ///Users/danlabotz/Downloads/360-Texto%20do%20artigo-1109-1-10-20180926%20(1).pdf.

La Botz, Daniel H. 1998, ' "Slackers": American War Resisters and Communists in Mexico, 1917–1927', PhD dissertation, University of Cincinnati.

'Las Últimas Huelgas Según Seis Industriales Prominentes' August 1920, *Boletín de la Confederación de Cámaras Industriales*, 10–11.

Lau, Ana, and Carmen Ramos 1993, *Mujeres y Revolución: 1900–1917*. Mexico: Instituto National de Estudios de la Revolución Mexicana.

Lear, John 2001, *Workers, Neighbors, and Citizens: The Revolution in Mexico City*. Lincoln: University of Nebraska Press.

Lemon, W.J. May 1921, 'Mexico; Its Government and Labor Movement', *The Industrial Pioneer*, 23–7.

Lempérière, Annick 1992, *Intellectuels, états et société au Mexique: Les clercs de la nation (1910–1968)*. Paris: Editions L'Harmattan.

Lenin, Vladimir 1964–68, *Collected Works*. Moscow: Progress Publishers.

Lens, Sidney 1969, *Radicalism in America*. New York: Thomas Y. Crowell.

Lerner, Warren 1970, *Karl Radek: The Last Internationalist*. Stanford: Stanford University Press.

Leverstein, Harvey 1971, *Labor Organizations in the United States and Mexico: A History of Their Relations*. Westport, CT: Greenwood Publishing Company.

'Levine Dismissed by School Board' 13 July 1917, *The Call*.

Levine, Herman December 1920, 'The Mexican I.W.W.', *The One Big Union Monthly*, 57.

'Lewis Corey Dies; Writer, Ex-Red, 61' 17 September 1953, *The New York Times*.

Lida, Clara E., and Carlos Illades Jul-y–September 2001, 'El anarquismo europeo y sus primeras influencias en México después de la Comuna de París: 1871–1881', *Historia Mexicana* 51, no. 1, 103–49.

'Limit of Law for Objectors to Draft' 14 June 1917, *The Call*.

Lloyd, Brian 1997, *Left Out: Pragmatism, Exceptionalism, and the Poverty of American Marxism. 1890–1922*. Baltimore: Johns Hopkins University Press.

Lloyd, Trevor 1971, *Suffragettes International: The World-Wide Campaign for Women's Rights*. New York: American Heritage Press.

Lombardo Toledano, Vicente 1994, *Obra Histórico-Cronológica*. Tomo I, vol. 3. Mexico: Centro de Estudios Filosóficos, Políticos y Sociales 'Vicente Lombardo Toledano'.

Lomnitz, Claudo 2014, *The Return of Comrade Ricardo Flores Magón*. New York: Zone Books.

London, Jack 1912, *Revolution*. New York: The Macmillan Company.

Lorwin, Lewis L. 1929, *Labor and Internationalism*. New York: The Macmillan Company.

Ludlow, Daniel H. 1992, 'Mexico, Pioneer Settlements in', *Encyclopedia of Mormonism*, available at: http://contentdm.lib.byu.edu/cdm/ref/collection/EoM/id/3926.

Luxemburg, Rosa 1951 [1913], *The Accumulation of Capital*. New York: Modern Reader Paperbacks.

Luxemburg, Rosa 1976, *The National Question: Selected Writings by Rosa Luxemburg*. New York: Monthly Review Press.

Luxemburg, Rosa 1967, *The Russian Revolution: Leninism or Marxism*. Ann Arbor: University of Michigan Press.

Lytle Hernández, Kelly 22022, Bad *Mexicans Race, Empire and Revolution in the Borderland*. New York: W.W. Norton.

'Lynn A.E. Gale' 15 August 1940, *New York Times*.

Macías, Anna 1982, *Against All Odds: The Feminist Movement in Mexico to 1940*. Westport, CT: Greenwood Press.

MacLachlan, Colin M. 1991, *Anarchism and the Mexican Revolution: The Political Trials of Ricardo Flores Magón in the United States*, with a Foreword by John Mason Hart. Berkeley; University of California Press.

Madero, Francisco 1910, *La sucesión presidencial*, available at: http://www.memoriapolit icademexico.org/Textos/6Revolucion/1910LSP.pdf

Marcy, Mary E. 1914, 'Whose War Is This?' *International Socialist Review* XIV, no. 12, 729–31.

Marchand, C. Roland 1972, *The American Peace Movement and Social Reform*. Princeton: Princeton University Press.

Mariátegui, José Carlos 1982, *Obras*. 2 vols. Havana, Cuba: Casa de las Américas.

Márquez Fuente, Manuel, and Octavio Rodríguez Araujo 1973, *El Partido Communista Mexicano*, Segunda Edición *(en el period de la Internacional Comunista: 1919–1943)*. Mexico: Édiciones El Caballito.

Martin, Jay 2002, *The Education of John Dewey: A Biography*. New York: Columbia University Press.

Martínez Múgica, Apolinar 1976, *Primo Tapia: Semblanza de un revolucionario*. Morelia: Ediciones del Gobiemo de Michoacán.

Martínez Verdugo, Adolfo 1985a, *Historia del comunismo en Mexico*. Mexico: Grijalbo.

Martínez Verdugo, Adolfo 1985b, 'De la anarquía al communism', in Arnoldo Martínez Verdugo, *Historia del Communism en México*. Mexico: Grijalbo.

Matute, Álavro 1983, *Historia de la Revolución Mexicana: La Constitución de 1917* (vol. 16 of the Colegio de Mexico's Historia de la Revolución Mexicana). Mexico: El Colegio de México.

Matute, Álavro 1995, *Historia de la Revolución Mexicana. 1917–1924 Las dificultades del nuevo estado* (vol. 18 of the Colegio de Mexico's Historia de la Revolución Mexicana). Mexico: Colegio de México.

McAlpine, E.W. 22 March 1918, 'Russian and Japanese Socialists Join Hands despite Looming Clash', *The World* (Oakland, CA), 1 and 5.

Medvedev, Roy A. 1971, *Let History Judge: The Origins and Consequences of Stalinism*. New York: Vintage Books.

Melgar Bao, Ricardo, and Javier Torres Parés (eds) 2006, *El Libertador. Órgano de la Liga Antiimperialista de las Américas. 1925–1929*. Edición facsimilar digital. Mexico: UNAM.

'Mexican Notes' October 1916, *Mother Earth* XI, no. 8.

'Mexican Communists' October 1919, *Industrial Worker*.

'Mexico' February 1906, *International Socialist Review* VI, no. 8, 498.

Mexico 1917, *Constitución política de los Estados Unidos de México*. Mexico: Imprenta de la Secretaría de Gobernación.

Meyer, Jean June–September 1971, 'Los obreros en la revolución mexicana: los "batallones rojos"', *Historia Mexicana* 81, 1–27.

Meyer, Jean 1973, *La revolution mexicaine: 1910–1940*. Paris: Calmann-Levy.

Meyer, Jean 1994 [1971], *La Cristiada*. 3 vols. Mexico: Siglo Veintiuno Editores.

Michels, Tony 2005, *A Fire in Their Hearts: Yiddish Socialists in New York*. Cambridge, MA: Harvard University Press.

Middlebrook, Kelvin 1995, *The Paradox of Revolution: Labor, the State and Authoritarianism in Mexico*. Baltimore: Johns Hopkins University Press.

Mijangos Díaz, Eduardo Nomeli 1997, *La Revolución y el poder político en Michoacán 1910–1920*. Morelia, Michoacán: Universidad Michoacána de San Nicolas de Hidalgo.

Miller, Richard U. 1974, 'American Railroad Unions and the National Railways of Mexico', *Labor History* Spring, 15.

Miller, Robert R. 1989, *Shamrock and Sword: The Saint Patrick's Battalion in the US-Mexican War*. Norman: University of Oklahoma Press.

'Minneapolis Teacher Charged with Being an I.W.W. Is Dismissed', 22 September 1917, *The Call*, 9.

Mitchell, Stephanie, and Patience A. Schell (eds) 2007, *The Women's Revolution in Mexico, 1910–1953*. New York: Rowman & Littlefield Publishers, Inc.

Moguel Flores, Josefina 1995, *Venustiano Carranza: Primer Jefe v Presidente*. Mexico: Secretaria de Gobernacion.

Molina Enríquez, Andrés 1991 [1909], *Los grandes problemas nacionales*. Mexico: Ediciones Era.

Molyneux, Maxine 1986, 'No God, No Boss, No Husband: Anarchist Feminism in Nineteenth Century Argentina', *Latin American Perspectives* 38, no. 1, 119–45.

Monzón, Luis G.J. 1924, *Algunos puntos sobre el comunismo*. Mexico: Talleres Linotipograficos 'Soria'.

Morales Jíménez, Alberto 1982, *La Casa del Obrero Mundial: Ensayo Histórico*. México: Biblioteca del Instituto Nacional de Estudios Históricos de la Revolución Mexicana.

Morones, Luis N., and J.H. Retinger 1985, 'La evolución del movimiento social en México', *Cuadernos del CIHMO* 189–223.

Mowat, Charles Loch 1968, *The Shifting Balance of World Forces 1898–1945*. New York: Cambridge University Press.

Murray, John March 1909, 'Mexico's Peon-Slaves Preparing for Revolution', *International Socialist Review* IX, no. 9, 641–59.

Murray, John April 1909, 'The Private Prison of Díaz', *International Socialist Review* IX, no. 10, 737–52.

Murray, John May 1909, 'The Mexican Political Prisoners', *International Socialist Review* IX, no. 11, 863–5.

Murray, Robert K. 1964, *Red Scare: A Study of National Hysteria, 1919–1920*. New York: McGraw-Hill.

Nettl, Peter 1966, *Rosa Luxemburg*. 2 vols. New York: Oxford University Press.

'Objector to Draft Agrees to Register' June 1917, *The Call*, 7.

'Observations and Comments' June 1911, *Mother Earth* VI, no. 4, 99.

'Observations and Comments' July 1911, *Mother Earth* VI, no. 5, 131.

'Observations and Comments' August 1911, *Mother Earth* VI, no. 6, 162.

'Observations and Comments' February 1914, *Mother Earth* VIII, no. 12, 355–6.

'Observations and Comments' May 1914, *Mother Earth* IX, no. 3, 67.

Office of the Historian n.d., 'Venezuela Boundary Dispute', United States Department of State, at: https://history.state.gov/milestones/1866-1898/venezuela

Ojeda Reyes, Felix 1987, 'Colonialismo sindical o solidaridad internacional? Las relaciones entre el movimiento obrero puertorriqueno y el noreteamericano en los inicios de la Federación Libre (1898–1901)', *Revista de Ciencias Sociales* 26, 1–4, January–December, 311–46.

Olcott, Jocelyn 2005, *Revolutionary Women in Post-Revolutionary Mexico*. Durham, NC: Duke University Press.

Orozco, Wistano Luis 1975 [1895], *Legislación y jurisprudencia sobre terrenos baldíos*. Mexico: El Caballito.

Ortega Aguirre, Maximinio 1979, *Bosquejo de la historia del movimiento ferrocarrilero (1890–1973)*. Mexico: Centro de Estudios Políticos, Falcultad de Ciencias Politicas, Universidad Nacional Autónoma de México.

Ortíz Hernán, Sergio 1988, *Los Ferrocarriles de México: Una visión social y económica*, 2 vols. Mexico: Ferrocarriles Nacionales de México.

Owen, William C. February 1910, 'The Russianizing of America', *Mother Earth* IV, no. 12, 394–6.

Owen, William C. April 1911, 'Viva Mexico', *Mother Earth* VI, no. 2, 42–6.

Owen, William C. 11 June 1911, 'Mexico's Hour of Need', *Mother Earth* VI, no. 4, 106.

Owen, William C. September 1911, 'Mexico and Socialism', *Mother Earth* VI, no. 7, 202.

Owen, William C. May 1912, 'What Mexico's Struggle Means', *International Socialist Review* XII, no. 11, 741 and 742.

Owen, William C. April 1914, 'What of Mexico?' *Land and Liberty* I, no. 1, 4.

Owen, William C. September 1914, 'What's What and Why', *Land and Liberty* 1, no. 5, 11.

Owen, William C. August 1914a, 'Huerta and After', *Land and Liberty* 1, no. 4, 4.

Owen, William C. August 1914b, 'Revolutionary Notes', *Land and Liberty* 1, no. 4, 3–4.

Owen, William C. September 1914, 'War? Then We Fight It Out', *Land and Liberty* 1, no. 5, 1–2.

Owen, William C. October 1914a, 'The Social Revolution', *Land and Liberty* 1, no. 6, 6–7.

Owen, William C. October 1914b, 'Against Invaders Only War', *Land and Liberty* 1, no. 6, 1–2.

Owen, William C. November 1914, 'War and Sinews of War', *Land and Liberty* 1, no. 7, 1–4.

Owen, William C. January 1915, 'Remove the Boulder!' *Land and Liberty* 1, no. 9, 1–3.

Owen, William C. February 1915, 'Our Letter Box', *Land and Liberty* 1, no. 10, 3–4.

Owen, William C. July 1915a, 'Where Ireland Stands', *Land and Liberty* 1, no. 15, 11–15.

Owen, William C. July 1915b, 'Firing on Fort Sumter', *Land and Liberty* 1, no. 15, 6.

Owen, William C. June 1916, 'The Modern Robin Hood', *New Review: A Critical Survey of International Socialism* 177.

'Pan-American Federation of Labor' 1918, *The Federationist* 26, 1–2, 601–5.

Pani, Alberto J. 1936, *Mi contribución al nuevo régimen: 1910–1933*. Mexico: Editorial Cultura.

Parker, Rev. T.A. 1918, *Billy – And the Slacker*. High Point, NC: W.A. Barber Printing Co.

Parsons, Lucy April 1914, 'Dominant, Not Dying', *Land and Liberty* 1, no. 1, 3.

Partido Socialista del Sureste 1977, *Primer Congress Qbrero Socialista. celebrado en Motul. Estado de Yucatán: Bases Que Se Discutieron y Aprobaron*. Mexico: Centro de Estudios Históricos del Movimiento Obrero Mexicano.

Passmore, John 2000 [1922], *The Perfectibility of Man*. Third edition. Indianapolis: Liberty Fund, at: https://oll.libertyfund.org/titles/670

Patsouras, Louis 1978, *Jean Grave and French Anarchism*. Dubuque: Kendall/Hunt Publishing Company.

Peterson, H.C., and Gilbert C. Fite 1957, *Opponents of War. 1917–1918*. Seattle: University of Washington Press.

Phillips, Charles Francis 4 June 1919, 'The End of the Great Austrian Empire', *El Heraldo de México*.

Phillips, Charles Francis 16 June 1919, 'The Tampico Strike', *El Heraldo de México*.

Phillips, Charles Francis 15 June 1919, 'Woman Suffrage and States Rights', *El Heraldo de México*, 2.

Phillips, Charles Francis 21 June 1919a, 'Suffrage is Certain in States', *El Heraldo de México*, 2.

Phillips, Charles Francis 21 June 1919b, 'Editorial', *El Heraldo de México*, 2.

Phillips, Charles Francis 17 June 1919, 'Red Rule Grips Tampico as Strikers Riot', *El Heraldo de Mexico*.

Phillips, Charles Francis 19 June 1919. 'Tampico, Not Juarez, Is the Point Of Attack', *El Heraldo de México*.

Phillips, Charles Francis 6 August 1919, 'Write At Once to Your Home Newspaper', *El Heraldo de México*.

Phillips, Charles Francis 7 August 1919, 'Why Machinery Leads to Intervention', *El Heraldo de M México*.

Phillips, Charles Francis 8 August 1919, 'Americas Here Must Not Be Silent', *El Heraldo de México*.

Phillips, Charles Francis 13 August 1919, 'How American Can Help Mexico', *El Heraldo de México*.

Phillips, Charles Francis 14 August 1919, 'Mexico's Reply to the American Notes', *El Heraldo de México*.

Phillips, Charles Francis 21 August 1919, 'Have the Dark Forces Won in the US?' *El Heraldo de México*.

Phillips, Charles Francis 22 August 1919 'US Trade Will Lose by Intervention', *El Heraldo de México*.

Phillips, Charles Francis 24 August 1919a, 'A Law Sermon for Americans Here', *El Heraldo de México*.

Phillips, Charles Francis 24 August 1919b 'Intervention a Shame', *El Heraldo*.

Phillips, Charles Francis 28 August 1919, 'The Importance of Students Here', *El Heraldo*.

Phillips, Charles Francis 30 August 1919, 'Americans in North Here Oppose Intervention', *El Heraldo de México*.

Phillips, Charles Francis 31 August 1919, 'Non-Partisan League and Its Aims', *El Heraldo de México*.

Phillips, Charles Francis 2 September 1919, 'Chicago Socialist Congress Expels Militant Lefts', *El Heraldo de México*.

Phillips, Charles Francis 7 September 1919, 'The Actors' and Car Strikes in New York', *El Heraldo de México*.

Phillips, Charles Francis 10 September 1919, 'League of Nations and Mexico', *El Heraldo de México*.

Phillips, Charles Francis 11 September 1919, 'Sec. Baker Favors Plumb Plan for Workers: Self-Government By Workers Has Been Proven Success', *El Heraldo de México*.

Phillips, Charles Francis 14 September 1919, 'Mexico's Hope Lies in the US Labor Movement', *El Heraldo de México*.

Phillips, Charles Francis 19 September 1919, 'India's Reward for Her Part in the War', *El Heraldo de México*.

Phillips, Charles Francis 23 September 1919, ''Pro-Mexico Society' Formed by Americans in Torreon', *El Heraldo de México*.

Phillips, Charles Francis 24 September 1919, 'Industrial Struggle Between Labor and the US Steel Corporation On', *El Heraldo de México*.

Phillips, Charles Francis 30 September 1919a, 'Negroes Warn Senate Against Race War: Peace Treaty Must Protect Dark Races They Say', *El Heraldo de México*.

Phillips, Charles Francis 30 September 1919b, 'Negro Lynched and Courthouse Burned in Race Riots', *El Heraldo de México*.

Phillips, Charles Francis 4 October 1919, 'Negroes Fire on Governor of Ark. And Military Commander', *El Heraldo de México*.

Phillips, Charles Francis 31 October 1919, 'Self-Determination as Applied to Egypt', *El Heraldo de México*.

Phillips, Charles Francis 1 November 1919, 'The Negro Challenges Civilization', *El Heraldo de México*.

Phillips, Charles Francis 4 November 1919, 'American Railroad Man Comes Out Against Intervention', *El Heraldo de México*.

Phillips, Charles Francis 5 November 1919, 'The American labor Party of Greater New York', *El Heraldo de México*.

Phillips, Charles Francis 18 November 1919, 'No Bolsheviks in Mexico', *El Heraldo de México*.

Phillips, Charles Francis 23 November 1919, 'The Jenkins Case', *El Heraldo de México*.

Phillips, Charles Francis 29 November 1919, 'On Intervention', *El Heraldo de México*.

Phillips, Charles Francis 3 December 1919a, 'The Mexican Feminist Council', *El Heraldo de México*, 2.

Phillips, Charles Francis 3 December 1919b, 'The Advent of Feminism in Mexico: Mexican Council of Women Formed to Aid Social, Economic and Political Reconstruction', *El Heraldo de Mexico*, 2.

Phillips, Charles Francis 17 December 1919, 'Intervention Scare and Its Effect on Business', *El Heraldo de México*.

Phillips, Charles Francis 18 December 1919, 'Has the US A Real Case Against Mexico?' *El Heraldo de México*.

Phillips, Charles Francis 15 January 1920a, 'Poor Persia Is Saved by England', *El Heraldo de México*.

Phillips, Charles Francis 15 January 1920b, 'Cuban Independence', *El Heraldo de México*.

Phillips, Charles Francis 13 June 1920, 'This World Has Had Enough of War', *El Heraldo de México*.

Phillips, Charles Francis 'Autobiography', Jaffee papers, Archives, Emory University.

'Phillips Sticks to IBs Vow Not to Register', 6 June 1917, *The Call*.

Pittenger, Mark 1993, *American Socialists and Evolutionary Thought, 1870–1920*. Madison: University of Wisconsin Press.

Polenberg, Richard 1987, *Fighting Faiths: The Abrams Case, the Supreme Court, and Free Speech*. New York: Penguin Books.

Pratt, Norma Fain 1979, *Morris Hillquit: A Political History of an American Jewish Socialist*. Westport, CT: Greenwood Press.

Puente, Ramón 1994 [1933], *Hombres de la Revolución: Calles*. Mexico: Fondo de la Cultura Económica.

Prezioso, Stéfanie 2017, *Contre la guerre 14–18: Résistances mondiales et révolution sociale*. Paris: La Dispute.

Quataert, Jean H. 1979, *Reluctant Feminists in German Social Democracy, 1895–1917*. Princeton: Princeton University Press.

Quirk, Robert E. 1962, *An Affair of Honor: Woodrow Wilson and the Occupation of Veracruz*. New York: W.W. Norton & Company, Inc.

Raat, W. Dirk 1981, *Revoltosos: Mexico's Rebels in the United States, 1903–1923*. College Station: Texas A&M University Press.

Rauschenbusch, Walter 1917, *The Social Principles of Jesus*. New York: The Women's Press.

Rawson, Hugh 1989, *Wicked Words: A Treasury of Curses, Insults, Put-Downs, and Other*

Formerly Unprintable Terms from Anglo-Saxon Times to the Present. New York: Crown Publishes, Inc.

Reed, John 1969, *Insurgent Mexico*. New York: International Publishers.

Reed, John 1987, *John Reed for 'The Masses'*, ed. by James C. Wilson. Jefferson, NC: McFarland & Company, Inc.

Retana, T. Reyes October 1920, 'Los Sindicatos', *Boletín de la Confederación de Cámaras Industriales* 62.

Retinger, J.H. 1925, *Morones of Mexico: A History of the Labour Movement in that Country*. London: The Labour Publishing Company Limited.

Retinger, J.H. 1926, *Tierra Mexicana: The History of Land and Agriculture in Ancient and Modem Mexico*. London: Noel Douglas.

Retinger, J.H. 1972, *Memoirs of an Eminence Grise*, ed. by John Pomian, with a foreword by H.R.H. Prince Bernhard of the Netherlands. Falmer: Sussex University Press.

Reyna, Manuel, Laura Palomares, and Guadalupe Cortez 1972, 'El control del movimiento obrero como una necesidad del estado de México (1917–1936)', *Revista Mexicana de Sociología* (34) July–September and October–December, 785–813.

Reyna Muñoz, Manuel (ed.) 1996, *Actores sociales en un proceso de transformación: Veracruz en los años veinte*. Mexico: Universidad Veracruzana.

Reynolds, Alfred W. 1953, 'The Alabama Negro Colony in Mexico, 1894–1896', *Alabama Review* 5 (October), 243–68 and 6 (January), 31–58.

Ridge, Jr., Michael Allen 2012, 'A Country in Need of American Instruction: The US Mission to Shape and Transform Mexico, 1848–1911', PhD Dissertation, University of Iowa.

Riddell, John 2018, 'The League Against Imperialism (1927–37): An Early Attempt at Global Anti-colonial Unity', at *Marxist Essays and Commentary*, 9 July, available at: https://johnriddell.com/2018/07/09/the-league-against-imperialism-1927-37-an-ea rly-attempt-at-global-anti-colonial-unity/

Redkey, Edwin S. 1969, *Black Exodus: Black Nationalist and Back to Africa Movements. 1890–1910*. New Haven: Yale University Press.

Rivera, Diego, and Bertram D. Wolfe 1934, *Portrait of America*. New York: Covici-Friede.

Rivera, Diego, and Bertram D. Wolfe 1937, *Portrait of Mexico*. New York: Civici-Friede.

Rivera Castro, José 1981, 'La CROM y el movimiento obrero internacional', manuscript (copy available in the library of the Colegio de Mexico, Mexico City).

'Roberto Haberman Dead at 79: Founder of Mexican Labor Unit' 1962, *New York Times*, 5 March, 23.

Rodea, Marcelo N. 1944, *Historia del Movimiento Oberro Ferrocarrilero en México (1890–1943)*. Mexico: n/.p.

Rodríguez José Refugio 1920, 'The Working Class Movement in Mexico', *The One Big Union Monthly* II, no. 6, 26–7.

Rodríguez, Miguel 1980, *Los tranviarios y el anarquismo en México (1920–1925)*. Puebla: Editorial Universidad Autónoma de Puebla.

Rosenstone, Robert A. 1975, *Romantic Revolutionary: A Biography of John Reed*. New York: Random House.

Rolland, M.C. July 1917, 'Why is a Government Needed in Mexico', *International Socialist Review* XVIII, no. 1, 48–50.

Rolland, Modesto C. September 1916, 'Petroleum in Mexico', *International Socialist Review* XVII, no. 3, 149–51.

Rolle, Andrew F. 1992, *The Lost Cause: The Confederate Exodus to Mexico*. Norman: University of Oklahoma Press.

Rosenberg, Rosalind 1992, *Divided Lives: American Women of the Twentieth Century*. New York: Hill and Wang.

Rothwell, Robert, Ian Drummon, and John English 1987, *Canada. 1900–1945*. Toronto: University of Toronto Press.

Roy, M.N. [n.d. 1935?], *Revolution and Counter-Revolution in China*. no place: no publisher. *Memoirs*. Delhi: Ajanta Publications.

Roy, Samen 1986, *Twice-Born Heretic: M.N. Roy and the Comintern*. Calcutta: Firma KLM Private Limited.

Ruíz, Ramón Eduardo 1978, *La revolución mexicana y el movimiento obrero*. Mexico: Ediciones Era.

Salas, Elizabeth 1995, *Soldaderas en los Ejercitos Mexicanos: Mitos e Historia*. Mexico: Editorial Diana.

Salazar, Rosendo 1962, *La Casa del Obero Mundial. Mexico*: Costa-Amic.

Salazar, Rosendo 1972, *Rosendo Salazar*. 2 vols. Mexico: Partido Revolucionario Institucional.

Salvatore, Nick 1982, *Eugene V. Debs: Citizen and Socialist*. Chicago: University of Illinois Press.

Sánchez Díaz, Gerardo 1990, 'Los Pasos al Socialismo en la Lucha Agraria y Sindical en Michoacán 1917–1938', *Tzintzun: Revista de Estudios Históricos* (Morelia. Michoacán) no. 11 (January–June), 105–24.

Sánchez, Martín 1994, *Grupos de poder y centalización política en México. El caso Michoacán 1920–1924*. Mexico: Instituto Nacional de Estudios Históricos de la Revolución Mexicana and Secretaría de Gobemacion.

Sandos, James A. 1992, *Rebellion in the Borderlands: Anarchism and the Plan of San Diego, 1904–1923*. Norman: University of Oklahoma Press.

Sarabia, Manuel June 1914, 'The Situation in Mexico', *International Socialist Review* XIV, no. 12, 735.

Sariego, Juan Luis 1988, *Enclaves y minerales en el norte de México: Historia sodal de los mineros de Cananea y Nueva Rosita. 1900–1970*. Mexico: CIESAS Casa Chata.

Schorske, Carl E. 1972, *German Social Democracy, 1905–1917*. New York: Harper.

Schou, August 1919, *Histoire de L'Intemationalisme*. Vol. III, by Christian Langue, Du congrès de Vienne Jusqu'a La Premiere Guerre Mondia. Oslo: H. Aschehoug & Co. [W. Nygaard].

Serge, Victor 1972, *Ce que tout révolutionnaire doit savoir de la répression*. Paris: Maspero.

Serge, Victor 1984 [1951], *Memoirs of a Revolutionary*. New York: Readers and Writers Publishing, Inc.

Shannon, David 1955, *The Socialist Party of America*. New York: Macmillan.

Shipman, Charles [pseud. of Charles Francis Phillips] 1993, *It Had to Be Revolution: Memoirs of An American Radical*, with a Foreword by Harvey Klehr. Ithaca, NY: Cornell University Press.

Shteppa, K.F. 1962, 'In Stalin's Prisons: Reminiscences', *Russian Review* 21, nos. 1 and 2 (January and April).

Silva Herzog, Jesus 1994 [1963], *Trayectoría ideológica de la Revolución Mexicana*. Mexico: Fondo de la Cultura Económica.

Sklar, Martin J. 1988, *The Corporate Reconstruction of American Capitalism, 1890–1916*. Cambridge: Cambridge University Press.

'slacker' s.v. 1978, *The World Book Dictionary*.

Snow, Sinclair 1960, 'Samuel Gompers and the Pan-American Federation of Labor', PhD dissertation, University of Virginia.

Soto, Shirlene 1990, *The Emergence of the Modern Mexican Woman: Her Participation in Revolution and Struggle for Equality, 1910–1940*. Denver: Arden Press Inc.

Spenser, Daniela 1994, 'Encounter of the Mexican and the Bolshevik Revolutions in the US Sphere of Interests, 1917–1930', PhD dissertation, University of North Carolina at Chapel Hill.

Spenser, Daniela 1998, *El Triángulo Imposible: México. Rusia Soviética y Estados Unidos en los años veinte*. Mexico: CIESAS and Porrua.

Spenser, Daniela 1999, *The Impossible Triangle: Mexico, Soviet Russia, and the United States in the 1920s: American Encounters/Global Interactions*. Durham, NC: Duke University Press.

Spenser, Daniela 2007, 'Emissaries of the Communist International in Mexico', *American Communist History* 6, no. 2, 151–70.

Spenser, Daniela 2011, *Stumbling Its Way Through Mexico: The Early Year of the Communist International*. Tuscaloosa: The University of Alabama Press.

Spenser, Daniela 2018, 'Bolsheviks Encounter with the Mexican Revolution', *Tensões Mundais* 13, no. 25 (September).

Stamm, George W. April 1914, 'Hinges on Land Monopoly' 1, no. 1, 3.

Steel, Ronald 1981, *Walter Lippmann and the American Century*. New York: Vintage.

Steffens, Lincoln May 1916, 'Into Mexico and Out', *Everybody's Magazine*, 533–47, Hathi Trust Digital Library, available at: https://babel.hathitrust.org/cgi/pt?id=mdp.39015 006994548&view=1up&seq=685

Steffens, Lincoln May 1958 [1931], *The Autobiography of Lincoln Steffens*. 2 vols. New York: Harcourt, Brace & World, Inc.

Steffens, Lincoln May 1938, *The Letters of Lincoln Steffens*. 2 vols. New York: Harcourt, Brace and Company.

Steffens, Lincoln May 1957 [1904], *Shame of the Cities*. New York: Hill and Wang.

Steffens, Lincoln May 1909, *Upbuilders*. New York: Doubleday, Page & Company.

Stein, Harry H. 1975, 'Lincoln Steffens and the Mexican Revolution', *The American Journal of Economics and Sociology* 34, no. 2, 197–212.

Sturges, Herbert October 1912, 'History, Mexico, and American Capitalism', *International Socialist Review* XIII, no. 4, 332, 35.

Taibo II, Paco Ignacio 1986, *Los Bolshevikis: Historia narrativa de los orígenes del communism en México: 1919-1925*. Mexico: Joaquín Mortiz.

Taibo II, Paco Ignacio 2006, *Pancho Villa: Una biografía narrative*. Mexico: Planeta.

Tannenbaum, Frank 1966 [1933], *Peace by Revolution: Mexico After 1910*. New York: Columbia University Press.

Taylor, Lawrence Douglas 1992 *La campaña magonista de 1911 en Baja California*. Tijuana: El Colegio de la Frontera Norte.

Taylor, Lawrence Douglas 1993, *La gran aventura en Mexico*. Mexico: Consejo Nacional par Cultura y las Artes.

'Teacher Who Resisted Draft Content in Jail' 3 September 1917, *The Call*.

'The Arrest of the Magón Brothers' April 1916, *Mother Earth* XI, no. 2, 492.

'The Mexican War Between Socialists and Communists' March 1920, *The One Big Union Monthly*, 44.

'The Rangel-Cline Case' June 1914, *Mother Earth* IX, no. 4, 111–15.

'The Rangel-Cline Case' August 1914, *Mother Earth* IX, no. 6, 201–2.

Thönnessen, Werner 1973, *The Emancipation of Women: The Rise and Decline of the Women's Movement in German Social Democracy*. London: Pluto Press.

Torres Pares, Javier 1989, *La Revolución sin frontera: El partido Liberal Mexicano y las relaciones entre el movimiento obrero de México y el de Estados Unidos: 1900-1923*. Mexico: UNAM and Ediciones Y Distribuciones Hispanicas.

Trachtenberg, Alan 1962, *The Incorporation of America: Culture and Society in the Gilded Age*. New York: Hill and Wang.

Traven, B. 1962, *Die Baumwollpflucker*. Hamburg.

Trent, Roy Evelyn 1 August 1919, 'La mujer mexicana y el movimiento feminista mundial', *El Socialista* 38.

Tridon, André 1913, *The New Unionism*. New York: B.W. Huebsch.

Trotsky, Leon 1957 [1931], *History of the Russian Revolution*. 3 vols. Ann Arbor: University of Michigan Press.

Trotsky, Leon 1976, *Leon Trotsky on China*, ed. by Les Evans and Russell Block. New York: Monad Press.

'Two Students Fined $500 and Day in Custody' 13 July 1917, *The Call*.

Tull, Jewell Bothwell 1917, 'The Slacker: A Play in One Act'. Boston: Walter H. Baker & Co.

Tunón Pablos, Esperanza, 1992, *Mujeres que se organizan: El Frente Único pro derechos de la mujer: 1935–1938*. Mexico: UNAM.

Turner, John Kenneth 1984 [1910], *Barbarous Mexico*, with an introduction by Sinclair Snow. Austin: University of Texas.

Turner, John Kenneth December 1910, 'The American Partners of Díaz', *International Socialist Review* XI, no. 6, 321–8.

Turner, John Kenneth 1911, 'The Revolution in Mexico', *International Socialist Review* XI, no. 7, 421.

Turner, John Kenneth June 1914, 'Why I am for Zapata', *New Review* 323–6.

Turner, John Kenneth May 1916, 'Marching Through Mexico', *International Socialist Review* XVI, no. 11, 652–6.

'Two Arrested At Objectors' Meeting' 28 September 1917, *The Call*.

'Tyranny in Texas' February 1914, *Mother Earth* VIII, no. 12, 377–9.

'Una lección provechosa?' June 1922, *México Industrial* 145–6.

Uriéstegui Mirando, Pinadaro 1987, *Testimonios del Proceso Revolucionario de México*. Mexico City: Instituto Nacional de Estudios Históricos de la Revolución Mexicana.

Valadés, José C. 1985 *Memorias de Un Joven Rebelde*. 2 vols. Mexico: Universidad Autónoma de Sinaloa.

Valadés, José C. 1988, *Historia general de la Revolución Mexicana*. 10 vols. Fourth Edition. Mexico: Gemika.

von Mohrenschildt, Dimitri S. 1945, 'Lincoln Steffens and the Russian Bolshevik Revolution', *The Russian Review* 5, no. 1 (Autumn), 31–41.

Vasconcelos, José 1993 [1936], *Memorias*. 2 vols. Mexico: Fondo de la Cultura Económica.

Villa, [Francisco] Pancho 21 March 1914, 'General Villa's Ultimatum to President Wilson', *The Appeal to Reason* 1.

Villegas, Abelardo, 1993, *El Pensamiento Mexicano en el Siglo XX*. Mexico: Fondo de la Cultura Económica.

Villegas de Magnón, Leonor 1994, *The Rebel*. Houston: Arte Publico Press.

Vizcaíno, Rogelio 1984, *Memoria roja: Luchas sindicales de los años 20*. Mexico: Ediciones Leega/Jucr.

Volin [V.M. Eikhenbaum] 1974 [1947], *The Unknown Revolution*. New York: Free Life Editions.

Wallace, Mary McOuat November 1916, 'Misunderstood Mexico', *Bulletin* 16, The Board of Foreign Missions of the Presbyterian Church, 1.

Walling, Willian English 1927, *The Mexican Question*. New York: Robins Press.

Weinstein, James 1967, *The Decline of Socialism in America*. New York: Monthly Review Press.

Weinstein, James 1968, *The Corporate Ideal in the Liberal State, 1900–1918*. Boston: Beacon Press.

Whittaker, William George 1968, 'The Santiago Iglesias Case, 1901–1902: Origins of American Trade Union Involvement in Puerto Rico', *The Americas* 24, no. 4, 378–93.

Wilkie, James W., and Edna Monzon Wilkie 1995, *Frente a La Revolución Mexicana: 17 protagonistas de la etapa constructiva. Entrevistas de historia oral*. Mexico: Universidad Autónoma Metropolitana.

Williams, William Appleman 1966, *The Contours of American History*. Chicago: Quadrangle Books.

Wilson, Woodrow 1981, *The Papers of Woodrow Wilson*. Princeton: Princeton University Press.

Wimer, Javier 1996, 'Cumpleaños del 33', *La Jornada* (Mexico) 30 January, 1.

Winton, George B. 1913, *Mexico To-Day: Social, Political, and Religious Conditions*. New York: Missionary Education Movement of the United States and Canada.

Wolfe, Bertram D. 1981, *A Life in Two Centuries*, with an Introduction by Leonard Shapiro. New York: Stein and Day.

Woodcock, George 1962, *Anarchism: A History of Libertarian Ideas and Movements*. New York: World Publishing.

Woods, Kenneth F. 1964, 'Samuel Guy Inman and Intervention in Mexico', at: http://academic.brooklyn.cuny.edu/history/johnson/Samuel%20Guy%20Inman.htm

Woodward, C. Vann 1979, *Tom Watson: Agrarian Rebel*. New York: Oxford University Press.

Yeager, Gertrude M. 1994, *Confronting Change, Challenging Tradition: Women in Latin American History*. Wilmington, DE: SR Books.

'Young, Robert Ralph' 1947, *Dictionary of American Biography. 1956–1960*, Supplement 6; *Current Biography*, 696.

Zertuche Muñoz, Fernando 1995, *Ricardo Flores Magón. El Sueño Alternativo*. Mexico: Fondo de Cultura Económica.

Zogbaum, Heidi 1992, *B. Traven: A Vision of Mexico*. Wilmington, DE: SR Books, Scholarly Resources Inc.

Zoraida Vázquez, Josefina, and Lorenzo Meyer 1982, *Mexico frente a Estados Unidos: Un Ensavo histórico 1776–1980*. Mexico: El Colegio de Mexico.

Zumoff, Jacob A. 2014, *The Communist Inteernational and US Communism, 1919–1929*. Leiden: Brill.

Dissertations, MA Theses, Unpublished Papers, and Oral History

Adelson Gruber, Steven Lief 1982, 'Historia Social de los Obreros Industriales de Tampico, 1906–1919', Doctoral Dissertation, Colegio de Mexico.

Andrews, Gregory A. 1988, 'American Labor and the Mexican Revolution, 1910–1924', PhD Dissertation, Northern Illinois University, 27 April.

Beals, Ralph 1977, 'Anthropologist and Educator: Ralph L. Beals', interviewed by Diane
    L. Dillon, Oral History Program, University of California, manuscript copy in Ban-
    croft Library, University of California at Berkeley.

Buford, Camile Nick 1971, 'A Biography of Luis N. Morones, Mexican Labor and Political
    Leader', PhD Dissertation, Louisiana State University.

Caulfield, Norman 1987, 'The Industrial Workers of the World and Mexican Labor, 1905–
    1925', Master of Arts Thesis, Department of History, University of Houston.

Christopulos, Diana K. 1980, 'American Radicals and the Mexican Revolution: 1900–
    1925', PhD Dissertation, State University of New York, Binghamton.

Fowler, Heather 1970, 'The Agrarian Revolution in the State of Veracruz, 1920–1940: The
    Role of Peasant Organizations', PhD Dissertation, American University, Washing-
    ton, D.C.

La Botz, Daniel 1998, '"Slackers": American War Resisters and Communists in Mexico,
    1917–1927', PhD Dissertation, History Department, University of Cincinnati.

Ridge Jr., Michael Allen 2012, 'A Country in Need of American Instruction: The US
    Mission to Shape and Transform Mexico, 1848–1911', PhD Dissertation, University of
    Iowa.

Index